A Di...ary of

...es

WITHDRAWN
UTSA LIBRARIES

⊕ SEE WEB LINKS

Many entries in this dictionary have entry-level web links. When you see the above symbol at the end of an entry go to the dictionary's web page at http://www.oup.com/uk/reference/resources/sportsstudies, click on **Web links** in the Resources section and locate the entry in the alphabetical list, then click straight through to the relevant websites.

Alan Tomlinson is Professor of Leisure Studies and Director of Research in the Research & Graduate College of Sport, Chelsea School, at the University of Brighton, UK. He has authored and edited numerous works on the social history and sociology of sport, leisure, and consumption. He has developed and delivered programmes on the history and cultural analysis of sport, and on sport media and journalism, for International Programmes at Pembroke College, Cambridge. His research interests cover the political economy of the modern sporting spectacle and event, the varied sport cultures of modern Europe, the place of investigative research in sports studies, and interdisciplinary methodology including the overlapping interests of the social sciences and the humanities.

Oxford Paperback Reference

The most authoritative and up-to-date reference books for both students and the general reader.

ABC of Music
Accounting
Allusions
Animal Behaviour
Archaeology
Architecture and Landscape
  Architecture
Art and Artists
Art Terms
Arthurian Literature and
  Legend
Astronomy
Battles
Better Wordpower
Bible
Biology
British History
British Place-Names
Buddhism
Business and Management
Card Games
Century of New Words
Chemistry
Christian Art
Christian Church
Classical Literature
Classical Myth and Religion
Classical World
Computing
Contemporary World History
Countries of the World
Dance
Earth Sciences
Ecology
Economics
Education
Encyclopedia
Engineering
English Etymology
English Folklore
English Grammar
English Language
English Literature
English Surnames
Environment and
  Conservation
Euphemisms
Everyday Grammar
Family and Local History
Finance and Banking
First Names
Food and Nutrition
Foreign Words and Phrases
Geography

Humorous Quotations
Idioms
Irish History
Islam
Kings and Queens of Britain
Law
Law Enforcement
Linguistics
Literary Terms
London Place-Names
Mathematics
Medical
Medicinal Drugs
Modern Design
Modern Quotations
Modern Slang
Music
Musical Terms
Musical Works
Nicknames
Nursing
Philosophy
Physics
Plant Sciences
Plays
Pocket Fowler's Modern
  English Usage
Political Quotations
Politics
Popes
Proverbs
Psychology
Quotations
Quotations by Subject
Rhymes
Rhyming Slang
Saints
Science
Scientific Quotations
Scottish History
Shakespeare
Ships and the Sea
Slang
Sociology
Space Exploration
Statistics
Superstitions
Synonyms and Antonyms
Weather
Word Histories
World History
World Mythology
World Religions
Zoology

A Dictionary of
Sports Studies

ALAN TOMLINSON

OXFORD
UNIVERSITY PRESS

OXFORD
UNIVERSITY PRESS

Great Clarendon Street, Oxford OX2 6DP

Oxford University Press is a department of the University of Oxford.
It furthers the University's objective of excellence in research, scholarship,
and education by publishing worldwide in

Oxford New York

Auckland Cape Town Dar es Salaam Hong Kong Karachi
Kuala Lumpur Madrid Melbourne Mexico City Nairobi
New Delhi Shanghai Taipei Toronto

With offices in

Argentina Austria Brazil Chile Czech Republic France Greece
Guatemala Hungary Italy Japan Poland Portugal Singapore
South Korea Switzerland Thailand Turkey Ukraine Vietnam

Oxford is a registered trade mark of Oxford University Press
in the UK and in certain other countries

Published in the United States
by Oxford University Press Inc., New York

British Library Cataloguing in Publication Data
Data available

Library of Congress Cataloging in Publication Data
Data available

Typeset by SPI Publisher Services, Pondicherry, India
Printed in Great Britain
on acid-free paper by
Clays Ltd., St Ives plc

ISBN 978-0-19-921381-8

1 3 5 7 9 10 8 6 4 2

Preface

A Dictionary of Sports Studies draws upon multidisciplinary and interdisciplinary perspectives that illuminate the nature and significance of sport, and in particular its social and cultural meanings, at levels from recreational participation in everyday life through to high-performance competition in international events. For this, it is necessary not merely to gather together sociological concepts and evidence, and historical examples, but to draw upon politics, economics, geography, philosophy, and the scientific approaches that are combined, and sometimes synthesized, in sports science and sport psychology. From this almost unbounded array of potential sources, I have selected particular perspectives and core terms that will enable the sports studies scholar or academic to make sense of the meanings of sport, in both contemporary society and past societies, and to both the individual and the social collectivity. This particular approach gives most space to how we think about sport, its place in society, and its importance to people in different times and places. It is not a 'how to' manual, a technical compendium, or a comprehensive encyclopaedia; the term 'sports studies' means exactly what it says, referring to how we can go about studying and understanding sport.

The most extensive subcategory within this dictionary is therefore concepts and theories, providing an interpretive framework, from sociocultural studies, for understanding sport cultures; it accounts for over a third of the dictionary. To show the sheer range of sporting formations that have been produced by past and present societies, the dictionary offers sports and games as its second largest category of entries, taking up almost a quarter of the text. Too often sports studies is drawn to the big events of the day, those implanted in public consciousness by unadventurous media institutions. But the sporting life has been much more varied than that, and the selections in the sports and games category are reminders of—or forms of potential awakening to—the diversity of sporting forms and practices. The third largest category is biographies, not just of sporting champions or innovators, but also of administrators and organizers, philosophers and politicians, novelists and educators: people who have taken a view on sport and its place in society, and whose view has influenced sporting trends and formations, how others see sport, or how sport is perceived in relation to other cultural forms; these biographies make up 15 per cent of the dictionary. Following a widely accepted—though not universally adopted—convention of Oxford University Press dictionaries, only dead figures are granted individual entries. As others have argued before me, setting boundaries of significance around living figures is a fruitless task, and too often establishes a fragile sense of topicality or contemporariness. Of course this creates good debating points, if not anomalies. How, for instance, can *A Dictionary of Sports Studies* not have an entry on Muhammad Ali? Or David Beckham? And of course, in world-historical terms, who could argue that the former is not of vastly wider significance than the latter?

Such debating points, engaging as they might be among the sporting public, could be indefinitely extended, and so the pragmatics of life or death are adhered to here on the question of eligibility for inclusion as a separate entry. But the dictionary instances the significance of such figures in entries on, for instance, boxing, and celebrity.

Other categories that have framed the dictionary are science (the majority of entries on which have been written by contributing adviser Professor Jonathan Doust), taking up 8 per cent; economics, around 4 per cent; policies, 2 per cent; organizations and institutions, 9 per cent; and terminology/language, 1 per cent. In all entries there is a definitional dimension, and where appropriate an accompanying contextualization or illustration, and a commentary on the impact of the person, concept, sport, or study. Dictionaries, right from Samuel Johnson's pioneering achievements in 18th-century England, have offered more than just definitions, and etymologies are like excavations of the origins of communication. Dictionaries have been signposts, invitations to explore, and it is in this spirit of beginnings that *A Dictionary of Sports Studies* is designed. Someone else would have designed the dictionary differently, but the interdisciplinary scale and scope is essential for the continuing maturity of sports studies as an established field of academic study and research. It is not a rival to specialist disciplinary dictionaries, or to remarkable collections such as John Arlott (ed.) *Oxford Companion on Sport and Games* (Oxford University Press, 1975), and J. A. Cuddon (ed.) *The Macmillan Dictionary of Sport and Games* (Macmillan, 1980). To reiterate, it is a volume designed to clarify the nature and challenges of sports *studies*. If you want to know how to play a sport, go to a manual or an instructional website; if you want to know about records and particular sporting idols, go to a specialist almanac of the sport of your choice; but if you are interested in what sports have meant in human history and society, and in the interpretive vocabulary that illuminates those meanings, then *A Dictionary of Sports Studies* offers many directional possibilities. These include a wide range of sports beyond the dominant forms of the day, and an open mind on the ways in which those sports are understood; thus, extended space is given to previously neglected (and sometimes misrepresented) topics, sources, and concepts, in order to alert readers and scholars to the scope of the field.

Acknowledgements

I am grateful to generations of students and academic and administrative colleagues at the University of Brighton (particularly in the Chelsea School) for their stimulation and support throughout the last thirty-four years; to US students on International Programmes at Pembroke College and King's College, Cambridge, particularly those who have taken my 'The British and their Sports' course over the last eight years, and instructed me wisely on the distinctiveness of the USA's sporting culture; to editors at the Oxford University Press who have supported this proposal with unusual combinations of skill, tact, and firmness; to the dictionary consultants/advisers on economics (Professor Stefan Szymanski) and internationalism (Professor Toby Miller); to the contributing consultant/adviser on sport and exercise science (Professor Jo Doust); to the always supportive and positive promptings and responses of Professor Jim McKay; and to the Tomlinsons and Kirranes who have put up with the reports on the progress of the project for too long, whilst reluctantly picking up snippets of sport-based knowledge when dictionary detail began to spill over into family life. Alys and Rowan have supported me as always in commitments such as this work. Bernie was calmness personified as the manuscript took shape, spotting tonal excesses and effusive indulgence, and displaying the combined skills of pacifier and classifier. Sinead went coolly about the business of compiling three of the appendices. Jo and Ita were cheerfully supportive, the latter unfailingly asking after the progress of Alan's A–Z. Despite all such forms of support, there are inevitably definitional nuances and interpretative comments in the dictionary with which some readers will no doubt want to take issue; I welcome any such responses, and will be grateful if they could be transmitted to the publisher.

Professor Alan Tomlinson
Brighton, East Sussex
Campillergures, L'Hérault/Languedoc
July 2009

Contents

ABC TV A US national television network broadcaster that has been one of the major investors—along with CBS and NBC—in sports programming in the USA. These three network broadcasters dominated much of the USA's sport coverage into the 1970s and 1980s, aided by a regulatory framework of the Federal Communications Commission. Their rivalry also raised the value of some sports events, most notably the Olympic Games; the broadcasting rights for the Summer Olympics in Los Angeles in 1984 were US$287 million, those for Atlanta in 1996 US $898.2 million, and for the 2000 Sydney Games US$1,331.5 million. The proportion of overall Olympic broadcasting rights coming from the US market was still more than half (52%) for the 2008 Beijing Olympics.

From the 1980s, with the emergence of cable television, and from the mid 1990s with the emergence of the direct-to-home satellite platform (DTH), the power of the three network broadcasters has been reduced, and specialist providers such as *ESPN provided what economists saw as much-needed competition. The relaxation of regulations also saw the emergence of a fourth network broadcaster, Fox, in 1994. ABC and the other network providers have remained committed to the sports profile in this more mixed market, which remains nevertheless what economists call a situation of oligopoly; for instance, the broadcasting rights of the National Football League (NFL) between 1998 and 2005 were worth over US$17 billion, jointly shared by ABC, CBS, Fox, and ESPN.

Abrahams, Harold Maurice (1899–1978) An English athlete and athletics administrator, who both epitomized and challenged the prevailing ethos of *amateurism. Born in Bedford, England, Abrahams was the youngest of four sons of Isaac Klonimus (1850–1921), an immigrant to Britain from Russian-occupied Poland who declared his origins to be those of a Lithuanian Jew. Klonimus changed his name to Abrahams (the given name of his father) in 1880. His son Harold attended Cambridge University, studying law at Gonville and Caius College, already an accomplished athlete, holder of the national public schoolboy titles in the long jump and the 100 yards (the 'dash'). In his time at Cambridge he won an unprecedented number of sprint races and jumping events, and, after completing his Cambridge studies, won the 100-metres gold medal at the 1924 Olympic Games in Paris, prepared under the intense and rigorous tutelage of his north-east English coach, French Arab Sam Mussabini. Abrahams retired from competitive athletics the following year, having sustained an injury in an attempt to beat his own English long-jump record, which was to survive for more than thirty years.

On retirement, Abrahams took up a career in law, also engaging—with widespread influence nationally and internationally—in athletics administration, broadcasting on the sport for the BBC, and working in economic policy during World War II, and in urban planning. From 1950 to 1963, he was secretary of the National Parks Commission. In 1954, he was the official who confirmed Roger Bannister's sub-four-minute mile at Oxford University's Iffley Road track. Abrahams's athletic achievements were immortalized in the film *Chariots of Fire*, which compressed parts of his career into the Cambridge years, and placed an emphasis on a motivating anti-Semitism at the university that was never confirmed by Abrahams himself. The film also pivoted around Abrahams's rivalry with the Scottish runner Eric *Liddell.

Abrahams was significant for straddling the amateur–professional divide, in his use of a coach to support his Olympic campaign and victory. In 1948, on the eve of the Olympic Games in London, Abrahams wrote: 'I was lucky enough in 1924 to win an Olympic title, and I realise to the full that the praise showered upon me was out of all proportion to the occasion. I am not going to pretend that I did not train extremely hard, but I realize to the full that luck played an enormous part.' Abrahams pleaded for more consideration of and praise for those at the Olympics who did not win. Ironically, given his professionalized approach in the 1920s, he became a bastion of the amateur establishment, though doing much to modernize the format, profile, and administration of athletics.

acclimatization Refers to the biological adaptations that take place in the body in response to extremes of pressure, heat, and cold. The body adapts acutely and chronically. The extent of the adaptation depends on the environmental factor involved and the level of exposure. An acute adaptation, for example, would be peripheral vasodilatation in response to a hot environment. The response is rapid, a matter of seconds or minutes, and the increased flow of blood close to the body surface allows an increased heat loss. An example of a chronic adaptation would be the increase in the number of red blood cells on exposure to high altitude. This increases the oxygen-carrying capacity of the blood in response to the lowered partial pressure of oxygen in the atmosphere. The response takes many weeks to be fully complete. Adaptations are greatest in response to altitude and heat. The human is only weakly adaptable to the cold and shows no adaptation to high pressures such as those experienced in underwater diving. Combined environmental stress, such as exercising in hot and humid environments, can be particularly challenging and fatalities can occur. Wherever possible, simple behavioural adjustments are the primary means to avoid environmental stress, such as clothing or indoor air-conditioning.

achieved status See ASCRIBED AND ACHIEVED STATUS.

achievement orientation In psychology, the state of an athlete in relation to a competitive or evaluative situation, ranging from a competitive drive for success and excellence to the fear of underachieving or failing. More generally, accounts have pointed to achievement as a central principle of life in competitive modern societies. Psychologist David McClelland's study *The Achieving Society* (1961) linked the achievement principle, a form of aspiration to succeed, to the level of the economy. Marxist accounts of sport—for instance, Bero Rigauer's *Sport and Work* (1969, English translation 1981)—have adapted the concept to account for the

nature of high-performance sport in modern industrial capitalist societies. Accounts
of sport influenced by Max *Weber—these include Steven J. Overman's *The
Influence of the Protestant Ethic on Sport and Recreation* (1997) and Allen
Guttmann's *From Ritual to Record* (1978)—have also seen sport as a form of striving,
and have drawn upon McClelland's work.

action research Research designed to affect the context of the study, to feed
back into the way an organization works, for instance, or the manner in which an
activity is undertaken. The action researcher is explicitly an agent of change, and
such research is often accomplished in relatively short time-frames. The founding
figure of action research, Kurt Lewin (1890–1947), identified a 'spiral of steps' in
which action research acts as a form of intervention and so generates new practices
as well as knowledge; each step is made up of a 'circle of planning, action, and
fact-finding about the result of the action' ('Action Research and Minority
Problems', *Journal of Social Issues*, 1946). Action research is often applied in
professional contexts, and the subjects are invited to contribute to the identification
of the research problems, and of potential solutions. Sport policies and sport
development initiatives are highly suited to action research approaches, and the
interventions and studies fostered by the UK government and associated bodies
(reported in *Leisure and the Quality of Life*, Her Majesty's Stationery Office, 1977)
are an illuminating example of the method at work in relation to local cooperation
and community involvement in evaluating and potentially initiating public policy
on sport and the arts. The principles of action research also have their radical
variants in research by and for social movements, and committed forms of research
designed to have a social application or impact on a transformative level.

addiction *See* EXERCISE ADDICTION.

Adidas A multinational corporation specializing in sports goods that, founded as
a small shoe company in Germany in 1920, became 'Gebrüder Dassler,
Sportschufabrik, Herzogenaurach' in 1924, and, when the Dassler brothers who ran
that company split, the separate company 'Adidas' in 1948. Adolf (known as Adi)
Dassler (1900–78) started Adidas, a compound of his abbreviated names; his
brother Rudolf (1898–1974) started the rival firm Puma. The initial company had
prospered in the Nazi years in the 1930s, as sport became a popular pursuit
associated with the goals of the *Hitler regime, Adolf Dassler joining the Hitler
Youth in 1935 as sport coach and supplier; he also crafted the spiked two-striped
shoes worn by Jesse *Owens at the 1936 Berlin Olympics. Adi Dassler's son, Horst
*Dassler, became a major figure in the remaking of the international sports economy.
    Adidas has been a pioneer in sport branding (its simple three-stripe logo,
registered in 1949, adorning sports products worldwide) and in product
development, from the innovative running-shoe spikes and studded football boots
developed by the Dassler brothers after World War I, to sports clothing of all
conceivable kinds, and the 'starball' soccer ball used in the annual *UEFA
Champions League. As a 20-year-old, Horst Dassler travelled to the 1956 Olympic
Games in Melbourne, Australia, with consignments of green-striped Adidas spiked
running shoes, which, in a masterful marketing stroke, he distributed to competing
athletes at no cost. The consignment of Puma shoes sent by his uncle, Rudolf

Dassler, remained locked in the Melbourne Docks, lacking clearance from Australian customs officials; no definitive documentation exists on how the Adidas consignment was released, the Puma one blocked. Horst Dassler went on to mastermind Adidas's emergence as a provider not just for individual athletes, but for events and national and international associations and federations.

Not just an up-front sponsor such as *Coca-Cola but also a behind-the-scenes operator, Adidas with its network—including *International Sport and Leisure—was among the major influences upon the power dynamics of international sport: FIFA (*Fédération Internationale de Football Association) president from 1998, 'Sepp' Blatter, was an Adidas trainee; International Olympic Committee (IOC) president Juan Antonio Samaranch was promoted and supported by Adidas in his emergence as the successful candidate for the IOC presidency. Its continued success in the wake of the emergence of *Nike and Reebok has been based upon its association with and sponsorship of superstar figures such as David Beckham, and prominent football clubs such as Real Madrid, Bayern Munich, and Russian oligarch Roman Abramovich's English football club, Chelsea, as well as the exploitation of fashion trends such as retro in the early 1990s, and brand clothing designs by figures such as Stella McCartney and Yohji Yamamoto. Its three stripes have also been sported by rock stars such as Jamaica's Bob Marley, and the Gallagher brothers of British band Oasis.

In 2005, Adidas bought one of its main competitors, Reebok, for a figure in the region of US$3.8 billion. Reebok chief executive Paul Fireman and his wife Phyllis, owners of approximately 17 per cent of the company, gained around US$800 million. The deal was designed to allow the two brands to continue as near-independent operations, but in the light of complementary strengths and markets. The origins of Reebok went back to a British-based athletics shoe retailer that, under the name Joe Foster, had been trading since the beginning of the century, and adopted the Reebok name in the 1950s. Reebok emerged as a market leader in the 1980s, after Boston entrepreneur Fireman acquired the US rights for the firm in 1979. Fireman sold 55 per cent of the company to British investor Stephen Rubin, as the venture hovered on the edge of bankruptcy. But a shoe called the Freestyle, with a soft-leather look, captured the women's market during the *aerobics boom; Reebok global sales of US$300,000 in 1980 became $12.8 million in 1983, $1.4 billion in 1987. Along with Nike's spectacular success, this undermined Adidas's place in the US market, and by the mid 1980s, from a market share of more than half, Adidas had plunged to fourth place behind Nike, Reebok, and Converse. Reebok was still among the top three global brands in the sports-shoe/trainer business in 2004, sponsored top US basketball players, including Chinese NBA star Yao Ming, and had made deals with some football clubs, including English club Liverpool. The bold acquisition of Reebok by Adidas could help the latter's profile in the USA, and the former's in the rivalry with world leader Nike. At the FIFA World Cup in Germany in 2006, Adidas and its arch-rival Nike, along with a resurgent Puma, consolidated their positions as multibillion conglomerates dominating the sporting goods markets of the world. The Adidas story is told in a colourful piece of investigative journalism by Barbara Smit (*Pitch Invasion: Three Stripes, Two Brothers, One Feud; Adidas, Puma and the Making of Modern Sport*, 2006).

(⊕) SEE WEB LINKS

• The official site of the company, promoting its products and its brand identity.

Adorno, Theodor W. (1903–69) A German philosopher, aesthetician, and social theorist who was one of the most prominent individual members of the Frankfurt School of *critical theory. Adorno fled Germany in 1938 to escape Nazi persecution, and lived and worked in the USA until returning to Germany in 1949. Much of his thinking was shaped by his response to his US experience, and his hostility towards mass culture and popular cultural forms. In his book *Prisms* (1967) he wrote that: 'Modern sports . . . train men all the more inexorably to serve the machine. Hence sports belong to the realm of unfreedom, no matter where they are organized.' For Adorno, artistic works are the source of the reaffirmation of individual existence in the face of the forces of domination in mass society: 'the greatness of works of art lies solely in their power to let those things be heard which ideology conceals', he wrote in the journal *Telos* in 1974. Sport, on the other hand, was increasingly a part of the *culture industry, a force working against the possibility of freedom and individuality. In *The Culture Industry* (1996) he observed that sport is 'not play but ritual in which the subjected celebrate their subjection'. For Adorno the modern sports that prompted his comments were essentially ideological, serving the interests of the forces of domination. *See also* NEGATIVE DIALECTIC; UTOPIA.

adrenaline A hormone that, secreted by the adrenal ductless glands, affects muscular action and creates more energy. In sport, adrenaline rush—the process of intensifying the release of adrenaline into the system—refers to both the physiological and psychological state of increased determination or enhanced physical competitiveness in an encounter. An adrenaline rush is therefore a condition of body and mind that the competitor seeks, or might hope to achieve, at critical points of the contest or performance. As Ellis Cashmore has noted, though, such effects might be sought through drugs such as the widely banned pseudoephedrine, which is contained in decongestants and remedies for the common cold, and 'mimics the adrenaline rush . . . Five different types of the stimulant were found in the urine of Argentina's soccer player Diego Maradona when he was tested at (and subsequently banned from) the 1994 World Cup championships' (Ellis Cashmore, *Sport Psychology: The Key Concepts*, 2002).

adventure sports A term widely used but rarely defined, relating to broad and imprecise categories of outdoor activity and what are also referred to as *lifestyle sports or activities characterized by elements of risk. While some activities—such as white-river rafting—combine adventure and risk, many others—such as supervised climbing and canoeing in shallow waters—entail minimal risk or danger. Rather like theme-park rides, the latter type offers a sense of adventure with virtually no risk; but the category 'adventure' remains attractive to promoters and consumers alike. In terms of analytical precision, though, the term adventure sports is of little value to sports studies. *See also* EXTREME SPORTS.

aerobic A term describing the metabolic pathway that involves the breakdown of carbohydrate, fat, and to a lesser degree protein, in the presence of oxygen.

Energy is captured in the phosphate bonds of adenosine triphosphate (ATP) for subsequent use in muscular contraction. During exercise, the rate of aerobic energy use is determined as the oxygen uptake measured in units of litres of oxygen consumed per minute. As the intensity of exercise increases the oxygen uptake increases proportionately until a maximum is reached—the maximal aerobic power. This maximum power is often used as a measure of fitness. It can be determined by direct measurement in the laboratory or estimated indirectly by a number of fitness tests such as the 20-metre shuttle (bleep) test. The maximum aerobic power is an individual characteristic and its size depends on a number of factors such as active muscle mass and inheritance. Maximal aerobic power is lower in women than men by about 10 per cent. In both sexes it can be improved by physical training and average increases of about 20 per cent are usually seen although there is considerable inter-individual variation in the response. The capacity of the aerobic system is essentially infinite as from the moment of birth to the moment of death the body is metabolizing aerobically.

aerobics A non-technical term for forms of exercise regimes based on improving health and fitness by causing cardio-respiratory adaptations as a result of stressing the various physiological systems associated with aerobic energy production. Aerobics came to prominence in the late 1960s to early 1970s from the work of Kenneth Cooper (author of *Aerobics*, 1968) in the USA at a time when the role of regular exercise in the prevention and treatment of heart disease was becoming recognized. Cooper developed the first exercise scheme to have mass impact on the general population. Cooper's aerobics awarded exercise points according to the intensity and duration of activities such as walking, jogging, and cycling. The points derived from the aerobic energy demands of these activities. Cooper's scheme was well founded in experimental science. Since that time, the boom in popular exercise schemes has led to the term being used more and more loosely. The original close connection to aerobic energy pathways has been lost. The term is now used, meaninglessly, in association with virtually all forms of exercise from t'ai chi to weightlifting.

aerodynamics *See* FLUID DYNAMICS.

aeroplane racing One of the two earliest forms of competitive sport with aeroplanes (along with record-breaking distance flights), established in France in the first decade of the 20th century. In England, the Aerial Derby introduced the spectacle of a race around London in the sky, and in 1922 the King's Cup air race further encouraged sporting aviation in the UK. The 1930s, despite the Great Depression, were known as the 'golden age' of US air racing. In 1970 the Formula One category—or class—of air racing was held in Britain (Isle of Man) for the first time, and this became the main class to be recognized in the international calendar by the Fédération Aéronautique Internationale.

aesthetics A branch of philosophy concerned initially, in German 18th-century philosophy, with the study of forms of understanding achieved by the senses and the intellect (the Greek *aisthetikos* means 'perceptive'). The new science, though, came to focus upon poetry and the arts, and the theme of beauty. Aesthetics has been applied widely to forms of performing arts, less so to the performative aspects of sport, though competitive sports based on the scoring of a performance (gymnastics, ice skating, diving, synchronized swimming) have been talked of with a superficial language of aesthetics; and specialist journals in the philosophy of sport have explored technical aspects of the performing sporting body from aesthetic points of view. A stimulating invitation to an aesthetics of sport is Hans Ulrich Gumbrecht's *In Praise of Athletic Beauty* (2006). The journal *Sport in History* dedicated a special issue (28/1, 2008) to responses to and debates with Gumbrecht.

aetiology The study of the causes of a medical condition, disorder, or disease. In sport science and sport medicine this can focus in specialist detail upon a particular sporting practice or physical action, and the unusual stress upon the body or particular parts of the body of that action.

AFC (Asian Football Confederation) Formed in 1954 with twelve founder members, the federation representing the national football (soccer) associations of Asia; the first president was Sir Man Kam-loh from Hong Kong. By 2007 the confederation had 46 member associations, and, as its official website claimed, represented 'over half of the world's football fans', 3.7 billion people, making it 'the most populous of FIFA's six federations' (for FIFA *see* FÉDÉRATION INTERNATIONALE DE FOOTBALL ASSOCIATION). As general secretary Peter Velappan wrote in 1996, the diversity of this membership has created huge challenges to a confederation comprising oil-rich states of the Gulf region, major economies ranging from Japan to China, and less well resourced and sometimes corruptly administered South-East Asian states—as well as five former Soviet republics which entered the confederation in the 1990s.

In its fiftieth year the AFC described football as 'Asia's unifying passion', confirming its commitment to the Asia Cup (for national teams) and the AFC Champions League, and confirming the implementation of its Vision Asia mission. An element in this mission was demonstrated in March 2007 when English football club Chelsea signed an agreement which, in Chelsea chief executive Peter Kenyon's words, 'fits with Chelsea's strategy of being recognized internationally by 2014 as the world's number one club. Achieving that is not possible without considering Asia in a serious and holistic way.' While the AFC could send young talent to train at the club, Chelsea could brand itself in the extensive Asian (including Chinese) market, anticipating unprecedented sales of club-related merchandise.

The headquarters of the AFC were moved to a purpose-built facility, AFC House, in Kuala Lumpur, Malaysia, in 2000. The president in 2007 was Mohamed bin Hammam of Qatar; the general secretary was Dato' Paul Mony Samuel of Malaysia, carrying on Malaysia's commitment to the AFC as represented in long-serving former general secretary Dato' Peter Velappan. Criteria of membership remain quite fluid; Israel is a member of the European federation, while Australia left Oceania to join the more competitive AFC (which also had more World Cup qualification places to compete for).

SEE WEB LINKS
- The official site of the AFC (Asian Football Confederation), including membership details, schedules, and statutes.

affect control The process, identified by Norbert Elias, whereby social constraints are brought to bear upon feelings, emotions, and associated behaviours. In the first volume of his *The Civilizing Process* (1939), subtitled 'the history of manners', Elias charted the developing inhibitions in social conduct that characterized the period in Western Europe of the emergence of the nation state and its accompanying bourgeois class: eating habits, sleeping conventions, urinating, and breaking wind were all subject to what Elias called 'the pattern of affect control' which regulated and transformed 'what must and must not be restrained': 'bourgeois society applies stronger restrictions to certain impulses'. In the sphere of sport, a range of examples from 19th-century Britain—from restrictions on bare-knuckle boxing to legislation against cruel animal sports, from moves against unrestrained violence in street football to the moral disapproval of frog-hunting by early public schoolboys—illustrates how forms of intervention and regulation combined with the internalization of more restraining forms of affect control, to reform and transform the boundaries of acceptability relating to bodily practices and the new formalized forms of sports and games-playing. *See also* CIVILIZING PROCESS; ELIASIAN.

African Nations Cup A football (soccer) tournament played every two years between national sides of the *Confédération Africaine de Football.

agency A term relating to the capacity of human beings—also often called actors, or agents—to determine their own lives and futures, rather than being merely the product of determining influences. People's sporting preferences, in whatever level of participation or spectatorship, might be understood as either the choices of particular individuals (an outcome of human agency) or as the product of influences beyond the control of the individual or a combination of the two. Agency is often discussed alongside structure, this latter being the source of determining influences. *See also* STRUCTURATION THEORY.

agents Representatives of sportsmen and -women, whose role is to negotiate contracts with employing clubs or commercial sponsors. The agent has come to have a notorious image in some sports, particularly those where television rights have generated unprecedentedly large revenues and players are transferred between clubs/teams and contracts, agents taking a substantial percentage of any transfer fee.

aggressiveness The disposition of offensiveness, in which a forceful approach to sporting encounter is adopted in contest and competitive play, but with no intent to harm or likelihood of harming another player or opponent. It is a term used in sport commentating in referring to the qualities of a winner, so that former Wimbledon champion John McEnroe can talk of a top player as unlikely to become a multi-champion if he plays a cautious game from the back of the court; in so doing, in lacking an 'aggressive game', such a player concedes the initiative to the braver opponent. Aggressive play can also be manifest in forms of *gamesmanship, such as the ways in which Muhammad Ali would verbally goad his boxing opponents before and during a fight; or cricketers can crowd around a batter and barrack the player.

aikido A form of Japanese martial art derived by Morihei Ueshiba (1883–1969), in part from the established and ancient principles of *ju-jitsu. The term comprises three elements: *ai*, meaning joining or harmonizing, *ki*, meaning life, energy, or spirit; and *do*, meaning way or path. It is translated as 'the path of the harmonious spirit', expressing the combination of the physical and the spiritual that characterizes much in Japanese physical culture. The key feature of the practice is that the defender responds by drawing in and upon the strength of the attacker, so redirecting the attacker's force against its source but also showing concern for the attacker; it specializes in training the practitioner to repel multiple attackers. The ideal outcome of an encounter in aikido is that neither the defending individual nor the attacker is harmed: quite an accomplishment given the presence of weapons such as short staffs, wooden swords, and knives. The stretching and warm-up exercises stress suppleness and balance, and the martial art is established in numerous training centres (*dojo*), particularly in the USA, France, Britain, and Australia, which were targeted by Ueshiba's disciples.

airplane racing *See* AEROPLANE RACING.

airsports An umbrella term for the sports of hang gliding and paragliding, and nine other disciplines that are included in the portfolio of the Fédération Aéronautique Internationale (FAI, established 1905 in France, based latterly in Lausanne, Switzerland). Hang gliding and paragliding became popular in the later 20th century, the first after US enthusiasts saw the potential of some wing technologies developed by scientists at the USA's space operations and research centre NASA (National Aeronautical and Space Administration). Paragliding took root in Europe but the two activities soon attracted worldwide participants. The two practices are serious commitments, and national associations do much in the way of training and health and safety preparation. Appealing to an age-old fantasy that humans might fly, they are also thoroughly modern activities in that their demands on time and money make them exclusive, undertaken in highly individualist and self-expressive fashion. The FAI also oversees aeromodelling, aerobatics, astronautic records, *ballooning, general aviation, *gliding, *microlights, *parachuting, and rotorcraft. In 2009, in Torino, Italy, the World Air Games generated a champion in each of these ten disciplines in what the governing body immodestly anticipated as the 'largest and most prestigious aviation event on the planet'.

alienation A concept describing the individual's separation from other individuals, or from a particular set of circumstances or conditions. Much of the debate on the concept refers to the writings of Karl *Marx, whose early writings of a markedly philosophical style and later economic analyses placed alienation at the centre of his work. One problem with the concept is the breadth of application of the term. Richard Schacht (*Alienation*, 1971) noted that in his early writings Marx employed the term 'in connection with a wide variety of things, including labor, the product, the senses, communal life and other men, and man himself'. This made difficulties for any specific application. Nevertheless, the notion of alienation linked to the labour process has suggested four forms of alienation that might be experienced by workers (Richard Kilminster, 'Alienation',

The Blackwell Dictionary Of Modern Social Thought, 2003). First, workers are alienated from their product, by the very fact that it is not theirs: in sport, consider how sport performers are bought and sold in the marketplace. Second, workers are alienated or estranged from their work itself, which might be forced upon them as little more than a means of survival: this may be less applicable to the sports sphere, as many declarations that 'I am paid for what I love doing' by sport professionals and sport journalists testify. Third, workers can be alienated from themselves, when their activity in work is not their own, or felt as their own: this feeling of self-estrangement can certainly develop in the disillusioned testimonies of athletes for whom sport-as-work has become a cross between routine and drudgery. Fourth, workers can become alienated from fellow workers, as each individual establishes his or her commodity value in the workplace: sport professionals are certainly vulnerable to this form of alienation, as they locate themselves in the financial hierarchy of the club or team's pay structure. Alienation is therefore a concept of persisting value to the social, psychological, and economic analysis of sport, in particular the nature of the sport worker's experience within the labour process and the sports industry.

al kora A traditional ball game played in North African Arab societies such as Morocco, Algeria, and Tunisia, where, as Allen Guttmann has noted, governments have supported the preservation of such traditional sports as a way of confirming local cultural identity in the context of increasing *globalization (*Sports: The First Five Millennia*, 2004). *Yalla nil'ab kora* translates, from the Arabic, as: 'let's play ball', cementing the language of tradition into the language of everyday life.

alterity From the Latin, alterity refers to difference, diversity, and otherness. In literary studies it has been a concept used in relation to the recognition of the possibility of dialogue, and the basis of the existence of the other in the dynamic of exchange. Postcolonial theory has used the concept to reinforce the position that there is always a 'possibility for potential dialogue between racial and cultural others' (P. Childs and R. J. P. Williams, *An Introduction to Post-Colonial Theory*, 1997). Where scholars have talked, in rather reductionist and often stereotyping fashion, of the difference in national styles of playing, it is more analytically useful to see respective sports and ways of playing as forms of culturally specific exchange and articulations of alterity. *See also* BRICOLAGE; CULTURAL DIFFUSION; HYBRIDITY.

alternative sports A term that has been loosely applied to forms of sports—or the way in which a particular activity is undertaken or sport played—that challenge the conventions or principles of an orthodox or dominant sporting form or practice. An example is *frisbee, which in its aesthetic and style represented many values in stark contrast to the claimed values and benefits of organized team games or competitive sporting competition; its stress on spontaneity, participation, inclusivity, and informality proved attractive to many, particularly the young. Alternative sports are sometimes equated with particular subcultures and lifestyles, as in the more general case of alternative subcultures that act in ways critical of and counter to the mainstream dominant culture. Alternative sports, though, are usually, if persistingly popular, commercialized and organized into competitive forms linked to expanding consumer markets—as in the case of *snowboarding.

altitude The vertical distance above sea level. Barometric pressure, temperature, and air resistance drop with altitude. The oxygen concentration of the air remains constant (20.93%) but because of the drop in barometric pressure the partial pressure of oxygen progressively drops from 159 mmHg at sea level to 52 mmHg at the summit of Everest (8850 m). At lower altitudes (below about 1700 m) the body is able to maintain oxygen supply because of the sigmoidal shape of the oxyhaemoglobin dissociation curve. At higher altitudes haemoglobin saturation begins to fall, less oxygen is transported to the active musculature, and physical performance declines. At the summit of Everest maximal oxygen consumption of a fit mountaineer is about 15 ml.kg.min or a quarter of the sea-level value. Short-duration athletic performance is not compromised by altitude since the energy source is predominantly *anaerobic. Indeed, the lower air density advantages sprinting and cycling.

The body adapts to altitude through a number of acute and chronic responses. Acute responses to maintain oxygen supply include an increased heart rate, and hyperventilation. Dehydration and an alkalosis result and at higher altitudes there is a risk of acute mountain sickness and pulmonary/cerebral oedema. In the longer term increases in red cell number and haemoglobin concentration improve oxygen transport, and acid–base balance is normalized. Acclimatization to altitude takes 2 to 6 weeks but does not fully restore function. Altitude training is widely used by endurance athletes for whom performance when competing at altitude is improved and some advantage at sea-level may also accrue.

altruism The kind of social act or behaviour that is motivated by disinterestedness, in which the consideration of others is of paramount importance. In sport, altruistic acts on the field of play counter a ruthless 'win-at-all-costs' approach, and in charity-based cases such as the London Marathon the individual competitive element is dwarfed by the voluntarist and participatory basis of the event.

amateurism The approach to the playing of sport that insisted that the game must be played for love rather than money (from the Latin, 'to love'), and according to a particular code of behaviour and conduct. Early definitions of amateurism in later 19th-century Britain—the earliest was related to *athletics, in 1866—were as much about exclusion, and forbade anyone who had accepted a prize in competition, or money, or had taught sport for remuneration, 'or is a mechanic, artisan or labourer' from participating in amateur events or joining an amateur association. The claims made on behalf of amateurism were articulated in many sports. Eustace Miles (*Let's Play the Game: The Anglo-Saxon Sporting Spirit*, 1904) claimed that cricket could illustrate eleven lessons for life: 'such valuable ideas as co-operation, division of labour, specialisation, obedience to a single organiser (perhaps with a council to advise him), national character, geography and its influences, arts and artistic anatomy, physiology and hygiene, ethics, and even—if the play can be learnt rightly—general educational methods'. Tony Mason (*Association Football and English Society, 1863–1915*, 1980) documents the arguments used by the amateur opponents of the professionalization of football (soccer): the nature of a voluntary leisure activity would be corrupted by turning it into a business; professionalism would undermine the survival of all but larger, wealthier clubs and so threaten local rivalries; professionalism would destroy amateurism because the latter would not be able to compete on equal terms; professionalism would produce an overemphasis on winning at any cost; the football professional was not really a 'professor' at all, having no teaching responsibilities.

The middle classes sought to defend the amateur code because it was 'good for the physique. It helped to build character, it perhaps led to diminution in drinking, it brought the classes together', wrote Mason. Some of these defences generated passionate responses. E. Ensor wrote, in 'The Football Madness' in *Contemporary Review* (November 1899), condemning the 'mighty influence' of the emerging professional form of football, and calling the competitive professional form 'thoroughly evil', its recruitment processes 'savouring of bribery and corruption'. Loretto school head H. H. Almond talked of the 'accursed money element' that threatened the sport of football: 'The football scrimmage is a great educator' that can 'foster that virtue which is most closely allied to purity, and without which no nation can be either great or truly prosperous; viz. the virtue of courage' (*Nineteenth Century*, 34, December 1993).

Definitions of the amateur were not all as explicitly excluding as the 1866 athletics one, but the amateur code was without doubt an expression of the privilege and dominance of a social class. Richard Holt, in an essay on 'Cricket and Englishness: The batsman as hero' (*International Journal of the History of Sport*, 1996), wrote of the amateur ideal which in its full-blown form combined 'older notions of honour and chivalry with an evangelical belief in the purity and moral purpose of competition and physical endeavour'. Amateurism's influence was long-term and widespread, the *International Olympic Committee not abolishing its insistence that Olympic athletes must be amateur until into the 1980s. Lincoln Allison (*Amateurism in Sport: An Analysis and a Defence*, 2001) has discussed the currency and applicability of the spirit of amateurism in the contemporary sporting world: he postulates the survival of a sporting culture not on any basis of class or privilege, but in a form sustaining the spirit of amateurism as a sporting activity in which what matters to the players 'on the field of play' continues to matter hugely to them, even if it is of no concern to anyone else. *See also* ATHLETICISM; CHARACTER BUILDING; FAIR PLAY; SHAMATEURISM.

ambush marketing The use of a sporting event to profile or advertise a brand or a business when that brand or business is not an official partner or approved sponsor of the event or the organization staging the event. Sponsorship of high-profile events such as the men's soccer World Cup, the Olympic Games (*see* OLYMPIC GAMES, MODERN (AS GLOBAL CULTURAL EVENT)), or the *UEFA Champions League (soccer) comes at a very high price, and organizations seek to guarantee their exclusive and chosen sponsors as full a profile as possible. Therefore organizers of such events condemn ambush marketing as unethical, and control and monitor the spaces of the events, even proposing that fans entering a stadium must not be admitted if their apparel bears the logo of a clothing company that is a rival of one of the approved sponsors. As the cost of sponsoring high-profile events rises, ambush marketing is a strategy considered by an increasing number of companies.

American College of Sports Medicine (ACSM) The national body in the
USA for the promotion of research into sport medicine and sport injuries. It was
founded in 1954, and established its National Center in Indianapolis in 1984. Its
mission is to promote and integrate 'scientific research, education, and practical
applications of sports medicine and exercise science to maintain and enhance
physical performance, fitness, health, and quality of life'. It is the largest
organization of its kind in the world, and holds an annual conference for its 20,000
regional, national, and international chapter members at which research into all
aspects of sport performance is presented by scientists from across the world.

(⊕) SEE WEB LINKS

• The official site of the ACSM, including its Health and Physical Activity Reference
  Database.

American exceptionalism Adapted from a political analysis of the USA's
foreign policy stances, and insightfully developed by Andrei S. Markovits, the notion
of American exceptionalism in sport highlights the cultural distinctiveness of the
Big 4 sports in USA *sport space, and the relative marginality of what is widely seen
as the world's most popular sport—soccer—in that sport space. Historian Eric
Hobsbawm (*Age of Extremes*, 1995) wrote that in 'the field of popular culture the
world was American or it was provincial' but with one exception: 'The unique
exception was sport'. The 'genuinely international' sport of (soccer) football
'made its way through the world entirely on its merits', but not in the USA. The
specifically US-based sports of American football, baseball, and basketball, and the
North American sport of ice hockey, did not become as widely adopted as soccer,
thus further supporting the notion of an American exceptionalism in the sphere
of sport. The analysis has been challenged by numerous theorists, and remains
controversial as a theory, in that in relation to sport it can be argued that *baseball
derived from *cricket, and it can be shown that football (soccer) is widely popular
in the USA, though occupying a different cultural space from that occupied by
the Big 4.

American Express A US company specializing in global financial services,
based in Manhattan, New York City, with a tradition of using celebrities in its
advertising campaigns. Founded in 1850, an arm of the Wells/Fargo name, it
dominated shipping and express businesses in the later 19th and early 20th
centuries, and when its near monopoly of the industry was ended by federal
government intervention, it moved into broader financial, travel, and insurance
services. Its primary global market became users of travellers' cheques, and then
credit and debit cards during phases of globalization matched by the explosion of
consumer culture. In 2007, *Business Week* and Interbrand ranked American Express
as the fourteenth most valuable brand in the world, estimating it to be worth
US$20.87 billion. Its brand has been sustained in award-winning advertising
campaigns featuring well-known individuals from popular culture—film, television,
and sport. The 'Don't leave home without it' slogan, coined in 1975 for its
advertisements for travellers' cheques, and then used for its credit cards, was one
that fitted the image of cosmopolitan, world-travelling sporting superstars such
as Spanish golfer Sevvy Ballesteros in the 1980s. The slogan was revived in 2005. In

a

2004 the company launched its 'My life. My card' campaign, again using sporting celebrities, including golfer Tiger Woods, Duke University basketball coach Mike Krzyzewski, snowboarder Shaun White, tennis players Venus Williams and Andy Roddick, and the then English soccer club Chelsea manager José Mourinho. The financial crisis of 2008 led to the company accepting federal support to bolster its finances, but its continuing image of individualist consumption blended with cosmopolitan glamour was a strong basis for the continuing impact and profile of its global brand.

American football An eleven-a-side field game played by men, with historical connections to *Rugby Union football and association *football. Some forms of football were played by students at Princeton, Yale, and Harvard in the first half of the 19th century, but playing the game on the public greens was banned by the college authorities at *Yale (1858) and *Harvard (1860). Columbia and Rutgers played the sport in the 1870s, when Harvard removed its ban. McGill (Montreal) also played rugby-style matches against Harvard. Different codes were played, veering between the rugby and what was to become the association form, and between teams of eleven or fifteen players. A meeting at Princeton in 1876 formed the Intercollegiate Football Association and adopted the rugby code. Yale's representative at that meeting was Walter C. Camp (1859–1925), who in 1880 began to change the form of the sport by introducing distinctive rules and a more developed tactical dimension to the play and strategic framework for preparation. The number of players was confirmed at eleven, the pitch size was reduced, and territorial dimensions were emphasized by marking the field with white lines at five-yard intervals, in order to clarify the new system of 'downs' that was introduced to vary possession. Looking like a gridiron (the parallel metal bars on which fish or meat is cooked over a fire), this gave the new sport its moniker: the 'gridiron game'. Camp also introduced the position of quarter-back, and a numerical scoring system; and in the 1880s the signalling of planned 'plays' was introduced.

By the beginning of the 20th century the game had become established nationally across the USA's college system. American football could be rough, and eighteen players died in the 1905 season, prompting the president of the country, Theodore *Roosevelt, to intervene and tell representatives of Yale, Harvard, and Princeton, invited to the White House, that the sport must be reformed. At the end of that year 28 colleges met in New York City to form the forerunner of the *National Collegiate Athletic Association, and a rules committee for regulation and reform of the game. The following year the forward pass was introduced, thus changing the cadence and pace of the sport in territorial terms. It is widely acknowledged that American football has become the most specialized team sport, and commentators have noted it as a case of the application in sport of Frederick W. Taylor's *scientific management. The professional form of the sport developed in tandem with the collegiate form during the 1920s. Professional games had been played from the 1890s, mainly on the east coast, and in 1919 an American Professional Football Association, precursor of the National Football League (NFL, 1922), was established, and the game began to spread to Chicago, and across the Midwest. Eastern and Western divisions were established in 1933, the national champion being decided in a one-off title match between the divisional champions, a principle underlying the initiation of the *Super Bowl in 1967.

The position of the NFL was challenged in 1960 by Texan Lamar Hunt (1932–2006), who established a rival American Football League (AFL) that struggled initially but then secured lucrative television revenue from the National Broadcasting Company (NBC) and initiated a star system in signings and recruitment. The merger between the two leagues in 1966 preceded the inauguration of the Super Bowl, and in 1970 the League divided into the National and the American Conferences, which provided the Super Bowl contestants. An important source of connection between the college game and the professional game has been the *draft system, which began in 1936; the bottom team of the professional league was given first choice in recruitment of players graduating from college. Weak teams could therefore build on the basis of recruitment and trading, and re-establish competitive strength. The system was also adopted by *basketball.

American football has been introduced into other countries but with limited impact, though transnational enterprises continue to search for global markets for the sport, as the fixtures of the NFL outside the USA have shown; in 2005, 103,467 attended Arizona Cardinals versus San Francisco 49ers in Mexico City. In October 2007, the Miami Dolphins played the New York Giants at Wembley Stadium, London, in the first regular season NFL match to be played outside North or Central America. NFL owners had voted to play up to two games outside the country per season, for the five years from 2007 to 2012. NFL commissioner Roger Goodell claimed that 'the international popularity' of the sport grows year on year, as 'the far corners of the world watch Super Bowl'. But in Britain, the short-lived sporting lives of the London Monarchs and the Scottish Claymores showed that a one-off spectacle of the world's best was a different, more attractive, and more lucrative proposition compared to watching lesser performers in routine schedules. In its home territory of the USA, the gridiron game has been supported by the state, as well as indirectly but essentially by the college system; the teams play relatively few competitive matches in the seasonal calendar, yet a short life expectancy has been reported for numerous players. The distinctiveness of the institutional character of the sport in the USA may go some way to accounting for its failure to develop a worldwide playing or participatory base. *See also* AMERICAN EXCEPTIONALISM; NORTH DALLAS FORTY.

(⊕) SEE WEB LINKS

• The official site of the National Football League, replete with statistics and minutiae on the game.

America's Cup A challenge competition for racing yachts, in which (from 1970) eliminating rounds have been followed by a one-to-one race between the challenger and the holder of the Cup, held 33 times from its inauguration to 2009–10. The race is named after the schooner yacht *America*, launched in 1851, sailing across the Atlantic and defeating British yachts in the event's first ever race at the Isle of Wight, England, the same year, and seen by sailing historians as the most important and influential single vessel in the development of yachting. The Cup itself was donated in 1857 to the New York Yacht Club by the syndicate that had built *America*. Britain and Canada were the only challengers until 1962 for a trophy dominated by the New York Club until 1983, when Australian yacht *Australia II* defeated the US holder of the title. The USA regained the title through the four-time winner the San Diego Yacht Club, after which New Zealand took the trophy on two occasions before losing to a Swiss challenger backed by a pharmaceutical billionaire. The America's Cup is not just a race; it has always been a stage for the display of a combination of national pride and entrepreneurial flair. The leader of New Zealand's two victories, Peter Blake (1948–2001), was knighted by the British and anointed by the British press as its own national hero, in interesting elisions of national belonging comparable to the British response to the ascent of Everest by New Zealander Edmund *Hillary; Blake's death—he was murdered by Brazilian pirates when on an expedition concerned with environmental exploration—was a tragic reminder that the oceans are more than the playgrounds of the rich.

anabolic steroids A group of synthetic steroid hormones used by competitive athletes to aid performance. Anabolic steroids have a range of medical uses including treatment of patients with hormone deficiencies, muscle-wasting diseases, old age, and osteoporosis. Their broad effect is similar to that of *testosterone, the male sex hormone. Anabolic steroids cause an increase in muscle mass and strength along with masculinizing characteristics. The increased aggression ('road rage'), competitiveness, fatigue resistance, and faster rate of recovery associated with steroid use allow an increased volume of training. Anabolic steroids do not improve *aerobic power. Use of anabolic steroids is associated with a number of side effects and, since the dosage used by athletes may be from ten to one hundred times the normal medical prescription, the risk is considerable. Liver function is particularly vulnerable since the liver is the site where the hormones are metabolized. In men testicular atrophy can arise since the exogenous provision suppresses normal endogenous production and infertility results. Also in men there is a growth of the breasts (gynaecomastia) and in women increased facial hair and a deepening of the voice. Psychological risks include increased aggression, and depression when use stops.

In most sports anabolic steroid use is considered to confer an unfair advantage and their use is banned on ethical grounds by the sports governing body. In some countries possession of anabolic steroids is illegal. Scientific understanding of how anabolic steroids affect sports performance, and the risks involved, is imprecise because their illegal or unethical use has limited well-controlled scientific experimentation. Steroid use in sport first developed in the 1960s. Increasingly widespread use through this decade and the next was accompanied by concerns over side effects and debate about the fundamental ethics of performance-enhancing substance use in sport. In particular widespread use by Eastern bloc countries, covertly supported by official agencies, led to considerable concern in sports agencies. As a result 'drug testing' through analysis of urine samples began to be developed. The complexities involved in collecting and assaying urine samples, combined with the continual development of effective but new and subtly different chemical analogues of steroids which were not detectable by existing assay techniques, have resulted in a continuing skirmish between sports administrators and athletes seeking a performance edge.

anaerobic Anaerobic, literally without oxygen, energy pathways are of two main forms. In the first form, phosphate bond energy from adenosine triphosphate (ATP) and cricopharyngeal muscle (CP) is utilized for muscle contraction in the very short term (a matter of seconds). In the second form, the anaerobic glycolytic pathway metabolizes glucose in the absence of oxygen. Energy is captured in the phosphate bonds of ATP and lactic acid produced as an end product. Anaerobic systems have high power (measured as the rate of ATP per second). Peak power output will be many times the maximal *aerobic power. But the capacity for anaerobic energy generation is very limited since the total amount of ATP-CP in the body amounts to just a few grams and the acid conditions resulting from anaerobic glycolysis inhibit continued catabolism of glucose and muscular contraction. Maximal anaerobic capacity is drained with a minute or so of maximal intensity exercise.

anaerobic threshold A measure of exercise intensity around 50 to 60 per cent of the maximal aerobic power which indicates the intensity at which exercise can continue for a fairly lengthy period of time, about 45 to 60 minutes. At this intensity a 'steady state' can be achieved. Metabolic rate is around ten times the resting level, heart rate around 150 bpm, and blood lactate concentration below about 4 mmol.L-1. Broadly, the rate of energy use is in equilibrium with the rate of aerobic energy production. Exercise at this intensity is only limited by other factors such as temperature regulation, the size of carbohydrate fuel stores, and central nervous system regulation. At higher intensities, although aerobic energy production can increase further, it cannot increase in proportion to the energy demand and anaerobic glycolysis becomes progressively important, limiting how long exercise can be sustained.

The concept of the anaerobic threshold has been subject to considerable research and debate since it was first identified (Owle's point) in the 1940s. Numerous names have found favour, including the lactate threshold, critical power, the ventilatory threshold, the ventilator breakpoint, the aerobic threshold, the lactate turnpoint, and the onset of blood lactate accumulation (OBLA). These names derive from either the experimental method by which they are determined or the theoretical construct to which they are linked. For a review, see Jones, A. M., Vanhatalo, A. T., and Doust, J. (2008), 'Aerobic Exercise Performance', in R. G. Eston and T. Reilly, eds, *Kinanthropometry and Exercise Physiology Laboratory Manual: Tests, Procedures and Data*, vol. 2, 3rd edn, London: Routledge.

anatomical movements A number of terms are used to help describe the movement of the major joints of the body. The terms can be used with precision although, because movement is occurring in a three-dimensional space, precise use requires identification of dimensional axes and planes. More commonly the terms are used with greater regard to practical meaning than anatomical theory and a selection of terms can provide a reasonable description of most movements. Terms are usually paired to distinguish movement in one direction from the reverse. Flexion is a movement that decreases the angle between the body part and the adjacent segment (e.g. the upper and lower arm). Extension is the reverse movement. Hyper-extension, extending the limb beyond its normal range, is possible at some joints and well illustrated in gymnasts and swimmers. Abduction is the movement of a body part upward and away from the midline (e.g. the arm at the shoulder). Adduction is the reverse. Plantar flexion refers to the ankle joint and is the movement of pointing the toes down. Dorsiflexion is the opposite. Inversion refers to turning the soles of the foot inwards so the soles point towards each other. Eversion is the opposite. Rotation is the twisting of a bone around its own long axis and this may be medial rotation (inwards, towards the midline) or lateral rotation (outwards, away from the midline). Elevation refers to the movement of a body part upwards and depression the reverse, such as the shrugging of the shoulders. Circumduction is a movement that combines flexion–extension–abduction–adduction so the end of a limb or bone moves in a circle.

androcentrism The inclination towards male bias in institutions and organizations, and towards an undervaluation or marginalization of the contribution of women. The history of male sporting institutions and the slow pace at which gender-based inequalities have been eroded in policy and provision testify to the androcentric nature of the culture of modern sport. *See also* FEMINISM; MASCULINITY; SEXISM.

angling The sport of catching fish with a rod and a hook. Well established in Britain by the later Middle Ages, angling was a leisure activity of the landed elite and also for urban merchants, and a form of supplement for the diets of the working class (John Lowerson, 'Angling', in T. Mason, ed., *Sport in Britain: A Social History*, 1989). The angler has been romanticized in various literary writings, from Izaak *Walton's *The Compleat Angler* in the 1650s to George *Orwell's menopausal protagonist Fatty Bowling in *Coming Up for Air* (1939) in the English tradition. Angling as a leisure pursuit expanded during the period of industrialization and urbanization. Wealthier classes fished and competed in game waters stocked with trout and salmon; other freshwater fish were collectively labelled coarse fish. In late Victorian Britain, sea fishing was established, the mainly middle-class British Sea Anglers' Society being established in 1893. Working-class clubs had grown and prospered in urban centres in the last quarter of the 19th century, particularly centred on the city of Sheffield in Yorkshire: as Lowerson observes, 'the sport's popularity grew in a world of male bonding, of workplace and street-life relationships focused on small pubs'.

The different forms of the sport have waned in profile and popularity in relation to national emergencies such as war or economic crisis, but the social distinctions in which the sport was anchored have persisted: it has been overwhelmingly male, and 'few recreational spaces have been as socially zoned as riverbanks', adds Lowerson. Claims concerning the participation rates should be carefully scrutinized: reporting the National Angling Survey of 1980, Lowerson wrote that there were 3,380,000 anglers in England and Wales, and 354,000 in Scotland; in 2005, though, Sport England's survey of sport participation reported a mere 281,083 anglers in England. Whatever the discrepancies in survey methods or data analysis, the decrease in anglers indicated an erosion of traditional male, and particularly working-class, sporting forms.

anomie A state of normlessness, in which individuals are neither rooted in traditional values and collective relationships, nor have adapted to new values in

a

unfamiliar social and cultural settings. The term was used in Greek writings (*anomos* meant 'lawless') and the sociological notion was developed in the works of French sociologist Émile *Durkheim, often associated with social breakdown and crisis. In *The Division of Labour in Society* (1893) Durkheim wrote that the 'state of anomie' is a condition in which the 'entire sphere of collective life is for the most part removed from the moderating action of any rules': in the absence of moral presence or authority, Durkheim added, anarchy may ensue. Anomie is a powerful concept for contextualizing and accounting for the growth of sporting clubs and associations in situations of cultural transition and social change: Irish Catholic football supporters in late 19th-century Manchester, Polish immigrants' sport and leisure groups in post-World War II Britain, and black Caribbean cricketing groups in the 1950s and 1960s in England are just some of the sporting groups whose formation can be seen as a positive collective response to a condition of anomie.

anorexia nervosa *See* EATING DISORDERS.

Anquetil, Jacques (1934–87) A French professional road-racing cyclist, born in Normandy, whose dominance in the sport in the late 1950s and early 1960s was combined with an unorthodox personal life and an honesty about his training methods. He was the first rider to win the *Tour de France five times, four times in succession from 1961 to 1964, often gaining his advantages in the shorter, sprint-like time trials. With blonde hair and blue eyes Anquetil had the look of a playboy and the concomitant lifestyle, arriving at his competitive venues at the wheel of a sports car. He drank alcohol and smoked, and was clear about his preparatory methods, stating that 'You can't ride the Tour de France on mineral water'; French president de Gaulle brushed aside questions about doping, noting the national significance of Anquetil's achievements, and that he got the Marseillaise played in other countries. Anquetil's private life included fathering children by his stepdaughter, and by the wife of his stepson. Retiring in 1969, he farmed and worked as a newspaper correspondent, radio broadcaster, and race director. His continuing work was illustrative of both his achievement and popularity, and the less invasive nature of mediated celebrity, particularly in a French context in which the public and the private were seen as separate dimensions of an individual's life.

anthropometry The scientific study of the size, shape, and structure of the human body as it relates to movement. Kinanthropometry is often used as an alternative term with the 'kin' emphasizing movement. The measurement of body shape and fatness formed the foundation of the subject. The founding of the International Society for the Advancement of Kinanthropometry (ISAK) in 1986 helped establish standards of measurement and a wider academic perspective. Modern anthropometry includes consideration of physical growth, maturation, body image, and physical activity as well as developing the measurement of body composition and handling of data. *See* BODY COMPOSITION.

anxiety An emotional state of apprehension, worry, or dread usually accompanied by physical symptoms such as restlessness, fast heart rate, changes in breathing, excessive sweating, and 'butterflies' in the stomach. Anxiety therefore has two components—the mental component (cognitive anxiety) and the physical component (somatic anxiety). Anxiety is also further conceptualized into state and trait components. State anxiety refers to the level of anxiety at any moment in time, a level that may change continuously throughout a competitive sports match such as football—rising, for example, when taking a penalty but lowering during a steady period of mid-field play. Trait anxiety refers to a fundamental part of the personality of an individual and the extent to which an individual is predisposed to perceive a particular circumstance as worrying. For example, a football player with a high trait anxiety is likely to show a higher level of state anxiety to the challenge of a penalty kick than a player with a low trait anxiety. Although anxiety is usually considered to negatively affect performance, an individual's interpretation of anxiety symptoms is also important since they may be interpreted as harmful to performance (debilitating) or as helpful to performance (facilitating). Sports psychologists have developed a number of techniques to help control anxiety, such as self-talk, *imagery, or focused breathing exercises.

apartheid This Afrikaans word means 'apartness' or 'separateness'. It became the label for the official government policy of racial segregation in South Africa from 1948 to 1989. It was a legislative confirmation of the racist principles and beliefs of the white government. Legislation from 1948 to 1950 prohibited mixed marriage, regulated and registered populations and districts and regions, reformed educational programmes, and suppressed political dissidence. Sport teams were already segregated, black sportsmen overlooked and ignored. As Sam Ramsamy noted ('Apartheid, Boycotts and the Games', in Tomlinson & Whannel *Five Ring Circus*, 1984): 'South Africa's first participation in the Olympics was in London in 1908. Since then, it has participated in all the Games up to 1960. The South African National Olympic Committee was exclusively white right through to its final expulsion in May 1970. Blacks were never given the opportunities nor the facilities to train for Olympic participation.' Clearly, then, apartheid was consolidating a system of discrimination, formalizing an already well-entrenched racist ideology. When South Africa became a republic in 1961, its racial laws were tightened and there were even fewer possibilities for black sportsmen and -women. In the early 1970s South Africa had separate administrative bodies for Indian soccer, African soccer, coloured soccer, non-racial soccer, and white soccer, the latter claiming to be the recognized voice in the international soccer arena. This was, in Mihir Bose's words (*Sporting Colours*, 1994), 'a unique South African Solution: a wonderfully abnormal sporting solution for an abnormal society'.

Apartheid generated international disgust and organized protest, including *boycotts of the Olympics by Black African countries (twenty withdrew from the 1978 Montreal Olympics), and the expulsion of South Africa from international sports (following Montreal, from athletics, swimming, and soccer). The anti-apartheid movement involved activists and egalitarians worldwide, bolstered by the Gleneagles Declaration of 1977 in which Commonwealth countries condemned 'the evil of apartheid' and called for the excommunication of South Africa from all international sporting arenas. Sportsmen—cricket was prominent in this—were offered high levels of remuneration to tour South Africa on official or 'rebel' tours or engagements, and sport became the focus for the debate about the injustices of the apartheid regime. Although the term apartheid was rejected by the incoming prime minister, P. W. Botha, in 1978, the legislative unravelling of the system took almost another decade and a half. The scars of apartheid still taint South Africa's sport, in which the legacy of the policy of enforced separateness continues to influence if not wholly shape the profile of the country's sporting institutions and culture.

aquafit   A combination of swimming and exercise in which the principles of *aerobics are applied in water. The aquatic setting provides a context for fitness, fun, and therapy that has made the activity popular among exercisers of all ages, especially, in the organized context of health and exercise clubs, women.

Arc de Triomphe, Prix de l'   France's most prestigious horse race, run over one and a half miles at Longchamp, Paris. First run in 1920, it takes place in October. In 2007, the Qatar Racing and Equestrian Club signed a five-year partnership contract with the Arc, and this racing classic became known as the 'Qatar Arc de Triomphe'.

archery   The practice of shooting arrows at a target from a bow. The practice was integral to the military effectiveness of innumerable ancient societies, and to the military strategies of European societies into the Middle Ages. The use of gunpowder in warfare superseded archery, and archery was maintained thereafter as a recreational practice; the archery meetings that had previously had a military rationale turned, in the 16th century in various countries in mainland Europe, into 'major urban festivals, combining a number of different sports with pageants, banquets, dances, drunkenness, buffoonery, and the randy pleasures of illicit sex' (Allen Guttmann, *Sports: The First Five Millennia*, Amherst, University of Massachusetts Press, 2004, p. 60). Such festivals might also be linked to religious occasions, or the celebration of royal marriages. Societies of recreational archers flourished in the 18th century, in Scotland and England. In the 19th century, in England and the USA, the sport was a middle- and upper-class activity, and in some discontinued forms featured in several early Olympic Games. The UK organizing body, the Grand National Archery Society, was founded in 1861.

The Fédération Internationale de Tir à l'Arc (FITA) was founded in 1931, in Poland, by seven countries: France, the Czech Republic, Sweden, Poland, the USA, Hungary, and Italy. It is based in Lausanne, Switzerland. Archery was reintroduced into the Olympic programme from 1972. Feeling its place in the programme under threat, FITA evolved a strategy for 2007 to 2011 called 'The Connection', to simplify and unify the identity of international archery, to connect more strongly with its partners, to make its events more attractive to spectators, to strengthen financial partnerships, and to sustain international expansion. These five targets reflected the pressure that traditional, low-profile sports have come under in the age of media and sponsorship influences, and a multimedia age of consumer selectivity in which new generations of sport fans can pick and choose according to taste, regardless of the traditions of an event or a particular sports discipline.

archival sources Sources of research data in which documents and artefacts have been saved, collected, and/or classified. Archives can range from modest collections of unique documentation (such as that of individual sporting entrepreneurs or athletes) to highly formalized collections (such as the files of meetings and correspondence of the International Olympic Committee, housed in the Olympic Museum in Lausanne, Switzerland; or the collection of Olympic Games posters collected and classified in the Victoria and Albert Museum, London, UK). Care must be taken by the researcher to authenticate the archival source, or locate corroborating data or evidence. Finding a unique archival source is the dream of the sport historian, but careful scrutiny is still essential to contextualize such sources alongside complementary sources of data and alternative accounts or bodies of evidence.

SEE WEB LINKS

- The online resource of *The Times* newspaper.
- The Times Digital Archive 1785–1985, available on personal subscription, and at subscribing libraries, including public libraries in the UK.
- The archives section of the official website of the BBC (British Broadcasting Corporation).
- A database provided by the British Library on sport research, and some sport-related collections including football fanzines.
- Web guidance on the British Library's newspaper collection at Colindale, London.

argot A use of words or way of speaking distinctive to a particular group or *subculture, constituting a specialist form of language and communication. Becoming familiar with a sporting argot is a sign of the introduction of an individual into the inner circles or layers of the sporting subculture. An argot may be developed—by ticket touts (or, in US terminology, scalpers)—in ways not understood by their potential clients, an extreme case of the way in which an argot is designed to be excluding, and so confirming the insider status of its users.

arousal A heightened state of psychological and physical activation. The state of arousal lies on a continuum and is an intensity of activation; towards one end would lie sleep, to the other end would lie intense agitation. It is generally believed that the level of arousal influences the level of sports performance and the relationship between the two has been subject to considerable investigation by sports psychologists. A number of theories have been proposed. Initial recognition was given to drive theory, which proposed that as arousal increases so does sports performance. The inverted U-theory based on the work of Yerkes and Dodson proposed an optimum level of arousal for peak sports performance with diminished performance in states of low or high arousal. The optimal level of arousal is associated with ideal physiological function (such as muscle force production and coordination) and ideal psychological function (such as attention and concentration). The optimal level will vary according to the individual athlete and the specific sports task. The catastrophe theory of Hardy linked physiological arousal and cognitive anxiety, predicting that in states of high anxiety there is a threshold in the level of arousal needed for peak performance and just beyond this optimal arousal level there will be a sharp decline—a catastrophe—in

performance. Kerr applied reversal theory to sports performance to draw out
the importance of the individual's interpretation of the level of arousal, not just the
level per se, and to show that this interpretation can reverse between a positive
and a negative one from moment to moment. As with *anxiety, sports psychologists
have developed a number of techniques to help the athlete achieve an optimal
level of arousal.

arrogation The process whereby a cultural product or ideal, such as 'Olympism',
has attributed to it meanings that are not contained within the core principles of
the ideal. As Alan Tomlinson (*Sport and Leisure Cultures*, 2005) has argued:
'allegedly universal values such as the "Olympic ideal" are reworked in different
times and places, necessarily arrogated, as particular histories and cultures are
brought to bear in the restating of the ideal'. In this process, too, 'values are
inevitably reshaped, while being claimed as preserved'. For example, although each
Olympic host city claims to sustain and even enhance the core ideals of Olympism,
it articulates in its own rhetoric and symbolism its own purportedly unique
contribution to the Olympic project; and, simultaneously, the Olympic moment
allows the telling of a particular metropolitan, regional, or national history.
Somehow, the uniqueness never threatens the core values of the Olympic message:
that is the art of the (necessary) process of arrogation, a process that makes the
predictable sporting spectacle sufficiently distinctive to attract both those wishing to
host it and the audiences upon which the future of such events ultimately depends.

ascribed and achieved status An individual's position in a culture and
society is the outcome of a combination of ascribed status characteristics—physical
features, age, sex, ethnicity—and achieved status that might be gained through
education or competition with others. Competitive sport, understood as an open
meritocratic field of human endeavour, is by such definition a field in which
achieved status is gained as a consequence and form of personal accomplishment.
Yet in some sports—basketball is an obvious example—physical qualities are an
important determining dimension in the career trajectory of the athlete; and in
historical terms, some sports have been used as markers of a particular given status
(ascribed and inflexible) reinforcing, for instance, divisions of social class and
gender.

Ashe, Arthur (1943–93) An African-American born in Richmond, Virginia, USA,
who showed precocious tennis talent from the age of 8. He attended UCLA
(University of California Los Angeles) on a tennis scholarship (where he graduated
in business administration) and at the age of 20 was the first black player to
represent the USA in the *Davis Cup. In 1968 he won the US Open, and in the
same year delivered a speech in Washington DC against racism, and spoke out in
protest against South Africa's *apartheid system. A late flowering of his competitive
career won him the Wimbledon title in London, England, in 1975 and in the
early 1980s he took on the leadership and coaching of the US Davis Cup team.
    Retiring from the professional game, Ashe undertook a variety of reformist and
philanthropic initiatives, even as, in 1988, he had to have brain surgery in an
operation in which a blood transfusion resulted in him getting the AIDS virus.
He hid the fact of this condition from the public for several years, founding a

programme for deprived black youngsters, and visiting Nelson Mandela in South Africa (1991). When the newspaper *USA Today* threatened to run with the revelation that Ashe, vulnerable in part through a heart problem, had AIDS, he announced, in April 1992, the nature of his condition, and founded the Arthur Ashe Aids Foundation before dying of the illness just ten months later.

Ashe also acted as a tennis broadcaster, occasional newspaper columnist, and university teacher. One offer was forthcoming from Yale University, but Ashe chose to offer a course at what he himself called 'Yale's polar opposite: Florida Memorial College (FMC), a historically black school of some twelve hundred students'. His experience there prompted him to instigate the production of the three-volume *A Hard Road to Glory: A History of the African-American Athlete* (1988), on which he spent $300,000 of his personal money; and to campaign to raise standards of education for US university athletes. His activism and his use of his sport 'as a way to gain and hold the attention of young people in the inner cities and other poor environments so that we could then teach them about matters more important than tennis' (*Days of Grace: A Memoir*, by Ashe and Arnold Rampersad, 1993) marked Ashe out as a thinking and reflective sport star of the modern period, for whom sport was a form of cultural politics and personal growth, success in which both embodied opportunity and generated social responsibility.

Asian Football Confederation *See* AFC.

Asian Games A multi-sport event staged every four years for national teams of athletes, alternating with the Olympic Games, and featuring Olympic disciplines and a wider range of characteristic Asian sports. They have been organized since 1951, first by the Asian Amateur Athletic Federation, then by the Olympic Council of Asia.

Asian Nations Cup The competition held every two years between national soccer sides that are members of the *AFC (Asian Football Confederation). The dominant teams in the history of the tournament have been South Korea, Saudi Arabia, and Japan, though an extraordinary result in 2007 saw Iraq win the title.

asset stripping The purchase of organizations or institutions or infrastructure with the intent of selling off most of the assets for a swift *profit, and either keeping the core resource or moving into another sphere of business for profit maximization. In sport, saviours who profess their love of a sport for a club and then use it to profiteer or diversify are in essence asset strippers.

assimilation A process, often noted in inter-ethnic and inter-racial relations, in which the marginal, minority, or subordinate group adapts to the culture of the dominant group(s), and abandons or loses the characteristics of its own culture. In sport, the attempt by the apostles of *rational recreation to reform the sporting culture of the urban working class in 19th-century Britain was a strategy of assimilation: get these people to play the games of their betters and they will be integrated into the overall society. The neutral-sounding language of assimilation, though, masks a process of incorporation, in which the sporting practices of the subordinate group—or the distinctive sporting culture of the immigrant

group—are morally condemned, socially disapproved of, and culturally and
politically undermined.

association football *See* FOOTBALL, ASSOCIATION.

associativity The principle of association by which people act in collective,
self-organized ways in organizing their cultural life. Associativity is a crucial element
in *civil society. French political scientist Alexis de Tocqueville (*Democracy in
America*, 1840) observed that Americans formed 'a thousand different types' of
associations for all aspects of civil life, and saw 'the art of association' as central
to a civilized and democratic life. English cultural and political critic George *Orwell
commented, in his essay 'The Lion and the Unicorn' (1940), on an English fixation
with 'hobbies and spare-time occupations' that reflected what he called the
'privateness' of English life, but not a closed individualist approach to life. Orwell
called the English 'a nation of flower-lovers, but also a nation of stamp-collectors,
pigeon fanciers, amateur carpenters, coupon snippers, darts-players, crossword-
puzzle fans'. He added that 'truly native' English culture is immersed in activities
that 'are communal but not official'—such as in the domestic garden or fireside,
or the pub or the football match. This is associativity without interference, an
expression of the individual right to construct 'your own amusements'.

  More generally, Stefan Szymanski has argued that modern sport developed out
of new forms of associativity created during the European Enlightenment. For
Szymanski, the club is the fundamental unit of modern sport; these club-based
associations 'developed autonomously in Britain during the eighteenth century
following the retreat of the state from the control of associative activities. The
evolution of modern sports thus formed part of the expansion of private associative
activity that occurred in the Anglo-Saxon world.' Szymanski contrasts this process
with the situation in countries such as France and Germany where 'associativity
continued to require the explicit or implicit license of the state', often fitting the
'objectives of the state, most notably the need to maintain military preparedness'.

AT&T Corporation The giant US telephone and communications company
that in 1982 was announced, in the words of Peter Ueberroth, president of the Los
Angeles Olympic Organizing Committee, as 'the official sponsor of the 1984
Olympic torch relay'. Ueberroth saw AT&T as having 'the depth, reach, and
nationwide network of affiliates unmatched by any other company' that would be
needed to promote and sell the idea of a torch relay across the USA. Ueberroth
recalled after the Games that 'Jerry Foster, regional vice-president of Pacific Bell,
the western affiliate of AT&T, was wild about the relay and convinced AT&T
executives in New York to sponsor it'. As the Los Angeles committee was negotiating
with the company, a US federal judge, in an antitrust lawsuit, ordered that AT&T
be deregulated, and broken up. In fact, going through with the relay sponsorship
allowed AT&T to retain its national brand throughout the restructuring process.
Greek Olympic officials had opposed this sponsorship of the Olympic flame, calling
it an unacceptable form of commercialization. But the International Olympic
Committee (IOC) accepted the proposal when informed that all the projected
$10 million raised by charging for individual runners' participation would go to
charities of their choice in the community. This was a pivotal moment in the history

of sport sponsorship, showing how an individual corporate brand could generate almost immeasurable exposure while the purported ideals of the Olympic spirit were enhanced rather than jeopardized. AT&T provided and paid for vehicles, maintenance, and manpower, and a squad of runners to carry the torch when no local runners or donors could be found. The IOC learned much from the Los Angeles case, and by the year following the LA Games had initiated its own sponsorship scheme, TOP (The *Olympic Programme).

athlete The term that was used, in Greek ('āthlētēs') and in Latin ('athleta') versions, for the contender for a prize at the public games of ancient Greece and Rome. In the 19th century it came to mean a physically developed performer of feats of physicality and strength. Gradually, the term developed in the USA and in other modern societies as the generic term for the individual sportsman or -woman, who through talent and/or training, whatever the sport, focuses upon the competitive experience; so that the term 'student athletes', in USA college sports parlance, refers to high-level participants in any activity, from swimming to equestrianism, American football to track-and-field.

athleticism A term describing the belief that sport and physical activity, and team games in particular, have character-building capacities. As a *belief system or an *ideology it emerged from the reformed physical education curricula of British public schools in the 19th century. J. A. Mangan's *Athleticism in the Victorian and Edwardian Public School: The Emergence and Consolidation of an Educational Ideology* (Cambridge, 1981) is the classic study of athleticism, and identifies four educational goals at the core of an ideology premised on the belief that physical activity could cultivate moral values: the goals were to foster (i) moral and physical courage, (ii) loyalty and cooperation, (iii) the capacity to act fairly and take defeat well, and (iv) the ability to both command and obey. As an idealized set of values, athleticism influenced *amateurism, and the origins of the modern Olympic Games (*see* OLYMPIC GAMES, MODERN (AS GLOBAL CULTURAL EVENT); OLYMPIC GAMES, MODERN (HISTORY OF THE SUMMER GAMES, 1896–2008)). Many contemporary appeals to the core values of sport echo the spirit and principles of athleticism. The United Kingdom's Conservative government, for instance, in its 1995 policy document *Raising the Game*, claimed that sport could teach lessons about competition that lasted for life, show how to be both a winner and loser and play by the rules and accept the outcome 'with good grace', demonstrate how to live with others via the experience of being in a team, improve health, and create friendships. In the harshest of competitive settings in modern professional sport, athleticist values remain relevant to the sporting agenda.

athletics The form of organized sport, based in running, throwing, and jumping, that emerged in the 19th century in Britain and the USA (where it became known as track-and-field), and superseded traditional forms of rural-based competitive activity of comparable types. Forms of athletics existed in organized physical contests and performance in earlier and ancient societies, most notably in Greece, where regular physical contest and display, including the ancient *Olympic Games, comprised a mix of bodily performance, religious observance, and military mimicry: 'a Platonic essence of athletics in ancient Greece . . . approximates as closely as possible to the tumult of battle stations', writes Spivey (2004: 24) of the *Pyrrhichê*, an armed dance practised in Athens by men carrying spears and shields.

In Britain, the Amateur Athletic Club was formed in 1866, staging the first organized athletics championship of the modern period, and formulating an influential definition of the amateur athlete, as: 'Any person who has never competed in open competition, or for public money, or for admission money, or with professionals for a prize, public money or admission money, and who has never, at any period of his life, taught or assisted in the pursuit of athletic exercises as a means of livelihood, or is a mechanic, artisan or labourer'. This definition was soon loosened and a more general definition identified the amateur as a 'gentleman who has never competed'. The notion of the club was central to this development, countering the competitive individualism of *pedestrianism. Clubs were formed by privileged males from the public schools, universities, professions, and business. In 1880, three former *Oxford University athletes founded the Amateur Athletic Association (AAA, pronounced 'three As'), which revoked the 'gentleman' clause, but was to consistently oppose professionalism; in 1883 and 1899 respectively, it excluded from its membership professionals from cricket and football, and pursued legal action, for fraud, against anyone breaching its ban. The AAA became the dominant force in the growth of athletics in England. In 1899 it authorized payment of travel expenses to athletes, and by the 1920s the gentleman amateur dominated British athletics.

Women's athletics had emerged in the USA at the turn of the 19th and 20th centuries, and the first national governing body for women's athletics had been set up in France in 1917. The first women's athletics club to be formed in England was the London Olympiads Athletics Club, established by women returning from Women's Olympiads in Monte Carlo (1921) and Paris (1922); the Women's Athletic Association was founded in 1922 (Hargreaves, 1994).

In the USA, athletics or track-and-field was influenced by Scottish Americans and later Irish Americans, on the East Coast. A meet was organized in 1836 by the Highland Society of New York, and Caledonian clubs were established in Boston in 1853 and New York in 1857 (Guttmann, 2004: 125). This Scottish influence, drawing on the *Highland Games as well as the newer sporting culture, also informed the pioneers of US college sports as they were established in the 1870s, and the New York Athletic Club in 1868 (the Amateur Athletic Union emerging from the latter in 1888). In these institutions, defendants of the amateur, socially privileged model of sport were dismissive of the aspirations of people of lower status, but a meritocratic strand in US culture contributed to an opening up of opportunities for ambitious and talented athletes: 'a win-at-all costs approach to sports began to topple the exclusionary barricades. The stellar athletic achievements of working-class Irish Americans shone too brightly to be overlooked when an Olympic team had to be assembled' (Guttmann, 2004: 126). The support of track-and-field by *college sports in the USA ensured that performance sport at its highest level would be 'working-class, multi-ethnic and multi-racial'. In 1912, Cambridge University athlete Philip *Noel-Baker wrote disapprovingly of how 'the American athlete specializes in one or two events', trains in a dedicated fashion before races, has a coach (also often a professional), and is supported by an organization and system with sound financial resources (Crump, 1989: 52). This tension between the all-round athlete adopting amateur values, and the more ruthless approach to competitive achievement of the full-time specialist, is captured beautifully in the film *Chariots of Fire.*

Athletics in its amateur form had been strengthened by the growth in profile and influence of the modern Olympic Games, though as the sport expanded in its international scope and impact, athletes began to question the premises of the amateur model, and in the second half of the 20th century disputes over payments and sponsorship highlighted the problem of *shamateurism. In the period following World War II until the beginning of the last decade of the century, the international profile of athletics was consolidated by the Cold War, with the USA and the Soviet Union competing for position at the top of (Summer) Olympic medal tables, and other international meetings and events providing a platform for the national rivalry of the two superpowers. A regular US–USSR athletics match started in Moscow in 1958, though interrupted when the Soviet Union withdrew from the Los Angeles event in 1966. College-sponsored athletes from the USA competing with prominent state-sponsored athletes (with token positions in the military or some other appropriate state institution) symbolized the distance that athletics had travelled from the amateur ideal. Athletics, along with other sports, was used as a strategic tool in the *Cold War.

This explicitly political influence was eclipsed to some extent after the collapse of the Soviet Union and associated states. Forces of *commercialism and the media had been influencing the move towards open professionalism and now changed the economic and cultural basis of athletics. More opportunities became available on the international arena for sportsmen and -women from poorer countries, and African runners, from Kenya and Ethiopia for instance, consolidated their dominance of middle-distance running. By the Beijing Olympics of 2008, the International Olympic Committee included 47 men's and women's events in its 'Athletics' category, confirming the centrality of athletics to the programme of the Summer Olympics. It recognized four sub-areas: track, with 14 forms of racing; field, made up of 8 forms of throwing or jumping, including pole-vaulting; road, comprising marathon and walking; and combined, the heptathlon and the *decathlon. Women's events in *pole-vault and throwing the hammer were not included in the programme until the Sydney 2000 Games. Despite the economic excesses of the sport, the controversies of drug scandals, and political dynamics and machinations underlying the management and organization of athletics, the elemental nature of running, throwing, and jumping contests has continued to appeal to local, national, and worldwide audiences in thrall to what Hans Ulrich Gumbrecht (2006: 51) has called the *focused intensity of the athletic performance.

References

Crump, J. (1989) 'Athletics', in T. Mason (ed.), *Sport in Britain: A Social History*, Cambridge: Cambridge University Press; Gumbrecht, H. U. (2006) *In Praise of Athletic Beauty*, Cambridge, Mass.: The Belknap Press of Harvard University Press; Guttmann, A. (2004) *Sports: The First Five Millennia*, Amherst: University of Massachusetts Press; Hargreaves, J. (1994) *Sporting Females: Critical Issues in the History and Sociology of Women's Sports*, London: Routledge; International Olympic Committee, website on 'Athletics' consulted February 2008; Spivey, N. (2004) *The Ancient Olympics*, Oxford: Oxford University Press.

Atlas, Charles (1894–1972) An Italian-born bodybuilder who transformed himself from a skinny weakling into the most famous muscleman of his time and,

due to the successful advertising campaign for his system, into a long-lasting icon of
the bodybuilding culture. Born Angelo Siciliano, Atlas emigrated to Brooklyn, New
York, in 1905, and began calling himself Charles, changing his surname in 1922,
after a friend commented on his resemblance to a statue of Atlas on the roof of
a hotel in Coney Island, New York. His company, Charles Atlas Ltd, was founded
in 1929. Atlas was inspired by figures such as Eugen *Sandow and, as a young
leather worker, coped with bullying by joining the *YMCA and developing his
physique. Winning competitions for the perfectly formed physique, and appearing
as a circus strongman, Atlas expanded into publishing. His course of lessons in
what he called his Dynamics-Tension programme sold many millions worldwide,
and the print advertisements of the 1940s featuring the '97 lb weakling' bullied
on the beach, but transforming himself and returning to humiliate the bully
(and win back the girl), have been hailed as one of the most effective advertising
campaigns in the history of the business.

audience effect A change in sports performance due to a crowd of spectators.
Based on drive theory, Zajonc proposed that an audience will improve performance
due to an increase in *arousal. In sport, however, the audience is seldom passive
so the interaction between players and the crowd becomes important and the
situation is complicated further by the audience usually comprising home and away
fans who will differ in their response to the same event. There is clear evidence of
a home advantage in sport results. Varca suggests home advantage may result
from the home team's increased level of arousal improving functional assertive
behaviour, whereas in the opponents the crowd stimulates dysfunctional
behaviour. The crowd size and density increase the home advantage, although if
the home team is performing poorly and the crowd becomes hostile then the
advantage may be reversed. David Runciman, writing in *Observer Sport Monthly*
(February 2008), links home advantage to *testosterone levels and the
concomitant raised aggression levels of some home teams.

Australian Institute of Sport (AIS) A specialist institute for the study and
promotion of elite sport performance, based in Australia's capital city, Canberra.
It was formed in 1981, after a review of Australia's disappointing performance at
the 1976 Montreal Olympic Games, where it won no gold medals, just one silver and
four bronze. At the Los Angeles Olympics—albeit without the Soviet Union and
other boycotting nations as opponents—Australians won four gold, eight silver,
and twelve bronze medals. At Atlanta in 1996 Australia was seventh in the
medal table, and on home territory at Sydney four years later—with sixteen gold,
twenty-five silver, and seventeen bronze—it took fourth place in the table behind
the USA, the Russian Federation, and China; this fourth place was secured again
at the 2004 Athens Games. Much of this success has been attributed to the work
of the AIS, and to associated policies for the development of better forms of support
for sportswomen.

The AIS's stated aim has been to achieve 'supremacy in sport'. The secret of
the AIS's success has been selected 'supremacy', in targeting performance-sport
development for Olympic sports and non-Olympic sports of national significance
that also have an international focus (such as *netball, at the *Commonwealth

Games). The Institute's staff covers the main sports science disciplines and all phases of the performance cycle from preparation to rehabilitation, and many scholarships are offered to athletes. It has been seen as a model for the organization of high-performance support schemes, features widely in sport development and policy study programmes across the world, and, as a part of the Australian Sports Commission, is recognized as a pioneering and influential state-sponsored organization.

SEE WEB LINKS

• The official site of the Institute, including valuable guidance on nutrition for athletes.

Australian Open Tennis Championship *See* GRAND SLAM (TENNIS).

Australian Rules football An eighteen-a-side game played on an oval pitch of indeterminate size for the duration of four quarters of 25 minutes each. The aim is to kick the oval ball between centre posts or behind posts at the end of the pitch. The ball may be moved by any part of the player's body, whether it is kicked, handled, or held while running (if the latter, the ball must be periodically bounced); but the ball must not be thrown. The game is fast and can be violent, and it has prospered for more than a century and a half after its first documented staging, in Melbourne, Victoria, Australia. It has drawn crowds of up to 120,000 for matches in the final stages of its major tournaments, often between Melbourne-based sides, and the fans comprise families, women as well as men, and straddle the ages. It was devised as a purely Australian game, though believed by some to be of Aboriginal origin, and derived in part from *Gaelic football which was played by Irish troops, gold diggers, and immigrants. It has prospered most in the southern and western states of Australia, though it has developed a national profile beyond its traditional stronghold in and around Melbourne, becoming the most popular code in all states and territories except Queensland and New South Wales; six of the sixteen teams, by 2008, were from outside Melbourne, and since 1990 ten Grand Final champions were from outside of the city or area.

Spectators respond keenly to the pace of the game, its tough physical contests between players, the multiple skills demanded of the players, and the high scoring. Though the game is played professionally only in Australia, the Australian Football League (AFL) Grand Final claimed, from 2005, to be the most highly attended club championship event in the world, dwarfing attendances for the USA *Super Bowl and the European UEFA Champions League (UCL). This did not make the clubs or the AFL rich, though, as its media audiences were tiny compared to the aforementioned events with their much bigger national and global broadcast audiences. This has generated a developmental and policy dilemma for Australian Rules: how to expand its markets without losing its identity? One response has been to create encounters with Gaelic football sides, but any further dilution of the game would risk alienating its native and loyal audience base.

authoritarian personality A book of this title (1950) was published by Theodor *Adorno and his associates during their time researching in the USA. The book, based on interviews with more than two thousand respondents, identified several facets of the authoritarian, also dubbed *ethnocentric, personality type: these included submission towards the authority of the in-group, hostility towards outsiders, obedience, intolerance of ambiguity, and prejudice. This could almost be a description of the traditional but also parochial and narrow-minded sport fan or the loyal team member, or of the focused motivator figure, the sport coach. The term has entered everyday language, but retains a seductive applicability to some of the core dynamics of a sporting culture and to some of the individual personalities within that culture.

autobiography The story of an individual life as told or written by the individual him- or herself. Lives of sportsmen and -women written in popular, accessible style constitute an established sub-genre of popular publishing. Many such autobiographies are ghostwritten, by commissioned professional writers and journalists, and there are several recurring motifs in the narratives of sporting lives as so told: the parental sacrifices made to support the nascent sporting star; the rags-to-riches theme; the hero–villain vicissitudes of a sporting career; the contribution of the understanding and long-suffering partner. Whatever the production process and principles underlying the making of an autobiography, and the literary merits of the written product, autobiographies can be a valuable source for the study and analysis of sporting cultures and the individual career trajectories of individuals. Even if the autobiography says little about the individual life itself in any credible or reliable way, it can still be a source of understanding of the reading tastes—and so cultural values—of a public; thus Leo Lowenthal's studies of magazine trends in the 1920s and 1930s in the USA showed the biographies of sportsmen and -women to be prominent in the switch from what he called 'idols of production' (politicians, industrialists) to 'idols of consumption' (film stars, singers, popular cultural celebrities). Autobiographies are at their least useful—though in this very characteristic can still be revealing—when seeking to offend the least, as in the bland narrative of English footballer David Beckham's *My Life* (ghosted by television soap opera actor turned sportwriter Tom Watt).

autocratic leadership *See* COACHING STYLES.

autoethnography The use of personal experience as data in the study of a selected topic such as *socialization, or *gender relations. For example, the homophobic characteristics of rugby can be illuminated by someone who has experienced the culture itself as a young player, and writes that personal experience into the account and the analysis of the culture. Such use of personal data can be revealing, even revelatory, but also raises difficult questions concerning the representativeness and generalizability of the self as a data-source. Autoethnographers also run the risk of running out of material, as individual experience is by definition limited, though it can be argued that forms of reflective practice constantly renew the individual's experience, and the sense that is made of that experience. The journal *Auto/Biography* is dedicated to analyses and accounts based on such approaches.

backstage A concept referring to the concealed or protected social spaces or regions in which social actors prepare cultural performances, as opposed to the *frontstage or front region in which social interactions take place more publicly. The term was developed by Erving *Goffman in his analysis of 'regions and region behaviour' in his 1959 study *The Presentation of Self in Everyday Life*. Backstage, 'action occurs that is related to the performance but inconsistent with the appearance fostered by the performance'. The unflappable batsman in cricket, for instance, may be a bundle of nerves back in the dressing room, but it is pivotal to the sporting performance and the team goals that he or she retains a cool demeanour when walking to the crease.

badger-baiting A barbarous sport in which a tough terrier was matched with a caged badger. The sport was popular in England across several centuries, along with *bull-baiting and bear-baiting. As Robert Malcolmson notes, badgers were easier to attain and, consequently, more often baited. Malcolmson quotes Henry Alken, an observer of 1839, on the objective of the sport, which was to see how many times 'the dog will draw the badger from his box, within a given space of time', and how effectively a 'well-bred and thoroughly trained dog' could accomplish this (*Popular Recreations in English Society, 1700–1850*, 1973). Badger-baiting attracted gambling, and cases were still being prosecuted at the end of the 19th century (in Preston, Lancashire, for instance, in 1897) despite the successful campaigning of the reformers who opposed such forms of cruelty to animals practised in the name of sport.

badminton An indoor racket game played in singles or doubles on a court divided by a five-foot-high net, and with a shuttlecock, made of feathers or nylon, rather than a ball. It has been played by men and women, and in mixed doubles. The name 'badminton' is taken from the name of the English Duke of Beaufort's estate of Badminton in Gloucestershire, where the game is said to have been developed circa 1870, as an adaptation of the old children's game of battledore and shuttlecock, though its sporting ancestry has been said to include the French *jeu de volant* and, in ancient China, a form of shuttlecock kicking. The sport became popular among the privileged classes, and military officers played a version of the game outdoors in India, establishing laws and rules in Poona in the mid 1870s. Its popularity grew back in England, particularly in the holiday season at seaside resorts, and in 1893 the Badminton Association was founded by fourteen clubs meeting at Southsea, Hampshire.

The International Badminton Federation was founded in 1934, recognizing England, Ireland, Scotland, and Wales as separate national organizations and including Denmark, New Zealand, and the Netherlands, with India joining two years later. Canada and Denmark were early international growth areas for the game in the 1920s and 1930s, when it also began to be organized competitively in India. In the mid 20th century, Indonesia, Japan, and Malaysia emerged as forces in the international game. Recognized as a full Olympic discipline in 1992 (it had been a demonstration event at Munich in 1972), the sport's outstanding Olympic competitors and champions have been from Indonesia, South Korea, and China. The sport has continued to appeal to participants at recreational level in local clubs and community groups, as well as at the international elite competitive level, at which speeds exceeding 270 kilometres per hour have been recorded for the flight of the shuttlecock.

Bagot Stack, Mary Meta (Mollie) *See* STACK, MARY META (MOLLIE) BAGOT.

Baillet-Latour, Henri de (1876–1942) The third president (1925) of the *International Olympic Committee (IOC), on to which he had been elected in Belgium in 1903. He had founded the Belgian Olympic Committee in 1904, contributed to Belgium's participation in the London 1908 and Stockholm 1912 Olympics, and secured the 1920 Games for Antwerp, in his home nation. Baillet-Latour opposed commercialism, arguing consistently for the retention of core Olympic ideals, but was overtaken by the political momentum of the 1936 Berlin Olympics, and died in 1942 before the re-emergence of the Olympics after World War II. A very severe, almost melancholic-looking, Baillet-Latour was photographed at the opening ceremony of the 1936 Winter Olympics at Garmisch-Partenkirchen, sandwiched between Rudolf Hess and Adolf Hitler.

Baker, Josephine (1906–75) A black US entertainer who found great success on the French stage in the 1920s, performing dances and singing virtually naked or in exotic costumes (such as one made of bananas). Baker was extending the boundaries of physical performance at a time when the sporting body was still, apart from in explicit shows such as *bodybuilding or emerging events such as ice dancing, very much clothed, covered, and little displayed. As part of the Harlem Renaissance in New York City, she attracted much attention, and her appearances in Paris from 1925 coincided with the loosening of some of these bodily restrictions, pioneered in tennis by Suzanne *Lenglen. Baker also starred—the first African American woman to do this—in feature films, worked for the French resistance movement in World War II, and was active in the worldwide civil rights movement. Ernest *Hemingway, another US expatriate in Paris in the 1920s, called her 'the most sensational woman anyone ever saw'. She took French citizenship, and is commemorated in Place Josephine Baker in Paris's Montparnasse district. Baker's contribution to the public display and wider acceptance of body performance and cultures is contextualized and evaluated in Jayna Brown's *Babylon Girls: Black Women Performers at the Threshold of the Modern* (2008).

Bakhtin, Mikhail (1895–1975) *See* CARNIVALESQUE.

Balfour, Arthur James (1848–1930) A prime minister of Great Britain, philosopher, and sports enthusiast, born into an aristocratic and high-achieving family including a brother who, professor of animal morphology at Cambridge, died mountaineering at the age of 30. Balfour's particular sporting loves were tennis and golf, and at Cambridge (Trinity College, 1866–9) he played court tennis. Inheriting a vast private fortune, Balfour constructed his own private golf course at one of his homes in Whittinghame, Scotland, captained the Royal & Ancient Club at St Andrews (1894), and dedicated his Septembers to playing the game. In his early life Balfour concentrated upon academic philosophy and was a leading member of the intellectual, aesthetic group the 'Souls'. Balfour's political career began when he entered parliament in 1874 as a Conservative member, devoting his energy to the Ireland question, education policy, and, increasingly, wider foreign affairs. He was prime minister—succeeding his uncle Lord Salisbury—from 1902 to 1905; and served in ministerial positions in Britain's war government during World War I, making influential contributions to international diplomacy thereafter.

Balfour sustained his commitment to sporting diversions throughout his career, playing tennis regularly until 1928, and regularly praising the benefits of a balanced sporting life. In 1897, *Fortnightly Review* (LXI, new series) printed his address to a university audience in Edinburgh, noting how sport contributed to the experience and feeling of community. Education, lectures, and study could do this, 'but no influence fostered it more surely and more effectively than that feeling of common life which the modern athletic sports, developed in modern places of learning, gave to all those who took an interest in such matters, whether as performers or spectators'. 'Every class of the community', he urged in 1909, should have the opportunity to spend a 'Saturday half-holiday . . . in the open air' playing golf.

balle au tambourin A traditional ball game in France which is instanced by Allen Guttmann (*Sports: The First Five Millennia*, 2004) as a survival of a traditional sport, though on a relatively insignificant scale; as Guttmann noted, in 1995 the French Football Federation could boast 2,055,610 members, the national federation for *balle au tambourin* a mere 720.

ball leaping An activity, more novelty item than sport, in which the individual leaps from one big ball to another. It calls for physical dexterity but also much luck, as the position of the ball is highly unpredictable. Ball leaping has a knockabout, carnival flavour to it, more in common with the challenges of events at pre-modern fairs and festivals than the conventions of organized modern sport.

ballooning The discipline of 'lighter-than-air' flight, in hot-air or gas balloons, or airships. In Britain, it is overseen by the British Balloon and Airship Club, founded in 1965; internationally, the discipline is governed by the Fédération Aéronautique Internationale (founded in France in 1905). Ballooning is, unsurprisingly, the most minority of minority sports, and many people who experience it do so for a one-off experience rather than to become a trained pilot. But it has a secure place in the popular consciousness, as will be confirmed by anyone who has craned his or her neck as a balloon floats into vision over a white mountain peak or a grey metropolitan skyline.

bandy An eleven-a-side team game played on ice-covered ground, with a ball rather than a puck. It originated in England at the turn of the 18th and 19th centuries, and an English-based team hosted a club from Holland in the winter of 1890–91. A National Bandy Association was founded in 1891, and published the first set of rules. But lack of regular ice constrained the growth of the game in Britain, and indoor *ice hockey developed as an alternative. Nevertheless, bandy did flourish in several countries where snow could be relied on: Finland, Sweden, Norway, Estonia, Latvia, Russia/the USSR, Mongolia. The International Federation of Bandy was established in 1955, by Finland, Norway, Sweden, and the USSR. This was renamed the Federation of International Bandy (FIB) in 2001, when bandy gained preliminary recognition as a sport by the International Olympic Committee. Bandy gained full acceptance as a recognized sport by the IOC in 2004, from which point the federation lobbied for inclusion in the programme of the winter Olympics. The FIB increased its membership in the early 2000s. World championships are organized every two years, at which at least four nations must compete. No nation other than the founding members of the FIB had won the championship in the first half-century of the federation's existence. In 2008, the United Arab Emirates became the federation's twenty-seventh member, indicating—along with fellow snowless member Australia—that bandy's development need not be confined to the outdoors and natural weather conditions, and showing the continuing attraction of sport as a means of asserting national prestige.

Barclay, Captain (Robert Barclay Allardice) (1779–1854) A Scottish-born landowner and aristocrat, whose passion for physical sporting challenges and feats of strength and endurance echoed the interests and activities of his father, and further popularized the sport of *pedestrianism. Known as 'Captain' from his time in the local militia in his late teens, Barclay entered Trinity College, Cambridge, in 1798. At the university, he engaged in no formal studies towards examinations or a degree, but hunted, fished, went shooting, and played numerous sports and games including cricket, swimming, jumping, battledore and shuttlecock, and swinging on ropes. Clubs, and dining and drinking groups, also took up much of Barclay's time. Cock-fighting, horse racing, and associated betting were popular among students, along with sparring in boxing gloves.

Barclay left Cambridge after less than two years at the university, on reaching his age of majority, when he could assume his position as head of his family and his late father's estate. He dedicated himself to his athletic interests and, in 1809, walked one thousand miles in one thousand hours, for one thousand guineas, at Newmarket. For a little under six weeks, Barclay drew unprecedented crowds to the area to witness what he and the sporting press constructed and claimed as the greatest human feat ever attempted. To achieve this, he had to walk one mile each hour throughout days and nights, with no break, over that six-week period. To make the feat possible, Barclay illuminated the Newmarket Heath course of his walk with innovative gas lamps, employed a former boxing champion as bodyguard, and armed himself with pistols. Peter Radford's *The Celebrated Captain Barclay: Sport, Gambling and Adventure in Regency Times* (2001) catalogues Barclay's extraordinary life, and estimates that the wagers laid on Barclay's feat amounted to the equivalent of £40 million at end of the 20th century values. Barclay went on to feature prominently in the national sporting culture of Britain, regularly sparring with other boxing enthusiasts, and training English champion Tom *Cribb. Barclay's sporting legacy includes a recognition of the value of training with regular and intense preparatory exercise, and attention to diet and nutrition, in sporting performance and achievement.

baseball A bat-and-ball game played between nine-a-side teams, mainly by men, and widely popular among men of all ages in the USA, and in Canada (where the Toronto Blue Jays represent the North American professional game, and won successive World Series titles in 1992 and 1993). The game has also established cultural profiles in the Dominican Republic, Puerto Rico, Mexico, Cuba, Japan, Taiwan, and Korea. Baseball, many argue, was developed in the USA as a version of the traditional English sport of *rounders, though its greatest entrepreneur, Albert Spalding, generated a foundation myth concerning its origins, attributing its invention to Abner Doubleday, in Cooperstown, New York, in 1839. The game survived match-fixing scandals, and inter-league and business rivalries, to eclipse other sports (such as cricket) and become a national sport in the USA, thriving at Little League (local and junior), amateur, college, and professional levels. Baseball was also introduced into the Summer Olympic Games in 1992, Cuba taking three of the five titles (the USA and Korea the other two) before the event was omitted from the programme after Beijing 2008; within Olympic networks, it had been argued that the sport—along with *softball—was insufficiently international to warrant its continued inclusion on the programme (these became the first sports to be cut from the Olympic programme since polo, which last featured in 1936). Also connected to that 2005 International Olympic Committee decision and vote was the refusal of Major League Baseball (MLB) to release top US players for Olympic competition.

Baseball in the USA has provided legendary figures to the national sporting pantheon, among whom the most notable are Babe *Ruth, Lou *Gehrig, and Joe *DiMaggio, batters of great distinction. Writer Paul Gallico (1897–1976) wrote of Ruth: 'There has always been a magic about that gross, ugly, coarse, Gargantuan figure of a man and everything he did' (*Farewell to Sport*, 1938). That magic, and the rise of radio, ensured the survival of the sport as a mass spectator attraction throughout and beyond the Great Depression of the 1930s. The sport had also overcome the match-fixing crisis of 1919, when eight members of the Chicago White Sox accepted pay-offs to lose the World Series championship play-offs to the Cincinnati Reds; the federal judge of Chicago's circuit court, Judge Kenesaw Mountain Landis (1866–1944), was appointed to the specially created post of commissioner of baseball, and the structure of the game reworked on the basis of a National Agreement giving the commissioner far-reaching powers, making him 'absolute dictator of the baseball community' (Leverett Smith, Jr, *The American Dream and the National Game*, 1975); Landis had control over both national leagues, the minor leagues, and the national association of professional clubs. Babe Ruth's emergence as the game's new hero at the same time also contributed to the restoration of the game's credibility. The World Series had begun in 1903, with champions from the two national leagues playing off for the overall title. The National League had begun in 1876, and this is sometimes claimed as the formation date of the MLB, which effectively became the single overarching body for the sport in 2000, when the two existing national leagues were dissolved as legal entities.

The MLB has had to examine the changing media context, in 2008, for instance, the broadcasts of the World Series on Fox Television attained an audience of only 8.4 per cent of US households, an all-time low, and programmers looked to bring coverage earlier into the evening schedule, pre-8 p.m., in order to retain the young audience across the nation's time zones. The MLB's list of eighteen official sponsors (2009) confirms its continued rootedness in US sporting consciousness: Anheuser-Busch; Bank of America; Bayer (One a Day); FIA Card Service, NA; Frito Lay; Gatorade; Gillette; General Motors (Chevrolet); InterContinental Hotels Group (Holiday Inn); KPMG; MasterCard International; Nike; Pepsi-Cola; Quaker Oats; Sharp; State Farm; Taco Bell; XM Satellite Radio. Despite match-fixing crises, economic fluctuations, and drug scandals, baseball has retained its place in the popular US imagination, a version of a sporting pastoral continuing to infuse its audiences and following with its mix of national distinctiveness and popular nostalgia, and its capacity to be immortalized in statistics and the quantification of performance records.

Baseball's roots in Japan stem from the enthusiasm of a US teacher at Tokyo University, who introduced students there to the game in 1873. Played informally and in non-standardized fashion for a quarter of a century, the sport was organized more systematically in Japan's elite universities from the end of the 19th century and in the first decade of the 20th century. By the 1920s, baseball was widely established in Japanese schools and colleges. An all-star US team, including Babe Ruth, toured the country in 1934, and a professional baseball league was established in 1936. Baseball in Japan has been seen to symbolize traditional values of harmony and order, but it also represented the modern world, Japan's own adaptation of an emerging US culture.

In Cuba, baseball was introduced by Cubans returning from the USA, the first such claim citing its introduction in Havana in 1864; a professional league was organized by 1878, though it did not prosper. In 1917, a more effective professional league was organized and players moved between Cuba and the USA. The Cuban revolution, abolishing professional sports in 1962, nevertheless prioritized the sport, stimulated by its political significance in the country's relationship with the USA, and Cuban teams have been dominant in world championships, winning twelve of the thirteen baseball World Cups between 1976 and 2005. The persisting prominence of baseball in Cuba shows the cultural hold that a sport can have despite social and political changes, and the sport continues to have an important influence upon identity formation, and to make a contribution to the retention of Cuban identity—*cubanidad*—in a volatile political world. The first two World Baseball Classic events, in 2006 and 2009, promoted by the MLB, were, however, won by Japan.

SEE WEB LINKS

• The official site of the Major League Baseball organization in the USA, including exclusive stories, schedules and statistics, interviews, and audio-visual clips.

basketball A five-a-side ball game invented in the USA in 1891, with a 21st-century claim to being the most popular participant sport in the world. The origins of the sport are linked to fitness initiatives in colleges and youth associations, the desire to create a challenging game of skill more interesting than formal gymnastics, and the inventor's ingenuity: Canadian-born Dr James Naismith (1861–1939), *YMCA instructor in Springfield, Massachusetts, could find no square wooden boxes, so adapted a peach basket for the point-accumulating target. The first game was played in 1892, and the Young Women's Christian Association asked for copies of the rules in 1895, adapting these to formulate the complementary new sport of *netball. Basketball was also adopted in women's colleges, introduced at Smith College, Massachusetts, in 1892. A photograph of early players (Mid-Manhattan New York Public Library Picture Collection, 'Sports Collegiate' §22,656) shows five women in frocks and short-sleeved blouses with numbered fronts, posing in an action shot of blocking and shooting: 'Students of Smith College . . . take to the court in a converted gym, where the net hangs over a fireplace'. US women's colleges across the country adopted the sport, and by 1930 it was reported that 95 per cent of the colleges provided facilities. By 1901 the sport had been widely adopted across the USA's colleges, and the first inter-collegiate conference was staged. By 1914, the Original Celtics professional team was branded as 'World Champions'. The exhibition troupe of players Harlem Globetrotters was organized in 1927 and gave a glamorous image of the game to crowds worldwide.

Basketball was no longer the prerogative of the USA, though, and the sport was recognized by the International Olympic Committee in 1930. An international governing body, the Fédération Internationale de Basketball Amateur (FIBA), was established in Geneva in 1932: European championships were held in 1935 (with Latvia the first winner); basketball (for men) appeared in the schedule of the Summer Games at Berlin in 1936, and for women at the 1976 Montreal Games; a men's world championship was established in 1950, a women's in 1953; in Europe, a cup competition for champions' clubs was established in 1958. At the Olympics, early US domination of the men's tournaments was challenged by the famous and controversial victory by the Soviet Union over the USA at the 1972 Olympic Games in Munich, ending the USA's 62-match winning streak at the Olympics. In 1989, the FIBA voted to allow professional players from the USA's National Basketball Association to participate in the Olympics (also then dropping the word 'amateur' from its name), and US hegemony was reasserted after the Soviet Union had again won gold at the 1988 Seoul Games, though when the majority of the squad choices turned down the prospect of competing at the Athens Games of 2004, Argentina took the gold. The hastily assembled US squad had arrived with a 109–2 match record in Olympic competition, and lost in Athens to Puerto Rico and Lithuania. Women's basketball at the Olympics has been dominated by the USA–Soviet Union rivalry at the heart of the *Cold War, the USA amassing six gold medals to the USSR's three up to the Beijing 2008 Olympics.

The professional game, though, has been dominated by men, and in the USA was a pioneer in the commercialization of modern sport. The Basketball Association of America (founded 1946) and the National Basketball League (founded 1937) merged to form the National Basketball Association (NBA) in 1949. Within the US consciousness, the sport has embodied equality of opportunity, offering a route to riches and fame for players from African-American backgrounds in particular, and embodying a kind of street style that could resonate with the interests and preoccupations of youth culture. Michael Novak has written that players and teams are 'free to elaborate' as 'the spirit' moves them: 'Basketball is jazz: improvisatory, free, individualistic, corporate, sweaty, fast, exulting, screeching, torrid, explosive, exquisitely designed for letting first the trumpet, then the sax, then the drummer, then the trombonist soar away in virtuoso excellence' (*The Joy of Sports: Endzones, Bases, Baskets, Balls, and the Consecration of the American Spirit*, 1976). For Novak, basketball is also a game conducive to black culture and experience, 'full of leaps and breakaway fluid sprints . . . a game of feint, deception: put-on'. Nelson George (*Elevating the Game: Black Men and Basketball*, 1992) reaffirmed the musical analogy, comparing the African-American player's relationship to basketball with the 'African-American musician's affinity for the saxophone', and linking 'basketball moves with rapping, sermonizing, and soloing' in the manifestation of a particular, shared 'African-American aesthetic'. The college system in the USA is linked to the professional tier of the game by a *draft system, in which the lower teams in the NBA have first choice of the emerging college stars.

Corporate sponsors have been attracted to basketball by the image of individual stars, the most famous of whom has been Michael Jordan, whose clients included Gatorade, *Coca-Cola, McDonald's, and *Nike. The latter created the Air Jordan sports shoe, and studies have corroborated that the endorsement of a product by a figure such as Jordan can generate huge financial profits, stimulating market capitalization of millions and even billions of dollars. Jordan has been frank about his stance on sponsorship: when questions of ethics, civil rights, and politics were put to him in the context of political candidates, he remarked that 'Republicans buy sneakers too'. Nothing, it seems, should compromise the economic power of the Jordan brand. Ira Berkow, reviewing David Halberstam's *Looking over Jordan* in the *New York Times* (January 31 1999), wrote: 'The "Michael Factor" meant a variety of things: he could elevate a struggling shoe company, Nike, to head-spinning heights; he could lead a team to six championships in the 1990's; he could make the difference of nearly nine million more television viewers during the National Basketball Association finals. And, as Halberstam says, citing a Forbes magazine estimate, Jordan's persona "helped generate $10 billion in revenues for the game, its broadcasters and for his varying corporate partners"'. The Women's National Basketball Association (WNBA) inaugurated a national US league in 1997, but has not rivalled the men's game in the marketplace. Men's basketball is the one of the USA's Big 4 sports to attain a global popularity to rival soccer.

((⊕)) SEE WEB LINKS

• The official site of the National Basketball Association in the USA, comprising statistics, schedules, player profiles, multimedia, news, and features.

Baudrillard, Jean (1929–2007) A French social theorist and cultural analyst whose main themes in his writings on media culture and consumption included the notions of *simulation and the *simulacrum. In an essay collection on the topic of 'extreme phenomena' (*The Transparency of Evil*, 1993), Baudrillard commented that the most striking thing about the 1985 *Heysel Stadium crowd tragedy was not the violence of the event itself, but the way in which the television coverage of that violence 'turned into a travesty of itself'. What he calls the 'real referent' diminishes in contemporary culture, as increasingly 'the only event occurring is strictly televisual in nature'. In *America* (1986), in 'I did it!' (a play on the *Nike symbol 'Just do it!'), he wrote that the 'New York marathon has become a sort of international symbol of . . . fetishistic performance, of the mania for an empty victory'.

bayonet charging An activity promoted by the physical education initiatives of the government of the People's Republic of China during the early years of Communist rule, when a national priority of national defence stimulated physical education and fitness programmes. As Allen Guttmann notes: 'Young Chinese were trained and tested in conventional track-and-field sports. They also acquired proficiency in firing rifles and in charging with bayonets' (*Sports: The First Five Millennia*, 2004). The Chinese authorities also embraced parachute jumping and drills within its definition of sports, and even generated a national champion for throwing hand-grenades. These, albeit extreme, cases highlight sport's potential to frame and underpin strategies of *military preparedness. *See also* COMMUNISM, SPORT IN.

beach volleyball An Olympic sport for both men and women, played on sand by teams of two players, though in recreational encounters numbers can vary widely. The sport began to be played on the beaches of Santa Monica, California, in the 1920s, and competitions for trophies were held after World War II. In 1960, the first Manhattan Beach Open (Southern California) was held. The sport was held as a demonstration sport, an attractive focus on the newly restored beaches of Barcelona, at the 1992 Olympics, and has been on the Olympic programme since 1996. Brazil and the USA have dominated the men's events at the Olympics, though an Australian women's pair won the gold at Sydney in 2000. At that tournament, matches on Sydney's Bondi Beach drew many spectators new to the sport, attracted by the combination of physical prowess in performance and the sexual allure of the contestants. The international organizing body, the FIVB (Fédération Internationale de Volleyball), confirmed in its guidelines for women athletes competing in Athens in 2004 that 'briefs should be a close fit and be cut on an upward angle towards the top of the leg. The side width must be maximum 7cm'; and tops had to 'fit closely to the body'. Men's shorts were baggier. 'Sand, Sun and Sky—get involved' was the running head of the FIVB in the run-in to the Beijing 2008 Olympics. The fourth 'S' was of course implicit: the successful profile of beach volleyball testifies to the popularity of the voyeuristic, sexual side of sport spectating.

behaviour How a person responds in act and thought to a stimulus. Some early models of behaviour were based on the classic stimulus–response work of Pavlov and Skinner but in the human context such a simplistic model neglects the cognitive element. Contemporary models in sport psychology place emphasis on cognitive interpretation between a stimulus and a response and, in consequence, how behaviour can be modified to ensure an athlete can remain focused on the task and motivated in training and competition. Behavioural models can also be applied to other topics such as helping people incorporate changes to their lifestyle to ensure an adequate level of habitual physical activity, or assisting an athlete in recovering from an injury.

behaviourism A form of social science in which environmental factors are said to be the paramount influence upon human actions. The Russian psychologist Ivan Pavlov, in late 19th-century experiments on dogs, claimed to prove that reflexes could be conditioned. To accept a behaviourist approach to the study of the psychology and social psychology of sport performance would be to reduce the human actor to the conditioned status of the Pavlovian dog. There is little case for the adoption of the behaviourist approach in a context in which the structure-agency couplet and dynamic (*see* STRUCTURATION THEORY) is accepted as a more credible model for the understanding of human behaviour. Even so, some elements of a behaviourist approach might still cast light on the conduct of athletes who have claimed not to know that they were being drugged, or the rationale of the arthritic former gymnast whose adult body is not equipped to cope with the effects of the pubescent peak performances.

belief system The set of *values or beliefs characterizing a particular society or culture. The term could refer to all of the beliefs and associated knowledge in the society or culture, so that one might talk of a belief system of *capitalism or *communism, and the place of sport in such a system. The term can be used in such a generalized fashion that it loses any precise meaning, though it has had a wide application to religion, and to the fundamental principles of behaviour and conduct expected of a particular belief system. Thus one can talk of the meaning of sport in relation to the *Catholic Church, or Protestantism, as an overarching belief system.

Belmont Stakes *See* HORSE RACING.

benchball A game played in school settings designed to cultivate skills that later can be further developed in *netball and *basketball. It is a simple team game used by sport and physical education teachers with young children, as a way of introducing core skills of ball handling and spatial awareness in an unthreatening way. Two teams have exactly five passes to get the ball back to their own goalkeeper who is standing on a bench in their own half of the playing area. Physical education teachers have reported successful adaptations of this basic format, and it has clear developmental value for the learning of teamwork and effective positional awareness.

Bentham, Jeremy (1748–1832) An English political and legal philosopher, and social reformer, who, expanding on the dictum 'the greatest good of the greatest number' encountered in Joseph Priestley's *Essay on Government*, became a leading advocate of utilitarianism, a philosophy that for its time was a radical and egalitarian stance, with practical implications manifest in forms of liberal reformism and constitutional reform. Two of Bentham's ideas that have been applied to or adapted in the analysis of sport cultures and sport institutions and spaces are the *panopticon, his vision of the perfectly functioning prison, and the notion of *deep play, as developed by anthropologist Clifford Geertz.

Bergman Österberg, Martina Sofia Helena *See* ÖSTERBERG, MARTINA SOFIA HELENA BERGMAN.

Best, George (1946–2005) A Belfast-born football player best known for his playing skills in his early professional years with Manchester United Football Club, with whom he won the European Cup in 1968, when he was also named the European Footballer of the Year. Best's nickname the Fifth Beatle indicated his level of popularity and fame, and his personal life became bigger news than his sporting feats. His alcoholism and his glamorous, turbulent, and sometimes violent domestic life kept him in the headlines of the UK press well beyond his prematurely terminated playing career. Best's fall from the highest levels of his talent was dramatic. Although in his thirties he had effective spells playing for Los Angeles Aztecs and San José Earthquakes, he failed to score in any of his last ten competitive professional games, for Bournemouth in England, Brisbane Lions in Australia, and Tobermore United in Northern Ireland. Best died of a kidney infection after abusing through drink a liver transplant. His death was reported at the beginning of the weekend in which new expanded opening hours were introduced in England for the consumption of alcohol, thus guaranteeing the still popular figure extensive national press coverage in death, on morals as much as sporting achievements. At his funeral in Belfast, an estimated 100,000 people turned out on the streets of the city. Best never had the opportunity to demonstrate his talent at a World Cup, as his national side Northern Ireland never qualified for a Finals tournament during his playing career. He thus lacked the appropriate stage for the display of what many believe to be one of the greatest all-round talents in the history of the game. Nevertheless, the communications technology of his later life and beyond has assured him of increasing and long-lasting fame among football fans worldwide, as those exploits that were captured by the media of his day have been replayed and appreciated on YouTube and secured countless numbers of new admirers.

best value A term used in some sport and leisure public services to describe the aspirations of public sector provision, implying that better service provision in terms of both customer care and physical infrastructure will create a stronger customer base. Adherence to best value, though, runs the risk of disenfranchising the core constituencies of such providers, the members of the public for whom even the most basic provision could be life-enhancing and transforming.

bharatiya kushti A traditional form of wrestling linked to the Hindu pursuit of a holy life, still practised in the north of the Indian subcontinent. The wrestlers do knee-bends and push-ups that are recognizable to Western athletes, but accompanied by the chanting of mantras. The instructor also supervises the controlled breathing (*pranayama*) of the wrestlers, as well as their diet and sex life. Allen Guttmann (*Sports: The First Five Millennia*, 2004) notes that in some respects the sport transcends the normal rules of caste, the system of social stratification central to Hindu culture; in a search for bodily purity, the rules might allow physical contact—in foot massage, for instance—between practitioners from lower and higher caste backgrounds.

biathlon An event combining running and swimming introduced in 1968 by the Modern Pentathlon Association of Great Britain, as a preparatory and developmental underpinning for potential pentathletes. It was reasoned that a strong basis in swimming and running could be complemented later by the acquisition of the other three skills of the *modern pentathlon.

Bikila, Abebe (1932–73) An Ethiopian runner who twice won the Olympic marathon, initially working as a shepherd but picked out by a Swedish coach hired by the Ethiopian government to develop athletic talent. At the Summer Olympics in Rome in 1960 he became the first black African to win an Olympic gold medal, winning the marathon barefoot, and defending his title (this time wearing running shoes) in Tokyo in 1964. A car accident rendered him disabled in 1969, and he died at the age of 41 of complications related to his condition. Bikila established a profile for Ethiopian runners that has been sustained in the nation's production line of long-distance running champions.

billiards A board and cue game played on a large table with three balls, based on the player's capacity to deflect a ball off the other two balls and when appropriate into one of the six pockets that hang from the edge of the table. The game was popular in 19th-century Britain, particularly prominent in the gentlemen's clubs of the elite, but the slow pace of the game and the tactical caution that underlies long encounters have not been conducive to the maintenance of a wide spectator base. It has been eclipsed in popularity by forms of *pool and other *cue sports. It has continued, nevertheless, to operate at the level of the enthusiastic amateur, the English Amateur Billiards Association affiliating to the UK's Central Council for Physical Recreation in 2009.

BINGO Business-based international non-government organization. A term and description applicable to large-scale and high-profile sport-based organizations such as the *International Olympic Committee (IOC) and the *Fédération Internationale de Football Association (FIFA), whose missions may have been outstripped by their commercial growth and the business rationale upon which their survival and expansion have been secured. Such organizations are non-profit-making, and may have charitable status or its equivalent, but remain the source of personal aggrandizement and are largely unaccountable to nation-states or to any body or authority representative of their international constituencies.

biofeedback A technique to teach people to control the responses of the autonomic *nervous system in order to reduce anxiety. It requires a device to monitor a physiological response such as the heart rate (*electrocardiogram), muscle activity (*electromyogram), brain activity (EEG), skin temperature, or galvanic skin response (GSR). The output from the device is turned into sound or a visual display and the individual seeks to reduce the signal by such means as trying to relax, think pleasant thoughts, or engage in positive self-talk. The successful strategy can then be initiated at times of need away from the biofeedback machine.

biography The *life course of a living being, as a literary genre documented in written form by another person. The biography of the individual athlete can reveal much about the social conditions of the time and the cultural significance of sport in the wider culture, as well as the psychological dimensions of sporting competition and achievement. It can provide a form of *case study valuable in the analysis of the meaning of sport, though some biographies of people in the world of sport can be little more than hagiography, the celebratory rendition of the celebrity life (hagiography was originally the written life of a saint). *See also* AUTOBIOGRAPHY.

(⊕) SEE WEB LINKS

• The online version of the *Oxford Dictionary of National Biography*, comprising biographical profiles of 'the people who shaped the history of the British Isles and beyond' (subscription, available via many institutional and public libraries in the UK).

biomechanics The study of the mechanics of movement in living creatures. In sport and exercise the term is also used to include the study of how equipment, surfaces, and clothing affect performance. Biomechanics is based on fundamental physical laws such as those concerning energy, motion, acceleration, or force and how these laws affect the way the body moves. The study of the subject is often divided into five broad and interrelated mechanical topics: linear and angular kinematics (describing motion), linear and angular kinetics (describing forces), and fluid dynamics (describing the effect of motion through air or water). The mechanical principles are used in analysis of sports techniques with the intention of improving performance. Sophisticated instrumentation aids this analysis. Common techniques include the description of motion using high-speed 3-D video, and the precise measurement of ground reaction forces using a force plate. High computing power is required to handle the mass of data, and complex models of movement can result. Understanding the mechanics of bones, joints, and soft tissues is important to knowledge of how the body behaves under load, with implications for acute and chronic sports injuries. The mechanics of drag, lift, and spin are important when considering the flight of projectiles such as a ball or a javelin. The properties of materials and their interaction with human motion have wide-ranging implications, from manufacturing innovations in golf club design, to the elasticity of a running track or the construction of protective clothing.

biorhythms A rather loose term referring to cyclical changes in the body. Cycles of mental, emotional, and physical well-being starting from the date of birth are fancifully derived with no theoretical or evidential basis. In contrast, there are many true biologically-based rhythms. Chronobiology is a more formal term used for the study of true biological rhythms. Rhythms usually follow a sinusoidal pattern. The most common cycle length is one day (circadian, e.g. body temperature), but cycles may be shorter (ultradian, e.g. deep/REM sleep cycles of about 90 minutes) or longer (infradian, e.g. the menstrual cycle at one month). Rhythms are driven by biological processes setting the fundamental frequency but they can be influenced, to an extent, by external factors such as environment and behaviour. The body can adapt and adjust its internal clock but this may take several days and performance may be compromised during this adaptive period. This is commonly seen when travellers cross time zones or when a worker changes shift pattern. The diminished performance is due to a combination of biological and psychological factors (particularly concentration and attention).

For sport, there are two main consequences to these rhythms. The circadian rhythms may affect performance depending on the time of competition. The physiological peak usually occurs between about 16.00 and 20.00 h and function is about 5 per cent greater than at the nadir between 3.00 and 5.00 h. International travel and jet lag can affect performance. In both cases, deterioration in performance is lessened by nutrition and hydration strategies appropriate to the new time, and through psychological skills training. The infradian rhythms, most notably the menstrual cycle, may affect performance although the evidence is equivocal.

black economy The unofficial economy that is not visible to the accountant's scrutiny, and is based on the circulation of counterfeit or stolen goods. When rationing determined how much meat an individual might have in wartime, a black economy immediately sprang up in the trading of meat. In sport, when tickets are expensive and in limited supply, a black economy emerges to cater for desperate fans; when official merchandise is offered by clubs at excessive costs (for, say, a replica football shirt), the black economy for counterfeit shirts mushrooms. Although the black economy is for the most part illegal, buyers in the black market are complicit in the transaction and do not see themselves as necessarily exploited, such is their desire for the experience or the commodity.

Blankers-Koen, Fanny (Francina Elsje) (1918–2004) A Dutch athlete who set twenty world records in her career. At the Olympics in London in 1948 she became the only female athlete to win four gold medals at a single Olympics, winning the 100 metres, 200 metres, 80-metre hurdles, and 4 by 100 metres. She competed too at the 1936 and 1952 Games. In 1951 she set a world record for the newly revised pentathlon event. In 1999 the *International Association of Athletics Federations (IAAF) voted her female athlete of the 20th century. Blankers-Koen was a 30-year-old mother of two when she competed in London in 1948. She was criticized by some for neglecting traditional and maternal responsibilities, as was English mountaineer Alison *Hargreaves more than four decades later. Blankers-Koen's performances were extraordinary too in that she was running in a hostile climate for women athletes; after the 1936 Games, Avery *Brundage, a member of the International Olympic Committee at the time and its president in 1952, commented that he was 'fed up to the ears with women as track and field competitors' as in that context women's 'charms sink to less than zero. As swimmers and divers, girls are beautiful and adroit, as they are ineffective and unpleasing on the track.' Blankers-Koen, nicknamed 'The Flying Housewife' in the Netherlands, demonstrated the absurdity of Brundage's comments in her achievements, winning huge popularity at home in the Netherlands, and across the expanding international sporting audience, for her unprecedented feats.

blues, Oxford and Cambridge Sportsmen or -women who have represented one of the ancient English universities in an annual fixture between the two institutions. A 'blue' (Cambridge is known as the 'light blues', Oxford as the 'dark blues') is a badge of status with continuing impact in post-university social and professional networks. Blues were also seen, in the age of the amateur domination of English sport, as people of particularly strong character and quality, traits more important to the needs of *colonialism than academic or intellectual qualities. In 1829, at the first Oxford–Cambridge boat race, also the first sporting competition between the two universities, the rowers of Oxford from Christ Church wore dark blue, their college colours, though the Cambridge crew was in pink or scarlet; the following year the Cambridge boat was adorned with a light blue ribbon (possibly a colour adopted from the public school Eton). These shades of blue became the official colours of the crews, and the language and recognition were adopted in other sports, and the tradition and convention of the 'blues' established.

boating A term referring to the relatively informal and casual activity of sailing in boats, rather than to more formal, organized, and competitive activities such as *rowing or *sailing. The term has the associations of idling along the river, *punting being one such variant; and it is evoked in the name given to the classic leisure headgear, the 'boater'.

boat racing *See* Oxford–Cambridge Boat Race.

bobsleigh Also called bobsledding, a winter sport in which women compete in two-crew events, and men in two- and four-crew teams. The sled is steered down a specially constructed high-sided, steeply banked, as well as bending, track of solid ice; no braking is permitted in competition, and speeds have exceeded 200 kilometres per hour. Originally made of wood, bobsleds have become technologically sophisticated products. Bobsleigh courses have been constructed in the European Alps and in New York State, USA (Lake Placid), most of them initially for an Olympic Games.

The sport originated among English visitors to the Alps in the 1860s, and as a more organized but still informal activity on specifically designed tracks in the 1870s, in St Moritz, Switzerland, where local tourist entrepreneur Caspar Badrutt provided winter sports opportunities for new international tourist markets. It developed distinctly from *tobogganing and, after being staged competitively on the Cresta Run in 1998, from the one-man bobsleighing of the Cresta (*see* TOBOGGANING, SKELETON). The world's first separate bobsleigh run was built in 1902 in St Moritz. Its international governing body was formed in France in 1923, inspired by Franz Reichel, a sport journalist for *Le Figaro*, though the federation covered tobogganing too, and went on to be based in Milan, Italy; men's four-crew featured in the first winter Olympics in 1924, men's two-crew being added in 1932.

Bobsleigh has featured in every winter Olympic Games since, apart from in 1960. Switzerland, Italy, and Germany have been the most successful and high-profile nations in international competition, with Austria, Canada, and the USA also featuring prominently. Two-woman crew events were held at the Olympics from 2002 onwards. The sport achieved widespread publicity when the film *Cool Runnings* (1993) was made, featuring the far from competitive—and therefore highly appealing—exploits of Jamaica's first-ever bobsleigh Olympians at the 1988 Calgary (Canada) Olympics.

body, sociology of the A burgeoning area of study in the last two decades of the 20th century, with obvious relevance to work on sport. Sport locates the performing body centrally in the competitive encounter, and media coverage of sport foregrounds the athletic body in its coverage, often sexualizing the body in close-up, in the cases of both male and female performers. The journal *Body & Society*, established in 1995, reflected the expanding interest in the body, fuelled by feminist theory, gay studies, medical sociology, cultural studies, and the widespread impact of the work of Michel *Foucault on the disciplining of the body. In their introduction to the inaugural issue of the journal, Mike Featherstone and Bryan Turner included the sociology of sport as one of the six areas in which the body has been given considerable attention, citing the work of French sociologists George Vigarello and Pierre *Bourdieu, and the latter's protégé Loïc Wacquant's work on professional boxing. As well as such work on the body as 'incorporating practice', Featherstone and Turner noted the possibility provided by sport for the losing of one's body in a collective euphoria of the physical.

Pioneering work on the body was also produced by John Hargreaves, on the physical education curriculum's disciplining of the young body, in his *Sport, Power and Culture: A Social and Historical Analysis of Popular Sports in Britain* (1986); and a neglected cultural studies contribution to understanding the sporting body was in part rectified by Andrew Blake's *Body Language: The Meaning of Modern Sport* (1996). A sociology of the sporting body also raises questions about the sexual, sometimes voyeuristic and frequently narcissistic, dimension of sport spectating and sport fandom. In his *Sportsex* (2001) Toby Miller acknowledges the significant positive aspects of sporting spectatorship and participation, but reminds us that 'narcissism, a high component of commodification, intense sexist pressure about body image, and unpleasant associations with militarism and Tayloristic discipline are dominant' in the sporting culture.

bodybuilding A form of physical culture in which (mainly) men and (some) women develop muscular bodies for competitive display. It achieved levels of international popularity in the later 19th century and into the 20th, in the burgeoning visual and print media where the musculature of the strong man or the bodybuilder could gain unprecedented levels of attention, in magazines and related self-help products that focused upon the development of the individual body as a means of personal transformation, and in live touring spectacles of physical display. Bodybuilding has also had a fascinating subcultural dimension, related to the forms of drug-taking necessary for the physical development of the body, and to the complex gender and sexual dynamics sometimes characteristic of its practitioners and followers. The classic study of the cultural base of the practice is Alan M. Klein's *Little Big Men: Bodybuilding Subculture and Gender Construction* (1993). *See also* ATLAS, CHARLES; SANDOW, EUGEN.

body combat A frenetic form of fitness and exercise activity that emphasizes 'cardio fitness' and claims to be inspired by *martial arts. It has been described by some of its promoters as 'empowering' with the capacity to 'totally unleash' the participant, in an intoxicating mix of fighting sports from both the West and the East—with none of the traditional blend of the physical and the spiritual that marks many Japanese physical disciplines, for instance. Body combatants usually train to 'driving music', and web images designed to attract participants foreground the aggressive muscular male looking venomously towards his invisible target or opponent. Body combat illustrates the way in which a body culture can seek to make respectable a form of aggression-based physical masculinity that in other spheres of social life would be unacceptable.

body composition A quantification of the main structural components of the body relevant to sport and exercise, i.e. fat, muscle, and bone. Assessment of body composition is valuable in sport to monitor the impact of training and to help identify the optimal lean body mass. The simplest approach is to determine height and weight, and tables of this ratio have long been used by insurance actuaries to determine mortality risk. Height and weight tables provide only a very coarse measurement, particularly in sport, since they do not reflect the composition of the body and an increased muscle mass is indistinguishable from an increased fat mass. The body mass index (BMI) provides a slightly improved measure. The BMI is the mass (kg) divided by the height squared (m). Large-scale epidemiological data provide standards for underweight, normal, overweight, and obese. The BMI provides a very simple and cheap means of measurement but it remains coarse since it does not account well for body composition nor does it reflect the distribution of fat.

A number of other measurement techniques can be used to determine body composition. Hydrostatic (or underwater) weighing utilizes Archimedes' principle to determine the density of the whole body and then the Siri equation to determine the percentage of fat and the percentage of non-fat mass. The Bod Pod utilizes air-displacement plethysmography to determine body fat percentage in a similar manner to hydrostatic weighing. Skinfold measurement uses a pincer-like caliper to determine the thickness of subcutaneous fat at a number of sites around the body. The thicknesses can then be used directly to assess relative fatness in different areas or between different individuals, or they can be used in special equations to estimate the overall body fatness. Girths can be used in a similar manner. Similarly, ultrasound, X-rays, computerized axial tomography (CAT scan), and magnetic resonance imaging (MRI) have been used to determine the bone/muscle/fat composition of specific regions and the whole body. Bioelectrical impedance analysis relies on the principle that the impedance to an alternating current flowing between two electrodes is related to the water content of tissues and estimates body fat percentage based on the relative differences in hydration, and therefore current flow, between fat, bone, and other tissues.

body language An everyday term used to describe or capture the physical demeanour of the sportsman or -woman. It is used in a fairly unsystematic way, by onlookers and commentators alike, to account for the performance of the competitor. Body language discussed in this way has generated predictable clichés: the 'heads have gone down' of the dispirited losing side; the double-faulting tennis player is explained by the imprecise 'the body language tells it all'. Some kinds of body language have been absorbed into pre-match or pre-contest practices: the *haka* of the New Zealand rugby union players, for instance, or their equivalents among other rugby countries such as Fiji and Tonga; the hostile stare of the boxers as they touch gloves before the bout. A more systematic attempt to study and understand what is talked of as body language has been developed in the social psychological study of *non-verbal communication.

body mass index *See* BODY COMPOSITION.

Bosman The surname of a Belgian footballer, Jean-Marc Bosman, whose case concerning contractual freedoms was heard by the European Commission's Court of Justice in December 1995. Based on the interpretation of Articles 48, 85, and 86 of the European Economic Community Treaty, the ruling introduced two significant changes: the legality of foreign player restrictions anywhere in the European Union (EU) was ended in cases of players with citizenship of an EU country; and the right of any EU player to move anywhere in the EU at the end of his contract, and with no transfer fee, was confirmed. 'Getting him on a Bosman' soon entered the lexicon of the football industry.

Bourdieu, Pierrre (1930–2002) A French anthropologist and sociologist whose influence on the analysis of sport's social and cultural significance has been widespread and immense. His initial specialist research was in the anthropology of work and gender in peasant societies, particularly Algeria. His broader interests included the sociology of taste, art, the media, and sport, framed by the general theme of power and culture's relation to power and privilege. In his book *Distinction: A Social Critique of the Judgement of Taste* (1986) he identified sport as a major source of prestige and social position. Based on questionnaire surveys carried out in 1963 and 1967–8, on a sample of 1,217 people, this study established the close link between cultural practices, including the opinions and attitudes embodied in those practices, and upbringing and social origin. As part of this, the analysis in *Distinction* showed that participation in sports was determined by *social class. Therefore, at that time in France, boxing, football, rugby, or body-building could be said to evoke the working class; tennis and skiing the bourgeoisie; and golf the upper bourgeoisie. His concepts *habitus, capital, and field were central to this perspective. Capital is a core notion for Bourdieu; though not systematically defined, it is identified in its economic, cultural, educational, and symbolic forms. A field, for Bourdieu, is a 'network, or a configuration, of objective relations between positions' (Bourdieu and L. J. D. Wacquant, *An Invitation to Reflexive Sociology*, 1992: 97), and he talks recurrently of the artistic, religious, or economic fields: to this can be added the field of sport, the sport field relating to particular sets of relations between agents engaged in the same activity.

bowling stones A traditional sport played in the villages and surrounding countryside of pre-industrial England and surviving into the early 20th century. Its popularity was based on its cheapness, as stones were gathered from the countryside and 'bowled' along outdoor routes, and on the accessibility of the matches to keen gambling publics. Such an activity was of clear threat to urban settings in which trade, commerce, and residential respectability were at the core of the new industrial and commercial social order. Bowling stones was, by the 1920s and 1930s, legislated out of official existence in English urban areas.

bowls A ball game played in both indoor and outdoor (lawn bowls) forms in the UK, with variants in other cultures and societies in which it can be played on rough outdoor surfaces, such as boules (*jeu provençal*, or **pétanque*) in France. The essential form of bowls is to aim one ball of a larger size at a target smaller ball, with players having numerous attempts to place one of their balls nearest to the target ball. In the UK, the most widespread modern form of the sport is played on flat greens (there are, though, regional variants such as **crown-green bowls). The game offers extensive opportunities for participation, as it can be played between individuals, or teams of two, three, or four (the latter sometimes called 'rinks').

Bowls enthusiasts claim the sport as 'the oldest of British games with the exception of archery', as written by the English Singles Champion of 1925 (H. P. Webber, *Bowls*, 1948). Joseph Strutt (*Sports and Pastimes of the People of England*, 1801) traced the English game back to the 13th century, when the target was cones rather than a ball, and the sport had much in common with **skittles. It was one of the sports that, in the mid 16th century, was banned by statute, but that people, including the English monarch, continued to play, and at that time bowls with bias were first introduced. English historical legend also relates that naval commander Sir Francis Drake (1542–96) was playing bowls on Plymouth Hoe, Devon (in England), when the invading Spanish Armada was sighted. The game was also popular in Scotland and at the Edinburgh court in the 16th century.

In its modern form, bowls was codified with standard rules in the mid 19th century in Glasgow, Scotland, and more gradually in England. The International Bowling Board was established in 1905 in Cardiff, Wales, and the game spread in popularity in the UK in both private clubs and clubs based in municipal parks. A century on, the organization World Bowls (now affiliated to the Confédération Mondiale des Sports de Boules, and via that body to the International Olympic Committee) reported that it represented 52 national associations in 46 member nations, and sought to 'develop a distinct and modern persona for the game'. This was its biggest challenge, as the sport for several generations had not appealed to new constituencies of younger player, and in many parts of England at least, the number of volunteers needed to run the game at its formal club level was decreasing dramatically. *See also* TENPIN BOWLING.

boxing In its modern form, fist-fighting with gloves in a roped-off ring over an agreed period of timed 'rounds'. These timings vary in amateur and professional fights, or bouts, and the amateur format that is an Olympic event is shorter, and scores in different ways, prioritizing touch and skill, from the professional sport. The professional heavyweight boxer has had the highest international profile, for two reasons: the attraction of the atavistic nature of the encounter to expanding media audiences (and traditional constituencies of gambler and betting fan); and the symbolism that has been attached to boxers as representatives of a nation, ethnic group, or race. The moral controversy over boxing is simple: how can an activity whose primary goal is to render an opponent defenceless and senseless be considered an acceptable form of sport in a civilized age? A legal ban on boxing in Sweden in 1970 was questioned and reframed 35 years later, and live boxing bouts can still fill halls in large cities and provide lucrative schedules for international broadcasts.

Prior to the codified form of the sport, bare-knuckle boxing provided bloody spectacles for gentry and common people alike, peaking in Britain in the late 18th century and early 19th century. John Sholto Douglas, ninth marquess of Queensberry (1844–1900), while at Magdalene College, University of Cambridge, for two years from 1864, engaged in hunting, steeplechasing, running, and cricket, and became interested in sport promotion, visiting the USA in 1866 with fellow Cambridge student J. G. Chambers (1843–83) and noting that the essentially disreputable sport of boxing was in need of reform. Returning from that trip, Douglas lent his titled name to the Queensberry Rules (1867), specifically to supersede the very open-ended London prize-ring rules of 1839. These twelve rules specified the dimensions of a ring for a stand-up encounter; that no wrestling or hugging be allowed; that rounds should last three minutes, with a one-minute break between rounds; the conditions of a count and a knockout; that 'hanging on the ropes' helplessly should be treated as being 'down', on the floor; that no seconds (assistants) or other persons be allowed in the ring; that the referee could rearrange a fight, or continue it, should a contest 'be stopped by any unavoidable interference'; that gloves should be worn, 'fair-sized' and 'of the best quality and new'; that burst or slipped-off gloves should be replaced; that a fighter on one knee should be deemed to be 'down', therefore not strikeable; that no shoes or boots should contain springs; and that otherwise, the contest should be 'governed by the revised rules of the London Prize Ring'. Queensberry, famous too for his legal victory over Oscar Wilde (1854–1900) relating to the playwright's homosexual relationship with his son Lord Alfred Douglas (1870–1945), left a legacy that modernized boxing, though it was not until the early 1880s that the world championship was settled according to the Queensberry Rules (and not until the 1890s with gloves). A Women Boxing Archive Network (see web link below) has compiled a chronology of women's boxing (primarily in the USA and Britain) from the 18th century to the later 20th century, when women challenged bans on their participation in the sport, and activists promoted the rights of women to engage in the so-called 'manly art'.

The draw of the boxing ring has been based in the one-on-one intensity of the boxing encounter, and testimony to its continuing worldwide popularity into the later 20th century and beyond is the status as one of the most famous, respected, and charismatic sportsmen of all time, Muhammad Ali, the former Cassius Clay, US heavyweight champion several times over. Despite the obvious ways in which numerous results have been 'fixed'—at Olympic Games, notoriously in Seoul in 1988, and in match-based television deals with individual fighters—the boxing ring and the atavistic nature of the encounter have continued to attract extensive audiences and so to sustain a prominent place in the global sporting consciousness.
See also BARCLAY, CAPTAIN; BURNS, TOMMY; CARPENTIER, GEORGES; CORBETT, JAMES J. ('GENTLEMAN' JIM); CRIBB, TOM; DEMPSEY, JACK; JEFFRIES, JAMES JACKSON (JIM); JOHANSSON, INGEMAR; JOHNSON, JOHN ARTHUR (JACK); LISTON, CHARLES L. ('SONNY'); LOUIS, JOE; MARCIANO, ROCKY; PATTERSON, FLOYD; RICHMOND, BILL; SCHMELING, MAXIMILLIAN ADOLPH OTTO SIEGFRIED; SULLIVAN, JOHN LAWRENCE.

SEE WEB LINKS

- The site of the Women Boxing Archive Network, cataloguing incidences and the survival and growth of women's boxing.

boycott The act, or policy, of cutting off relations with an individual or a social entity, such as trade, commercial, or sporting relations with a particular country (the term derives from the English land agent Captain Boycott who was treated in this way by the native Irish in the 1880s). Boycotts in sport have been used as forms of international diplomacy to bring a policy such as *apartheid into disrepute, or as ways of expressing diplomatic disapproval of non-sporting acts such as military aggression or war. The US president Jimmy Carter led one such boycott in 1980, urging non-Communist nations to boycott the Moscow Olympics in protest at the USSR's invasion of Afghanistan in December 1979. Carter threatened to revoke the passports of any US athlete who tried to get to Moscow the following summer, and 65 nations boycotted the event. The Soviet Union led a retaliatory boycott of the Los Angeles Olympics of 1984: only fourteen nations stayed away, but those nations had won 58 per cent of the gold medals at the 1976 Games in Montreal (the bulk of the medals in *weightlifting and freestyle *wrestling, for instance, and many of those in *gymnastics and women's athletics). At the Montreal Games, 22 African nations refused to participate, boycotting in protest at New Zealand's rugby union tour of South Africa. Ten years earlier, at the football World Cup in England, the North Korea football team got in to the tournament without playing a qualifying game; the African and Asian confederations boycotted the qualifying competition in protest at the disproportionate allocation of places for their federations in the final tournament. In some cases, these boycotts have changed stubborn and reactionary attitudes, and sport can claim much credit in the fight against apartheid. The 1966 boycott was also significant in the shifting power base of the administration of world football. The Cold War boycotts of 1980 and 1984 were simply superpower games, but one price that international sport has to pay for its enhanced global profile is the fact that agencies, institutions, and nations recognize that cultural politics are as much a part of sport as the contest on the track or in the auditorium.

Bradman, Sir Don (Donald George) (1908–2001) An Australian cricketer whose batting statistics set groundbreaking world records, for single-innings scores, for aggregates of runs in match series, and for the number of centuries (a score in a single innings of 100 or more) in all his international (Test) matches. He became a major celebrity in Australia, and in other cricket-playing countries, attracting, throughout his playing career from 1927 to 1949, record attendances and crowds across the world. At his last Test match, in England in 1948, he failed to score the four runs needed to achieve an average Test score of 100 for his career (it was 99.94). Bradman worked in cricket administration after retiring from competitive play, and in the year of his retirement was awarded a knighthood, the first Australian cricketer to receive the honour. Many—and not just Australians—believe Bradman to be the greatest cricketer of the 20th century. This of course is unprovable, but nevertheless the stuff of sporting gossip that sustains the profile of the game and its players in the public's imagination and consciousness.

Brasher, Christopher William (1928–2003) A British Guiana-born English amateur athlete of the mid 20th century. Brasher lived in Jerusalem before, at the age of 7, moving to England, and attending preparatory school, Rugby School, and St John's College, Cambridge. At Cambridge, he was an outstanding middle- and long-distance runner, representing the university and the Achilles Club (the club, formed in 1920, for past and present members of the Cambridge and Oxford athletics clubs). Brasher was pivotal to the success, in May 1954, of English runner Roger Bannister in breaking the *four-minute mile barrier, and went on to personal glory at the Melbourne Olympics in 1956, winning the gold medal for the 3,000-metre steeplechase. Retiring from competitive athletics after his Olympic triumph, Brasher worked in sport journalism, serving four years as sports editor of _The Observer_, and then working as a freelance writer, broadcaster, and sports promoter. A keen outdoor all-rounder, he founded the British Orienteering Federation in 1966, and diversified into business—sport equipment chain Sweat Shop, and his own-brand Brasher Boot—as well as organizing London's first marathon in 1981, two years after running the marathon in New York City. Allegations of financial mismanagement of the London Marathon were made against Brasher by Channel 4 television and the magazine _New Statesman_, but he successfully defended himself against these in the courts and gained considerable damages. Brasher also supported initiatives for the protection of the countryside and open spaces, combining the legacy of a high-performance career with a continuing commitment to the benefits of physical exercise for all.

bread and circuses A term referring to the potential of spectator sports and mass spectacle to divert populations or factions of a population away from the weightier business of politics and society, and to entertain them with amusements and physical contests. It is a term used in, and widely mistranslated from, the writings of the Roman satirist *Juvenal. The key idea of the phrase is that, to cite a more contemporary source, Neil Postman, following novelist Aldous Huxley's _Brave New World_: 'people are controlled by inflicting pleasure' (_Amusing Ourselves to Death: Public Discourse in the Age of Show Business_, 1985). Television—in which 'much of our public discourse has become dangerous nonsense', Postman asserts—has become the new arena to which the 'bread and circuses' argument can be applied. _See also_ MAGNIFICENT TRIVIA.

bricolage In French, do-it-yourself; the most prominent do-it-yourself chain store in modern, and patriarchal, France has been _Monsieur Bricolage_. In cultural analysis, the term derives from work in French anthropology, and refers to the process of the formation of a 'new' cultural object on the basis of the appropriation and combination of different cultural elements; mixing images into new formations can challenge and change meanings. The concept was applied to youth subcultures by researchers at the University of Birmingham's Centre for Contemporary Cultural Studies: John Clarke interpreted skinhead practices and values as the 'magical restoration of working class community', so portraying them as cultural _bricoleurs_ (_Resistance through Rituals_, ed. Stuart Hall et al., 1976); Dick Hebdige, in his influential _Subculture: The Meaning of Style_ (1979), took it as a core concept for the analysis of punk style. The concept is an important one for accounting for cultural change and cultural interventions with the capacity to subvert established meanings: in sport, the clothes and style of the snowboarder are deliberately adopted as a challenge to the orthodox and established skiing culture; in histories of sport more generally, the development of sports (both through time and across cultures) can be seen as a process of cultural formation based upon pioneering and sometimes subversive interventions by *bricoleurs*. *See also* ALTERITY; CULTURAL DIFFUSION; HYBRIDITY.

Brighton Declaration A declaration—also called a 'Declaration of Principles'—made by an international meeting of sport activists, progressive women scholars, policy-makers, and practitioners, on the urgent need to challenge the persistingly patriarchal framework of sport culture and international sport administration. The declaration is so called because it was drafted and formulated at a meeting in the Grand Hotel, Brighton, England, in 1994. Its general commitment statement was: 'It is in the interests of equality, development and peace, that a commitment is made by governments, non-governmental organizations and all those institutions involved in sport to apply the Principles', of which there were ten, all of which should be more fully applied to women worldwide: equity and equality; facility provision; school and junior sport development and provision; developing participation; support and development for high performance; leadership; education, training, and development; information and research on and for women; resources for all levels of involvement; and domestic and international cooperation. The Brighton Declaration was a milestone in the women's sports movement, transcending feminist factions and formulating the challenges and aspirations that could feasibly challenge 'malestream' sport.

(((∰))) **SEE WEB LINKS**

• Background on the declaration by the International Working Group on Women and Sport.

Brookes, William Penny (1809–95) An enthusiast for the notion of the revival of the ancient Olympic Games. Son of a surgeon and a surgeon himself in turn, Brookes was born in Much Wenlock, Shropshire, and studied medicine in London, Padua, and Paris, taking over his father's practice in his hometown in 1831. Covering a large rural area, Brookes was known to ride up to seventy miles a day on his medical duties. Botanist and linguist, and master of Greek, French, and Latin, Brookes was also interested in the benefits of physical education. An active citizen in Much Wenlock, he is most famous for combining his classicist and physical educational interests into annual games, beginning in 1849, 'for literary and fine-art attainments, and for skill and strength in athletics'. These were expanded into the Shropshire Olympian games (1861), and Brookes and others went on to form the National Olympian Society (1865), whose first games were held at Crystal Palace in 1866, attracting over 10,000 spectators. It has been stated that this prompted the formation of the Amateur Athletic Club (later Association). Pierre de Coubertin, founder of the modern Olympics, visited the Wenlock Olympian Games in 1890, after Brookes responded to de Coubertin's newspaper announcement in the English press promoting his Paris Congress on Physical Training, and has acknowledged the vision of Brookes, and its influence upon his own thinking.

Brundage, Avery (1887–1975) A US athlete, Republican politician, and self-made businessman turned sport administrator, Brundage was born in Detroit,

Michigan. His competitive event at the 1912 Stockholm Olympics was the
decathlon. He was the 84-year-old president of the *International Olympic
Committee (IOC) at the time of the Munich terrorist tragedy in 1972. Brundage was
president of the US Olympic Association and Committee from 1929 to 1953; and
vice-president of the International Olympic Committee from 1945 to 1952, then
assuming the presidency for two decades until 1972.

Brundage was a defendant of amateurism, opposed the commercialization of the
Olympics, and cultivated an authoritarian presence in international sporting
administration. He insisted that sport should transcend politics—captured most
controversially in his announcement on 6 September 1972 in Munich, after the
murder by Palestinian terrorists of eleven Israeli athletes:

> We have only the strength of a great ideal. I am sure that the public will agree
> that we cannot allow a handful of terrorists to destroy this nucleus of
> international cooperation and good will we have in the Olympic movement.
> The Games must go on and we must continue our efforts to keep them clean,
> pure and honest and try to extend the sportsmanship of the athletic field into
> other areas.

At the meeting of the IOC executive board the day after the announcement, it was
business as usual for the Olympic committee members, Brundage condemning as
'disgraceful' the commercialization of athletes wearing rival manufacturers' shoe
brands. Brundage also summarized the four options that had been considered
before deciding to continue the event, and it was generally agreed that 'there would
be no large occasions until the end of the Games, i.e. no receptions, no music, a
short Closing Ceremony and it should be emphasised that the teams were staying
solely for the sake of sport'. For the sake of sport alone? Yet the Games must go on
because of their influence 'into other areas'. In this central tension and
contradiction Brundage personified the arguments that have surfaced and
resurfaced for many years between the purportedly apolitical idealist and the
activists and scholars for whom sport itself is a form of cultural politics.

Brundage, widowed in 1971, once joked to a German friend 'that his ambition was to
marry a German princess' (Allen Guttmann, *The Games Must Go On: Avery Brundage
and the Olympic Movement*, 1984). Retiring from his IOC position after Munich, in
1973 at the age of 85 he married the 37-year-old daughter of the ruler of a tiny German
principality, and bought a house in Garmisch, Germany—site of the 1936 winter
Olympics—where he died of heart failure in 1975. He had argued consistently that the
best ever Olympic Games had been those of 1936 in Germany, and he was a long-term
member of a freemason's lodge in Chicago. For someone arguing for the capacity of
sport to transcend politics, he had a very well-defined political position and profile,
also opposing the expansion of women's sports in athletics/track-and-field. *See also*
BLANKERS-KOEN, FANNY; COMMERCIALIZATION; INTERNATIONAL OLYMPIC COMMITTEE.

SEE WEB LINKS
• An inventory of the Avery Brundage collection at the University of Illinois Archives.

bulimia *See* EATING DISORDERS.

bull-baiting A form of animal-baiting, or blood sport, in which a bull was tied
by rope to an iron ring fixed to a stake in the ground, and then set upon by a bulldog,

usually prior to being killed by the local butcher. The practice was widely established in the calendar of holidays and wakes in 18th-century England, often supported by the local parish or borough corporation. Opposition to such practices developed in the early decades of the 19th century, when they were condemned as cruel and increasingly perceived as disreputable. As Robert Malcolmson writes: 'The movement against popular blood sports was at its peak during the first forty years of the nineteenth century; by the 1840s most of them had been almost entirely eliminated' (*Popular Recreations in English Society, 1700–1850*, 1973).

bullfighting *See* CORRIDA DE TOROS.

bureaucracy Etymologically (French and Greek), a term referring to the power of deskwork, or what we would call administration. It is widely recognized that a key stage in the formation of modern sports is the setting up of a bureaucratic organizational and administrative base for the sport, capable of formulating rules and shared understanding of the nature of the sport and its staging and scheduling. For Allen Guttmann, 'bureaucracy' is one of the seven characteristics defining the nature of modern sport. The term was developed in its sociological form by Max *Weber, for whom bureaucracy—as an *ideal type—was the organizational means of effecting rational action and authority, and had six characteristics: it was ordered by rules or administrative regulations; it rested on a clear, ordered, hierarchical system of the supervision of lower office by higher ones; modern office procedures and management were based on written documents, in the form of accessible files; office managers must be trained; in the fully developed bureaucracy or office, the official worked full-time; office procedure and management followed general rules, the learning of which required technical training. Weber also catalogued aspects of the bureaucratic official's position: for instance, the job was a vocation, often a career for life; and rank and status followed on from the official's position.

Many sports were developed in their modern organizational forms at precisely the time at which Weber was writing about bureaucracy, in the early years of the 20th century, and have further developed, in their professional and commercial forms in particular, the characteristics of ideal-typical bureaucracy that he outlined. One especially interesting dimension of sport bureaucracies is the pace at which they have or have not assumed these modern dimensions, and the extent to which officeholders have retained their positions in the organization regardless of the efficiency with which they have conducted the bureaucratic business or the organizational tasks. In this sense bureaucracies can begin to work against the very objectives that were the basis of their formation. Interestingly, an earlier use of the word (1848) is found in the writings of English philosopher and political scientist John Stuart Mill, who considered it unwise to concentrate organized action and power 'in a dominant bureaucracy'. Ruling bodies of sport, at both national and international levels, are interesting case studies on the basis of which Mill's assertion might be tested.

burnout The state in which an athlete, in either an individual contest or an overall career, no longer performs to his or her potential, and competitive effectiveness and achievements deteriorate consistently and even drastically.

Burnout is a consequence of both physical and psychological influences, and the complex interplay of such influences. Burnout can occur in relatively young athletes, for whom a *celebrity status creates more problems than advantages, and the balance between public life and consistent performance is a turbulent one; in champion athletes such as tennis players for whom the relentless international circuit of the professional game becomes an intolerable bubble, a pressurized cocoon; or in ageing performers who realize that their feats of earlier years are now beyond them, and for whom all the psychological preparation in the world cannot compensate for declining physical condition and capacity. The determinants, states, and consequences of burnout are difficult to identify with absolute precision, but it is a lay term with undeniable resonance in the experience and individual careers of sportsmen and -women.

Burns, Tommy (1881–1955) Born Noah Brusso, Burns is the only Canadian-born boxer to hold the world heavyweight championship, which he defended eleven times within two years from 1906 to 1908. One of thirteen children, he left his home territory of Ontario, Canada, to begin his prizefighting career at Detroit, Michigan, in the USA. Extraordinarily short (5 feet 7 inches) for a heavyweight, Burns was the first champion to accept a challenge from a black boxer, losing his title to Jack Johnson of the USA in a bout in Sydney, Australia. After his boxing career he ran a speakeasy in New York but lost much of his fortune in the Great Crash of 1929, and went on to become ordained and to work as an evangelical preacher in Canada, though he was buried in an unmarked pauper's grave.

buyer's market A situation in which the value of a product has fallen, and the buyer may acquire the product with the strong likelihood of accruing high profits. In sport, the product is inherently volatile, and so the market for, say, players or clubs may exhibit great internal variation. If a football club in England, for instance, falls out of the top division, its value can plummet so that a current owner may be desperate to offset the losses accrued, so creating a buyer's market for that particular club.

buzkashi A traditional game of the nomadic peoples of central Asia, which has been seen as an antecedent of modern equestrian *polo. It has survived into the 21st century in an Afghan form, 'characterized by a dusty melee in which hundreds of mountain tribesmen struggled to seize the headless carcass of a goat' (Allen Guttmann, *Sports: The First Five Millennia*, 2004). In one variant the single victor was the individual who could get hold of one of the animal's legs and drag it clear of the rest of the horsemen. The sport is considered to be the Afghan (male's) national sport, and attracts crowds of thousands, justified by its practitioners and apologists as a means of teaching the riders not just equestrian skills, but principles of communication and teamwork.

Byzantium, sport in From the early 4th century to the crusades and the conquering of Constantinople by the Turkish Sultanate, the eastern empire of Byzantium, centred on the metropolitan capital of Constantinople, continued some of the sporting traditions of the Roman Republic and Roman Empire. The Hippodrome was a racetrack laid out at the heart of the imperial city, along the lines of Rome's *Circus Maximus. Turkish baths were versions of the Roman institution, and both public and (many more) private baths were installed early in the city's history. Travel writer and popular history writer Robert Byron called the Hippodrome the 'pivot of popular recreation in Constantinople' (*The Byzantine Achievement*, 1929): 'Sharing the central tableland of the city with St Sophia, and topping the declivity of the Great Palace, it completed the triple symbolism of Emperor, Patriarch and People at the core of the Empire.' The Hippodrome was the focus for 'all the passion of popular leisure' concentrated on the chariot races and public games. Factions from the city had different levels of membership: those who paid annual subscriptions; the drivers and racing personnel themselves; and, as Byron put it, 'the unregistered masses'. The factions were highly organized, each with 'its president, stables, stud-farms, chariots, employees and supporters/ mummers'. The factions adopted colours, and became known as the Reds and the Greens. Betting on the races was widespread, initiated in the imperial box itself. Crowds could be threatening and uncontrolled, and on one occasion rioted across the city. Within the upper levels of Byzantine society, contests took place within laid-out sports arenas—albeit on a more modest scale than the Hippodrome— within the palace precincts, where a form of polo borrowed from Persia was played.

What Byron calls the 'cult of the stable' reached its peak in the 9th and 10th centuries: one emperor, Michael III the Drunkard, raced chariots himself, and the Hippodrome remained fully used until the fourth crusade. It was used by the Sultans themselves for public ceremony before remaining elements of it were used in constructing the Sultan Ahmet (Blue) Mosque in 1610. The spatial scale of the Hippodrome is still clearly discernible in modern Istanbul, at the heart of the old city. *See also* CHARIOT RACING.

caber tossing A traditional sport of the Scottish Highlands, a long-established competition event for professional Scottish athletes and participants in traditional games meetings. The caber is a tree trunk or pole, stripped of its bark, of no set proportions, size, or weight, though usually around 17 feet (5 metres) long and weighing somewhere near 90 pounds (40 kilograms). The aim of the sport is to turn the caber in a certain way, rather than aim for distance: it is arguably, therefore, more concerned with technique than brute strength. It is an event exclusive to Scottish *Highland Games, and its cultural distinctiveness includes the sartorial condition that the male contestant must wear a kilt.

caddie A person who accompanies the golfer on his or her round, carrying the clubs that the golfer will choose to use for respective shots. The word reputedly derives from the masculine noun in French, *le caddie* (the junior/youngster). Early professionals in the amateur golfing world were skilled all-rounders from modest social backgrounds, who often began as caddies, developing observational experience and technical knowledge about the course and equipment, and the best choice of shot and club, and evolving into club professionals. The caddie is a vital part of the modern professional golfer's support team, offering a combination of technical advice and personal and psychological support to the individual contestant.

Caesar, Julius Gaius (100–44 BC) From 49 to 44 BC, the ruler of the Roman Republic as its 'dictator for life'. He had secured power and popularity on the basis of his military conquests, and, like his successor Sulla, usurped powers of a dictatorial kind for his own ends, so contributing to the conditions leading to the downfall of the republic. He recognized the utility of sport and spectacle in the consolidation of political power. Caesar was a supporter of *gladiatorial games on a grand scale, and owned his own school of 5,000 gladiators. In 65 BC, he had arranged an event in honour of his father involving 320 pairs of gladiators, bedecked in silver armour; a century earlier, the equivalent event had drawn upon only 25 pairs. He saw and exploited skilfully the political potential of mass spectacle, staging a combat in memory of his daughter, and enhancing the scale of the *Circus Maximus. Roland Auguet credits Caesar with the creation, 'at least in embryo', of 'the amphitheatre and the imperial *ludi*, realizing that it was necessary to endow the authorities with the means of contenting a mob ever more greedy for this kind of spectacle' (*Cruelty and Civilization: the Roman Games*, 1972).

CAF *See* Confédération Africaine de Football.

Caillois, Roger (1913–78) A French scholar whose study *Man, Play and Games* (1969) includes a fourfold classification of play/games: Agon/competition; Alea/chance; mimicry/pretence; and Ilinx/*vertigo. This has been adapted to numerous sport contexts and the relevance of the classification has been reaffirmed by the emphasis in some sports upon the thrill of the moment, and the experience of balancing challenge and control in physical activity. Caillois also emphasized the importance and attraction of the uncertain element in play and sports that was guaranteed to offer a source of excitement away from the routines of everyday life. He wrote of the human need to feel the body's stability and equilibrium temporarily destroyed, in order to escape the 'tyranny of perception'. One anthropologist, Shirley Prendergast, has described the playing of stoolball, by women in an English village in East Sussex, as 'the pursuit of vertigo' (in *Women's Studies International Quarterly*, 1, 1978).

calcio An early form of football played in 16th-century Florence, Italy, that became known as the Florentine kick game (*calcio* means 'kick'). Its documented rules allowed the use of hands as well as feet, and specified teams of 27. The formulation of a game of this sort so early has led historians to dispute the claims made by many that Britain is the birthplace of football/soccer. Some of these discussions are of little value, though, as the *calcio* game, played initially by the privileged elite, did not sustain a strong cultural profile, and so can hardly be seen as a precursor or antecedent of the modern organized form of soccer. Revivals of the sport date from the 1930s, but these are marginal practices within Italy's sporting culture. The term has been used by some to lend a distinctive national historical dimension to the term soccer, though this establishes no credible historical lineage.

Calcutta Cup A trophy competed for annually between the *rugby union national sides of England and Scotland. It was first played for in 1879, having been presented to the Rugby Football Union the previous year by the Calcutta Rugby Club, which had been formed in India in 1873 after a game of rugby between twenty Englishmen and twenty Scots or Celts. When the club disbanded, it used its funds to commission the cup, which has in the 20th century been contested within the programme of the Six Nations tournament.

calf roping A *rodeo event, also known as 'tie-down' roping, in which the horse-mounted rider is timed as he catches a calf by throwing a rope around its neck, dismounting, and tying three legs of the calf together. It derives from the working practices of cowboys in North America in the 19th and 20th centuries, and has been recognized by most professional rodeo organizations. The event has been the focus of animal rights protesters, who have reported injuries to and the maiming of calves; authorities have agreed in some cases, the event being banned in Rhode Island and in the city of Baltimore, USA. The survival of the event is evidence of the enduring influence of masculinist working practices in the sport entertainment sphere, and of an atavistic attraction to human–animal contests (though some would argue that this is barely a contest) on the part of the spectators.

Calgary Stampede Billing itself as 'The Greatest Outdoor Show on Earth', an annual ten-day event in Calgary, Canada, widely recognized as the world's largest outdoor *rodeo. The event combines races between wagons, exhibitions, concerts, and agricultural competitions, as well as the rodeo events, and attracts more than 1.2 million visitors. It is a celebration of the image of the cowboy and the nostalgic tradition of the outdoor horseman. Critics point to danger, death, and animal cruelty, but traditionalists argue the values of continuity and community; the event claims a history from 1912, and gave its name to the prominent professional football team the Calgary Stampeders.

Californian sports A term—*les sports californiens*—used by French sociologist Pierre *Bourdieu to refer to individualized and usually outdoor sports (that have also been called '*whiz sports' by Nancy Midol in France), many of which emanated from the west coast of the USA. Bourdieu contrasted these Californian sports— trekking by foot, pony, cycle, motor-bike, or boat; canoeing; archery; windsurfing; cross-country skiing; sailing; hang gliding; microlights—with what he called 'classical sports' that represent an 'organized, signposted, cultivated nature'.

callisthenics A term (US spelling 'calisthenics') referring to the practice of relatively simple forms of exercise that use the exerciser's body as a source of movement and resistance, usually without weights or equipment, and are designed to enhance body strength and develop flexibility. Its development can be compared to the history of *gymnastics, of which it is in some ways a variant. Push-ups, pull-ups, and sit-ups are common exercises, and various forms of callisthenics have been seen to be predominantly participated in by women; Allen Guttman observes that in the modern—or at least modernizing—period, women's sports were 'for the most part, not sports at all; they were noncompetitive physical activities like calisthenics or a day at the seaside' (*Sports: The First Five Millennia*, 2004). Some would find this comment too dismissive of what many groups—such as, in the UK, the *Women's League of Health and Beauty—see as a strength-inducing and health-promoting activity with both physiological and psychological benefits. Proponents of callisthenics point to its aesthetic dimensions, and comparisons have been made with what evolved as the Olympic discipline of rhythmic gymnastics.

calorie A measure of energy expressed as heat or the performance of work and defined as the amount of heat necessary to raise the temperature of one gram of water from 14.5° C to 15.5° C. In human terms this is a very small quantity of heat so the kilocalorie is more commonly used, equal to 1,000 calories. Calories are used in sport and exercise science to measure the energy obtained from the various foods in the diet and the energy expended during physical activity. For example, a typical human will consume about 2,500 kilocalories of food a day; a gram of fat in a food will provide the body with 9 kilocalories; an athlete might expend 10 kilocalories a minute playing football. In common talk the word 'calorie' is used as shorthand for kilocalorie, as in '125 calories in a slice of cake'. The joule (J) is the correct *metric or SI unit for energy and 1 calorie equals 4.186 joules.

calorimetry A method by which to determine the energy expenditure of an organism in order to assess the intensity of physical activity and the calorific requirement from food. In 1780, Lavoisier and Laplace demonstrated the direct relationship between heat and respiration by measuring the amount of ice melted by a guinea pig in a small chamber. The first human calorimeters were sealed chambers to measure heat production directly. Understanding of the fundamental thermodynamics of respiration, notably by Atwater and colleagues, allowed the development of indirect calorimetry. In this form, measurement of the volume of oxygen consumed and the volume of carbon dioxide produced allows precise determination of energy expenditure and the proportion of carbohydrates, fats, and proteins used to provide that energy. The gas volumes can be determined by collecting expired air. The development of small, lightweight mouthpieces and valves allowed air to be collected with ease in the laboratory from an exercising individual. More recently, advances in microelectronics have led to rapid-response integrated systems for the laboratory (on-line gas analysis) and relatively lightweight portable systems for ambulatory monitoring.

calva A throwing game played, predominantly by men, in regions of Spain. The game is said to derive from pre-Roman diversions of shepherds, who for their amusement threw stones at bulls' horns. Played in parts of cities such as Madrid and Barcelona, as well as more rural regions across the country, the game is now based upon aiming a cylinder of iron or steel (the *marro*) at a wooden target protruding from the earth. The name *calva* is possibly derived from the word describing an open field or space in which there are no obstacles that would impair the game. The game is obviously cheap to play and conducive to spontaneous forms of playing and adaptations. These factors may well account for its survival among poorer sections of the population.

Cambridge Rules The codification of the laws of the game of football (soccer), initially in 1848 and revised in the mid 1850s, and then articulated in the Cambridge University rules, drawn up by a committee of Trinity College football enthusiasts convened in October 1863, and published the following month. In these rules, harmony was sought and compromise reached between different conventions of play that had characterized the football codes of the different public schools that the players at the university had attended, such as Eton, Harrow, Westminster, Marlborough, Shrewsbury, and Rugby. Undergraduates had played a version of football in a Cambridge University team since the early 1840s, playing matches on Parker's Piece in the south of the city, and as the game grew more popular, standardization was required so that players from different traditions and colleges could accept a single set of laws. The 1863 rules became the basis of the modern game (rather than the Sheffield Rules that had been developed in the industrial football culture of Sheffield, in Yorkshire). They were developed coterminously with the foundation of the FA (Football Association) at a meeting in London at the end of October 1863, where all the representatives of clubs 'were strongly in favour of Eton-Harrow-Cambridge principles; that is of the "dribbling game"', Percy M. Young writes (*A History of British Football*, 1968). Although these club representatives did not negotiate adequately with the football-playing public schools and with Cambridge, and took no account of the provincial model in Sheffield, it was the Cambridge model and its maturation into the Association code that was to prevail and confirm the framework for what became recognizably the sport of modern football (soccer).

Cambridge University, sport at From recreational sport to elite international competition, the University of Cambridge, with its collegiate structure and the legacies of its public-school-educated undergraduates, has fostered a distinctive sporting culture, comparable to that of *Oxford University. The pedestrian Captain *Barclay, the enthusiasts for the game of (association) *football, Olympic sprinter Harold *Abrahams, and the runner Chris *Brasher all benefited from the environs and culture of sport of their times at the university. *See also* BLUES, OXFORD AND CAMBRIDGE; BOXING; CAMBRIDGE RULES; NOEL-BAKER, PHILIP JOHN; OXFORD–CAMBRIDGE BOAT RACE; STEPHEN, LESLIE.

camel racing A traditional sport in countries of the Gulf States, such as Saudi Arabia, Bahrain, and the United Arab Emirates, and some north African states such as Mauritania, where the modern form of the activity has been promoted as a traditional cultural practice. More commercialized versions of the sport have been based on betting and gambling, and mired in controversies relating to alleged child labour (the use of children as lighter jockeys).

camogie The all-female version of the male Gaelic sport of hurling, first played in public at a Gaelic League Fair in Meath, in 1904. Teams of twelve, from squads of fifteen, played with the stick (the camán) and a ball-like object (the sliotar) in matches of two halves of 30 minutes each. The full-size Gaelic Athletic Association pitch, for fifteen-a-side teams, was adopted in 1999. The object is to propel the sliotar into the opponent's goal, for which three points are awarded; or in between the posts that rise above the goal, for one point.

Camus, Albert (1913–60) An Algerian-born writer and left-wing activist whose writings addressed artistic and sporting issues as well as direct political matters, embodying his belief that ethical and moral affairs were the stuff of everyday life and the daily imagination. His literary and philosophical works explored the conditions of absurdity in the human condition, yet he committed himself to rational political causes such as the French resistance during World War II. He played football, in the goalkeeping position at a high level, boxed and swam in his youth, and wrote (*France Football*, 1957) that sporting encounter and competition gave him important ethical lessons: 'What I know most surely in the long run about morality and obligations, I owe to football.'

Canadian football A version of football played in Canada, with much in common with *American football, though differences include the game being played with twelve players on each side (reduced from fourteen in 1921), on a larger pitch, and without time-outs. The Canadian game thrives at college and professional league levels, and shares the same look—in player uniforms and attire, and the actual ball—as the game in the USA, but on a smaller scale.

Canetti, Elias (1905–94) A Bulgarian-born German sociologist, essayist, novelist, and dramatist. Recipient of the Nobel Prize for Literature in 1981, Canetti's most widely known work in the sociological area is *Crowds and Power* (1960), a study recognizing no disciplinary boundaries and locating sport as an important manifestation of the mass phenomenon of the crowd. *See also* CROWDS, BEHAVIOUR OF.

cannabinoids A category of drug banned by the International Olympic Committee (IOC), referred to by the IOC/WADA (*World Anti-Doping Agency) as 'prohibited narcotics'. These include hashish and marijuana, consumed for whatever (recreational or performance-enhancing) purpose.

canoeing A water sport in which the canoeist propels a small craft by either sitting or kneeling in a central, forward-facing position, and using a single- or double-bladed paddle; the canoe is pointed at both ends. If the canoeist sits and uses a double-bladed paddle, this is kayaking; in Canadian canoeing, the canoeist adopts a half-kneeling position and switches the single blade from side to side. Canoeists engage in slalom canoeing (where there are artificial barriers or 'gates'), wild or rough-water canoeing, long-distance racing, sprint racing, or canoe sailing. Canoes were used by Native Americans, and kayaks by the Inuit of Greenland and Alaska. In its organized form, canoeing's origins lie in the formation of the Royal Canoe Club in England, in 1866, though Germany provided technological advances in the early 20th century, and the event (for men) was introduced into the Olympic Games at the 1936 Berlin Olympics, in both its kayak and its Canadian canoe forms. German and East and Central European nations have excelled in high-performance competitions such as world championships and Olympic Games. In the Olympics, by 2008, there were twelve kayak and Canadian specialist disciplines for men and four kayak disciplines for women. Kayaking in not-so-wild water has become a popular recreational sport for outdoor holiday enthusiasts, particularly in mountainous areas with rocky rapids that provide thrills but negligible danger.

canoe polo A variant of the sport *polo, in which contestants are in specially designed canoes. The sport is one of eight forms of canoeing recognized by the British Canoeing Union, which says: 'Polo combines paddling and ball handling skills with an exciting contact team game, where tactics and positional play are as important as the speed and fitness of the individual athletes.' The ball can be thrown by hand or flicked by the paddle, and the aim is to score goals in the opponent's net, suspended two metres above the water. In 2009, British men were the world champions, though the sport was not established on an extensive worldwide basis.

canyoning The activity of travelling through canyons by a variety of means: scrambling, swimming, jumping, climbing, abseiling, and walking. It is distinct from mere canyon hiking in that it usually involves technical descents requiring equipment and specialist technical skills—*parkour, the use of rope, or water techniques. Rugged mountain environments with flowing water constitute the ideal conditions for canyoning, which, consequently, is a select sport for participants of adventurous disposition. It can be dangerous, and in 1999 twenty-one tourists drowned in a flash flood in Switzerland's Saxetenbach Gorge; these included thirteen Australians, and young people from Switzerland, the United Kingdom, South Africa, and New Zealand. The tragedy generated court cases and debates about the commercial pressures that allowed inexperienced guides to lead the fatal expedition when weather warnings had anticipated the thunderstorm that produced the flash flood. Such a tragedy also highlights the need in such sports for serious preparatory training and extreme caution.

capillary power (sociology) The capacity of power to circulate throughout a society. In his discussion of the nature of power in *Sport, Power and Culture* (1986) John Hargreaves recognized the different forms that power relations might take: physical violence used, or threatened, to obtain compliance; economic sanctions and other types of coercion; assertion of authority; powers of persuasion of respective individuals and groups. But there is no single kind of power, or power relation: 'Power in societies like ours is diffused and circulates throughout the social body. It is precisely this "capillary" quality that has enabled power to be expanded so effectively in the modern age, to be applied routinely at appropriate points in the social order, and to be reorganized, refurbished and elaborated periodically.' As sports are transformed, modernized, adapted, changed, serving one set of interests or another, or a particular alliance of interests in a particular historical moment, it is the capillary movement and circulation of power that must be recognized for any adequate analysis of the relation of the sport culture or institution to the society or culture of which it is a part.

capitalism A type of society and economy that emerged in its earliest developed form out of the industrial revolution of the 18th and 19th centuries in Western Europe, and in the USA in the later 19th century. In his *Capital*, Volume 1 (1867), Karl *Marx began with the declaration that the wealth of capitalist societies is manifest in 'an immense accumulation of commodities', the basis of the capitalist system being the 'single commodity' and the multiple and expanding production of the commodity. In Marx's analysis the principal means of production—factories, for instance—are owned by the bourgeoisie, and the labour power of workers is bought or sold, itself a commodity. Marxist-influenced analyses of capitalism have therefore been particularly concerned with the nature of the economy (seen as the basis of the whole society) rather than with the nature of the superstructure (religion, art, and the like, the sphere in which cultural forms, including sport, would be located). In this model of capitalism, sport is therefore little more than a minor element in the overall economic system. Marx never wrote on the place of sport or specific leisure forms in capitalism, seeing recreation as merely a space in which the labour power of the worker is, literally, re-created for its continuing contribution to the commodity-producing process.

The primary characteristic of capitalism was identified by English historian Arnold Toynbee (1884) as 'the substitution of competition for the mediaeval regulations which had previously controlled the production and distribution of wealth'. The new kind of society featured rapid population growth, huge changes to agricultural land systems, the enclosure of commons and wastelands, technological invention and manufacturing initiatives, advances in the means of communications, the expansion of trade, and the substitution of a 'cash nexus' for the more traditional human tie. In this seismic social and cultural context it is hardly surprising that capitalism would generate new forms of leisure and sport, and E. P. Thompson's brilliant essay on 'Time, Work-Discipline and Industrial Capitalism' (1967) captured the pivotal change in the way that 'Time is now currency: it is not passed but spent'. Thompson listed seven ways in which new work patterns and approaches to time were imposed: 'by the division of labour; the supervision of labour; fines; bells and clocks; money incentives; preachings and schoolings; the suppression of fairs and sports'.

In the new industrial capitalism the popular recreations of an earlier period would be perceived as inappropriate, creating the cultural space for the development and imposition of newly organized forms of sport, and the economic space, as capitalism further developed, for the expansion of *commercialism in the sport and leisure sphere. For Marx, capitalism also generated a central conflictual dynamic of *class struggle, and raised, for the reformist and revolutionary alike, the question of *class consciousness. Marxist and neo-Marxist scholarship continues to explore class-based and economic dimensions of sporting institutions and cultures, and the contribution to overall social relations of sport as *ideology, *hegemony, and as a form of *alienation. Some of these ideas remain as important as ever in their insights as capitalism has continued to expand on an increasingly globalized level.

capoeira A combat sport or martial art fusing elements of fighting, music, and dance. Evidence of such fight-dancing has been identified in engravings in Cuba, but the activity was formed in 19th-century Brazil, by erstwhile African slaves. Contenders for the etymological roots of the practice include a *capa*, a basket worn on the head of a slave for carrying merchandise for sale; and the Kikongo word *kipura*, referring to a struggle or a fight, and sharp fluttering movement. Capoeira is contested and performed within a circle of onlookers, and generates an interactive, dialogic dynamic. It was outlawed in Brazil in 1892, and survived initially as a form of *contra-culture, on the margins of mainstream society, the combatants and participants adopting secret nicknames. Some forms upheld religious and spiritual rituals and meanings. Contact was feigned as much as sought, and the practice is a demonstration of skill, cunning, evasion, and survival as much as a physical confrontation. It has proved suitable to appropriation in the popular cultural sphere, having featured in computer games, and sharing some characteristics with break-dancing.

carbohydrate A molecule of the general formula $(CH2)_n$, generally classified as monosaccharides, oligosaccharides, and polysaccharides. The monosaccharides are the basic units of carbohydrates and include glucose, fructose, and galactose. Oligosaccharides are formed of a small number of monosaccharides joined together (Greek *oligoi*, 'few'), of which the most common are sucrose or table sugar (a glucose and a fructose molecule joined together) and lactose or milk sugar (a glucose and a galactose molecule joined together). Polysaccharides are formed from multiple monosaccharide units, from a few to many thousand, in long straight or branched chains. The most important polysaccharides include starch, the storage form of carbohydrate in plants; glycogen, the storage form of carbohydrate in humans; and fibre, a plant structural polysaccharide forming part of leaves, seeds, and roots.

Carbohydrate in the form of glucose derived from stored glycogen is an important fuel during exercise. The human has only limited capacity to store carbohydrate and about two **hours** of steady exercise will deplete the stores. Consequently, carbohydrate provision before, during, and after exercise becomes a key factor in any sport which requires a long duration of effort, such as a marathon race, or in coping with the rigours of day-to-day training and competing. Carbohydrate is often supplied in specially formulated drinks which allow the athlete to simultaneously hydrate and fuel the body. The rate at which carbohydrate taken in at the mouth appears in the bloodstream as glucose is described by the glycaemic index. The amount and form of carbohydrate in the diet is also important to health. A high proportion of simple sugars and refined carbohydrate and a low proportion of complex carbohydrates including fibre are associated with poorer health.

Cardus, Neville (1889–1975) A Manchester-born writer who spent most of his professional life from 1917 onwards as cricket correspondent and music critic of the *Manchester Guardian* (later, *The Guardian*). He had been assistant cricketing coach at Shrewsbury School from 1912. In his autobiography, Cardus called the newspaper 'a dear tyrant' from which 'I have never been able to break free'; the 'credo' of *Manchester Guardian* editor C. E. Montague—'To bring to the day's diet of sights and sounds the wine of your own temperament'—was his guiding principle, as he established sport writing as a respected sub-genre of journalism within the mainstream quality press in the UK.

career Two senses of career are relevant to the analysis of sport cultures. 1. The formal professional or occupational positions occupied in a *life-course—for instance, competitive athlete, coach, administrator. This first sense raises important issues concerning the long-term future of competitive, professional athletes, for most of whom the high-performance career is by definition a short-term one. 2. The stages through which the individual passes in entering a culture, seen as stages of a career path contributing to the notion of becoming. This second sense has a social psychological emphasis, recognizing that what Anselm Strauss (*Mirrors and Masks*, 1959) called 'transformations of identity', planned or unanticipated, occur in the process of individual life-courses; people come 'to new terms' and in doing so become 'something other' than they once were. People are often also forced to recognize that they are not the same as they were or used to be, and Strauss argues that 'critical incidents constitute turning points in the onward movement of personal careers'. Sport performers feeling the ageing process, or players injured in mid-career, will recognize exactly what Strauss means about critical incidents; sport fans passing through stages of subcultural membership also experience these career phases.

Carlyle, Thomas (1795–1881) A Scottish historian and essayist, Carlyle popularized epochal historical events, such as the French revolution, and provided condemnatory critiques of the mechanistic materialism of industrializing 19th-century Britain. His solution to the woes of the age was to call for the emergence of more strong individuals, and his lectures on heroes and hero-worship (1840) celebrated the world-shaping impact of selected religious, artistic, political, and military figures. His ideas have had some currency in sports studies in the consideration of the emergence of the sporting hero, but he never mentioned sporting figures. His particular model does little to illuminate the subtleties and contradictions of the relationship between the sporting hero and his or her public, though Richard Holt and J. A. Mangan have observed that 'it is scarcely to be doubted . . . that if he were alive today in Ecclefechan he would have added "futballer" to his list' (*European Heroes: Myth, Identity, Sport*, 1996).

carnival A popular festival staged in public and drawing upon a range of popular cultural forms, characterized by flamboyant display in parades and processions and sustained hedonism and feasting. It has been widely studied by cultural historians and anthropologists, and its culturally symbolic and political significance depends upon its historical and geographical context. French historian Emmanuel Le Roy Ladurie's 1979 study *Carnival* showed, in the context of 16th-century south-eastern France, the place of carnival as a form of popular expression and sometimes protest, there being in effect two carnivals in one in Romans (the village he studied), one of and for the 'plebeians' and one of and for the 'notables'. The event included staged, rigged foot races of upper-class men, the winner of which would assume a title of Carnival King; as he writes:

> Fixing games like this was a common practice in urban sporting and folk events. Carcassonne's archery and shooting match, for example, was always won by the town consuls: the best shots in town would let one of the consuls kill the snake or eagle effigy, even if he were a dotard . . . so nearsighted that he pointed the gun at his own face.

For both of Romans's factions the carnival was also bound up with the expression of a local cultural and political identity; festivities and folk gatherings, often linked to saints' days or religious rites, operated as *reynages* (carnival-based forms of association rooted in the construction of 'kingdoms'), in which a communal, religious core was confirmed, the prize for races was election to a symbolic status of king or queen, and entertainments (horse as well as foot races) were staged. This form of carnival acted as a social tool that 'allowed the lower classes to express themselves, their mockery, and sometimes even their grievances. Plebeian political tendencies that were repressed during the rest of the year came to light during the festivities', Ladurie observes.

French historian Hippolyte Taine visited the English classic horse race the Derby at Epsom in May 1861, and likened the rowdy, festive atmosphere of the 200,000 racegoers to the carnival, in stark contrast to the bucolic tranquility of the rail journey across the English suburbs and countryside from Waterloo Station in London; Derby Day for Taine creates, in 'the vast area, . . . all the disorder of the human carnival', which carries over back in London where at Hyde Park Corner revellers still gather, knowing that 'Today everything is allowable, it is an outlet for a year of repression' (John Carey, *The Faber Book of Reportage*, 1987).

More orchestrated forms of carnival have been shown to have close links with sport in more recent cases. The established form of carnival in Rio de Janeiro, Brazil, in the first half of the 20th century was based on the spontaneous parades of black communities through the city, in which a degree of informal competitiveness set groups apart from each other. In 1931 Rio's first (and short-lived) daily sports paper, lacking material and copy for its second issue, transformed the carnival into a more explicit competitive form, judged by an appointed committee. The enterprising editor of that newspaper, Mario Filho, also encouraged the cultivation of the carnival spirit at Brazilian football matches. In 1934, as *O Globo*'s sports editor, he 'launched a competition between supporters of Flamengo and Fluminense. He encouraged fans to bring drums, instruments, coloured streamers and fireworks to matches—with the winner the side that put on the most exhilarating display' (Bellos, 2002).

Another country in which carnival has been central to public cultural life is Trinidad. Carnival began to take on its modern form in Trinidad in the 1840s:

> Carnival ... was made their own by the former slaves. They transformed it from what it had become in Trinidad, a genteel and coquettish diversion of the Roman Catholic upper classes, into what such a celebration had been in antiquity, a living folk festival in which the participants could purge themselves of emotions held in check for the rest of the year ... Carnival gave the Negro Creoles the chance to express a corporate pride in their own values and at the same time to ridicule the pretensions of the upper classes. Its fantasies enabled them to be kings for the day and to assume for a short time the "*person*" of other beings, real or imaginary, with envied attributes. Its opportunities for unrestricted behaviour left the emotions spent and satisfied. (Wood, 1968).

The history of carnival in Trinidad has been a story of repression, remaking, adaptation, contestation, and consensus. No sport was included by Wood in his seminal study, although Cowley (1996) has traced the historical minutiae of carnival ritual and practice, including a burlesque cricket match documented at the 1869 carnival. For Mason (1998), carnival 'brings together nearly all aspects of Trinidad's cultural identity and speaks volumes about its attitudes to religion, music, language, humour, folk traditions, politics, male–female relations, its lively ethnic mix and even its food and sport'. It has kept alive African roots and helped define a 'complex cultural and national identity after independence'. On the positive side, such a reading of carnival has demonstrated how 'a resilient people have managed to create a healthy society out of adversity'. In the case of Trinidad and Tobago, the motif of the uninhibited carnival tradition was evoked in the marketing of the country's national football side up to and at the football World Cup Finals in Germany in 2006, echoing the public relations profile and cultural presence of Jamaican supporters at that country's appearance at the 1998 Finals in France. *See also* CARNIVALESQUE.

References
Bellos, A. (2002) *Futebol: The Brazilian Way of Life*, London: Bloomsbury; Cowley, J. (1996) *Carnival, Canboulay and Calypso: Traditions in the Making*, Cambridge: Cambridge University Press; Le Roy Ladurie, E. (1979) *Carnival: A People's Uprising at Romans, 1579–1580*, London: Scolar Press; Mason, P. (1998) *Bacchanal! The Carnival Culture of Trinidad*, Philadelphia: Philadelphia Press; Wood, D. (1968) *Trinidad in Transition: The Years after Slavery*, London: Oxford University Press.

carnivalesque A concept developed by Russian literary scholar Mikhail Bakhtin (1895–1975) to describe the irreverent folk-culture of medieval society. In *Rabelais and his World* (1984), Bakhtin's interpretation and development of François *Rabelais's notion of carnival is rooted in the recognition that 'ritual spectacles' and feasts may be integral to the religious calendar, but that their carnivalesque elements are not *of* the religion: rather, the festive, comic elements of the carnival 'offered a completely different, nonofficial, extraecclesiastical and extrapolitical aspect of the world, of man, and of human relations; . . . a second world and a second life outside officialdom'. For Bakhtin, carnival and the comic embodied a 'two-world condition' that could not be legislated out of existence or simply eroded by an official, dominant culture. Carnival is 'lived in' by the people, and during carnival 'there is no other life outside it . . . life is subject only to . . . the laws of its own freedom'. Bakhtin's carnival has a 'universal spirit' and is 'a special condition of the entire world', and fuels 'revival and renewal'. The carnivalesque inverts authority, having a logic of the 'turnabout' or the 'inside-out'. For Bakhtin, 'Carnivalesque spirit is political: it derides serious, "official" thought and behaviour; it brings the high low' (Samuel Kinser, *Rabelais's 'Carnival': Text, Context, Metatext*, 1990).

The idea of the carnivalesque has been widely applied to popular cultural contexts and—Bakhtin also noted the grotesque realism of Rabelais's depictions of bodies—in the burgeoning field of studies of the body. Formal modes of competitive sport hardly lend themselves to elements of the carnivalesque, but some sport fans and spectator cultures assume behaviours and ritualistic practices that embody modified variants of the 'idiom of carnival forms and symbols', as Bakhtin put it. At cricket matches in the Caribbean, and football World Cup Finals at which Jamaica (1998) and Trinidad and Tobago (2006) competed, feasting, music-making, dancing, and singing are as much a part of the fan's experience as watching the sporting action on the field of play.

Bakhtin wrote in the USSR of Lenin and Stalin in the 1920s and the 1930s, and his work on Rabelais was not published until 1965. His reading of Rabelais has to be placed in this context, in which identification of a vibrant culture from below can be seen as a source of hope and freedom in the bleakest of times. As Kinser observes: 'Bakhtin's carnivalesque interpretation of Rabelais's communalism was a supremely political act of communication'. Any use of Bakhtin's work in relation to sporting cultures should acknowledge the context of Bakhtin's own work, and the influence of this upon his theoretical claims for the importance of the carnivalesque spirit. *See also* CARNIVAL.

Carpentier, Georges (1894–1975) A French professional boxer who began fighting professionally at the age of 14, and fought at all eight weights throughout his career. He held the world light heavyweight title, and stimulated an extensive popular following, including among women fans. He is best remembered for his fight with heavyweight champion Jack *Dempsey in 1921, the first one-million-dollar gate in the sport. A war hero as an airman in World War I, as well as a sporting champion, he personified the emergingly suave image of the sportsman in a transformative phase of the internationalization of sport by the new media of radio and film. On retirement, he worked in vaudeville in England and the USA and appeared in several movies, before becoming the proprietor of a successful bar in Paris.

Carpentier was a catalyst for the intensifying influence of US culture upon Europe, calling French boxing a blend of 'English science' with 'American ruggedness' (see Kasia Boddy, *Boxing: A Cultural History*, 2007), winning his light heavyweight title in New Jersey and befriending his conqueror Dempsey for life. In his autobiography, Dempsey referred to the Frenchman as 'dapper Georges Carpentier': 'He was thinner than I expected and chalk white. He looked like a graceful statue. I looked like a street fighter.' The ruggedness from the USA, profiled in the big-money events increasingly transmitted worldwide, proved too much for the grace of Carpentier, but his own contribution to the internationalization of sport, in mediating the US influence in Europe, was considerable.

cartel An alliance of organizations or businesses that make an agreement, which can be informal or formalized, to restrict competition within the alliance. This might be by specifying particular spheres of marketing, as is negotiated by national or international sports organizations with exclusive partner sponsors; or agreeing similar levels of pricing for comparable products, as is sometimes informally done by some professional sport leagues. A cartel is a form of *monopoly of the sporting product. It is often based upon a horizontal agreement between companies engaged in the same activity, relating to (a) minimum sale price if the cartel is in the business of supply, or maximum purchase price if it is a demand cartel, and (b) the quantity of the product that is exchanged. A sporting league or federation operates as a supply cartel when it is the sole holder of negotiating rights for the sale of broadcasting coverage to television. A group such as the European Broadcasting Union (EBU) operates as a demand cartel by representing the international interests of numerous countries in negotiating with sports organizers.

Cartels affect the basis of open competition: USA television chiefs in the later 1980s, beginning to pay unprecedentedly high sums for Olympics broadcast rights, teased the chief of the BBC, Billy Cotton Junior (1928–2008), that his company got the Games for an unrealistically low sum that the EBU was willing to pay on behalf of its members; just a few years after that, the EBU showed its competitive inefficiency when it failed to mount a bid to UEFA's agents for the television rights for the newly formatted UEFA Champions League, one consequence of which was that the agency TEAM exceeded all predictions for the generation of those rights as they were sold separately to broadcasters in individual national markets. Nevertheless, the EBU, able to guarantee a European viewing market of almost seven hundred million viewers, was the preferred partner of the International Olympic Committee for the 2000, 2004, and 2008 Olympics, though it had bid considerably less than had the Murdoch Group. Cartelized practices, though, run foul of regulatory rules on open and free competition, and are constantly challenged by non-cartel rivals. *See also* COLLECTIVE SELLING.

case history In sport medicine and science, a statement of an athlete's or individual's history of injury or disease. Also known as *anamnesis*, such a personal record is an essential basis for diagnosis of sport injury, and for informed planning of *rehabilitation and training schedules.

Casement Park A sports stadium in Belfast, Northern Ireland, that is the primary stadium of the Gaelic Athletic Association (GAA), and stages matches of *Gaelic football, and *hurling. It was opened in 1953, named after Irish Republican hero Sir Roger Casement (1864–1916). Knighted by Britain for his contribution to bettering the lot of the oppressed peoples of the South Americas, he returned his decorations in 1915 and dedicated himself to the political and nationalist cause of what he called 'the white Indians of Ireland'. He travelled to Berlin the following year, unsuccessfully seeking arms supplies from Germany to support the Irish nationalists. Returned to Ireland's west coast by German submarine the following year, he was immediately arrested and hanged for treason in London in 1916. The naming of the GAA's stadium is powerful testimony to the political and cultural significance that can be attached to sporting sites and spaces.

case study A study of a single case justified by (i) the importance of the case itself (this can range from, say, an individual sporting *biography to the consideration of the sporting culture or system of a single country) or (ii) the demonstrable representativeness or typicality of the case (such as a metropolitan professional sports team, or school sport in a school with a particularly dominant ethnic composition).

casino capitalism A term coined by the political economist Susan Strange, referring to the resemblance of the Western financial system to a 'vast casino', in which 'the gamblers in the casino have got out of hand, almost beyond . . . the control of governments' (*Casino Capitalism*, 1997). In such a situation, Strange contends, people experience an increased sense of uncertainty, and luck triumphs over dedication, application, and hard work. Highly commercialized forms of competitive sport can be seen as forms of casino capitalism: the supranational media moguls financing world sport; the largely unaccountable and often corrupt officials of international governing bodies of sport; the owners of football clubs for whom the team is a plaything in a larger financial empire. In sport's form of casino capitalism, the passion and the values of the fan are at the mercy of the gamblers in the casino.

caste A system of *social stratification based on hierarchically ordered and inflexible social strata. Hinduism in India has been seen as the most developed form of the caste system, based on religious criteria. Membership of such strata is given at birth (ascribed), and in its purest form the caste system permits limited contact between ranked strata, allows no possibility of mobility between them, and enforces endogamy (compulsory marriage within the groups). A caste system of this kind is a conservative force and would obviously reproduce the inbuilt inequalities of the system, including 'the unequal distribution of facilities and resources for leisure activities and pursuits' and sports (Scott Fleming, '*Home and Away': Sport and South Asian Male Youth*, 1995).

catastrophe theory Emanating from the work of French mathematician René Frédéric Thom (1923–2002), a theory based on the analysis and classification of surfaces on the basis of their shape, with elements of the theory dealing with abrupt changes generated by changes reaching a critical point. Psychologists have drawn on the theory in accounting for outbursts of temper following on from intensifying expressions of anger. Sport psychologists have used catastrophe theory to demonstrate that *stress in athletic competition is the product of an interaction between mental anxiety and physiological arousal. Catastrophe theory has had scarce visibility in sociological analyses of sport, though it may well illuminate particular points of pivotal change in sport policies or systems, such as the collapse of the Soviet-style sport performance systems in several Eastern European states in the early 1990s; or the underachievement of a nation in the sporting arena, such as Canada's lack of any gold medals at the 1976 Montreal Olympics, which was seen in terms of the breakdown and failure of the high-performance sport system in the host city's nation.

catcall A shrill whistle expressing disapproval of a public performance, for instance in the theatre or at the sporting arena. It is acceptable to express such disapproval in large crowds watching team sports, or some individual sports such as boxing; but not around the tennis court or on the golf course, unless a player is perceived to have exhibited a form of bad sportsmanship. The catcall, like other forms of verbalized disapproval such as booing, is a part of the dynamic of sporting performance culture; where sporting etiquette deems it unacceptable, this can be traced to class origins and a more refined model of sporting conduct.

catharsis From the Greek for 'cleansing', a term that emerged in relation to dramatic performance that could be seen as purging built-up or suppressed emotion. Sport can also be seen as a source of cathartic expression and outpouring: competitive performance has been linked to the need to find an outlet for levels of aggression either inherent or cultivated in individuals (in sports emphasizing physical superiority, or in the verbal or physical conduct of sport fans, for instance); or in the *achievement orientation that social psychologists and sociologists have identified as a core feature and value system of modern societies in particular.

Catholic Church, attitude towards sport in the Religion numbers among the influences that can give a sport culture a distinctive character, particularly in a context in which a local, regional, or national culture is shaped by a dominant religion. Historically, in early 17th-century Lancashire in the north of England, some traditional cultural forms such as processional rituals, religious plays, and associated physical activities survived longer in the least Protestant parts of the country. It was these that prompted James I to issue The *King's Book of Sports in 1617. Medieval Catholicism relied greatly, for the transmission of its messages, on images and traditional rituals. These were undermined in those regions and countries in which the Protestant-based Reformation took hold, and such practices were condemned in the institutionalization of anti-Catholicism in England during that period.

In some social and cultural contexts, religion has combined with particular linguistic, cultural, and geographical influences to demarcate popular cultural and leisure practices. In Switzerland, for instance, local events such as festivals, sports meetings, and village or neighbourhood fetes have been more popular among French and Italian speakers than German speakers, a product in part of the more hedonistic and communal public culture of Catholic communities. More explicitly political, the case in Ireland of the Gaelic Athletic Association highlighted the close link that can be established and nurtured between religious, sectarian interests and sporting institutions. In the ascendancy of fascism in 20th-century Italy, popular sport and its famous figures and personalities could be used to symbolize the claimed values of the Catholic Church, after its compromise with the fascist state, in the1930s, and in its self-representation in rivalries with communist elements and institutions after World War II. Cycling champion Gino Bartali, as Stefano Pivato's 1996 essay (*International Journal of the History of Sport*) has shown, was appropriated by the Catholic Church in its 'systematic exploitation of the pious Bartali . . . as a model Catholic'. His 1938 triumph in the *Tour de France was seen as the embodiment of the core Catholic values of stoicism, charity, and chastity, and of a form of Christian courage expressed in his readiness to 'turn the other cheek in contrast with Fascist glorification of aggression and arrogance'.

More generally, the Catholic Church has proved less willing than other religious bodies to exploit sport, particularly in comparison with evangelical groups, which can be found campaigning, recruiting, and converting at large-scale sports events such as the Olympics. Nevertheless, in 2005 the then Pope, John Paul II, established an office in the Vatican called Church and Sport, and the Pontifical Council for the Laity also held an international symposium on sport as a global phenomenon. This has further supported Catholics who have sought to find religious messages in sport, and mobilize sport as a means of recruitment to the faith. Robert Feeney, author of *The Catholic Ideal: Exercise and Sports* (2005), cites St Thomas Aquinas's claim that 'exercise is the medicine of the soul'. The symposium focused on sport as a 'field of Christian mission' and its proceedings (2006) included summaries of two round table discussions. As the Vatican website stated:

> The first deals with 'problems and challenges of sport today' offering a brief overview of the polemical relationship of sport with business, violence, doping, and the media. The other round table, 'Sport: frontier of the new evangelisation' explores how Catholic sports associations, sport chaplains, pastoral care at major sports events, and the Christian presence in sports institutions offer the Church opportunities to permeate the world of sport with the gospel.

Pope Benedict XVI, less of an enthusiast for sports than his soccer-playing predecessor, nevertheless allowed the office to continue its mission, though with scant evidence of active follow-up to the 2005 initiative.

caving The recreational sport of cave exploration. Within the caving constituency it is known as 'spelunking', a term adopted among US cavers in the 1940s and 1950s. Caving as a leisure pursuit and athletic challenge is an activity of the modern era, dependent upon technological equipment and scientific knowledge of the cave; it is not romantic exploration. Climbing and crawling are necessary skills for the caver, and have been since the pioneering cavers of late 19th-century France developed appropriate techniques. France provided the first national association for the overseeing of caving, the national Société de Spéléologie Society being founded in 1895 along with a specialist journal. A variant in the north of England, referring to vertical caves, is 'potholing'. Classified as one of what sociologists and sport analysts have called *extreme sports, caving is seen by its committed practitioners as more established, more responsible, and more mature than that label implies.

CBS TV *See* ABC TV.

celebrate humanity A slogan used in the later 1990s by the International Olympic Committee to encapsulate its principles and ideals. The combination of celebration and universalism that is evoked in the slogan can be seen as a form of reductionism that misrepresents the nature of the social and political world, the stress on the all-embracing notion of 'humanity' diverting attention from the social and cultural realities of a complex, and often conflict-ridden, world.

celebrity A phenomenon in which exceptional attributes—such as glamour, sustained fame, beauty, talent—are recognized and associated with an individual, whose cultural profile is then often reproduced not necessarily in terms of the attributes but on the basis of the celebrity status itself. Increasingly, in a media age characterized by Daniel Boorstin's epigram that such individuals are becoming well known for being well known (*The Image*, 1961), celebrity feeds off itself. In the USA, sociologist Leo Lowenthal (1944), in a *content analysis of biographies of US figures, identified the 'heroes' of the first three decades of the 20th century as 'idols of production', from the worlds of business, industry, and the natural sciences, without 'a single hero from the world of sports' ('The Triumph of Mass Idols', reprinted in *Literature, Popular Culture, and Society*, 1961). The first biographies of sportspeople were accounts of the technical side of the sport or the sports feat, written for a knowledgeable audience, not yet seen as 'a special phenomenon which demands almost undivided attention'. By the early 1940s magazine heroes of biographies are 'idols of consumption', from the world of entertainment, sport, and communications, whose life stories stress 'hardships and breaks'. Lowenthal identified, in the popular readership of print magazines, the emergence of the self-referencing celebrity phenomenon.

Chris Rojek, in a broad historical sweep (*Celebrity*, 2001), sees celebrity as a result of the democratization of society and the decline of organized religion, bound up with the commodification of everyday life. Celebrity status also 'always implies a split between a private self and a public self', Rojek asserts, though this is frequently threatened by the intrusion of those media determined to blur or shatter the distinction, or by individual celebrities eager to both control access to their image management and secure the best financial return on their celebrity. English footballer David Beckham is a revealing case of celebrity in the late 20th and early 21st centuries. His career with English soccer club Manchester United and Spanish club Real Madrid and then, in 2007, his move to play for LA Galaxy in the USA's Major League Soccer (MLS) reflected a changing balance between sporting achievement and celebrity profile. His marriage to a successful pop star, 'Posh Spice' Victoria Adams, launched him into the most marketable sphere of national and international celebrities. In the English press 'Posh and Becks' became known as a kind of popular royal couple. Their marriage in 1999 was represented in the British media as more splendid, more regal than the royal wedding of Prince Edward and his bride Sophie Rhys-Jones the previous month: 'QUEEN POSH TAKE THEE KING BECKS' ranted the *Daily Mail* on 5 July. The Beckhams sold media rights for their wedding to *OK!* magazine. Garry Whannel shows how the celebrity phenomenon pervades the media: politicians commented on, presenters alluded to, and comedians joked about the Beckhams, all drawn towards the Beckham story and the Beckhams drawn into all aspects of the media 'as if by a vortex' ('The Case of David Beckham', in D. Andrews and S. Jackson, eds, *Sport Stars: The Cultural Politics of Sporting Celebrity*, 2001). David Beckham continued to play and compete at the highest level over the ensuing years, but was as prominent in fashion and gossip pages, and male fragrance and underwear advertisements, as on the football field. The commercial opportunities for top sportsmen and -women, endorsing multiple products or developing their own business lines as did the US tennis sisters Venus and Serena Williams, have increased the celebrity profile of such figures, and burgeoning media outlets have exacerbated and exploited their celebrity potential. *See also* ROLE MODEL; VORTEXTUALITY.

Central American and Caribbean Games A competitive multi-sport event first staged in 1926, held every four years, and continuing to promote itself as the oldest such regional games in the world. In 1960, in the build-up to the IXth Games in Kingston, Jamaica (1962), the Central American and Caribbean Sports Organization (CACSO) was formed to represent on a more stable basis the sporting interests of countries in the region. The 2010 Games held in Mayagüez, Puerto Rico, is the XXIst event. By the 2006 event in Colombia, 29 nations had won medals at the games, the top five medal-winners being Cuba, Mexico, Venezuela, Puerto Rico, and Colombia. The Games have had an important role in profiling the region's sporting identity and aspirations, and providing a rehearsal platform for athletes between Olympic Games. Although the Games preceded the Cuban Revolution by more than a third of a century, Cuba was prominent in the early history of the Games, staging the 1930 event in Havana; the Games have since the early 1960s offered Fidel Castro's post-revolutionary nation a vehicle for the display of the nation's qualities, with its haul of 3,060 medals.

Central Asian Games A subregional multi-sport event promoted by the Olympic Council of Asia to promote competitive international sport among smaller nations in central Asia. The Games are organized by the host nation, as there is no specific association that takes responsibility for them. Held every two years, they were first staged in Tashkent, Uzbekistan, and attract in particular the smaller nations that had previously been a part of the USSR (Union of Soviet Socialist Republics).

central fatigue *See* FATIGUE.

centre–periphery A model employed in sociology to distinguish between the dominant centre and the subordinate periphery, widely applied to the economic profile of countries and the relations between established capitalist societies and developing countries. The centre–periphery model could be applied to national sporting cultures as well as in the international and global context. The recruitment of players from sub-Saharan African nations to the top clubs in Western European soccer leagues is an example of how the periphery might remain underdeveloped in relation to domestic sport institutions. David Runciman ('They can play but they can never win', *New Statesman*, May 2006) notes the 'equality of luck' that determines whether one African nation or another reaches the final stages of a men's soccer World Cup. The established European clubs thrive with African-born star players, but the grass roots remain unchanged and the infrastructure undeveloped in the player's home country. The centre prospers; the periphery stagnates or deteriorates.

ceremony Forms of performance—that can be private, as in secret societies, or public, as in the coronation of monarchs or the opening of parliament or a sporting festival—that transmit or confirm established values, and/or act as forms of *ritual or *status passage for individuals. *See also* OLYMPIC CEREMONY.

Cerutty, Percy Wells (1895–1975) An Australian running teacher, as he
preferred to call himself, who coached and trained a number of world-beating
Australian middle-distance runners. These included John Landy, one of the men at
the forefront of the athletes threatening to the break the *four-minute mile barrier in
1954, and Herb Elliott, whose winning margin in the 1960 Rome Olympics in the
1,500 metres astounded the world of sport. Cerutty was a post-office worker turned
athletic guru, whose athletes attributed to him an extraordinary capacity to
inspire in words. Elliott, interviewed on Radio National Australia in January 2001,
recalled Cerutty's

> magnificent ability which very few people have got, some of the great
> speakers in history I guess, Winston Churchill had it, I guess King had it, I
> guess maybe to some extent, JFK. He just had the ability to transfix you with
> words, and lift you 20 feet into the air. I mean he had a wonderful eloquence,
> an inspiring eloquence about him.

Elliott added that Cerutty got his athletes interested in using their sport 'to develop you
into a better human being', not just to aspire to 'become a world champion'. Cerutty,
seen by many as wacky and eccentric, specialized in urging his trainees, or pupils, up
precipitous sand dunes, and encouraging what were at the time seen as strange
health-food diets. Graeme Kelly's *Mr Controversial: The Story of Percy Wells Cerutty*
(1965) collects anecdotes about and memories of Cerutty's Portsea training camp
south of Melbourne, Australia, and documents some of the games of the psyche that
Cerutty would play with his athlete pupils to instill in them the will to win.

   The success of his athletes generated a revolution in training methods, despite
the mocking depiction of him by traditionalists and sporting authorities. Roger
Bannister, four-minute mile pioneer, reviewed Cerutty's *Athletics: How to Become a
Champion* in the *Sunday Times* (15 May 1960), observing that Cerutty's written
words might spark scepticism and ridicule, but that his personal dynamism and
actual achievements must be acknowledged as revolutionary for their times. As
Bannister observed, 'a diet fortified by nuts, raisins and raw oats' was combined
with strength training, 'quick thinking, intelligent planning', and tactical
competitive courage, in a formula that produced undeniably successful results.

Champions League *See* UEFA CHAMPIONS LEAGUE.

Channel swimming The act of swimming the English Channel, the strip of
water separating England and France (in France, *La Manche*). The idea of crossing a
channel is not of course exclusive to this strip of sea, and channel swimming
has developed in California, in Santa Barbara and (from 1927) the Catalina Channel;
but the English Channel swimming challenge was an early challenge that
gripped the popular imagination of the 19th-century public. The first person to
swim the English Channel (from England to France) was Matthew (known as
Captain) Webb (1848–83), an English merchant seaman who, reported as
swimming against dogs as well at times in his youth, swam the Channel on his
second attempt in 1875. He was accorded instant heroic status, and made
appearances in endurance events. Charles Sprawson writes: 'Webb's triumphant
return to London brought business to a close at the stock exchange, and bonfires
illuminated the valleys of his native Shropshire' (*Oxford Dictionary of National*

Biography, 2004). But Channel swimming had made him a hero without security, and financial needs drove him to attempt to swim downriver beneath the Niagara Falls, where he drowned.

Swimming the Channel could be an international news event. When Gertrude Ederle (1905–2003), 1924 triple Olympic medallist, became the first woman to swim the Channel (from France to England) in 1926, her time of 14 hours 39 minutes broke the men's record by two hours. She was welcomed home to New York with a ticker-tape parade. W. W. McGeehan had anticipated her feat, writing in the *New York Herald Tribune*:

> If there is one woman who can make the swim, it is this girl, with the shoulders and back of Jack Dempsey and the frankest and bravest pair of eyes that ever looked into a face. She told me of her last attempt, when she swam for an hour on instinct alone, blinded, deaf, and only half conscious. She remembered only the humour of the trip. This girl keeps her even temper. I felt that I would sooner be in that tug the day she starts than at the ringside of the greatest fight or at the arena of the greatest game in the world, for this, in my opinion, is to be the greatest sports story in the world.

In the preparation for the swim, Ederle was actually contracted to the *New York Daily News* and the *Chicago Tribune*, which refused access to the tug for writers from other papers, such as McGeehan. After her achievement, Ederle appeared in a movie, and launched an unsuccessful career in entertainment (purportedly mismanaged and defrauded), though a song-and-dance step was named after her. Becoming fully deaf in the 1940s (measles had affected her hearing as a child), she worked thereafter as a swimming teacher to the deaf. Californian Florence May Chadwick (1918–95) was the first woman to make two crossings, in 1951 and 1953, from England to France.

Channel swimming over this strip of sea has continued to attract much publicity, and demonstrates the human challenge that is stimulated by the natural environment. It is estimated that fewer than 10 per cent of those attempting the swim have succeeded, but one of the most successful of these, in July 2006, was English comedian David Walliams, who completed the swim in 10 hours 34 minutes, raising over a million pounds for charity, associated with the Sport Relief/Comic Relief event of that year. The challenge also continues to attract endurance swimmers, and a hundred and thirty years after Webb's first crossing, some English swimmers had completed three dozen individual crossings.

Chapman, Herbert (1878–1934) A Yorkshire-born Englishman who became a leading manager-coach in professional football in the 1920s and the 1930s, leading Huddersfield Town to two (1924–5) and Arsenal to two (the first in 1931) league titles in England's Football League Division 1. The three successive Arsenal titles from 1933 to 1935 (the second and third of these after his death) equalled his old club Huddersfield's record that had been achieved the season after he left for Arsenal. Chapman was born into a working-class family and received a technical education but combined this with playing football at top amateur and also professional level (including a spell in London playing for Tottenham Hotspur), and moved into management with Northampton Town and Leeds City, where charges of illegal payments to players tarnished his success (the Leeds club became the first club ever to be expelled from the League). He re-emerged, though, in 1921 to take the manager's job at Huddersfield, and was then attracted to the job at Arsenal (where again, financial irregularities were proven, but Chapman escaped personal censure).

Chapman was a brilliant adapter—though not inventor—of modern tactics (exploiting the changes in the offside law, for instance), and combined image-building and marketing initiatives with his determined team building, insightful coaching, and dictatorial disciplinary philosophy; he introduced team talks, golf as relaxation, and medical conditioning. Tony Mason calls him one of the greatest modernizers of football and the football business:

> Chapman certainly embraced football modernity; his broadcasts and journalism were full of ideas about the future development of the football business. He was in favour of floodlights, of numbering players' shirts, and of making Arsenal stadium more attractive for spectators. One of his shrewdest moves was to persuade the London Electric Railway in 1932 to change the name of their Piccadilly Line station adjacent to Highbury from the mundane Gillespie Road to the charismatic Arsenal. He was among the first to recognize the growing threat of European football to British superiority. He thought the size of the selection committee of the England team should be reduced from twelve to three. He had a European-wide reputation and looked forward to a European nations' championship. (*Oxford Dictionary of National Biography*, 2004).

A confirmed workaholic, Chapman died suddenly of pneumonia after catching a cold. A bust by Jacob Epstein stands in the lobby of Arsenal's new stadium, The Emirates, to which the club moved in 2007.

character In psychology, the aggregation of traits (relatively consistent and distinguishing patterns of behaviour) that constitutes the individual and separates one person from another. In sociology, studies of national character have become unfashionable if not discredited, accused of perpetuating *stereotypes, though anthropological studies have shown that the meaning of a sport in one society or culture (baseball in Japanese culture, for instance) is different from the meaning of the sport in another (say, the USA); and that these differences can be accounted for by the different character formations brought to bear on the sport by players and fans. Social and historical analysis of sport has demonstrated too that sports and the way in which they are played has been widely associated with *character building.

character building The process whereby a particular activity develops desirable values in an individual. Sport has frequently been claimed to be a way of character building. Through learning to play in teams, cooperate with others, and the like, it is seen as not just a reflection of wider social values, but as generative of such values. Although there is scepticism about the role of sport in character building, historical analyses have shown the place that sport played in this sphere. In Britain in 1864 the Clarendon Commission stated that 'cricket and football pitches . . . are not merely places of amusement; they help to form some of the most valuable social qualities and manly virtues, and they hold, like the classroom and the boarding house, a distinct and important place in public school education'. Loretto School's headmaster H. H. Almond wrote in 1893, in *Nineteenth Century*, that football could educate its players in a 'spirit of chivalry, fairness and good temper'. Modris Eksteins sees in this British model of sportsmanship a dual moral and physical purpose, captured in Sir Henry Newbolt's 1898 poem *Vitai Lampada*, which 'transported the sporting mentality' into the imperial context: '"Play the game!" That's what life is about. Decency, fortitude, grit, civilization, Christianity, commerce, all blend into one—the game!' (*Rites of Spring: The Great War and the Birth of the Modern Age*, 1989). It was the sporting spirit that marked the British approach in the early years of the war, and that was condemned by one French observer as 'too calm and inclined to a who-gives-a-damn attitude', seen as an expression of *l'égoïsme anglais*.

Not all educational idealists and sport reformers would succeed in their character-building missions: team games could breed selfishness and brutishness; *rational recreation providers could see their initiatives appropriated by social groups who wanted to play in different ways. But despite the scepticism of some psychologists and empirical social scientists, testimony—such as the biographies of boxers from deprived social circumstances, or the reciprocal respect of international contestants in the Olympic arena—confirms that there is more to the character-building capacity of sport than mere rhetoric or wishful thinking. *See also* AMATEURISM; ATHLETICISM.

chariot racing A form of horse racing immensely popular in the ancient civilizations of Greece, Rome, and Byzantium, with some predecessors in the privileged cultures of earlier civilizations, such as in Syria, where chariot-based hunting parties of aristocrats offered a model for the adaptation of the chariot to the competitive racing form. In Greece, two-horse chariots were initially used. Homer dedicates almost 700 lines of the *Iliad* to description of the sporting contests held in mourning for the dead hero Patroclus, in the ninth year of the siege of Troy, 60 per cent of which is dedicated to chariot racing. Five competitors steered their chariots, and the organizer, Achilles, provided prizes. Chariot racing of this kind remained the preserve of a small elite, performing and competing as an enhancement of their already well-established reputations for courage, and in acknowledgement of their physical expertise, though it could generate excitement among spectators. A four-horse chariot race—the *quadriga*—was established in the Olympic Games in Greece in 680 BC. Four-foal and two-foal chariot races were added in the 4th century BC. The course at Olympia could take sixty or more chariots at once. The expansion of the facilities at Olympia had included the creation of a special course, the hippodrome. At one particular festival, the Panathenaea, held in Athens in celebration of the city's goddess-protector Athena, and staged on a large scale every four years, chariot races were combined with athletic feats; *apobatai*, drivers wearing only a shield and a helmet, would descend from their chariots and run alongside them before remounting.

Chariot racing became a major cultural event in the early Roman Empire, and races were illustrated on the walls of tombs and vases; historians claim that competitive chariot racing was brought to Rome by Etruscans who had come from eastern civilizations on the continent of Asia, where there is evidence of the embryonic sporting form. It was in purpose-built facilities such as the *Circus Maximus that regular *ludi circenses* (games in the circus) were held as a form of popular celebration. Young riders were trained and strong affiliations emerged for particular factions, associated with one colour: red, white, blue, or green. It has been estimated by archaeologists that 300,000 Romans could get in to the Circus's 600 metre by 100 metre plus, and mile-long, elliptical space. The Emperor Augustus, from close to his house atop the Palatine Hill, could gaze down at the contests that brought together the disparate elements of the Empire in a symbol of collective expression and enthusiasm.

Chariot racing was the one sport of the ancient world to survive the collapse of the western Roman empire and civilization, prospering in the eastern empire in the 6th and 7th centuries, where, in Constantinople, an elaborate hippodrome catering for 100,000 seated spectators was constructed. This space was a focus for public protest and rioting, reflecting the deep-rooted economic, political, social, and religious tensions of the Byzantine Empire. One such set of circumstances sparked the Nika Revolt in 532, put down only at the price of 30,000 dead. Chariot races were established, nevertheless, as part of court ceremonial and as a direct expression of imperial power, and Christian attacks on the sport stopped once the emperor, who was also head of the Byzantine church, had such direct control over them. Chariot racing remained prominent in the Byzantine Empire throughout Europe's Middle Ages, until undermined by Crusaders' temporary control of Constantinople en route from Europe to Jerusalem. *See also* BYZANTIUM, SPORT IN.

Chariots of Fire A 1980 film based upon the athletic achievements of Englishman Harold *Abrahams in his time as a Cambridge student, and Scottish preacher and missionary Eric *Liddell, culminating in their medal-winning performances at the Paris Olympics of 1924. Scripted by Colin Welland and directed by David Puttnam, the film won the Oscar for best film. The aristocratic hauteur of the English amateur is depicted in the character of Lord Lindsay, loosely based upon the figure of David George Brownlow Cecil (1905–81), sixth Marquess of Exeter and Baron Burghley (the 'hurdling lordship'). The scene in which Lindsay practises his hurdling technique with glasses of champagne balanced on the hurdles is contrasted with the analytical training methods of Abrahams, the mechanistic training drills of the US athletes, and the elemental hill-training of the sabbatarian Liddell.

charisma A term used in contemporary everyday parlance, by journalists, cultural commentators, and the general population, to refer to the extraordinary and/or heroic qualities of an individual. The term is a Latin one, and also derives from Greek, and came in 17th-century English to refer to favour and grace dispensed by God. In the work of Max *Weber, charisma is linked to the capacity to wield authority over individuals, one of three, more routine or mundane, forms of domination that he analysed. Charisma is a form of domination or authority based, in Weber's words (c.1918), in 'the provisioning of all demands that go beyond those of everyday routine', and characterizing 'natural leaders' who are 'holders of specific gifts of the body and the spirit', gifts believed to be supernatural, not accessible to everybody. In Weber's sociology of charismatic authority, such leaders are usually cultural heroes or religious visionaries: 'The holder of charisma seizes the task that is adequate for him and demands obedience and a following by

virtue of his mission.' Without such a following, there is no charisma; and
'charisma lives in, not *off*, this world', rejecting 'rational economic conduct'. The
concept has illuminated historical studies of political leaders (for instance, Ian
Kershaw's *Hitler, 1889–1936: Hubris*, 1998, in which he states his debt to Weber's
insight that charisma rests in the perceivers' view of the charismatic figure). Other
spheres in which the concept has been applied include the world of business
leadership.

   In comparison to religion, politics, and business, sport is a relatively insignificant
sphere for the discussion of the charismatic figure and his or her followers.
Despite the diluted everyday use of the term, in what real way do golfer Tiger Woods
or all-time Olympian gold medal-holding swimmer Michael Phelps exert
charismatic authority? Weber's 'god-like strength of the hero' may seem apparent
as Woods closes in on the title on the fourth day of a tournament, or Phelps turns
defeat into victory with a superhuman last length of the pool. But their opponents
know that they are also human, vulnerable in competition; and the great
sporting triumph does not translate into any dynamic of authority over followers.
Such sport triumphs are better understood as examples of the *celebrity, or in
relation to the notion of *role model.

charivari In popular culture, a cacophonous but organized medley of sounds
performed in public as a sign of disapproval or of cultural defiance; the term is
derived from the French, meaning a serenade, made with pans and trays, to an
unpopular person. It is what E. P. Thompson, in his article on 'Rough Music' in
Customs in Common (1993), referred to as a 'rude cacophony', sometimes with and
sometimes without ritual, used to express hostility towards or to mock anyone who
had offended the collective or group values. Thompson notes too that illiterate
people can be very rational actors, self-aware and deliberate in their superficially
random actions, or what we might call their charivariesque choruses. The
apparently mindless chants and songs of fans at sport stadiums might be better
understood as charivari-like statements against the interests of the powerful owner
and the pampered but underperforming superstar.

Charles, William John (1931–2004) Born in Swansea, Wales, United Kingdom,
a professional footballer for English club Leeds United, for which he signed on his
seventeenth birthday after two years as a trainee at his local Swansea Town
Football Club. Charles was a strong, muscular player—he boxed with some success
during his National Service in the army—and his great quality was that he could
play with equally impressive effect in both attacking and defensive positions.
Charles moved to play with great success for Juventus of Turin (Torino) where, in
1957, the club doctor commented that 'I have never seen a better human machine
in a lifetime in medicine'. Obituarists wrote lyrically in 2004 of these physical
qualities, and despite this physical prowess Charles's demeanour in play was such
that in Italy he acquired the nickname 'The Good (or Gentle) Giant' (*il Buon
Gigante*); in a quarter of a century of competitive matches, he was never cautioned
or sent off. Charles's career in Italy made him a rich man but his later years were
blighted by declining stature in the game (as player and then manager), business

misadventures, relative poverty, and illness. In 1997, nevertheless, Juventus fans voted him their greatest ever foreign player.

charreada A Mexican event based upon horseback parades and contests, established as a way of preserving the traditions of the *charros* (cowboys) in the period of the break-up of the haciendas after the Mexican Revolution. The national association was established in 1921, and the genre was featured in the emerging film industry, so profiling (and romanticizing) the practices of the traditional horseman in modern entertainment forms. The event is judged rather than timed, and is primarily amateur, with modest prizes.

cheating The deliberate and intentional violation of clearly formulated, reciprocally understood and shared rules of competition and engagement in sporting encounters. Cheating does not, as philosophers of sport have clarified, signal the end of competition, as the rationale for cheating is based upon a notion that cheating will gain the competitor an advantage within the game or contest itself. Although cheating can be seen as culturally relative and temporally or historically contingent—the notorious 'Hand of God' goal by footballer Maradona for Argentina against England in the 1986 football World Cup was widely admired as a successful form of street cunning by many of the player's home fans; banned drugs were not always banned—the revelation that a competitor has cheated is widely perceived to warrant the disqualification of that competitor. *See also* CORRUPTION; MORAL LABORATORY.

cheerleading A combination of exercise, acrobatics, and dance performed by teams of predominantly young women in the context of team sports, before and during breaks in team sport contests, these latter usually being the sporting encounters of males; the performances are intended to rouse the crowd into noisy enthusiasm and vocal support for the team. Organized cheerleading dates from the late 1800s in US universities (initially, the University of Minnesota) when all-male groups urged on the college football side; in 1898, it began to be organized more formally on the basis of supportive chants in the crowd led by what became a yell-leader. In the early 1920s, cheerleading women were organized in US universities. Latterly, cheerleading has laid claims to the status of a competitive physical activity in itself, with teams in the USA entering national competitions, and the National Cheerleaders Association (founded 1948) espousing the values of the activity: its web welcome in 2009 thanked the association's founder, Lawrence Herkimer, and declared a commitment to

> hold dear his vision of creating an atmosphere to cultivate the whole cheerleader. We embrace our rich heritage as the first cheerleading company and continue to pioneer the way with innovative Camp curriculum, industry-leading Championships and Special Events that reward the hard-working, well-rounded cheerleaders in America today!

As the web declaration shows, cheerleading has spawned a serious business drawing in large numbers of young enthusiasts. The more cut-throat and damaging end of the competitive variant of the activity has been exposed in Kate Torgovnik's *Cheer!: Inside The Secret World of College Cheerleading* (2008). Sociological study has shown that there is also an interesting gender dynamic underlying the activity. Laura Grindstaff ('Cheerleading and the Gendered Politics of Sport', *Social Problems*, 2006) has shown how male cheerleaders want to perform separately from female practitioners, because their association with the feminine side of the activity has branded them as gay. Controversies abound on the potentially injurious effects of the activity, but it has prospered at school, college, and even professional level in the USA. The practice has been adopted in schools and in the context of some professional sports in numerous countries beyond the USA, and particularly well-organized mixed cheerleading groups (*Ōendan*) of both male and female Japanese fans are visible on the international sporting stage, at events ranging from softball matches at the Olympic Games, to men's football games at the FIFA World Cup. Whether cheerleading is a sport or not remains an unanswerable question; it is certainly an established form of public, performative body culture, in its organized forms drawing on committed participants, and requiring discipline, training, physical skill, coordination, and collective cooperation. The meaning depends on the context, for in the support role in the stadium, as opposed to the self-contained competitive variant, it can also be redolent of sexism, voyeurism, and nationalism.

Cheltenham Gold Cup *See* HORSE RACING.

chess The most cerebral and least obviously physical 'sport' to be included on the International Olympic Committee's Recognized Sports List, a game with a long and complex global history that in its modern competitive form materialized in Europe in the 19th century. The World Chess Federation was established in 1924, and 85 years later had 165 affiliated national members. As a board game with a history of over 1,500 years, chess has intrigued players and intellectuals alike with its intense one-to-one format. It is in this confrontational mode that commentators and writers find parallels between chess competitors and sport combatants. George Steiner's account of the world chess contest between Robert J. (Bobby) Fischer of the USA and Boris Spassky of the USSR, in Reykjavik, Iceland, in the summer of 1972, acknowledged these parallels in the title of his memoir: *The Sporting Scene: White Knights of Reykjavik* (1972). Famous for his idiosyncrasies and irrational behaviour, Fischer prompted Steiner to comment on 'the abundant impulses to paranoia and unreality in chess itself, in the violence and autistic patterns of the game'. Chess, for Steiner, is

> a radically sterile form of play. The problems it poses are at the same time very deep and utterly trivial . . . What needs emphasis is the plain fact that a chess genius is a human being who focuses vast, little understood mental gifts and labours on an ultimately trivial human enterprise.

Its practitioners show symptoms of 'nervous stress and unreality'. Steiner observes that only two other human pursuits—mathematics and music—have seen creative achievements by young children, and in this chess is of course very different from a physical pursuit such as sport; but the young prodigy's behavioural patterns are comparable in both endeavours. Describing the 19-year-old Fischer, Steiner wrote of his lack of 'ordinary human contact and emotional maturity', and an 'almost pathological one-sidedness to Fischer's outlook and personality'. He was a young man of nineteen with the chess brain of a complete master and the emotional, intellectual reserves in all other regards of a raw adolescent.' Some of these character assessments might have been written of the young US tennis prodigy John McEnroe who emerged on to the international tennis circuit just a few years later.

Chicago School A name applied to sociologists at the University of Chicago's Department of Sociology in the first half of the 20th century (especially the 1920s and 1930s), whose pioneering and often *qualitative research on urban life used the city itself as a laboratory for human enquiry, and focused upon distinctive urban cultures. Major analytical themes of the Chicago School were the ecology and culture of modern urban living, involving detailed studies of particular figures and places such as the hobo and the taxi dance-hall. Such studies can still be seen as templates for the study of sport and leisure cultures, combining as they did the close observation of relatively invisible facets of city life and urban culture as, methodologically, researchers prioritized detailed and sustained fieldwork into the cultures of the city. A more social psychological dimension of the School's work led to the formulation of *symbolic interactionism and sociologically rooted interactionist accounts of social life. *See also* MEAD, GEORGE HERBERT; WIRTH, LOUIS.

children's sports and games In his *Sports and Pastimes of the People of England* (1801) Joseph Strutt included a whole chapter on children's games, many of them simple in conception, dependent upon little or no equipment, and involving running, jumping, catching, chasing, and the like. These would be played in the outdoors, and at fairs, and in later years in school playgrounds. Forms of such pre-modern children's games survived into the 19th and 20th centuries, in schools and some smaller communities, but modern urban conditions, mass communications, and media-based leisure forms have changed the context in which such games flourish. In contemporary sporting culture of the early 21st century, children's games are associated with very young children, and the public culture of children's game-playing is all but obsolete. *See also* STREET GAMES.

choker A player or athlete whose performance suddenly deteriorates at a critical point in performance or competition, and whose confidence decreases, so that the contest is not 'closed out' when the player is on the point of victory. The golfer with the critical championship putt and the tennis player on match point can exhibit such losses of form and confidence, and the onset of uncontrollable nerves, and become perceived as chokers. The term derives from the meaning of the word 'choke', to suffocate, or to become blocked. Psychologists have explored the phenomenon in both team sports and individual sports, but no definitive explanation has been established as to why one individual rather than another becomes a choker, or what set of circumstances produces the *anxiety and nerves that constitute choking.

chuiwan A racket game enduringly popular among women during recorded Chinese history. The game claimed to represent the principles of fairness and harmony, and exhibited elements of contemporary golf and billiards, involving striking a wooden ball towards holes indicated by coloured flags. See Allen Guttmann's *Sports: The First Five Millennia* (2004). It was played by women of the privileged classes, bedizened in elaborate costume, and was clearly a form of *conspicuous consumption as well as gentle exercise.

cinema, sport in Sport has featured in film and the cinema in a variety of genres, rather than constituting any single identifiable genre of the sporting film. These have included the biopic, the treatment of the biography (or a selected part of the life) of a single individual; the documentary, reconstructing and analysing a particular event or experience; the adaptation of a fictional text; the (approximate) historical reconstruction of famous deeds or achievements in their social and cultural context; and the newsreel. Recurrent narrative motifs in sport films have been the failure–success dynamic and the process of the comeback; the rags-to-riches story of sporting achievement; the identity politics that sporting cultures can address, in terms of gender, sexuality, and ethnicity; and the athlete–coach relationship. The sporting context itself—the action and the contest—is far from easy to capture on screen, though there are cases where the boxing match or the athletics race has been conveyed credibly; but the most effective sport-based film is frequently the one where the sporting action is a context and a backdrop against which wider themes and motifs are played out. *See also* Chariots of Fire; North Dallas Forty; Olympia; One Day in September; Personal Best; Seabiscuit; This Sporting Life; Triumph of the Will; Visions of 8.

circuit 1. A course or a track in sports such as *motor racing or *horse racing. 2. A series of tournaments or competitions in different places, sometimes now called 'the tour' by professionals. 3. In reference to circuit training, a term used to refer to a set of exercise routines designed to be done in succession, and repeated a number of times, often at increased intensity without pausing, sometimes done until a particular time period has elapsed.

Circus Maximus The most magnificent of the Roman circuses. The Etruscan king of Rome, Tarquinius Priscus, laid out a sports ground for the celebration of the victory of the Etruscans over the Latins, and erected tribunes for the higher-class spectators. The last Etruscan king, Tarquinius Superbus, rebuilt these, thus laying the foundations for the Circus Maximus where Roman Games were staged. Sculptured into the slopes of the depression in the Murcia valley close to central Rome, between the Palatine and the Aventine hills, its layered seating could accommodate more than a quarter of a million spectators: the *podium* was reserved for the most privileged, and wooden structures at the top of the structure accommodated slaves and visitors/strangers. Booths surrounded the Circus, with salesmen of the day offering merchandise of all kinds, including astrological forecasts and the services of prostitutes. Julius *Caesar modernized the venue, enlarging it to 621 metres long, and 118 metres across. Twelve starting gates—*carceres*—dominated one end of the site, out of which the horses raced; at the other end of the course a triumphal gate welcomed the winning unit. The Circus was later the source of the fire through which the Emperor *Nero, as legend but not definitive history relates, fiddled.

The sexes were not segregated, and in the early years of the first century AD a day at the races was established as not just a betting venue and a holiday fair but also a meeting place; Ovid refers to the site as a source for finding potential partners. There were up to 24 races staged throughout the day, and disappointed out-of-pocket gamblers might be compensated with free raffle tickets or snacks. In the fourth century AD the writer Ammianus Marcellinus wrote of the importance and significance of the games for the Roman populace:

> Now let me describe for you this mass of people, unemployed and therefore with too much time on their hands. For them the Circus Maximus is temple, home, social club and centre of all their hopes. You can see them beyond the city, arguing about the races . . . and declaring that the country will come to ruin unless their favourite wins in the next races. And on the day they all rush to the circus even before daybreak, to secure a place.' (cited in Vera Olivova, *Sports and Games in the Ancient World*, 1984).

The Circus Maximus became a model for the hippodrome in contemporary Istanbul, north of the Blue Mosque and close to the Topkapi Palace. In both Rome and Istanbul, the spaces of these racing venues remain identifiable, powerful testimony to the profile in imperial cities of this blend of popular culture and political control. The Circus area itself hosted the free rock concert of the band Genesis in 2007, in front of 500,000 people; and the victory of the Italian national side in the 2006 men's football World Cup was celebrated by 700,000 people there.

citizenship In its modern form the notion of citizenship refers to what Tom Bottomore (*The Blackwell Dictionary of Twentieth Century Social Thought*, 1993) calls formal citizenship, widely recognized as membership of a nation state, and substantive citizenship, 'the possession of a body of civil, political and especially social rights'. Social rights have usually been guaranteed in written constitutions or delivered in systems of welfare capitalism. In relation to sport and leisure, the issue of citizenship is whether leisure—in the form of resources and facilities, and access of a reasonable nature—is a right of the citizen. Should municipal provision of, for instance, swimming pools and training gyms be supported on the rationale that they will be health-inducing and could generate valued forms of sociability? These are difficult questions to which to find neutral answers, as they clearly enter the realm of political commitment and decision-making.

Alan Clarke, in a 1992 essay responding to the process of Compulsory Competitive Tendering of the management of UK public sector leisure facilities, argued that such changes afforded the opportunity for a revitalization of the model of citizenship. Rather than seeing citizenship provision as something apart from self-determination or free-market supply, he argued, such a moment could 'open the provision of public services after the welfare state to the public themselves . . . build on the notion of citizenship a fuller sense of rights and responsibilities'. In this model of citizenship, the sport and leisure participant is also less passive, and more than a mere recipient of the state's beneficence: the citizen 'takes on an active and determining character', and citizens become 'active agents, commissioning their own performances'. Such a participatory vision of leisure and sport as an expression of public citizenship remains to be realized; and sport and leisure as an element of substantive citizenship look increasingly fragile next to the burgeoning sport industry and leisure market.

cityscape The urban equivalent of the notion of landscape. A cityscape focusing upon sport stadiums and leisure and consumption facilities would be a form of conceptual mapping of public and observable spaces in the urban setting. An exercise mapping the movement of sport stadiums from city centres to out-of-town sites could be informed by systematic cityscapes of respective zones of the city.

civilizing process A process identified by the sociologist Norbert Elias. 'In the course of a civilizing process', Elias and Eric Dunning wrote, 'the character and the whole balance' between 'pressures and restraints' and 'special leisure areas for relieving and loosening them' changes: restraints on people's behaviour become more all-embracing (*Quest for Excitement: Sport and Leisure in the Civilizing Process*, 1986). These restraints become internalized, providing a 'personal armour' operating as a means of 'self-control'. This effects a transformation in sport and leisure activities, from more violent to less violent ones, for instance; though counter-movements (sometimes called 'de-civilizing spurts') are detectable in the long-term civilizing process, in activities such as sports or music or drama, as compensatory forms of excitement countering 'the restraint of overt emotionality in our ordinary life'. But even in these counter-movements the activities 'are themselves tempered by civilising restraints'.

Dunning and colleagues have produced seminal and hugely influential works applying the theory of the civilizing process to the history and sociology of sport, and in particular to the English context of *football hooliganism. Dunning has also outlined a five-point agenda for the application of the theory of the civilizing process to the question of sport and gender. The civilizing process can illuminate, or begin to explain, (i) the persisting meanings of sport for 'traditional male identities and roles'; (ii) the relative empowerment of females, allowing them to challenge bastions of male preserve; (iii) changes in what is seen as acceptably 'feminine' behaviour; (iv) reactions of some males to what they see as female 'encroachment' into their male preserve; and (v) the 'motivational sources' leading increasing numbers of females to take up sport, and their reactions to those seeking to block their entry (*Sport Matters: Sociological Studies of Sport, Violence and Civilization*, 1999).

There has been widespread debate on the scope and validity of the theory of the civilizing process. Is it implicitly linear, simplifying theories of cultural change and social development? Is it inherently functionalist, with its emphasis on the chains of interdependency of configurations that hold a society and culture together? Adherents of the theory have mounted robust defences, and the Eliasian legacy remains without doubt one of the most influential general theories seeking to account for the sociocultural genesis and significance of modern sport forms. *See also* AFFECT CONTROL; ELIASIAN.

civil rights The rights of any individual to be treated as an equal and with dignity, regardless of ethnic or racial background, gender and sexuality, or any other defining characteristic. The most famous case of civil rights activism in international sport was the podium demonstration by the three medal winners in the 200-metre race at the 1968 Olympics in Mexico City. In the year in which the black leader of the civil rights movement in the USA, Martin Luther King, was assassinated, two black US athletes and one white Australian shocked the sporting establishment by mounting the medal podium wearing civil rights badges. The Californians Tommie Smith and John Carlos, fellow students at San José State College, were also barefoot, and Carlos wore beads around his neck to symbolize the lynching of blacks in the USA; Smith wore a black scarf around his neck. Both bowed their heads and raised one black-gloved hand in a Black Power salute when the US national anthem was played. The bare feet, they said later, were a symbol of black poverty in the USA; the salute represented the unity and strength of black culture; the bowed head was to protest that the anthem's theme of freedom was true only for white people in the USA. Australian Peter Norman explained later that as a believer in human rights and an opponent of 'White Australia' immigration policy, he was wholly in support of the protest. Threatened by the International Olympic Committee with the expulsion of the whole national track-and-field squad if Smith and Carlos were not banned from the Games, the United States Olympic Committee capitulated. The two Californians, also members of an organization of athletes opposing the treatment of blacks in the USA (the Olympic Project for Human Rights), met with widespread disapproval in their own country after the Games, and it was several years—and broken marriages each—before they found stable employment in coaching and youth development; Brent Musburger, a Chicago sports writer, had branded them 'black-skinned storm troopers'.

By 1982, though, the reactionary establishment had been superseded by a more enlightened administration in US sport, and Carlos worked for the Los Angeles Olympic organizers promoting the 1984 Games and liaising with black constituencies and communities. The Black Power salute was a pivotal moment in the cultural politics of sport, as well as the civil rights movement. Carlos pointed out the inherent politicization of the Olympics with its uniforms, anthems, and Cold War rivalries. In this context the 1968 gesture showed that peaceful protest was possible and powerful, and that sport should not be allowed to gloss over the cleavages of an unequal social fabric. Touchingly, when Australian Norman died in 2006, both Carlos and Smith were pallbearers at his funeral. Carlos had commented in 2000 that Norman's participation was not merely peripheral: 'To wear the badge as a white individual... made the statement even more powerful.' This lifelong respect between black and white embodied both the civil rights concerns that brought these three athletes together, and the potential of sport to transcend the barriers that the protest was designed to expose.

civil society A sphere of social organization and cultural activity that is neither market-led nor state-provided, and that takes place in public life rather than private spheres such as the family. It is associated with *voluntary sector organizations and activity and other forms of public participation, straddling political and non-political forms of association and *associativity. A strict definition might include in civil society organizations such as corporations or businesses, but in the analysis of sport's contribution to civil society it is the emphasis on participation that has been dominant, concerning sport as an expression of *citizenship or, in another version of the debate, an articulation of *social capital. It is in civil society that what Michael Sandel (*Democracy's Discontent*, 1998) calls the politics of the common good might be found, as 'persisting civic aspirations' manifest themselves in sport groups and other forms of human cooperation and expression that counter the 'anxieties of the time' and, potentially at least, revitalize the 'civic strand of freedom'.

class In its most general sense, the social and cultural expression of an economic relationship. Classes are made up of individuals who are located and identified on the basis of their contribution to economic production, their access to and control over resources, and their articulation of particular and distinctive class cultures and lifestyles. In modern societies social classes are based on the individual's and the group's place in the industrial and economic process, with the most significant measures of class distinction being wealth and occupation. Sport is a significant contributor to relations of social class in that people in elite groups have the resources to organize and maintain games on their own terms and in spaces inaccessible to others. This ultimately serves to reproduce social and economic distinctions and preserve the power and influence of those who control resources in society. The growth of modern sports cannot be adequately understood unless this key influence and core dynamic is fully recognized.

Class in history Forms of inequality and exploitation characterized the civilizations of the ancient world, where participation and spectatorship in Greek festivals and Roman games were based upon position and rank in the social and economic order. In the European Middle Ages, when the military rationale of the jousting tournament receded, it was maintained by despotic rulers as a spectacular public display of power and a form of theatre in which participation and spectatorship were based on social status and class position.

In comparable ways, a structure of social differentiation based on class characterized the emergent social order of the West's early modern period as industrialization and urbanization reshaped the basis of society and culture. *Ascribed status, leaving little option for social mobility, was superseded by achieved status that, in theory, held the promise of a change in status, according to the individual's economic position and potential. Social standing came to be defined in terms of what people did to make a living and how they publicly displayed their acquired economic status rather than in terms of inherited status and prescribed opportunities. Yet in practice, social class defined primarily in terms of economic status and its associated cultural dimensions reproduced the status quo and contributed to the consolidation of power relations and cultural distinctions.

Social histories of sports in Britain have vividly demonstrated how the emergence and the evolution of modern sports forms were rooted in class relations. Association football in its amateur form was championed by the middle and upper classes, and developed in its professional form by the working class and lower middle classes. The attitudes and beliefs embodied in the ethos of particular sports expressed class-based status and values. The middle classes, for instance, believed that the amateur code of football built character, strengthened the body, discouraged drinking, and unified social classes (Mason, 1980: 229). Rugby football's 'Great Schism' of 1895 saw the split between the Northern English mass spectator form of the game, and the amateur, Southern English-based Rugby Football Union (Dunning and Sheard, 1979: 198–200). Class patronage shaped many forms of sports provision, in particular societies such as the UK, the United States and in advanced societies generally (Cross, 1993: 102–3). *See also* CLASS CONSCIOUSNESS, CLASS DIVISIONS; CLASS HABITUS; CLASS MOBILITY; CLASS STRUGGLE; CULTURAL CAPITAL; CULTURAL CONTESTATION.

References
Cross, G. (1993) *Time and Money: The Making of Consumer Culture*, London and New York: Routledge; Dunning, E. and Sheard, K. (1979) *Barbarians, Gentlemen and Players: A Sociological Study of the Development of Rugby Football*, New York: New York University Press; Mason, T. (1980) *Association Football and English Society, 1863–1915*, Sussex: The Harvester Press.

class consciousness The expression of the interests of a particular social class, conceived in Marxist terms as a question of how a class-in-itself that has no common consciousness can develop into a class-for-itself that does have a common consciousness. Political institutions (organized labour in the form of trade unions) can provide a vehicle for the articulation of a common consciousness, and sport certainly has the potential to mobilize common interests, though not in accordance with any general pattern. Particular sporting preferences have been more likely to express the conservative elements of the class culture.

class divisions Differences of values and interests between social groups based upon their location in the *social class system and the cultural and economic relations of that system. Sport, despite its aspirations to meritocratic, egalitarian bases has usually continued to express social and cultural divisions according to *gender and *race, and social class. National surveys of *sport participation in the UK, for instance, confirm the way that sport reproduces class divisions, acting as a form of *cultural capital. The same is true for spectator sports, and for all levels of sport, examples abound across societies and cultures: *NASCAR as blue-collar culture in the USA; *Rugby League with its strong working-class base in England and Australia; *polo as an upper-class enclave in England, the USA, and Argentina. *See also* CLASS.

class habitus A set of dispositions which generate practices and perceptions. For Pierre *Bourdieu, the notion of habitus is central to the analysis of class-based cultures. He notes (1978) that sports emerged in exclusive English public schools, where the sons of wealthy, powerful, and aristocratic families appropriated popular games and changed their function to suit their interests. He connects the rationalization of games into modern sport forms with a class-based philosophy of *amateurism that expressed the moral ideal and the ethos of the most powerful segments of the bourgeois class. Playing *lawn tennis or *golf, riding or sailing, as Bourdieu argues, bestowed upon the participant what he called gains in distinction (1978: 828). Sports in which lower middle class or working-class people participate develop as spectacles created for the people as mass commodities. Sports, therefore, are not self-contained spheres of practice, and it is class habitus that defines any meaning conferred on sporting activity, and any social value that is associated with the sporting practice (Bourdieu, 1978: 835). From this perspective, then, sports participation is not a matter of personal choice or individual preference; it depends upon the financial resources available to the potential participant, the social status of those prominent in that activity, and the cultural meaning of a sport and the individual's relationship to those meanings.

Far from being an open sphere of limitless possibilities, sport is a social phenomenon and cultural space that operates in Max *Weber's terms as a form of social *closure, in which potential entrants are vetted and excluded to suit the incumbent gatekeepers. At the same time, the inner world of the sports culture is tightly monitored and controlled, as in golf or tennis club membership committees, and in other sports institutions in which formal or informal entry requirements are barriers to open participation.

The recruitment and induction processes into such clubs are operational expressions of and examinations in cultural capital. For example, entrance into a tennis club requires that newcomers must communicate competently with the gatekeepers of a club; read the social interactions and etiquette and conventions of a club; comply with the dress code; be equipped with relatively sophisticated technology; and have the ability to play at an acceptable level of competence. This apparently open choice is in reality a possibility or trajectory based upon what Bourdieu recognizes as the power of economic and cultural capital, so that class variations in sporting practice can be understood as shaped not just by the basic financial costs of an activity, but also by the perceived benefits that will accrue, either immediately or later, to the participant. Sporting practices, and associated physical and body cultures, are therefore aspects of the class habitus (Bourdieu, 1986: 212). Practices, in the Bourdieuian framework, are articulations of habitus (ibid., p. 172).

Bourdieu is sensitive to the fact that classes are not monolithic. He argues that there can be divisions within classes and these too can be reflected in sports. An interesting example that he uses is that of the gender dimension of the class habitus that produces a sexual division of labour that in turn affects participation in particular sporting activities (1986: 218). But in general, for Bourdieu, the analysis of sport is a form of class analysis. Sport acts as a kind of badge of social exclusivity and cultural distinctiveness for the dominant classes; it operates as a means of control or containment of the working or popular classes; it is a potential but unlikely source of escape and mobility for talented working-class sports performers; it articulates the fractional status distinctions which exist within the ranks of larger class groupings; and it reveals the capacity of the body to express social principles and cultural meanings, for physical capital (Wacquant, 1995) to connect with forms of economic and cultural capital. Bourdieu described his study *Distinction* as an attempt to think through *Marx and *Weber's rival conceptions of *class and *status (1986: xii), and his major achievement was to connect the study of class position and concomitant lifestyles and statuses. The lesson here for the sociologist of sport is to recognize the need for a complementary and integrated analysis of both the class dimensions of a sport and its associated lifestyle dimensions.

References

Bourdieu, P. (1978) 'Sport and Social Class', *Social Science Information*, 17/6: 819–840; Bourdieu, P. (1986) *Distinction—A Social Critique of the Judgement of Taste*, London and New York: Routledge & Kegan Paul; Wacquant, L. (1995) 'Pugs at Work: Bodily Capital and Bodily Labour among Professional Boxers', *Body & Society*, 1/1: 65–93.

classical sports A term used by Pierre *Bourdieu to contrast established, organized forms of sport with the more modern, individualistic and lifestyle-based sports that he sometimes called *Californian sports. In such classical sports, 'there is respect for forms and for forms of respect, manifested in concern for propriety and ritual and in unashamed flaunting of wealth and luxury'. Bourdieu was talking here of the established sports of the dominant classes, and the way in which they represented the values of the social order and acted as forms of *conspicuous consumption.

class mobility The movement, between generations, of people across social classes, in either an upward or downward direction. Success in sport can be the basis of dramatic forms of mobility, so that English footballer David Beckham, who was born into the working class of east London, can achieve, through his sporting success and accompanying commercial profile, a status within a different social class, or a social stratum almost outside of the *social stratification system, as do movie stars, rock stars, and supermodels. More modestly, sport has provided a form of professional work that has been a means of escape from situations of limited opportunity: examples include black boxers escaping the ghetto; working-class footballers playing in early English and Scottish professional leagues; and footballers from underdeveloped countries prospering in the highly commercialized and rich leagues of Western Europe.

class struggle The struggle between social classes—usually defined according to economic criteria—whose interests lie in different social and political objectives and usually incompatible visions of the way in which society must be ordered. Karl *Marx (with Friedrich Engels, 1820–95) identified the ruling class, or the bourgeoisie, and the proletariat as the two primary social classes whose essential relationship, based on the former's exploitation of the latter, was one of struggle. In *The Communist Manifesto* (1848) the opening line posited class struggle as a universal, cross-temporal dynamic: 'The history of all hitherto existing society is the history of class struggles.' Attempts to understand the history of sport in such terms have had a partial credibility in that there are cases of workers' sports with a distinct political motivation; but the more complex dynamics and meanings of sport are better accounted for by more subtle analyses of class relations, such as provided in *hegemony theory.

clay-pigeon shooting A form of shooting devised when the shooting of live birds was made illegal in some countries. Early forms of spring mechanism were employed in the late 1800s, to catapult artefacts made of clay into the sky to be shot at. A Clay Bird Shooting Association was established in Britain in 1903, the sport having featured as a men's event at the 1900 Paris Olympics under the name of 'trap' shooting (where all top six competitors were French). The trap event for women was introduced at the 2000 Sydney Olympics. Competitors use a 12-gauge shotgun in aiming at the artificial birds (or 'saucers', more recently made of pitch and chalk rather than of clay). It is a sport resonant of the hunting sports of the privileged classes, and the prowess of the military, but in a peculiar way is an event that evokes a spirit of the triumph of the amateur in the modern age.

Clayre, Alasdair George S. (1935–84) A British academic, Prize Fellow of All Souls College, Oxford, whose publications included *Work and Play: Ideas and Experience of Work and Leisure* (1975). This was an innovative attempt to identify the importance of an aesthetics of everyday life in which forms of play are central to human expressivity. Clayre cited sympathetically the German philosopher Friedrich Schiller (1759–1805), whose *Aesthetic Letters* sought to show that 'the source of our energy and our wholeness, even in aspects of our life that seem to have no connection with "play", may lie in an unpossessive relationship to something loved, outside ourselves and . . . detached from our practical interests'. For Schiller, one paradigm of play is the making of art and its enjoyment. Forms of games and sports undoubtedly have the capacity to express such pleasures, to express humanity and wholeness, as opposed to the fragmentary and alienating activities of everyday working life.

climbing *See* MOUNTAINEERING.

closure, social The process whereby a social group can close and shut off social and economic opportunities from outsiders. Max *Weber's term was developed by Frank Parkin in his discussion of strategies of social closure employed in class relations and formation (*The Social Analysis of Class Structure*, 1974). Parkin identified two forms of social closure: the power of exclusion and the power of solidarism. The discriminating golf club committee using undeclared criteria for membership would represent the first; the partisan home-supporting sport crowd embodies the second. In both cases, closure occurs and the club or the crowd effects the exclusion of many, in the name of a collectivism of the few. Strategies of social closure are also the reason why progressive theories of sport development so often have little effect, as sport institutions and groups close ranks against the egalitarian initiatives of sport policymakers and providers.

club The basic organizational unit, in which and through which competitive sports are played, from amateur and recreational levels through to high-performance professional competition. Clubs based in the free association of its members are also the institutional manifestation of a *civil society, though the paradox of the club is that it has the power to exclude as well as include. In the historical development of sport, clubs have both reflected and reproduced social exclusiveness, moving for example from one activity such as cycling to another, such as motoring, when the cycle became a less exclusive item. Different models of the club—the professional football club as a members' club, as in Barcelona; the all-sports clubs dominated by a particular activity, such as the German *Turnen* clubs—illustrate the wide-ranging social and political significance of this apparently mundane cultural formation. Continuing study of sport clubs and their social composition remains crucial to the understanding of sport's place in a society and culture.

coach and horses Also known as 'coaching', this was a sport in which the early 19th-century nobility in England raced their coach and horses against each other. Exclusive clubs were formed and rich members of the leisure classes preened their status in parades, and in races and competitions on which large sums might be wagered. The most famous of such clubs was the Coaching Club, established in 1871 by the eighth Duke of Beaufort, and still staging the Coaching Club Drive at the Royal Windsor Horse Show in London into the 21st century.

coaching styles A description of the behaviour and leadership approach taken by a coach. Traditionally, there are two broad types of coaching style: democratic and autocratic. The democratic style is cooperative and athlete-centred, seeking to develop the intrinsic motivation of the athlete and willing to share control and decision-making. The autocratic style is tightly structured, controlling, and task-orientated. Both categories of coach are widely seen in sport and neither style is inherently superior. This bipolar categorization is considered by many theorists as too simple and sports psychologists have developed more sophisticated approaches, such as Chelladurai's multi-dimensional model or Smoll and Smith's leadership behaviour model.

Coca-Cola A transnational corporation with a long association with sport sponsorship. The Coca-Cola company is proud of its association with football's (soccer) ruling body the *Fédération Internationale de Football Association (FIFA), whose (2008) website noted: 'The Coca-Cola Company is one of the longest-standing corporate partners of FIFA, with a formal association since 1974 and an official sponsorship of FIFA World Cup™ that began in 1978. Coca-Cola has had stadium advertising at every FIFA World Cup™ since 1950.' The company has signed up with FIFA through to 2022, for the pinnacle events of the men's game in South Africa (2010) and Brazil (2014) and wherever FIFA awards the following two Finals in 2018 and 2022. It also supports

> the broad spectrum of FIFA-organized events around the globe, including the FIFA World Cup™, FIFA Women's World Cup, FIFA World Youth Championship, FIFA U-17 World Championship, FIFA Beach Soccer World Cup, FIFA Club World Championship, FIFA Interactive World Cup, FIFA U-20 Women's World Championship, FIFA Futsal World Championship, and the FIFA Confederations Cup.

The soft drink magnate also sponsors FIFA's world ranking system for the men's and the women's national sides.

Coca-Cola established itself early in international sport sponsorship. Hundreds of its posters advertised the company and its product around the stadium at the 1928 Amsterdam Summer Olympic Games, and it supplied equipment to the Olympic squad at its living quarters aboard the SS *Roosevelt*. The following year its publication *Red Barrel* combined the contemporary with the classical: 'Coca-Cola is now found within the bull fight arenas of sunny Spain and Mexico, at the Olympic Games stadium below the dykes of Holland, atop the Eiffel Tower above "Gay Paree", on the holy pagoda in distant Burma, and beside the Coliseum of historic Rome.' With this pedigree Coca-Cola was ready for the expanding football market. When Brazilian Dr João Havelange won the FIFA presidency in 1974, the organization had virtually no budget for the implementation of his manifesto. Aided by *Adidas boss of the time, Horst *Dassler, and English marketing pioneer Patrick

Nally, FIFA targeted Coca-Cola. Havelange, advised by Dassler, flew in to Coke's Atlanta headquarters in his private plane. As Nally observes, the ambitious soccer development programme needed a big corporate player and, 'if you're into Coke, you're into the biggest bluechip company on a global basis'. Coca-Cola was in at the beginning, branding events on the African and Asian continents, and then the 1978 World Cup in Argentina: 'The sums were so vast that lots of companies couldn't touch it but it was a lot easier to work with the few who could', Nally recalls. The deal changed the face of world sport and the basis of the economics of sports mega-events. It also provided a smokescreen for the activities within FIFA itself. Nally again:

> Coca-Cola if you like legitimized the industry, the amount of money that was
> going in to soccer . . . but I don't think ever quite realized the importance of
> their association and how it . . . enabled this club, this whole mafia going on
> within sport, to be really supported by them because they gave it all
> credibility.

On the road to South Africa 2010 fans were invited to 'enjoy "Football on the Coke Side of Life"', to share, whatever their background, 'their mutual passion for football in a positive way'. Coca-Cola's activities in the context of the World Cup have included grass-roots programmes; local promotional activities by Coke's bottling partners; a World Cup trophy tour across 29 nations; international football camps; a Coca-Cola football camp at the host nation; flag bearers and referee escorts at opening ceremonies; and in 2006, 900 German youths—the Coca-Cola Ball Crew—aside the pitch at every match. Coca-Cola also sponsored UEFA's European Championship, and other mass market sports such as *NASCAR in the United States, individual institutions such as Georgia Tech (in Atlanta, Georgia, location of its own headquarters), and individual sports stars with national and international profiles. As the most serious global economic crisis for a generation worsened in 2008, Coca-Cola's president of European operations, Dominique Reiniche, confirmed that Coca-Cola would not turn its back on sport: 'we stay firm on our fundamentals and supporting the core sports like the Olympics and football is an essential part of what we do and will continue no matter what happens'. Speaking to Reuters, she also emphasized Coca-Cola's commitment to grass-roots initiatives and partnerships with national football associations for instance, linking these to the worldwide concern with obesity among the young, a cause that International Olympic Committee president Jacques Rogge was putting at the centre of his platform for re-election.

((⊕)) SEE WEB LINKS

- The official website, comprising a mix of self-promotion, brand affirmation, and institutional history.

cock-fighting A form of animal-baiting or blood sport practised in ancient cultures and widely popular from the 14th century in Britain, in defiance of a public proclamation banning the sport in 1366. *Henry VIII (1491–1547) added a cock-pit to his palace at Whitehall; James I (1566–1625) watched the sport twice a week. It became established as a fashionable pastime for the gentry, and for the poorer sections of the population who could gain access to a cock-fight at an inn if not a more exclusive cock-pit: 'Cocking, in fact, was one of the diversions which cut sharply across class lines', Robert Malcolmson writes (*Popular Recreations in English Society, 1700–1850*, 1973), attractive as an elemental spectacle and as a focus for betting. Pairings were the most common form of the event, cocks being bred and classified by weight; but a match-play competition called the Welsh main could include 32 cocks, from which only one would survive.

From the mid and later 18th century, opposition to the sport—and to the more working-class sport of 'throwing at cocks'—as a cruel and barbaric practice grew, and the Royal Society for the Prevention of Cruelty to Animals mobilized opinion against the sport (though not until most gentlemen had stopped backing it), successfully prosecuting numerous cases between 1838 and 1841. Cock-fighting has resurfaced notoriously when illegal gambling rings have been detected and exposed, revealing an atavistic masculine violence that links to the attraction of betting. The cock-fight has been popular in numerous societies, as a cheap and accessible—however cruel—form of public entertainment, as testified by Clifford *Geertz in his famous analysis of the cultural significance of the Balinese cock-fight.

coexistence through sport, promotion of Forms of intervention designed to bring together disparate groups or communities in sporting exchanges and experiences, with the objective (at least for the moment) of transcending conflict and difference, and pointing towards future forms of reciprocal understanding. Initiatives of this kind have included the bringing together of children from Catholic and Protestant backgrounds in Northern Ireland, in football tours away from the country; and the use of football as a peace-enhancing tool in building bridges between children, families, and institutions from neighbouring Jewish and Arab towns and villages in northern Israel. John Sugden, who has led initiatives in both these settings, has argued that 'pragmatic and grass-roots interventions' can build such bridges 'between otherwise divided communities'. Incremental efforts and interventions in the cultural field can, Sugden claims, help 'smooth the way' to political resolutions: 'the chances of achieving . . . peace may be enhanced, but also the day to day existence of those labouring in the shadow of conflict might also be improved' ('Teaching and Playing Sport for Conflict Resolution and Co-existence in Israel', *International Review for the Sociology of Sport*, 41/2, 2006).

cognition The higher mental processes, such as memory, attention, language, and reasoning. While some aspects of sport, such as simple movements, muscle contractions, or reactions, are fairly automatic, overall performance is significantly mediated by cognition. Cognitive influences impact on every aspect from the learning of new skills, *anxiety, and the perception of exertion through to *team building, *exercise adherence, and *coaching styles.

cognitive dissonance The perceptual response by individuals and groups to the recognition that *behaviours or *cognitions comprise competing or contradictory elements. The theory of cognitive dissonance, generated by Leon Festinger (1919–89) in general writings and studies of religious sects, seeks to account for how people adapt their view of circumstances when those circumstances contradict all that they believed—when a sport team loses the final or the deciding match, the fan can say that it's all to the good, that it was a learning experience: 'There's always next season or the next match.' Cognitive dissonance is an attractive way of accounting for how sport fans and performers make sense of unpromising situations, construct a coherent account in the face of rationality and logic: in sport psychological terms, it shows how hope fuels the *commitment to the sporting moment.

COI (Comité International Olympique) *See* INTERNATIONAL OLYMPIC COMMITTEE (IOC).

Cold War The rivalry between the two world superpowers, the Soviet Union and the USA, and their allies, in the second half of the 20th century. It dominated international politics from the end of World War II to the end of the 1980s, when the Berlin Wall was dismantled and, from 1991, most of the satellite states of the Soviet Union rejected the reigning political ideology of communism. The term has been attributed to US politicians and journalists in the late 1940s, but was also used by English writer George *Orwell to refer to the clash of capitalist and communist ideologies. In sport, the history of the Olympics in the second half of the 20th century was dominated by Cold War strategies and rivalries, and sport systems in both ideological blocs were fostered and supported in order to prepare Cold War warriors for the battlefields of international sport.

collective selling A transaction in which a set of rights owners—the member clubs of the English football Premier League, for instance, or of the National Basketball Association in the USA—sells the rights to broadcast coverage of its matches collectively, and the income is subsequently divided up among all of the member clubs. Collective selling might be in principle favoured by the smaller clubs, with the larger, dominant clubs arguing that the principle and practice curtail their profit-maximizing potential (compared with, say, the potential of themselves, as an individual company, selling coverage of all of their games). Economists observe, though, that collective selling works against the interests of small clubs, by boosting the already strong profile of leading and high-profile clubs, and limiting the exposure to potentially new markets (or fans) of the relatively low-profile clubs. *See also* CARTEL.

college sports (USA) Organized sports within the university setting, from specific US team sports such as basketball, American football, and baseball, to track-and-field, and individual sports from tennis to golf and swimming. In the USA, college sports have been long-established routes into professional sporting competition. Golfer Tiger Woods and tennis player John McEnroe both attended Stanford University. Sporting scholarships were available in most US universities for promising athletes from the early 20th century onwards, and a common route became to excel at the Olympic Games as an amateur and then pursue a professional career. For team sports such as basketball and American football, college sports have become feeders for the professional game. Controversies have arisen over athletes' rights and questions of exploitation in relation to the purported academic programme that student athletes follow. Novelist Tom Wolfe's *I am Charlotte Simmons* (2005) took Stanford as a model for his biting and satirical depiction of 'Dupont University', where less well-off academic students sold their skills to athlete superstars from the basketball team, writing their essays for them and tending them through academic assessment hurdles. College sports have become an essential part of the US sport culture and system, in turn talent-spotting for stars of the future, and generating giant revenues linked to old university rivalries and *alma mater* nostalgia. *See also* NATIONAL COLLEGIATE ATHLETIC ASSOCIATION.

colonialism The rule of one country by another, based on annexation or military victory by the invading country. Such countries acquired by extensive imperial powers have become colonies of that power. In the dynamic within colonialism, sport has often featured prominently in colonizer–colonized relations, as in the introduction of, for instance, *cricket by the English and the British in the colonies, whether in Philadelphia and other east coast parts of its North American colony, the Indian subcontinent, Australia, South Africa, or the Caribbean. Spanish colonization of regions of the South and Central Americas has also left sporting legacies, in the *corrida or bullfight. Such sports were introduced as a means of cultural conciliation, often intended to displace indigenous sports, but one of the most interesting and captivating international sporting dynamics has been when the colonized (or formerly colonized) defeat the colonial power at what was the latter's own sport. In football, Brazil has habitually achieved this in relation to Portugal; in cricket, dominant West Indies cricket teams in the 1970s were motivated by this in contests with the English cricket team, as have been Australian cricketers in contest with England.

Sport was widely seen by the British colonialists as a better preparation for running the colonies than a book-based academic education: recruiters to the civil service to work in the Sudan (Africa) in the early 20th century targeted Oxford and Cambridge sportsmen (known as *'blues' if they competed in an annual inter-university match), who were seen as the 'right sort of chaps' to rule the unruly. In an extraordinary admission of the racist convictions of this ruling class, the Sudan became known as 'the land of Blacks ruled by Blues' (J.A. Mangan, *The Games Ethic and Imperialism*, 1985). Recognition of the ideological dimensions of the colonialist project has informed illuminating work on the post-colonial context of sport in former colonial territories of the world.

Colosseum Opened in AD 80 as the Flavian Amphitheatre, this Roman template for modern stadiums then became known as the Amphitheatrum Caesareum. In the 11th century the name Amphitheatrum-Colyseus was adopted, derived from the colossal bronze statue of *Nero, at 120 feet tall the largest bronze statue ever made, that then still dominated the immediate vicinity of the site. The Colosseum provided Rome with its first large-scale, custom-built facility for its spectacles, particularly its *gladiatorial games. These had been staged in temporary wooden buildings that had replaced the city's first amphitheatre, the latter having been destroyed by fire in AD 64. Construction, begun by Vespasian in AD 72, was completed by his son Titus eight years later. The inauguration of the amphitheatre lasted for 100 days. As an engineering feat, it was a phenomenal achievement, the arena occupying in total 3,357 square metres. It is estimated that, including standing room in the upper areas, its capacity was 73,000 spectators, and it could be emptied of people, through the aptly named *vomitoria*, with efficiency.

Entrance to the public spectacles at the Colosseum was free, and citizens received tickets with precise details of where they would be seated. Stands were divided into sections on the basis of social categories, and the positioning of different social classes was carefully regulated. Senators had front row seats on the podium; the Vestal Virgins and magistrates had their own special section; soldiers were separated from civilians; young people, schoolteachers, and priestly cults had special seats; foreign ambassadors or diplomats had reserved places. A sophisticated network of ramps and passageways both enabled the swift and easy flow in and out of the Colosseum of the crowd, and reaffirmed the distinct social divisions upon which the seating arrangements were based.

The grandeur of the Colosseum transcended the grubby and often brutal functions for which it was designed. The venerable Bede recorded a saying of the 8th-century Saxon pilgrims to Rome (as translated in Byron's *Childe Harold*): 'While stands the Coliseum, Rome shall stand; When falls the Coliseum, Rome shall fall; And when Rome falls—the world.' The trails of tourist queues at the site in contemporary Rome, and the tribute to the ancient model embedded in the naming of the stadium at the heart of the 1932 and 1984 Summer Olympic Games in Los Angeles, are testimony to the persisting resonance of the Colosseum in contemporary consciousness, not just as a relic of ancient culture, but as a symbol of the appeal of sporting spectacle to the authorities and the public alike. There are debates and arguments as to whether what went on in the Colosseum can justifiably be called sport. What is beyond argument is the political significance of such a structure and site, consolidating the power and status of individuals and the state; and symbolizing both the established hierarchy of the social order, and the common interests in the spectacle that could bind together disparate social groups. For a full cultural history of the Colosseum, see Keith Hopkins and Mary Beard, *The Colosseum* (2006).

combat sports Contests based upon direct combat between individuals, often involving direct physical encounters of strength and skill with no mediating implement, such as *wrestling and *boxing, but also embracing contests using such implements, as in *fencing, the pre-industrial folk sport of *cudgelling, and medieval *jousting. The term has come to relate widely to the *martial arts stemming from Japanese and Chinese traditions of unarmed combat.

comeback A lay term referring to the process of recovery from what looks like a hopeless position in a match or contest, to win the game; or to the return of an athlete or player to competitive performance after a (usually prolonged) absence, often following injury, or retirement.

comfort zone A psychological space or mental zone in which the competitor or performer feels in control of the performance environment and the nature and outcome of the performance dynamic and/or competitive encounter. This is not to say that the comfort zone is a sphere of easy or effortless performance; the player may be stretched competitively, but confident—as in key points in tennis matches, for instance—that opportunities will arise for making the winning move, and will be taken.

commercialism A system of social and economic organization in which
financial profit is valued above any other criterion or consideration. In English, from
the 16th century, the word 'commerce', initially from the French and the Latin,
referred to trade, and also to the relationships and deal-making between those who
traded. By the mid 19th century, 'commercialism' was the noun used for the
economic dynamic at the core of the newly industrializing society. The principles of
commercialism underpinned the development of professionalized forms of sport,
and so came into conflict with those central to amateur conceptions of sport.
Debates within the *International Olympic Committee (IOC) even as late as the
1980s made reference to commercialism and the threat that it represented to the
perceived values of Olympic sport. At the IOC's 86th session in New Delhi in
1983, Polish IOC member Włodzimierz Reczek could still argue that national
Olympic committees and international federations should be urged to 'respect the
status of amateurism' as 'amateurism was the protection against commercialism'.
FIFA (*Fédération Internationale de Football Association) president João Havelange
responded that the word 'amateur' had been taken out of the Olympic Charter
a decade earlier. And the following year the Los Angeles Summer Olympic
Games confirmed that commercialism could provide a new basis for the
economic organization of the Olympic Games. This formal move away from
non-profit-making amateur models confirmed the emerging dominance of
commercialism in sport: confirmation of unprecedentedly high costs for television
rights, and for sponsorship status for top events, consolidated this model. What has
been seen as the 'golden triangle'—of sport, media organizations, and *corporate
sponsorship—then came to dominate the economic organization of top-level
competitive sports, from the Olympics through to the reconstituted European Cup
in football, the *UEFA Champions League. *See also* COMMERCIALIZATION.

commercialization The process whereby *commercialism, and its *raison
d'être* of financial profit, becomes the underlying economic basis of sports
organization. It can be a gradual process, as in the case of established amateur
sports in which the athlete might accept commercial contracts to advertise
goods, or when the organizing body negotiates over time with the forces of
commercialization. The spectre of commerce was conspicuous in its absence at
the first Olympic Games staged after World War II. The president of the
International Olympic Committee (IOC), Avery *Brundage, was a right-wing
businessman from the USA; but he opposed with a messianic vehemence any
moves to develop the Olympics on a more commercialized footing. Even at the
time of his retirement, at the Munich Olympics in 1972, Brundage was still declaring
that the IOC 'should have nothing to do with money'. Stepping down as
president, he observed that arguments over the distribution of money were
destructive, threatening to 'fracture the Olympic Movement'.

The modern Olympics had been from its inception vulnerable to the influence
of commercial forces. De *Coubertin, speaking at the University of Lausanne in
1928, even opposed the escalation in the construction of stadiums: 'Almost all the
stadiums built in recent years are the result of local and, too often, commercial
interests, not Olympic interests at all.' The idealistic founder of the Olympics spoke
against 'athletics as a show', implying that commercially-based large-scale events

would corrupt the amateur spirit: drawing upon promotional budgets and generating large crowds to justify the investment in the event, 'these oversized showcases are the source of the corruption at the root of the evil'. Yet de Coubertin himself knew that his project needed to attract sponsors, and he was not averse to accepting some forms of commercial support. His publication *Olympic Review*, the IOC's official bulletin, sported a full-page advertisement from a Parisian sporting goods manufacturer in the January 1901 issue. And alcohol helped him fund the October 1902 issue, when the French brandy maker Benedictine paid for a comparable advertising spread. In 1924 in Paris the Olympic stadium was bedecked in advertisements for Ovalmaltine, Dubonnet, Cinzano, and many other commercial product labels; and the French Organizing Committee published a 320-page guide to the Games containing advertisements on 256 of its pages, including ones for sporting goods and specialist alcoholic brands.

But the IOC was naive and innocent in terms of the commercial exploitation of its product, which of course in a pre-television age was hardly a global brand. This was to leave the Olympics open to exploitation by bodies with a more basic commercial rationale. The case that alerted the IOC to the dangers of leaving its product unprotected was that of Helms's Olympic Bread. Paul H. Helms, head of Helms Bakeries of Los Angeles, founded in 1931, was a well-placed businessman who secured a contract from the Los Angeles Organizing Committee to supply bakery goods for the Olympic Village at the 1932 Olympic Games. But he also registered the marks of the Olympics in all states of the USA, for his own exclusive use: these included the five-ring symbol, the Olympic motto, and the word 'Olympic' itself. Neither the IOC nor any other body had ever looked to register ownership of these marks. Carl Diem, manager of Germany's Olympic team in Los Angeles, recommended Helms as the supplier for the Berlin Games of 1936. In 1948 Helms was the supplier in London. From 1938 Brundage did all he could to prevent Helms from continuing with his branding, but to little avail, as the visionary baker had watertight legal rights to what nobody else had sought to claim in law. Helms himself gave up his rights in 1950, and his generosity allowed the IOC both to defend its products from commercial exploitation and, when the media potential of the event became clearer, to exploit its products more fully for its own financial interests. Entrepreneurial operators from outside the IOC were the ones to see the potential of the commercialization process. In a later phase of this story, it was the German shoe-manufacturer Horst *Dassler, of *Adidas, setting up the company *International Sport and Leisure (ISL), who revolutionized Olympic finances, when the IOC had also established a commission for the exploration of new sources of funding and so was receptive to such forms of economic reform. *See also* COMMERCIALISM.

References

Barney, R. K., Wenn, S. R. and Martyn, S. G. (2002) *Selling the Five Rings: The International Olympic Committee and the Rise of Olympic Commercialism*, Salt Lake City: The University of Utah Press; N. Muller (ed.) (2000) *Pierre de Coubertin, 1863–1937: Olympism, Selected Writings*, Lausanne: International Olympic Committee.

commitment In sociology, the sense of a strong affiliation to a social or cultural group and its associated beliefs, values, and practices, so that one might talk of the culture of commitment characteristic of a highly focused and dedicated subcultural group for whom the focus of the members' commitment is a prominent and sometimes primary element of their overall lifestyle. In psychology, commitment is an attribute of the individual athlete or competitor, and the degree of commitment to the accomplishment of the set task will obviously affect the potential and success of the athlete.

commodity There are different definitions of, and levels of thinking about, commodity. The word initially referred to 'a quality or condition of things in relation to the desires or needs of men', and to 'the quality of being "commodious"; conveniency (*OED*, s.v., sense 1a). As economics and markets reconstituted social and cultural boundaries and definitions of needs and desires, the notion of commodity came to mean, as in everyday economic life, simply a product in the marketplace, an item of purchase: 'an article or raw material that can be bought and sold, esp. a product as opposed to a service' (*Oxford English Reference Dictionary* (*OERD*), 1996: 291). Large-scale modern sports have in this latter sense always been a commodity, in that entrance fees were set, products were put on display (the events), and financial transactions underpinned the event itself and associated phenomena, from betting to player endorsement of commercial products.

There is, though, another level on which the commodity can be conceptualized, drawing upon critical analyses of the fundamental economic dynamic of market capitalist societies as analysed by Karl *Marx in *Capital*, in his discussion of *commodity fetishism; and as developed in Harry Braverman's neo-Marxist exploration of the expansion of the market (in *Labour and Monopoly Capital: The Degradation of Work in the Twentieth Century*, 1974). Braverman commented: 'How capitalism transformed all of society into a gigantic marketplace is a process that has been little investigated, although it is one of the keys to all recent social history.' National and supranational sport, driven by mixtures of political, economic, and social forces, have had their part to play in such a transformation, as have sports that have developed worldwide markets and global audiences. The *OERD* definition above and the Marxist perspective both see commodification as the process in which commodities are produced for their value in exchange, and not merely for use by the producer. In sport, the non-profit-making club in the voluntary sector produces a different product from the top-level competitive and profit-generating professional organization.

commodity fetishism The attribution of special meanings to the commodity product. In Karl Marx's first volume of *Capital*, where the use-value of an object is distinguished from its exchange-value (its worth in the market, or price), the idea of the commodity fetishism is also introduced. The notion of fetishism refers to how the commodity—a sporting event for instance, or a particular item of sporting clothing—has meanings attached to it that are not seen as related to the actual labour that created it. So objects and products appear to have special values; an almost 'phantasmagorical' dimension is attributed to them. At sporting events, the brand name of a corporate sponsor is associated with the profile, history, or tradition of the event, and the sporting occasion and the marketplace for the particular product become one.

common land Land available for recreational, sporting, and leisure purposes and use to any member of a population. The recognition, or provision, of common land or freely available spaces was the basis of many pre-modern popular recreations or folk sports, and its modern equivalent is the rural landscape to which the public has access, and the urban park. Common land allows collective, public spontaneity in play and sports, and permits innovation and experimentation in sporting practice. The provision of such spaces retains, or re-establishes, the basis for a public physical culture.

Commonwealth Games An organized athletic competition between the self-governing nations of the former British Empire and Commonwealth, first staged in Hamilton, Canada, in 1930, in London in 1934 (when women's events were first included), and then at four-yearly intervals (barring 1942 and 1946). The event was originally called the Empire Games (1930–50), then the British Empire and Commonwealth Games (1954–66), the British Commonwealth Games (1970–74), and finally the Commonwealth Games, from 1978. Commonwealth Day officially replaced Empire Day in Britain in 1958, the term 'Commonwealth' having become more generally applied after Word War II. It referred, in the later 19th century, to the status of the dominions, that is, self-governing former colonies within the British Empire, the first of which was Canada, given its dominion status by the British North America Act in 1867 (dominion status was granted to Australia in 1900, New Zealand in 1907, and South Africa in 1910).

The Commonwealth Games Federation's 'role-statement' expresses a 'will to dynamically promote and celebrate a unique, friendly, world class Games', around its core ideals of 'Humanity', 'Equality', and 'Destiny'. The Commonwealth's two billion people comprise approximately 30 per cent of the world's population, and the Games broadened its programme beyond core athletics disciplines to team games—hockey (field), cricket, netball, rugby 7s—in 1998. Seen—in implicit comparison with the *gigantism of the Olympics—as 'The Friendly Games', the Commonwealth Games has shown in the sporting sphere what historians have called 'the strong but elastic link of former ties to Britain'. This sporting embodiment of the British Commonwealth of Nations—the network of self-governing states and their dependencies formerly within the British Empire—illustrates the story of the end of Empire and the capacity of sport to contribute to the remaking of national culture in a post-colonial context.

communication Initially a noun referring to the communication or imparting of something, the term then came to refer also to an object through which the communication was imparted. In the early industrial period in Britain the term was extended to refer to the means of communication. As Raymond Williams observes (*Keywords*, 1976): 'In the main period of development of roads, canals and railways, **communications** was often the abstract, general term for these physical facilities.' Such facilities were integral to the growth and expansion of modern forms of sporting competition, and expanding forms of spectator sport contributed in turn to their use and further development. Sport was also closely bound up with the means of communication—written/print, and then broadcast—in the new communications industry in the late 19th century and throughout the 20th century, as sporting encounters provided a ready-made public focus for those media. More generally, communication refers to the process of meaning-making and transmitting in human culture, between either small groups of interacting individuals or more formal groups or established organizations. As much of sport is experienced by people through the media, and not in face-to-face interaction, the study of means of communication, and the interpretive response of audiences and constituencies (fans and followers) is, by default if not definition, of central concern in sports studies.

communism, sport in The use of sport in the political project to build communist society by inculcating values of the society in the individual, and at the level of the group (the collective) and the nation. The most prominent states to use sport in this way in the 20th century were the Union of Soviet Socialist Republics (the USSR) and communist China. Societies associated with, or all but annexed by, the USSR in the broader communist project also used sport in this way: prominent among these were the German Democratic Republic (the GDR, or East Germany), Bulgaria, and Romania. In the Caribbean, Fidel Castro's Cuba also employed sport in support of the construction of the new socialist and then communist society.

These communist projects and initiatives have shared several characteristics, or as some would observe, claims: the use of sport to build the fitness and health of a previously neglected and often abused populace—in Cuba, the principle of *massivity; the connection of sporting development to the military, by cultivating particular skills and practices and also providing (often bogus) employment positions to protect the amateur status of the athlete—Romanian tennis player Ilie Nastase was, officially, an officer in the army; the facilitation of women's participation in top-level sport and therefore the recognition of sport as a means of women's emancipation—seen by some societies somewhat pragmatically as a relatively sure way to secure world titles and Olympic medals as more women's events were accepted into athletic programmes; the aspiration to construct, through sport, a model new citizen steeped in communist values; and more generally, the use of international and particularly Olympic sport as a means of exhibiting the qualities of the new society over those of the societies of the capitalist world—stimulating, for much of the second half of the 20th century, international sport's version of the *Cold War.

Not all of these characteristics or aspirations were or are exclusive to communist societies, as sport's contribution to nationalism in just about any societal context has demonstrated. But they became a particularly powerful concoction of influences informing national policy in those communist states. When the USSR emerged from its sporting isolation at the 1952 Helsinki Summer Olympics, Western nations were overwhelmed by the power and professionalism of the competitors, and it went on to vie with the USA for top position in the medal table for the following forty years until the full impact of the fall of the Berlin Wall (1989) and the disaggregation of the Soviet Union in the early 1990s. With the absence of the USA at the Moscow Games of 1980, the top four nations in the table were the Soviet Union, the GDR, Bulgaria, and Cuba. Romania, defying the USSR's lead in its tit-for-tat boycott of the 1984 Los Angeles Games, came second to the USA in the table. China, emerging into the capitalist world at the end of the 20th century but preserving its communist polity, challenged the USA for top spot in the Olympics medal table in Athens in 2004, and—on the basis of golds won rather than all medals won—pushed the USA into second place on its home territory at Beijing in 2008.

The price of such achievements is high, in investment and human effort. The use of performance-enhancing drugs, the identification of young talent and the recruitment of mere children into specialist schools, the lack of substance to the claims about mass participation—these are just some of the criticisms that can be laid against the sport policies of such communist societies and regimes. Perhaps the biggest criticism of all is a moral one, relating to the shaping and use of the individual by the state: in *capitalism, it can be argued that the individual is more of a free agent (though an equally powerful argument can be made that such freedom is illusory for the majority). The great theorist of communist society, Karl *Marx, with his intellectual partner Friedrich Engels (1820–95), envisaged a different kind of life-balance in the ideal society: in the communist society the individual would not have an 'exclusive sphere of activity' on which he or she depends for a 'means of livelihood'; rather, one could 'do one thing today and another tomorrow . . . hunt in the morning, fish in the afternoon, rear cattle in the evening, criticise after dinner', just as one chooses, 'without ever becoming hunter, fisherman, herdsman or critic' (*The German Ideology*, 1846)—thus fulfilling the essence and potential of what Marx saw as humanity's species-being. On artistic talent, they commented that in a 'communist society there are no painters but at most people who engage in painting among other activities'. The USSR's waif-like 17-year-old gymnast Olga Korbut, 4 feet 11 inches tall, from Belarus, was talent-spotted and trained by a sometimes physically abusive coach, who scrutinized and made notes on young married couples in Korbut's town of Grodno, with a view to training any gymnastic prodigy that a young couple might produce. It is unlikely that Korbut, catapulted to global fame at the 1972 Munich Olympics, was permitted the balanced existence of which the philosophers of communism so seductively wrote. *See also* MASSIVITY; SPARTAKIAD.

communitarianism A view that a social, public, and moral order 'without Puritanism or oppression' can be based upon shared values, the renewal of social bonds, and the reform of public life. This has been given wide international and political currency in the work of sociologist Amitai Etzioni in his *The Spirit of Community* (1994). Talking of how such a community might be realized, Etzioni turned to extracurricular activities (school games and team sports). An exclusive focus upon winning at the expense of an adherence to teamwork, camaraderie, and playing by the rules would, he argued, produce people who are 'aggressive, maladjusted members of the community'. Rather, people must be taught that they have obligations as well as rights. Communitarians have claimed significant political influence in the USA and Britain in the 1990s, in stressing the importance of mobilizing the community to work towards a common good, but their philosophies and proposals can appear rooted in an outmoded notion of *character building and cultural conservatism.

communitas A concept referring to, in the words of cultural anthropologist Victor Turner (1920-83), 'a perception of shared emotional states . . . a direct, spontaneous and egalitarian mode of social relationship'. It is linked to the phase or condition of *liminality. For Turner, liminal states of communitas are potentially transformative, constituting a kind of cultural time-out in defiance of normal influences or determinants. In sport, to be hugged by strangers in a crowd of spectators is to experience some degree of the state of communitas.

community A concept referring to types of social relationship that bind people together, and provide valuable and often enduring sources of *identity. A concern with community was central to the interests of numerous founding figures in the field of sociology in the 19th century, concerned as they were with the changing basis and parameters of social experience in a world under the increasing influence of industrialization and urbanization. Émile *Durkheim and Ferdinand Tönnies (1855-1936) were especially concerned with how, in such changing times, individuals could feel part of a wider whole. Sport contributes prominently to expressions of community, be it in pre-modern forms of popular recreation or more modern forms of organized and institutionalized sport such as clubs, societies, and associations. Although the concept of community has been criticized for a tendency to generate nostalgic evocations of the past, or for evoking a sense of idealized collective stability, a revitalized notion of communities (in the plural) has recognized that the core concept has much to say about how people connect to each other and express collective values. Zygmunt Baumann, for instance, has written of 'cloakroom communities' constituted at cultural spectacles such as theatre—to which one could add sport—and of the 'thin' rather than 'thick' bonds of community in late modernity. From this perspective, the sport participant or spectator can be a member of multiple communities, none of which need lay claim to be the sole source of personal identity. For an accessible and insightful overview of such debates see Adam Brown, Tim Crabbe, and Gavin Mellor's work (2006-7) on football and its 'communities', at the web link given below.

(((·))) SEE WEB LINKS

• The site of the UK-based consultancy and research group Substance, containing reports on the theme of community and football.

comparative studies (comparative analyses) Studies which take at least two cases—of, say, a sporting institution—and attempt to show the contrasts and differences in their structure, practices, cultural character, and sociocultural meanings and significance. Take, for instance, the notion of the sports club. This will be differently established in Spain, Britain, and Germany, with different notions of membership and varying legal and economic bases and parameters. But the clarification of difference can point to the specificity of the single, distinctive cases, and so illuminate sport's contribution to community life or the local culture. Indeed, it can be argued that social scientific analysis is by definition comparative, since single cases are rarely studied in total isolation from related or comparable cases. Important comparative work on sport policy and policy communities and networks in Australia, Canada, the Republic of Ireland, the UK, and the USA has been produced by Barrie Houlihan (*Sport, Policy and Politics: A Comparative Analysis*, 1997); and general informed and accessible discussions of comparative method (for which there is no single template) can be found in Else Öyen's edited volume *Comparative Methodology: Theory and Practice in International Social Research* (1990). Öyen does though identify 'purists', who believe that researching across national boundaries is simply one way of doing sociological work; 'ignorants', who ignore questions concerning the complexity of cross-national analysis; 'totalists', who recognize the problems of cross-national research but give no special consideration to accompanying challenges of hypothesis-testing; and 'comparativists', who argue for the recognition of the distinctive characteristics of comparative studies. It would be a rather narrow, even parochial model, of sports studies that excluded these sorts of considerations about comparative cases. Difficulties recur in identifying features or variables for controlled comparative analysis; but the insights provided by comparative study of selected cases outweigh the methodological challenges.

competition A formal contest in which, on the basis of shared understanding and procedures, a winner emerges. In sport, the matching of opponents is essential for a fair or balanced contest, giving rise to the phrase 'a competitive encounter'. More generically, competition is an activity or a dynamic in which an individual seeks to establish a position of recognized superiority over the other. In sport development and associated professional fields, important and controversial debates have considered the effects of too much competition on young children, given sport's dependence upon principles of cooperation.

competitive balance A condition of competitive equilibrium within competition, such that consumers will be satisfied by the uncertainty of outcome, so that demand will then be sustained. To protect competitive balance in professional team sports, it has been widely argued, particularly in the USA, that teams be permitted to enter collusive agreements such as recruitment and the *draft, limits on rosters or squads, and *revenue sharing.

competitive sport A form of sport based upon *competition, in which it is recognized that opponents' performances are judged in relation to each other. Competition as a character attribute can also be expressed on an individual basis, in, for example, the lone runner's aspiration to better his or her previous best time (*personal best).

Compton, Denis (1918–97) An English professional cricketer who combined an entertaining style and improvisational approach with consistent achievement with the bat. Compton was also an accomplished bowler, and played football at the highest level for the London club Arsenal. In 1950, on returning from a tour of South Africa where in one innings he scored a triple century, he played in Arsenal's winning (soccer) side in the FA Cup Final at Wembley Stadium, so embodying the all-round qualities of the amateur ideal as well as the application of the professional. His glamorous image also appealed to an English public rooted in post-World War II austerity. Known as the 'Brylcreem Boy' through his lucrative contract with the hair-oil company, he could effortlessly switch from cricket flannels to formal evening attire and dance with film star Anna Neagle at high-profile social events. Compton's image and style made him a pioneer of sporting *celebrity in the second half of the twentieth century.

CONCACAF (Confederación Norte-/Centroamericana y del Caribe de Fútbol; The Confederation of North, Central America and Caribbean Association Football) The federation representing the national associations for soccer in the Caribbean, and Central and North Americas. Formed in 1961 with just a few members, by 2007 the federation had 35 full members, forming a powerful lobby in world football politics when delivered as a block vote on issues such as the election of FIFA (*Fédération Internationale de Football Association) presidents. Although organized football associations in the region dated from the early 20th century (Guyana 1902, Haiti 1904, Trinidad and Tobago 1908, Jamaica 1910, Barbados 1910, Canada 1912, and the USA 1913), as one official CONCACAF publication of 2002 stated: 'up until recently, football in CONCACAF wallowed in a sea of mediocrity, and was considered more as a pastime than a competitive sport requiring excellence'.

CONCACAF had been dominated in its early days by Mexican interests and the influential figure of Guillermo Caedo, though based in Guatemala City. In 1971, the then FIFA president, Sir Stanley *Rous, addressed a CONCACAF congress in Caracas and called for the administration (though the president and the secretary general of the confederation were not present at the address) to 'see that all financial resources were used to best effect', warning too that 'bad administration, which was out of touch and spent money in the wrong ways' was wasteful; clearly the confederation was perceived as unaccountable, self-serving, and more corrupt than naive. Rous also questioned refereeing appointments and noted the lack of representativeness in the confederation's committee and decision-making processes. Nevertheless, three years later delegates from CONCACAF national associations were to play an important supportive part in Dr João Havelange's successful challenge to Rous for the FIFA presidency.

In 1990, Jack Warner of Trinidad and Tobago won the presidency and the confederation relocated to Port of Spain, Trinidad. Warner was elected on a manifesto stressing grass-roots development and more effective national associations in wider football politics; within a decade, 72 persons from the confederation were on FIFA's 21 standing committees, and Warner himself was on FIFA's executive committee. Despite the post-1990 developments, controversy has continued to surround the confederation's business, with Warner's business interests and personal networks overlapping with confederation business.

(⊕) SEE WEB LINKS
- The official site of the Confederation of North, Central America and Caribbean Association Football, comprising news, competition schedules, and a member directory.

concentric *See* MUSCLE ACTION.

concept-construction The process whereby concepts are developed as a means of developing knowledge in a field, or contributing to the fuller theoretical understanding of the field. For Max *Weber, the science of sociology was what he called a series of successive 'critiques of concept-construction'. For instance, he identified a particular set of characteristics of *bureaucracy; further studies should identify whether those particular features accounted for organizations in some other or later context. An organization would not need to share all of the established analysis's features for it still to be an example of a bureaucracy. Similarly, the phenomenon 'sport' is not conducive to an all-or-nothing conceptual description. It changes from time to place, and place to time, place to place, and time to time, constructed by particular influences and contexts. Weber helps us see how a sophisticated analytical approach to sport should be a continuing critique of the construction of the concept of sport.

Confédération Africaine de Football (CAF) (Confederation of African Football) The federation representing the national soccer associations of the continent of Africa. Formed in 1957 in Khartoum, the CAF was initiated by the only four independent nations in Africa at that time: Egypt, Ethiopia, Sudan, and South Africa. CAF was initially opposed by *CONMEBOL, the South American confederation, which viewed it as a potential stool pigeon of the colonial masters. In 1958, South Africa insisted on sending either an all-white or an all-black team to the first African Cup of Nations in Khartoum, and was suspended. With just three members, CAF was a minor force in world football politics until independence and post-colonial autonomy created an expanded membership. When membership increased, CAF members' votes were sought by candidates for the FIFA presidency, and the confederation became increasingly significant in global power structures of football. Fifty years on from its formation, CAF had 53 members and had proved itself a powerful player in FIFA (*Fédération Internationale de Football Association) politics. Cameroonian Issa Hayatou was president from 1988 onwards.

(⊕) SEE WEB LINKS

- The official site of the Confederation of African Football, comprising its history, scheduled competitions, regulations, and contacts.

configuration A set of interrelating factors or influences creating the specific character of a cultural moment or phenomenon. For instance, China's success in heading the gold-medal tally at the 2008 Beijing Olympics can be seen as the outcome of economic, political, and cultural influences gelling at national and international levels, creating a configuration in which no other single nation could rival its ambitions, preparations, and projections.

conflict theory A generic term for sociological theories stressing that the core dynamic in society is one of conflict between sets of interests or groups. These theories might be very diverse, though, placing economic relations (Karl *Marx) or power/status relations (Max *Weber) at the centre of the analysis. Accounts of sport as a catalyst for conflict have also been produced in *cultural studies-style analyses of sport, in which *cultural contestation is seen as characterizing the social and cultural dimensions of sport. Whatever the particular emphasis on the determining source of the conflict, conflict theories stress the divided and divisive nature of societies, in contrast to structural *functionalism, which assumes consensus and integration to be the basis of society.

Confucianism A 2,500-year-old Chinese philosophy based on the teachings of
Confucius concerning individual morality, ethics, and power. There are
numerous branches of Confucianism in Asian societies, with complex variations
relating to the individual and the self. Its concern with the balance between the
individual's spiritual and physical self has informed numerous forms of physical
practice and martial arts, and has had widespread influence in societies beyond
China (in Korea, in particular). Confucianism informed the Chinese conceptions
of physical and body culture before the communist revolution, and successful
how-to manuals on the Confucian legacy have sold in their millions in
contemporary China. For the sports studies analyst, the key question has to be this:
has a real sense of Confucian legacy underpinned the inexorable—yet still
extraordinary—rise of Chinese athletes to the apex of world sport and the Olympics;
or is Confucianism a convenient mask for the central powers of a still communist
polity for whom sport is an irresistible vehicle for the articulation of world status?

**CONMEBOL (Confederación Sudamericana de Fútbol; South American
Football Confederation)** The federation for the national football (soccer)
associations of South America. Inaugurated in 1916, CONMEBOL was the first of the
six continental football federations to be formed, giving shape to the ambitions of
aspiring football nations beyond the then-Eurocentric world governing body,
FIFA (*Fédération Internationale de Football Association), which was founded
twelve years earlier by just six European nations. With ten member nations,
CONMEBOL has been the joint smallest confederation in FIFA (with political
minnow *Oceania) in sheer voting numbers, but has had power and influence
proportionate to its sporting achievements: three of its members—Argentina, Brazil,
and Uruguay—have won the men's football World Cup more than once each.
Brazil has won the trophy more times than any other nation. The confederation's
grandiose headquarters in Asunción, Paraguay, are testimony to the symbolic
profile of football in less economically developed societies. Festering tensions
between CONMEBOL and FIFA, particularly in the period after World War II
when FIFA was led by Frenchman Jules *Rimet, Belgian Rodolphe *Seeldrayers,
and Englishmen Arthur *Drewry and Sir Stanley *Rous, led to the successful
challenge and campaign of Dr João Havelange to become the first and so far only
non-European president of FIFA, in 1974.

(((SEE WEB LINKS

• The official site of the South American Football Confederation.

conscience collectif A term, meaning 'collective conscience', used by Émile
*Durkheim to define the beliefs and feelings that are common to members of a
society. The collective conscience of a people or population is defined by its
social and cultural context, and can vary from region to region, and within regions
themselves. Irish and Scottish Catholics following football in industrial
Manchester, England, would follow the United club once a tradition of affiliation
was established. So the collective conscience might not be the same for all of a
complex and fragmented society. Durkheim therefore saw new forms of social
and cultural organization—though he showed no interest in sport—such as the firm

or the corporation as new forms of dispersed, but nevertheless mutually reinforcing collective conscience.

consensus theory A generic term for sociological theories positing the core principle of social life as consensus, and seeing common experiences, interests, and values as the defining characteristic of a population or a society. A consensus theory approach sees sport as a source of collective harmony, a way of binding people together in a shared experience. In sociological debates, consensus theory has been seen as in opposition to *conflict theory. The perspective gained much currency in the mid 20th century in the works of Harvard sociologist Talcott *Parsons, for whom equilibrium of the social system and integration of its various elements were the foundations of the social system. Most sociologically open-minded approaches to the place of sport in society will recognize that sport can embody both consensus and conflict, as well as one or the other, and that detailed empirical analysis of context and locale will generate cases illustrating the different balances of these elements.

conservation An ethos and a movement that looks to protect and preserve the environment, and so opposes particular sports that are seen as a threat to the environment—skiing, for instance, or sports for which a new stadium is needed which it is said would deface the countryside or the natural environment. The conservation argument has much in its favour, but has tended to be mobilized to protect the status quo and dominant interests, and to oppose any form of cultural change. *See also* COUNTRYSIDE ALLIANCE.

conservatism The belief in the value of traditional institutions and practices, and the maintenance of the existing societal order. Conservative approaches to sport have usually reaffirmed the status quo in sport, though enlightened political conservatives in Britain, for instance, such as Arthur *Balfour, have argued the benefits of expanding sporting participation to all of the population. Conservative approaches to sport will usually, though, argue against state provision, favouring the dynamics of the market to provide for what is needed (conservatives, by definition and experience, usually being favourably placed in the market).

conspicuous consumption A concept introduced by the economic and social commentator and analyst Thorstein Veblen (1857–1929) in *The Theory of the Leisure Class* (1899), referring to the way in which people of particular privilege in the financially well-off classes use their sports, leisure, and pastimes as a form of status display. He compared such display with more ritualized forms of public behaviour in more primitive societies. Veblen was commenting on the *fin-de-siècle* USA, and stressed that people in the ruling class recreated imagined lifestyles of the elites from previous times and constructed a life of leisure that set them apart from lower classes and less privileged groups. Veblen explained that the accumulation of wealth and conspicuous consumption in sport and leisure were inextricably linked. As the leisure and consumer economies of the 20th century consolidated and expanded, this link would become increasingly important for social classes who could balance work–leisure choices, and not just for those who could afford to dispense with paid work or employment altogether. Veblen's notion of conspicuous consumption has wide cross-cultural and cross-historical applicability: the parvenu bourgeois of early 19th-century Britain adopting *hunting with hounds as a symbol of their establishment pedigree, the later middle classes adopting new forms of transport from the bicycle to the car, and the fashionably dressed rich in attendance at particular cultural or sporting occasions are all engaging in the expression of conspicuous consumption.

Constantine, Learie (1901–71) A West Indian cricketer, born in Trinidad, who played for Nelson Cricket Club in the Lancashire League in the north of England from 1929 and through the 1930s. He was a noted all-rounder who attracted wide popular support, and linked his sporting profile to a progressive political commitment, mentoring the writer and political activist C. L. R. *James. His sporting prominence led him into political life in the Caribbean, and then public life in Britain: he was the first black rector of St Andrew's University, the first black governor of the BBC, and the first peer of African descent when becoming Baron Constantine of Nelson and Maraval in 1969.

consumer culture A culture in which consumer goods are widely available to all, and in which increasing numbers of people work in order to acquire consumer goods that act as markers of the consumer's power in the marketplace and concomitantly as badges or markers of status. An advanced consumer culture combines the mass distribution of goods (very often manufactured in less affluent parts of the world) with the production of less widely distributed luxury. Sport, from the televising of events to the apparel of fans, contributes prominently to the profile of consumer culture. The abstract and volatile figure of the consumer (Raymond Williams, *Keywords*, 1976) has displaced the personalized regular customer in a discourse invented by the manufacturers of new consumer goods and their advertising strategists. Initially the term consumer culture or consumer society had a pejorative ring to it, implying the waste inherent in a throwaway society. The dynamic of the consumer culture has come to prioritize renewal— new replica shirts, associated with new sponsoring brands, in seasonal supersession of far from worn-out items. For a fascinating dissection of the football shirt as an item of consumer culture, see Claudio Benzecry's study of the Argentinian football club Boca Junior's changing designs and styles, as determined by sponsors and the demands of the branding process ('Azul y Oro: The Many Social Lives of a Football Jersey', *Theory, Culture & Society*, 2008). *See also* CONSUMPTION.

consumption Any act of consuming, or using, goods or services. In sociological and cultural studies it has come to refer in particular to the analysis not of basic necessities of subsistence and survival, but of the scale and significance of consumer products in fields such as fashion, transport, design, and leisure more generally, including sport. The widening access, in more affluent societies, to such spheres of consumption, has stimulated the study of the meanings of consumption as opposed to the study of the processes of production of the consumer object. In *Consumption, Identity and Style* (edited by A. Tomlinson, 1990) the significance of consumption is discussed in relation to the 'aura of the commodity'. It is this emphasis that sets apart the newer sociology of

consumption from an older emphasis on the general act of consumption. What are
the meanings attributed by the user to the act and the objects of consumption?
This is a relatively modern question of interest to both market researchers and
academic researchers, though first highlighted by Thorstein Veblen (1899) in his
classic study *The Theory of the Leisure Class*, where he showed the emerging
prevalence of *conspicuous consumption. *See also* CONSUMER CULTURE.

contact sport A game or sport in which physical contact between players is
permitted, and the use of such contact to hinder an opponent is accepted. The
amount and nature of such contact varies, according to the conventions of the
sport as combat or contest. Individual contact sports include *wrestling, *boxing,
and *judo. Team-based contact sports include *American football, *rugby union,
and *rugby league.

content analysis A technique invaluable for the rigorous analysis of sport
media and sport-related texts. It comprises the systematic counting and
classification of topics, subjects, words, or themes in, say, newspaper sport pages;
or the counting of column inches dedicated to particular sports or sports
performers, and their visual representation. Its roots lie in mid-20th-century
communications science in the USA, and the analysis of political propaganda.
Content analysis of newspaper coverage of sport has revealed the persisting
prominence in sport reporting of dominant male sports. Content analysis is often
contrasted with *semiology, the interpretive analysis of visual images, but in truth
meaning is conveyed by the juxtaposition of word and image. For a full
understanding of how sport is portrayed in media, integrated analysis is needed
of the recurrent verbal motifs and the visual conventions employed alongside these.

contest As a noun, the formal version of a sporting encounter or fixture between
individuals one-to-one, or groups of specified numbers, in which physical
prowess, skill, or a combination of such factors leads one individual or side to
victory. *See also* COMPETITION.

contest and sponsored mobility Forms of cross-generational progression
through the ranks of society (in the upward direction): contest mobility is based
upon open meritocratic channels, in contrast with the selected basis of sponsored
mobility. American sociologist of education Ralph H. Turner identified these forms
of mobility in the early 1960s, claiming that contest mobility characterized US
institutions, while selective education was more characteristic of British society,
in which movements or progressions of this sort are controlled by the dominant
groups in a society. Contest mobility is said to offer numerous openings and
opportunities for the achievement of high status through contest. Certainly, talent
and outstanding performance have been, for some sportsmen and -women,
a means of acquiring dramatically enhanced position and status in society. But this
has also often been on the basis of selection, institutionalized forms of talent-
spotting and recruitment. Sport champions making dramatic ascents of the social
ladder have often represented both forms of mobility simultaneously.

contra-culture A practice or activity, usually of a group or a network, in
which the values expressed by the participants are inherently critical of or out of line

with the dominant or mainstream culture. Contra-cultural sport forms might be created by changes in the law and legislation, as happened with forms of folk football in early industrial Britain; or may be connected to recurrent social habits such as gambling.

contradiction In sociological terms, a condition of a system, structure, or practice in which incompatible trends and forces are in tension. The theoretical roots of the term lie in forms of Marxist thinking in which one social condition has within it the elements of its own demise, to be replaced by another; so one can talk of the contradictions of a capitalist system which is purportedly based in market economics and the creation of wealth, yet generates unprecedented levels of poverty. Sport's place in society has been considered in terms of the contradictions that are integral to it: it is supposed to be open and meritocratic, yet can be based on sheer strength and privilege; it is conceived as play, yet is put to serious political purposes; it represents the power of an established elite, yet can create blissful, even utopian moments. Along with other forms of popular culture, sport shows how such contradictions both expose yet contribute to the perpetuation of a society or a social system.

Cooley, Charles Horton (1864–1929) A philosopher and sociologist whose work at the University of Michigan engaged with the question of the relationship of the individual to society. In *Human Nature and Social Order* (1902) Cooley wrote: 'In the study of society we must learn to see mankind in psychical wholes, rather than in artificial separation. We must see and feel the communal life of family and local groups as immediate facts . . . '. Cooley generated the concept of the primary group as the formative basis of social life, and the idea of the *looking-glass self. Sporting experiences in intimate group relations are 'immediate facts' that have the currency of 'physical wholes'.

Corbett, James J. ('Gentleman Jim') (1866–1933) The world heavyweight boxing champion in 1892, winning the title in the first gloved championship bout fought against champion John L. Sullivan under the Queensberry Rules, at the Olympic Club, New Orleans. Corbett was given little chance in the betting odds, but brought an approach to the contest 'based on his abilities as a scientific boxer, not on barroom brawling' (Elliott J. Gorn, *The Manly Art: Bare-Knuckle Prize Fighting in America*, 1986). Corbett held the title for five years, adding an air of respectability to the sport, and acquiring the nickname Gentleman Jim (the press also labelled him 'Handsome Jim' and 'Pompadour Jim'). Corbett had attended college, and worked as a bank clerk; he trained in sparring clubs and fought with gloves, according to the new rules. The fight with Sullivan also attracted coverage in the respectable press, reaching out to, as Gorn puts it, the 'large potential audience for the newly sanitized sport'. The fight can be seen as the first truly modern heavyweight boxing match, transformational in its consequences; in this sense Corbett transcended the ring in symbolizing this emerging modernity, his professional image of the pugilist superseding the image of the bruiser and brawler of the bare-knuckle era.

Corinthian spirit An approach to sporting encounter rooted in the amateur philosophy of football in late 19th-century England, when the Corinthian (Casuals) club was formed in 1881 as a riposte to the emergence and rise of (initially concealed) professionalism in the sport. (A lively non-academic account is provided in D. J. Taylor, *On the Corinthian Spirit: The Decline of Amateurism in Sport*, 2006.) Paradoxically, the club's founding rationale pointed to an aspiration to improve the performances of the English football team at national level, but the core motivation lay in the preservation of an amateur ethos outlined in its 1883 constitution declaration that Corinthian players 'shall not compete for any challenge cup or any prize of any description'. This was loosened for entry into a charity shield tournament, but friendly matches were the purist norm. The club produced teams that could beat early professional champions, and provided many players for England XIs in the late 1800s.

The 1906 *Annals of the Corinthian Football Club* called its members 'missionaries of the Empire', linking British sportsmanship to international understanding as well as the bringing together of colonies and the 'Mother Country'; prioritized charitable causes; and emphasized that a game should be a game, opposing competitive glory-seeking and trophy-hunting. Brilliant but selfish players, in the words of veteran Corinthian G. O. Smith (1872–1943), should not be tolerated. The Corinthian spirit of fair play was embodied in the famous principle that if a penalty was awarded against the team, the goalkeeper must vacate the goal to allow the opposition to score and take its just rewards for the Corinthian team's violations of the rules (and the spirit) of the game. The Corinthian spirit came, in British football and sport, to represent a byword and shorthand for the golden age of *amateurism and its associated values.

cornhusking One of a category of activities noted by Allen Guttman as derived from the transformation of domestic activities into forms of competition (*Sports: The First Five Millennia*, 2004). A National Cornhusking Association, with a membership based on nine Midwest USA states, has continued to sponsor an annual competition to find the 'best person at picking corn by hand'. Cornhusking was at its peak in the 1920s, 1930s, and 1940s. A crowd of 50,000 was reported to have witnessed southpaw (left-handed) Carl Seiler win the 1932 Illinois State title; he went on to win the national championship in the same year. Such crowds for such local and traditional activities illustrate the persistence of local cultures, and the limits of the reach of consumerism, at the time of the Great Depression.

Cornish wrestling A form of wrestling in Cornwall, England, in which the physical encounter was based traditionally upon the 'hug' (in which a wrestler could grip the garment of an opponent) rather than kicking or tripping, which was more characteristic of the Devon style. Joseph Strutt (*Sports and Pastimes of the People of England*, 1801), quoting Carew's *Survey of Cornwall* (1602), noted that wrestling was learned early in a young man's life in Cornwall, and that the inhabitants of Cornwall (and Devon) 'are universally said to be the best wrestlers in the kingdom'. Devon champion Abraham Cann (1794–1864) challenged the much larger Cornwall champion, publican James Polkinghorne (b.1788), in a drawn match in 1826 that attracted 12,000 spectators, almost none of whom, having backed their favourite to win, could then take home any winnings. It was a controversial outcome, not least because of the lack of clarity concerning the permissible moves and styles. Cornish wrestling continues to attract its devotees, and a Cornish Wrestling Association, established as late as the 1920s, organizes regular events and championships. Its survival is based on a mixture of cultural pride, Celtic revivalism, and heritage tourism in which the distinctively regional practice can be rebranded as a cultural novelty.

coronary heart disease (CHD) Also known as ischaemic heart disease, CHD is caused by a build-up of fatty material in the lining of the coronary arteries (atherosclerosis), leading to a narrowing of the arteries and a reduction in oxygen supply to the heart muscle. This can cause a number of cardiac problems, such as angina (pain in the chest and surrounding areas, particularly when exercising or stressed) or myocardial infarction (a heart attack). Heart disease is a leading cause of death in the UK, with over 100,000 people dying each year. Even if not fatal, CHD may significantly affect a person's quality of life through physical incapability.

Understanding of the risk factors associated with CHD has led to the development of many preventative health initiatives such as those designed to promote improved diet, smoking cessation, or increased levels of exercise. Preventative strategies are of two forms. Primary CHD prevention is designed to prevent cardiac events in individuals with no clinical evidence of heart disease. These strategies are usually targeted at young people and younger adults. Secondary CHD prevention is designed to improve the longevity and quality of life of individuals with clinical signs of CHD. Both primary and secondary strategies may be targeted at a policy level, such as transport planning to increase cycling and walking, or at an individual level to encourage people to change their behaviour and reduce their personal risk factors.

Exercise is a key component of primary and secondary CHD prevention. Seminal studies in the 1950s by Morris and colleagues used elegant epidemiological techniques to demonstrate the role of an active lifestyle in reducing the risk of CHD. Morris demonstrated a lower incidence of CHD in the bus conductors compared to the bus drivers of London double-decker buses, and of postmen compared with telephonists or office workers. Subsequent research has repeatedly demonstrated the beneficial effect of exercise as well as explaining its mechanistic basis. Exercise can also have a positive impact on a number of other modifiable CHD factors, including obesity, diet, smoking, and stress.

Cardiac *rehabilitation in the UK provides a four-phase structure to assist the recovery of individuals after a cardiac event such as a heart attack or heart surgery. Phase I is the in-patient phase and includes medical treatment, assessment of physical capacity and risk factors, support and education. Phase II is the early post-discharge phase. It provides home-based support and education and lasts about three months. Phase III starts after 8 to 12 weeks and involves an exercise class twice a week with a specially trained exercise leader, often a cardiac nurse. Educational, psychological, and group support is provided. Phase IV provides a programme to promote long-term maintenance of physical activity and reduction of other risk factors.

corporate sponsorship Sponsorship of a particular sport institution or sport event by a commercial organization, corporation, or business. Sponsorship is about product placement and brand awareness, and large sums are paid by national and international firms to gain exclusive sponsorship rights. Whereas corporate sponsorship may once have been thought of as a variant of philanthropy, it is now a core and very visible element in the contemporary political economy of sport, and corporate sponsorship is talked of as a kind of partnership. The marketing department of the International Olympic Committee (IOC) expresses gratitude for the

> help of our Worldwide Corporate Partners: Not only do these companies understand the importance of the Olympic Movement, but they have provided food, shelter, training facilities and more to the world's athletes. We thank them for their dedication and ask the world to return the favour by supporting the companies that advance the spirit of the Olympics. (<http://www.olympic. org/uk/news/media_centre/press release, accessed 28 Jan. 2004).

Michael R. Payne, then IOC marketing director, could write after the 2000 Sydney Games that 'new and innovative programmes' by the sponsors had enhanced spectators' experiences, and that 'the marketing programmes were presented with a new focus on promoting and enhancing the Olympic spirit, in a commercially-controlled, ambush-free environment'. It is in such marketing speak, eliding the claimed ideals of Olympism with the goals of profit-hungry multinationals, that corporate sponsorship is now discussed and justified. *See also* Adidas; Coca-Cola; commercialism; commercialization; sponsorship.

corporeal Referring to the body. The term corporeal culture can therefore refer to a society's cluster of institutions and practices related to physical education and performance as well as sporting practices. The corporeal culture can vary widely according to a wide range of social influences. The French sociologist Pierre *Bourdieu and his associates identified differing and sometimes rival forms of corporeal or body culture as crucial markers of distinction, or hierarchized social difference. *See also* body, sociology of the.

corrida de toros Spanish for the 'running of the bulls', a more accurate term than the English 'bullfighting', as in the *corrida* there is no equal contest between fighter and bull; this raises the definitional question, in the absence of the dynamic of the contest, of the extent to which the practice can be described as a sport. The *corrida* flourished most, and has continued to exist, in Spain, with variations of the form in Portugal, parts of south-west France, and some regions and countries of Central and South America. In the French variant, the bull is not killed and the aim is to remove a kind of rosette harnessed to the bull's horns. Nevertheless, in the classic Spanish form, it is more than a mere display, in that the human protagonist whose role it is to kill the bull (the matador) is often injured or gored, sometimes killed. The *plaza de toros* (bull ring) has been a potent symbol of Hispanic public culture for centuries. The specialist language of the techniques, performance, costumes, and equipment of the *corrida* led writer Ernest *Hemingway to produce a 64-page 'explanatory glossary of certain words, terms and phrases used in bullfighting' (*Death in the Afternoon*, 1932). Hemingway was particularly interested in the often neglected victims of the doomed bull, the horses—'the death of the horse tends to be comic while that of the bull is tragic'—and wove a moral narrative around the 'well-ordered . . . ritual' of the event.

Another US writer, Norman Mailer, was also attracted to the event (*The Bullfight—A Photographic Narrative with Text*, 1967), finding in 'the mystery of the form . . . the record of a war'. Matadors for whom Mailer had little initial respect or admiration nevertheless illuminated 'the paradox that courage can be found in men whose conflict is caught between their ambition and their cowardice'. In the case of both Hemingway and Mailer, the *corrida* was as much about their search for the essence of themselves—and the nature of manhood—as the inherent artistic or sporting merits of the practice. Mailer romanticizes the fight as an elemental way of a man showing 'what he was intended to be . . . in his greatest moment', rather than being judged on what he is every day:

> It is a romantic, self-pitying, impractical approach to the twentieth century's demands for predictable ethics, high production, dependability of function, and categorization of impulse, but it is the Latin approach. Their allegiance is to the genius of the blood. So they judge a man by what he is at his best.

corruption The process whereby a pure or ideal form of something is tainted or distorted. Applied to human affairs, corruption refers to a range of immoral or dishonest practices by individuals or agencies seeking self-aggrandizement and personal gain, often while purporting to embody pure ideals. Corruption has not been a primary theme in writings and commentaries upon the nature of modern sport. But discussions on the transformation of the values of modern sport, analyses of different forms of *cheating in sporting competition, and studies on administrative malpractices in sports organizations are three areas that have at least raised the question of the extent to which corruption can be said to be a more than occasional characteristic of contemporary sports culture.

Transformation of the values of modern sport The seminal work of Allen Guttmann (1978) generated a comparative framework for understanding the different values expressed in sport in societies of different types. The seven characteristics of sport in modern societies included, for Guttmann, an unprecedented preoccupation with measurement, records, money, and forms of rationalization. The characteristics conjure up an image of a previously existing, more spontaneous form of sport in a less complex social setting. Sport in an earlier age could be seen as a less compromised form of play, expressive of a more localized or even organic culture. A form of thinking taken too far—not by Guttmann himself—in this direction might see modern sport, in all its developmental complexity and variety, as inevitably tainted, a kind of corrupted ideal. The amateur condemnation of the emergence of professional sport might be seen as evidence of one such form of thinking.

The founder of the modern Olympic movement, Baron Pierre de *Coubertin, was inspired by the amateur model of sport, on his visits in England to Rugby School and Cambridge and Oxford universities, as well as the Ivy League universities of Harvard and Princeton in the USA. As professional sports challenged the dominance of athleticism and the amateur model, it could be said that the ideal of amateur sport was being despoiled or corrupted, in a swing away from doing sport for the love of it towards doing sport for financial reward. De Coubertin wrote to athletic associations in 1894, rallying them in support of his idea to revive the ancient Greek Olympic Games: 'Imperfect humanity has ever tended to transform the Olympic athlete into the paid gladiator. But the two things are incompatible. We must choose between one formula and the other' (cited in British Olympic Association, 1909, pp. 16–17). Historical debates in Britain addressed this issue widely in sporting circles as the tensions between the amateur code and professionalism became manifest in many sports. Defences of the amateur code against professional models of payments to performers and officials were championed by the *International Olympic Committee (IOC) throughout the majority of the 20th century. These constituted rearguard actions against what were seen as the corrupting influences of commercialism, and of illicit forms of professionalism such as those that dominated the *college sports system of the United States, the statism of the Soviet Union and other state-centrist communist societies, or the *shamateurism of so-called amateur athletes.

Cheating in sporting competition A core tenet of the modern sports cultivated in the public schools (those attended by the social elites of the time) of 19th-century Britain was the notion of *fair play. It is a term that was exported and/or adopted worldwide, and for which other languages—French, for instance—sought no direct translation. It meant respecting your opponent, playing by the rules, not seeking to take unfair advantage, and accepting the result of a sporting encounter in good spirit. It became almost synonymous with the values and principles of the amateur philosophy of sport, or the ideology of athleticism (Mangan, 1981). But a closer look at sporting practices themselves shows that the fair play principle was always open to challenge and abuse, and gamesmanship and outright cheating entered early into the pantheon of modern sport.

W. G. *Grace played with an ego that more than matched his talent, and could defy the judgement of cricketing umpires in his vanity, claiming that sporting crowds had gathered to see him bat, not officials make decisions in favour of his opponents. Roger Bannister's famous breakthrough in middle-distance running, the *four-minute mile, was at the time (May 1954) seen by some as based upon a dubious practice—pacing—rather than genuine open competition. Bannister himself was quick to detach himself from any 'paced time trial' that 'could hardly be called a race' (Bannister, 1955: 175, 176) when sporting authorities condemned some of his times in the 1953 season, but his career was in its entirety as much a successful series of experimental trials as romantic triumphs of natural human endeavour. As Bale puts it: 'Most of Bannister's key performances were not competitions: rather, they were scientific tests' (2004: 124). W.G. Grace may have been guilty of gamesmanship, Bannister of disrupting the true spirit of competition. Such threats of corruption of an ideal spirit of sport are widespread in competitive sport.

Administrative malpractices in sports organizations Many sports organizations were founded as classic forms of voluntary bodies, but in a world in which high-performance sport is at the centre of the global marketplace and is a worldwide media product, the commitment and motivation of sports administrators have changed radically. In the case of two of the world's most prominent international sport federations, the *International Olympic Committee (IOC) and the *Fédération Internationale de Football Association (FIFA), this transformation took place when new leaders such as Juan Antonio Samaranch at the IOC (1980–2000) and Dr João Havelange at FIFA (1974–1998) assumed the presidency of those bodies, and worked with Horst *Dassler of *Adidas and his collaborators at *International Sport and Leisure (1982–2001). The marketing programmes and television bidding wars transformed the financial infrastructure of modern international sport, and rendered it vulnerable to the ambitions and visions of ambitious entrepreneurs. Financial dealings of FIFA and the IOC have been notoriously difficult to pin down in these circumstances (Sugden and Tomlinson, 2003).

At the national level, these forces have also intensified tendencies towards financial corruption. In English football (soccer), for instance, the riches flowing into the game in the 1990s came from new levels of television revenue and sponsorship and exacerbated what Bowker (2003) has catalogued as an endemic condition of corruption. Football men claimed that off-the-pitch activities were irrelevant to, say, effective coaching: in 1994, the England Football Association could thereby appoint Terry Venables as coach to the national side at the very moment that illegalities and financial malpractice were coming to light with regard to his conduct at his former club employer Tottenham Hotspur: 'in the football fraternity, there was no sense of shame or blame, but a singular desire to enjoy their sport and its social life' (Bowker, 2003: 77).

Corruption in sport is unlikely to be eradicated, given the popular passion for the drama of the contest, the excitement of gambling, and the high rewards that can accrue to both competitively successful sportsmen and -women and to other practitioners and opportunistic entrepreneurs for whom high-profile sport provides such a potentially lucrative source of personal aggrandizement and rich profits.

References

Bale, J. (2004) 'Scientific and Romantic: The Rhetorics of the First Four-Minute Mile', *The International Journal of the History of Sport*, 21/1: 118–26; Bannister, R. (1955) *First Four Minutes*, London: Putnam; Bowker, T. (2003) *Broken Dreams: Vanity, Greed and the Souring of British Football*, London: Simon and Schuster (Pocket Books); British Olympic Association (1909) *Official Report, London 1908, 'The Fourth Olympiad'*, drawn up by Theodore Andrea Cook, issued under the authority of The British Olympic Council; The British Olympic Association: London; Guttmann, A. (1978) *From Ritual to Record: The Nature of Modern Sports*, New York: Columbia University Press; Mangan, J. A. (1981) *Athleticism: The Emergence and Consolidation of an Educational Ideology*, Cambridge: Cambridge University Press; Sugden, J. and Tomlinson, A. (2003) *Badfellas: FIFA Family at War*, Edinburgh: Mainstream.

cost–benefit analysis The evaluation of the identifiable costs and benefits of an event in the light of the balance between them, so enabling the analysis of the event's outcomes as either negative or positive. Related approaches such as studies of *economic impact are central to the evaluation of large-scale mega-sports events in particular. Cost–benefit analysis looks to specify event-induced effects in cost and benefit categories that include impacts of intangible and indirect kind (such as volunteer labour). It also contextualizes the costs and the benefits in the medium to long term, seeking to establish the value of the outcome of the event.

Cotswold games *See* Dover, Robert.

Coubertin, Baron Pierre de (1863–1937) A French aristocrat whose passion for the educational and diplomatic potential of physical education and sport stimulated him to inspire a revival of the ancient *Olympic Games. A congress in Paris in 1894 was followed by the first modern Olympic Games in Athens in 1896. De Coubertin opposed the participation of women in the Games, and combined his vision of international cooperation through sport with traditional elite, aristocratic, ethnocentric, and male-dominated attitudes. *See also* CORRUPTION; LIMINALITY; Olympic ceremony.

counter-culture A culture in which the values expressed and promoted are in potential or actual opposition to those of the dominant culture, sometimes amounting to a wholesale rejection of that culture. The term became particularly prominent in the 1960s as a label for the radical culture of the hippies, and for particular variants of popular culture such as rock music. In sport, alternative physical practices or activities such as *frisbee have sometimes been seen as counter-cultural in relation to the dominant culture of mainstream sports. Such activities are often, though, swiftly appropriated by the sports industry, organized into competitive and commodified forms, and so shorn of their counter-cultural potential.

Countryside Alliance An organization in the United Kingdom whose stated objectives are to represent the interests of country dwellers, to work 'for everyone who loves the countryside and the rural way of life'. This includes campaigning, lobbying, and seeking to affect legislation and public policy, in particular concerning hunting, shooting, and angling. The Alliance reports research that reveals a widespread misunderstanding about gun training for instance, members of the public thinking that such training does not make gun abuse less likely in the future. It has opposed what it sees as an 'unjustified ban on broadcast advertising of firearms', saying that the respectable sport of shooting has been unfairly bracketed with prostitution and brothels. From the Alliance's web literature, it is clear that it seeks not only to overturn the 2004 Hunting Act that banned fox hunting with hounds in England, but also to shift the ground of politics itself by continuing 'to campaign for a more tolerant and balanced House of Commons'. The Alliance was set up in 1997, the year in which the New Labour government took office and political power after eighteen years of Conservative administration, and its political—not merely sporting and conservationist—agenda is clearly stated in this anti-constitutional objective. The Alliance does much of its face-to-face campaigning at race meetings at countryside tracks, where its uninhibited pro-hunting commitment is even more forcefully expressed than in its web rhetoric.

(()) SEE WEB LINKS

• The Alliance's official site, mixing sporting enthusiasm with conservative politics.

country sports 1. In a generic sense, an overarching term for sports that are on a local, non-urban scale in a rural and traditional setting. The country fair of the late 18th and early 19th centuries, as recalled by the protagonist of *Tom Brown's*

School Days (1857), included 'wrestling, and the boys jumping into sacks, and rolling wheelbarrows blindfolded; and the donkey race'. Such sports and games, linked to traditional feast days and holidays, overlapped with what are often called folk games, or the popular recreations of a traditional pre-industrial society, as brilliantly evoked by Robert Malcolmson in his seminal study *Popular Recreations in English Society, 1700–1850* (1973). Thomas *Hughes, author of *Tom Brown's School Days*, was already noting that 'gentlefolk and farmers' were becoming less involved in such sports, neither subscribing to the prizes, nor going down to the village fair 'to enjoy the fun'. The integration of the different groups within the community was being replaced by a 'further separation of classes' brought about by economic and cultural changes. 2. In a more specific usage, 'country sports' has referred to the sports of hunting, shooting, and angling. In the UK the *Countryside Alliance has been a defender of (fox) hunting with hounds: in this appellation, the defendants of such practices envelop their interests in a mystique of tradition, countryside, and community. The Alliance, formed in 1997 from an alliance of the British Field Sports Society, the Countryside Business Group, and the Countryside Movement, states that it 'works for everyone who loves the countryside and the rural way of life. Our vision is of a vital, working and thriving countryside for the benefit of the whole nation.'

county championship In Britain, a form of regional sporting competition based upon fixtures between teams representing counties, politically designated and named areas (such as Somerset, or Yorkshire). County championships have been organized in various sports such as *hockey, *rugby union, and *cricket. English first-class cricket in particular was organized, from 1890 onwards, on the basis of its County Championship, a form of the game played over three days (from 1993, four days). The profile of this form of the game has diminished in the context of international fixtures and the rise of one-day and evening-based forms of competition. In 2008, data from the British Market Research Bureau confirmed the popularity of the Twenty20 format over the County Championship: 23 per cent of English adults (9.6 million) reported having followed Twenty 20, only 20 per cent still following the traditional County Cricket Championship.

coursing The pursuit of game—especially hares and rabbits—by greyhounds that hunt in pairs by sight not scent. Enthusiasts date the sport to ancient civilizations in the region of the Nile valley as long ago as 1500 BC, and its appeal has combined the twin rationale of hunting and recreation. Competitive forms in Britain were organized in the 16th century, but the sport was not institutionalized formally until the creation of the National Coursing Club in 1858, based on a membership comprising landowners and aristocracy. Its social base was slightly broadened when *greyhound racing devotees were attracted to the sport from other social groups. Legislation in England and Scotland, in 2004, made coursing of hares illegal, and the coursing of rabbits legal only if the landowner's permission was granted. Coursing hare has remained legal in some parts of the USA, and (in Europe) in Spain and Ireland, for instance.

covert observation Observational research in which the observer is not known to, and the study not known about by, the potential subjects of the study. This

necessitates a form of *participant observation in which the researcher finds
a role within the context of the setting or institution or activity that is being studied,
and conceals the purpose from most if not all of the people under observation.
Covert observation must be justified ethically, as it does not recognize the right of
subjects to consent to being subjects of a study. Such justifications include the
arguments that access would not normally be granted for the study of a topic that is
in the public interest, and that the covert role guarantees that the research setting
and the behaviour of subjects remain unaffected by the presence of the researcher.
Some covert observation is undertaken in a compromised form, in that a
gatekeeper (the individual enabling access for the researcher) might know that
the research is underway, but colludes with the researcher in granting and
facilitating access and a particular identity and role adopted by the researcher.

Revealing studies of sport cultures based, in whole or in part, on covert
observation include John Sugden's work on boxing in the USA, Northern Ireland,
and Cuba (*Boxing: An International Analysis*, 1996) and Alan Klein's study of the
culture of body-building gyms in Southern California (*Little Big Men: Bodybuilding
Subculture and Gender Construction*, 1993). Sugden's *Scum Airways: Travels in
Football's Underground Economy* (2002) is an example of covert observation
sanctioned by a gatekeeper. One problem with studies based on covert observation
is that, on publication, subjects who feel that they have been used by researchers
will deny future access to other researchers. Nevertheless, some forms of research—
including *investigative research—rely heavily upon fieldwork strategies in which
covert observation is essential.

crazy golf A form of entertainment popular at seaside locations and attractions in
which the golf club known as the putter is used to strike an orthodox golf ball,
but along hazardous obstacle-strewn routes laid out in mini-walled routes
towards the hole into which the ball must be struck. It is a game of fun and random
luck, rather than controlled skill, but this has not prevented the formation of a world
Minigolf Sport Federation, which organizes world championships for different
classes (in adventure golf as well as crazy golf), subscribes to the international
association of world sport federations, and adheres to the principles of the
*World Anti-Doping Agency (WADA). This level of organization for such an activity
is either evidence of the limitless potential of sport tourism, or an index of the
triumph of bureaucratic logic in the contemporary world.

Cribb, Tom (1781–1848) A British boxer who became prize champion of
England in 1809, and retired in 1822. His fights with Tom Molineux, a black
American freed from slavery in Virginia who had arrived in England in 1809,
established the popularity and appeal of international boxing matches. They fought
twice, in 1810 in Sussex and the following year in Leicestershire. Cribb won both
fights, though the first one with the help of an invasion of the ring by spectators
supporting and betting on Cribb, and dubious inputs from his seconds. A century
on, one writer characterized the encounters as a confrontation between the
'superior science' of the Englishman and the strength of the 'hurricane fighter'
with a 'perfectly Herculean frame' from the New World (Ralph Nevill, *Sporting Days
and Sporting Way*, 1910). Both fights attracted large crowds, estimated at more than

5,000 and 20,000 respectively, and from all social backgrounds: in Nevill's words, the 'assemblage of sporting characters, from the peer on the coach-box to the more gentlemanly-looking pickpocket, was very complete'. The fights also generated high levels of gambling, and profits for entrepreneurs. Cribb's patron and trainer, Captain *Barclay, won the then huge sum of £10,000 on the second fight.

The popularity of Cribb and Barclay was on a national scale. As Barclay and Cribb travelled north to Scotland to train for the fight, they did so as the two most celebrated sportsmen in the nation. As Peter Radford states:

> They were not merely sporting curiosities—they were heroes . . . Wellington was struggling to establish his superiority in Spain, and Britain had been at war almost without a break for 18 years. Cribb and Barclay were welcomed as much needed proof that British manhood was still the best in the world, and they were greeted with a mixture of curiosity, enthusiasm and awe. (*The Celebrated Captain Barclay: Sport, Gambling and Adventure in Regency Times*, 2001).

In London, sporting enthusiasts celebrated the Englishman's victory as a symbol of national qualities against a backdrop of threats to the status and stability of the nation: the struggle with Napoleon was still at its height; social disturbances were intensifying with the emergence of the machine-breaking Luddist protesters; and the economy was volatile (the following year, the British Prime Minister, Spencer Percival, was assassinated by a bankrupt businessman from Liverpool). Cribb held on to his title, though never defending it again after the second Molineux fight, living off a coal business and his reputation. Molineux died destitute, at the age of 34.

cricket A bat-and-ball team game, reputedly created by shepherds on the Sussex Downs in the south-east of England, played in villages and towns of that region of south-east England by the common people mixing with other social groups. It was organized and codified in its dominant form for men in the late 18th century, in particular in the famous Hambledon Club (David Underdown, *Start of Play: Cricket and Culture in Eighteenth-Century England*, 2000). The MCC (Marylebone Cricket Club), founded in 1787, standardized the laws of the game, which established a strong base in the emergent public schools of Britain, and became one of the main team games which were believed to contribute to *character building. Cricket became strongly established in these schools and in the ancient universities of Oxford and Cambridge, and was further developed at national and international levels.

As the British Empire expanded, in India, the Caribbean, South Africa, and Australia for instance, cricket was widely established in the educational institutions of British colonies. It was believed that the sporting values learned on the cricket field could transfer to other spheres of life such as work and war; cricket was central to the cultivation of *athleticism, the belief that sporting activity and team games could have such significance beyond the field of play. Cricket exhibited, at the national level in England, many of the snobberies and prejudices of a class-ridden system: gentlemen amateurs were kept apart from working-class players and professionals in the changing facilities of grounds, were referred to differently in team-sheets, and used separate gates to enter the field of play. Yet it could also act as a focus for different strands in a community, a bonding mechanism for members of the different social strata (equally capable of being used as a form of *social control, in which people are reminded of their place in the order of things).

The game is played between two teams of eleven players, and can last for an afternoon in its local, village amateur form, or its modern, professional one-day encounter; for four days (from 1993 onwards) in the English championship between county sides; or for a full five days in international contests between national sides. It is a matter of persisting mystery to people from non-cricketing nations that, after five days, there may be a draw (not a tied result) and no outright victor. Cricket became very popular in the colonized countries of the British Empire and the *Commonwealth, and was used in the most dramatic of ways to assert the cultural equivalence and superiority of the indigenous population against a side representing the imperial invader, most notably in Australia during the bodyline series in the 1930s, in the Caribbean where a supranational composite side of West Indian islands became in the 1970s the dominant world side, and in the Indian subcontinent where world-class performances by India, Pakistan, and Sri Lanka have humbled English (and more recently, Australian) touring sides.

Cricket was catapulted into the world of modern sporting finances by the Australian entrepreneur Kerry *Packer, who in the later 1970s defied the international and national cricketing authorities and organized his World Series Cricket (WSC) initiative, bringing together the world's top players and staging televised matches in a more commercial and business-like fashion. Players were better remunerated after the Packer revolution, when cricketing authorities came to recognize the potential of the sport in the world marketplace. International cricket thrives on traditional rivalries, among the most celebrated of which is the Ashes, the series of encounters between Australia and England. Cricket has generated inestimable amounts of writing in the English press and one of its champions was the revered English cricket and music commentator Neville *Cardus. In England, the sport carries with it some of the symbolic weight that baseball has in the consciousness of US sports fans. The balance between the sport's traditional form—the five-day long Test match between international sides—and new forms of competition such as Twenty20 and the Indian Premier League (with its star players on each roster) remains precarious.

In the first decade of the 21st century, the battle between Indian television money and the broadcasters in the heartlands of the cricketing establishment looked to be swaying towards the former. Peter Wilby ('The Empire Strikes Back', *New Statesman*, 6 July 2009) commented that 'the rise of India has changed everything', the subcontinent generating 70 per cent of world cricket's revenues: this power, he added, 'represents an astonishing reversal of history'. In 2005, too, the International Cricket Council relocated from Lord's (the cricket ground in north London, England), to Dubai, in the United Arab Emirates, where the Council had been offered generous tax-free benefits and privileges. Also motivating the move was the perception that the world body should be nearer the centre of power of the game: in 2010 an Indian succeeds to the top position at the Council, confirming the supremacy of India in the administration of the game, and the victory of the Asian countries in the struggle to control the future of world cricket.

See also COMPTON, DENIS; CONSTANTINE, LEARIE; COUNTY CHAMPIONSHIP; CRONJE, HANSIE;

FRY, C. B.; GILLETTE CUP; GRACE, W. G.; HOBBS, SIR JACK; RANJITSINHJI, VIBHAJI; WOMEN'S CRICKET; WORRELL, SIR FRANK MORTIMER MAGLINNE.

((()) SEE WEB LINKS

• A site with extensive detail and commentary on cricket, including access to the Wisden Almanack and the Wisden Monthly Archive.

crip theory A strand of critical cultural analysis that, alongside 'queer perspectives and practices', has 'been deployed to resist the contemporary spectacle of able-bodied heteronormativity', as Robert McCruer (*Crip Theory: Cultural Signs of Queerness and Disability*, 2006) puts it. Dominant conceptions of able-bodiedness in sport are vulnerable to critique in the sense that they have often matter-of-factly assumed the ideal body to be the platform for and pinnacle of sporting excellence. The term 'crip' emerged in disability movements, as an adaptation and reworking of the derogatory word 'cripple'; as McCruer states, the term's 'positive valences are . . . multiple'. Crip theory and practice entails sustained forms of coming out, and the recognition that another, more accessible world is possible in which disability is no longer the raw material against which imagined and sometimes liberationist worlds are formed. Crip theory has its own radical and critical agenda, draws much upon personalized narratives, and has generated illuminating readings of films and other popular cultural forms. It is likely that a crip-based reading of the relationship between able-bodied and disabled sport, or between the Olympic Games and the Paralympic Games, would be discomfiting reading for sport administrators and organizers.

critical power The intensity of exercise that can be sustained for a long period. Monad and Scherrer in 1965 developed the application to sport of the hyperbolic relationship between power output and time shown previously in single muscle fibres. Expressing this relationship in terms of total work done and time to exhaustion allows the identification of critical power, i.e. the power output, or the intensity of exercise, that can be sustained for a long period without exhaustion. The critical power output is typically around 60 per cent of the maximal aerobic power and can be sustained for 30 minutes or more. The critical power has been determined in cycling, running, and swimming and can be used as a measure of fitness and to set training loads. It is a construct well based in theory and relates closely, but not exactly, to the physiological measures of *anaerobic threshold. The important distinction is that the critical power is a measure derived theoretically and empirically from how power output varies over time, whereas the anaerobic threshold is derived theoretically and empirically from how physiological responses vary over time.

critical theory An approach to sociology and social theory widely associated with the Frankfurt School. Critical theory takes the stance that *positivism serves the interests of the authoritarian system. 'How is critical theory possible?', Gillian Rose asked in an article in *Political Studies* in 1976, subtitled 'Theodor W. Adorno and Concept Formation in Sociology'. Her answer was ambivalent, but her sympathy for the project clear. She summarized *Adorno's distinction between critical sociology and a non-critical sociology:

> Critical sociology or theory is oriented to the idea of society as a subject in spite of all experience of reification, and critical sociology gives direct expression to that experience. Non-critical sociology, on the other hand, accepts reification, repeats it in its methods, and thereby loses the perspective according to which society and its laws reveal themselves.

Rose notes that Adorno writes recurrently of the complete reification of society and consciousness of society—reification being 'when a relation among men appears in the form of a property of a thing'. So the role for critical theory is to expose the hold of what Adorno labelled the cultural industry upon what we would now refer to as the processes of meaning production, cultural practice, and identity-formation. For Adorno, much of popular culture, including passing references to sport and the stadium, is implicated in the domination of the consciousness of the masses: his critical theory must, then, question the reification characterizing the present state of society, and offer a form of thinking differently—this is his notion of the negative dialectic, in which a critique of the reified nature of the current situation and relations of domination celebrates artistic and cultural innovation, and points to the (utopian) possibilities of a different future and an alternative consciousness. To be critical here, across the complex and wide-ranging body of Adorno's work, means to read the relations of mass production and ideological domination into the products and practices of mass culture. It is to find the politics—a populist authoritarian one—in the everyday practices of the culture; so for Adorno there is little point in studying close-up the meanings of an act—a sport contest, a form of popular music—for its meanings are simply those of the wider characteristics of the society.

Take an example from the world of sport, the English Premier League and the Championship. If Adorno were in England at the end of the first decade of this century he would see the big money, the dazzling marketing, the corporate profiles, the interdependence of sporting contest, fashion, and consumption. He would be able to offer critical analyses of the increasing commodity form of the game, the reach of *capital, the reification of consciousness; his negative dialectic would label the sport as oppressively ideological. But he would know nothing of the tradition, the passion, the life-affirming dramas of the matches; nothing of the aesthetics of the body; nothing of the patterns of fandom, of regional identity and the symbolic expression of locality; nothing of the wit and riposte of sport gossip between encounters. Critical theory has made a telling contribution to the analysis of relations of domination in *consumer capitalism, but its insights are restricted by the triumph of theoretical postulation over empirical open-mindedness.

critique A verb or a noun referring to the informed evaluation of the meaning or the nature of a cultural, or sporting, phenomenon or practice. It derives from the notion of criticism, and the judgement-making capacity of criticism, particularly from the late 17th century in relation to literature and the arts. But it has come to have a particular negative, or derogatory, connotation, so that to critique a sport has come to imply that there are faults to be found in that sport. Pierre *Bourdieu's brilliant study *Distinction*, in homage to the philosopher Immanel Kant (1724–1804), was subtitled 'A Critique of the Judgement of Taste', a usage which could be said to capture both senses of criticism and critique. But in widespread useage, critique is taken to be a more pejorative position or analytical stance, and so has been used to point to social injustices in sport, or sport's more controversial and polemical dimensions. *See also* CRITICAL THEORY.

Croke, Thomas William (1824–1902) A Roman Catholic archbishop of Cashel, born in Cork, Ireland, and educated at an endowed school in Ireland in his teens, where he was outstanding in sport and in handball in particular. Further study in Paris (the Irish College) and Rome (the Gregorian University) was followed by his return to Ireland as curate of various parishes, where he preached on behalf of the poor, and in the 1850s began to write articles on Irish nationalism in the organs of an emergent nationalist movement. His condemnation of the English effect on Irish culture was passionate and all-embracing, as he berated 'the ugly and irritating fact that we are daily importing from England, not only her manufactured goods . . . but her fashions, her accents, her vicious literature, her music, her dances and her manifold mannerisms, her games also and her pastimes, to the utter discredit of our grand national sports'. When the Gaelic Athletic Association (GAA) was formed in 1884, to champion and revive genuine or native Irish sports, and so promote a concomitant Irish nationalism and separatism, Croke accepted the position of patron of the organization. This blend of the religious, cultural, and political became a powerful alliance and force in the development of the Irish nationalist cause. Croke's contribution is commemorated in the naming of the GAA's national sport stadium in Dublin, *Croke Park, in 1913.

(((⊕))) SEE WEB LINKS

• The full text of Croke's letter that is seen as the rallying call for a kind of sporting reformation under the aegis of the Gaelic Athletic Association.

Croke Park (Páirc an Chrócaigh) A sport stadium in Dublin, Ireland, named after Archbishop Thomas *Croke, where the Gaelic Athletic Association (GAA) has traditionally staged its *Gaelic football and *hurling matches. On the afternoon of Sunday 21 November 1920, British Auxiliary security forces opened fire among the crowd at a Dublin versus Tipperary Gaelic football match. This was a military response to the killing of twelve British spies in Dublin that morning. Thirteen people, including the Tipperary captain Michael Hogan, were killed in the stadium. Revoking its Rule 42 that banned foreign sports, in February 2007 the GAA permitted the Ireland rugby union side to play its fixtures there in the Six Nations Rugby Union tournament, against first France, and then England. That the Ireland side's record-breaking victory over the English passed without political incident or controversy is testimony to sport's capacity to symbolize cultural and political meanings and processes.

Cromwell, Oliver (1599–1658) A Puritan convert in the 1630s, and a parliamentarian (MP for the city of Cambridge) from 1640–42 who, after leading parliamentary forces against royalist armies, rose to the head of the successful revolutionary movement, assuming the role of 'Lord Protector of England, Scotland and Ireland' in 1653. Cromwell entered Sidney Sussex College, Cambridge, two days before his seventeenth birthday, but left after only fourteen months immediately following the death of his father. His early adult life was one of fluctuating fortunes as dispossessed landowner, yeoman farmer, and re-instated landed gentry (via inheritance). His commitment to God—following the Battle of Marston Moor in 1644, he wrote of the royalist forces that 'God made them as stubble to our swords'—motivated his extraordinary political rise and his approach to the reform of parliament that also included the execution of King Charles I in January 1649. In 1653, following brutally accomplished military successes in Ireland and Scotland, Cromwell became lord protector, a position he held for the four and three-quarter years until his death, resisting offers and attempts to make him King Oliver, though adopting increasingly king-like attire and the trappings of a monarch.

His overriding vision for a Protestant nation was what was called the 'reformation of manners', the tighter enforcement of legal constraints on what were unambiguously for Cromwell sinful activities: gambling and drunkenness, Sabbath breaking, and fornication. His religiously driven vision had a social goal as much as any political vision, that of reforming a populace to live a godly life unstained by inappropriate leisure pursuits or bodily practices. The attribution 'Cromwellian' might best in the history of leisure and sport be seen as a cultural interregnum, matching the political climate of the times, in which the suppression of purportedly degenerate and debasing physical practices were inscribed in law: Peter Borsay, in his *periodization of English leisure history, sees the Cromwellian protectorate as the apogee of this tendency. English Puritan preacher and poet John Milton (1608–74) recommended an hour of physical education a day for the education of young men, and recognized the worthiness of physical strength as long as 'it is used to good purpose'. But if the moral worth of the physical activity was unclear, time was better spent in more constructive and productive activity, potentially contributing to the reformation of manners that became the declared mission of Cromwell's protectorate years. *See also* CATHOLIC CHURCH, ATTITUDES TOWARDS SPORT; KING'S BOOK OF SPORTS, THE.

Cronje, Hansie (Wessel Johannes) (1969–2002) A South African cricketer who captained the national men's cricket team in the 1990s. Cronje was an all-round sportsman of excellence in his schooldays, representing the Orange Free State at both cricket and rugby. He came from a prominent cricketing background, his father and elder brother having played the first-class game. Cronje's distinguished playing record, as both batsman and captain, was ruined by his admission in April 2000 that he had accepted up to $15,000 from a bookmaker in London, England, for what he termed 'forecasting' results of one-day matches in India. In June of that year he confessed to receiving monies from other bookmakers during the previous four years; by October of that same year he was banned from playing cricket for life. He was killed in a plane crash in 2002, the only passenger on a cargo flight. Rumours have circulated that his death was ordered by a betting syndicate. Cronje's downfall is a reminder of the less romantic side of cricket, in which the game is embroiled in corrupt practices and held—and this relates particularly to the one-day game in which outcomes can be manipulated and matches are of short duration—in the ruthless grip of gambling organizations.

croquet A game played with balls and a wooden mallet on a grass court on which are laid out six or nine metal hoops (with square, not rounded, tops) through which the ball must be knocked; a wooden peg is also implanted in the court, and must be 'scored' after all the hoops have been 'scored' in both directions. Croquet can be played by single players or by doubles, and four balls are always used, blue and black for one side, yellow and red for the other. Evidence suggests that croquet was played in parts of London in the 16th century, and its name and terminology indicate some French origins. Sports goods manufacturer John Jaques made the first set and wrote a book on the game in 1857, and a decade later the first croquet championship was held in Evesham, Worcestershire, England. This championship was transferred, in 1870, to the All-England Croquet and Lawn Tennis Club at Wimbledon, and the rules standardized. Lawn tennis eclipsed the popularity of croquet, though, and it was not until 1896 that the Croquet Association was formed. Records of the 1900 Paris Olympics show the participation solely of French women contestants, France taking first place in both singles and doubles.

Croquet has been for the most part contained in private clubs, the preserve of a privileged elite, and the ideal social sport for that elite's garden-party culture. In its recreational form it can be played as garden croquet or golf croquet, adapted to the mood and disposable time of the participants; the competitive international form is association croquet. 'Croquet' remains inscribed in the nomenclature of surviving grass-court tennis clubs, but is invisible to the wider public and flourishes in the 21st century only on the manicured lawns of Oxford and Cambridge colleges, genteel and discreetly located hotels and stately homes, and exclusive private clubs. The UK's Croquet Association continues to sponsor national championships and tournaments, and the United States Croquet Association reported, in 2008, a mere 3,000 members in 300 clubs. Outside the United Kingdom, croquet has had some popularity in the white Dominions (Australia, New Zealand, and South Africa), and in Australia provided a valuable sporting outlet for women of relatively privileged backgrounds.

cross-country running A foot race held over either (i) a natural outdoor route in the countryside containing natural obstacles such as hedges or streams or ditches, or (ii) a route that includes manufactured obstacles such as hurdles. Races were run in England in the later 1800s by rowing clubs in order to enhance and sustain the fitness of oarsmen, and wealthy landowners had staged such races in the 18th century, wagering between each other on the racing performance of their footmen. The first English championship was run in the Epping Forest in 1876, and the first men's international contest was between England and France in 1898, the first women's international being between the same nations in 1931. The individual (from 8,000 to 12,000 metres) cross-country event was held three times at the Olympic Games, in 1912, 1920, and 1924. It might have been acceptable at Stockholm in 1912, the top seven finishers coming from Finland or Sweden. But on one of Paris's hottest-ever days in 1924, only the legendary Paavo *Nurmi could finish comfortably, the first home of 15 finishers from a field of 38. Others were still missing hours later, and sunstroke and vomiting decimated the field. Cross-country running was never included in the Olympic programme again.

The International Cross-Country Championship, inaugurated in Scotland in 1903, was dominated in its early years by English runners and teams, France becoming the first international team to defeat England, in 1922. The International Athletics Association Federation's world championship replaced that event in

1973, and though runners from Europe and the USA were prominent in early contests, the event has become increasingly dominated, in both men's and women's categories, by Ethiopian and Kenyan runners. Winners of the women's event who have come from the British Isles include South African expatriate Zola Budd (1985–6), Englishwoman Paula Radcliffe (2001–2), and Sonia O'Sullivan (1998) from Ireland. Cross-country running continues to appeal to endurance runners and the athletics public alike, in its elemental natural appeal and its defiance of the controlled, measured criteria by which much of contemporary athletic performance is gauged—though a not always welcome reminder for generations of school-goers of the miseries of the enforced cross-country run on a wet and windy winter afternoon.

cross-country skiing *See* SKIING.

crowds, behaviour of Crowds were first studied by social psychologists whose interests lay in the collective behaviour of large groups or mobs, particularly in explicit political situations. Gustav Le Bon's *The Crowd: A Study of the Popular Mind* (1895) offered a speculative classification of types of crowd as either heterogeneous (framed by nationality or 'race') or homogeneous (in the form of sects or other smaller collectivities). Elias *Canetti (*Crowds and Power*, 1960) considered the sports crowd as an example of the 'stagnating crowd', closely compressed and dense, relatively passive and waiting, for the match or the fight or the event. In the sport crowd, people are 'so closely jammed together, they are felt to be one'. Canetti also notes that within the stagnating crowd at the sports event, 'anything may happen'; it can be loud and boisterous, but also comfortable, knowing that after its 'final disintegration' there will always be the next match or scheduled game. So for Canetti, the sporting crowd is stagnant and controlled, but not necessarily passive.

Analysts of crowd behaviour agree that individuals behave differently in the context of the crowd than in other situations or in more individual, personal, or institutionally formal contexts. The individual is drawn in by the momentum of the crowd, the collective pressure of the group, and a shared excitement in the sphere of common commitment to a cause or an activity. Bill Buford's *Among the Thugs* (1991) evokes this spirit and momentum of the less controlled football hooligan crowd as it draws in the individual towards acts and behaviours that might be threatening to the everyday social order. He identifies stages in the emergence of such a crowd. First, individuals must choose to cease being individuals, and make an 'intensely conscious' choice to become a crowd, crossing a threshold from individual to crowd 'by the willed consent of everyone there'; a second stage, and the first law-threatening one, is reached when the crowd runs rather than marches; a third stage is reached when the crowd becomes violent, in Buford's case towards the police; the final stage is 'complete lawlessness'. The more orderly crowds such as Canetti's stagnating crowd also legitimate conduct and behaviours that would not be condoned on the street or in everyday life; chants at sporting events express an inoffensive or sometimes abusive sentiment about opposing individuals or teams. More positively, and in a spirit of collective playfulness, a crowd of opposing fans can cooperate in the acting out of the Mexican wave. *See also* FOOTBALL HOOLIGANISM; HOOLIGAN.

crown-green bowls A variant of the outdoor version of *bowls, in which the bowler must negotiate not just the lie of the grass green and the weighted bias of the balls (or woods), but also a built-in camber as the green rises to the centre and falls away to the edges. In crown-green bowls, the jack—the ball at which the woods are aimed—is also biased. The sport was widely popular in the midlands and north of England for much of the 20th century, both for playing at all levels, and for betting by spectators at organized professional competitions, the most famous of which was at the Talbot Hotel at the seaside resort of Blackpool, Lancashire, in the north-west of England. Crown-green bowls provides the focus for a central chapter of Brian Jackson's *Working-Class Community: Some General Notions Raised by a Series of Studies in Northern England* (1968), in which he noted that the bowling club (in his case-study town of Huddersfield, Yorkshire) constituted a 'society of members . . . part of the network of community'; expressed the pride and skill of the working class, as against the 'snootiness' of middle-class sports; and gave status to the older generation in the community—the green, 'itself so aggressively green and fresh to look at and yet paradoxically so old and cherished, is a very special setting where an old man, for a brief spell, feels young again'. The crown-green game also caught the attention of Mass-Observation researchers in the 1930s, for whom the bowlers appeared to associate magic and superstition with the demands of the game.

In the early 21st century, crown-green bowls continued to feature in the municipal parks of the north of England, but new generations were emerging on nothing like the scale of the mid 20th century. The British Crown Green Bowling Association labelled the sport a 'Sport for all Ages', emphasizing the enjoyment to be had at club, county, or national level: 'All the family can play Crown Green Bowls, from grandchildren to grandparents and it is a great sport for making new friends. It is a non-contact sport which is enjoyed by all, including people with disabilities.' But the less populated and increasingly neglected greens of the public parks—due to, among other factors, rises in hiring costs and a lack of new volunteers to take on the responsibility of running the clubs—were testimony to the fading significance of the sport in local communities and the sporting landscape.

cudgelling A combat sport, or form of duel, played between individuals (usually one-to-one, but sometimes in teams) armed with two staves, one for attack and one for defence. The sport was popular in English rural communities of the 18th century, when bouts could be organized for stakes, and prize money could be considerable. Joseph Strutt (*Sports and Pastimes of the People of England*, 1801) cited a 1711 publication describing a cudgel contest at a country wake, in which the author found 'a ring of cudgel-players, who were breaking one another's heads in order to make some impression on their mistress' hearts'. It could obviously be seen as little more than violent sport, but was also without doubt one in which status was accrued and honour defended. In such contests 'the young men of the village demonstrated their masculinity' in what could be 'a bloody and dangerous sport' (David Underdown, *Start of Play: Cricket and Culture in Eighteenth-Century England*, 2000). A triumphant cudgel-player might also win a few guineas, 'a goodly sum for an agricultural labourer'; but deaths were not unknown in the 1730s. *Jackson's Oxford Journal*, in 1753, announced the basic head-breaking aim of the sport: 'No Head to be deemed broke unless the Blood runs an inch' (Robert Malcolmson, *Popular Recreations in English Society, 1700–1850*, 1973). The sport also attracted aristocratic sponsorship in the first half of the 18th century, and such events guaranteed even higher prize monies. Singlestick contests were, as the name says, a version of cudgelling based on use of just one staff, and, like cudgelling, revived in popularity after the Napoleonic wars, though the processes of urbanization and industrialization, along with increased regulation of public life, were to render cudgelling obsolete.

cue 1. In psychology, a signal—verbal or visual (including bodily signs or gesture)—to a performer or actor to begin a particular performance or action. The hand-signals of a footballer taking a corner-kick, or of a rugby player throwing the ball at a line-out, are common examples in team sports. 2. In more everyday exchanges a cue is an indication or hint of the behavioural expectations in a particular situation. In this latter sense cues relate to the etiquette of performance and the way that opponents relate to each other in competitive exchanges.

cue sports Sports played on a rectangular table (which may or may not have pockets) with balls, played by individuals who strike the ball with a long tapered stick called a cue. *See also* BILLIARDS; POOL; SNOOKER.

cuju An individual or team-based ball game played in ancient China, claimed by some as a forerunner of modern association football (soccer). The *ju* was a sort of rubber ball, leather on the outside, and stuffed with feathers, or with an animal bladder inside the sewn skin. *Cuju* means 'to kick the ball with the foot'. The game had a religious symbolism during the Wei dynasty (AD 220–65), when 'the football field seems to have symbolized the earth while the ball represented a heavenly body' (Allen Guttmann, *Sports: The First Five Millennia*, 2004). During the earlier Han dynasty (206 BC–AD 220) the game had featured in poetic writing and a handbook was written on it, and evidence suggests that it could be officiated by a referee, and had a general recreational profile as well as a military rationale. *Cuju* societies were formed during the Tang period (618–907). Accounts vary over when the game also used two goals and set numbers of players in a team, but during the Northern Song Dynasty (960–1126) the game became established as an urban sport of the newly expanding cities. Fixed playing pitches were laid out, and a *cuju* match could embellish the birthday celebrations of the emperor. Professional teams—of both men and women—were formed at the imperial palace, and this popularized the sport for the general populace. By the Ming Dynasty (1368–1544) and the Qing Dynasty (1644–1911), equestrian sports were preferred, particularly by the Manchurian rulers of the latter period.

   Cuju's precise origins are unclear, but it is claimed that an organized, rule-based form was played in the city of Linzi, capital of Qi state in the Shandong province, in China's Spring and Autumn Period (770 BC–476 BC). Joseph 'S' Blatter, president of world football's organizing body *Fédération Internationale de Football Association (FIFA), attended the Third Chian International Football Exhibition in 2004, and stated that football originated in China, with Linzi the birthplace of the game. In 2006, officials from Linzi began to lobby UNESCO and China's culture ministry to seek status for the city as a 'world nonmaterial heritage' site. As part

of this, *cuju* courses were established in primary and middle schools in Linzi and
its district, and 5,000 players were reported to be active in the sport. This labelling
of the game's heritage, linked to forms of regional revitalization and cultural
renaissance of traditional practices, is an illuminating case of the power of sport
to contribute to the heritage industry.

cultural assimilation The process whereby one culture (usually a minority
one) is absorbed into another culture (usually a dominant one), so that the cultural
distinctiveness of an indigenous sport (*lacrosse is an example) is diluted and
sometimes eliminated by the development of the sport in the institutional confines
of the dominant culture. *See also* ASSIMILATION.

cultural capital A notion derived from Pierre *Bourdieu, referring to the tastes
and values that are inherited (that is, predispositions) and can be mobilized by
particular social groups in the expression of their status and their social position.
Studies of sport continue to pose the question of how much influence cultural
capital, linked in particular to social class, has upon participation and/or
spectatorship. A Canadian study (White and Wilson, 1999) reports the primary
influence of socio-economic status upon sport spectatorship; a Scandinavian
study (Thrane, 2001) questions this, disputing any linear influence of household
income upon spectatorship, and claiming a further complexity by seeking to
measure the influence of education, cultural capital, and sport participation.
Unsurprisingly, the more that is measured, the more confusing the picture
gets. But analysing data from the US General Social Survey, in 1993, and drawing
upon Bourdieu's concept of cultural capital, Thomas C. Wilson is much more
analytically unequivocal: cultural capital enables people to do more sport, and
social class provides the knowledge, tastes, skills, and preferences that motivate
individuals towards particular types of sport consumption (Wilson, 2002: 13).

An overemphasis upon the potential of sport to offer social mobility to a few
can distort this picture of sport's reproductive capacity. It is often thought that
working-class males take up boxing in order to get out of the ghetto. Some do; a few
more may. But Sugden's (1987) insightful ethnography of the Burnt Oak boxing
gym shows how, for the majority who will not graduate to the professional ranks,
boxing is a form of exploitation, giving them little more than survival skills,
honing skills and fuelling hope, but confirming their ghetto culture. It does not
provide them with the cultural capital to move beyond their cultural and class
location.

In societies such as Britain, *sport participation in a general sense has
demonstrated a relative stability and has acted as a form of cultural capital,
sustaining patterns of privilege whether in terms of gender or class privilege.
National participation figures are notoriously difficult to unravel in completely
reliable ways, but it is clear that there was no boom in participation during the
1990s. In fact, sport participation rates and the patterns of participation among
different social groups have remained largely unchanged since the early 1970s,
with the exception that more women now participate in fitness activities (Rowe,
2004: 2–3). The 2002 General Household Survey in Britain showed enormous
differences between groups classified by socio-economic criteria: 20 per cent of

adults in the higher occupational cum economic groupings did keep fit-yoga; for those not working, or long-term unemployed, it was 4 per cent; 59 per cent of the former group took part in at least one physical activity in the four-week reference period compared with 30 per cent of those in routine jobs (Fox and Rickards, 2004: 9). One in 10 of the top occupational group had played golf, the same figure for running/jogging; only 1 in 50 of those in routine jobs had participated in these activities (ibid.: Table 9, p. 29).

National studies confirm such persisting patterns of class-based inequality; local and regional studies provide parallel confirmation, as in analyses of urban space and sport and leisure consumption (Tomlinson, 2005). Twenty-first-century consumer society without doubt offers numerous opportunities for the expression of experimental identities, for a kind of project of the self to which sport can be one contributing source, as work on lifestyle and extreme sports has shown (Wheaton, 2004). Cultures can and do change, but as Raymond Williams (1977) noted, in subtle ways in which the dominant, residual, and emergent elements sometimes intermesh. Dominant cultures resist transformation, however, and in this wider context sport at its various levels of performance, participation, and spectatorship continues to show how *class habitus and cultural capital remain major determinants of everyday practices and cultural institutions.

References

Fox, K. and Rickards, L. (2004) *Sport and Leisure: Results from the Sport and Leisure Module of the 2002 General Household Survey*, London: TSO; Rowe, N. (ed.) (2004) *Driving up Participation: The Challenge for Sport (Academic review papers commissioned by Sport England as contextual analysis to inform the preparation of the Framework for Sport in England)*, London: Sport England; Sugden, J. (1987) 'The Exploitation of Disadvantage: The Occupational Sub-Culture of the Boxer', in J. Horne, D. Jary, and A. Tomlinson (eds), *Sport, Leisure and Social Relations*, London: Routledge & Kegan Paul, pp. 187–209; Thrane, C. (2001) 'Sport spectatorship in Scandinavia—A class phenomenon?', *International Review for the Sociology of Sport*, 36/2: 149–63; Tomlinson, A. (2005) 'Patterns of Consumption in Sport and Leisure Cultures—Urban Space and Suburban Fears', in *Sport and Leisure Cultures*, Minneapolis: University of Minnesota Press, pp. 159–182; Wheaton, B. (ed.) (2004) *Understanding Lifestyle Sports*, London: Routledge; White, P. and Wilson, B. (1999) 'Distinction in the Stands', *International Review for the Sociology of Sport*, 34/4: 245–64; Williams, R. (1977) *Marxism and Literature*, Oxford: Oxford University Press; Wilson, T. C. (2002) 'The Paradox of Social Class and Sports Involvement: The Roles of Cultural and Economic Capital', *International Review for the Sociology of Sport*, 37/1: 5–16.

cultural change How cultural forms emerge, and are then influenced, reproduced, or changed is a central question for sports studies scholars combining historical and sociological approaches. Change can be influenced by numerous factors, such as social, economic, religious, and political influences that in turn have been stimulated by historical situations and circumstances. Change rarely occurs overnight, apart from in political coups or unforeseen disasters. It took decades for the *International Olympic Committee (IOC) to formally recognize professional athletes as participants in the Olympic Games; and the sporting cultures of many countries remain male-dominated in terms of both general participation and high performance. Cultural change may come about through educational policies or policy interventions in the sporting field (Title IX, legislating (1972) against sex discrimination in sport in educational contexts in the USA, is a good example of this), and sometimes on the basis of changes in awareness of issues that can take generations.

Cultural change can be incremental or dramatic, but is usually relatively gradual, as elements of the culture embody the power interests of rival groups and interrelate in tension. In his *Marxism and Literature* (1977) Raymond Williams noted that a dominant culture is not all-embracingly dominant. It may coexist with a residual culture, or face challenges from an emergent culture. It is useful to think about the Olympic programme of events as an illustration of this point; the modern pentathlon (residual in any seriously cultural sense) and beach volleyball and snowboarding (emergent forms of lifestyle sports) exist alongside the core track-and-field events at the Summer Games and the main skiing events at the Winter Games. Behind these survivals and changes lie complex institutional dynamics and national rivalries. *See also* CULTURAL CONTESTATION; CULTURAL CONTINUITY; CULTURAL DIFFUSION.

cultural contestation The process whereby values and meanings of social actions are disputed, rather than merely accepted, often referring to aspects of *class struggle. Karl *Marx said nothing about sport or its relationship with social class, but neo-Marxists have explored the nature and histories of class dynamics and ideological struggles. E. P. Thompson's (1968) historical interpretation of the making of the English working class describes how sport and leisure were often sites for class struggle, as the social forces that pioneered the development of capitalism emerged, and sought to shape the ideological and cultural production of the new age. The establishment of capitalism and the inexorable rise of an industrial and commercial bourgeoisie demanded a disciplined and reliable labour force. A priority for the new ruling class was the reformation of the working rhythms of those whose experience of labour was based on past rural rhythms and seasonal cycles. Necessarily, the non-work habits of the masses formed part of the equation of reform, for what people did in their spare time had implications for how they related to the process of production. Thompson showed how an emergent bourgeoisie in England used its influence, both in government and within the church, to carry out a legal and moral crusade against the recreational habits of the lower orders. He also explained that new labour habits were established though the imposition of time-discipline; a division of labour; the supervision of labour through the use of fines, money incentives, and bells and clocks; the words of preachers and teachers; and the suppression of fairs and sports (Thompson, 1967). The incipient working class did not willingly surrender long-established customs and leisure practices. Such reforms succeeded only through processes of resistance and struggle between classes and class fractions. For example, Delves's (1981) study of the decline of folk football in the English city of Derby illustrated how new cross-class alliances—the emergence of newly dominant class fractions with common interests in commerce, change, and reform—accounted for the demise of the traditional form of folk football, and the rise of horse racing—a more regulated, enclosed, civilized, and profitable form of sport. *See also* RESISTANCE.

References

Delves, A. (1981) 'Popular recreation and social conflict in Derby, 1800–1850', in E. Yeo and S. Yeo (eds), *Popular Culture and Class Conflict, 1590–1914: Explorations in the History of Labour and Leisure*,

Sussex: The Harvester Press, pp. 89–127; Thompson, E. P. (1967) 'Time, Work Discipline and Industrial Capitalism', *Past and Present*, 38: 56–97; Thompson, E. P. (1968) *The Making of the English Working Class*, Harmondsworth, Middlesex: Penguin.

cultural continuity The transmission of the meanings and values characteristic of a culture, down through time and generations. Individuals make sense of their lives in relation to supra-individual contexts and situations in which shared experiences and characteristics—a language, a history, a tradition, a country—are recognizable, familiar, and accessible. Sport has provided one such experience, and the social and cultural history of sport (in Britain at least, according to Richard Holt's *Sport and the British: A Modern History*, 1989) confirms the subtle balance between continuity and change in the making and remaking of sporting culture(s). Sports may also lean towards continuity in that too much change threatens the identifiable base and framework of the sport itself. Pressures towards change, though, can affect the tempo and length of an encounter, or the style and flow of a match: Rugby League's rule changes in the early 21st century made for a more fluid style of play; the tie-break in tennis reduced the potential length of a match; limited-overs cricket introduced a new style of excitement into the game, attracting new audiences. Change can be too sudden though, and proposals to make the goal bigger in football (to stimulate higher scores) and play the match in four quarters (to allow more advertising on television coverage) before the US 1994 men's soccer World Cup Finals were, thankfully, not accepted by the football authorities. Nevertheless, such debates can generate evaluative review, and certainly affected the change in the soccer offside law that was designed to favour creative attacking players. Wholesale change to a sport would make it not just unfamiliar, and possibly unrecognizable, to its established fan base, but would also render inter-generational debates difficult, and undermine the historical traditions that fuel so much sporting gossip and discourse. Sport elites are often conservative, even reactionary, in defence of a sport's traditions. But sport cultures themselves are inherently culturally conservative, contributing in important ways to forms of cultural continuity that serve to hold societies together. *See also* CULTURAL CHANGE.

cultural diffusion The spread of a particular cultural form or practice—such as sport, or music, or food—from one social and political context to another, on the basis of contact between different societies. In sport, it has been widely asserted that an Anglo-Saxon or British model of sport was, through the formal Empire and political rule, and the informal Empire and trade networks, diffused worldwide. The assumption of the diffusion approach is that contact equates with spread, in an almost automatic or organic way. But cultural forms develop differently according to sets of interests, and this affects how cricket is developed or remade in Australia or the Caribbean; or helps explain why cricket did not develop a stronger cultural base in the USA. In a bold and ambitious article in *American Sociological Review* (2005), Orlando Patterson and Jacob Kaufman review diffusionist literature and argue, on the basis of the case of cricket, that research on diffusion needs to recognize particularities of influence, such as the precise nature and interests of influential groups and the role of change agents and adoptees, and avoid the implications of the diffusion model in which cultural effects are said to happen almost naturally or automatically. One might also add that a recognition of *ideology in the process of sport formation in cross-societal settings also exposed the limitations of the more naive diffusion model.

cultural politics The blend of cultural analysis and political activism, often directed towards intervention in some social or political issue of the day. Some theoretical approaches to the analysis of sport—*Marxism of a particular kind, or *feminism—closely link the identification of, say, discrimination or exploitation in sport with arguments about action and reformist change. This can create difficulties for the position of the researcher, whose analytical objectivity (or at least, critical distance) might be compromised by the adopted role of lobbyist or political campaigner.

cultural relativism A position, relating to the understanding of a culture or a society, arguing that there is inevitable cross-cultural variation in concepts and theories that are used to understand the society or the culture. The concepts and the theories are themselves seen as social constructions. 'Modern sport' is a case in point; modern for whom? 'Advanced' societies of the West, with a self-referencing sense of developed-ness and modernity, may quite simply lack the conceptual toolkit to understand the meanings and cultural significance of an indigenous sporting practice in a non-Western context. It is undeniable that, to understand a sporting culture, one needs to learn the specialist language of that culture and the conventions of the performance form. Extreme variations of the argument imply that some cultures might be so different that inter-cultural understanding is next to impossible. More realistically, a recognition of cultural relativism can be complemented by an anthropological approach to understanding 'other' sport cultures, and the adoption of careful and sensitive fieldwork approaches such as *ethnography.

cultural studies An interdisciplinary area of academic study and research which blends sociological, historical, and literary concerns, and has prioritized the study of everyday life, popular culture, and working-class experience, often on the basis of qualitative forms of enquiry. Cultural studies has had an immense effect on the humanities and the social sciences in, among others, the UK, the USA, Canada, and Australia. The major early academic base for such work was in the UK at the University of Birmingham's Centre for Contemporary Cultural Studies (CCCS). The Centre was established with Richard Hoggart, author of *The Uses of Literacy* (1957), as its first director in 1964. His study was an exploration of the nature and parameters of everyday working-class life and leisure, and its relationship to new forms of mass entertainment and leisure, much of this influenced by *consumer culture in the USA, and typified by the juke-box culture of the emerging youth market. But Hoggart also recognized that 'great boxers and footballers and speedway riders naturally become heroes' to 'working-class sports lovers': 'very modified modern counterparts of the heroes of saga, who combined natural physical gifts with great application and cunning in the use of them'. Away from professional sports, Hoggart also lauded the collective culture of working-class sports such as cycling: 'valuable evidence that working-class people can still react positively to both the challenge of their environment and the useful possibilities of cheap mass-production'.

Stuart Hall succeeded Hoggart as director in 1968, and stimulated a prolific generation of scholars and studies, these latter often collectively conceived, produced, and authored. Early contributions from CCCS considering sport and leisure were produced on women, sport, and ideology (Chas Critcher and Paul Willis), a typology of post-war football cultures (Chas Critcher), and the culture of adolescent femininity (Angela McRobbie). Garry Whannel, in a later phase at CCCS, produced his seminal work on television and sport. CCCS work helped place *consumption at the centre of the research agenda, and elevate the study of everyday life to a major concern for both the humanities and the social sciences. The University of Birmingham closed the CCCS in 2002, but the innovative work achieved there has continued to have major worldwide impact, not least in interdisciplinary and critical approaches to the analysis of sporting culture developed by individuals and groups across the globe. For the range of themes covered in the field (in the UK at least), David Morley and Kevin Robbins's *British Cultural Studies: Geography, Nationality, and Identity* (2001) provides a valuable overview, including a chapter (by Alan Tomlinson) on 'Sport, Leisure and Style'. *See also* CULTURAL TURN.

cultural turn The tendency in sociology and social history to give more attention to the nature of *culture, by studying the contribution of cultural forms to the formation of *identity, and recognizing the importance of everyday life and popular culture in processes of meaning-making (including their effects as *ideology). In social historical work on sport, this has stimulated the application of literary notions such as *narrative to the practices of sporting encounters, and to their representation in the media; and raised the question of the nature of historical reconstructions, showing many of these to be particular forms of *discourse rather than objective, fact-based accounts. Work within the cultural turn has also included studies of the body, though the analysis of selected cases has not always provided a basis for a more general understanding: a recurring difficulty, and challenge, of the cultural turn is to locate sophisticated interpretations of particular sport or body cultures in the wider framework of their making. In this sense, the cultural turn should not abandon work on production, but should blend such work with the deep level of reading of the cultures of consumption that has been achieved. The cultural turn has in this way generated comprehensive frameworks for rethinking the sociocultural meaning of sport; as David Chaney has put it (in *The Cultural Turn: Scene-Setting Essays on Contemporary Cultural History*, 1994), sport is commercial entertainment characteristic of modernity, but it simultaneously 'provides a focus for class and community identifications', and a 'form of drama' within the modern diet of mass communications. *See also* CULTURAL STUDIES; DEPTH HERMENEUTIC; BODY, SOCIOLOGY OF THE.

culture Raymond Williams (*Keywords*, 1976) called culture 'one of the two or three most complicated words in the English language', given its range of meanings and applications, from the 'tending of natural growth' in husbandry, to the full range of practices and beliefs that make up the way of life of a people. Grandiose conceptions of culture sometimes combine these different elements. Alfred Kroeber's *Configurations of Culture Growth* (1944) is one example, though his only mention of sport in the book was as a degraded form of public theatre, drama deteriorating into mere 'spectacles of sport'. A dominant modern use, Williams notes, has been the description as 'culture' of the 'works and practices of intellectual and especially artistic activity'—music, literature, painting, sculpture, theatre, and film. This is how common-sense understandings of the term have been and are still widely employed. Sport can now be added to such a list, but should be linked to the notion of the way of life of a people or a group of people.

The fundamental meaning of the word is based in the recognition of the meaning-making capacity of human beings, and in this sense culture is everything in society that is humanly made or socially produced, rather than biologically given. The scope of the term is so vast, therefore, that limits must be introduced, and so we can talk of sport *subculture or other smaller units of the cultural such as *contra-culture. This is important because, although culture refers to the full set of meanings and values in a society, cultures are far from homogeneous, and tensions within the larger unit must be recognized. Sport, for instance, quite as much as expressing the views of the dominant culture, can embody the tensions of *cultural contestation. Anthropological studies of particular smaller units—the rugby or football club in the Welsh context, the body-building gym in France or the USA—show the value of focusing upon the discrete culture of the particular sporting form, but also situating this in the wider social context of, say, the local economy, or gender relations and sexual identity construction.

culture industry The industry that produces cultural goods such as fashion, popular literature and music, movies, and sport as entertainment. This formulation of the culture industry was popularized by writers of the Frankfurt School, and in particular Theodor *Adorno. With Max Horkheimer (1895–1973), Adorno wrote *Dialectic of Enlightenment* (1941), in which the culture industry is presented as serving the interests of the dominant culture—and its model of rationality—of late capitalism.

Cumberland and Westmorland wrestling A traditional form of *wrestling in north-west England and southern Scotland, and parts of north-east England, known for its uninhibited and little-regulated form of combat. Wrestlers are male, the contest is fought on grass, over the best of three falls, and in the world championships the contestants must wear white long-john pantaloons. Traditionally, in the 19th and 20th centuries such contests were a source of cash gain and local status. Organized championships were first held in 1904, and the Cumberland and Westmorland Wrestling Association celebrated its centenary year in 2006, by which time aspects of the sport were not just organized in local academies, but coaching was provided and public sector facilities made available for training. In the mid 20th century, as observed by anthropologist W. M. Williams in his case-study village of Gosforth (a rural parish in West Cumberland), the wrestling was still very traditional in form and organization. Though Gosforth had its own Wrestling Academy, re-established in 1946 after a 20-year gap, the skills of the local style were still orally transmitted and learned by practical demonstration. Wrestling prowess guaranteed more prestige than proficiency in football or cricket, and though practised in Gosforth 'almost entirely' by farmers' sons and farm labourers, a keen interest in the activity was 'shown by people of both sexes from all occupational and social levels' (see W. M. Williams, *The Sociology of an English Village: Gosforth*, 1964).

curling A sport—often known as '*bowls on ice'—played outdoors or on purpose-built ice rinks, based on the propulsion of stones by hand, aimed at a target called a 'tee' that is located at the centre of an area known as a 'house'. Visual evidence in the form of 16th-century paintings in Holland testify to its longevity, but its strongest and most sustained profile was in Scotland, where archaeological evidence of its existence dates to the 16th century (1511). In 1795 the Duddingston Curling Society was founded in Edinburgh; the Grand Caledonian Curling Club advanced the sport in 1838, the prefix 'Royal' displacing 'Grand' after an exhibition in front of Queen Victoria and the Prince Consort in 1843. That organization formalized the rules, and became the international governing body of the sport. Scots had introduced the sport in Canada, and the Royal Montreal Curling Club was founded in 1807. It grew rapidly in Canada, and was also introduced in the USA (Michigan) and Switzerland (St Moritz); its popularity further spread in various European countries (such as Germany, Austria, Denmark, Sweden, the Netherlands, and Italy) in the 20th century. The first purpose-built indoor arena for the sport is said to have been constructed at an ice rink in Southport, Lancashire, England, in 1879.

Curling featured early in the Olympics, as a demonstration sport at the first Winter Games and for several succeeding Games, consolidated in the Olympic programme at the 1998 Games, and retrospectively recognized as a full, official Olympic event from those first Games in 1924. The sport is a combination of theatricality and intuitive science, in that members of a team can precede the launched stone, employing a brush or broom to sweep away ice or inhibiting debris from the path of the missile. The sport is strong in its own distinctive *argot; the captain of a team, for example, is called the skip of a rink. Canada has dominated the sport at the highest performance level, though Scottish women won gold at the Torino 2006 Winter Olympics, achieving wide acclamation for their enthusiasm and the truly amateur basis on which the team had prepared and competed.

custom Established practices and beliefs engaged in and held by members of societies or smaller units of societies. W. G. Sumner (1840–1910; author of *Folkways*, 1906) believed that customs were the primary forces binding people together in collective and social life (though he saw these, in extreme determinist fashion, as natural laws). Custom and customs are indeed important in how societies and communities reproduce themselves: the middle-aged leather-jacketed male alumnus at the Buckeyes' annual match in the Ohio State University football stadium; the replica football shirt-wearing soccer fan at a big European game; the Little Leaguer in the neighbourhood baseball tournament. Customs are by definition inherently conservative, though in a cultural rather than an explicitly political way. Sport, in its leaning towards tradition and preservation, and its inclination towards nostalgia, is widely based upon, and in turn generative of, established customs.

cybernetics The study of how communication, and particularly feedback, occurs between machines and human beings, and in biological systems. The term derives from the Greek word *kybernetes* ('steersman'), implying control and direction. Large-scale sports organizations might well be better understood—in terms of their knowledge of and working relationship with their different constituencies, for instance—if a cybernetics approach was applied to them.

cycling The act of riding a bicycle, or in France *un vélo*, for recreational, health-based, or competitive purposes. As a competitive sport, it includes a variety of tests of endurance, skill, and speed. As a recreational activity, it can be a means of fun, exercise, and adventurous mobility. The Olympics included the 1,000-metre match sprint (for men) in the first modern Games in Athens 1896, and for women in 1988 in Seoul. Cycling events have traditionally been on track (outdoor and indoor) and road, but at the Atlanta Games (1996) mountain biking was introduced, and in Beijing in 2008, BMX (bicycle motocross) racing was introduced as a means of linking the Olympic programme to more recent sporting innovations and the global youth market. At indoor events in the velodrome, track racing is a focus of the most precise forms of sport science as winning margins are tiny, and issues of technological equipment design and aerodynamics are primary determinants of race results. The Union Cycliste Internationale was founded in 1900 by cycling federations from France, Belgium, Switzerland, Italy, and the USA, and located in Paris (moving to Switzerland in 1965); the Union also recognizes *cyclo-cross, para-cycling, time-trialling, a category of cycling for all, and, as specialist forms of indoor cycling, artistic cycling (most popular in Germany) and cycle-ball. On the road, the top event in the world remains the *Tour de France.

Cycling was revolutionary in its impact when the first low-wheel bicycles were invented in the second half of the 19th century, replacing the *vélocipède* ('boneshaker' or 'penny-farthing') built by the Michaux family firm of coachbuilders in Paris in the 1860s. Technical innovations and breakthroughs—for instance, pneumatic tyres, all-steel machines—from the 1880s (Coventry, England, had become an influential centre of design and production) and through into the next century established the bicycle as an object of consumer status and fashion, and as an exciting new form of sporting participation. Its initial and enduring attraction was speed combined with endurance, and cycle racing was rapidly established in European countries and North America. Road races in France linked towns and cities: the first from Paris to Rouen was won by Englishman James Moore in 1869; in the 1880s some races exceeded 200 kilometres; in 1891 Frenchman Charles Terront was greeted by thousands of fans when he arrived at the Porte Maillot in Paris after completing the 1,200-kilometre Paris–Brest–Paris race 'in 71 hours and 35 minutes, averaging 400 kilometers a day over three days without rest' (Christopher S. Thompson, *The Tour de France: A Cultural History*, 2006). Professional events in England began in the 1870s, and a cement track was laid in south London in 1891, the same year that a six-day race was introduced in New York. By 1896, more than three-quarters of a million bicycles were being produced annually in seven hundred British factories. In Britain, the National Cycling Union banned road racing in the 1890s, after debates concerning the hazardous impact of the cyclist on other road users, although road touring was organized, the Tour of Britain starting in 1903.

As mass production increased, the bicycle became significant both as a form of essential personal mobility for many working people, and as a means of recreational exercise and competition encouraged by and organized in clubs and by institutions such as the Youth Hostels Association. The continuing innovations in design, the reach for new consumer markets, and the evolution of new forms of cycling competition have sustained cycling's profile in the modern, international sporting landscape, despite some loss of integrity and credibility at its sporting apex, in exposure of the normality of the use of performance-enhancing drugs among numerous top-level professional competitors. As in many other high-profile competitive sports, the top performers are increasingly remote from the fan base or the mass of participants. US cyclist Lance Armstrong, motivated by his successful fight against cancer and remarkable consequent successes in the Tour de France, has noted this: 'Too many athletes live as though the problems of the world don't concern them. We are isolated by our wealth and our narrow focus, and our elitism' (*It's Not About the Bike: My Journey Back to Life*, 2001). But the persistence in the popularity of cycling is in part due to the continuing accessibility of the activity: anyone can stand by the roadside to catch a glimpse of the Tour de France; England's London–Brighton bike ride can accept 27,000 riders from the age of 14 to 80 in a collective, mid-summer festival-style activity sponsored by the British Heart Foundation. It is these accessible events, linked to everyday experiences and possibilities, that make cycling such an inclusive sporting activity. *See also* ANQUETIL, JACQUES.

cyclo-cross A form of winter-based bicycle racing practised on cross-country courses, in which the cycle may have to be carried rather than ridden across particularly rough terrain. The sport's origins have been identified in France, in the early 20th century, and in the industrial midlands of England in the early 1920s. It became popular in parts of northern Europe, Eastern Europe, and the USA. A first world championship was held in 1925, officially recognized from 1950 by the Union Cycliste Internationale, which recognizes cyclo-cross as one of its disciplines: riders do circuits of 2.5 to 3.5 kilometres that include 'clearings, roads, country lanes and paths through forests'. Several laps of the circuit are accomplished within the prescribed period of one hour.

dance The act of leaping, skipping, hopping, or gliding 'with measured steps and rhythmical movements of the body, usually to a musical accompaniment' (*The Shorter Oxford English Dictionary on Historical Principles*, 1987). This definition applies to the so-called 'aesthetic' sports that are not a matter of measuring heights, lengths, or times, or finishing first-past-the-post; rhythmic gymnastics, *ice skating, and *synchronized swimming are the main Olympic disciplines in which dance skills and principles are at the core of the practice. They are also the sort of event (along with points-based boxing) in which judgement and scoring can be most disputed and discredited. Sport and dance have been said to have much in common—in spurious, and yet recurrent, comparisons of the footballer to the ballet dancer for instance—but a more cautious sense of the definition of dance can guard against such misplaced interpretations. Dance as an alternative source for and articulation of body culture is a more interesting question, through which issues could be raised concerning the sensuous rather than mechanistic dimensions of corporeal culture. Both sport and dance are high-profile contexts for public bodily display; the differences in their meanings and impacts can show much, in relation to sexuality for instance, about the nature of the wider culture.

darts A throwing game, played primarily indoors in clubs and drinking places, in which the players aim a cross between a javelin and an arrow on a very small scale at a marked circular board. Joseph Strutt's (1801) study of the sports and pastimes of the people of England noted that holidaying young Londoners in the 12th century threw 'darts' and stones, among other 'missive weapons'. Throwing darts or javelins was also seen as a military activity or skill, and so was not prohibited by Edward III's act of the mid 14th century, designed to encourage *archery. It was, nevertheless, sometimes practised as a feat of strength, the winner being the one to throw the dart the longest distance or beyond a stated boundary, rather than at a specified target. Strutt also cites descriptions of some 16th-century children's games, including 'blow-point', 'probably blowing an arrow through a trunk at certain numbers by way of lottery'. The early forms of 'dartes' were long like daggers, designed for archers to throw in close-quarters fighting. Darts players in Britain still refer to their darts as 'arrows', and late in the 19th century the clock board was established as the target and forms of metal darts on modern dimensions were patented.

In Leeds, England, in 1908, a magistrate adjudged that darts was a game of skill, not chance, after an impressive demonstration by a local publican; and darts was established as a legally acceptable target game in British public houses, seen by one commentator, W. E. Simnett, as perhaps 'a degenerate descendant of the ancient English sport of archery or toxophily' (*Leisure*, 1946). In the second half of the 20th century, degenerate or not, darts established itself as a massively popular sport among working-class males in particular. A National Darts Association formed in 1924 by licensed victuallers standardized rules and equipment, though the association folded and it was the newspaper the *News of the World* that provided a platform for high-level competitive darts tournaments after World War II, stimulating up to 300,000 entries in its national individual championship. Winner in 1964 and 1965, 57-year-old Tom Barrett could report prize monies of £500, as well as television appearances. Barrett competed in smart cardigan, and collar and tie, more casual than the 1948 champion Harry Leadbetter, who sported a pin-striped suit and waistcoat in his final.

The combination of media interest and increased sponsorship awareness of the game (tobacco companies were early sponsors of the *News of the World* tournament) catapulted the sport into the public consciousness. In 1972 Independent Television's *World of Sport* showed the first live coverage of the *News of the World* Finals, from London's Alexandra Palace. Other television providers moved into the field, and in 1978 BBC2 covered the new Embassy World Professional Championship. Champion of that inaugural contest Leighton Rees recalls that the nightly coverage was at first weak, but that the introduction of split-screening, focusing on both thrower and board, generated new audience levels; 2,750,000 watched the final Friday night broadcast. Darts was now established as a television sport with a common man's touch, and larger-than-life personalities contested its boom years of the 1980s.

Although the governance of the game has undergone splits and schisms, darts sustains a high profile in the media landscape. The women's game has also been elevated within the national and media context. Winners of the British Darts Organisation's Lakeside World Professional Championships in 2008 were 24-year-old Welshman Mark Webster and 23-year-old Russian Anastasia Dobromyslova. The BBC viewing figures for the men's final reached 4.1 million, and the event was transmitted on Eurosport and to 70 countries via BBC Worldwide. The casual clothing style, comfortable celebrity profile, and substantial winner's cheques of Webster and Dobromyslova evidenced the transformation of darts into a mainstream media event.

Dassler, Horst Rudolf (1936–87) A German sports equipment entrepreneur who brokered influential marketing and sponsorship deals in the 1970s and 1980s that established a new basis for the financing of high-profile international sporting events such as the Olympic Games and the men's football, or what became known as the FIFA, World Cup. Dassler, son of Adi Dassler, founder of the firm *Adidas (a title adopted in the late 1940s) that began making sporting footwear in the 1920s, became head of the company in 1984, though he had by then worked influentially for many years. His innovation was to develop a network of contacts among the international sporting world, and to bring together the interests of sporting administrators and potential corporate sponsors. This could include lending support to individuals in gaining powerful positions in international organizations. Denis Howell, veteran British sport politician and former football referee, chaired a committee investigating the nature of sport sponsorship, and recalled asking Dassler to 'give me any justification as to why a football boot manufacturer should wish to decide who should become the president of FIFA and control world football'. Dassler replied simply that his computerized networks were available to all who approached him. He did not say at what price this availability could be secured.

Dassler had been groomed in the world of subterranean sport marketing, paying athletes to wear the Adidas brand at Olympic Games, and he knew who to target and how to impress. He got FIFA's new President, João Havelange, to impress Coca-Cola executives at the world headquarters in Atlanta by flying there for talks on a private plane; he provided lavish hospitality for sport administrators, including a restaurant with a variety of services in Montmartre, Paris; the Adidas complex at Landersheim, Alsace, France, trained company loyalists, including Joseph Blatter who was to become FIFA president, succeeding Havelange, in 1998; he gave individuals, such as loyalist Harry Cavan from Northern Ireland, bogus and lucrative retainers, such as 'shoe consultant'. Dassler was the man behind the emergence of the marketing company *International Sport and Leisure (ISL), which was to dominate sponsorship and marketing deals with FIFA and the IOC from 1983 until its bankruptcy in 2001. The Dassler legacy, alongside the model established by Mark *McCormack for sport promotion, was hugely influential in the remaking of the finances of world sport, but also in the development of a model of sport administration and organization lacking in ethics and morals, and conducive to abuse and corruption.

Davis Cup An annual tennis tournament between national teams of four men and a non-playing captain, officially called the International Lawn Tennis Trophy, but named after its founder, Dwight Filley Davis (1879–1945), a Harvard graduate and prominent player at the time of his donation of the trophy in 1900. Davis also became an advocate of municipal provision of sporting opportunity, promoting and providing golf, baseball, and tennis facilities. The Davis Cup, though, was for international teams, initially the USA and the British Isles (the USA winning 3–0 in 1900), but from 1903 including more nations, and dividing into geographical zones for qualifying stages. The USA (32 titles up to 2008) and Australia (28 titles) have dominated the event, with France and Great Britain enjoying dominant spells (and 9 titles each), mostly in the 1920s and the 1930s (France also taking the title in 1991 and 2001; Britain's last triumph was in 1936, before Fred *Perry turned professional). Other nations to have won the Cup, up to 2008, are Sweden (7 times), Germany and Spain (3 times each), Russia (twice, first in 2002), and Croatia (2005), the Czech Republic, Italy, and South Africa once each. The Cup is a truly international competition, having had up to 139 national entries, and an example of how sporting competition based on national pride can transcend the mercenary individualism of professional sport.

decathlon From the Greek meaning 'ten prizes', an event in athletics comprising ten activities, four track and six field. Day one includes the 100 metres, long jump, shot-put, high jump, and 400 metres; day two includes the 110-metre hurdles, discus, pole vault, javelin, and 1,500 metres. The event was first introduced at the 1904 St Louis Olympics, won by Ireland's Thomas Kiely (1869–1951), but was omitted from the London 1908 programme. Reinstated at the 1912 Stockholm Olympics, it was won by the USA's Jim *Thorpe. Norway and Finland also produced champions (as did Sweden retrospectively, when the International Olympic Committee stripped Thorpe of his title). But the USA dominated the event for decades, with occasional winners from the Germanies and the Soviet Union, and Britain's Francis 'Daley' Thompson (1980 and 1984). Latterly, in the three Olympics up to and including Beijing 2008, East European nations have produced the champions (Estonia, the Czech Republic, and Belarus). The decathlon continues to have appeal to spectators because of the dogged commitment needed to compete in such a range of events in such a limited time-scale.

decoding *See* ENCODING AND DECODING.

deconstruction An approach to critical analysis in which the meaning of a word or a statement is seen to be inherently unstable, bearing no clear and unambiguous relationship to the thing to which the word or statement refers; meanings are therefore multiple and non-definitive, depending upon the context of the word or statement. Deconstruction has its philosophical roots in the work of French literary theorist Jacques Derrida (1930–2004). More generically, it has come to refer to the process whereby texts or statements can be interrogated to probe their deeper—sometimes deliberately hidden or concealed—meanings. It does this too by critiquing binarism (that is, the view that oppositional couplets are the basis of cultural formations) and insisting on the logocentric interdependence of apparent opposites. Deconstruction reminds us, essentially, that things are not always as they appear. Consider the sporting champion who smuggles a mention of a fast-food sponsor into a post-race interview; or the sporting organization whose slogan might be 'for the good of the sport'. In both cases a deconstructionist approach to such public utterances would reveal the disingenuousness—and often hypocrisy—on which such statements are actually made.

deduction The analytical process on the basis of which a general proposition leads to the facts, or a hypothesis (derived from previous evidence and theory) provides the foundation for the exploration of particular cases or facts. Deduction is the form of reasoning and logical method underpinning the bulk of research in sport and exercise science, in which the planned laboratory experiment or the field test is designed to elicit detailed results on specific functions or effects.

deep play A term adapted by anthropologist Clifford Geertz from the writings of Jeremy *Bentham in *The Theory of Legislation* (1802, French translation; English retranslation 1840, 1864), and used in his influential study of the meaning of the Balinese cock-fight. Bentham employs the term in a footnote to a section concerned with the relationship between equality, wealth, and the chance of happiness. Bentham was examining the proposition that a loss of a portion of wealth would produce a level of defalcation (reduction) of the loser's total happiness, 'according to the proportion of the part lost to the part which remains'. His footnote cites a gaming/gambling example:

If you have just a thousand pounds and the stake is five hundred and you lose, your fortune is diminished by a half; but if you win, the gain is only a third. If the stake is a thousand pounds, and you win, the doubling of the gain in fortune is not matched by a doubling of happiness; but if you lose, your happiness is destroyed; . . . [you] are reduced to indigence.

For Bentham, this all-or-nothing stake constitutes 'the evils of deep play', undesirable in its high-risk threat to the condition of pleasure or happiness; his liberal-reformist position, therefore, would exclude deep play from the 'principles of the civil code' (the overall chapter heading). Geertz recognizes something more than evil in the way that higher amounts of money are staked in the Balinese cock-fight, creating a deep play element in which symbolic status and not just money is also on the line, in a very public context. So for Geertz the deep play is not so much a practice that threatens the culture; rather, it enriches it, symbolizing 'the dramatization of status concerns'. For Bentham, then, deep play is irrational; for Geertz, citing Max *Weber, it is about creating significant meaning. Uses of the term have too often ignored the specific nature of the 'deep' element, using the term deep play as an unsubstantiated rationale for arguments supporting the notion of the seriousness of play-forms, sport or leisure.

definition of the situation   A social psychological concept associated with *symbolic interactionism, and first used in the study *The Polish Peasant in Europe and America* (1918–20), by W. I. Thomas and Florian Znaniecki. It refers to the serious consequences of the subjective meaning given to a situation by a person. Regardless of the purportedly objective nature of a situation, a person's subjective understanding of that situation will have consequences for all the people involved. If a Player A believes, contrary to all statistical evidence and match analysis, that Player B never passes the ball when a throw to basket or a shot at goal is on, Player A will in all likelihood begin to move around the court or the pitch in different ways; the situation is (inaccurately) defined and understood by Player A, but the consequence of the player's understanding and response will resonate throughout the whole team.

dehydration   A process whereby the amount of total body water is reduced from the normal level (euhydration) to a lower level (hypohydration). Water comprises around 60 per cent of the total body mass or around 40 litres in an average adult. There is considerable inter-individual difference due to body size or composition since different tissues have different water content; adipose tissue is about 10 per cent water whereas muscle is about 70 per cent water. A little over half the body's water is contained within cells and the rest around the cells, in blood, lymph, kidney, gut, etc. An average adult requires about 3 l of water a day to maintain a euhydrated state. About 1 to 1.5 l is consumed as drink with the rest obtained from the water in foods and as a result of metabolism.

Exercise places a demand on water balance since sweating is a major mechanism for heat loss. The evaporation of 1 l of sweat removes 580 kcal of heat from the body; an athlete exercising hard may produce up to 2 l of sweat per hour and a further 0.5 l per hour may be lost as moisture in the expired air. The rate of water loss during exercise varies with the environmental conditions, with hot, dry, or high-altitude environments increasing water loss. Fluid intake cannot normally occur at a rate sufficient to prevent dehydration, although under normal conditions a typical bout of exercise will result in hypohydration of less than 0.5 l and will not affect performance. In more challenging conditions involving lengthy exercise in adverse environments, a hypohydration in excess of 1.5 l ($\approx$ 2 per cent of body mass) may occur and performance is diminished. Paradoxically, in mass-participation public marathons, hyperhydration, and consequent disruption of sodium balance, can be a major problem; slower runners sweat less due to a lower metabolic heat production but consume too much water at the many drinks stations along the race route.

delinquency Antisocial and/or illegal behaviour, most widely associated with adolescent or young adult males (thus the term 'juvenile delinquent' that was widely used in criminological and policy studies of the mid 20th century). Sport has been seen in many places and at many historical moments to be a means of deterring or diverting young males from delinquency acts and the ambience—often of the gang—in which such acts are expected and commonplace. Boxers such as Mike Tyson, it has been said, traded the delinquent gang for the training gymnasium; but as his subsequent life story indicates, the alternative activity is not guaranteed to eliminate deviant or delinquent tendencies in behaviour.

demand The level of consumer interest in a particular market; without demand, the production of particular goods would cease. In relation to consumer goods and the sports goods industry as a sub-sector of the consumer market, consumers make up a segmented market, with diversified and numerous sporting practices within the marketplace. In sport, therefore, there can be a high volatility of demand; yesterday's trailblazing trainers can soon become today's charity-shop donation. Variables determining the level, growth, and size of the demand for sports goods include contemporary taste and fashion, the use to which the good can be put, its actual purchase price, consumer income and disposable income of families and individuals, and the life-cycle of the sports good itself. A keen amateur tennis player may well play with the same racket for decades, restringing it a few times; the football fan drawn to wearing replica club shirts will be tempted to renew (both home and away) shirts at the beginning of each season. Where the demand is for top performance, and an ailing or failing team or franchise loses its projected sustained and loyal following, a sudden slump in demand can follow, particularly in a context such as *depression or *recession.

democratic leadership *See* COACHING STYLES.

democratization The process of opening up access to political influence and power to all members of a community, though the precise contours and characteristics of a democracy in the contemporary world defy classification. In sport history and the sociology of sport, democratization has come to refer to the expanding possibilities of participation in a sport for all the members of a population, regardless of wealth, status, race, gender, age, or any other potential source of division. Many sports will claim to have democratized, but are accessible in principle only; in practice, who can afford the horses for the polo matches at Cowdray Park, England, or the yachts for the marina in Monaco?

Dempsey, Jack (William Harrison) (1895–1983) A US boxer who held the world heavyweight title from 1919 to 1926. Five of his fights generated revenues of more than one million dollars. Dempsey had come to professional boxing from the bar-room and dance-hall circuit, and his aggressive style gained him the nickname 'The Manassa Mauler'. His successful defence against French fighter Georges *Carpentier in 1921, watched by 91,000 in Jersey City, was boxing's first gate of more than a million dollars, remarkable in the pre-television age, and successfully exploiting the new medium of radio in the US's first national broadcast. Dempsey's parents mixed English, Irish, and Choctaw/Cherokee Native American ancestry and this multi-ethnic background widened his appeal. His ruthless demolition of champion Jess Willard in 1919 established his reputation for merciless and brutal attack, and he exploited his new status with circus appearances, exhibitions, and some appearances in Hollywood movies, marrying film actress Estelle Taylor and hobnobbing with film stars. Losing his title to Gene Tunney in 1926, before more than 120,000 spectators, he reportedly explained to his wife: 'Honey, I forgot to duck.' In Chicago in 1927, a rematch with Tunney generated a gate of more than two million dollars for what became known as 'The fight of the long count', in reference to the time that was given to Tunney to recover from a knock-down, justified in terms of Dempsey's failure to abide by new rules concerning the conditions of the count.

Dempsey served with distinction in World War II, which countered allegations that he had avoided service in World War I, and he went on to run successful businesses, such as his Manhattan restaurant. In his *Dempsey: The Autobiography of Jack Dempsey* (with stepdaughter Barbara Piatelli Dempsey, 1977), he concluded with a paean to the USA and to the rags-to-riches trajectory of the sporting champion:

> Looking back on a full life with all its ups and downs, I wouldn't change it for anything. Five wars, fifteen presidents, the advent of the automobile, the airplane, motion pictures, political assassinations—and an unbelievable landing on the moon. I lived it my way, and if I were asked, I would do it all over again.

He also recalled staying in Berlin's Adlon Hotel on a European tour, 'where German women tried to tear my clothes off'. Other German women he encountered—female boxers he was taken to see—were, he recalled, 'the most savage and offensive athletes I had ever seen'. Dempsey straddled the worlds of sport and showbusiness, celebrity politics and stardom, in ways made possible by the new reach of an internationalizing media, and the increasing emphasis on sport champions as figures representative of national pride and global ambitions.

depression In relation to the economy, a sustained downturn in consumer demand and spending, with associated reduction in production. When this downturn generates increasing *unemployment, consumer markets shrink, though this may stimulate revived or new forms of associational activity or public sporting culture, as in the Great Depression of the 1930s. *See also* KNUR-AND-SPELL; RECESSION; SEABISCUIT.

depth hermeneutic An integrated method for the study of cultural phenomena, in which different phases in the production, construction, and consumption of a cultural or sporting form or practice are recognized, but can be studied in an interrelated fashion. First articulated in communication and media studies, the depth hermeneutic was fully formulated by John B. Thompson (*Ideology and Modern Culture: Critical Social Theory in the Era of Mass Communication*, 1990), as a way of linking 'different types of analysis' on 'the path of interpretation'. In relation to a sporting event, a depth hermeneutic approach would study, first, the circumstances of social production of the event (its organizational structures, its funding, its cultural or political genesis); second, the constructed product itself, its dominant themes and motifs, and its essentially performed context, often in the form of lived ritualized performances as well as artefacts—this is a formal/discursive analysis of the features, patterns, and relationships characterizing the event; and finally the method would be concerned with, in Thompson's words, 'the creative construction of meaning . . . an interpretive explication of what is represented or what is said'; it would explore the modes and varieties of reception and interpretation of the event, how it is consumed, and in what ways meanings and understandings are generated in that act of consumption. Full depth hermeneutic studies can be daunting, requiring teams of experienced researchers competent in a variety of research techniques. The attraction of the method is clear though, offering analysis of the sport and its meanings at all phases from production to consumption, including the (theoretically) limitless cycles of interpretation. *See also* HERMENEUTICS.

Derby *See* CARNIVALESQUE; HORSE RACING.

deviance An attribute or act perceived as varying from the norms of acceptable conduct or behaviour, often associated with rule-breaking and law-breaking. The difficulty in establishing a systematic and robust sociology of deviance is that it is also widely recognized that the boundaries of deviant and non-deviant behaviour and acts are malleable and flexible, and that acts described as deviant are often social constructions, frequently the product of the media's contribution to *moral panics, and a consequence of a spiralling process of labelling, creating *deviance amplification. In sport, the raucous spectator in the stadium can engage in vocal—if not physical—forms of conduct that would not be acceptable on the high street; the competitor in contact sports can employ physical tactics that would lead to criminal charges away from the field of play; a banned performance-enhancing drug may be last year's booster before the race; a ruling body's policy on ticket distribution may be more iniquitous than the redistributive activities of ticket touts. Nevertheless, the conceptual agenda of the sociology of deviance, and its indication of issues and topics where these analyses and debates can be established, provide an illuminating framework for understanding some of the complexities and contradictions of sport and sport culture.

(((∰))) SEE WEB LINKS

- The proceedings of the Old Bailey court sessions, 1674–1913 (London), including searchable subjects and bibliography, showing how boxing, cricket, football, wrestling, and the (horse) races linked to law-breaking.

deviance amplification A process usually instigated by the organs of the mass media, which report an act of *deviance in an exaggerated form, so intensifying awareness and often fear of that act, and even stimulating further occurrences of the act. The media coverage then becomes the instigator of the deviance that it purports to report. Teams of broadcasters at international football tournaments have been known to goad groups of fans into unruly public behaviour, so contributing to the spiralling perceived significance of the deviance.

diaulos The race at the ancient Greek Olympic Games of a duration of two lengths of the stadium, seen as roughly similar to the modern 400-metre race. *See also* OLYMPIC GAMES, ANCIENT.

Didrikson, Mildred Ella ('Babe') (1911–56) A multi-talented US athlete who won two athletics/track-and-field gold medals (in javelin and hurdles) at the Los Angeles 1932 Olympic Games, excelled in competitive basketball and golf, and also dived, roller-skated, and bowled at a high level. Born in Texas, Didrikson acquired the nickname 'Babe' (after Babe *Ruth) when she showed precocious talent as a baseball batter; as a young woman she worked as an employee for a Dallas insurance firm but was effectively a full-time basketball player and athlete in the company's representative sides. This prepared her for the 1932 Olympics, after which she played in exhibition basketball tours, headed by her name, before taking up golf and dominating the US circuit, as amateur and then professional, winning every title available there and throughout the world. In 1950 Didrikson achieved the *Grand Slam by winning the three available titles in the women's game in the USA. She died at the age of 45, of colon cancer, still a competitive force as she battled the phases of the fatal illness. Her marriage gave her the name Zaharias, but the marriage bore no children, and speculation has been widespread that she was bisexual or lesbian. Her strong, muscular style revolutionized the women's game, and her all-round prodigious sporting talent was an important counter to the prejudice against competitive women's sports that was still dominant in her time. On her death, the US President Eisenhower paid tribute 'to Mrs. Zaharias as a woman who had won the admiration of all Americans both in her sports career and in her fight against cancer': she had 'put up one of the kind of fights that inspired us all', Eisenhower added (*New York Times* obituary, September 28 1956).

Diem, Carl (1882–1962) A German sport administrator and pedagogue whose lasting legacy in the educational sphere is the German Sport University (Cologne), founded in Berlin in 1920 as the German College of Physical Education, and revived in Cologne in 1947. It is now recognized as the largest sport university in the world. But Diem's more notorious legacy is linked to his commitment to Olympism; he was the primary organizer of the 1936 Berlin Olympic Games, which became widely known as the Nazi Games. Although he had assumed responsibility for German Olympics before Hitler came to power, in 1936 he presided over what has been recognized as a mass political spectacle, at which he took the opportunity to introduce the 'tradition' of the torch relay and the torch ceremony. In 1938, Diem began editing the *Olympic Bulletin*, and he remained an ardent champion of Olympism despite the political excesses to which the ideal could clearly be put. Most commentators conclude that Diem was not explicitly a Nazi sympathizer, but neither did he do anything to deflect the patronage of Adolf *Hitler and his inner circle.

diffusion *See* CULTURAL DIFFUSION.

DiMaggio, Joe (Joseph Paul) (1914–99) Born Giuseppe Paolo DiMaggio, a US baseball player whose 'hitting streak' of 1941—hits in 56 consecutive American league baseball games, in a season when his team the New York Yankees won the league pennant (i.e. title) and also the World Series—entered the language of popular culture, everyday life, and the arts. Les Brown's big-band hit *Joltin' Joe DiMaggio* made him the most talked-about person in the country during the run, and decades later athletes on a run of victories or scores have talked about their 'DiMaggio streak'. Ernest *Hemingway wrote of 'the great' DiMaggio in *The Old Man and the Sea*, in a reference to the player's Sicilian forebears' fishing background; the song *Bloody Mary*, in the Hollywood musical *South Pacific*, included the phrase 'skin tender as DiMaggio's glove'; singers Paul Simon and Art Garfunkel, in their song *Mrs Robinson*, asked 'Where have you gone, Joe DiMaggio? A nation turns its lonely eyes to you'. DiMaggio had played for the Yankees from 1936 to 1951, with an interruption for war service, and led them to nine titles in thirteen years.

After retirement, the 39-year-old DiMaggio married his second wife, 27-year-old Marilyn Monroe, after a whirlwind romance and elopement. A separation followed after only nine months, after a tempestuous relationship in which his jealousy and possessiveness failed to cope with Monroe's public, sexual, and flirtatious persona; even so, several years later DiMaggio was talking of remarriage just days before her death in August 1962. The painting of Monroe that DiMaggio kept on display in his home after her death portrayed the 'innocent curiosity' of 'a simple girl', as Gay Talese wrote ('The Silent Season of a Hero', *Fame and Obscurity*, 1981). DiMaggio saw Monroe as 'a warm big-hearted girl that everybody took advantage of'. DiMaggio turned his back on the Hollywood, Los Angeles elite and lived mostly in San Francisco for the rest of his life. In the 1980s he became known, on the basis of his endorsement career, as 'Mr Coffee'. His *life history is a fascinating case of the construction of *celebrity and the way in which sporting achievement enters the language of a time and a culture.

disability sports Specific competitions for athletes grouped into classes defined by the degree of function. There are six main classes: amputee, cerebral palsy, visual impairment, spinal cord injuries, intellectual disability, and a group of all others. The classes are defined by each sport and often have subclasses to make competition equitable. Participation in disabled sport has grown significantly over the past years. A major step was taken by Dr Guttman who, in 1948 on the same day as the opening ceremony of the London Olympics, organized a sports competition at Stoke Mandeville hospital for World War II servicemen with spinal cord injuries. The Paralympic movement was subsequently established. A considerable science has developed investigating the particular challenges faced by the disabled athlete and how training may be adapted and performance enhanced. *See also* PARALYMPICS.

discourse analysis A method of qualitative research concerned with the analysis of texts and verbal interactions. The notion of discourse also often infers ideological and power interests, so that texts and statements (this can be particularly the case in the policy field) can be shown as serving ends that are not explicitly stated in the documents or transcripts/recordings of interactions or conversations. Discourse is treated as a construction of reality rather than a faithful representation of it. Reading sport *biographies, therefore, the discourse analyst would be less interested in the veracity of the reported life narrative than in the way in which the life is constructed, and the primary themes around which the story is told. A version of the approach, critical discourse analysis (CDA), emerged in the late 1980s and the 1990s, outlining more fully an analytical framework recognizing but oscillating between 'a focus on structure and a focus on action', and comprising a five-stage analytical model: the focus upon a social problem with a semiotic aspect—this might be sexist representation of the female sporting body; the identification of obstacles constraining the tackling of the problem, by analysing, for instance, the sporting networks in which sexism is embedded, and the discourse itself; consideration of how or whether the sporting networks and practices acknowledge or see any problem at all; identification of ways past the obstacles; and critical reflection on the analysis accomplished in those stages (Norman Fairclough, 'Critical Discourse Analysis as a Method in Social Scientific Research', in Ruth Wodak and Michael Meyer, eds, *Methods of Critical Discourse Analysis*, 2001). CDA offers much to the study of the capacity of sport to reproduce itself within the power dynamics of a particular social context or cultural setting, but brings a 'positive critique' to bear on an issue by pointing to unforeseen possibilities in how problems might be tackled. In the example instancing the method, CDA makes possible not just a critique of sexism in sport, but an understanding of the conditions of its making and remaking, and so a potential challenge to its dominance. *See also* DECONSTRUCTION; SEMIOLOGY.

discrimination Prejudiced attitudes towards or treatment of a person or a group. Established sporting institutions have been widely culpable of sexual discrimination, in protecting their sporting spaces as male-only or predominantly male preserves. Racial discrimination has also been widespread in the frequent stereotyping of the black athletic body.

discus A throwing event that was included in the early ancient Olympic Games, and has been long established as a core field event in athletic competitions and meets worldwide. The discus is a circular object made of wood, tapering out from a thick centre, with metal plates set into the rim. Thrown with one hand, and constant in conception and shape since its Olympic origins, it has symbolized the longevity of the fundamental act of throwing an object; the Greek sculptor Myron's statue of Discobolos (*c.*460–450 BC) has come to stand for the resilience and universality of athletic motion. It featured centrally, as a motif or an inspiration, in the official Olympic posters of the 1920 Antwerp and the 1948 London Olympic Games, and was the astoundingly beautiful moving image linking classical past and modern present at the beginning of the Leni *Riefenstahl film of the 1936 Berlin Olympics, *Olympia*. The discus is also one of the ten events in the *decathlon.

In the men's Olympic competition, the USA dominated the event for many decades from the 1896 Games until the later 1970s, after which East European nations and Germany, and then, especially, Lithuania (three golds from 1992 to

d

2004) and Estonia (gold in Beijing in 2008) produced the champion throwers. In the women's event, inaugurated in Amsterdam in 1928, East European and Soviet athletes began to dominate after 1952, when the Soviet Union first entered the Games. In the 2004 Games at Athens, gold was won by Russian Natalya Sadova, who two years later was banned for two years by the *World Anti-Doping Agency (WADA) after a positive drugs test for the anabolic steroid methandinone. At Beijing 2008, the gold was won by a US athlete. These fluctuating national fortunes have clearly been intertwined with the use of performance-enhancement drugs, and the advances that have been made in both their detection and their masking. The same broad story—though not quite so emphatically—can also be told about the shot-put, particularly in the women's event, which did not begin until 1948; though victories for Cuban and New Zealand athletes in 2004 and 2008 respectively broke the East European stranglehold on the event. Tamara Press of the Soviet Union/ Ukraine won gold in Rome (1960) and Tokyo (1964), also taking the gold for the discus throw at Tokyo. Press disappeared from competitive athletics and international competition, though, when sex tests were introduced at international events. *See also* GALEN; GREECE, ANCIENT, SPORT IN; GYMNASION; OLYMPIC GAMES, ANCIENT.

diuretics A class of drugs designed to alter the function of the kidneys and promote the loss of water by increased production of dilute urine. Medically these drugs are used in a variety of conditions, notably as a treatment for high blood pressure since the increased water loss reduces the volume of plasma and therefore the pressure in the cardiovascular system. In sport, diuretics are mainly used in two circumstances. In weight-classified sports such as judo, wrestling, and horse racing, athletes may take diuretics prior to the weigh-in to achieve a temporary reduction in weight and fit into a lower category. Adverse effects of this artificial reduction include impaired cardiovascular and thermoregulatory capacity. Diuretics may also be used in an attempt to disguise drug taking since the more dilute urine will show a lower concentration of illegal drug metabolites.

diving A form of aerial *gymnastics in which an individual or pairs plunge into water either directly, or after performing some bodily manoeuvres while in the air. Diving has been an element of physical recreation or informal performance in any culture in which water-based recreation was established. But in its modern form it emerged from German and Swedish gymnastics, and has featured in the Summer Olympics programme from London 1908. The USA was for most of the 20th century the dominant nation in both men's and women's events across the four subdisciplines of springboard and platform (individual and synchronized), challenged at some Games by Soviet/East European nations, also Sweden and Australia, but increasingly—to the point of eclipse—by China. At the Beijing 2008 Games, Chinese divers won all four women's gold medals, and three out of four men's. Diving has also, like *swimming and *weightlifting, been a route into showbusiness; 1928 Amsterdam double Olympic (springboard and platform) champion, Canadian-born Ulise Joseph 'Pete' Desjardins (1907–85), 5-foot-3-inch Stanford graduate, turned professional and performed billed as 'The Little Bronze Statue from the Land of Real Estate, Grapefruits and Alligators'.

division of labour A classic social scientific concept, with its roots in the analysis of the economy of the capitalist system, but having relevance to the structural analysis of any society's production relations. Émile *Durkheim was particularly interested in the moral implications of the division of labour in the workplace, in how it related to the everyday conduct and values of members of the society. In sport, the term is a useful one for identifying the respective roles in a complex team operation, or the hierarchy of tasks and responsibilities in the sports club. It has also become generally acknowledged, in the later 20th century, that myriad social systems have functioned on the basis of a gender-based division of labour between the sexes. Patriarchal sport systems are unimaginable without the support of a domestic division of labour, and numerous anthropological studies have shown how sporting men have been serviced in their leisure by women acting as unpaid laundresses or volunteer caterers or in some other servicing capacity.

Dod, Lottie (Charlotte) (1871–1960) An English all-round sportswoman whose myriad achievements in a range of sports and longevity of performance embodied the enthusiasm and ethos of the amateur code and era. Born into a wealthy northern English family of merchants and bankers, Lottie, the youngest child, was raised in a culture of privilege, inducted into a life of leisure, and had an independent income for life. Her cocooned family life as a child and a young woman included private education by hired tutors and governesses, and regular sporting encounters in country house games such as bowls, billiards, archery, croquet, golf, skating, and tennis. Her brother William was a gold medal winner for archery—aged 40—at the 1908 London Olympics. Playing tennis from the age of 9, Lottie Dod was challenging the champion of Wimbledon at a north of England tournament at the age of 13, becoming Wimbledon champion herself at the age of 15. Dod retired from competitive tennis in 1893, having won five titles, though choosing not to defend her title in 1889, as she was already committed to a yachting holiday. As traditionally amateur and privileged as her background might have been, Dod nevertheless dominated through modern techniques of play, mixing volleys, overheads (smashes), and spin in an athletic approach to the game for which, to enhance mobility, she wore shorter skirts than was the orthodoxy of the time.

After her tennis career, Dod took up cycling and golf; and wintered (1895–6) among the fashionable upper classes in the Alps, tobogganing and mountaineering. Persevering at golf, she won the British Ladies' Championship in 1904. She had also played hockey for England in 1899 and 1900, before adopting archery prior to the London 1908 Olympics, where she took the silver medal. After her competitive sporting life, Dod mixed service to sport in a voluntary capacity for clubs and associations with involvement in musical circles, also undertaking youth work; she lived a life of privileged leisure and disinterested altruism to the end, reputedly listening to the broadcast of the Wimbledon tournament on her deathbed. Dod's precocious and prodigious achievements can be seen as both epitome and apogee of the amateur ethos in women's sport.

dolichos The 'long race' run at the ancient Olympics in Greece, introduced in 720 BC, and comparable to the modern 1,500- or 5,000-metre events. *See also* OLYMPIC GAMES, ANCIENT.

domination The exercise of *power over another, or the rule of one person or group over another. Max *Weber identified three types of accepted domination, or authority: rational-legal, traditional, and charismatic. This classification is useful for considering the relational basis of authority figures in sport, such as coaches or club/team managers. *See also* CHARISMA; CULTURE INDUSTRY; FOUCAULT, MICHEL; HEGEMONY; LEADERSHIP.

Dover, Robert (1581/2–1652) An English legal practitioner and founder of the Cotswold Olimpick Games. Dover attended Queens' College, Cambridge, at the age of 13 or 14, but took no degree. He qualified in law in London, and practised his legal work in the Cotswolds or the Vale of Evesham, England. He began his Cotswold Olimpick Games in 1612, in all probability as a part of some traditional festivity, and they were staged until 1644, the decade of the ascendancy of Oliver *Cromwell. Contemporary poets wrote about these events,

> and all were enthusiastic about Dover's character, referring to him as jovial, generous, mirth-making, heroic, and noble-minded . . . The games offered activities for all levels of society—horse-racing, coursing, backswords, wrestling, jumping, tumbling, spurning the bar, throwing the sledge-hammer, and pike exercises—with dancing for ladies as well as feasting in tents on the hillside. A castle was erected from which guns were fired to introduce events. Competitors and spectators came from more than 60 miles around, and prizes included Dover's yellow favours which as many as 500 gained in any year.' (F. D. A. Burns, *Oxford Dictionary of National Biography*, 2004).

Dover called his sports 'honest and harmless', explicitly criticizing Puritan attitudes towards games, and so supporting The *King's Book of Sports. Revived after the Restoration, the games continued until 1852, when 'rowdyism' was cited and used by religious opponents—clearly proponents of *rational recreation—as the reason for closing them down. Games of 1812 and 1849, where they continued to be described as 'Olimpick', advertised (on surviving posters) 'horse-racing, wrestling, backsword fighting, jingling, dancing, leaping, and running in sacks'. Revived again for the Festival of Britain in 1951, the games became an annual event in 1966. Dover's Cotswold games provide a fascinating barometer of the political, religious, and cultural times that can reshape a recreational and sporting culture, and of the way in which cultural revivals of sports contribute to the heritage industry.

doxa From the Greek, the shared opinions or widespread beliefs held by people; the word 'orthodox' derives from the term. Doxa was a concept used by the philosophers of ancient Greece, and adapted by Pierre *Bourdieu, in his *Outline of a Theory of Practice* (1972), to refer to what people take for granted: to 'what goes without saying because it comes without saying' in a 'natural and social world' that 'appears as self-evident'. Feminists have adapted the concept to account for the persistingly patriarchal nature of many sports; a basis of male domination of the sporting world is that it is simply assumed that boys play rugby or football, that male sports dominate the pages of the sporting press and the schedules of the broadcasters. To examine the conditions of the attainment and reproduction of sporting doxa is a vital step in demonstrating the social constructedness of the doxa itself.

draft In the USA, the recruitment of players from college sports into the professional ranks, on a basis not merely of market forces, but in terms of evenness of playing strengths of the different professional teams.

dragon boat racing An ancient Chinese sport combining, as Allen Guttmann puts it, 'aesthetic and agonistic impulses' (*Sports: The First Five Millennia*, 2004). Impromptu races developed, in the Tang dynasty (618–907), into major commemorative events honouring public figures. Paddle-fuelled dragon boats are used in modern China as a form of cultural heritage, and by diasporic Chinese populations as a form of preservation and assertion of cultural identity.

Drewry, Arthur (1891–1961) A President of the FIFA (*Fédération Internationale de Football Association) from 1956 to his death in 1961, after acting as interim head for six months following the death of Rodolphe William *Seeldrayers. With his successor Stanley *Rous, he worked with long-term FIFA president Jules *Rimet to bring the British football associations back into FIFA after World War II, and was appointed vice-president of FIFA by Rimet. Drewry served as president of the English Football League (1945–54) and as chairman of England's Football Association (1955–61). Working closely with Rous, and holding the positions of both FIFA president and FA (*Football Association) chairman at the time of FIFA's decision to award England the 1966 World Cup Finals, Drewry was an experienced football administrator. He had chaired the FA's International Selection Committee in 1945. A fish-processing businessman from Grimsby, England, Drewry married the daughter of Grimsby Town Football Club's chairman (the fishing business was his father-in-law's) and became in turn chairman of the Grimsby club. Drewry's name is little-known, but he had a widespread influence on the administration of soccer in both England and the international setting. England's victory in 1966 prompted some commentators to call for more representative participation in the World Cup Finals. Dr A. Foni, coach to the Swiss national team, contributed to FIFA's technical study of the event and wrote that the premises for the English victory 'were created well in advance: selection of a definite ground, longer breaks between games, decisions by referees that were slightly but very clearly favourable'. Although written half a decade after Drewry's death, this is a condemnation of the international legacy of the Drewry years, Foni adding that the necessary reform would raise 'the moral and athletic level of the World Cup'.

drill A form of exercise based upon mass standardized movement, stemming from military forms of fitness training, but also employed in schools and educational institutions as a way of training the young person's body. Reginald Brabazon, twelfth Earl of Meath (1841–1929), founded the Lads' Drill Association (1899–1906), which was then incorporated into the National Service League. Concerns in Britain after the second Boer War (1899–1902) over the fitness of the nation identified low levels of physical condition among recruits, and led to educational initiatives to provide drill in state schools, a poor substitute for the organized team games provided to their privileged public school counterparts.

drum dance A body cultural event of the Inuit (Eskimo) peoples, from Greenland, Canada, Alaska (USA), and Soviet Siberia: 'the ancient centre-piece of Inuit festival culture, a dance of laughter and enjoyment, play and display, as well as an instrument of conflict resolution (by duel dancing) and a technique of shamanic ecstatic healing' (Henning Eichberg, *Body Cultures: Essays on Sport, Space and Identity*, 1998). The use of such a dance in the late 1980s in the context of the cultural politics of Inuit identity achieved a corporeal expression of collective identity, showing how traditional, indigenous body cultures and sporting practices could generate new meanings beyond the novelty value of a culture of nostalgia.

Duncan, Isadora (1877–1927) A US dancer, born in California, who innovated and championed a primitivist form of expressive dance that challenged the canon of classical dance. Patricia Vertinsky ('Isadora Goes to Europe as the "Muse of Modernism": Modern Dance, Gender and the Active Female Body', *Journal of Sport History*, 2010) quotes Paul Magriel: 'It was Isadora . . . who first brought to Europe and then to her own country, a new attitude—her own vision of America Dancing.' Making her home in Europe for most of her adult life, Duncan based herself in Paris, Berlin, and St Petersburg. As Vertinsky writes: 'En route she captivated audiences with her barefoot dancing, indulged in free love, took up with political radicals and leading artists of the day, experienced more than her fair share of personal tragedies and earned the nickname "Isadorable Drunken" for her excesses.' Duncan died in a tragic car accident, all but strangled by one of her own flamboyant scarves. While women in sport were still restricted by conventional dress codes and patriarchal and puritanical views of the female body, Duncan—also bisexual— broadened the boundaries of acceptability of performative bodily cultures.

Durkheim, Émile (1858–1917) A French, philosophy-trained and hugely influential force in the founding of the discipline of sociology. Durkheim's major studies were concerned with the changing basis of religious and social life and the individual crises that might stem from such ruptures to a traditional way of life: *The Elementary Forms of the Religious Life* (1912), *The Division of Labour in Society* (1893), and *Suicide* (1897). He was particularly interested in the ways in which industrialization undermined the basis of traditional collective living, a process which he described as a shift from mechanical solidarity to organic solidarity. In his study of the social conditions of and influences upon suicide, he proposed that in a time of rapid social change an individual's uncertainty in relation to norms of behaviour could create a crisis of *anomie, or of normlessness: some forms of suicide could therefore be accounted for not merely as an individual act, but as a 'social fact'. Durkheim's work on religion identified too the issue of collective consciousness (*conscience collectif).

Critical sociologists have dismissed Durkheim's work as *functionalist, and so have too often given less attention to some of his core conceptual and analytical concerns. A sense of sport's contribution to the making of new collective groupings and cultures in industrializing societies can only be strengthened by a close reading of Durkheim's work on the sources of social solidarity; and the use of sport to express collective ideals in communist or state socialist societies has been seen (see Jim Riordan, 'Outside North America—Soviet Muscular Socialism:

A Durkheimian Analysis', *Sociology of Sport Journal*, 1987) as an equivalent to the function of religion as a kind of social cement in more traditional societies. Scholars accounting for the capacity of sport or play to feed into the moral forces of society have also cited Durkheim, drawing upon his discussion of the Aboriginal 'corroboree' in *The Elementary Forms*. For Durkheim, the 'slavishness of daily work' was in marked contrast to the effervescence often expressed in religion, and this latter had the capability to fuel a renewal of morality. Durkheim paved the way, in this analysis, for Victor Turner's notions of *liminality and *communitas. Looking at 'fun spaces' such as cricket at its 'level of Pakistani mass cultural stardom', Pnina Werbner has demonstrated the capacity of sports to occupy symbolic spaces in ways potentially transforming of established cultural and ethnic practices and their accompanying moralities.

dynamometer An instrument for measuring the power or force resulting from a muscular contraction. A common example is the handgrip dynamometer where the grip compresses a spring which rotates a pointer and the force exerted may be read from a calibrated scale. The development of small force transducers and microprocessors has allowed considerable progression in the sophistication of dynamometers. In cycling, for example, the SRM power crank system utilizes sets of force transducers embedded in the cranks, the output of which is processed to provide the cyclist with an instantaneous measure of power output displayed on a small unit mounted on the handlebars. This tool is used to monitor training performance or to guide pace during a race. *See also* ISOKINETIC DYNAMOMETER.

dystopia A counter-notion to *utopia, this is a neologism of English philosopher John Stuart *Mill. It refers to an imaginary place in which every aspect of the world is as bad as can be imagined. The idea has some currency and potential in relation to preparation for performance in sport, as a way of imagining the opposite of the ideal. More sociologically, it is interesting to think of a sporting world of performance extremes led by drug-enhanced preparation and performance and excesses of commercialization and commodification as a dystopian scenario. *See also* UTOPIA.

E

eating disorder An abnormal pattern of food consumption leading to a range of physical and psychological problems. Anorexia and bulimia are the two most prevalent forms of eating disorder in sport, most commonly seen in females, with between 5 and 20 per cent of performers showing a disorder compared with 2 to 3 per cent in the general population. Anorexia is characterized by a body mass at least 15 per cent below the expected mass, weight loss induced by behaviours which avoid food intake, a body image distortion, and amenorrhoea. Bulimia is characterized by recurrent episodes of binge eating with a lack of control over how much is consumed, followed by compensatory behaviours to prevent weight gain, such as vomiting, misuse of laxatives and enemas, and excessive exercise. Body image is also distorted. In women, anorexia and bulimia, combined with osteoporosis, are termed the female athlete triad. The combination of disordered food intake, excessive exercise, and amenorrhoea results in a range of health risks and an increased mortality. In weight-category sports like horse racing, martial arts, rowing, and boxing, there is intense demand to 'make the weight'. And for women athletes in sports such as distance running there is a considerable performance premium to be gained by a light weight. The behaviours of many athletes in these types of sport display an altered body image and an obsession over food intake, not at the extreme that would necessarily lead to a clinical diagnosis of an eating disorder, but that may do so.

economic classification of physical and sporting activities An overview of sports enabling the breaking down of the sports economy into discrete economic accounts. A nine-class classification of physical and sporting activities (CPSA) has been produced by Brigitte Belloc and colleagues in France, working on data relating to twelve criteria: the type of practice (individual, dual, team); the required equipment; participant numbers for 15- to 75-year-olds; gender proportions of those participating; number of registered participants; age of registered participants; proportion of young people within those registered participants; number of participants practising at a high level; budgets of federations; federation budgets dedicated to professional practice; total broadcasting coverage on terrestrial television; and press coverage in *L'Équipe* (France's daily sports newspaper). Applying these criteria to previous classifications of activity, a nine-class CPSA was produced: independent leisure activities requiring equipment (such as bodybuilding, fishing, rock climbing, roller skating, ten-pin bowling); social and leisure activities (such as badminton, bowls, dancing, table tennis, and walking); highly organized activities (such as aeronautical sports, fencing, judo/martial arts, and shooting); individual sports requiring special equipment (such as canoeing, golf, ice skating, rowing, and waterskiing); equipment-intensive open-air sports (such as sailing and horse riding); individual mass-participation activities (such as cycling, gymnastics, swimming, track-and-field/athletics, winter sports); motor sports; semi-professional sports (basketball, combat sports, tennis, volleyball, other team sports); and professional sports (football, rugby) (Wladimir Andreff, 'Sports Accounting', in Wladimir Andreff and Stefan Szymanski, eds, *Handbook on the Economics of Sport*, 2006). Any CPSA is only as strong as the statistical data and sector information and intelligence upon which it is based; and the classification will be culturally, socially, and politically distinctive from country to country. Sophisticated modelling such as this, however, demonstrates the range of sporting practices that coexist in any society, and the relative socio-economic significance of those practices.

economic impact The value of a sporting presence or event to the community or other identifiable constituency. This is best assessed by independent bodies or individuals, as it is highly unlikely that an organization with a vested interest in the impact and success of an event or activity could guarantee an adequate level of objectivity to measure or evaluate its economic impact. Identifying economic impact is also difficult, as instant returns are wanted and looked for, though short-term impacts are frequently superseded by medium- or long-term shifts in impact. Many large-scale international sporting events, for instance, have reported a boost in the awareness of a venue, or an increase in tourist figures in the season or year after the event. But when the eyes of the world turn to the latest venue or event, the previous one fades in the international tourist consciousness.

Nevertheless, economic impact analysis is a widely applied methodology. It is based on the estimation of the attendance at a sporting event, analysis of survey respondents' declaration of spending associated with the event, and the application of a multiplier that indicates the level of circulation of monies throughout the economy after the event. Victor Matheson ('Economic Impact Analysis', in Wladimir Andreff and Stefan Szymanski, eds, *Handbook on the Economics of Sport*, 2009) gives the example of *Super Bowl XXVIII in Atlanta in 1994: 306,680 visitor days at US$252 expenditure per individual per day equalled a direct impact of $77.3 million. An economic multiplier identified an additional, indirect impact of $88.7 million. The total economic benefit was therefore identified as $166 million. Simon Chadwick, in a report for UEFA sponsor Mastercard (*Heart of Sports Commerce*), has applied the economic impact model to the *UEFA Champions League final in Rome in 2009, for the match between Barcelona and Manchester United. The event was said to be worth €310 million to the European economy (Moscow the previous year was estimated to be worth €267 million), with even the losing side benefiting by up to €65 million, from combinations of image enhancement, increased squad value, prize monies, and sponsoring benefits. The Mastercard report argued that the global economic downturn had a positive effect upon the event, creating a new community of football fans (presumably, via the broadcast transmissions) excited by an event of which they had previously little or no experience. For Rome itself, the event was said to be worth €45 million, in expenditure in bars, clubs, shops, attractions, accommodation; the final in Athens two years earlier was estimated to be worth only €26 million to the city.

Many economists remain sceptical about claims relating to economic impact, which are seen as significantly overstating the true economic benefits of professional sports and particular costly sporting events. In Matheson's words, 'analysts tend to overstate benefits, understate costs and misapply multipliers'. Additionally, analyses of economic impact usually fail to account for activity that '*does not* occur due to an event'. This is a critical point. If a population, dreading the prospect of the arrival in its neighbourhood of thousands of visitors, simply leaves town, how are the economic consequences of that to be factored in to the economic impact analysis? In Rome, for the Champions League final, a last-minute municipal edict banned the sale of alcohol from 11 p.m. on the Tuesday night to 6 p.m. on the Thursday morning. How does that fit in with the projections and the estimates of expenditure, or with the informal economy that enabled some visitors and fans to find a drink before and/or after the match?

economy and efficiency The ratio between the mechanical work produced and the energy expended. Efficiency is usually expressed as a percentage where:

% efficiency = (mechanical work accomplished ÷ energy input) × 100.

The efficiency of the human walking, running, or cycling is around 20 to 30 per cent. However, determining the mechanical work accomplished during a complex movement such as walking is very difficult in practice since the various body parts are each moving in a complex manner and much of the work being done is non-propulsive. The term economy is often used when considering human movement as an alternative to the engineer's precise use of efficiency in the study of machines. Economy is defined as the energy cost of moving at a certain speed. For example, the typical energy cost of running at 3 $m.s^{-1}$ is about 0.18 kilocalories per kilogram per minute.

Economy of movement is affected by skill, limb length, mass, gender, age, and equipment. Trained athletes may have a running economy that is 10 per cent better than an average runner, and in highly skilled sports such as swimming an elite swimmer may require half the energy to swim at a particular speed compared with a recreational swimmer. Two forms of external factor, both related to resistance, can considerably affect the economy of movement during sport or recreational activity. First, the energy cost of overcoming air resistance is relatively modest when moving slowly on a calm day but can impact considerably during fast motion or in a headwind, an effect vividly displayed by the echelon formations of the Tour de France peloton when a crosswind affects a stage and the riders adopt a formation that attempts to minimize additional effort. The second effect relates to the mechanical properties of equipment. A major influence in the design of sports equipment is the minimizing of resistance, as seen in the skintight suit of a swimmer or the aerodynamic helmet of a cyclist.

ectomorph *See* SOMATOTYPE.

Ederle, Gertrude *See* CHANNEL SWIMMING.

Edström, J. Sigfrid (1870–1964) A Swedish engineer, industrialist, and sport administrator who became the fourth president of the *International Olympic Committee (IOC). As a student in Gothenburg, Edström was a sprinter. After studying in Switzerland, at Zurich's Federal Institute of Technology, he became Sweden's most prominent sport administrator, important in the organization of the 1912 Stockholm Olympics, a landmark event in the expansion and modernization of international sporting competition, and its representation. At that event Edström also set in process the formation of the *International Amateur Athletics Federation (IAAF), becoming its first president, and holding that position until 1946 when he assumed the IOC presidency. The 1912 event's poster mixed the nationalistic with the physical—too explicit and allegedly erotic for some countries, which banned the poster. Edström had headed the Swedish delegation at the 1908 London Games, and carried out that role at the five summer Games from 1920 to 1936. His IOC profile was high right from his initial membership in 1920, to his election to the executive board the following year, and his later appointment to a vice-presidential role.

Controversially, in his capacity as IAAF chief, he disqualified the Finnish runner Paavo *Nurmi from the 1932 Los Angeles Olympics, amidst allegations that the Finn was paid to run. Edström also held back women's participation in Olympic events. During World War II, Edström, from his base in a neutral country, maintained contact with as many IOC members as possible, and convened the first post-war meeting of the executive board, which accepted London's offer to stage a Summer Olympics in 1948; as vice-president, he was made president by acclamation in 1946, the incumbent president, Count de *Baillet-Latour, having died in 1942, when Edström assumed the role of acting president. Edström retired in 1952. His contribution to the modern organization and the survival of the Olympics was immense, embracing a principled criticism of the lack of accountability of the founder, Pierre de *Coubertin, and a determination to sustain the idea and the ideals of the Olympics during wartime.

efficiency *See* ECONOMY AND EFFICIENCY.

ego One of the elements developed by Sigmund *Freud in his theory of psychoanalysis as formulated in the 1920s. His theories of the self and the mental world placed the ego within the structure of *id–ego–*superego, the ego referring to both the conscious mind as it is constructed by the individual in relation with reality and the external world, and some less conscious and potentially anxiety-inducing elements. In sporting competition the degree of self-awareness necessary to understand competitive contexts requires that the individual has this developed sense of him- or herself in the broader context. In common-sense understanding, ego has come to refer to an individual's sense of self-esteem ('the athlete's personal best in training boosted his ego before the big competition') or to the degree of self-importance displayed by an individual (English football manager Brian Clough called himself 'Old Big Head' and was regularly accused of egocentrism and egomania).

elective affinity A relationship of connectedness between two phenomena in which neither phenomenon is the determining influence. In sociological and historical analysis there is a recurrent challenge to establish the relation between observable but separate phenomena, such as a sporting institution and an economic system, or the participatory culture of a sport and the main family structure of a society. These cannot by any means always be established as causes (A produces B), and the term elective affinity was Max *Weber's way of seeking to account for parallel processes that are connected, but neither or none of which can be said with certainty to be the determining cause. This is how Weber framed his analysis of the complementary systems of capitalism (an economic system) and Protestantism (a religious belief-system). Weber's studies were to some degree framed as a methodological and epistemological debate with what he saw as a form of economic determinism in the work of Karl *Marx. An elective affinity could be identified, Weber proposed, between, say, a set of religious beliefs and a particular social group or system (Weber, 1948: 62–3), so identifying a correspondence between sources of meaning that may not initially seem to be connected, and generating a process of reciprocal, mutual self-referencing and justification. This notion is central to Weber's analysis of *The Protestant Ethic and the Spirit of Capitalism* (1905).

A sport-based example of the use of the concept takes the Beijing 2008 Summer Olympics as a case: 'there is an *extraordinary convergence*, or *elective affinity*, between modern Olympism and the *ideals and tendencies* of modern market capitalism' (Close et al., 2007: 1–2, 117). The Beijing Olympiad and Olympics are seen, in this light, as a catalyst 'in the re-alignment process of the global political economy' (ibid.: 2, 117), as well as a focus for some potential internal reform, in relation to human rights. Adapted to the Olympic context, the argument for the use of the concept goes that the Olympic Ideals or Movement converge with the spirit of contemporary market capitalism. The implication here is that neither one determines the other, but that the values of the two meaning-systems are conducive to a kind of reciprocal development. Close et al. offer the synonyms, for elective affinity, of 'mutual attraction' and 'irresistible mutual desire' (2007: 118). When referring to Beijing as a catalyst they refer to how the city/event and the period (the Olympiad) leading up to the event will contribute to re-alignments of both the overall global political economy (p. 2) and the 'political economy arena of Chinese society' (p. 117).

Close et al. highlight five developments: deepening institutionalization, on a global scale, of Olympism; a global spread of the doctrine of individualism, in Western terms; global scales of advance in liberal democracy and market capitalism; a consolidation of global society within the continuing progress of globalization; and China's emergence as a superpower and player in the political economy, in both regional and global terms (pp. 2–3, 117–18). These developments are said to share 'a formidable array of elective affinities' (p. 2). All five developments are presented with the adjectival label 'global', which seems to be the core feature of the meaning-systems that are claimed as converging in the period of the Beijing Olympiad and Games. This is a bold claim: that one sporting mega-event crystallizes political, economic, cultural, and social changes at all conceivable levels of social organization.

The boldness of the conception may blur the specifics of the analysis, though, and the temptation in the application of the concept is to find more and more corroborating cases of affinities. Nevertheless, the concept has sustained a high profile in historical and sociological research, as it warns against premature claims of determinacy and encourages the recognition of important forms of connectedness of belief-systems across different spheres. There is a lesson here for historically-minded sport scholars for whom the (always valuable) close analysis of a sport culture or sporting institution is sometimes accomplished without the location of the analysis in the broader social and cultural context.

References

Weber, M. (1948) *From Max Weber*, edited by H. Gerth and C. Wright Mills, London: Routledge and Kegan Paul; Close, P., Askew, D. and Xin, X. (2007) *The Beijing Olympiad: The Political Economy of a Sporting Mega-Event*, London: Routledge.

electrocardiography (ECG) The recording of the electrical signals produced by the contraction of the cardiac muscle fibres. The small voltages produced (*see* ELECTROMYOGRAPHY) are picked up by electrodes on the body surface, amplified, and displayed on a screen or printed on to paper (the electrocardiogram). The four chambers of the heart contract and relax in a precise sequence which results in the characteristic pattern of the ECG. The electrical waves of the ECG are closely related to the mechanical events of the cardiac cycle. Stated broadly, the P wave represents atrial contraction, the QRS complex represents ventricular contraction, and the T wave represents ventricular relaxation. The rhythm and shape of the ECG signal is of great value in the diagnosis of certain forms of heart disease. Diagnosis is taken from a 12-lead ECG. An electrode is attached to each wrist and each ankle and a further six electrodes are placed on the surface of the chest in a semi-circular pattern running from the sternum to the left armpit. The voltages from the electrodes are summed in various combinations to, in effect, 'view' the heart from different directions to increase the diagnostic potential. In the healthy body the main value of electrocardiography is to provide an accurate count of the heart rate. The largest voltage arises from left ventricular contraction and produces the R-wave spike of the electrical signal, which can be easily discriminated from the other waves or electrical noise and conveniently counted. Short-range telemetric devices (so-called heart-rate watches) use a chest strap with two electrodes to obtain an ECG which is crude but adequate for rate determination. Microprocessors in the chest strap transmit the heart rate to a data-logging unit worn on the wrist.

electromyography (EMG) The recording of the electrical signals produced by muscle action. When a muscle is stimulated by a nerve impulse there is a reduction in the electrical potential of the muscle cell (polarization) as the muscle is activated, followed by repolarization as the muscle recovers. The sum of these voltage changes from all the fibres in a muscle, over time, gives rise to the EMG signal. The EMG signal is usually measured by placing pairs of electrodes on the skin directly over the particular muscle under investigation. EMG is an extremely valuable tool for recording activity in muscles since it provides an objective recording of whether a muscle is active, it provides some quantification of the extent of activity, and it can be used to help determine which muscles are active in various movements. However, the practical use of EMG is fraught with difficulties. The small voltages (10 μV to 2 mV), high frequencies (25 to 20,000 Hz), electronic noise, and movement artefacts necessitate careful signal processing. Furthermore, a surface electrode will pick up voltage not only from the closest muscle but also from adjacent ones. Interpretation of the EMG signal is not always easy and, although a theoretically sound measurement technique, the practical use of EMG is mainly restricted to controlled laboratory conditions.

Eliasian Referring to the work of sociologist Norbert Elias (1897–1990), in particular his theory of the *civilizing process and his overall project to establish a figurational or process-sociology approach to the study of society, in which sport was a primary focus for his empirical investigations. *See also* AFFECT CONTROL; CIVILIZING PROCESS; FOOTBALL HOOLIGANISM; HABITUS; PLEASURE; PROCESS SOCIOLOGY; SPORTIZATION.

(⊕) SEE WEB LINKS

• A site dedicated to the works and the legacy of Norbert Elias and his project to establish a figurational, or process, sociology.

Eliot, T. S. (1888–1965) A US-born editor, cultural critic, and poet who spent most of his adult life in England. In his *Notes Towards the Definition of Culture* (1948) Eliot included sport and popular games among his list of 'the characteristic activities and interests of a people'. Of the thirteen items or events in that list, six were sports and two were games: the Derby Day horse race, rowing at the Henley Regatta, sailing at Cowes, the twelfth of August beginning of the grouse-shooting season, a (in most likelihood football) cup final, and dog races; the pin table and the dartboard were the games. In listing both elite and popular sporting practices and events, Eliot recognized the cultural significance of the sporting sphere.

elites Groups in a society that are by definition small and influential, with interlocking relationships and interdependent interests and networks; these networks might straddle politics, business, and other spheres of social and public life, such as sport or the arts. Much of the control and administration of sport can be seen to be rooted in such networks. The term elite was established by the 19th-century Italian Vilfredo Pareto (1848–1923), following up the ideas of his compatriot Gaetano Mosca (1858–1941), in his application of the term to the ruling few. Pareto's study *The Mind and Society* (1935) also borrowed the categories of the lion and the fox from Niccolò *Machiavelli. Lions have strength and courage and stimulate change, while foxes are cunning and compromising and have the qualities to rule by stealth rather than mere strength. In attributing such qualities to types of necessary elite, and the circulation between them, Pareto showed how elites, in compositional adjustments, can sustain their ruling power.

Elite theory is highly neglected in sports studies, and has much potential to illuminate the study of sport organizations and sport business. Consider the ease with which minority elite sports gain prestigious sponsorship deals; or the overlapping membership of bodies such as the *International Olympic Committee and other sports organizations such as the *Fédération Internationale de Football Association (FIFA); or the invitations that might be made across networks, such as FIFA's (accepted) invitation to Sebastian (Lord) Coe, leader of London 2012's successful bid to host the Summer Olympics, to chair its inaugural 'independent' ethics committee in 2006. A study of the way in which high-profile sport administration and organization actually operate would without doubt benefit from situating such cases in the context of elite theory and analysis, and even considering their modus operandi on the basis of the categories of the lion and the fox.

emic and etic analysis Categories in linguistics adapted as analytical terms in anthropology. Emic refers to those values seen as indigenous to a particular culture or society; an etic analysis recognizes the relevance of more generalized modes of understanding, in which values are seen to characterize numerous cultures and/or societies. Emic and etic analysis has had limited recognition in sports studies, but has much potential for sharpening analytical understandings of sport's culturally specific formations alongside its increasingly cross-cultural and global profile.

emotion A psychological state arousing feelings such as happiness, fear, excitement, anger, love, etc. For each emotion there is (a) subjective experience of that emotion, (b) physiological change, such as a racing heartbeat or flushing of the skin, and (c) behaviour, such as smiling or running away. How these interrelate is the subject of much psychological theorizing. Sport can elicit extremes of emotion before competition (e.g. *anxiety), during competition (e.g. frustration or anger at the referee or an opponent), and after competition (e.g. depression following a poor performance). *Sport and exercise psychology has developed a range of techniques to help athletes cope with these demands.

empathy The quality of understanding the experiences and feelings of another person or culture. This was a central principle for Max Weber's concept of *Verstehen. An ability to understand the other is a fundamental premise for comparative and international analysis of sport, though it is disputed by some arguments favouring *cultural relativism. The capacity to empathize is also significant for interpersonal relationships and dynamics in sport, in both team dynamics and personal performance; the efficacy of a coach–athlete relationship would be undermined by a coach's failure to see the athlete's perspective, and seek to identify with his or her emotions.

empirical A term referring to evidence based in observations, experiments, or evidence-generating studies such as surveys, rather than isolated discrete theory or mere speculation. The term has been use in an exaggerated and misleading fashion to equate with *empiricism. Empirical data-generation is vital for any adequate understanding of the place of sport in contemporary culture, an understanding of the place of sport in the minds of individuals and the collective expressions of groups, and for analysis of the physiological and biomechanical factors affecting, framing, and constraining performance. All empirical evidence needs also to be located in adequate conceptual and theoretical frameworks, and contextualized in terms of its limitations. But evidence—empirical data—is central to the informed understanding of sport and sport performance; to deny this is to retreat into the realms of indulgent speculation.

empiricism Although the term 'empiricism' has its roots in British philosophy of the 16th and 17th centuries, referring to the testability of knowledge by empirical observation (obviously a radical, secular intervention), it has come to have a narrower meaning: a concentration on the generation of empirical knowledge—facts and data—and often the sophisticated statistical elaboration and manipulation of those facts and their interrelationships. Such preoccupation with the facts has often been seen to be at the expense of conceptual analysis and theoretically informed interpretation. The US sociologist C. Wright Mills (*The Sociological Imagination*, 1959) identified abstracted empiricism as an extreme form of this tendency: an undoubted skill, in which a myriad of facts is produced but little contextual knowledge. In other words, we know more and more about less and less. A good test of whether rigorous empirical work has passed over the boundary and entered empiricist territory is to ask the 'So what?' question: we know so much about who plays what sport and where but so what?; we know more and more about the limits of endurance in *aerobic activity, but so what? If this cannot be answered with some conceptual clarity or theoretical insight, then the data sets and the facts will be marooned in empiricist isolation.

employment A contract between two parties, the employer and the employee, pertaining to the nature of and remuneration for a specified form of work or labour. In high-performance sport, the nature of employment, the employees' rights, and the contractual detail on remuneration (payment by results, or bonuses on achievement) have come to dominate sport's equivalent of employment law. Most sport enthusiasts, participating in sport at lower levels, are neither employer nor employee, and the sporting encounter and relationship is a different one in which sociability and reciprocal voluntary labour are the core of the social dynamic and human exchange. The etymology of the term 'employment' is rooted in the sense of putting something or someone to use in accomplishing a task of the employer's making; in sport culture, particularly in a competitive encounter in the classic amateur mode, the human dynamic is different—cooperative, reciprocal, (in principle) more equal. Employment in businesses in which sport is the main activity are clear forms of employer–employee contact, related to three main forms of employment: technical jobs, in training, teaching, organizing, and developing the sport; administrative, management, and commercial employment managing facilities, sport associations, and clubs; and work in maintenance (groundsman of the football field or the tennis court) and service provision (the health-club receptionist). *See also* FULL EMPLOYMENT; UNEMPLOYMENT.

encoding and decoding 1. In psychology, encoding is the ability to convert information into a different but retrievable form, usually in the memory; it is unsurprisingly critical to game plans or performance strategies. 2. In cultural and media studies, encoding is the way in which texts are put together, and decoding the way in which these can be disassembled for their meaning; the approach has been widely used in analyses of sport media and the juxtaposition of the visual and the printed word in those media. Stuart Hall's 'Encoding and Decoding in Television Discourse' (University of Birmingham Centre for Contemporary Cultural Studies, Stencilled Paper no. 7, 1973) was highly influential in developing a cultural analysis of media forms that was not based in the concept of the circulation circuit or the loop. Hall argued that moments of encoding and decoding are '*determinate* moments' (original italics), so that raw historical events are not simply transmitted by the television newscast: 'Events can only be signified within the aural-visual forms of the televisual discourse'. As Hall puts it, an event must become a 'story' before it becomes a communicative event. This emphasis on the structuring of the media form highlighted the role of the media in constructing sport discourse and narratives, not merely relaying the action from the site of the live action to the viewer. *See also* DECONSTRUCTION.

encounter From the Old French *encontrer*, 'to meet face to face', the term can refer to any such meeting between two or more people. It has also come to refer to sporting competitions, as a kind of synonym for 'match' or 'competitive event'. In social psychology, Erving *Goffman, in his brilliant but idiosyncratic observational style, demonstrated the richness of the concept, and its potential for understanding relatively small-scale interactions in everyday life.

enculturation US cultural anthropology has used the term to refer to the learning processes whereby an individual becomes a full member of a group, *culture, or *subculture. The term refers to the same process that sociologists call *socialization. Enculturation can involve formal inductions into the culture, for instance registering as the member of a sports club on the basis of an understanding of documented rules, and informal knowledge acquisition, such as following non-verbal cues or picking up the *argot (the specialist language) of the sport and sport culture.

endomorph *See* SOMATOTYPE.

endurance exercise Endurance is the time for which a specified power output, force, or speed of movement can be maintained. Endurance exercise refers to sports and activities such as marathon running which are maintained for a lengthy period of time, typically 30 minutes or more. The great majority of the energy required is derived from *aerobic pathways.

energy expenditure The rate at which the body uses energy, usually expressed in *calories per minute or per day. The body's daily energy expenditure comprises the resting metabolic rate (the minimal amount of energy required to support physiological functions, about 1,600 kilocalories or 65 per cent of a normal person's total daily energy expenditure); the thermic effect of a meal (the increase in metabolism needed to digest and metabolize food, about 250 kilocalories or 10 per cent of the daily total); and the energy required for voluntary activity (daily life plus sport and exercise, about 650 kilocalories or 25 per cent of the daily total). The energy expenditure of sports and exercise varies with their intensity. Activities such as golf require a relatively low energy expenditure of about 6 kilocalories per minute compared with football (10 kilocalories per minute) or jogging (14 kilocalories per minute). The highest rate of energy expenditure is seen in Olympic endurance athletes, where a cross-country skier or a heavyweight rower might achieve up to 30 kilocalories per minute. The MET has proved a popular alternative means of describing energy expenditure since it takes a person's size into account and provides simple numbers. The MET is defined as a multiple of resting metabolic rate; for a 65-kilogram person 1 MET would be equal to an energy expenditure of about 1.1 kilocalories per minute. Walking might require about 4 METS and leisure swimming about 6 METS.

In some sports the primary desire is to maximize the rate of energy expenditure (e.g. running as fast as possible) and this is achieved as a result of *training and *economy and efficiency of movement. In some sports, such as football or rugby, the relationship between energy expenditure and performance is more complex, since these sports require skilful technique and an optimal balance between tactical positioning and movement around the pitch. In other sports, such as bowls or golf, the rate of energy expenditure is largely irrelevant. In health terms, energy expenditure is important in *weight control and *obesity.

epidemiology Originally the scientific study of epidemics, locating the time and place of diseases and illnesses. More generally, this has come to refer to the study and analysis of patterns of illness and disease. In relation to sport and exercise science, an epidemiological dimension can map the distribution of sport injuries, complementing the *aetiology, which concentrates upon causes.

epistemology The branch of philosophy dealing with the nature of knowledge, from the Greek *epistēmē*, meaning 'knowledge'. Epistemology is of central relevance to any academic enquiry, as it addresses the question of how we know what we know, and demands thought-through and rigorous answers concerning the status of knowledge claimed for and within any academic discipline or research. In sports studies, sport and exercise science is, as a discipline within the natural sciences, widely concerned with the testing of theories on the basis of indisputable or proven empirical data, and with the goal of explanation; sociocultural studies are often more concerned with a wider variety of approaches to knowledge generation, and the development of forms of understanding (*Verstehen*) and interpretation. These approaches share the legacy of the scientific revolutions of the Enlightenment, however, in that knowledge (about sport and associated phenomena) is a form of transcendence, or supersession, of dependence upon beliefs, opinions, or prejudices.

An awareness of epistemological issues does not constitute a necessary affiliation to one epistemological camp or another. A perfectly valid study of, say, the motivations, performance, and culture of a group of veteran distance runners could include the objectives of both explanation and understanding, using robust physical measures of performance, questionnaires on the runner's reasons for and perceived benefits of running, and observation of the subculture of the group. Such multi-method work in an integrated study renders traditional splits between rationalists (for whom knowledge is based on pre-established categories or concepts) and empiricists (for whom direct experience of the world is the basis of all knowledge) irrelevant if not obsolete. *See also* INTERPRETIVISM; METHODOLOGY; POSITIVISM.

equality The state of being equal, though this can vary greatly as to whether the question is one of, say, equality of opportunity or equality of outcome. It is a complex interdisciplinary concept, drawing on philosophy, politics, and economics as well as sociology. In sport, a sort of equality is assumed so that genuine competition can take place. Boxing has weight categories; golf has handicaps (as did many early forms of track racing); sports have leagues based on achievement and mobility (and of course resources). Allen Guttmann (*From Ritual to Record: The*

Nature of Modern Sports, 1978) listed 'equality' in his seven-fold typology of the characteristics of modern sport, though all the processes and possibilities underlying an equality that is fundamental to the sporting encounter are often based on structurally rigid forms of *inequality in a society or culture.

equestrianism The training of horses for specific performances or tasks, which can be for the purposes of hunting, racing, agriculture, war, or display/exhibition as in the equestrian event in the modern Olympics, from 1912 onwards. Three forms of competition within the equestrian event are dressage, show jumping, and endurance (three-day event). The term 'dressage' is from the French meaning 'to train' or 'to break in', linked to the preparation of horses for military operations, and then adapted in the splendour of display units such as Vienna's Spanish Riding School, built in 1729–35. Other cavalry schools in France, Germany, Switzerland, and Sweden cemented this tradition within Europe, and it was Swedish influence that gained the recognition of the event at Stockholm's 1912 Olympic Games (Sweden also won the individual dressage event in 1912, and at the 1920 and 1924 Games). Show jumping or leaping emerged in the latter half of the 19th century in the USA, France, Russia, and Britain, and was also adopted as an Olympic sport under the Swedish influence, and featuring the military. The three-day event derived also in part from military traditions of long-distance cavalry training. In the Olympics, riders must wear formal dress unless they are members of a military organization or a police force, in which case they can wear uniform. The event is the only one in which animals feature at the Summer Olympics, and in which men and women have competed routinely against each other on equal terms. Only rarely have non-Europeans or non-North Americans triumphed; in one case Brazilian Rodrigo Pessoa was upgraded to the gold medal for the Athens 2004 individual jumping event, on the disqualification of Ireland's Cian O'Connor after his horse Waterford Crystal had tested positive for doping substances known to be used to calm a horse's nerves. Equestrianism is a costly sport; its place in the Olympic programme is a reminder of the legacy of the privileged upper classes and the military to the sporting calendar.

Équipe, L' A French daily newspaper dedicated to sport, founded in 1900 as *L'Auto-Vélo*, reflecting the popularity of motor vehicles and *cycling, and from 1903 the promoter of the *Tour de France, the success of which rapidly established the paper as France's primary sport-based publication. The spectacular initiative of the Tour undermined the dominance of *Le Vélo*, which had been founded in 1892 and had established popular long-distance bicycle races between French cities. Legal action by *Le Vélo* led, ironically, to *L'Auto-Vélo* dropping the second term from its name in the same year as the inaugural Tour, and as *L'Auto* driving *Le Vélo* out of business the following year. The editor of the paper, Henri Desgrange (1865–1940), represented powerful economic and political interests on the centre-right of the political spectrum, and though the initial daily circulation figure of the paper was 20,000, with the advent of the Tour its daily sales rose to 30,000 during the build-up to the event, and 65,000 during the race; by 1913, its average daily circulation was 120,000, and in 1914 during the race itself in July its average daily circulation was 320,000, a pattern sustained up to World War II. *L'Auto* organized the Tour from 1903 to 1914, and 1919 to 1939.

Association of the newspaper with the German occupation saw the title banned in post-war France, but in 1946 one of Desgrange's chief assistants of the 1930s founded *L'Équipe*, which, following national legislation, bought up the assets of *L'Auto* and acquired half of the rights to the Tour. The other half was owned by a Parisian daily paper (*Le Parisien Libéré*) with which *L'Équipe* organized the event for close to two decades, until in 1964 *L'Équipe* was bought by Éditions Émilien Amaury, owner of *Le Parisien*. The Amaury Group established the Société du Tour de France to run the Tour and other races (Christopher S. Thompson, *The Tour de France: A Cultural History*, 2006). *L'Équipe* has also stimulated international sporting competitions in football (soccer), basketball, and skiing: drafting a template in 1955 for the football European Champion Clubs' Cup, popularly known as the European Cup, and then the *UEFA Champions League, first contested in 1955-6; providing the trophy for the European Cup for Champion Clubs, an annual inter-club competition for basketball clubs first staged in 1957-8; and innovating and sponsoring (jointly, with a mineral water company) the World Alpine Ski Cup in 1967.

The longevity of the dominance of *L'Équipe*, despite challenges from rivals and dips in circulation figures, constitutes a form of *monopoly; economists identify market dominance when a company secures at least 50 per cent of sales, and in France at the end of the 1990s Amaury/*L'Équipe* held more than 70 per cent. In this sense the group defies any neoclassical model of perfect competition, representing a 'compulsory partner for readers, for the sports movement and for advertisers; . . . even more so, since this hegemony is enduring, even growing' (Frédéric Bolotny and Jean-François Bourg, 'The Demand for Media Coverage', in Wladimir Andreff and Stefan Szymanski, eds, *Handbook on the Economics of Sport*, 2009). In achieving this hegemony, *L'Équipe* has exploited to the full its combination of quality production and low price (there was no increase in daily price between 1988 and 2002, and sometimes prices were actually lowered). Defending its monopoly in 1987 when a potential rival *Le Sport* was launched, it introduced layout changes, new headings, colour, more pages, and added to its staff and correspondents throughout the world. By 2003, its sales stood at 327,000, and the Amaury group was embracing rather than jeopardized by the internet; its website L'Équipe.fr was a market leader with sixty million hits per month. Amaury also established specialist titles for football, tennis, and cycling, as well as its magazine edition, and its own television channel. It could generate as well as report the sports news; and at special moments, such as the victory of the French men's national football team at the 1998 World Cup, achieve astronomical one-off sales of more than a million and a half. The story of *L'Équipe*'s dominance in its national market, and its role in the emergence of international sporting competition for more than a century, is an illustration of the economic and entrepreneurial influences on the making of modern sport culture.

equity A form of justice based on the perceived fairness of a situation. The term has been widely appropriated in sport policy and interventionist critique of institutionalized sport practices which appear to be based upon privilege and tradition, favouring particular social classes, genders, or other social groupings. In equity theory, fairness is based upon an understanding and recognition that outcomes should be based upon inputs in ways that do not privilege individuals and groups by skewing inputs in their favour. If unfairness is perceived, resource distribution or access to opportunities should be adjusted. Sport has a real challenge in this area in the sphere of performance sport, as the competitive dynamic must favour the few over the many; the construction of fair conditions and circumstances is of course an elusive, probably unattainable goal, though. Who is to say whether US tennis player John McEnroe, in his time at Stanford University, had a more advantageous launching pad than Arthur Ashe at UCLA (University of California Los Angeles)? Sport equity may be more achievable at levels of participation and recreational sport, by the sustained commitment to open up access to sports and teaching and coaching expertise to people of all backgrounds. That of course is next to impossible; therefore, sport equity remains a worthy aspiration, but a doomed policy.

ergogenic aids A broad-ranging term, derived from the Greek *ergon* ('work') to cover substances, techniques, and equipment that improve sports performance. The main focus in the study of ergogenic aids has been on the manipulation of the body's physiology to enhance energy output. A wide range of drugs have been used to stimulate training or performance. Sport is peppered with examples, from Thomas Hicks, the 1904 Olympic marathon victor who received strychnine and brandy during the race, to the ignominious history of substance abuse in the *Tour de France. The *International Olympic Committee bans several categories of drugs due to their ergogenic effect, including *anabolic steroids, analgesics, beta blockers, *cannabinoids, *diuretics, glucocorticoids, peptide hormones, and stimulants, all of which improve performance by conferring a physiological advantage. In more recent years, growth hormone and erythropoietin (EPO) have featured. There are several pharmacological procedures which are not banned but which do result in an ergogenic effect. Caffeine is a controlled drug in Olympic competition, but only above a threshold level. In more modest doses it still creates an ergogenic effect through increasing arousal and by stimulating fat metabolism. Ingesting sodium bicarbonate to induce alkalosis increases the buffering potential of the body and delays the build-up of acid during anaerobic exercise, so allowing a greater power output. Ingesting creatine in the form of a powder providing many times the normal intake for several days increases the stores of the energy compound phosphocreatine and improves high-intensity activities such as sprinting.

Non-pharmacological ergogenic physiological manipulations include *warm-up and *carbohydrate loading. More recently, exposure to hypoxia (low oxygen level) has been of particular interest. *Altitude training has been the traditional approach but training at altitude poses practical difficulties for many athletes, which has led to the development of individual 'hypoxic' tents and chambers where an athlete can train or sleep to gain the same effect as travelling to a mountain. Other ergogenic procedures arise from sports psychology and sports technology. Sports psychologists have developed a battery of psychological skills training techniques to help athletes in competition (e.g. *relaxation, *imagery, and *anxiety control). Developments in sports technology are legion, from the golf club and the running shoe to the fibreglass vaulting pole and the artificial hockey pitch; all have a significant effect on sports performance.

Central to the discussion of ergogenic aids is the question of morality, and legality as defined by the specific rules of each sport governing body. In some cases, for example the replacement of wooden rackets by metal ones in tennis, the ergogenic advantage is readily embraced by a rule change and the sport continues as before. In other cases an ergogenic aid, such as the use of beta blockers by snooker players to improve precision by reducing tremor and slowing down the heart rate, opens up a challenging ethics debate since, for some players, the drug is an essential medical treatment for heart disease. In other sports, such as cycling, the governing body places tight restrictions on the design of a cycle but it is considered entirely honourable to use sophisticated engineering to work within these rules to gain a mechanical advantage over other cyclists. In some cases, such as the use of hypoxic training to improve endurance performance by stimulating red blood cell production, the ergogenic technique is recognized as 'natural' and therefore acceptable, whereas the same effect produced by a drug is outlawed. Overall there is little logical pattern to what is, and what is not, an allowable ergogenic aid.

ergonomics The scientific study of the interrelationship of machines and human beings, based in approaches to understanding factors affecting industrial production, efficiency, and output at the workplace. In industrial psychology, it has broadened into the analysis of how particular jobs, and the work environment, fit people with certain physiological characteristics. In sport, ergonomic approaches look at engineering possibilities and solutions for athlete–equipment relationships, in the design of racing machines on land and water (racing cars, bicycles, sailboats, and canoes for example).

espionage and sport Sport and spies appear at first an unlikely pairing, but the incipient and then expansive internationalism of sport make it ideal for the apparently innocent global movement of selected individuals; and within certain societies, the sport club or the leisure outing may be the informal setting in which cautionary fronts are dropped and reportable sentiments uttered. At the heart of the *Cold War, the tense political rivalry between the US-led capitalist West and the USSR-led communist world, international teams and squads could cross borders unscrutinized, including advisers, alleged medical specialists, attachés, shadowy diplomatic figures in the Olympic circus. International relations experts have been known to train in specialist institutes in Washington DC, and then appear in the line-up of the Olympic team's personnel. One US academic close to the Olympic movement has asked, but requested not to be quoted on this: 'Are there spies in American sport?' In the Cold War at least, the answer would have been an unequivocal 'yes'. The US's international relations with China have warmed in recent decades, as have in recent years even those with Cuba, but the rationale for the use of sport as a vehicle for espionage retains some currency. With relation to forms of intra-societal surveillance—spying within the community, or even the family—the former German Democratic Republic's *Stasi remains the most notorious case.

ESPN A US cable television network established in 1979 and specializing in sports coverage, positioning itself as 'The World Leader in Sports'. ESPN is the acronym of Entertainment and Sports Programming Network, and the channel broadcasts 24 hours a day in a successful mix of live coverage, playback and highlights, features, sport gossip, and match analysis. Its website also provides fantasy games for fans. The SportsCenter slot has broadcast more than 30,000 times, and runs its own web and blog profile in a self-referencing cycle of fan chat, video highlights, and celebrity gossip. The company has created and not just reported sports, instigating the annual Summer X Games (Extreme Games) in 1994, and the annual Winter X Games from 1997. In September 2009, ESPN covered the US Open Tennis Championship live for the first time and has also covered English Premier League soccer, consolidating its increasingly dominant place in the sport-media marketplace.

essentialism The tendency to explain or account for a phenomenon in terms of just one influence or factor, whether sociological, psychological, or physiological. For instance, to say that sport is *only* about money, or to claim that play is *only* about pleasure, or to propose that performance is *only* about diet, is to reduce a complex phenomenon to a single essence. Essentialist accounts have been sought by rigorous scientists intent on establishing definitive theoretical truths, but in social science the term is usually now reserved for flawed accounts that claim too much in far too certain a fashion.

ethics, codes of 1. For performers in modern sport, intangible codes of conduct based upon the reciprocal respect of competitors. When an athlete does something particularly ethical, such as over-ruling a line judge in tennis, or deliberately refusing to score a goal in football when an opponent lies prostrate and injured, this makes headlines, demonstrating the lack of any developed ethical code. 2. For sports studies researchers, ethical codes abound, discipline by discipline. Scholars and researchers should consult these as appropriate, but always considering for whose protection the code is written—the subject/respondent, or the researcher and his/her employer. In matters of public interest, as in the ethical reminders of the UK's National Union of Journalists, an ethical decision is taken in terms of the interests of the public, not the protection of any individual subject.

(⊕) SEE WEB LINKS

- The site of Britain's National Union of Journalists, with an ethics subsection listing its professional code of conduct.
- The site of the American Psychological Association, including its ethical framework based on its five core ethical principles.
- The site of the UK's Social Research Association, including its statement on the four fundamental obligations of the researcher.
- The site of the British Sociological Association, including its 61 points comprising its Statement of Ethical Practice.

ethnicity A distinctive set of characteristics or features that allows a particular grouping of individuals to set themselves apart from another group. These might be cultural characteristics such as religion, politics, or language, and sources of ethnicity are much wider than those of biologically determined race. In the southern Pyrenean areas of France and Spain, for instance, a Rugby League club was formed in the early 2000s, playing in Perpignan, France, but called the Catalans Dragons, evoking the ancient kingdom of Catalunya in a contemporary political revitalization of that geographical, linguistic, and cultural identity. In the religiously divided context of Northern Ireland, sectarian groups following different football clubs and sporting cultures could also see themselves as discrete ethnic groups.

ethnocentricism The tendency to evaluate an unfamiliar culture in terms of one's own culture, values, and individual experience. Avoiding ethnocentrism is one of the defining features of the *sociological imagination, according to Anthony Giddens (*Sociology: A Brief but Critical Introduction*, 1982). For ethnocentrism is the social scientific sin of studying other cultures and societies on the basis of one's own experiences and perspectives. An ethnocentric judgement has also often attributed an inferiority to the society or culture under scrutiny. Proper social scientific understanding must, though, be anchored in a recognition of the specific nature of the culture and the society under scrutiny, in their own contexts. Understanding sporting cultures in unfamiliar social and cultural contexts requires that, however different the sport or the fan culture might be, it is interpreted in its own terms. Bullfighting, for instance, must be located in the histories, traditions, and choices of those aficionados for whom it is a major cultural practice; fox hunting should be understood as a particular preference of a privileged class and its cross-class countryside-based supporters. Of course, as these examples have been chosen deliberately to highlight, the extreme version of a commitment to avoid ethnocentrism means the suspension of judgement and the elimination of moral evaluation and critical intervention from the social scientific framework.

ethnography In early anthropology, the study, from a basis of close observation and adequate immersion, of a selected culture, initially in classic anthropological fieldwork focusing upon whole individual human societies. Ethnography is both the act of undertaking such a study, and the written account that is produced of the society or culture. Outstanding sport-based ethnographies include Alan Klein's study of bodybuilding culture in California (*Little Big Men: Bodybuilding Subculture and Gender Construction*, 1993); John Sugden's comparative studies of boxing cultures in the East Coast USA, Havana, and Northern Ireland (*Boxing and Society: An International Analysis*, 1996); Loïc Wacquant's 'Pugs at Work: Bodily Capital and Bodily Labour among Professional Boxers' (*Body & Society*, 1995); and Belinda Wheaton's study of windsurfing culture (*Journal of Sport & Social Issues*, 1998). All of these studies required convincing entry into the culture under study, and close and regular interaction with the people in the sport culture (whether the researcher role was declared or not). Controversies may arise as to the authenticity and credibility of the ethnographer's account, and reported-on subjects in particular settings have sometimes disputed this account. But this is both the strength and weakness of the ethnographer's position: unless someone revisits the setting in a systematic fashion, the ethnographer's account can claim indisputable validity.

Too often the term ethnography is used interchangeably with *participant observation, when the latter could be achieved on a much shorter-term and partially focused basis. Ethnographers do recognize that long-term immersion

might be impractical for a number of reasons—such as the demands of an academic
career, or the difficulty of entry if, for instance, the ageing researcher is interested in
youth culture—and so have talked (not altogether convincingly) of ethnographic
interviewing, ethnographic visiting, or ethnographically flavoured fieldwork
excursions. Ethnographic writing has also been challenged by postmodern-inspired
debates about the privileging of the ethnographer in the production of the
ethnographic report or analysis. Despite these difficulties, doubts, and challenges,
ethnography still has much to offer the study of sport in its focus upon sheer detail
and its capacity to portray the distinctive make-up of a particular sporting culture.

ethnomethodology A once popular and very controversial approach to the
study of everyday life, which emerged in the 1960s through the studies of US
sociologist Harold Garfinkel (1917–87). The term itself derived from the Greek,
ethnos, meaning a nation or a people, combined with 'ology' as the study of, and
'method' as the methods of everyday life; ethnomethodology was therefore the
study of people's methods of everyday accomplishments. It embraced a range
of empirical foci, from sophisticated analysis of recorded conversations to
observational studies of how people walking along a pavement ensured that they
did not bump into each other. Garfinkel was urging that study of the practical
logics of everyday social life become the core focus of sociology.

   Ethnomethodology has had few champions in sports studies, and no sustained
application to sporting situations. One exercise that Garfinkel famously gave his
students was to continually and stubbornly ask 'What do you mean?' in
conversations, the assumption being that stimulating a breakdown of the tacitly
agreed social order would reveal the essential nature of that order. In sport, of
course, to make such an intervention would be to end the sporting encounter before
it had begun; and in sport, the rules are more explicit than in some of the cases
of practical everyday logics that ethnomethodologists set out to illuminate.
Therefore it is unsurprising that the approach has had little impact in sports studies,
though its emphasis on the social significance of talk and conversation has been
recognized as of value in the broader sociological field. It is in this area—the
study of fan talk, web-exchanges, *sport chatter—that ethnomethodology may yet
have an impact upon the study of sport culture.

etic *See* EMIC AND ETIC ANALYSIS.

Etruria, sport in Etruscan society, based in the geographical region of what
became northern Italy, pre-dated and was coterminous with classical Greek
(Athenian) civilization, and overlapped with the emergent Roman republic. Often
absorbed into generalized accounts of classic Mediterranean culture and
civilization, the Etruscans were actually considered by Greek and Roman writers
to be different from other societies of their time. Scholarly consensus recognizes
that Etruscans have prehistoric antecedents in Etruria itself, and that Etruscan
civilization was influenced by Greek society (though Etruscans, classified as
'barbarian', were barred from the Greeks' four-yearly athletic festivals). Sporting
events in Etruria were widely associated with death and represented in funerary art.
Funeral games may have included brutal and unequal struggles between human
victim and animal, and illustrations of forms of boxing, wrestling, and tug-of-war

have been preserved in Etruscan tombs. The Etruscans took other sports from the Greeks, such as discus-throwing. At pan-Etruscan festivals, a range of activities was staged, as depicted on an Etruscan black-figure amphora of the later 6th century BC. One probable Etruscan legacy to Roman sporting culture, scholars agree, was the notion of the public sporting event. The first laying out of the *Circus Maximus at Rome may have been modelled on Etruscan precedent, and Roman *chariot racing drew on Etruscan practice, including the use of three-horse teams and the attire of the charioteer. (*See* G. Barker and T. Rasmussen, *The Etruscans*, 2001.)

European Cup (European Champion Clubs' Cup) *See* UEFA CHAMPIONS LEAGUE.

European Union (EU) A supranational and intergovernmental organization, previously known, up to 1993, as the European Community, and before that as the European Economic Community (EEC). Its more colloquial name was the Common Market, based as it was in forms of pooling of coal and steel resources in 1951–2 by six European nations (Belgium, France, Italy, Luxembourg, the Netherlands, and West Germany). These nations founded the EEC in 1958, based on the previous year's Treaty of Rome. Trade, commerce, and economic policy were the bedrocks of the EEC; the work and politics rather than the sport and leisure of the members' populations was the driving force in its formation. But as numbers have increased— to 25 in 2004—stronger emphases have emerged on cultural policy and mobility of members' citizens, and in this context sport has been found a place on the agenda of the Council of the European Union (and its Commission), one of the legislative bodies of the EU (the other being the directly elected European Parliament). From the 1990s onwards, lobbyists have developed a higher profile for sport in the policy-making deliberations of the EU and its Council, the *Nice Declaration and successive debates and statements seeking to articulate the distinctiveness of a European model of sport.

SEE WEB LINKS

- The vast, expansive official website of the European Union, detailing its missions and aims and those of its constituent elements, including cultural policy initiatives.

event study The study in detail of a particular case, and from an economic perspective all of the financial dimensions of that case, in particular in terms of projections, stated and hidden costs, and outcomes. From the annual local sports tournament in the community to the national final between professional teams, and through to the big international spectacles of world sport, such focused and balanced study is necessary for any informed understanding of the benefits and impact of the event. *See also* COST–BENEFIT ANALYSIS; ECONOMIC IMPACT.

exercise addiction A psychological dependence on regular exercise, usually daily but also more frequent. The addicted exerciser suffers mood disturbances such as anxiety and guilt if prevented from exercising. The addict will often still exercise even when injured or ill and will manipulate social and family arrangements to ensure they are able to complete the day's exercise bout. The form of exercise is usually non-competitive, simple, and individual, such as running or a gym class. A common path to addiction is shown by a previously sedentary adult who takes up exercise and finds the increased fitness, loss of weight, and improved self-esteem to be positively reinforcing. What is initially a positive health-enhancing habit is taken to excess and the exercise addict continues to believe that their level of exercise is essential and will lead to further improvement in health despite objective evidence to the contrary. Exercise addiction can be associated with *eating disorders since the physical work involved in exercise is a potent means of burning calories and reducing body fat. It has been proposed that exercise addiction has a physiological basis, by stimulating an increase in the level of endorphins which reduce pain and produce a sense of euphoria, but the evidence is mixed.

exercise adherence The adoption and maintenance of a regimen of exercise. Adherence is of particular relevance to exercise for the purposes of health and well-being in the general population. Despite widespread public knowledge and understanding of the benefits of regular exercise, over 75 per cent of the general UK population (2008 data) take insufficient exercise (i.e. less than the recommended minimum of 5 × 30 minutes of moderate exercise per week). Furthermore, typically more than half of the people who start an exercise programme discontinue within six months. The factors influencing adherence are many; they include personal factors such as age, attitudes, motivation, and prior experience, and environmental factors such as social support from family and friends, access to facilities, and cost.

Several psychological theories attempt to explain exercise adherence in terms of planned behaviours, stages of change, and social cognition. The theory of planned behaviour suggests that exercise intentions derive from an individual's attitude, their perception of their own ability to undertake exercise, and social norms. The transtheoretical model of changes proposes five stages of behavioural change: precontemplation, contemplation, preparation, action, and maintenance. Individuals progress through these stages and movement between them may be cyclical because efforts to establish and maintain an exercise habit may not be successful. Social cognition theory proposes that personal, behavioural, and environmental factors are interacting determinants. An individual's belief that they can successfully perform a behaviour (level of self-efficacy) is a key attribute and a high self-efficacy is associated with a high likelihood of engagement in the behaviour.

The clear benefits of exercise to *health, and the immense social and medical costs associated with inactive lifestyles, have led to considerable efforts by governments to engineer public health policies which encourage exercise adherence. The main settings for initiatives are in schools, workplaces, and the community, and through the promotion of recreational opportunities and modes of active transport such as walking and cycling.

exercise physiology The study of the function of the human body during exercise; also sometimes known as sports physiology or work physiology. Physiology is concerned with the structures of the body (such as muscles, bone, heart, and lungs), the metabolism of the body (such as the biochemistry of energy supply), and the coordination of processes (through the nervous system and hormones). Exercise physiology places a particular emphasis on responses to acute situations (single bouts of exercise, such as running a race or playing a football match) and to chronic situations (repeated bouts of exercise, such as over three months of a physical training programme), and in the context of both the high-intensity efforts of competitive sport and the moderate-intensity efforts of exercise for health. The primary biological systems involved are nutrition, energy metabolism, muscle, the heart and circulation, the pulmonary system, fluid balance, thermoregulation, neural control, growth, and ageing.

The key contexts to which exercise physiology is applied include maximizing power, endurance, and effective muscle action during competitive sport; the adaptations resulting from training; nutrition, energy supply, and weight control; growth and ageing; disease; and coping with unusual environments. Exercise physiologists use a wide range of techniques such as *calorimetry, *electromyography, *electrocardiography, and *fitness testing in their work. Exercise physiology is a theoretical and an applied subject. To the theoretician, exercise is a useful means of stressing the body systems, thus allowing improved investigation of their form and function. To the practitioner, exercise physiology is about working with athletes, coaches, and health professionals to develop strategies and techniques to improve performance and fitness.

exercise prescription A structured programme of physical training designed for a specific purpose or individual. The use of 'prescription' in a quasi-medical sense arises from the recognition that a regimen of exercise can be a valuable contribution to the treatment of a number of medical conditions such as *coronary heart disease, hypertension, and *obesity. A preliminary *fitness test is used to establish the individual's capabilities and the prescription will detail a progressive regime for a period of around 12 weeks tailored to the individual's medical condition and fitness. Exercise prescriptions are common in *exercise referral schemes.

exercise psychology *See* SPORT AND EXERCISE PSYCHOLOGY.

exercise referral schemes A system which links general practitioners and primary health care professionals to public leisure facilities. Referral schemes were developed in the UK as a means of promoting exercise as an adjunct to medical treatment. The schemes are based on the argument that 95 per cent of people will consult a medical practitioner within any three-year period and over 70 per cent of these people are likely to be insufficiently active. Health professionals are therefore ideally placed to promote physical activity since they are trusted by patients and an *exercise prescription can be a valuable part of medical treatment. However, while time, facilities, and expertise are limited within a health care setting, they are available in leisure facilities where qualified professionals can lead structured exercise programmes. Exercise referral schemes are a partnership between health care and exercise professionals.

A typical scheme is designed around twice-weekly exercise for 12 weeks. It takes place at a leisure centre and includes gym activities, swimming, and aerobics. The nature and intensity of the exercise sessions are customized to the individual patient and his or her condition. The programme may also include educational sessions concerning diet and stress management. Referred patients are typically those with conditions such as hypertension, diabetes, *osteoporosis, and a high risk of *coronary heart disease. Exercise referral schemes have been enthusiastically received in the UK and hundreds of thousands of patients have participated. The fundamental structure of a referral scheme is sound but in practice their overall effectiveness is limited. Systematic reviews identify that referral schemes have only a small impact on increasing physical activity, with fewer than 1 in 10 referred patients becoming habitually active. The key problems are the low take-up rates of the *exercise prescription and poor *exercise adherence.

explanation An account that seeks to attribute causality to an identified influence or determinant. Sport and exercise science research aspires to such explanatory accounts so that particular factors can be isolated and understood in their effect upon performance; such explanation is achieved through statistical procedures applied to rigorously generated and observed *empirical data. In sociocultural studies of sport, explanation may be relevant in relatively large-scale surveys, but in *qualitative research accounts are often more provisional, and researchers provide interpretive accounts rather than watertight explanations.

extreme sports Forms of physical activity that either challenge or trangress mainstream and dominant models of sport, or are constructed by the media as a category of thrilling sporting experiences that have dramatic televisual presence and appeal to a cosmopolitan youth market. The US television cable channel *ESPN categorized such sports—BMX biking, *skateboarding, *snowboarding, street luge, for instance—in its creation of the 'X/Extreme Games' (Kyle Kusz, 'Extreme America: The Cultural Politics of Extreme Sports in 1990s America', in Belinda Wheaton, ed., *Understanding Lifestyle Sports: Consumption, Identity and Difference*, 2004). The energy-sustaining drinks company Red Bull, which has a Formula One motor-racing team, launched *The Red Bulletin* ('an almost independent monthly magazine') in 2008: this offered revisionist interpretations of traditional sports such as *hurling, on the passions and myth of 'the fastest field sport in the world', and features on rising stars in activities such as kitesurfing. The activities and sports clustered into such a category are sometimes also called *lifestyle sports, or *whiz sports, and such discussions have echoes of Pierre Bourdieu's labelling of *Californian sports.

Eysenck, Hans Jürgen (1916–97) One of the most influential and widely cited psychologists of the 20th century, Eysenck spent his career in London, England, after fleeing Nazi Germany. His work on intelligence and personality was world-leading, though his claims concerning the relationship between genetics and personality sparked much controversy. His model for the analysis of personality and for the identification of traits has been applied in sport psychology, and the distinction between extrovert and introvert personalities has informed the analysis of athlete behaviour and performance.

FA *See* FOOTBALL ASSOCIATION.

FA Cup The Football Association Challenge Cup, established by England's
*Football Association (FA), and first contested in season 1871–2. It was conceived as
a competition open to 'all clubs belonging to the Association', and based upon a
knock-out principle. Harrow-educated C. W. Alcock (1842–1907), secretary of
the FA, would have played in House Matches at Harrow based on knock-out
contests, and establishing the eventual winner as 'Cock House'. In July 1871 Alcock
and six fellow upper-class *football enthusiasts and organizers met in London at the
offices of the *Sportsman* newspaper and adapted the public school model to an
adult and national scale. This created the first formal, inclusive, knock-out Cup
competition, a format unaltered since, and inspiring countless imitations: 'The
whole joy of the Cup is that it is the most democratic of contests. The giants cannot
stand aloof in their own class' (Geoffrey Green, 'A priceless inspiration', in
Association Football, edited with A.H. Fabian, 1960).

fair play An ethos emanating from the cult of team games and *athleticism in the
British public schools and the universities, often evoking a sense of moral
superiority. Tony Mason writes that 'the dominant sporting ideology in the late
Victorian and Edwardian periods, perhaps 1870–1914, was that of fair play and
the joy of taking part' (*Sport in Britain*, 1988). Its influence was long-lasting, and
J. A. Mangan quotes Sir Thomas Cook, author of *Character and Sportsmanship*
(1927), on the link between an enthusiasm for games and a sense of Anglo-Saxon
superiority: 'We must be worthy of our heritage. We shall keep it by that sense
of fair-play which is bred in our bones and courses through our blood, which makes
a boy play the game' (cited in *Athleticism in the Victorian and Edwardian Public
School: The Emergence and Consolidation of an Educational Ideology*, 1981).
In 1928, a German author, Rudolph Kercher, published his *Fair Play*, equating the
Anglo-Saxon way of playing games with the principles of honour, dignity, and
respect for the rules. In 1976, the International Council of Sport and Physical
Education, along with the *International Olympic Committee, and supported by
UNESCO, produced a *Declaration on Fair Play*, emphasizing that sport's
contribution to the quality of life and to 'the accomplishment of man' was only
possible 'if it is practiced in full accordance with the ideals of fair play'.

As an ethical code, fair play may have been challenged by win-at-all-costs
approaches to sporting competition, but it has continued to attract adherents.
A fair play award committee was established in Paris in 1963 to make Pierre de
*Coubertin Awards to the most deserving athletes and publics; this committee or
bureau was formalized as the International Fair Play Committee in 1973, dedicated

to the 'world-wide defence and promotion of fair play'. International sporting bodies and national sporting associations continue to make much of the fair play ethos, also establishing fair play awards to counter the excesses of 'gamesmanship' and *cheating. *See also* SPORTSMANSHIP.

false consciousness A concept derived from the work of Karl *Marx on the inbuilt inequalities of the capitalist system, relating to the ways in which people might make sense of their place in that system, but in doing so work against their own interests. For example, a late 19th-century factory worker might go to a football match to watch his local team and feel part of a cross-class community as the middle-class administrators look on, the aspiringly socially mobile players perform, and the workers in the crowd cheer. For Marx, such a form of community identification would be a form of false consciousness, as, in any objective view of the capitalist system and its concomitant class structure, the factory worker is exploited and alienated. Beyond the specific Marxist case, the concept has come to refer to broader situations in which an individual's perception of his or her position is not matched by another's reading or interpretation of the objective context. The Marxist concept remains the more powerful variant, in that it suggests that sport (for those who have applied this concept to sport) is a major means of confirming subordination, rather than promoting emancipation. What the Marxist notion lacks is an awareness that subordinated groups can be very aware of their subordination, and know what the outcomes of their sporting commitment might be, but choose to continue (often in negotiated ways) with that with which they are familiar. A more nuanced understanding of such issues was therefore prompted in the thought of Antonio Gramsci and his thinking on *hegemony.

fandom The disposition to follow a particular sport or representative of a sport— either a team, a group, or an individual—with demonstrable, and even extreme, levels of commitment and dedication. The novel *Fever Pitch*, by Nick Hornby, was on its first publication in 1992 subtitled 'A fan's life', and Hornby's self-declared obsession with football provided a focus for writing 'about being a fan', more than a mere *spectator—not just loving the sport, but relating to it in the ways that the Latin basis of the word evokes (*fanaticus* means 'enthusiastic' or 'frenzied'). Sociological work on fandom has focused upon the *subcultures of fans, or the conditions of fandom that have superseded subcultural formations: for instance, Steve Redhead, in *Post-Fandom and the Millennial Blues: The Transformation of Soccer Culture* (1997), wrote of a condition of 'post-fandom' into which we 'are now manifestly born'. He linked this to 'the accelerated hyper-modern culture' that allows the post-fan to relate to the object of adulation in increasingly mediated ways: 'the fragmentary, self-conscious, reflexive, mediated, "artistic" . . . , "style-surfing" . . . notion of what it means to be a fan of soccer, music and fashion'. Social psychological work on fans has explored the attitudes underlying fandom and fan behaviour, and the place of fandom in the constitution of personal and cultural identity.

Fangio, Juan-Manuel (1911–95) An Argentinian-born winner of five World Championships in *motor racing's Formula One/Grand Prix, the son of Italian immigrants. His first racing car was a Model T Ford, a later one a Chevrolet. In racing these innovative new products, he symbolized the glamour and excitement of technological modernity, and as he entered the European racing circuit—sponsored by the Argentinian government—was the figurehead of the new sport that had inaugurated the first World Championship in 1950, winning his five titles between 1951 and 1957.

farm system A system of recruitment and nurturing of young sportsmen and -women in which a smaller club might be supported by a larger club to bring on the talent of the player or athlete prior to a move up to the bigger stage of competition. It is an inhumane term, with overtones of factory-farming and ruthless production, but it is conceived as a relatively sensitive way of finding and grooming sporting talent.

fartlek A Scandinavian-derived term for the combination of fast and short bouts of running with slower and longer bouts, so increasing both *aerobic and *anaerobic capacity. *See also* INTERVAL TRAINING.

fascism, sport in Fascism emerged from the political currents of World War I and its aftermath in Italy. A patriotic and anti-communist movement took root at this time and culminated in the dictatorship of Benito *Mussolini in the 1920s. From that time and throughout the 1930s sport was a core part of the fascist state's project, not only at high-profile events such as the Olympics and at the two successful campaigns for the football World Cup, but as related to the everyday life of the people. Youth groups and university associations were targeted through sport to acclaim, reaffirm, and reproduce the values of the extreme right-wing state, with its inherent authoritarian and racist kernel. The term 'fascism' was taken from the Italian word *fascismo*, and that in turn from the Latin *fascis*, a bundle of rods with an axe in the middle that acted as an ensign of authority in ancient Rome. Thus Mussolini linked his movement to a classical heritage. Fascist movements elsewhere in Europe sought to emulate the Italian project—the blackshirts in England, for instance. And neo-fascist associations have linked sport and the extremist right state, as in the case of National Front leader Martin Webster in England in the 1970s, who saw in some English football hooligans the ideal recruits for his movement; strong and robust English lads, he saw them as, who would physically confront left-wing and any other groupings opposed to the Front's extreme right-wing agenda.

   Fascist states that have used sport explicitly to assert forms of national prestige include Franco's dictatorship after the Spanish Civil War, and Argentina in the 1970s. In both these cases, international football afforded the opportunity for such manipulation. The club side Real Madrid dominated the early years of the European Champion Clubs' Cup (the precursor of the *UEFA Champions League), winning the trophy five times in succession from its inauguration in the 1955–56 season. Franco insisted that the best players in the world be attracted to the club to play alongside the Spanish international Francisco Gento (Ferenc *Puskas from Hungary, Alfredo di Stefano from Argentina, Raymond Kopa from France). Argentina, so often the underachievers of South American football, won the football World Cup in 1978, under the regime of the Generals, in a climate of brutality and internal oppression of Argentinian liberals and dissenters, and amid suspicion that other nations were victimized and even bribed; the nationalistic frenzy that accompanied the victory was later directed towards the Generals' follies in its Malvinas escapade, the invasion of the Falkland Islands. Fascism in the first half of the 20th century proposed a doctrinaire ethos of physical culture in which the body as the armoury of the individual was little more than the tool of the state; in this, it has been observed that although fascism and communism were at the opposite ends of the political spectrum, their ideologies of sport and perspectives on the sociocultural and political value of sport ran along uncannily parallel lines. *See also* COMMUNISM, SPORT IN; NAZISM, SPORT IN.

fatigue The inability to maintain the required muscular force or power output. Fatigue is a complex phenomenon with multiple causes whose relative importance varies according to the specific exercise situation. Most conceptual models interpret fatigue in terms of the relative disruption of three broad constituent parts of the physiological adjustments to an exercise demand: the supply of energy fuels and oxygen, the nervous stimulation of muscles, and the accumulation of metabolic by-products. For example, during a 400-metre sprint fatigue may be predominantly, but not exclusively, due to the high rate of anaerobic metabolism causing acidic conditions within the muscle and a decline in contractile ability. Psychological factors influence fatigue, deriving from an individual's motivation, and external factors such as verbal encouragement from spectators. An alternative theoretical approach to fatigue argues that it is a central brain effect, not a peripheral physiological effect. The argument is that, since most people stop exercising before the physiological limits are reached, feelings of discomfort and fatigue must be conscious interpretations designed to halt exercise before physical damage is caused or before pain becomes intolerable. Furthermore, one particular central fatigue hypothesis provides a mechanistic explanation by demonstrating a relationship between increased brain serotonin and diminished exercise performance.

Fédération Internationale de Football Association (FIFA) Football's international ruling body, founded in 1904, in Paris, by representatives of sporting or football organizations of seven European nations: France, Belgium, Denmark, the Netherlands, Spain, Sweden, and Switzerland. The football associations of the UK were conspicuous by their absence; led as they were by the FA (Football Association [of England]), and controlling the rule-making body the International (Football) Board, they arrogantly declared that there was no need for any international organizational body. Two years later, though, with the new initiative faltering, the British associations did join, taking up the leadership role when an Englishman became the second of FIFA's presidents. FIFA's presidents have been Robert *Guérin of France (1904–6); Daniel *Woolfall of England (1906–18); Jules *Rimet of France (1921–54); Rodolphe *Seeldrayers of Belgium (1954–6); Englishmen Arthur *Drewry and Stanley *Rous (1956–61 and 1961–74 respectively); Brazilian João Havelange (1974–88), and Joseph 'Sepp' Blatter of Switzerland (1998 onwards). Unlike the reformed *International Olympic Committee, there is no limit to the number of elected four-year periods that a president can serve, nor any age limit for FIFA office-holders.

FIFA operated on a relatively low profile in its early years, but nevertheless contributed to sport's emergence as an expression of what Roland Robertson called the third phase of *globalization. FIFA was essentially dormant during the years immediately following World War I, and organizational development was more noticeable in mid-Europe, with the Mitropa Cup attracting Austrian, Hungarian, and other clubs to compete in an international tournament. Football was becoming increasingly internationalized, featuring (in its amateur forms) in early Olympic Games, the British initially dominant. As the game grew in popularity around the world, Uruguay's calculated football triumphs in the 1924 and 1928 Olympics challenged, and superseded, the performance and competitive levels of any purist or idealist model of *amateurism. The British associations, though, reviving their parochial insularity, withdrew from FIFA in 1926–8 in disputes over amateur status and Olympic eligibility.

FIFA's first World Cup in 1930 was both hosted and won by Uruguay, building on its double Olympic triumph. A South American federation, *CONMEBOL (with ten member associations in 2008), could by then claim to have been in operation for fourteen years. By 1930, the power struggles and rivalry between Europe and South America were framing the worldwide development of the game. Jules Rimet was stubbornly and effectively resistant to the formation of continental federations, wanting to keep the world game under the control of the single body, based since the 1920s in Zurich, Switzerland. The end of his third-of-a-century tenure corresponded with the growth of political autonomy and independence for many colonized nations and territories, though, and the foundation of other continental federations after World War II both stimulated the worldwide growth of football in new markets and for new or previously neglected constituencies, and simultaneously generated intensified worldwide rivalries in the politics of the game. The European federation, *UEFA, the Union des Associations Européennes de Football, dates from 1954 (53 member associations in 2008); as does the Asian federation, the *AFC or Asian Football Confederation (46 member associations in 2008); Africa's confederation, CAF, the *Confédération Africaine de Football, was established in 1957 (54 member associations in 2008); *CONCACAF, the federation for the North and Central Americas and the Caribbean, was inaugurated in 1961 (40 member associations in 2008); and the *Oceania Football Confederation, OFC, was recognized in 1966 (11 member associations in 2008). FIFA reported 208 members in 2008, and the higher total of all the listed member associations of the federations is explained by the lesser status of some member countries of the federations that do not qualify for full recognition in FIFA. How these member associations vote at FIFA Congresses determines the election of the president and matters of principle, statute, and policy, and some federation officers have pledged a commitment, and even boasted of an ability to deliver federation votes as blocs in favour of particular candidates. World Cup Finals are allocated by the FIFA Executive Committee, comprising 24 members.

With the expansion of the FIFA (*Fédération Internationale de Football Association) Men's World Cup Finals, and the *commercialization of the world game after Havelange succeeded to the presidency, there has been increasing scope for *corruption and *graft in the development and administration of the world game. Investigative academic research by John Sugden and Alan Tomlinson

(*Great Balls of Fire: How Big Money is Hijacking World Football*, 1999; *Badfellas: FIFA Family at War*, 2002) and investigative research by journalist Andrew Jennings (*Foul! The Secret World of FIFA: Bribes, Vote Rigging and Ticket Scandals*, 2006; and a trilogy of BBC Panorama programmes, in 1998, 2006, and 2007) have revealed the scale of hypocrisy and institutional manipulation in the organization and its affiliates. FIFA's motto was from 1996 to 2007 'For the good of the game'; this was replaced in 2007 by the slogan 'For the Game. For the World'. FIFA's mission statement lists its commitment to the principles of authenticity, unity, performance, and integrity, the latter said to embody a model of fair play, tolerance, sportsmanship, and transparency. But the history and underlying political dynamics characterizing the growth of FIFA and its relationships with global-regional federations and international associations shed light on the shifting politics of nationalism in the post-colonial period; and reveal opportunistic forms of personal aggrandizement shaping an increasingly media-influenced and globalizing world in which international sport was both a harbinger and an early reflection of these trends and forces. Corroborating this, in 2007/8 the organizational watchdog One World Trust reported FIFA to be one of the most unaccountable transnational bodies in the world. There has been no doubt that in the Havelange years FIFA's expansion brought more nations into the world picture than ever before, and FIFA's portfolio was genuinely revitalized by Havelange, with under-17 and under-20 international tournaments, a (however begrudging) recognition and embrace of women's football, and small-side and beach football; the outstanding, persisting question is whether the means by which these goals have been achieved are ethically adequate, and whether the price has been too high in terms of integrity and accountability.

(⊕) SEE WEB LINKS

• The official site of the world governing body of football, FIFA, including mission and policy statements and reports.

fell running A form of foot racing across the demanding terrain of the hilly country in the north of England known as the 'fells', and in mountainous regions of Wales and Scotland. It is an endurance event, across distances of up to forty miles. An ascent and descent of Great Britain's highest peak, Ben Nevis in Scotland, was first raced in 1895. The sport has attracted participants from an increasingly wide social and gender base, and in Britain the Fell Runners' Association coordinates the events, entries, and organization of runs, limiting entries as adverse weather conditions can expose participants to serious personal risk. Fell running is the equivalent of mountain running in many other countries, and its international dimension is overseen by the World Mountain Running Association (WMRA) and the International Association of Ultra Runners (IAUR). The WMRA staged an event with the winner receiving a 'World Trophy' from 1985, and was recognized by the global parent athletics body, the International Association of Athletics Federation, in 2002.

femininity, culture of A widely influential notion of how young women and girls collude in their own gender-based subordination. Angela McRobbie, in 'Jackie: An Ideology of Adolescent Femininity' (Stencilled Paper no. 53, published by the Centre for Contemporary Cultural Studies at the University of Birmingham, UK, 1977), looked at how the adolescent magazine *Jackie* constructed trajectories of young girls' lives. In order to throw off the shackles of authority, working-class girls retreated from the domesticity of the home and entered lives of consumption and pleasure. But these soon led to traditional male-dominated relationships and the reiteration of the feminine role. Femininity is both the escape and the mechanism of entrapment. The notion has been employed illuminatingly in the study of young girls' attitudes towards and experiences of sport, in the work of Sheila Scraton (*Sport, Leisure and Social Relations*, ed. J. Horne, D. Jary and A. Tomlinson, 1987).

feminism An intellectual and activist movement based upon the recognition that *patriarchy has privileged men and perpetuated the gendered or sexual division of labour. It has stimulated work revealing the nature of women's oppression, and the marginalization of women's achievements (which have been, in Sheila Rowbotham's memorable phrase, and book title of 1974, *Hidden from History*). There are numerous phases and variants of feminist work and perspectives, but feminist scholarship has successfully challenged and revised agendas in sports studies. First, it has highlighted the male-dominated nature of (particularly historical) overviews of sport, in which male team games and individual male champions have been widely celebrated, yet women pioneers and champions all but forgotten. Second, it has prompted policy interventions, such as Title IX in the USA, and the setting up of specific foundations and institutes dedicated to the promotion of sport for women. Third, it has contributed to the burgeoning field of the sociology of the body, by showing the sexualized construction of *both* women's and men's bodies in some sporting practices, and in much media representation and reportage of sport. Fourth, it has stimulated men's studies based on an unprecedented reflexivity about the nature of *masculinity, or at least a more reflexive approach to the study of sporting male preserves. Although, therefore, there are numerous feminisms generating debate and rivalry about the balance between theory and practice, critique and intervention, the accumulated impact of feminist scholarship has reshaped the agenda for an inclusive and comprehensive sports studies, if not yet all specialist disciplinary spheres of its practice.

fencing The use of a sword, wielded by hand, for attack and defence. Its origins lie in the military history of various societies—including England and Japan—with roots in chivalric codes of honour as well as military conflict. The foil, the *épée*, and the sabre have been the three predominant forms of weapon in fencing, and have their separate events in the Olympics for both men (from 1896) and women (from 1924). European nations, and the USA, have dominated the Olympic disciplines, and the Fédération Internationale d'Escrime was founded in Paris in 1913. Strong fencing competitors began to emerge from Central and South American countries as well as Asian ones, in the later 20th century. The International Fencing Federation, now based in Lausanne, Switzerland, oversees events at the world youth games, the Mediterranean Games, and world championships, as well as at the Olympic Games. Its aristocratic and soldierly legacy defies the federation's attempts to associate the sport with the youth of the world, though by the early 21st century there were 126 national associations affiliated to the federation. Fencing, as a form of swordsmanship, has an expansive history through numerous civilizations. In 17th-century imperial Japan, fencers, like archers but not so swiftly, moved 'from mortal combat to sports competition to spiritual exercise' (Allen Guttmann, *Sports: The First Five Millennia*, 2004).

Fever Pitch A book by the English writer Nick Hornby, cataloguing the vicissitudes in mood and emotions of a supporter of the London-based soccer club Arsenal. The book is a selective, confessional memoir of a self-confessed obsessive, focusing upon Hornby's own adolescence and young adulthood, and the importance of soccer as a form of identity, a constant form of comfort blanket. The book is based upon particular matches played by Arsenal, and by Cambridge United when the Hornby character was at university; matches and scores are springboards from which Hornby reflects on a myriad of topics and issues, witty and melancholy in turn. Published in 1992, the book spawned numerous imitators, and two films, one in the USA where soccer was replaced by baseball as the focus of the central character's obsession.

FIFA *See* Fédération Internationale de Football Association.

fitness tests Tests of physical performance used to measure the components of fitness necessary to be effective at a particular sport or physical activity. For example, a set of fitness tests for a rugby player might involve measures of the aerobic system, muscle strength, and speed. The purpose of fitness testing is fourfold. It breaks down the composite sports performance into component parts to allow the identification of strengths and weakness and thus baseline information for the design of a training programme; it can be used as a tool to monitor the effectiveness of a training programme; it can monitor the standing of an athlete after injury and guide whether he or she is fit to return to competition; and it can be used by a coach as a means of selection or by a sports organization as a means of identifying young athletes with potential.

Tests of fitness fall into two main categories. One category comprises relatively simple tests of physical performance, such as a timed 10-metre sprint. These may be undertaken in any suitable environment and are usually known as field tests. The second category comprises sophisticated tests, often carried out in a science laboratory, which are designed to determine underlying physiological function, for example a maximal oxygen uptake test (*see* aerobic).

Simple performance tests have a long history. They derive from a military need and are still in common use to set entry standards for the armed services: for example, the British Army entry fitness test comprises two minutes of sit-ups, two minutes of press-ups, and a 2.4-kilometre run. The perspective of German and Swedish pioneers such as *Ling brought educational gymnastics to the fore in the latter parts of the 19th century and influenced the subsequent development of physical education and fitness tests in a direction that was no longer just for military needs but also for purposes of sport, fitness, and health. In the middle of the 20th century, mainly in the USA, Kraus and Weber developed an extensive range of performance-based fitness field tests for the mass screening of American and

European youth. The poor scores of the Americans led to considerable political outcry and the establishment, in 1956, of Eisenhower's President's Council on Physical Fitness and Sports.

Field tests also began to be developed for individual sports and by the end of the century a wide battery was available. For example, in basketball a profile of a player's fitness could be recorded by the vertical jump test (leg power), the lateral slide test (defensive movements in the key), the suicide drill (speed endurance over about 30 seconds), the multistage shuttle test (aerobic endurance), the sit-and-reach test (flexibility), and body weight (fatness). These types of performance tests have considerable utility since they are easy to administer, closely reflect the physical movement patterns of a sport, and require little equipment. However, they are not very reliable, depend heavily on the skill and motivation of the athlete, and do not assess the underlying biological function.

Laboratory-based fitness tests offer considerably greater validity and reliability. Work by Robinson in the 1930s, Morse in the 1940s, and Astrand in the 1950s used techniques of indirect *calorimetry and ergometry to establish the basic characteristics of trained and untrained individuals and how these characteristics were related to sports performance. Roger Bannister, in his autobiography *The First Four Minutes*, describes his own research into oxygen uptake during treadmill running when inspiring various percentages of oxygen. Just three years later Bannister broke the *four minute mile barrier but he was still convinced that the complexity of human exercise physiology would defy detailed analysis for decades. Technological limitations and the complex laboratory environment were not welcoming from the athlete's perspective and advances were mainly limited to theoretical research rather than to the applied context.

From the 1970s microprocessors allowed instrumentation to be shrunk into compact units and a number of portable devices were developed, such as Polar-type heart rate data loggers, portable indirect calorimeters, and infrared timing devices. Laboratory-based fitness testing became more practical and in turn its benefits were recognized by coaches and athletes. Contemporary laboratory fitness tests provide a set of valid and reliable techniques for assessing many of the components of sports performance, including electromyography, lung function, haematology, cardiovascular function, aerobic and anaerobic power and capacity, thermoregulation, muscle function, body composition, and flexibility. Eston and Reilly provide a definitive guide (*Kinanthropomentry and Exercise Physiology Laboratory Manual*, 2nd edn, 2001). Laboratory testing of athletes is now routine and has played a highly significant role in the optimization of training routines and the enhancement of sports performance. Many national sports organizations have established specialized laboratories for this purpose, such as the British Olympic Medical Centre and the English Institute of Sport.

The same fundamental principles and techniques apply to exercise and health. Simple performance tests are widely used to assess individuals' fitness levels before they start an exercise programme. Laboratory tests are seldom used in healthy but unfit individuals since the sophistication is not merited. Performance tests are used clinically in a wide variety of patients, such as a timed stand-and-walk-10-metres test, since such tests provide a simple and practical means to assess functional incapacity or to monitor whether a treatment is working. Clinically, laboratory tests are used mainly in the assessment of patients with cardio-respiratory disease. The 'exercise stress test' is the most common example. This test involves the patient walking on a treadmill with the speed and incline raised progressively every couple of minutes. The controlled laboratory conditions allow real-time monitoring of the *electrocardiogram, blood pressure, breathing, and oxygen use along with the sampling of blood. The results have considerable diagnostic value.

fives A game of hand-ball played by pairs on a three-walled court, sometimes compared to squash, but without rackets, the ball being played by the palm of the hand. The court's design is based upon an area outside the chapel of the English public school Eton, where pupils played with bare hands and balls of varying composition. Other variants of the game stem from other public schools such as Rugby and Winchester. The Eton Fives Association continues, into the 21st century, to act as the governing body of the game, though it remains a preserve of the elite, with very few courts in existence in either England (in the early 21st century, there was only one public court in England, in London) or other parts of Europe and the Commonwealth, where it was introduced within, essentially, old-boy networks. Its most supported outpost remains Nigeria.

fixed costs Costs that do not change when there is a shift in the level of sales, either upwards or downwards. These are, in the budgets of organizations, largely associated with salaries, pay, and remuneration over time. Sport finances could be unbalanced in circumstances in which fixed costs persist against a declining financial trajectory. Take for example the case of English football club Newcastle United. At the end of season 2008–9, the club was relegated from the top tier of English football, the Premiership, yet fifteen players were reported to be on contracts of at least £50,000 a week that had no clause concerning a reduction of pay should the club not preserve its place in the Premiership (a scenario in which its income would drop dramatically). Adherence to fixed costs can prove financially disastrous in a downward financial spiral. It could prove profitable if sales and income rise, but at the cost of employee dissatisfaction based on the sense of having been excluded from the fruits of their successful labour.

Fixx, James F. (1932–84) A US recreational runner whose conversion to running prompted him to write the best-selling book *The Complete Book of Running* (1977), which sold more than a million copies and was a major influence on the rise and increasing popularity of exercise and recreational running. A chronic overweight smoker, Fixx did not begin running until aged 35, and in the ten years from that point to the publication of his book he gave up smoking and shed 60 pounds of weight. Further publications associated running and jogging with tension relief and stress reduction, though Fixx himself died of a heart attack after his daily run, aged only 52. His family, though, had a history of weak hearts in its males, and many have argued that Fixx's running conversion actually elongated his life rather than foreshortening it. *See also* JOGGING.

flexibility exercises *See* STRETCHING.

flow From the work of psychologist Mihaly Csikszentmihalyi (*Flow: The Psychology of Optimal Experience*, 1990), the concept of flow refers to an elevated state of experience characterizing a particular practice, activity, or performance so that the action or the performance comes to have what seems to be its own smooth and seamless momentum. The experience of flow can generate pleasurable feelings, as much as any end result or outcome. The first man to be recorded running a mile under four minutes, Roger Bannister, captured some aspects of this experience of flow in his autobiography (*First Four Minutes*, 1955):

> I remember a moment when I stood barefoot on firm dry sand by the sea...I...could not absorb so much beauty...In this supreme moment I leapt in sheer joy...The earth seemed almost to move with me. I was running now, and a fresh rhythm entered my body. No longer conscious of my movement I discovered a new unity with nature. I had found a new source of power and beauty, a source I never dreamt existed.

In performance and competition the state can be equated with *focused intensity and peak levels of performance, and with Susan Jackson, Csikszentmihalyi has identified the constituent elements of the experience and process of flow (*Flow in Sports: The Keys to Optimal Experiences and Performances*, 1999).

fluid dynamics The mechanical consequences of moving a body through a fluid medium—air or water in the case of sport. The primary effects relevant to sport include drag (force acting against the direction of motion), lift (force acting at right angles to the drag), and the Magnus effect (curved flight of a projectile as a result of spin). Important to the magnitude of these effects is the density of the fluid (water is about 820 times as dense as air) and the speed of movement. In most sports, most of the time, the effects produced may be effectively ignored because they are so small, or affect all competitors equally. For example, the mechanical consequences of air as the medium during walking or a shot-put are negligible. But in aquatic sports, fast-moving sports, and many ball sports, the effects are large and techniques to minimize or maximize the effects are an inherent part of the sport. Examples include swimming costumes to aid buoyancy and reduce drag, or drafting in cycling to reduce drag, or spinning a football to produce swerve or dip.

focused intensity A concept developed by cultural historian Hans Ulrich Gumbrecht, in his book *In Praise of Athletic Beauty* (2006). Gumbrecht relates the experience of Pablo Morales, a triple Olympic gold medal winner in 1984 and 1992. Morales was talking at a colloquium on the athlete's body at Stanford University in 1995, and was asked why he had returned to Olympic competition for the 1992 Games, where he won his only individual gold medal. He had not been selected for the 1988 Games, and could hardly bear to watch his specialist event, the 100-metre butterfly, on television; then, watching sprinter Evelyn Ashford in action in the 400-metre relay, Morales was drawn to Ashford's face, oblivious as she was to both context and rival: 'I saw her lost in focused intensity,' he recalled, and in a revelatory and cathartic moment Morales had to stop watching the race and began sobbing for the lost experience of such a special feeling. Gumbrecht develops this description of the special nature of the athletic moment, equating 'lost' with being in a world away from everyday life, 'intensity' with a 'heightening of qualities and impressions', and 'focused' with both the capacity to shut out distractions and an openness to the prospect of something happening. For Gumbrecht, to be lost in focused intensity marks 'a stunning, complex, precise formula through which . . . [the athlete] . . . links the fascination of watching sports with the motivation of performance' (p. 51). *See also* FLOW.

folkways *See* MORES.

football *See* AMERICAN FOOTBALL; AUSTRALIAN RULES FOOTBALL; CANADIAN FOOTBALL; CUJU; FOOTBALL, ASSOCIATION; FOOTBALL ASSOCIATION, THE; GAELIC FOOTBALL; RUGBY UNION FOOTBALL; RUGBY LEAGUE FOOTBALL; WOMEN'S FOOTBALL.

football, association An eleven-a-side ball game in which a round leather ball is controlled by, passed, and distributed without use of the arms or hands, apart from by the goalkeeper and for throw-ins: the ball is mainly controlled by the foot, though the head is also used to good effect. The sport is known as either 'football', particularly where it has become the dominant footballing code, or 'soccer', a derivation of 'association football' used widely in England's footballing circles of the late 19th century, and in the USA, where 'football' refers to the distinctive national sport of *American football. Forms of football have been reported in many pre-modern civilizations and cultures, and unruly forms of the folk game were documented extensively in early modern Britain, persisting into the mid 19th century: these, though, were predecessors of what was to become the *Rugby Union code. Association football emerged as a distinctive form of the sport when students at the University of Cambridge favoured the dribbling form of the game, and the (English) Football Association (FA) was established (1863) on the basis of agreed rules and playing procedures (in the initial form of these rules, all players were permitted to catch the ball, and the distinction between rugby and association codes was worked through fully over the succeeding decades). Former pupils of the English public school Shrewsbury School (whose alumni were known as Old Salopians) made important contributions to the evolution of football, stimulating the *Cambridge Rules of 1846: one of these, John Charles Thring, also formulated his ten rules of the 'Simplest Game' in 1862, and these were very much the basis of the 1863 developments. In industrial Sheffield, Yorkshire, the local Sheffield rules continued to be the basis of the game played by some of the oldest clubs in the country, unaware of the emerging framework of the Cambridge Rules.

The FA established a Challenge Cup for its members (the FA Cup) in 1871, and in 1872 a crowd of around 2,000 witnessed Wanderers' 1–0 victory over the Royal Engineers in the first FA cup Final at London's Kennington Oval. The teams that had entered were Barnes, Civil Service, Clapham Rovers, Crystal Palace, Donington School, Hampstead Heathens, Harrow Chequers, Hitchin, Maidenhead, Marlow, Reigate Priory, Queen's Park (Glasgow), Royal Engineers, Upton Park, and Wanderers. Of these fifteen entrants, thirteen were in, or in the hinterland of, London: Donington was in Lincolnshire, and withdrew from its second-round match with the Glasgow club Queen's Park, the latter withdrawing in turn rather than make the journey for a semi-final replay in London with Wanderers. The first FA Cup was therefore a haphazard, and essentially English metropolitan affair.

It attracted national attention, though, and teams and clubs sponsored and promoted by educators, employers, and evangelists—often initially as rugby clubs— were attracted to the association code: in the heart of the industrial north-west of England, the Lancashire FA was formed in 1878. The Sheffield Association had been formed in 1867, Birmingham's in 1875. In 1877, the Sheffield body was incorporated into the FA, and a united framework was achieved for the evolution of the modern game.

Organized and ambitious, the industrial clubs became increasingly effective in the FA Cup tournament. In 1882 Blackburn Rovers lost to Old Etonians, but the following year, the Blackburn Olympic side defeated the Etonians in a victory symbolizing the change in the power base of the game, from the south to the north, from the professional and upper classes to the working classes, and from the amateur ethos to an emergent professionalism. The elite clubs of the north-west and midlands of England, increasingly dominant, included players who had no other occupation, and professionalism became the battleground for the future of the English game, the FA accepting its existence as the 1885-6 season began. These dominant clubs soon organized into the (English) Football League, accepted by the FA when a breakaway and pan-British league was proposed should the FA not embrace this new competitive framework. The twelve clubs in the 1888-9 inaugural season of the Football League comprised six from Lancashire (Accrington, Everton, Blackburn Rovers, Bolton Wanderers, Burnley, and Preston North End), and six from the west and east Midlands (Aston Villa, Derby County, Notts County, Stoke City (arguably the north Midlands), West Bromwich Albion, and Wolverhampton Wanderers). The success of the League ensured further growth, with teams from big northern cities such as Manchester, Newcastle, and Sheffield soon joining an expanded divisional format.

The conservative, amateurist London Football Association kept the top southern English clubs out of the earlier national initiatives, though the Royal Arsenal, in 1891, turned professional and severed its links with the London FA, becoming the first southern club to play in the Football League, in season 1893-4. The following season, the new Southern League provided a foundation for the professional clubs in the south of the country; in 1920-21 its first division merged into a further expanded Football League with the formation of the League's Third Division (South). Promotion and relegation systems would over the ensuing years equalize in part the geographical distribution of clubs in the higher divisions. The game also developed an international dimension, with a goalless Scotland–England encounter in 1872.

It was in 1904, though, with the formation of the world governing body La *Fédération Internationale de Football Association (FIFA), that a truly international framework for international competition began to emerge, though domestic football satisfied many national associations and it was not until 1930 that the first men's football World Cup was held, in Uruguay. British associations had withdrawn from both the Amsterdam Olympics and FIFA in 1928, in relation to issues of Olympic eligibility and principles of amateurism, and it was mid-Europe's Mitropa Cup, from 1927, that provided organized international competition for clubs; in the same year, Austria, Czechoslovakia, Hungary, Italy, and Switzerland played for the Dr Gero Cup, in a tournament conceived as a Europe, International, and/or

Nations Cup. International competition had also flourished in South America, in particular between double Olympic champion (1924 and 1928) Uruguay and Argentina, and the South American federation ('CONMEBOL') had been established in 1916. In the absence of the self-isolating British, the growth of world football assumed an increasingly all-embracing international presence. The European association, *UEFA (Union des Associations Européennes de Football), was established in 1954, followed by other continental federations for Africa, Asia, the Central Americas/Caribbean, and Oceania.

The growth of the game worldwide—imported by military presence, migrant international workers, educators, and colonial elites—has been phenomenal, and (soccer) football, though with little in the way of definitive empirical corroboration, is widely recognized to be the world's most popular game, in terms of both participation and the fan-base for the professional game. Conservative authorities and associations have held back the development of *women's football, but the dominant men's form has become increasingly visible in the international spotlight. The *UEFA Champions League (UCL), and continent-wide competitions organized by federations, are high-profile events in the international sporting calendar. Star players such as Cristiano Ronaldo, of Real Madrid from 2009 onwards and formerly of Manchester United, excite global headlines for their sartorial choices as well as salary deals; effectively mobilized, their profile and image can galvanize worldwide markets for club products, as well as individual sponsors. While this might sway sporting judgements—it is difficult to see David Beckham's move to LA Galaxy in 2007 as anything but misjudged, by both player and employer—it also sustains football at the top of the sporting headlines and the hit-lists of global internet gossip sites.

Football's epithet 'The Beautiful Game' had emerged as a response to the dazzling skills of the all-conquering Brazilian sides of the 1950s and 1960s, and the country's World Cup winners of 1994 and 2002. From 1992 a combination of the reformatting of the European Cup into the UCL, the formation in England of the Premier League, and a sense of post-Cold War globalization of sport provided a set of interrelated economic, political, and cultural influences that reshaped the structure and the media profile of the game. In Europe, too, the *Bosman case accelerated international recruitment, and Rupert Murdoch's *Sky Television and competing broadcast providers invested unprecedentedly high levels of money in the sport. In turn, this has attracted investors from Russia, the Gulf States, and North America to invest in football, though with uneven results.

The continuing attraction of football lies in the core features of what the pioneer Old Salopian educator Thring called 'the simplest game': football can be played at its highest level of excellence by a short and stocky figure such as Argentinian Diego Maradona, or by physically deformed Brazilian *Garrincha, as well as by mercurial bad boys such as George *Best. Its principles are simple, its equipment minimal, its dramas flowing and focused. We all know what it is: and yet we can all argue over Brazilian or Argentinian style, German pragmatics, or French hubris, Italian ruthlessness or Dutch prima donna-ism, Cameroonian indiscipline or English doggedness. It brings players of varied cultural backgrounds together in teams of global appeal, a metaphor for cosmopolitanism and cross-cultural harmony, yet can still be a catalyst for local club loyalties and national passions.

The simple game, the beautiful game—the bountiful game?—feeds the diet of the fan worldwide. In media markets, soccer may have reached towards its international peak—yet still, the final frontier of the USA attracts the investor, and the saturation point that some commentators and analysts believe to have been reached continues to be stretched to new limits.

Nevertheless, the sense of belonging in football can be threatened by the extreme commodification of the game; English film director Ken Loach raised this theme in his 2009 film *Looking for Eric*, which starred former Manchester United Football Club's French star of the first half of the 1990s Eric Cantona, but also captured the disillusionment of United fans marginalized by the increasing cost of following the game: Loach observed that the 'idea of a group of people who club together is lost. The sense of identity is split between people who treat it as a club and those who treat it as an investment and a brand.' Loach is in the tradition of English novelist J. B. Priestley, whose opening pages of the novel *The Good Companions* captured the community and expressive base of professional football in the north of England in the 1920s. While such commentators might be accused of slipping into nostalgic romanticization of the sport, if top-level professional football does lose its *community base then its historical and cultural legacies will be seriously jeopardized. *See also* AFC (ASIAN FOOTBALL CONFEDERATION); AMERICAN FOOTBALL; AUSTRALIAN RULES FOOTBALL; CANADIAN FOOTBALL; CHUIWAN; CONCACAF; CONMEBOL; CONFÉDÉRATION AFRICAINE DE FOOTBALL; OCEANIA FOOTBALL CONFEDERATION; RUGBY LEAGUE FOOTBALL; RUGBY UNION FOOTBALL.

References
Giulianotti, R. (1999) *Football: A Sociology of the Global Game*, Cambridge: Polity Press; Goldblatt, D. (2006) *The Ball is Round: A Global History of Soccer*, London: Viking Penguin; Magee, J., Bairner, A. and Tomlinson, A. (eds) (2005) *The Bountiful Game?: Football Identities and Finances*, Aachen: Meyer & Meyer; Mason, T. (1980) *Association Football and English Society: 1863–1915*, Sussex: The Harvester Press; Priestley, J. B. (1929) *The Good Companions*, London: William Heinemann; Tomlinson, A. (1998) 'North and South: The Rivalry of the Football League and the Football Association', in *The Game's Up: Essays in the Cultural Analysis of Sport, Leisure, and Popular Culture*, Aldershot: Avebury.

(((⊕))) SEE WEB LINKS

• The site of the National Football Museum in Preston, England, claiming 'the finest and most significant football collection and body of associated evidence in the world' and a number of exclusive collections of ephemera and memorabilia.

Football Association, The An association established in 1863 as the authorized governing body of *football in England. It was established to unify the different football codes and the widely varying sets of local rules; representatives of eleven clubs met in London and formulated nine original rules for the playing of the game, and in succeeding years amended these rules in ways that led to the separate development of the association football and rugby union football codes. The FA has retained its position as the controlling body of the game in England, though its insular attitudes to international developments left it marginal to global initiatives such as the football World Cup in the first years of the existence of the *Fédération Internationale de Football Association (FIFA), the world governing body (founded in 1904), and from the later 1920s until after World War II, when again the FA was not a member of FIFA.

The FA continues to represent football in England at all of its levels from amateur to professional, and has primary responsibility for the national side and for bids to stage international tournaments (such as a World Cup). The FA Council includes representatives of English counties, the ancient universities, the armed forces, and the Women's Football Conference. Critics claim that this is unwieldy and anachronistic, resulting in unprofessional outcomes and lack of focused leadership. An alternative view is that the FA is a genuinely inclusive, all-embracing and fundamentally democratic body representing the interests of the game at all of its levels. It has certainly been a conservative and at times reactionary body. FA secretary Ted Croker (1924–1992), in post from 1973 to 1979, commented in 1988 that football is a 'hard, physical contest, a form of combat sport, a man's game' in which 'women have no place except to cheer on their men, wash and iron their kit, and prepare and serve refreshments'. In Croker's time (1983), the Women's Football Association had been invited to affiliate to the FA Council. A decade later, women's football began to be integrated more fully with the formation of a Women's Football Committee, followed by the FA taking on responsibility for the women's professional league, and its cup competition.

(⊕) SEE WEB LINKS

• The official site of England's Football Association (FA), containing background historical detail, general information, and contact details.

football hooliganism Group-based forms of aggressive and sometimes violent behaviour, widely but by no means exclusively associated with young, adult working-class males. Football hooliganism emerged as a recognizably collective phenomenon in British professional football crowds or groups of supporters in the late 1960s. Social psychological studies have stressed the ritualistic dimensions of football hooliganism, and the *career stages through which young hooligans pass in becoming inducted into the culture (Peter Marsh, in his Oxford studies, exemplifies this approach). Sociological studies, including figurational sociology, have emphasized the socio-economic context out of which hooligans emerge—the displaced generations, for instance, of de-industrializing areas and regions, for whom identification with the team in the aggressive hooligan fashion becomes an alternative source for the expression of manhood and a traditional tough form of masculinity (Eric Dunning and his colleagues in the Leicester School are the most prominent scholars taking this approach). Football hooliganism has been a real social issue, but it has also been the focus of *moral panics in the media and the wider society, and *deviance amplification, as its incidence and nature have been exaggerated. Some of the most interesting more recent research on football hooliganism has focused on international hooligan groups of 'Ultras', for whom the badge of the extreme hooligan—whether at Accrington or in Rome—appears to provide a sense of self-esteem not elsewhere available. Dunning, using and adapting *Eliasian theories, notes the paradox that football hooliganism represents a kind of throwback, given the overall tendency in modern Western society towards increased restraint in a context of the *civilizing process; this is accounted for by the observation that football hooliganism represents but one of a range of possible decivilizing spurts. The sociological question recurs of what social conditions and cultural circumstances combine to make such spurts possible. *See also* AGGRESSIVENESS; HOOLIGAN.

force platform A high-precision instrument used to measure the x,y,z direction and the magnitude of force over time. A force platform is used to investigate the biomechanics of human movement as a person stands, walks, runs, or jumps on the platform. A force platform typically consists of a metal plate about 1 m × 0.5 m set flush to the floor with a force transducer under each corner. The force transducer is typically either a strain gauge or a piezoelectrical device. The former is superior in measuring static forces and more suited to investigations such as postural control and sway when standing. The latter is superior in measuring dynamic forces and impact and is more suited to investigations of running and jumping. A force platform is a high-precision instrument, typically recording to a precision of 1 per cent and a frequency of 1000 Hz.

Formula One *See* MOTOR RACING.

Foucault, Michel (1926–84) A French philosopher-sociologist whose works on the history of sexuality and on the essentially power-laden nature of knowledge and its reproduction had worldwide impact in the social sciences in the last quarter of the 20th century. His notions of disciplinary power (picking up on Jeremy Bentham's notion of the *panopticon) and *governmentality have been applied in a variety of sport contexts, from analysis of the use of physical education systems to control the body, to discussion of the nature of governmentality as articulated in national and global strategies and policies for sport.

four-minute mile The running of a mile within or under four minutes. This was an elusive—and some believed unattainable—goal for many years. Swede Gunder Haegg held the mile record of 4 minutes 1.4 seconds for nine years until Englishman Roger Bannister broke through one of sport's most enduring sporting barriers when he ran the distance in 3 minutes 59.4 seconds, at the University of Oxford's Iffley Road track on 6 May 1954. Over the previous athletic season, Bannister had aimed to achieve this feat in an international rivalry with Australian John Landy and US runner Wes Santee. Landy lowered the record within six weeks. A combination of this international rivalry with the application of systematic training regimes, and tactical running that included the use of pacemakers, built up to the successful attempt by Bannister. His running and training partners were Chris *Brasher and Christopher Chataway (both graduates of the University of Cambridge; Bannister was a graduate of the University of Oxford when he became the first man to run the four-minute mile, while completing his medical education in London). In the historic race, Bannister was running for the Amateur Athletics Association in a token match against the Oxford University Athletics Club, and in a BBC documentary (*The Four-Minute Mile*, May 2004) Chataway reflected on the event as 'the last hurrah of amateurism'; on the fiftieth anniversary of the breaking of the barrier, the record for the mile stood at 3 minutes 43.13 seconds, set in Rome in 1999 by Moroccan Hicham El Guerrouj, and still the record ten years later. Not featuring in international competitions or the Olympic programme, the distance is decreasingly likely to be challenged. Multiple perspectives on Bannister's achievement are collected in a special issue of *Sport in History* (2006). *See also* ABRAHAMS, HAROLD MAURICE; BRASHER, CHRISTOPHER WILLIAM; TROPE.

fox hunting A blood sport in which the fox is chased and hunted down by mounted riders guided by a pack of trained foxhounds which, on catching the fox, savagely kill it. Accounts of fox hunting can be found in ancient Rome and in the 4th century BC in Persia, for instance, but it is sociologically more curious that fox hunting has prospered in more modern societies such as the industrial and post-industrial United Kingdom. It is a practice that has generated huge controversies concerning the treatment of the fox, but that has been defended as a part of national cultural heritage, a form of class conciliation (bringing the upper and the lower classes together in a shared enthusiasm), even as a form of environmental protection (ridding the countryside of one of its persistent pests). It has a powerful presence in the historical consciousness of parts of the British populace, though David C. Itzkowitz has shown how even in the period of fox hunting's first great expansion in the later 18th and early 19th centuries, the sport was seen in idealized terms as more than just a sport, almost as 'an institution of national and rural life' integral to the nation's sense of itself (*Peculiar Privilege: A Social History of English Foxhunting, 1753–1885*, 1977). Itzkowitz identified three factors that meant that the hunting field was open to all, and in the interests of all sectors of the population. First, the fox was vermin, unprotected by any game law, and so all were encouraged to destroy it. Second, as the fox was killed by the hounds, sportsmen were not in conflict over who won the prize or bagged the prey. Third, the hunt charged over the land of different landowners, making it the opposite of exclusive to landowners, and being premised on a shared tolerance of access. These factors have been mobilized in comparable fashion as argument in favour of fox hunting in the modern period. Itzkowitz also documents the colourful case of the chimney sweep who rode in the Duke of Beaufort's hunt in the 1930s, though as much a 'licensed entertainer' as a hunter; parallel stories could be told in the late 20th century of apologists and defendants of the hunt who argued for the event as a symbol and articulation of cross-class interests. The Hunting Act 2004 banned hunting with hounds in the UK, though the pro-hunting lobby continued to campaign vociferously for its restoration.

French Open Tennis Championship *See* GRAND SLAM (TENNIS).

Freud, Sigmund (1856–1939) An Austrian psychiatrist, founder of *psychoanalysis, whose work covered the interpretation of dreams, theories of the unconscious mind, and the repression of sexual desire. Core concepts in his theory were the *id, the *ego, and the *superego. Freud's work has had limited application in the sports sphere, as scientific psychologists have been dismissive of his case study-based approach and his idiosyncratic samples that could not permit replication of his studies. Peter Fuller's *Champions: The Secret Motives in Games and Sports* (revised edition, 1978) is one of the few attempts to take Freud's theoretical categories and use them in seeking to illuminate the nature of sporting aspiration, endeavour, and competition. The angler's fishing rod is seen by Fuller as compensation for a sense of penis inadequacy; such observations with scant if any empirical verification have done little to further the case for the use of Freudian thinking in the study of sport.

frisbee A game or sport in which a plastic disc is thrown from one person to another, initially in non-competitive and recreational forms, but also in organized forms in teams under the name of ultimate frisbee. From the later 1930s to the early 1960s various forms of frisbee were developed before its successful patented modern form in 1964. The name derives from the Frisbee Baking Company of Bridgeport, Connecticut, USA, whose tin pie-plates were whizzed through the air by college students. Its popularity in the 1950s and 1960s was also linked to burgeoning interest in unidentified flying objects (UFOs), and the vigorous marketing of the object as a universally accessible toy as well as a sophisticated piece of sporting technology. Ultimate frisbee, as a non-contact sport, has been championed by players seeing it as a way of setting themselves apart from the dominant sporting culture of heterosexual, white males, and as evoking in its manifesto 'The Spirit of the Game' a sense of the potential restoration of untainted, even spontaneous, play into the realm of sport culture.

frontstage A concept referring to the public social space or region in which social life is experienced by both those who make particular cultural performances, and those for whom such performances are prepared. It is defined in relation to the *backstage sphere or region in which less public, what might be called pre-performance, acts take place. The term was developed by Erving *Goffman, in his work on the ways in which catering professionals worked in a hotel in the Shetland Isles, Scotland. The public performance of the waiter contrasted with the working style alongside workmates when back in the hotel kitchen: the latter exhibited the crofters' culture in matters of working dynamics and status interaction, eating patterns, and modes of dress. Sport performance, particularly at the higher competitive levels, is managed and performed as a form of frontstage operation, premised on a sophisticated sphere of backstage activities in the treatment room, the dressing room, and the more closeted culture of the team and/ or the club.

Fry, C. B. (1872–1956) Charles Burgess Fry personified the all-round amateur ideal of the English gentleman in the late 19th and early 20th centuries. Fry played cricket for Oxford University and then England and was the most consistently prolific batsman in England for several years. But he also played for England at association football (playing in an FA Cup Final for the Southampton club), played rugby football at international level, and was joint holder of a junior long-jump record for more than twenty years. Fry was an accomplished Oxford classics scholar: cricket writer H. S. Altham wrote that 'Fry could . . . have stepped out of the frieze of the Parthenon'. Yet Fry was also a self-promoting one-man industry, starting *Fry's Magazine*, producing fiction and an autobiography, and acting as a model for risqué photographic shoots. Dabbling in parliamentary politics, and actually meeting German Nazi Party leader Adolf *Hitler, Fry tarnished his positive image, but a lifetime of image-management survived these political excesses.

full employment A state of the economy in which all eligible people who want to work can find employment at prevailing wage rates: 'full' does not necessarily mean 'total' or '100 per cent', as for some employment may be seasonal. The question of whether full employment is relevant to the sport labour market is an interesting one. In some professions—medicine, architecture, teaching—accreditation is carefully controlled, and recruitment fitted to planned and projected numbers. For individuals aspiring to make a living by playing sport, no such controls are applied: apprentice schemes attached to professional soccer in countries such as England are, in the knowledge that a tiny minority makes the grade, essentially academies for preparation to fail; college athletes in the USA know that only the exceptional few will be drafted into the professional leagues. Full employment of eligible professional performers is by definition unattainable (though in a command economy such as Cuba, it is claimed that every qualified sportsperson will be found work at some level of the sporting system, coaching and administering if not competing, or after a competitive career). In Western economies such as the UK, the number of people making a living out of playing sport and running professional sport at the end of the 20th century was not high (Richard Holt and Tony Mason, *Sport in Britain, 1945–2000*). If full employment is a built-in impossibility in sport work and sport labour, and associated work and professions, the question might also be asked: 'What sense does it make to qualify so many people in sport-related subjects, from sport development to sport coaching and management, from sport economics and general sports studies to sport journalism?'

functionalism A theoretical framework in sociology that draws upon an organic analogy to explain the role and place of different elements of the overall society and their contribution to the general workings of the society. Also known as structural functionalism, the approach recognizes that just as, say, a limb of the human body is not directly connected to another limb elsewhere in the body, then one part (an institution or a social group) of a society with no direct connection to many other parts of the society can nevertheless be seen as contributing to the overall structural stability of the society; its existence is functional to the workings of the overall structure. In this perspective, sport can be seen as one of society's institutions that serves the overall social order: it can stimulate collective identities and so counter individualism and fragmentation; it can provide expressive outlets for people's leisure and so refresh them for their continuing contribution to work and the economy; it can represent the claimed core values of a society, so strengthening social bonds across the society.

Functionalism was highly influential in mid-20th-century social science, and functionalist sociologists of sport were prominent in the USA and in the Soviet Union, where the inherent conservatism of the functionalist framework clearly served the wider ideological interests of the dominant interests in those societies. Its powerful analytical appeal also attracted early sociologists of sport in Germany. Functionalists have claimed to explain threats to the social order by arguing that, for instance, *deviance can be socially useful by prompting reaffirmations of the accepted, mainstream values of a society: in sport, for instance, the drug-using athlete who is caught flouting the rules—and the law—can be condemned in comparison to the athletes who uphold the official, mainstream values. Deviance itself can then be argued to have a social function. As this example shows, functionalism can justify many dysfunctional elements of a society or a system, and more critical sociological theories have questioned such levels of all-embracing explanation.

G

GAA (Gaelic Athletics Association) *See* CROKE, THOMAS WILLIAM; GAELIC FOOTBALL; HURLING.

Gaelic football A fifteen-a-side outdoor ball game played throughout the island of Ireland by male teams who combine the skills of handling, passing, catching, bouncing (or hopping), carrying, and kicking the ball, with the intent of scoring goals by propelling the ball between two posts, under a crossbar for three points, over it for one point. The sport is unusual for the range of skills that players can exhibit, defying the highly specialist *division of labour that has come to characterize sport performance at the highest level. In this, it shares characteristics with *Australian Rules football. Rough and less organized forms of the game were played in pre-modern Ireland as early as the 16th century, and a six-a-side match was documented in mock epic format by the poet Matthew Concanen (1701–49) in his *A Match at Football: A Poem in Three Cantos*. The game was rough and violent, as the approach of one player (Terence, satirically described as 'gentle') to an opponent (Swain) testifies: 'A Dextrous Crook about his leg he wound, / And laid the Champion Grov'ling on the ground' (lines 85–6). Forms of the sport played in the later 18th and early 19th centuries involved much brawling, in unbounded limits between villages as well as on prescribed, marked pitches (where there could be more than thirty players per side).

It was in 1884 that, stimulated by the growth of the nationalist movement, the sport was codified and, under the guidance of the Gaelic Athletic Association (GAA), transformed into a distinctive Irish cultural form, lowering the numbers on each side to 21, and introducing rules to curb excessive violence that could occur during tackling and wrestling. An All-Ireland Championship was first staged in 1887. During the 1890s, numbers were further reduced to 17 per side, and then 15 per side in 1913. In 1926, after Irish partition (1920), provincial and national leagues were instituted, with finals played at *Croke Park, Dublin, in the Republic of Ireland. Gaelic footballers continued to play for the county sides of their birth, so that the sport provided a strong sense of continuity of regional culture as well as a symbolic cultural recognition of the integration of the whole of the island in a distinctively Irish practice and heritage (what Thomas *Croke had called 'football kicking, according to Irish rules' in his 1884 letter to the Irish Republican brotherhood's Michael Cusack, who had been briefed to use the revival of traditional Irish sports as a tool of nationalist cultural politics, and became general secretary to the GAA). The sport championed most by Cusack was *hurling, but Gaelic football was successfully promoted to become one of the top spectator sports in Ireland, regularly attracting capacity crowds of more than 80,000 to All Ireland Finals at Croke Park in the early years of the 21st century.

(⊕) SEE WEB LINKS
• The official website of the Gaelic Athletic Association, including archives and its oral history project.

gait analysis A technique used in sports biomechanics to study the biomechanics of the leg and foot during walking and running. A *force platform and video cameras may be used to collect kinematic (movement) and kinetic (force) data to describe the motion of the limb segments, the angles through which the joints move, and the ground contact forces during footfall. The information may be used in research, for example to aid the design of cushioning in running shoes; or it may be used in the diagnosis and treatment of injury, for example the identification of ankle pronation and the provision of a corrective orthotic insert for a shoe.

Galen (AD 129–200) A gladiator and a trainer, specializing in medical advice, who became court physician to the Roman emperor Marcus Aurelius. His writings on exercise brought a new level of systematic thinking—or at least the commitment of this thinking to a written form—about not just the general health benefits of exercise, but the benefits of particular exercises, such as with the small ball. His general principle was that the best exercise is that which 'not only exercises the body, but also refreshes the spirit'. The first special advantage that he saw in 'exercise with the small ball' was its convenience: 'even the poorest man can play ball, for it requires no nets nor weapons nor horses nor hunting dogs, but only a ball and a small one at that... And what could be more convenient than a game in which everyone, no matter his status or career, can participate?' Small-ball exercise could also keep all parts of the body in motion, and vary the pace of the exercise as appropriate. Galen linked the benefits not just to health: 'You can easily understand that ball playing trains for the two most important maneuvers which a state entrusts to its generals: to attack at the proper time and to defend the booty already amassed.' Running did not impress Galen, being too weight-reducing and having no capacity to train people in courage; he saw running as an uneven, unbalanced activity. In contrast, 'exercise with the small ball' contributed to a balanced diet of exercise, causing 'neither excessive corpulence nor immoderate thinness': 'I especially favour that exercise which promotes sufficient health for the body, harmonious development of its parts, and *arête* in the spirit', he wrote, and ball-playing was the ideal exercise for this, gentle for the aged or the infirm, challenging and vigorous for those seeking simultaneous exercise of the body and the lungs. And Galen pointed out that his recommended exercise is also less dangerous than sprinting, horseback-riding, discus, or wrestling. Galen's recommendations went against the grain of the sporting legacy of Greece and certainly the excesses of Rome, but as Stephen G. Miller observes (*Arete: Greek Sports from Ancient Sources*, 1991), he reflects on practices that represent 'a change to a more scientific system of physical education which had evolved from the teachings of generations of *gymnasion* trainers'.

gamesmanship An approach to sporting competition in which contestants play by the rules, but not necessarily by the spirit of the rules. Examples include putting opponents off when it is their turn to strike the ball in, say, golf; verbally disturbing a player's concentration as in, say, fielders sledging a batting opponent;

or taking unnecessary injury or toilet breaks in, say, tennis. The place of gamesmanship raises challenging questions for philosophers of sport, who recognize in such examples the practice of cheating within the rules, but also pose the question, as Graham McFee puts it in *Sport, Rules and Values: Philosophical Investigations into the Nature of Sport* (2004), of how far gamesmanship can go before the shared assumptions of the contest are jeopardized. Gamesmanship is often seen, in moral terms, as the negative counterpart to the more morally acceptable ethos of *sportsmanship.

GANEFO Games of the New Emerging Forces, a short-lived alternative to the Olympic Games, led by Indonesia in 1962, and at the 1963 first Games attracting 51 nations, mostly newly independent and/or socialist states. Taiwan and Israel had been refused entry to the fourth *Asian Games in Jakarta, Indonesia, and the GANEFO was a politically explicit response. Athletes attending the event were banned by the International Olympic Committee from competing at the Olympics, and Indonesia itself was also suspended. A second event—called the First Asian GANEFO—was staged in Phnom Penh, Cambodia, in 1966, but the GANEFO did not sustain any long-term political momentum.

Garrincha (Manuel Francisco dos Santos) (1933–83) A Brazilian soccer player who played in Brazil's World Cup winning sides of 1958 and 1962. The name Garrincha means 'little bird', and is often given in Brazil to people with a disability; at times Garrincha was also given the nickname 'Joy of the People' or 'Angel with Bent Legs'. Born with a defective spine, an inward-bending right leg, and an outward-bending left leg that was also shorter than the other leg, Garrincha was raised in a deprived family and domestic setting in which his father was an alcoholic, and did not enter the professional game until 1953. His continuous alcohol and associated weight problems did not prevent him achieving a glittering career, almost wholly—apart from a few months in Colombia—in Brazil, mostly with the club Botafogo. The national team never lost a match in which Garrincha and Pelé played together, and his playing style and impact captured the fantasy and imagination of the population, particularly the poor and the oppressed. John Humphrey writes:

> Brazilians saw in his play the affirmation of Brazilian values over European, and also popular values over those of the elite. For many people in Brazil there was no better sight than a six-foot, blond, superbly-coached and tactically-trained European defender on a rigid calorie-controlled diet being made to look like a fool by the devastating artistry of an undernourished, anarchic black winger with two twisted legs who would have never got past the medical exam in European soccer. ('No Holding Brazil: Football, Nationalism and Politics', in A. Tomlinson and G. Whannel, eds, *Off the Ball: The Football World, Cup* 1986).

'Good legs and good luck' were Garrincha attributes, in the words of Eduardo Galeano, who notes too that the player 'had fun cracking jokes with his legs' (*Football in Sun and Shadow*, 1997). His farewell match in 1973, between a Brazil side and a World FIFA XI, attracted 131,000 spectators to the Maracanã stadium. Garrincha died of cirrhosis of the liver ten years later, in an alcoholic coma in Rio de Janeiro, having been in and out of hospital numerous times in the previous few months. Physical and mental deterioration obscured his later years, and as in the case of many such socially mobile sporting figures, his descent into such a condition, his fall from the celebrated to the neglected, was rapid. Garrincha is commemorated in a named sporting stadium in Brasilia.

Gay Games *See* GAY SPORTS.

gay sports Sporting encounters or events organized by and for gay people. Gay sports have been considered as an antidote to the hedonism of the gay club scene, but have also been seen as a way of countering the implicit and explicit heterosexual biases of mainstream sporting culture. Gay sports have also been seen as a source of sexual adventure or relationship: 'On lesbian and gay teams nationwide, every team-mate is a potential lover', observed Roxxie, in *Sports Dykes: Stories from On and Off the Field* (ed. Susan Fox Rogers, 1994). On the international level, the Gay Games provide what the executive director for the fourth such event in New York in 1994 called 'a tremendous opportunity for the international and lesbian community, and our friends, to eradicate prejudice, achieve our personal best and create a living legacy for millions of lesbian and gay youth in the years to come' (quoted in Jennifer Hargreaves, *Sporting Females: Critical Issues in the History and Sociology of Women's Sports*, 1994). The Federation of Gay Games emerged in 1989, out of the San Francisco Arts & Athletics initiative of the early 1980s, and after the first two events in San Francisco, the Games expanded across North America and internationally (Vancouver 1990, New York 1994, Amsterdam 1998, Sydney 2002, Chicago 2006, Cologne 2010). The founding principles of the Federation are 'Participation, Inclusion, and Personal Best', and in an interesting way the Games comment on, if hardly subvert, the performance principles of mainstream top-level competitive sport.

gaze A term used by Laura Mulvey in her essay, in *Screen* (1975), on 'Visual Pleasure and Narrative Cinema'. Her suggestion that women are subjected to a 'male gaze' identified three sources and manifestations of this gaze: how women are represented on the screen; how women are looked at by the camera; and the narratives in which women are situated and located. The notion of the gaze has its obvious applications in the spheres of mediated sport seen on screen, and spectatorship at the live sporting event; the attractive sporting body has been a focus for variously motivated gazes, in its public physical display. The male gaze has certainly framed the representation of sporting women and girls in aesthetic sports such as gymnastics and ice skating, and in the reporting of women's sporting achievements. But the gaze need be neither exclusively male, nor heterosexual. Allen Guttmann has noted the voyeuristic dimension of sport spectating in the attraction of young males' performance to adult men (*Sport Spectators*, 1986). Watching Martina Navratilova in pre-Wimbledon tennis tournaments at Eastbourne's Devonshire Park tennis venue in the 1980s became a pilgrimage for thousands of lesbian tennis enthusiasts. Mass Observation researchers in 1930s England documented the attraction of strong male wrestlers to the women in the audiences: 'No other sport has such fine husky specimens of manhood as wrestling. I find it such a change to see real he men after the spineless and insipid men one meets ordinarily', reported one woman (Charles Madge and Tom Harrisson,

Britain by Mass-Observation, 1939). In its Foucault-inspired adaptation by Mulvey, the concept of the gaze has much to offer sports studies, but its wider applicability to the pleasurable and the erotic in sports is yet to be fully developed.

GDP (gross domestic product) A basic measure of an economy's economic performance; an integral part of most countries' national accounting system, providing a measure of the total economic activity within a region, calculated on the basis of output, income, and expenditure. Economists have used GDP, alongside other factors such as a country's political system, population, climate, and home-advantage, to predict the achievement of gold medals at the Olympic Games (*Wall Street Journal*, blog, May 2008). Alternative tables of achievement can also be generated based upon medal count and GDP, that would put small, less wealthy nations at the top of a value-for-money Olympic medals listing. *See also* GNP.

Geertz, Clifford James (1926–2006) A US cultural anthropologist who, adhering to Max *Weber's notion of social science as an interpretive challenge, located meaning at the centre of his analytical agenda. Geertz had early pretensions to literary writing and his narrative-fuelled fieldwork reports and studies drew upon a wide range of sources and ideas in literature, philosophy, and political science as well as anthropology and sociology. He considered social relations and social institutions as 'an assemblage of texts', conducive to analysis and interpretation just as are documents and literary forms. His evocation of *thick description as the foremost and central anthropological task, and his analysis of the *deep play that really gave meaning to the ritual of the cock-fight in Bali, have been widely used—and at times misunderstood—in popular cultural and sports studies. Geertz urged that the accounts of the subjects in the culture under study must be given priority in anthropological accounts—one of his books was entitled *Local Knowledge*—and that the cultural anthropologist's task is to show not merely what cultures do, but what they mean; this of course raises a central tension in his approach, between acting as a conduit for the voices and experiences of his subjects, and representing these latter as the anthropologist's own interpretive representation. Eschewing the responses of research committees and peer-review scrutineers, Geertz stated, in the foreword to the 1999 reissue of *The Interpretation of Cultures*, that his main approach had been to go and do the anthropology, get the account, and then figure out what it was that he had found out. A multitude of sport-based cultures awaits the kind of cultural interpretation that Geertz brought to bear in his intellectually deep, inquisitive, and honest fashion.

Gehrig, Lou (Henry Louis) (1903–41) Born Ludwig Heinrich, a native of New York City, a professional baseball player for the New York Yankees in the 1920s and the 1930s. His outstanding durability as a hitter established long-standing records for Major League Baseball, including one still unbeaten almost seventy years after his death, for his 23 career grand slams (in baseball, a grand slam is a home run hit while all the bases are occupied, thus scoring four runs, the highest possible score from a single strike). His 'streak' of 2,130 consecutive games (1925–39) was also unequalled for 56 years. This endurance in top-level performance gave him the nickname 'The Iron Horse', but ironically, and tragically, Gehrig is best remembered for the neuromuscular disease that killed him, amyotrophic lateral sclerosis, popularly referred to in the USA as 'Lou Gehrig's Disease'. Gehrig left the game in an emotional and very public moment: his farewell speech at the stadium was captured on film, and his story and curtailed career and life have prompted Stephen G. Miller (*Ancient Greek Athletics*, 2004) to compare him with those athletic heroes of ancient Greece whose fame and heroism were bestowed on them for what they did or represented beyond their accomplishments in the stadium or on the field of play. The son of poor German immigrant parents, Gehrig gained entry to Columbia University and excelled in the baseball team, though not graduating after attracting the attention of professional scouts. This story of rags-to-riches, the modesty of the man as well as his sporting achievements, and his dignity at his early death make Gehrig a figure remembered and commemorated for more than just the strength of his batting arm.

(⊕) SEE WEB LINKS

• The official site of the baseball player, including his moving speech addressing fans when he knew that he was dying.

gender The social and cultural construction of masculinity and femininity, as opposed to the biological division of humans into male and female sexes. This has come to be understood as operating across individual, cultural, and social structural settings, so that the sporting body must be understood not as a solely biological product but, for the most part, as a sociocultural construction. As Jennifer Hargreaves states (*Sporting Females: Critical Issues in the History and Sociology of Women's Sports*, 1994):

> because gender is experienced through the body, 'masculinity' and 'femininity' seem absolutely intimate and fundamental ... Girls tend to be handled more gently; boys are tossed around and wrestled with more frequently and vigorously ... girls are restricted in methods used and distances covered when traveling; boys are allowed more freedom when traveling away from home for sports meetings.

It is in such mundanities and rhythms of everyday life that sporting cultures can be seen to be influenced by gender, as well as in the entrenched institutions of sport at its organized and administrative levels. Hargreaves sees gender as an 'organizing principle'—no mere influence—reproduced and disseminated in public and private settings across all social contexts, and pervading 'the cultural sphere'.

The recognition, initially in pivotal and challenging forms of *feminism, of the centrality of gender to the making of sport cultures has had an enormous effect upon research and scholarship previously dominated by men researching men. It has also stimulated radical re-evaluations of the patriarchal and often sexist basis of sport in what some have labelled pro-feminist men's studies. While some earlier concessions to the importance of gender might have considered women's sport in an extra chapter of a book dominated by a concern with male sport, or in an extended footnote, the gendered basis of much of sporting culture is now so widely acknowledged that such tokenistic or gender-blind approaches have become discredited.

gender differences The difference in sports performance between men and women as a result of physiological, psychological, and social factors. As a general approximation, female performance is around 10 to 20 per cent lower than that of males, although the exact difference ranges from 40 per cent lower in heavyweight weightlifting to 10 per cent lower in sprinting. Part of the difference derives from biology: haemoglobin level, lean body mass, heart size, and anabolic hormone levels are all greater in males, and body fat levels are lower. Psychologically, sports-related traits such as achievement orientation and aggression are higher in males. Socially, the nature of sport and societal factors may mean a lower rate of participation by women. It is important to note that in a population there is considerable overlap in the performance of men and women, and the average gender difference of 10 to 20 per cent is considerably smaller than the difference between the fittest and least fit, which is around 400 per cent.

gender relations The relationships between men and women on the basis of their masculine and feminine identities. Sport-based gender relations have often been perceived as biologically determined, and so separate sporting cultures of men and women have been claimed as evidence of natural differences. In fact, such gender relations must be seen as forms of gendered power relations, rather than accepted as an element of the natural order. *See also* FEMINISM; GENDER.

General Association of International Sports Federations (GAISF) A non-profit organization representing all international sport federations, developing from a bureau for the federations established in 1921, and growing into the General Assembly of International Federations (GAIF) in 1967, based in Lausanne. The GAIF became the GAISF in 1976, and the following year, stimulated by Horst *Dassler of *Adidas, moved from Lausanne to Monaco. The association had a membership of 104 organizations and associations by 2007. The GAISF statutes stress the promotion of information-sharing and harmony among the different sport organizations, and the identification and protection of the organizations' common interests. It has become a powerful lobbying body, a platform for ambitious sports administrators and bureaucrats, for example for Kim Un Yong of Korea to profile his own sport of *tae kwon do, from 1986 when he assumed the presidency to 2004 when jailed in his home country on conviction for corruption charges. It is also a way in to the corridors of influence and potential power in the world of the International Olympic Committee (IOC), and Kim succeeded in getting tae kwon do accepted into the Olympic programme. The GAISF claims to speak for the interests of all sports, but 'Mickey' Kim's corruption conviction tarnished its reputation. His successor, Hein Verbruggen, president of the International Cycling Union, took over from Kim in 2004, and has rebranded the annual meetings of the GAISF as SportAccord, held in parallel with meetings of the IOC's executive board.

Gibson, Althea (1927–2003) A US sportswoman who was the first African American woman to compete on the international tennis circuit, and became the first black woman to win one of the four top world titles, the French Championship, in 1956. Gibson won the Wimbledon title the following year, and was also a US champion and the recognized world number one in the women's game. Her childhood in Harlem, New York City, was an impoverished one, but she excelled in sport, including basketball and table tennis, and her talent at table, or 'paddle', tennis in particular marked her out to people in the Police Athletic League (PAL). As the *New York Times* obituary (29 September 2003) noted:

> In 1941 Buddy Walker, a Harlem bandleader and part-time P.A.L. supervisor, bought her two rackets and introduced her to friends at the Cosmopolitan Tennis Club, a predominantly black club that played on courts on 149th Street just a few blocks away but a world removed from the neighborhood she had known. Gibson was coached there by Fred Johnson, the one-armed club pro, and taken up by the club's members, who taught her some more important lessons.

Sponsored and encouraged in this way, and later supported by what was then a separate governing body for black players' tournaments, tennis became her means of personal development and social mobility. Her talent was used as a catalyst by black human rights activists to raise the issue of the segregation of black and white players, leading to her participation in the 1950 US Championships. A tennis and basketball scholarship enabled her to graduate from Florida A & M University (1953), and take employment as an athletic instructor in a university. Gibson retired from the amateur game in 1958, working as an exhibition professional, but also making a popular music album and a feature film. Sometimes labelled the Jackie *Robinson of tennis, for overcoming discrimination and racism in the sport, Gibson had won doubles titles with English Jewish player Angela Buxton, and one of their triumphs was greeted in the press as a victory for the 'minorities'. Buxton was to save Gibson from destitution in the early 1990s, helping raise monies that sustained her in her last years.

Gichin, Funakoshi (1868–1957) The creator of modern *karate, Gichin was from the island of Okinawa, and introduced karate to the Japanese mainland in 1921–2. Blending poetry, philosophy, and the bodily practice of karate, he attracted committed followers and in 1936 established his specialist (Shotokan karate) *dojo* in Tokyo. Gichin's philosophy was that in karate the individual could transcend the egotistical self:

As a mirror's polished surface reflects whatever stands before it and a quiet valley carries even small sounds, so must the student of karate render his mind empty of selfishness and wickedness in an effort to react appropriately towards anything he might encounter. This is the meaning of 'kara' in karate.

Gichin's beliefs challenged the nationalist hegemony of the established *martial arts, and he was the chief instructor at the Japan Karate Association when it was established in 1955, though he died two years later. His work *The Twenty Guiding Principles of Karate* has been reinterpreted by later practitioners, but is recognized as the founding text of the discipline.

gigantism A condition, in medical science, generating abnormally large growth caused by an excess of growth hormone during childhood. The term has been adopted in debates concerning the growth of large-scale sporting events, what are often called *mega-events, such as the Olympic Games (*see* OLYMPIC GAMES, MODERN (AS GLOBAL CULTURAL EVENT)) or the men's football (soccer) World Cup. These events have expanded in duration, size, and scale as global audiences and markets have been targeted; taking the medical analogy, the phase in which the Olympics were reshaped by new media and economic forces led to an abnormal and uncontrolled growth. The International Olympic Committee (IOC) expresses a concern that the Olympics has become too big, and uses this issue as a way of discussing limits on numbers of participants, and the possible elimination of particular events or sports. In the IOC view, sports should have a genuinely international popularity and a profile on every continent, to be included in the schedule. The IOC arguments are weakened by the inclusion of opportunistic but televisual events such as *beach volleyball, and it is unlikely that with its commitments to sponsors, media interests, and the international sporting network, the moral debate will lead to significant reduction.

Gillette Cup A knock-out cup competition in English cricket, sponsored by the company Gillette, an established sport sponsor of US boxing and radio features on sport. The cup began in 1963, devised as an initiative to counter the decreasing interest of the public in the *County Championship, and was an immediate success with both live spectators and the television audience. As a revolutionary form of limited-overs cricket, with matches scheduled for just the one day, the Gillette Cup was a transformative moment in the history of English cricket.

gladiatorial games Combat sports staged in ancient Rome as early as 264 BC, linked to the funeral of Brutus Pera, organized by his sons. Originally linked to rites and ancient ceremonies, or occurring in the days following funerals, the combat was between pairs of gladiators and took place in the Forum area of the city. Two factors influenced the transformation of gladiator games into a prominent form of spectacle: their great popularity, if not frequency; and the lack of state control of such forms of spectacle, allowing private individuals to stage displays celebrating their own status and prestige. It was not until the first century BC that gladiatorial games were recognized as official spectacles by the Roman Senate, and a special law of 61 BC was passed to curtail their use as forms of individual and political propaganda. The games then became part of the official and public culture of Rome, controlled by the emperors. In 22 BC the Senate authorities sought to limit the events to two a year, with no more than 120 gladiators. The events, though, expanded in scale, as politically motivated and calculating emperors saw the advantages of engaging the masses in such diversions and entertainments. Although it was 20 BC before a permanent stone-built amphitheatre was constructed in Rome, the Flavian Amphitheatre, latterly known as the *Colosseum, was inaugurated a century later in AD 80, and was used mainly for two types of spectacle, the mock hunts of ferocious and exotic animals—*venationes*—and the gladiatorial fights, known as *munera* from the earlier time in which they were conceived as offerings to the dead.

Gladiatorial combatants were usually slaves or former slaves, though some free men were attracted to the rewards of a successful gladiatorial career. It was a precarious choice, evidence suggesting that most survived for less than a year. Unfree gladiators surviving for more than five years were granted their freedom. Gladiators were specialized, highly trained, organized into different groups or *familiae* (scholars have identified at least fifteen) based upon the type of weapons and tactics used. Historians have agreed that contests between such protagonists could be seen as sophisticated professional combats, far removed from the midday fights or interludes that were often little more than 'summary massacres' of condemned criminals (Roland Auguet, *Cruelty and Civilization: The Roman Games*, 1972). The well-trained and successful gladiator could become valuable property, as Allen Guttmann observes (*Sports: The First Five Millennia*, 2004). Guttmann also notes that the successful gladiator could become an object of sexual desire for women, as well as the idol of the Roman masses. Christian emperors—beginning with Constantine in the early 300s—opposed the games, or combats, and they were suspended by Honarius later in the same century, and abolished by Valentinian in AD 438. The *venationes* lasted almost a century longer, last held in AD 523.

gliding The sport of flying a form of aeroplane that has no motor, according to principles based upon the systematic study of bird flight. France, England, and the USA produced pioneering gliders and experiments. For obvious reasons—cost, time, support—the sport is a minority one, though it can engender enthusiastic spectator followings. *See also* AIRSPORTS.

globalization The process whereby the world has developed from national and international dimensions into a single global system, in terms of social, economic, and cultural factors that often transcend political determinants. As Jeffrey Hill observes, it has been a 'profoundly influential process' on sport, based in 'the operation of economic and cultural interests and activities on a global rather than a national scale' (2002: 40). International sport certainly emerged in the 19th and 20th centuries, but control of sport was rooted in national contexts and bodies. At the end of the 20th century, sport embodied, and had arguably been leading, global developments and trends.

Robertson (1992) identified five historical phases of globalization, in relation to Western history at least. In the first, 'germinal' phase, from the early 15th to mid 18th centuries, national communities were formed, the idea of the individual emerged, and a scientific world view was developed. At this point sports cultures generally obeyed national boundaries, served military purposes, or provided amusement for the privileged classes. The less privileged classes engaged in popular recreations and traditional pastimes. The second, 'incipient' phase, from the mid 18th century to the 1870s, saw the consolidation of the nation state, and further developments in international relations, trade, and communications. Sport contributed to some of this in experimental international exchanges and contests, though in the UK at least was still taking shape in its modern forms under the influence of reformers, educators, and in particular the elite public schools. An English cricket side first toured Australia in 1861, and the first cricket *Test Match was played sixteen years later. It was in the third, 'take-off' phase, for a half-century after the 1870s, that sport emerged as a prominent global phenomenon. In this phase, worldwide agencies were established, global awards and prizes were initiated, and global communications enabled new levels of communication across the world. The *International Olympic Committee (IOC) was founded in 1894, and the world governing body of football FIFA (*Fédération Internationale de Football Association) was established in 1904, demonstrating sport's contribution to this formative phase. The late 1920s to the mid 1960s were for Robertson a phase of struggle for hegemony or control, predominantly in terms of the Cold War struggle between the Western powers and the Soviet Union and its satellite states. Certainly from the entry of the Soviet Union into the Olympic Games after World War II, the tussle between the USA and the Soviet Union to top the (summer) Olympics medal tables dominated the international sporting arena. Robertson's fifth stage, from the 1960s/70s onwards, constituted one of uncertainty, in which old certainties were threatened by the consolidation of the global media system, this latter intensifying global consciousness, and increasing multicultural and polyethnic dilemmas. At this stage, a new political economy of sport emerged, blending the corporate interests of international organizations with the ambitions and aspirations of supranational sporting bodies; and the sporting potential of the less developed countries was accelerated. Miller et al. (2001) claim that:

> the move towards a global sports complex is as much about commodification and alienation as it is to do with a utopian internationalism. We discern five simultaneous, uneven, interconnected processes which characterize the present moment in sport: Globalization, Governmentalization, Americanization, Televisualization, and Commodification (GGATaC) . . . (2001: 4).

Globalization has not always made things the same, or acted as a homogenizing force, yet 'many components of globalization are common across sites, leading to the acceptance of certain governing rules, media norms, and economic tendencies' (p. 4).

It is useful to ask what conditions might be necessary in order to characterize a particular phenomenon as a case of globalization. J. B. Thompson (1995) identifies three such conditions: first, a global arena where activities take place; second, a global scale of organization, planning, and coordination of activities; third, a reciprocity and interdependency of activities, with activities of a local kind around the world having the capacity to shape each other. Global sport events from motor racing's Formula One to the football (soccer) World Cup and international athletic meetings can be seen as matching these conditions. Some commentators see a momentum and an inexorability in the globalization of sport, Joseph A. Maguire commenting that 'the sportization of the planet seemingly knows no bounds' (1999: 207). Maguire also talks of the 'flows' that mark an increasingly global culture:

it is more difficult to understand local or national experiences without reference to these global flows. The flow of leisure styles, customs and practices from one part of the world to another, 'long-haul' tourism, and global events such as music festivals and the Olympic Games are examples of these processes at work. (1994: 400)

Jarvie (2006: 100) points to five different cultural flows that illustrate the development of the globalization of sport. First, sporting ethnoscapes involve the migration of sports personnel. Second, sporting technoscapes encompass goods, equipment, facilities, infrastructure, and transport of the technology. Third, sporting financescapes refer to the monies that flow across the world in relation to sporting goods, endorsements, prize monies, and the trade in players. Fourth, sporting mediascapes transmit sporting events across the globe and widely determine the scheduling and staging of those events. Fifth, sporting ideoscapes embody the values, ideologies, and philosophies expressed in sporting cultures and institutions.

Critics of globalization have raised important questions: Naomi Klein's anti-globalization study, *No Logo*, described *Nike's retail outlet in Manhattan, New York, as 'a shrine, a place set apart for the faithful, a mausoleum... a temple where the swoosh is worshipped as both art and heroic symbol' (2000: 56). Her study concludes with a discussion of 'consumerism versus citizenship'. Leslie Sklair questions the culture or ideology of consumerism in his *Globalization—Capitalism and its Alternatives*. In sport contexts, these critiques stimulate questions such as: does it matter who sponsors the Olympics or the (men's) World Cup? Or where matches are played, and contests staged? In 2007, an American Football NFL (National Football League) match was played at London's new Wembley Stadium in England, and the following year the English Premier League football organization proposed playing an extra round of matches at non-English worldwide venues. This latter proposal was vehemently opposed by FIFA president Joseph 'Sepp' Blatter, but the plans, along with the initiation in the same year of an Indian Twenty 20 cricket Premier League, highlighted the continuing globalization of sports seeking enhanced international presence and global profiles. Sport's capacity to reach worldwide media audiences and establish new consumer markets has consistently underpinned its contribution to the globalization of world culture. At the same time, sporting cultures are not completely remade and standardized in this process. Anthony Giddens, recognizing globalization as the general process of the spread of the modern across the world, talks of 'the dialectic of the local and the global' as central to any consideration of the nature of identity, self, and society in the late modern age (1991: 22). This dialectic continues to be a major feature of contemporary sporting cultures. Indeed, Robertson (1992) introduced the term 'glocalization' to describe the process whereby the global actions of, say, a transnational organization have impacts that are locally specific and that can themselves act back on the global system.

References

Giddens, A. (1991) *Modernity and Self-Identity: Self and Society in the Late Modern Age*, Cambridge: Polity Press; Hill, J. (2002) *Sport, Leisure and Culture in Twentieth-century Britain*, Basingstoke: Palgrave; Jarvie, G. (2006) *Sport, Culture and Society: An Introduction*, London: Routledge; Klein, N. (2000) *No Logo*, London: Flamingo/Harper Collins; Maguire, J. A. (1994) 'Sport, Identity Politics and Globalization: Diminishing Contrasts and Increasing Varieties', *Sociology of Sport Journal*, 11/4: 398–427; Maguire, J. A. (1999) *Global Sport: Identities, Societies, Civilisations*, Cambridge: Polity Press; Miller, T., Lawrence, G., McKay, J. and Rowe, D. (2001) *Globalization and Sport: Playing the World*, London: Sage; Robertson, R. (1992) *Globalization: Social Theory and Global Culture*, London: Sage; Sklair L. (2002) *Globalization: Capitalism and its Alternatives*, Oxford: Oxford University Press; Thompson, J. B. (1995) *The Media and Modernity: A Social Theory of the Media*, Cambridge: Polity Press.

global public good An idea that emerged within international debate and negotiations at the end of the 1990s, particularly in the context of questions concerning sustainable development. Global environmental problems, from climate change to North–South inequality, stimulated policy-makers to ask what conditions might create forms of responsible global governance. Issues of corporate social responsibility, and heightened awareness of fair trade consumerism, are two spheres in which notions of the global public good have been mobilized. Does sport, like education, or health, lie in the sphere of public goods, those goods which a market cannot produce and which are valuable regardless of the dynamics and autonomy of the market? Many governments and sport associations and federations would agree that it does, and the mission statements and objectives of such national governments and international bodies appeal to what might be termed the global public good: yet actions by such bodies appear limited, hypocritical, and constrained. Governments continue to negotiate with provenly corrupt agencies for the right to stage mega-sports events; sport federations and clubs continue to play with equipment made by exploited child labour in the poorest parts of the world. The tension between globally commercialized sport as a private good, and sport (often the Olympics is claimed in this fashion) as a heritage of the whole of humanity and therefore a public good, is embedded in the very structure and existence of international sport. This allows the 'global public good' argument to be appropriated by profiteers who speak for the world but work for themselves in the governance and administration of world sport. This is not to decry the argument for or the ideals that fuel the notion of the global public good; but it would be misleading to ignore the way in which the argument can be exploited, and the ideals hijacked.

glycogen The storage form of glucose. Glycogen is a polysaccharide comprising between a few hundred and many thousands of glucose units arranged in an irregular structure of straight and branched chains. The average adult stores about 500 g of glycogen, mainly in the muscles (400 g) and the liver (100 g). By the process of glycogenolysis, stored glycogen is broken down to the constituent glucose units which are then available for energy metabolism. The total stored glycogen is sufficient to sustain exercise for only about two hours and it can take more than 24 hours for stores to be replenished after exercise. Manipulation of the pre-exercise diet can enhance the amount of stored glycogen though a procedure known as carbohydrate loading, in which a diet high in carbohydrate is consumed in the days before a sports competition and endurance is increased.

GNP (gross national product) The total value of all finished goods and services produced within a country in a given year, including what domestic companies earn abroad. *See also* GDP.

goal setting A psychological theory about motivating change, used extensively by sports psychologists. Goals may be set as an outcome (such as winning a competition), a performance (such as a certain time in a race), or a process (such as a long follow-through after a tennis stroke). Goal setting results in improved performance by focusing the athlete's attention on key tasks, by increasing motivation and persistence, by helping the development of new learning strategies, and by increasing self-confidence and satisfaction. Goal setting is most effective when carefully structured, and the acronym SMART is often used as a guide: goals must be Specific, Measurable, Action-oriented, Realistic, and Timely.

Goffman, Erving (1922–82) A sociologist trained in the USA, whose formative fieldwork included *ethnography undertaken in the Shetland Islands, UK (see his *The Presentation of Self in Everyday Life*, 1959), and a mental health institution in Washington, DC, in the USA (see *Asylums: Essays on the Social*

Situation of Mental Patients and Other Inmates, 1961). His works are based upon the perspectives and frameworks of *symbolic interactionism, premised on close observation of the everyday world and immersion in the culture or institution that is the focus of study. His major conceptual contributions include *frontstage, *backstage, and *total institutions. In his emphasis upon the interactive dimensions of everyday life and what he also called 'relations in public', Goffman offers fascinating approaches to the study of the familiar and what he also called a sociology of occasions. In his *Interaction Ritual: Essays on Face-to-Face Behaviour* (1972), his essay 'Where the Action Is' was concerned with forms of chance-taking, cases of experience-seeking above the mainly everyday and routine. Commercialized competitive sport was one sphere in which such action could be found, where 'the activity is staged for an audience and watched for fun'; a second was 'non-spectator risky sports', 'vigorous sports [which] are dominated by solid, young-minded citizens who can afford the time, travel and equipment'; a third sphere comprised the commercialized places providing the 'safe excitement of thrills' (the gamble at the race-track or the casino, the 'vertigo' rides at the theme park); a final type in the classification was 'fancy milling', the act of consuming valued products.

Goffman's work has had enormous and widespread influence, sustaining the quest to establish a blend of sociology and social psychology. The study of sport from its recreational through to its high-performance levels and forms stands to gain much from the application of an informed Goffmanesque approach—though the difficulties of this are severe, in that Goffman's work is based on insight, different forms of *observation, and wide reading. A methodological template guiding the symbolic interactionist in empirical studies does not exist, but despite this his form of microsociology, often known as the dramaturgical approach, has continued to have immense influence.

golf A club-and-ball game for individual players or team formations, played on manufactured courses in open countryside, and known as 'links' when by the coast. The origins of the modern form of the sport have been identified in Scotland, though some make a case for the Netherlands as the birthplace of the game. In Scotland, in the 15th century the game was prohibited by royal decree. Nevertheless, it flourished among both the privileged and the general populace. The first golf club, in Leith in Scotland, dates from 1744, becoming the Honourable Company of Edinburgh Golfers, and in 1754 a similar group founded what became the *Royal and Ancient Golf Club, and also drew up a code of rules. The first club to be established outside Scotland was in Blackheath, London, where James I of England (1566–1625), formerly James VI of Scotland, had played on the Common.

Club-based events between local players and associations were the predominant mode of play throughout the first half of the 19th century, the first championship being staged in Prestwick, Scotland, in 1857. The 1860 competition was based on stroke-play between individual professionals, and this is acknowledged as the first British Open Championship. Scotland's tradition embraced the elite and the masses, whereas in England the game had more connotations of social class and exclusivity. In the second half of the 19th century in England, there were just a few clubs—estimates place this at little more than a dozen in the 1870s—'but by 1914 there were almost 1200 clubs playing over 1000 courses' (John Lowerson, *Sport and the English Middle Classes, 1870–1914*, 1993). Golf reflected the class structure in this boom, and was also related to patterns of suburban development. In both Scotland and England, the rise in popularity of the game was a consequence of the expansion of the middle class: golf provided a source of cultural identity and status, and the private golf club could foster a philosophy of exclusivity. Middle-class women formed ladies' clubs, and working-class players were allowed to play at specified and restricted times, as members of artisan clubs. Richard Holt's study of Stanmore Golf Club, founded in 1893 in the London suburbs, showed that one third of the membership comprised women in the years just prior to World War I. Holt recognizes these women as 'part of a pioneer movement for women's sport', but this was based on a small, privileged sector of the population. Women did compete in golf at the 1900 Paris Olympic Games (the only time the event was held, though it was accepted into the Olympic programme in 2009), won by a 22- year-old Chicago socialite who was in Paris to study art.

A broader social base was sought in England in the expansion of golf provision in the third quarter of the 20th century, but a survey across Great Britain in 1974 showed that 83 per cent of golfers were male, 81 per cent were married, and the average age was 43; 47 per cent were of professional middle-class occupations, and only 24 per cent in manual working-class occupations. Clubs emerged in the USA in the 1880s, and the game was further popularized by the exhibition tour of English professional Harry Vardon (1870–1937) in 1900, when he also won the US Open Championship. Vardon made two other US tours, and personified the emerging boom in spectator sports, and their international dimension made possible by the railway and new forms of mass communication. Golf has retained an aura of social exclusiveness, despite its rising profile as a spectator sport for the big events in the television age. Sponsors have been keen to be associated with global superstars playing in beautiful and televisual outdoor settings. Tiger Woods, following on from his golf scholarship at Stanford University, won three successive American Amateur titles (1994–96) and then, at the age of 21, his first Grand Slam title, the US Master's at Augusta, in 1997. He could then sign contracts with *American Express and Rolex, and clinch deals with *Nike and golf ball manufacturer Titleist. Woods was the most famous face of a global industry which centred on the four annual championships of the Master's, the US Open, the US PGA Championship, and the British Open, but which included millions of enthusiasts worldwide, including in Japan, where it has been reported that, at the Koganei Country Club near Tokyo, some paid three million dollars for membership in the last years of the 20th century. The environmental impact of the creation of golf courses worldwide, especially in the Global South, has also become an issue of debate and controversy.

governance 'Sporting governance is in the spotlight as never before', wrote Sunder Katwala in 2000 (*Democratising Global Sport*). He was writing at a time when the International Olympic Committee was defending itself against allegations of *corruption, about to change its leadership and embark upon a course of institutional and procedural reform. Football's world governing body, FIFA, had also been exposed as self-serving and largely unaccountable to any outside body in its administrative practices, voting procedures, and financial operations. Sporting governance therefore emerged on an international level as an issue for debate and a challenge for international policy makers and reformers. The notion of governance can refer to all levels of administration of the sport: the club, the regional body, the national association, the international federation, the world governing or ruling body. In some cases governance is an issue in the non-state sector; in other cases—such as the theocratic dynasties of some Gulf states—sport governance is inextricably linked to the established and hereditary structures of state power; in many cases, sport governance—in relation to bids to host major events, for instance—is rooted in cross-sector alliance and interests. The key question in discussing sport governance is that of accountability to the sport's constituency: is the sport governed in an open and transparent fashion? Are international governing bodies in any way accountable to the international community? Are the mechanisms of sport governance representative of the grass roots of the sport? In an era of global sport, international ownership of national institutions, and unforeseen levels of profit-making in media–sport alliances, questions of governance are unprecedentedly central to the critical analysis of sport and its organization and administration.

governmentality Sport has had a vital place in the policies of many nations, and it is the state and its governmental arm that has often framed sport policy. Two concepts have become central to thinking about the nature of this sport–state relation, and the wider question of how sport is structured, organized, and governed (in non-state sectors as well as the formal structures of government): *governance, and governmentality. The latter term was coined by Roland Barthes (*Mythologies*, 1957, English translation 1972), and is what he called 'a barbarous but unavoidable neologism' to refer to the influences and strategies of the government, as articulated in organs such as the press: '*governmentality*, the Government presented by the national press as the Essence of efficacy'. It is an adaptation of the word government but, crucially, evoking the mentality, not just the actions, of those who govern, and linked to the mechanisms by which the views, values, and intentions of government and the state are conveyed in other institutional spheres of life and soak through the cultural fabric of the society.

In a more historical context, Michel *Foucault, in his essay on 'Governmentality' from his later years, developed the concept within a critique of Niccolò *Machiavelli's *The Prince* and other meditations on political power. Five core questions concerned Foucault: how does one govern the self?; how is one to be governed?; how are others to be governed?; who will people accept as governing them?; and what makes the best possible governor? These questions and issues arose in a period of turbulence in European history, as economic and religious systems were under radical and revolutionary challenge. These changes, Foucault argued, led to the notion of governance infiltrating all levels of the society; families are managed like mini-states; bodies become managed as part of perceived state responsibility. All of the population, and all social and cultural activity, come into the embrace of the principle of governmentality; sport, leisure, the arts become more central elements of state strategies. Governmentality can account for the nature of everyday life in more advanced capitalist societies in two main ways, Foucault suggests: shared views of economics make efficient producers of us all;

and the government intervenes to ensure that we become efficient producers, with health strategies underpinning the individual body, and sport, for instance, providing one of the means whereby the population can make, at national level, public expressions of collective affiliation. Even progressive movement education as developed by women professionals in late 19th- and 20th-century Britain can be interpreted as a model of physical education that functions 'so that body management symbolized individual responsibility as the basis of a harmonious social order', as John Hargreaves put it (*Sport, Power and Culture: A Social and Historical Analysis of Popular Sports in Britain*, 1986). Fitness-related discourse is both part of a public health agenda, and an element in the state's surveillance of the population based on a statistical demographic analysis that can intensify the general scrutiny of the population (Pirkko Markula and Richard Pringle, *Foucault, Sport and Exercise: Power, Knowledge and Transforming the Self*, 2006).

Grace, W. G. (1848–1915) An English amateur cricketer who played for the county side of Gloucestershire each summer season from 1865 to 1899; and for the English national side for 22 games over 19 years, in 1880 making the first Test century to be made against Australia. In a review published in 1922 of a memorial biography of Grace, Neville *Cardus wrote that he was 'the most famous man of his day . . . the most recognised of all by the man in the street'. In that biography the Bishop of Hereford could even write that 'Had Grace been born in Ancient Greece the Iliad would have been different'. Grace prompted such lyrical praise to the point of hyperbole: the great cricketer *Ranjitsinhji wrote that Grace 'turned the single-stringed instrument into the many chorded lyre'. He is widely recognized as the inventor of modern batting techniques that allowed him to accumulate almost 55,000 runs, including 126 centuries. As a bowler he was also effective, capturing 2,876 wickets. Trained as a medical doctor, Grace played as an amateur but made money as if he was a professional, in part from the commercialization of his image and the marketing of his name. Stories abound of his competitive ruthlessness, and his flouting of the spirit of *fair play in imperious treatment of opponents and disputes with umpires.

Graeco-Roman wrestling A term referring to the men's Olympic discipline, based upon a form of wrestling established in the 1860s modelled upon the Roman style of wrestling: the use of the legs is prohibited, and no holds can be made below the hips. It is held at a number of weights and has been dominated throughout its Olympic years by Scandinavian and East European nations. While claiming a classicist pedigree for the Olympics in the modern media age, though in fact a modern creation, the sport draws few informed spectators. In the wrestling halls of the contemporary Olympics, audiences are as likely to be made up of school parties accessing some of the cheaper Olympic tickets, or groups of gay men for whom the contorted movements of the combatants clearly provide light relief and entertainment as much as sporting thrill.

graft Two senses of the word 'graft' are relevant to sports studies. 1. Hard work; a good trainer and all-out team player can be complimented as committed and hard-working. 2. Corrupt practice, fraud, or criminal activity in the unofficial economy; John Sugden's *Scum Airways: Inside Football's Underground Economy*

(2002) is an illuminating investigative exploration of the world of UK-based ticket touts (or scalpers, as the USA terms them) in the world of international football.

Gramsci, Antonio *See* HEGEMONY.

Grand National *See* HORSE RACING.

Grand Slam The achievement of winning all matches or tournaments in a given competition, year, or season. In the six-nations rugby union tournament, for instance, a team that wins all of its five matches achieves the Grand Slam. The term has also been used in relation to golf's major tournaments, and particular strikes in, for instance, baseball. *See also* GEHRIG, HENRY LOUIS; GRAND SLAM (TENNIS).

Grand Slam (tennis) The achievement of holding all four Grand Slam tennis titles at once, in the same year: the Australian Open Tennis Championship (January), the French Open Tennis Championship (Roland Garros, May), the All-England Lawn Tennis Championship (Wimbledon, June), and the US Open Tennis Championship (September). The Wimbledon championships were first held in 1877 (men) and 1884 (women); the US championships in 1881 (men) and 1887 (women); the Australian in 1905 (men) and 1922 (women); and the French in 1925 (men and women). Only two men have achieved the pure Grand Slam feat of winning the four majors in one calendar year: Don Budge of the USA, in 1938; and Rod Laver, of Australia, in 1962 and 1969. Three women achieved this: Maureen Connolly Brinker (USA) in 1953; Australian Margaret Court in 1970; and German Steffi Graf in 1988 (when she also won the Olympic gold medal).

Greece, ancient, sport in Donald G. Kyle (*Sport and Spectacle in the Ancient World*, 2007) writes that sport was an essential custom for the ancient Greeks, contributing to Greek identity and cultural distinctiveness, and the 'exportation of their cultures'. Evidence is widespread on the place of sport in the society and culture, coming from literature (history, myth, poetry, drama, philosophy); sites, buildings, and facilities; depictions in art (vase paintings, statues); prizes, equipment; dedications; inscriptions; coins. Drawing on all of these sources, Kyle writes (p. 7):

> It would be hard to overstate the cultural significance of athletics for the Greeks—what the contest, the victor, and the victory meant to them. As symbolic in Greece as in modern society, sport meant different things to different people, but it meant something to everyone. Sporting concepts, including contest, prize, excellence, glory, physical and moral beauty (*agon, athlon, arête, kleos, kalaokagathia*) were central to Greek culture. Greeks saw sport as an essential part of a good education, a way to establish social status and individual pre-eminence, an index of manliness, a therapeutic outlet for aggression, a preparation for warfare, and an appropriate way to honor gods and heroes in festivals.

Sport embodied a Greek male ethos expressing skill and excellence in war, sport, and hunting, and women were excluded from even watching the Panhellenic Olympics, though in the case of Sparta, women's athletics was more developed than in the other city-states. Sport events and organized games and contests were central to the Greek cultural calendar, and dominated by the Panhellenic Games, or 'crown games', of which there were four; and more local games in particular city-states, often called the *chrematitic* (or 'monied') games, such as the Panathenaic Games, in Athens. Regardless of type or scale, these were, as Kyle puts it, 'more public and interactive' than cinema or television; ancient sports and spectacles were 'communicative performances or displays that included mediation between viewers and viewed, actors and audiences'.

Athletic competition had begun as surrogate warfare, or funeral games to honour the dead hero, and later developed as homecoming festivals, to greet a returning hero such as Odysseus. In Book 8 of the *Odyssey*, games are organized for the shipwrecked Odysseus. He proves himself through deeds, winning the discus, and being willing to contest a foot race. The Archaic Age (*c*.750–500 BC) laid the foundation for modern athletics when athletic festivals complemented earlier funeral games, and by the mid 6th century Olympia (*see* OLYMPIC GAMES, ANCIENT) was the greatest of the four Panhellenic crown, or stephanitic, games (non-war games of crown festivals), the others being Delphi's Pythian Games, Corinth's Isthmian Games, and Nemea's Nemean Games. Kyle (2007: 75) writes:

> Victories in these four games, later known as the *periodos* or "circuit", brought the highest honour, and victor inscriptions listed games in order of prestige: the games of the *periodos* came first, the Panaetheaia topped local games, and chrematitic games were added at the end. States offered a vast array of local contests—in dancing in armour, chariot dismounting, torch racing, male beauty, wine drinking, cheese stealing, team events, and more, in various civic festivals throughout the year.

Early on, funeral games and cultic festivals were intertwined in local games, but they became increasingly distinct. City-states themselves also developed distinctive sporting and athletic cultures and institutions, the most famous of these being Athens and Sparta. In Athens, called by Kyle the 'city of contest and prizes', the Great Panathenaia games began in 566 BC, on a site resurrected for the inaugural modern Olympic Games in 1896: its embankments could accommodate 50,000, there were dressing rooms and a vaulted tunnel, and the stadium represented a form of advanced specialization in sporting facilities. The Athenian games had an expanded gymnastic programme and prizes (initially sacred olive oil in amphoras such as the Burgon amphora of *c*.560, featuring an equestrian motif); later ones featured athletic events, with prizes having 'material but also symbolic value'. Athletics were staged in the Archais Agora north of the Acropolis, which by the 6th century had a racetrack. In Athens, an institutionalized culture of the body matured in the *gymnasion (gymnasium) and the *palaestra* (wrestling schools), where athletic youths of physical beauty were courted. Some institutionalized settings remained relatively exclusive, but, Kyle observes, 'official games and performances were essential rituals of democratic Athens'.

Sparta was renowned for its sport and physical culture as integrated into the educational philosophy of the city-state. There is little written evidence from the laconic Spartans, but it is clear that their sport was that of a privileged elite, a physical culture based on nudity and homoerotic aspects. Physical education for Spartan males and females in classical Sparta was supervised by a magistrate with boys divided into age-groupings (*agelai*) or 'herds', performing exercises in the nude or in nude dances, and reviewed by older males. Teams of boys played a rough ball game or battle, *sphairomachia*, and a game based on cheese-stealing was linked to whipping rituals—these were public spectacles designed to toughen up the coming generation of young Spartan warrior. Sparta's women were trained for marriage and childbirth—this included public nude exercises, parades, choral dances, initiatory runs—in a less rigorous programme or regime than for the boys, and clearly geared towards the service of a male state. Sparta did not celebrate Olympic victory for any champion until that individual actually died a heroic war death for which his name was celebrated, allowing the Olympic victory to be added as a supplement; and Spartans left no victory odes for their Olympic champions. Other states gave Olympic victors material rewards and civic privileges, but in Sparta the champion won only the right to fight at the side of the king in battle; and sporting victories were not commemorated in statues.

Sparta provides the source for discussion of the first woman victor at an Olympic Games. Kyniska of Sparta is usually named as the first woman Olympic champion (for the four-horse chariot race in 396 and in 392); but the owner could enter without going, and she was pressurized by a royal brother, who, as Kyle notes, used his sister to show that the race could be won by wealth rather than manly prowess, 'in effect, emasculating the Olympic chariot race'. But Spartan women were without doubt physically striking, and set other city-state commentators talking and writing. Spartan women in particular had and showed off physical attributes in sport, and were associated with loose morals, talked about and known as *phainomerides* (thigh showers) as early as the 6th century (Stephen G. Miller, *Ancient Greek Athletics*, 2004). Euripides (426 BC) wrote for an Athenian audience, in his *Andromache*:

> A Spartan girl could not be chaste even if she wanted. They abandon their houses to run around with young men, with naked thighs and open clothes, sharing the same race tracks and *palaistrai* [wrestling schools]—a situation which I find insufferable. And if your girls are trained is it any wonder that your Spartan women grow up without knowing what chastity is?

Spartan women did the *bibasis*, for instance, jumping up in the air as many times as they could, while kicking their own buttocks with the heels of the feet, referred to by Aristophanes in *Lysistrata* (411 BC).

But despite the Spartan exception, women were not prominent in Greek sport or athletics. In Athens, some archaeological evidence has identified wrestling schools for girls and women in some localities, and there was more such activity than was documented, though the association of strong active womanhood with the Spartan case perhaps explains why that activity was given little documented profile in Athens; 4th-century authors such as Xenophon and Plato, more sympathetic to the Spartans, emphasized women's athletics more than their predecessors. And there are pictures of women swimming; one red-figure amphora in Paris's Louvre, dating from *c.*520 BC, shows four women oiling their bodies, swimming, diving in, and (probably) undressing. But this was, in Miller's words, 'a day at the beach rather than . . . athletic competition'. Overall, the Greek athletic world remained a male-dominated one, stressing excellence and reward in the competitive sphere, and contemplation, voyeurism, and status in the recreational institutions.

greyhound racing A form of dog racing in which the dog pursues a mechanical hare around a track that is circular or oval-shaped. An artificial hare was first used for this kind of racing in Hendon, north London, in 1876, though the sport was slow to expand, until an effective mechanical hare and circular track were developed in 1919 in Emeryville, California, and the International Greyhound Racing Association was formed in 1920. Betting was permitted, through bookmakers, and the sport prospered. In the 1920s, tracks were built in Manchester, England (the Bellevue Track), as well as London, and the sport attracted regular, large crowds in provincial towns and regions. It became a particularly popular venue for working-class males, though its association with gambling led to the term 'going to the dogs' as a way of describing deterioration and decline. In 1932, tracks in London attracted nine million spectators, according to the National Greyhound Racing Club, and *The Times* reported that by 1935 Britain (mostly England) had 230 tracks (Mike Huggins and Jack Williams, *Sport and the English, 1918–1939*, 2006). The sport thrived in Australia as well as in the USA, and was established in Spain. It did not sustain its level of popularity in the second half of the 20th century, though where it has survived it offers combined dining and betting experiences in improved facilities that cater for the special event consumer as well as the regular punter.

gridiron *See* AMERICAN FOOTBALL.

Griffith-Joyner, Florence (1960–98) An African American track-and-field champion, born Florence Delorez Griffith. Born and raised in Los Angeles, Griffith-Joyner rose to prominence at the Olympic Games in her home city in 1984, more noticed for her theatrical and showy fingernails than for her silver medal in the 200-metre event. Her nickname, Flo-Jo, became a shorthand by which her celebrity was fuelled and reproduced. After withdrawing into family and working life, she re-emerged to produce remarkable times in sprint races just prior to and at the 1988 Seoul Olympics, where she won three gold medals and one silver medal in individual and relay events. Sport writer Mike Collett recalls her emergence onto the athletic and celebrity scene at the World Athletics Championships in Helsinki in 1983: 'she had these incredible four-inch long fingernails painted blood red'. Collett also noted the difference in her appearance on her re-emergence: 'Her body was different. She's been a gorgeous, beautiful, elfin-like woman in the early 80s. By the late 80s she wasn't. She had a square jaw, the sort of acne you get from steroid abuse, and was totally different.' Griffith-Joyner retired abruptly from competitive athletics after her Seoul triumphs, on the eve of the introduction of random drug testing in 1989. She died from suffocation during a seizure in her sleep, in 1998, though Collett recalls her death and funeral as being a 'hush-hush' affair. The official coroner's line was that her body could not be tested for steroid effects, as no reliable or accurate test was possible. Her family reported that Griffith-Joyner had suffered several seizures, said to be the consequence of a congenital condition, in the earlier 1990s.

grounded theory An approach to sociocultural research, rooted in social psychological and microsociological studies, in which the conceptualization of the phenomenon under study develops in the course of the fieldwork, not from some predetermined conceptual agenda. Barney Glaser and Anselm Strauss (*The Discovery of Grounded Theory*, 1967) emphasized that theory emerges from the observational process itself, as the researcher both observes and interprets, generating sensitizing concepts, and then returns to the process of observation anew to begin the observation–interpretation cycle once more. Grounded theory is often linked to the *ethnographic method, and is a branch of *symbolic interactionism. It is widely employed in small-scale studies of sport cultures or subcultures, where the nuance of a style or the impact of a playing or performing technique could reveal the wider meaning and significance of the sporting action or encounter. The approach is a prominent inductive framework in which to undertake *qualitative research, but can be used confusedly and confusingly, as a masquerade for ignorance or lack of rigour in the fieldwork process.

Guérin, Robert (1876–1952) A French sport journalist, writing for *Le Matin*, and sport administrator, who became the first president of the world governing body of football, La *Fédération Internationale de Football Association (FIFA), in 1904. The founding constitution of the organization was signed in Paris. Guérin, aged only 28, was chairman of the Union des Sociétés Françaises de Sports Athlétiques, an umbrella association covering a wide range of sports in France. From this base in journalism and administration, Guérin had from 1902 advocated an international organizing body for football, with the primary objectives of clarifying and standardizing the rules of the game, recognizing one national association per country, and providing a framework for the organization of international matches and competition. There would inevitably be tensions here, as Great Britain claimed four 'national' associations, and ran the rule-making body the International Football Association Board. Guérin and his pioneering colleagues nevertheless continued negotiating with the British, including his successor *Daniel Woolfall, and in 1905 FIFA was recognized by the British. In 1906 Guérin resigned when his attempts to launch an international tournament were frustrated, and the English Football Association joined FIFA with Woolfall becoming the organization's second president. Guérin represents a French prominence and internationalist vision in sport administration, alongside the inventor of the modern Olympics, Pierre de *Coubertin. *See also* Rimet, Jules.

gusimbuka *See* Rwandan high jumping.

Guts-Muths, Johann Christoph Friedrich (1759–1839) A German founder of a system of gymnastics that was introduced into schools in Germany in the 19th century. Guts-Muths wrote several books and manuals outlining his system of gymnastics and exercise and targeting youth and young people (*Gymnastics for Youth*, 1793); he also studied theology and geography. His influence, combined with that of Friedrich Ludwig *Jahn, created a long-lasting nationalistic ethos of physical training within the German tradition. His belief in the power of exercise was as much a philosophy as a science, and his teachings constitute an influential European strand in a kind of secular theology of body culture. *See also* Turnen.

gymnasion Literally translated as 'the nude place', the location in ancient Greece where nude exercises took place. It was often physically connected to the *palaestra*, the wrestling school. The gymnasium was in essence a mini-stadium, a covered practice track next to an uncovered practice track; on this latter people trained for the javelin and the discus. Originally emerging on undeveloped sites on the edge of towns, gymnasia spread widely in the 5th century BC, stimulated by the increasing popularity and profile of gymnastics exercise and athletics, particularly for the social elite and the privileged strata of society. The gymnasium also became associated with the intellectual life, and schools of philosophy emerged alongside gymnasia; in the 4th century schools of philosophy arose linked to gymnasia (Plato spoke and taught at the Academy, and the Lyceum—whose name became the basis of the long-lasting French term for school, *lyceé*—was the site of Aristotle's school).

Gymnasia became central to the physical context of Athenian intellectual life. They combined the intellectual and the physical, the platonic and the erotic. Nigel Spivey (*The Ancient Olympics*, 2004) captures this in his description of the gymnasium as a place where 'exercise is undertaken in training for beautiful goodness'. In describing the archaeology and the practice of the gym and the wrestling school he teases out the dynamic of the 'philosophers and the pederasts', and the erotic dimensions of performance and courtship. Socrates called the supreme qualities of a young man 'beauty', things that could shake the soul: the images painted upon the cups used at the gymnasium were (as Spivey observes) of,

> boys with slim waists, broad shoulders, neatly proud buttocks, and springy thighs . . . Thousands upon thousands of such images and inscriptions were produced in ancient Athens, and they leave us in no doubt. Men were not born beautiful. They made themselves that way—in the gymnasium.

Athenian society was male-dominated but also bisexual, and Plato commented on how Olympic pentathlon victor Ikkos of Tarentum abstained from 'women and even boys' while in training. Gymnasia institutionalized pederasty, though this prioritized the principle of beauty and it is quite likely that in many cases contemplation and not sexual exploitation or desire was the main motivation of the elder participant.

gymnastics A form of exercise and physical performance with origins in military preparation (in ancient as well as more modern societies), and educational programmes for fitness and health. In many respects gymnastics (alongside classic team games) is the foundation of much of the physical education curriculum in the educational institutions of Western societies. It flourishes at the highest competitive level, in the Olympic Games, where fourteen gold medals are competed for; in the schooling systems of the aforesaid societies; and at club and associational level in neighbourhoods and communities. The British army formed an Army Gymnastic Staff in 1860. In its recognizable modern form, gymnastics arose as pedagogic and political initiatives of pioneering thinkers: *Guts-Muths and *Jahn in Germany, and *Ling in Sweden. Educational visionaries with Swedish and German backgrounds—*Österberg and *Wilkie respectively—promoted Swedish gymnastics, with its stress on rhythmic fluency rather than strength-building, in schooling and physical education for women in the later 19th century in England.

Olympic gymnastics was dominated by West European nations until the 1948 London Olympics, but the sport was revolutionized in conception and ambition by the Soviet Union; at the 1952 Helsinki Olympics the Soviet gymnasts won five of the seven men's titles, and four out of six of the women's. Russia and other East European countries have continued to dominate events in the discipline, especially so in rhythmic gymnastics, in which, in the words of David Wallechinsky and Jaimie Loucky, 'thin young women perform 75–90 second routines using various accessories: hoop, rope, clubs, ball, and ribbon' (*The Complete Book of the Olympics*, 2008). At the Olympics, gymnasts compete mainly in the team competition, individual all-round competition, and routines on individual apparatus. Gymnastics was a significant popularizer of the Olympics itself, in the groundbreaking impact of performers such as Olga Korbut (USSR) and Nadia Comaneci (Romania) at the 1972 and 1976 Olympics respectively. Allen Guttmann (*Sports Spectators*, 1986) recalls how when pony-tailed Olga Korbut 'slipped, fell, and wept', the ABC's sports director Roone Arledge 'ordered a close-up' and the American audience shuddered with empathy; after that, gymnastics was no longer 'an almost unknown spectator sport' in the USA. Such performers became genuine *role models for countless young women across the world.

habitus A concept first formulated by French philosopher and anthropologist Marcel Mauss (1872–1950), and then by Norbert Elias in 1939 in his major work *The Civilizing Process*, but most influentially developed in the works of Pierre *Bourdieu. For Bourdieu habitus was a defining principle or set of principles that regulate the actions of individuals; or a system based upon 'modes of perception, of thinking, of appreciation and of action'. The concept reminds us that sport cultures do not spring from nowhere; nor can they be made anew overnight—they are anchored in established values, ways of seeing, and practices. *See also* CLASS HABITUS.

Hagen, Walter (1892–1969) A US professional golfer whose achievements and profile in the first half of the 20th century did much to establish the basis and prominence of the sport. His eleven championship titles in the major competitions (four in the British Open, two in the US Open, and five in the Professional Golfers Association, or PGA, tournament) place him third in the all-time list of winners of the four major titles. His style of play was as important as his wins, for his swashbuckling play popularized the sport, and changed the image of the full-time golfer from that of the mundane workaday professional to the glamorous and increasingly popular figure. *See also* HOGAN, WILLIAM BEN.

haih à deux A sport encouraged by North African Arab states as a way of preserving traditional games and indigenous culture in the context of increasing globalization (Allen Guttmann, *Sports: The First Five Millennia*, 2004). It is similar to the traditional English sport *prisoners' base.

hallmark events *See* MEGA-EVENTS.

handball A team game played on an indoor court between five- or seven-a-side, or outdoors between eleven-a-side. It is a non-contact sport based on throwing, catching, and passing the ball with the aim of throwing it into the opponent's goal. It emerged from the German gymnastics tradition, invented by schoolteacher Konrad Koch (1846–1911) in the 1890s, though formalized, institutionalized (in educational settings), and popularized after World War I. Koch had also organized the first football match to be staged in Germany (in 1874), and wrote treatises on the moral value of sport and games, as well as promoting folk sports. Once established in the 1920s, the sport gained popularity across numerous countries and the International Amateur Handball federation was established in 1928, with Avery *Brundage (later president of the International Olympic Committee) of the USA as its first president. The seven-a-side indoor version was introduced into the Olympic Games (for men) in 1936, and for women in 1976. A world championship was staged in 1938. Soviet, East German, and East European teams have dominated the men's Olympic competition up until France's 2008 triumph, Scandinavian nations the women's.

handy-grips A traditional Irish sport included by Archbishop Thomas *Croke in his list of 'dead and buried... favourite exercises and amusements', some of which he noted were already 'entirely forgotten and unknown' (1884). Others were: 'Ball-playing, hurling, football kicking, according to Irish rules, 'casting', leaping in various ways, wrestling... top-pegging, leap-frog, rounders, tip-in-the-hat'. Handy-grips has been mentioned in passing in much of the commentary on and analysis of Croke's cultural manifesto for the Gaelic Athletic Association (GAA), but little has been written on the nature of the practice. It remains an oft-cited but little-understood footnote to the history of cultural revivalism in and through sports.

hang gliding *See* AIRSPORTS.

Hanot, Gabriel (1889–1968) A French footballer who played as a full back or winger, winning a first French cap at 19, but after a twelfth international was injured piloting a plane. Following World War II he became both football journalist and national team coach. After a 5–1 home defeat to Spain he wrote anonymously in the French sporting newspaper *L'Équipe* (*see* ÉQUIPE, L') demanding the coach's dismissal, and then resigned the coach position, following his own recommendation. In 1955, aged 65, and as football editor of *L'Équipe*, aided by the paper's editor Jacques Goddet and two other journalism colleagues including Jacques Ferran (b. 1920), he led the launch of the European football club tournament, the European Cup, remodelled and renamed the *UEFA Champions League in 1992. Ferran recalls that Englishman Sir Stanley *Rous was talking of a cup linked to cities and trade fairs, and so the leading European clubs hinted at a breakaway, which led to the *Fédération Internationale de Football Association (FIFA) insisting that *UEFA organize the new European-wide competition.

Hargreaves, Alison (1962–95) An English mountaineer who began a professional climbing career in her early twenties, having failed to gain a place to study geography at universities in good climbing locations. Joining British and American expeditions to the Himalayas in 1986 and 1987, she climbed the north face of the Eiger in 1989, while five and a half months pregnant. Hargreaves secured national coverage for her feat, the controversy over her portending motherhood overriding the uniqueness of her achievement in becoming the first British woman to make the ascent. Lacking secure sources of finance for her climbing, her economic problems escalated when her husband's outdoor equipment business went bankrupt in 1993. To escape creditors, they moved to the Alps with their two children, and Hargreaves embarked on high-profile solo climbs. This strategy was adopted too in 1995, this time without her family supporting her on the expeditions, in a plan to scale the world's three highest peaks in a single year. Climbing Everest alone in May 1995 gained her a book contract, and the funding to pay off her debts and plan the climb of K2. She reached the summit in July, but was killed in a storm during the descent, along with six others. The death of Hargreaves stimulated wide debate about the responsibilities of motherhood and parenting, and the gendered cultural politics of the professional sporting world more generally. Her husband's decision to take the children to visit 'mum's last mountain' in the autumn of 1995—accompanied by a BBC camera crew—sparked further commentary and controversy on the allegedly voyeuristic and maudlin exploitation of Hargreaves's death.

Harvard University A private, Ivy League university in Cambridge, Massachusetts; the USA's oldest university, founded as New College in 1636, renamed Harvard three years later. The annual rowing competition with *Yale University began in 1852, and is the oldest inter-university sporting event in the USA. Harvard–Yale rivalries on the sporting field also include *American football, and the inter-collegiate sporting competition between the two universities fuels a buoyant alumni culture.

Hawthorne effect The effect, in social scientific fieldwork, of the presence of the observer upon those under observation. The Western Electrical Company's Hawthorne Works, Chicago, was studied by Fritz J. Roethlisberger and William J. Dickson for their 1939 study *Management and the Worker*. The study, started in 1929 with 5 employee-subjects, escalated into a large-scale study of 20,000 subjects, focusing upon the factors affecting worker output, such as environmental conditions and material gain or remuneration. But the researchers found that worker output was also affected by the experiments themselves. Alongside their major finding that informal organization was often neglected, yet has serious influences and often positive effects on worker behaviour and plant performance, this insight produced a recipe for the development of personnel practice in the industrial organization, and what would later be more fully developed in *action research approaches. Therefore their findings showed the complexities of undertaking a case study of a large organization or institution, and the importance of building into the research design an awareness of researcher effect, and measures to control such experimental effects. An understanding of the Hawthorne effect is essential to any sensitively conceived study of sport cultures, institutions, and organizations.

hazing A term used predominantly in North America, referring to ritualistic and often humiliating induction processes that require newcomers to a sport subculture to perform acts or practices that can secure or confirm their membership of the group. Justified as a cultural process, these have often, in athletic or sports clubs, involved alcohol consumption in drinking challenges, and serve as a form of reinforcing the status of the established and veteran members of the group. In male sport groups hazing processes and rituals reinforce dominant forms of heterosexual masculinity, and can involve the verbal vilification of other groups such as homosexuals and women. In any kind of group, though, the hazing process can afford the opportunity for experienced and established group members to reinforce their status through oral, physical, or sexual abuse. In the USA, a 1999 study by Alfred University and the NCAA (*National Collegiate Athletic Association) identified that around 80 per cent of college athletes had been subjected to some form of hazing:

Half were required to participate in drinking contests or alcohol related initiations while two thirds were subjected to humiliating hazing. Additionally, much of the reported hazing in high schools occurs during initiations related to athletic teams with many problems arising during pre-season sports camps. (StopHazing.org, Educating to Eliminate Hazing website)

The NCAA, and the national professional body for college coaches in the USA, have made the reform of hazing practices a top priority. But hazing remains inadequately studied and widely tolerated, and reproduces itself in the manner of the rituals of a secret society.

health A state of soundness of body and mind with freedom from disease or illness. While 'ill health' is commonly understood as meaning a state of illness or disease, 'health' is generally used in a positive but nebulous sense. It derives from the Old English for 'whole' and has been defined by the World Health Organization as 'a state of complete physical, mental and social well-being, not merely the absence of disease or infirmity'. It is widely applied to indicate something that is believed to promote its attainment—a health food, a healthy environment, a health visitor. To an extent the broad concept of health has been reconfigured into the term *wellness although it is common to see the two terms linked, such as in the phrase 'health and well-being', in order to evoke both the alleviation of illness and the attainment of a positive state of being.

The role of exercise in the promotion of health has long been recognized, from the ancient Greek temples of Asclepius and the writings of Hippocrates, to an influential modern English medical treatise by Francis Fuller: *Medicina Gymnastica, or, A treatise concerning the power of exercise, with respect to the animal oeconomy and the great necessity of it, in the cure of several distempers (1705)*, which proved highly popular and passed through nine editions in the 18th century. But exercise mainly remained in the realm of the sportsman or fanatic until the middle of the 20th century, when a rapidly growing body of scientific evidence began to unravel the mechanistic basis to its health-promoting properties. The beneficial value of exercise shifted from being based on belief to being based on proven fact. Government health policies formally accepted the role exercise can play in preventing ill health, and there is almost universal individual belief that exercise promotes well-being, as evidenced by the explosive development of exercise and health clubs, products, and media.

The scientific evidence base is extensive and strong. Exercise impacts on many of the body's systems and reduces all-cause mortality although it does not extend longevity. Its main positive effects are on cardiovascular disease, skeletal health, type 2 diabetes, obesity, some forms of cancer, and mental health. Exercise can improve work capacity in adults and it can slow down the natural decline in physical condition that comes with age, allowing older people an improved quality of life and greater independence. While intense exercise is important to achieve peak fitness and sports performance, most of the health benefits accrue with relatively modest amounts and intensities of exercise—the standard recommendation is a minimum of five bouts of 30 minutes of moderate activity each week. There are some hazards of exercise. Sudden intense exercise can trigger a cardiovascular event in those with existing but undiagnosed heart disease; physical activity involves a risk of muscle or skeletal injury; and intense training can led to a susceptibility to infection, *eating disorders, and *osteoporosis.

SEE WEB LINKS

- The official site of the World Health Organization, with resource and publications databases.
- The official site of the UK government's Department of Health, including access to publications, reports, and policy statements on health care and public health germane to the study of exercise.

hedonism From the Greek word for 'pleasure', hedonism came to mean in the mid 19th century a system of ethics in which the primary good is pleasure; therefore, the goal of a good life should be to experience as much pleasure as possible. As a broader psychological theory, hedonism recognizes the pursuit of pleasure as a central motivating drive, and of course a particular conception of and attitude towards sport could be seen as hedonistically driven; though the work ethic necessary for success in performance sport, and the competitive momentum that dominates sporting encounters, work against the straightforward pursuit of pleasurable experiences. In competitively serious and high-performance sport cultures and environments, the term hedonist has come to have negative connotations, implying that the hedonistic approach and attitude is incompatible with the dedication and commitment necessary for sporting achievement.

hegemony 1. In international relations and political science, the condition of dominance of a particular state in the world order—Great Britain in the period of its global imperial domination, or the USA in the later 20th century and beyond. 2. In sociology and cultural studies, derived from the Italian Marxist activist and thinker Antonio Gramsci (1891–1937), a condition of dominance achieved by one group, such as a social class, over another, on the basis of a compliance rooted in a sense that the interests of the dominant group are also the interests of all other groups. Dimensions of hegemony include the process whereby ideological interests are rendered as common sense, as values that can be shared on the basis of negotiation. Thus, in the context of sport, the victory of a national sporting team can be claimed to be in the interests of the whole of a populace, and to represent the genuine enthusiasms of very varied groups. Critics have argued that the notion of hegemony has been applied in too limiting a fashion to the dynamics and relationships of social class. But there is no logical reason why the concept cannot be equally effectively applied to questions of gender, such as the persistence of male dominance in sport.

Hemingway, Ernest Miller (1899–1961) A journalist, short-story writer, and novelist raised in Chicago, USA, who spent time in Paris in the 1920s and civil-war-torn Spain in the 1930s, and lived his last years in Cuba, taking his own life with a gunshot in the mouth. Hemingway's writings often combined pastoral nostalgia with depictions of a life of tough outdoor masculinity, and hunting, fishing, boxing, and bullfighting feature prominently in his works. His famous prose style, characterized by plain English and realistic description, is based upon his premise, as he wrote in *Esquire* in 1935, that 'Good writing is true writing'; the writer must combine honesty with experience, and 'the more he learns from experience the more truly he can imagine'. This formula generated works in which fiction crossed over extensively with journalistic themes, whether these were concerned with war or sport. So bullfighting is covered in his 1927 novel *Fiesta* (also published as *The Sun Also Rises*) and his 1932 book on bullfighting, *Death in the Afternoon*; fishing and deep-sea fishing feature in his short stories and thinly disguised autobiographical pieces, and provide the core theme for his 1952 novella, *The Old Man and the Sea*. In *Fiesta*, the narrator Jake Barnes has a kind of neutrality as he has been rendered impotent by a war wound, and his athletic endeavours are now restricted to therapeutic swimming in the sea and observing the love life of his fellow expatriates in Paris; but the other male protagonists are boxers, or bullfighters, contrasted with less manly tennis players or focused cynical professional cyclists.

Hemingway's crisp, staccato prose is selective, based on the view that the writer can omit things that he knows so that, as he put it in *Death in the Afternoon*, the reader, 'if the writer is writing truly enough, will have a feeling of those things as strongly as though the writer had stated them. The dignity of movement of an iceberg is due to only one-eighth of it being above-water.' Hemingway claimed to be aiming to capture 'what really happened in action'. This could lead him to idealize male physical action, and Jake Barnes in *Fiesta* says to ex-Princeton boxing champion and novelist Robert Cohn: 'Nobody ever lives their life all the way up except bull-fighters.' The Hemingway realistic style, and a thematic range based on writing 'what really happened in action; what the actual things were that produced the emotion that you experienced', became known as a 'hard-boiled', and to some, limited approach. Fellow Nobel Prize winner Saul Bellow wrote, in *Dangling Man* (1944), through the words of his own protagonist Joseph: 'This is an era of hard-boiled doom. Today, the code of the athlete, of the tough boy . . . is stronger than ever . . . The hard-boiled are compensated for their silence; they fly planes or fight bulls or catch tarpon, whereas I rarely leave my room.'

Henie, Sonja (1912–69) A Norwegian figure skater whose gold medals at the Winter Olympics of 1928, 1932, and 1936, and an accompanying string of World Championships (1927–36) and European titles (1931–6), established the popularity of *ice skating in international competition. Born into an affluent Norwegian family, she was an exceptional all-round sportswoman as a child and competed at the first Winter Olympic Games (Chamonix 1924) at the age of 11. Her impact was stylistic as well as technical, introducing dramatic gestures of the head, and shorter skirts, speeded-up movements and spectacular leaps. Turning professional in 1936, she became a wealthy showbusiness star, combining ice revues with a Hollywood film career; her *One in a Million* (1936) was the first full-length skating movie (released in Germany through the patronage of Nazi propaganda chief Joseph Goebbels) and she made nine more films, all of which were lucrative money-making exercises, featuring Henie's outstanding skating skill and her petite, consciously feminine and sexualized image. Henie was also controversially close to Adolf *Hitler, accepting invitations to tea and displaying a signed photograph of him in her home in Norway. She amassed an art collection and lived the luxury life of the Hollywood superstar in Los Angeles, providing much material on her love life and liaisons for the voracious gossip columnists of the film world. Dramatic to the end, she died on board a plane on the way from Paris to Oslo, scheduled for specialist medical treatment for the leukaemia that killed her. Henie exploited with rare skill not only the stage of international sporting competition, but the sets of the 20th century's other most prominent popular cultural form, combining sexual appeal with performance skills in both of those spheres, and generating huge audiences for her blend of sport and entertainment.

Henry VIII (1491–1547) King of England from 1509, and of Ireland from 1541/2, Henry VIII is historically significant for his reformation of the church in a break with Rome, and remembered popularly for marrying six wives in succession in an unsuccessful mission to produce a male heir. But his sporting prowess was one of the qualities that contributed to an overall ebullient character and popular image, which fronted a ruthless and merciless authoritarian figure of state power and a strategy of increasing centralized governmental power. Public forms of spectacle were central to this strategy, and the young king cultivated the full-scale romantic tournament on an unprecedented scale, with associated pageantry and *spectacle. They were part of the expectations of Henry's public as he challenged the trappings of the church in public life. E. W. Ives (*Oxford Dictionary of National Biography*, 2004) observes that for his subjects,

> Henry was everything a king should be; he had all the monarchical virtues in full measure. The first was magnificence, immediately obvious in his personal appearance, whether excelling in the joust before a crowd of courtiers and commoners or grandly robed to dominate a diplomatic set piece.

On the French/Calais border in June 1520, Henry stage-managed a meeting between himself and Francis I of France, the central focus of which was a series of tournaments, designed to symbolize a possible end to Anglo-French hostility. Though this stated policy intent was unachieved, when in the following year England joined an alliance against France, the symbolism was long-lasting: 'The reputation of the Field of Cloth of Gold spread throughout Europe, not simply as a vastly expensive exercise in image building, but as regal glory in action', as Ives states. Henry had made his mark in the popular imagination by competing successfully in *jousting events, tournaments, and foot combat from 1510 to the late 1520s, and exhibiting a forceful physicality to political associates and rivals, the wider public, and diplomatic figures from foreign states. Though one might question the motivation and application of his stream of vanquished rivals, Henry's profile and image on the sporting field fuelled the perception of him as a figure of strength and magnificence.

hermeneutics In philosophy, and forms of social theory, this is the term for the systematic study of processes of understanding, and within that the interpretation of the meaning of both social actions and texts. For the meaning of sport practices, or actions, to be probed in any depth, or for the interpretive analysis of textual representations of sport (in media or literary forms, for instance), a hermeneutic perspective provides philosophical and theoretical foundations for any adequate exploration. *See also* DEPTH HERMENEUTIC.

Herrigel, Eugen (1884–1955) A German philosopher who, when visiting Japan, took up archery as a way of understanding the philosophy of Zen, in which the everyday mind must be attuned to the Unconscious. In Zen, aesthetic or artistic practices can be seen as a way of training the mind, of bringing the mind into contact with what is seen as the ultimate reality. In 1936 Herrigel gave a lecture to the German-Japanese society in Berlin, on 'The Chivalrous Art of Archery'. This circulated in translations in numerous languages and, asked to agree to a reprint of the paper, Herrigel expanded his thoughts into the little book *Zen in the Art of Archery* (1953), talking therein of swordplay as well as archery. The core claim in the book is that technical knowledge of how to practise an art or a sport is insufficient in order to master the art: the practitioner must, repeatedly, time and time again, 'take the road to the artless art', in a process of constant rebirth. Herrigel's reflections may seem irrelevant or fantastical to the calculating competitive athlete or coach, but the notion of shooting or combat being a form of training of the mind has much in common with Western assumptions about the values of games and physical education; and the idea that physical activity can be a matter of entering a particular spiritual state is important in certain psychological approaches to performance such as the notions of *flow and peak performance, or popular appeals to self-actualization such as the *inner game.

heuristics Etymologically, the process of finding things out by modes of trial and error, particularly by generating artificial constructs to account for selected social phenomena, constructs that might have some, but no certain or definitive, base in *empirical evidence. Social scientists engage in this kind of thinking as a way of theorizing complex phenomena, in an overarching yet possibly speculative way, such as in Max Weber's notion of the *ideal type. Definitions of sport that have been produced by theorists and philosophers are usually heuristic devices that can be challenged by close consideration—or generation—of further evidence; yet, challengeable as such heuristic devices are by definition, they remain useful, and some would argue necessary, for attaining any adequate level of conceptual clarity. Therefore one might not agree with all the aspects of a particular definition of sport, while continuing to recognize the value of the definition-seeking.

Heysel Stadium disaster A crowd disaster at Belgium's Heysel Stadium in Brussels on 29 May 1995 when 39 fans of the Italian football club Juventus died before the final of the European (Club Champions) Cup against English club Liverpool. A retaining wall collapsed on the terraces—widely believed to have been caused by the aggressive behaviour of some Liverpool supporters—and people were crushed or trampled to death in the aftermath. Controversially, the match went on to be played, the television schedules taking priority. English clubs were banned from European competition for the subsequent five years. *See also* BAUDRILLARD, JEAN.

high jumping An established athletic discipline in its own right, based on clearing a bar suspended by upright posts in an unassisted jump from a running approach (in several earlier Olympics, competitors jumped from a standing position), and also featuring in the *decathlon and the heptathlon. With its organized roots in mid-19th-century England, there is scant evidence of high jumping as an established activity in earlier societies and cultures of the West, including at the ancient Olympics. High jumping has given the history of sporting techniques one of its most famous names: at the 1968 Mexico Olympics US jumper Richard Fosbury superseded the orthodox 'straddle' technique, launching himself to the Olympic title in a head-first leap with his back to the bar and so revolutionizing the event with his 'Fosbury flop'. US and Soviet or Eastern European jumpers have dominated men's and women's Olympic events. Other forms of jumping showing the profile and appeal of the activity within a particular culture include *gusimbuka* (*Rwandan high jumping). This indigenous practice of young Rwandan men was photographed by Adolf Friedrich von Mecklenburg's photographer on an anthropological expedition in 1907. This famous picture portrayed an airborne shorts-clad young Tutsi male straddling a make-do rope and hurtling above the heads of two formally dressed Europeans. John Bale's *Imagined Olympians* (2002) and his *Sports Geography* (2nd edn, 2003) explore this—at least to modern Western eyes—extraordinary image, as both an expression of the Tutsi's sense of physical superiority over the majority Hutu, and an ordering of 'African corporeality' by the colonialist explorer.

Highland Games Traditional sporting and athletic events held in the Highlands of Scotland since the early 19th century, competitive in nature and often professional. Contests embraced standard athletic activities, and also tossing the caber (a tree trunk of an agreed size), tossing the weight (a metal sphere attached to a chain and ring, thrown up for height in one variant, and for distance in another), and stone-throwing. Dancing and bagpipe-playing would often feature in the schedule of the event. The Games were institutionalized in 1832 with the formation of the Braemar Royal Highland Society, and their influence was widespread, Scottish-Americans forming early athletics clubs on the east coast of the USA and Scottish expatriates influencing the formalization of athletics in Canada. Grant Jarvie writes of the social and cultural significance of the Games: 'The Scottish Highland Gatherings, through the reproduction of tartan symbolism, clan regalia and images of harmonious social relations, contribute to a certain image of Gaelic culture that was initially popularized during the reign of Queen Victoria', whose Scottish Balmoral estate had social links with the Braemar Society ('Highland Gatherings and Balmorality', *Sociology of Sport Journal*, 1992). Scottish-Americans continued to draw on the Highland Games as a source of cultural identity, and in 1981 the 'Association of Scottish Games and Festivals was founded . . . as a modern clearing house for information about American-Scottish Highland Games and Gatherings' (G. Jarvie, *Sport, Culture and Society: An Introduction*, 2006).

Hillary, Sir Edmund Percival (1919–2008) New Zealand mountaineer who, along with Sherpa *Tenzing Norgay, made the first ascent of Everest, the world's highest mountain, in 1953. The expedition was led by an Englishman, Sir John Hunt (1910–98), and, with the Commonwealth connection to New Zealand, Hillary's achievement could be claimed as a British triumph. Richard Holt (*Sport and the British: A Modern History*, 1989) summarizes the nature of this claim: Hunt read the *Oxford Book of Greek Verse* while organizing things; umbrellas were carried up to 13,000 feet; 'native' races were seen to be handled well and integrated; *The Times* compared the feat to Sir Francis Drake's circumnavigation of the globe; the Queen's speech spoke of the Commonwealth as a new kind of post-imperial cooperative entity 'moving steadily towards greater harmony between its many creeds, colours and races'. Hillary was knighted, but shunned celebrity for much of his life (which he called 'a constant battle against boredom'), sustaining his passion for and expertise in apiarism, and doing much to help develop educational and medical institutions and facilities for the communities of Nepal.

hillwalking *See* MOUNTAINEERING.

Hitler, Adolf (1889–1945) An Austrian-born German politician whose World War I military service was followed by a political career after joining the National Socialist German Worker's Party (the Nazi Party, in popular parlance). Hitler gained the leadership of the party and, on the basis of a manifesto combining racist doctrines of superiority with right-wing political extremism and fascist beliefs, became the chancellor of Germany in 1933, and its dictatorial head of state in 1935. In his book *Mein Kampf* (1925) Hitler referred to 'faultless, sports-trained bodies' and 'the breeding of bodies that are healthy to the core'; and the Nazi Party saw sporting themes as of political significance, noting in its 1920 party programme that 'powerful bodies' should be valued, held up against forms of 'physical degeneration' in the development of the ideal of 'racial equality' (cited in John Hoberman, 'Primacy of Performance: Superman not Superathlete', *The International Journal of the History of Sport*, 1999). Hitler, and in particular his propaganda chief Josef Goebbels (1897–1945), recognized the powerful ideological impact of sport, promoting the film-making of Leni *Riefenstahl at the 1936 Berlin Olympic Games, and cultivating the notion of the healthy and strong body as the basis of the collective articulation of the master race. *See also* NAZISM, SPORT IN; FASCISM, SPORT IN.

Hobbs, Sir Jack (John Berry) (1882–1963) England's first sportsman to be awarded a knighthood, born in Cambridge, the eldest of twelve children of the groundsman of Jesus College. Hobbs was the foremost professional cricketer of his time in England, hailed not just for his batting prowess but for his calm and modest personality. Nicknamed 'The Master', for the way in which he coped with all kinds of opponents in an unflurried fashion, Hobbs first played for England during the tour of Australia in 1907–8, and batted for the national side until 1930. Playing for the county side Surrey from 1905 to 1934, his performances—particularly in the 1920s when he had passed the age of 40—were remarkable, and by the mid 1920s he had overtaken W. G. *Grace's record of high scoring. Hobbs started a successful sport retailers' and business, and was knighted in 1953. The importance of Hobbs's modest demeanour yet prolific sporting impact was highlighted in the part that he played in England's 1926 win over Australia, a victory that regained the Ashes against a backdrop of the nation's General Strike and a sense of political turmoil. Hobbs, from modest roots but within an elite milieu, and adopting a deferential manner to his amateur peers, symbolized the reconciliation that might be made between the instrumental dedication of the professional and the traditional values of the amateur.

Hoch, Paul A US-born radical activist, writer, and critic whose *Rip Off the Big Game: The Exploitation of Sports by the Power Elite* (1972) provided a provocative 'historical materialist analysis of sports', as Hoch himself put it. His critical sweep included sport's role in reproducing military might, monopoly capital, sexism, and racism. Presciently, he noted that the use of performance-enhancing drugs, which shrink the testes of big muscular male athletes, has the ironic outcome of producing '*plastic Supermen with no balls*'.

hockey, field An eleven-a-side team game played with stick and ball, by men and women. Numerous cases of stick-and-ball games have been identified in ancient cultures, including in what is now Argentina, where early 16th-century European settlers documented a game called *cheuca* (meaning 'the twisted one') played by the Araucaño Indians; and the game has been associated with *hurling. Its organized modern form dates from the later 19th century in England: the London-based cricket club at Teddington, not keen on adopting football, developed hockey as its winter sport, and used the hard cricket ball. In Olympic competition, after English/British victories at the 1908 and 1920 tournaments, India and Pakistan dominated the men's event until the emergence of Germany, Holland, and Australia as world-class teams in the later 20th century and into the 21st. Great Britain's men won the title at Seoul in 1988, but could not sustain a competitive impact at succeeding Games. The inaugural women's event at the 1980 Olympics in Moscow produced an irresistible Olympics fairy story, as the Zimbabwe team triumphed in the absence of five of the six scheduled competitors, all withdrawn as part of the USA-led boycott. Australia (three victories), Holland (two victories), Spain (just the one at Barcelona in 1992), and Germany (at Athens 2004) shared the gold medals at the succeeding seven tournaments.

The International Hockey Federation had been formed in Paris in 1924, prompted by the omission of hockey from that year's Olympic programme (Fédération Internationale de Hockey sur Gazon). Its founding members were Austria, Belgium, Czechoslovakia, France, Hungary, Spain, and Switzerland, and before the next Olympics, Denmark, Holland, Germany, and India joined the federation. In 1970 the English Hockey Association (founded in 1886 in London) also joined the international federation, and its International Rules Board was incorporated into the federation, thus uniting world hockey. An International Federation of Women's Hockey Associations had been founded in 1927 by Australia, Denmark, England, Ireland, Scotland, South Africa, the United States, and Wales. These two bodies merged in 1982. Hockey was introduced into the Asian Games in 1958, and the Pan-American Games in 1967. A European Cup for men was inaugurated in 1970, won by West Germany, and was at the time the largest ever international tournament, with nineteen nations competing. Forty years later, the international federation had 127 affiliated national members, and oversaw a truly international game, though the sport's profile in the global media remained low: the speed of the ball, associations with privilege and exclusivity in some countries, and the relative inelegance and inflexibility of the playing position are not features that appeal to television producers or viewers.

Hogan, William Ben (1912–97) A US professional golfer whose post-World War II achievements included four US Open Championships, a (British) Open, two PGA (Professional Golfers' Association) titles, and two Masters. The nine victories place him joint fourth, with South African Gary Player (b. 1935), in the all-time list of winners of major titles, behind three other US players: Jack Nicklaus (b. 1940, 18 titles), Tiger Woods (b. 1975, 14 titles), and Walter *Hagen (11 titles). It is not just the achievements that immortalized Hogan, but the comeback legend that he became when recovering from serious injuries in a road accident in 1949, winning most of his major championships after that date. He also rose to the highest levels of the sport gradually, after a tragic childhood in which his blacksmith father committed suicide when Hogan himself was nine, and on the basis of a long period as a club professional, in his home-town area of Fort Worth, Texas, and then at the Century Country Club, Purchase, New York State. His hard-won career, doggedness and determination, and taciturn competitiveness made him an ideal example of sport as the fulfilment of the American dream, and in his national profile and popularity he represented what Leo Lowenthal (in an analysis of biographies in popular magazines, first published in 1944) called a 'triumph of mass idols', in the switch in popularity from 'idols of production' (industrialists, politicians, doers and makers) to 'idols of consumption' (film stars, singers, sports champions).

homophobia A fear of homosexuality, translated into discriminatory and hostile attitudes towards homosexuals, sometimes manifest within sport as abuse of the homosexual. In men's rugby football, for instance, a tradition of vilification of women and homosexuals has characterized the songs and jokes of the assertively heterosexual male dressing-room and clubhouse bar. Eric Dunning has observed that such obscene songs, 'mocking... effeminate and homosexual males', have been a means of stressing and reinforcing the rugby players' unambiguous masculinity (*Quest for Excitement: Sport and Leisure in the Civilizing Process*, 1986, with Norbert Elias). Where such aggressive reaffirmations of heterosexual masculinity are made, homosexual identities are unsurprisingly repressed, and the homophobic attitude and culture reinforced; this accounts for the large number of cases in which homosexual sportsmen and lesbian sportswomen have opted not to reveal their sexual identity. Famous exceptions include English footballer Justin Fashanu (1961–98), US diver Greg Louganis, tennis players Billie-Jean King (USA) and Martina Navratilova (Czechoslovakia/USA), and Australian Rugby League player Ian Roberts.

hooligan A word that came in the late 19th century to refer to members of unruly male youth groups. It had too a judgemental dimension, in that such groups were perceived as a threat to the established social order, and debate about hooliganism has often generated *moral panics. In sport, the term has been most widely used in relation to fans and their behaviours, and in particular the very public and visible profile and practices of members of *football hooligan groupings and gangs.

horse racing A spectator sport, in which riders—or jockeys—race horses against each other over a specified length of track, which sometimes has hurdles or fences over which the mounted horse must jump: the first is flat racing 'across the flat'; the second is 'over the sticks', either steeplechasing or hurdle racing. The sport is a focus for betting and gambling, and at its highest-profile events also a catalyst for displays of distinctive cultural status and fashion, a form of *conspicuous consumption. Wray Vamplew points out that even 'the minority who

attend race meetings are unusual among watchers of elite sport in that they have
no knowledge of the sport derived from personal participation at a lower level'
('Horse Racing', in Tony Mason, ed., *Sport in Britain: A Social History*, 1989). For
most people with an interest in racing, the 'quality thoroughbred . . . is . . . little more
than a betting mechanism'. Organized horse racing is also vulnerable to betting
scams and corruption, by either 'nobbling' horses or bribing riders and others in the
industry. It nevertheless provides appealing public events that can attract—often
culturally and economically zoned—wide sectors of the population, particularly to
annual events such as the *Arc de Triomphe in France, and its counterparts in
England and the USA. Horse racing has been a staple of the sports pages in the
British press, due primarily to its focus for betting, though the large crowds of the
first half of the 20th century declined from the 1950s onwards, and competing
attractions for the consumer's leisure pound—and the legalization of betting in
neighbourhood betting shops—made attendance at the track no longer a necessity
for the punter. It is a sporting spectacle, in many countries, where it is expected
that both the privileged elite and the hoi polloi attend, but do not necessarily
mix. While the aristocracy and royalty mingled, sometimes with international
guests, at sumptuous house parties before and after big races, the masses arrived
at the race on the day, for the drama of the event, the sightseeing, and the
excitement of the wager.

In England, the most important races 'over the sticks' (courses with jumps) are
the Cheltenham Gold Cup, first run in 1924 (though previously existing as a race
without jumps since 1819); and the Grand National, first run in 1839. The most
important race 'on the flat', claimed by some as the most famous horse race in the
world, is the one-and-a-half-mile Derby, run since 1780 and named after the
12th Earl of Derby. The popularity of the event as a form of *carnival, attracting
people of all social backgrounds, was commented on by French historian Hippolyte
Taine. The Grand National in particular, run over a little over four and a half miles
by forty or more horses on a course with thirty jumps, draws large numbers of
casual gamblers, many of whom make their sole appearance in a betting shop for
Grand National day. In the USA the three most prestigious races in the racing
calendar are the Belmont Stakes, over one and a half miles, founded in 1867, run in
June; the Preakness Stakes, over one mile one and a half furlongs, founded in
1873, run in May; and the one-and-a-quarter-mile Kentucky Derby, founded in
1875, and run earlier in May. These constitute the USA's triple crown in horse
racing, though no horse won the crown (that is, all three races) in the 31 years since
the achievement of Affirmed in 1978.Other forms of horse racing include trotting,
or harness racing, in which the horse tows the rider who occupies a small cart
(called a 'sulky'): this parody of Roman *chariot racing gained numerous
adherents in Australia and New Zealand in the 1930s and into the mid century, and
has a market and public in the USA and Canada, but it has scarcely a presence in
Britain in the 21st century. *See also* SEABISCUIT.

hot rod A term that originated in southern California in the 1930s to describe the
customized motor vehicles that were adapted to achieve the fastest possible
speeds on roads and streets—'drags', rather than purpose-designed tracks. The
term is of unknown origin, though could well refer to forms of burn-out of engine

parts. Such contests appealed in particular to young male adults or late adolescents, with speed and danger providing physical thrills characterized too by macho performative display and a spirit of youthful rebellion. On its professional level in the USA (National Hot Rod Association), the national champion from 2004 to 2008 was Tony Schumacher, nicknamed 'The Sarge' for his army look, and sponsored by the US Army. Schumacher, as the winner of more championships than any other driver, reaching speeds of over 330 miles per hour, was hardly resonant of hot rod's countercultural image, more a symbol of the sport's entry into the mainstream of US entertainment culture.

Hughes, Thomas (1822–96) Writer and social reformer, most famous as the author of *Tom Brown's School Days* (1857), a lightly veiled autobiographical account of life at Rugby School, where Hughes was educated from 1834 until going on to Oriel College, Oxford, in 1842. Charlotte Mitchell's *Oxford Dictionary of National Biography* portrait of Hughes cites his recollection of Rugby as 'a very rough, not to say brutal place when I went there, but much mended during those years'. And the mending was achieved in the famous reforms at the heart of which was the development of team games and their associated values, in collective contexts such as the houses into which the school was subdivided. This reform, as Mitchell observes, 'was to make Rugby world-famous; its essential characteristic was that older boys were given responsibility for disciplining the younger, in an atmosphere of moral earnestness and self-questioning'. Hughes captained the cricket team at Rugby, inviting the previously excluded local boys on to the school's playing fields. Hughes also recollected his Rugby years (in his *Fifty Years Ago*, 1891) as a 'training for a big fight' testing to the utmost the physical, intellectual, and moral powers of the individual.

At Oxford, Hughes was a keen rower, and developed reforming and political interests, leaving the university without a degree to study law in London. Instrumental in the foundation of the Christian Socialist movement, Hughes was an influential proponent of *rational recreation or *muscular Christianity, teaching boxing as well as law and the Bible at the Working Men's College founded by the group in 1854; and he helped establish the Working Men's Club and Institute Union in 1862. But it was as the author of *Tom Brown's School Days* that Hughes—initially unidentified when the book was published anonymously— became best known, the book going through 53 editions within 35 years. The book contains celebrated accounts of football and cricket matches, and of the value of boxing. Leadership by example is articulated on the football field; the 'true football king', Old Brooke, is Tom Brown's inspiration: 'His face is earnest and careful as he glances a last time over his array, but full of pluck and hope, the sort of look I hope to see in my general when I go out to fight' (Chapter V, 'Rugby and Football'). The early chapters (covering Tom's pre-Rugby years) evoke the bucolic harmony expressed in traditional recreations such as fighting, backswording, and running in the festivals of rural life, and Hughes himself, in later life, criticized the excesses of *athleticism, if it became too dominant.

Huizinga, Johan (1872–1945) A Dutch historian and pioneer of modern forms of cultural history. Huizinga's *Homo Ludens—A Study of the Play Element in Culture*

(1938, English translation 1949) is a study of the seriousness of play. Written as World War II was approaching, the book argues for the recognition of the centrality of play to human culture: play is not just marginal, rather it actually determines human expressivity. For Huizinga, certain forms of modern sport embody the 'mechanization of community life' and threaten the play element: in 'immense sport organizations' such as football and baseball, 'we see free youthful forces and courage reduced to normality and uniformity in the service of the machinery of rules of play and the competitive system' (*America*, written during World War I).

human capital The competencies, talents, skills, and knowledge embedded in people, and their ability to create and contribute to economic value through work and labour. This is widely recognized but difficult to measure, particularly as in sport so much necessary labour is accomplished by volunteers, from the local boules society in France to the neighbourhood bowls club in England, from the Little League committee in Midwest USA to the eighty thousand uncosted volunteers at a summer Olympic Games. Chicago's *The Journal of Human Capital* acknowledges the expanding importance of human capital in the contemporary knowledge economy, recognizing 'the role human capital plays in the production, allocation, and distribution of economic resources and in supporting long-term economic growth and development'. Sport, as is the case with many associated cultural industries, is dependent at many of its levels upon the input of human capital. *See also* SOCIAL CAPITAL.

hunting The pursuit by humans of animal prey for the purposes of pleasure and fun, rather than commercial profit, subsistence, or survival. In upper-class British culture in the later 18th century and into the early 19th century, the very word 'sportsman' could be seen as a synonym for 'hunter'. Ralph Nevill, in his *Sporting Days and Sporting Ways* (1910), catalogued the sporting enthusiasms—which might, he acknowledged, seem 'brutal' to the more modern eye and sensitivity—of 'the man of pleasure'. Sport, he noted, 'monopolised the attention of the majority of the upper class', and many country gentlemen were 'entirely concentrated upon it'. Military, imperialistic careers and cultures perpetuated this tradition of the hunt, and indeed it was sometimes claimed that an accomplished hunter could transfer his qualities to the roles and responsibilities of the cavalry officer. *See also* FOX HUNTING.

hurdles An activity in athletics that is an established event in all major athletics championships, its main formats being run over distances of 110 metres (100 metres for women) and 400 metres, during each of which there are ten flights of hurdles that runners must clear. Hurdles also feature in the *steeplechase, and the 110-metre event is one of the five challenges in the *decathlon. This combination of sprinting and jumping was first documented at the University of Oxford sports of 1864, where sheep hurdles were used. In earlier forms, hurdlers were disqualified if three or more hurdles were knocked over. This rule was abolished for the 1932 Olympic Games, at which the legendary US athlete 'Babe' *Didrikson numbered the then 80-metre hurdle race among her victories, reaffirming the hurdles as an event that would prove attractive to the ambitious all-rounder, and as a planned combination of pace and technique. In the men's event in 2008 a Cuban won the gold medal, but the USA has dominated, and by the end of the 2008 Beijing Summer

Olympics had won twenty gold, twenty bronze, and eighteen silver medals, while no other nation had won a tenth of that medal haul. In the women's event, first introduced at the Olympics in 1932, an early US domination was challenged by Europeans and, from the 1950s, by competitors from the USSR and other East European state socialist nations; 400-metre gold medallists have included a Moroccan (in Los Angeles 1984 in the inaugural event) and Jamaicans (in Atlanta 1996 and Beijing 2008).

hurling A fifteen-a-side team game played with sticks and ball, with a long-established pedigree in Irish history and culture. In Gaelic, the hurling stick is known as the *caman*, and the ball as the *sliothar*. Points can be scored by driving the ball into the opposition's goal either under (three points) or over (one point) a crossbar. The Irish Annals include a description of a hurling contest in the context of territorial battles and conquest in the 13th century BC, and the sport recurred in tales of heroic endeavour over the subsequent two thousand years. Colonizing Anglo-Norman Christians did not succeed in curbing the enthusiasm for the game, even when (in the 14th century AD) regional parliaments decreed that hurling be banned on common land. The game sustained a strong cultural hold in rural villages, games sometimes being played, literally, between neighbouring rival villages with three hundred a side starting a contest on the common boundary, the winner being the side to hurl the ball 'home' to their own village landmark. The Anglo-Irish gentry was attracted to the game, particularly in the 18th century, keeping estate-based teams and organizing wager-linked matches and contests.

The more modern, formalized version of hurling was stimulated by the formation of the Gaelic Athletic Association (GAA) in 1884, included by Archbishop *Croke as one of the 'racy of the soil...Irish sports and pastimes' that could be revived and promoted as a vital element in the nationalist movement. County-based clubs were formed, and an All-Ireland championship established. The number of players was reduced, from twenty-one in 1884 to fifteen in 1913. Hurling also contributed to the profile of Irish culture and nationalism on the east coast of the USA, where the Irish Athletic Club of Boston was founded in 1879, with the goal of promoting 'the preservation of the national games, sports and pastimes of Ireland' among the first-generation Irish immigrants of Boston (Paul Darby, 'Gaelic Games and the Irish Immigrant Experience in Boston', in Alan Bairner, ed., *Sport and the Irish: Histories, Identities, Issues*, 2005). Irish immigrants also promoted the game in Australia, New Zealand, South Africa, and Argentina.

In 2009, the 125th anniversary of the GAA, the association could claim hurling, often described too as a violent or brutal variant of *hockey, as 'Europe's oldest field game'. The game is played by men—*camogie is the women's version of the sport—and has continued mainly on an amateur basis (though with increasing controversies concerning payment for players): the sport has thus provided a robust basis for the articulation of both regional identity and national culture, and continues to be among the two or three most popular participation sports among Irish males. In February 2009, the GAA's investment in the game among US university/college students, stimulated by the formation of a Californian Collegiate Gaelic Athletic Association, led to a hurling match between Stanford and UC Berkeley Universities. Larry Beil, of ABC Channel 7 News, covering one of these

Californian matches, introduced it thus: 'It's like lacrosse, and rugby, with a little bit of soccer thrown in, and then some baseball too'. The multiple skills of throwing, running, kicking, and driving with the hurling stick continued to attract new enthusiasts, as well as reaffirm a distinctive Irish sporting culture.

Hurlingham Club A club established in 1869 in extensive grounds on the banks of London's River Thames, at which *clay pigeon shooting was organized, and where *polo became established from 1874, followed by lawn tennis (1877) and *croquet at the turn of the century. The club was as much a focus of and catalyst for the privileged leisure classes of the late Victorian era as a site of sporting competition; spectacular fetes were held for Queen Victoria's 1887 and 1897 jubilees. The Hurlingham Polo Committee is the governing body for the sport, though playing of the game ceased at Hurlingham itself after World War II.

hybridity A term referring initially to forms of interracial mixing that were disapproved of in a particular society, so that a dominant—often white—culture in a colonial setting could reassert its own allegedly pure identity with relation to mixed-race categories such as 'half-breed'. A more positive sense of the term has been developed by cultural theorists recognizing hybridity as a source of the development and articulation of identity, based on a creative fusion of different elements. Most prominent and influential among theorists of hybridity is Homi Bhabha (*The Location of Culture*, 1994), for whom hybridity is not merely a condition of the fusion of the different cultural elements, but is a transformational and counter-hegemonic process; transcultural forms, for Bhabha, are created in interdependence and a relation of mutual construction of their emerging subjectivities, and these have an inbuilt potential to challenge existing interpretations, representations, and authorities. Sport forms that have emerged as a consequence of the process of hybridization have been called 'hybrid sportoids', and the example given by John Bale and Mike Cronin of such a case, in their edited collection *Sport and Postcolonialism* (2003), is *Trobriand cricket. The concept is a valuable counter to approaches describing the diffusion of sports, as if the movement of sports across cultures is a natural process. *See also* BRICOLAGE; CULTURAL DIFFUSION; ALTERITY.

hypnotism The artificial production by one individual of a state resembling sleep in another individual, generating actions by the hypnotized subject on the basis of the external suggestion of the hypnotizer. Sport performers have used the technique—or had the technique used on them—in advance and anticipation of specific contests or encounters, as if what they have been told while in their trance-like state can be transferred to the context of post-hypnotic action. There is no credible scientific evidence to support a case for the reliable use of hypnotism in relation to sporting achievement, but its attraction even to the odd athlete or performer indicates a persisting belief in the power of the mind over the body.

Hyundai A South Korean company based in Seoul with interests ranging from departmental stores to motor vehicles, and a high profile as a sponsor of the men's football World Cup, the Euro (the championship for national teams), and the *UEFA Champions League. The value of its World Cup sponsorship at the 2006

World Cup in Germany included exposure, through perimeter board advertising in the stadium, to 'an accumulative TV audience of 34 billion in 239 countries at an average of almost 13 minutes per game' (Hyundai, *2006 FIFA World Cup Germany Sponsorship Report*). In the final match, board exposure was for twenty minutes. Its 'Hyundai Fan of the Match' was adjudged a success, an 'on/offline' integration delivering 'more excitement'. As the 'automotive' category of official partner for the World Cup, it also secured invaluable levels of exposure of its motor products. Hyundai's sponsorship strategy has successfully branded the company as a modern, dynamic corporate body, so showing the power of sport and its associations to overturn stereotypes and preconceptions concerning so-called less-developed, or developing, societies.

h

I

IAAF *See* International Association of Athletics Federations.

IBM *See* Olympic Programme, The.

Icarus Cup A free-flying festival that first took place in Saint-Hilaire du Touvet, in the Rhône-Alpes region of France, in 1974, claiming to be the oldest such festival in the world. It is held annually, in September, and attracts more than 8,000 pilots of aircraft ranging from hang gliders and paragliders to hot air balloons, and includes stunt kite demonstrations. The event lasts for four days and is as much carnival and festival as sporting contest, attracting 75,000 visitors. The event also includes a film festival and an aeronautical display by the French Air Force.

ice dancing *See* ice skating.

ice hockey A team sport played on ice comprising six players per team, originating in Canada and growing to one of the four most prominent professional team sports in North America, where the sport is known simply as hockey. Veterans of the Crimean War are said to have played a game with a puck, rather than a ball, on the frozen waters of Kingston Harbour, Ontario, in 1860. British troops were also reported to have played the game at Halifax, Nova Scotia, at around the same time. Rules were formulated in 1879 by students at McGill University, Montreal, and a university club was formed the following year. When US universities, led by Yale and Johns Hopkins, began to play the sport in 1893, leagues were already well established throughout Canada. In that year, too, the Governor General of Canada, Lord Stanley of Preston, donated a trophy that became ice hockey's chief honour, the Stanley Cup, first won in 1894 by a team from the Montreal Amateur Athletic Association.

The International Ice Hockey Federation (IIHF) was formed in 1908, by five founder members, all European: Belgium, Bohemia, France, Great Britain, and Switzerland; and the first European championship, held in Les Avants in the Swiss Alps, was won by Great Britain. The sport developed strongly in the UK in the 1930s, with many Canadian players, and the Great Britain team even defeated Canada, the dominant world force in the sport, for the Olympic and World Championship titles at the winter Olympic Games in Garmisch in 1936. The Soviet Union won the Olympic Gold at Cortina in 1956, and went on to dominate world championships, in part due to the stability of its full-time but technically amateur players; nine of the Soviet Union's players became the first ice hockey double gold medal winners in 1968, while rival nations had lost their top performers to professional leagues. Other countries where the sport has gained national popularity and international success include Finland, the Czech Republic, Slovakia, Sweden, and Switzerland, all of which have had some success at the IIHF world championships. Olympic honours and world championships in women's ice hockey have been dominated by the nations mentioned above, with the exception of Switzerland.

It is in North America that the professional game has flourished most successfully. The National Hockey League (NHL) was inaugurated in its modern form by four Canadian clubs in Montreal in 1917, and over the following decades included increasing numbers of US teams or franchises. The NHL comprised, in 2010, 6 Canadian and 24 US franchises, though Canadian players continued to outnumber US players. The commercial success and media profile of the NHL are explicable in relation to what Richard Gruneau and David Whitson have called the 'politics of accumulation' within a 'set of international dynamics involving urban growth and decline' (*Hockey Night in Canada: Sport, Identities and Cultural Politics*, 1993). Cities looking to secure major-league franchises and international sporting events see sport as a catalyst for economic growth. Having a hockey franchise is about more than tradition and cultural history, 'now best understood as part of a larger project in which corporate and civic elites struggle to establish and maintain their cities' status in a transnational economic and cultural hierarchy of cities'.

ice skating On indoor arenas, the aesthetic performances of figure skating and ice dancing; in the outdoors, long-distance racing and speed skating. Ice skating has strong and long-established recreational profiles in countries with appropriate weather conditions, such as Canada and the Scandinavian countries, but skates were adapted in various forms in innumerable European countries, including in the Netherlands where visual documentation exists of women skating at the end of the 15th century. The International Skating Union, the oldest winter sports governing body, was founded in the Netherlands in 1892 by fifteen delegates from European countries, twenty-nine years after the first modern speed skating competition was staged in Norway, ten years after the first international figure skating competition was held in Vienna, Austria, and three years after the first men's world championships (Amsterdam). Canada joined in 1894. Ice-skating disciplines became a staple of the Winter Olympics programme in the 20th century, not least because of the outlet that it offered to women performers such as Sonja *Henie, and the opportunity for spectators to see the female body in action. The combination of speed, balance, athleticism, and aesthetics has continued to ensure its niche in the winter sports calendar, though the popularity of recreational ice rinks receded in the later 20th century.

ICSSPE *See* INTERNATIONAL COUNCIL OF SPORT SCIENCE AND PHYSICAL EDUCATION.

id In the psychoanalytic theories of Sigmund *Freud, the id is one of three interrelated elements of the psyche, along with the *ego and the *superego. In particular, the id—described by Freud as 'a chaos, a cauldron full of seething excitations'—is seen as a wholly unconscious source of instinctual drives requiring immediate satisfaction. It is a tantalizing concept in its potential relevance to physical and sporting experience, but lacks any basis in scientific empirical study.

idealism Following Raymond Williams (*Keywords*, 1976), there are two modern senses of idealism. 1. A philosophical sense in which reality is said or understood to be based on or formed by ideas (so that sport is what the idea of sport says that it is, not some separate action-based experience). 2. A way of thinking wherein a judgement is made or an action proposed based upon a projected 'higher or better state'. In this second sense, sport—or particular models of sport such as *fair play—can be claimed as embodying a morally superior state of conduct compared to other spheres of cultural life or social action. *See also* IDEALIST.

idealist As a noun, an individual who subscribes and is committed to a particular set of distinctive values, and is resistant to change or compromise in the interpretation of those values. Notable examples in sport include defendants of the principle of amateurism, or believers in sport's power as a force for international understanding. An idealist viewed from the perspective of someone not sharing his or her values may well be seen more as an apologist or a propagandist.

ideal type In the work of Max *Weber, a *heuristic device for capturing the primary qualities of a subject under study; a kind of conceptual model, an abstraction from the concrete reality. A good example of this in Weber's own work was his notion of *bureaucracy. In his essay on '"Objectivity" in Social Science' (1904) Weber emphasized that the ideal type was conceived as an accentuation of reality, not a simple representation of it. Constructing an ideal type is part of the general process of analysis of social phenomena; so for Weber, sociology was a process of 'the critique of concept construction'. He called the ideal type 'a mental construct for the scrutiny and systematic characterization of individual concrete patterns which are significant in their uniqueness', for making explicit the 'unique individual character of cultural phenomena'. Take the very idea of sport; its character will vary from place to place and across historical periods, and according to the experiences and perceptions of the individuals and groups in a particular society or culture; its meanings, and definitions of what sport actually is, will be— and have been—widely argued over. People in ordinary, everyday life will say 'but that's not a sport' to others for whom a particular activity (darts or chess, for instance?) constitutes the essence of sport. Knowing this, though, does not lead us to altogether abandon the concept; there is still something recognizable, identifiable, and specific about the cultural phenomenon known as sport, and this fuels—in both everyday reflection and academic theory—the further construction of revised ideal types. Ideal types have been much criticized as being too vague, too dependent upon the subjective whims of the individual theorist; but they remain essential tools for making conceptual sense of a complex world, and for the informed conceptualization of selected phenomena.

identity A term referring to the identifiable, traditionally stable, characteristics of an individual or an institution. The Latin root *idem*, conveying continuity and sameness, is the source of the word. The term has been widely adapted and applied, in social psychology, cultural studies, and sociology, and can now refer to personal identity, cultural identity, social identity, and national identity. Long-standing debates question the extent of the stability of personal identity; Anselm Strauss's 1959 essay 'Transformations of Identity' emphasized the 'open-ended, tentative, exploratory, hypothetical, problematical, devious, changeable and only partly unified character of human courses of action', and considered numerous cases of 'movement in identity'. This social psychological perspective highlights the contingent and changeable nature of identity: a sport fan moving residence can begin to follow his or her 'new' local side; an 'early adult' extreme sport enthusiast might switch to golf or bowls in middle age; an ageing sport star—or one prematurely retired, through injury—may find the identity of star or celebrity to be a vulnerable and fragile one as performance levels fade or sponsors move on to newer younger clients.

This experiential, subjective source of identity needs to be balanced with determining influences of identity such as class, gender, ethnicity, and race. Sports have been widely and deeply linked to class, gender, ethnic, or race identities, and any careful observation of sporting practices and cultures will confirm the continuing relevance of such influences upon the structuring of identities, despite the undoubted identity transformations of which human subjects are capable. This interplay of the structuring influences and the subjective expression of one's identity generates in some cases new blends and this is recognized in the idea of the hybridity of cultural identities and practices; sport may be initially imposed on a colonized populace, but in playing and following the sport in its own style, that populace creates a new hybrid form. Sport has also provided an important site for forms of identity politics or symbolic contestation of taken-for-granted understandings, whether this be the black-power salutes of John Carlos and Tommie Smith on the Olympic podium in Mexico in 1968, the environmental activism of surfers in the early 2000s, or the public display of lesbian identity by fans of particular tennis players on the international circuit.

ideology A complex concept with a long pedigree in the social sciences, ideology is in its most general sense a set of ideas that can be seen to characterize a particular social group, on the basis of which that group makes sense of the world. Crucially, such ideas are seen to shape institutions, so that sport in 1930s Italy, for instance, can be seen as reflective of fascist ideology; sport in the USSR was constructed as a tool of communist ideology; and sport in the societies of Western Europe and North America could be seen as serving the interests of capitalist ideology. It is important to recognize this capacity of sport-based ideologies to serve the interests of particular groups or social formations. Used too loosely as a descriptive term for ideas, the concept can lack analytical focus. In the work of Karl *Marx and Friedrich Engels, ideology has referred to both a state of illusion, or *false consciousness, and to the set of ideas that are generated by identifiable interests. Such interests, from a Marxist perspective, are usually economic, and associated spheres of life such as politics, the law, religion, aesthetics, and philosophy (and one could add sport to their list) are what Marx called 'ideological forms'.

Crude Marxist approaches have reduced sport to little more than a sphere of false consciousness, serving the interests of the dominant ruling class. Jean-Marie Brohm, for instance, following the Marxist philosopher Louis Althusser (1918–90), sees sport, and particularly Olympic high-performance sport, as an 'ideological state apparatus' (an ISA). Sport may have some organizational independence in a society, but, from this perspective, it nevertheless transmits the dominant values of the society and the capitalist system, and contributes to the maintenance of social order: it mechanizes the body; it represses sexual drives; it establishes order and hierarchy; its competitive ethos equates with capitalist competition; it prioritizes productivity; and it dissects human performance as a means of celebrating the human species (Brohm, *Sport: A Prison of Measured Time*, 1976). More sophisticated and subtle analyses of the ideological sphere have been generated by adaptations of the work of Antonio Gramsci, using the concept of *hegemony.

imagery The process of recreating an experience in the mind, often as an element of mental practice or mental preparation. Imagery uses all the senses and is a form of simulation that recalls from memory pieces of information to create an image of a sports skill or setting, such as how a golf swing should be played. Imagery can enhance the learning and performance of motor skills although the explanation of its effectiveness is still subject to a number of theoretical positions. Individuals differ in their imaging ability and sports psychologists have developed programmes to improve the controllability and vividness of the images seen.

IMG *See* INTERNATIONAL MANAGEMENT GROUP.

individualism This can refer to any perspective placing the individual as an autonomous actor in social settings and contexts. In team sports, emphasis on the individual is often discouraged in the cause of the collective interests of the team. A more positive interpretation of individualism was provided by US sociologist David Riesman in his 1951 essay 'Individulism Reconsidered', where he argued against forms of conformity that threatened 'that margin of freedom which gives life its savour and its endless possibility for advance'. Individualism has fostered, Riesman noted (adding that it was far from fashionable to say this), one of the 'great cultures of history', in developing its 'arts of consumption' via innovations 'in architecture and design, in moving pictures and in poetry and criticism'. Sport may be conspicuously absent from this list, but has undoubtedly been a source for the articulation of relative autonomy and freedoms, and so has—paradoxically it might seem, given the collective base of so much of what is taken to be sporting culture—made some contribution to this more positive sense of individualism.

induction In contradistinction to *deduction, this is the process of thinking and analysis that proceeds from observation of particular phenomena towards *empirical generalizations. These generalizations are then fed back into the broader process of theory formation, discussed alongside all previous empirical cases that have informed the theoretical process. Take the example of a sport *subculture such as surfing. The researcher studying a particular group or community of surfers is unlikely to be ignorant of the existing knowledge about surfing and its adherents, but as data are gathered the developing interpretation and analysis is stimulated initially and primarily by the observations of the actions and behaviours of the surfers themselves (not thoughts about previous surfers or studies of other subcultures). These latter will be relevant when the empirical generalizations of the surfing culture being studied are contextualized more widely—in relation to the literature of lifestyle sports or water sports of fashionable youth, for instance.

inductive As in inductive reasoning or inductive thinking, referring to the analytical process of *induction.

inequality It is widely recognized that society is characterized by forms of inequality; this can be demonstrated in the spheres of gender, race, ethnicity, wealth, education, and hereditary status, for instance. Any familiarity at all with the world of sport confirms this, as *sport participation figures and studies of social class and social stratification have shown. Yet sport claims, in order to ensure an evenly matched and genuine contest, to rest upon principles of equality. The sociological fact of deep-rooted inequality therefore lies in some tension alongside this sporting ideal, and despite modern societies' aspirations to treat all of its members more equally and to promote *equality and *equity policies, inequality remains a major focus for sport researchers and analysts.

inferior good In consumer theory, a good for which demand decreases when consumer income rises. In technical economic terms, the inferior good has little 'elasticity of demand'; that is, consumers with more discretionary income move on to something perceived as affordable that they previously could not afford (the gastro-pub rather than the takeaway meal). This notion of 'inferiority' is about affordability and perceived value of products, and not necessarily any inherent quality of the 'inferior' product. Sport seems not to follow any law of the inferior good, as consumers make decisions that are not based purely on affordability: someone with more money at his or her disposal might choose to continue to watch lower-league football or village cricket rather than the top-level professional version that has become affordable, because of the sense of access, intimacy, and *community that the 'inferior good' continues to provide.

inflation The rise in the general level of prices of goods and services over time. If inflation rises beyond the rise in wages, then a worker will suffer a reduction in disposable, discretionary income, and leisure spending may well decrease. Subscriptions to gymnasia and health clubs are terminated when the family budget becomes more stretched; the price of the fortnightly professional sport fixture begins to look like a luxury. The leisure and sport industries are highly vulnerable in inflationary times.

informal economy Transactions and exchanges that are not formally identifiable in measures of economic activity. These may not be illegal, but neither are they logged in the formal accounting frameworks of organizations and economists. The collection at the sport club, for player or administrator, or the proceeds of the jumble sale, might be critical to the well-being of the individual and the collective; but they do not show in the bookkeeping procedures of the club or association. Where the informal economy operates in illegal ways, such as in ticket touting, it overlaps and is coterminous with the *black economy.

INGO International non-government organization, such as an international sport federation, or a body formed to support a particular conception of sport, such as the *International Olympic Committee. The status of INGOs is important, as by definition such bodies are not usually accountable to any political constituency at national or international level, and so their very constitution can raise issues and questions concerning the nature of sport *governance.

injuries *See* SPORTS MEDICINE.

inner game A mind–body theory of performance and coaching pioneered by W. Timothy Gallwey. In 1971, during a sabbatical from his work in higher education administration, Gallwey took on some coaching at a tennis club in California. Noticing blockages in the responses of players to his coaching, he 'began to explore ways to focus the mind of the player on direct and non-judgmental observation of ball, body, and racquet in a way that would heighten learning, performance, and enjoyment of the process'. His books on *The Inner Game of Tennis* (1974) and *The Inner Game of Golf* (1980) became best-selling texts, and he translated his insights into a formula: performance equals potential minus interference. Your performance improves by either developing your potential still further, or decreasing interference. Gallwey's performance philosophy is a form of mind-game, the inner game taking place 'within the mind of the player', and 'played against such obstacles as fear, self-doubt, lapses in focus, and limiting concepts or assumptions'. Gallwey's ideas have been applied beyond sport, in the area of business organization in particular. In his first book, Gallwey distinguished between Self 1, the 'conscious teller', and 'Self 2', the 'unconscious, automatic doer', that make up each individual player. Self 3 is Gallwey's primary goal, a form of self-knowing and liberating humanness in blended mind–body practice. Gallwey's book was dedicated not just to his parents, but to Guru Maharaj Ji, and academics express appropriate scepticism about his philosophy and formula. But these pseudo-psychological musings of a former Harvard tennis-team captain have had an extraordinary popular and worldwide impact.

SEE WEB LINKS
• A site dedicated to the works of W. Timothy Gallwey and their applications in numerous spheres of life beyond sport.

institutionalization A term describing a process whereby individuals become dependent upon the institution in which they reside or spend much of their time. It is usually used pejoratively, implying that the individual is no longer able to operate without the support of the institution. Such institutions might be the boarding school, the asylum, or the prison, but could also include the professional sports club, whose procedures and controlling practices have been said to infantilize the adult athlete or sportsperson. *See also* TOTAL INSTITUTION.

intentionality A term of psychological and philosophical pedigree, referring to actions undertaken or performed with intent or deliberately, as opposed to contingently or accidentally; in an athlete's game-plan or contest strategy, intentionality must underlie the planning and the execution, but is of course constantly challenged by the game-plans, or strategic intentionality, of opponents. More specifically, and in relation to the *phenomenology of Alfred *Schutz, the term refers to a process embracing the human being's anticipation of an activity, the choices available of what actions to undertake and so the identification of a 'preconceived project', and the accomplishment of the action. For Schutz, this was a way of understanding what he called 'projects of action'; a 'starting activity carries along an intentional horizon of later phases of activity which will fulfill or not fulfill what has been anticipated' (*Collected Papers 1: The Problem of Social Reality*, 1971). Schutz sought to apply the philosophical works of his mentor Edmund Husserl (1859–1938) to the social world. Husserl had in turn been taught by Franz Brentano (1838–1917), who identified the *intentional* character of all thinking, meaning that any of our experiences as appearing in our stream of thought must be referred to the object experienced. Schutz summarized this perspective: 'There is no such thing as thought, fear, fantasy remembrance as such; every thought is thought *of*, every fear is fear *of*, every remembrance is remembrance *of* the object that is thought, feared, remembered. The technical term coined by Husserl to designate this relationship is "intentionality".' A very underused term in sports studies, this has the capacity to illuminate planned courses of sporting action from a *career or *life course to the match strategies of teams, *goal setting, and the rehearsal of individual athletes.

interactionism A term with myriad formulations, all generally referring to the reciprocal influences and dynamics between at least two phenomena or elements, such as mind–body, human–machine, or individual–group. *See also* SYMBOLIC INTERACTIONISM.

interdisciplinarity The use of different academic disciplines in an integrated way in the exploration of a research problem or question, the systematic study of an area of enquiry, or the application of knowledge to a social issue or human activity. The best sports coach would be an authentic interdisciplinarian, using concepts and findings from numerous academic disciplines in planning the training and performance schedules of the athlete. Sports studies itself is an interdisciplinary field, in which the history of sport is not separate from the sociology of sport, or the politics of sport from the psychology of sport; rather, the disciplines are the sources of concepts that are brought to bear in an integrated fashion in the illumination of the phenomenon under study.

International Association of Athletics Federations (IAAF) The world governing body of athletics, formerly the International Amateur Athletics Federation. It was founded in 1912 by seventeen national members, in Stockholm, Sweden, in the year of the Stockholm Olympics, to standardize the athletic programme and equipment, and monitor and approve world records. By 2008 membership had risen to 213. It began to approve payments to athletes when introducing the *trust fund scheme in 1982, and dropped the word 'amateur' when changing its name in 2001. From 1912 to 2009, the federation had had only five presidents: Sigfrid *Edström of Sweden, 1912–46; Lord Burghley (1905–81) from England, 1946–76; Adriaan Paulen (1902–85) of the Netherlands, 1976–81; Primo *Nebiolo (1923–99) of Italy, 1981–99; and Lamine Diack (b. 1933) of Senegal, from 1999. Nebiolo moved the IAAF headquarters to Monaco in 1993. The IAAF stages ten regular athletics events, including the World Championships and the World Indoor Championships every two years; annual events include the World Athletics Final, and cross-country and half-marathon championships. The switch from the 64-year-long rule of the patricians Edström and Burghley to an African leadership pledging to 'benefit millions of youngsters around the world' is a reflection of the changing global politics of sport.

(⊕) SEE WEB LINKS

- The site of the world governing body for athletics, providing news, calendar, results, statistics, and links.

International Council of Sport Science and Physical Education

(ICSSPE) An organization founded in 1958 by UNESCO, as the International Council of Sport and Physical Education (the 'science' amendment was made to its title in 1982). It was founded by Philip *Noel-Baker, Nobel Peace Prize laureate, as a body representative of UNESCO's brief for both culture and education. *See also* UNITED NATIONS.

(⊕) SEE WEB LINKS

- The site of an international organization representing the interests of researchers and professionals worldwide.

International Management Group (IMG) A leading international

marketing group founded in the USA in 1960 by Mark *McCormack, when signing golfer Arnold Palmer as his client. Acquired in 2004 by Ted Frostmann, the company positions itself as 'the world's premier and most diversified sports, entertainment and media company', specializing in growing its clients' businesses through 'event properties, media production and distribution, talent brands, sponsorship consulting, brand licensing, sponsorship sales and other services'. It operates across thirty countries and is an independent sport-media producer in its own right, also targeting sports practitioners with its IMG Academies, which have been described in *Sports Illustrated* as 'the country's most comprehensive playground for athletes in training'.

International Olympic Committee (IOC) Founded in Paris in 1894, by

French aristocrat Pierre de *Coubertin, the IOC has been responsible for staging the Olympic Games every four years (a period known as an Olympiad) since then, apart from interruptions to the schedules during the two World Wars of the 20th century. The first Summer Olympic Games was staged in 1896, the first Winter Olympics in 1924. The IOC was not the first international sports organization of the modern period to be formed, but it was distinctive in that it was organized on the basis of an event, in which a variety of sports could feature. It is an international non-government organization (*INGO) with exclusive ownership of the Games; the right to control and oversee the Games was granted to the IOC at its Congress for the Renewal of the Olympic Games in Paris on 23 June 1894, by a coterie of international delegates mustered from enthusiasts and sport administrators from France, England, the United States, and nine other nations.

In its early years the IOC functioned little more than as an almost ad hoc club, de Coubertin and a few other idealists and enthusiasts meeting in irregular fashion or at the venues of the early Games. Jean-Loup Chappelet and Brenda Kübler-Mabbott, in *The International Olympic Committee and the Olympic System: The Governance of World Sport* (2008), have logged some of the history and described the structure and system underpinning this extraordinary organization.

No executive board was established until 1921, when de Coubertin as president established a fledgling administrative system. He had moved the headquarters to the Swiss city of Lausanne in 1915, in the early years of World War 1, and this confirmed the legal status of the organization, in Swiss law, as a simple form of association (not stated explicitly in the Olympic Charter until 1970). In 1981 the Swiss Federal Council acknowledged the IOC as having 'the specific character of an international institution', allowing it exemption from the levy of taxes on its revenues, and permitting it to recruit staff of any nationality for its administration. The IOC has continued to seek further privileges from the Swiss government associated with this international organizational status.

The IOC is the hub of a worldwide network of organizational interests and partners that can be understood as the overall Olympic system, operating towards a kind of negotiated equilibrium in an imperfect world. In this system different 'actors' or 'entities' make up the structure of the Olympic Movement. The core five actors are the IOC itself, the respective and relatively short-lived Organising Committees of the particular Games, the International Sports Federations, the National Olympic Committees, and the National Sports Federations. Four newer actors are governments and inter-governmental organizations, multinational sponsors, national sponsors, and professional leagues of teams or athletes. This 'new, expanded Olympic system' encompasses 'a broad range of partners: public, private and associative, and national, international and transnational'. Joint governance by this range of partners and interests is, not surprisingly, complex and volatile, so 'the equilibrium is a precarious one'.

Three regulating influences that the IOC has spawned are the *Court of Arbitration for Sport (1983), and the *World Anti-Doping Agency (WADA) and the IOC Ethics Commission, both founded in 1999 in a climate of controversy and crisis for the IOC amidst revelations of administrative corruption and escalating revelations of drug abuse by athletes and coaches. The IOC instituted reforms and new structures only in response to pressure from the world media, partner sponsors (US company John Hancock in particular), and US Congress investigations. The IOC has created an event, the Olympic Games, that is undoubtedly a significant cultural legacy and heritage on a global scale, and has striven to represent international peace and cooperation, Chappelet and Kübler-Mabbott argue; but they also acknowledge that much reform remains to be done, and list 'five major political and management principles' upon which a more developed model of adequate governance by the IOC might be based: transparency, democracy, accountability, autonomy, and social responsibility. They also, along with many other commentators, recognize three threats to the integrity of world sport: doping, violence, and corruption. Their solution is that the United Nations steps in with a global sport policy; and that the IOC stimulates a diplomatic conference to get as many countries in the world as possible to sign up to 'Lausanne Conventions' confirming sport as a public good, and 'the Olympic Games as a world heritage'.

Less sympathetic and more investigatively critical analysis of the IOC and its practices has been produced by Andrew Jennings in a trilogy of works. With Vyv Simson, he published the best-selling *Lords of the Rings: Power, Money and Drugs at the Olympic Games* (1992), exposing the fascist pedigree in Franco's Spanish regime of the then IOC president Juan Antonio Samaranch; his 1996 *The New Lords of the*

Rings: How to Buy Olympic Gold Medals revealed corruption at the heart of the
judging and competition of some Olympic events (particularly in boxing); and
in 2000, with Clare Sambrook, his *The Great Olympic Swindle: When the World
Wanted its Games Back* went into graphic detail on the corruption scandals
related in particular to the winning of the bid to host the Winter Games by
Salt Lake City, and the responses that forced Samaranch and the IOC to
introduce reforms.

In its first 115 years there were just eight presidents of the IOC: Demetrius
*Vikelas of Greece, 1894–6; Baron Pierre de Coubertin of France, 1896–1925;
Count Henri de *Baillet-Latour of Belgium, 1925–42; Sigfrid *Edström from Sweden,
1946–52; Avery *Brundage of the USA, 1952–72; Michael *Morris, Lord Killanin,
from Ireland, 1972–80; Marquess Juan Antonio Samaranch from Spain, 1980–2001;
and Count Jacques Rogge of Belgium, from 2001, and re-elected in 2009 for a third
four-year period. That Jacques Rogge won the presidency with the title of (medical)
Doctor, and was ennobled to the status of Count soon after election, says much
about the continuing elitist basis of the IOC, and its self-serving snobbery.
Nevertheless, the IOC's survival testifies to the powerful pull of its main product—
the Olympic Games—on the global imagination, as well as to the benefits that
accrue to commercial sponsors, broadcast organizations (when the audiences turn
up), national governments (when the medal table looks good), event organizers
and facility developers (if budgets are balanced), and national sports organizations
and Olympic Committees (which receive much of the redistributed revenue
generated by the IOC's commercial dealings). The IOC, though, continues to
present a self-aggrandizing image and mission to the world, Jacques Rogge insisting
throughout 2008 that the Beijing 2008 Summer Games was an opportunity for
the Olympic system or movement to change China. It was unlikely that this would
be the case once the IOC moved its focus and shifted its priorities towards
Vancouver 2010, London 2012, Sochi 2014, and Rio de Janiero 2016. *See also*
OLYMPIC GAMES, MODERN (AS GLOBAL CULTURAL EVENT); OLYMPIC GAMES, MODERN (HISTORY
OF THE SUMMER GAMES, 1896–2008); OLYMPIC GAMES, WINTER.

(((●))) SEE WEB LINKS

• The extensive site of the IOC, with history, reports, records of events, policies,
  and details of partners and overall finances.

• Independent website collating material, evidence, and discussions on the politics
  of the Olympic Games.

International Sport and Leisure (ISL) A marketing organization established
in 1982, in Lucerne, Switzerland, by *Adidas chief Horst *Dassler, staffed at the
top by Dassler's own personal assistant Klaus Hempel, and a recruit from Adidas
itself, Jürgen Lenz. ISL revolutionized the football (soccer) marketing business, acting
as the intermediary between La Fédération Internationale de Football Association
(FIFA, the governing body of world football) and the international companies most
likely to seek sponsorship opportunities in world sport. Targeting exclusive
sponsors for the World Cup, ISL generated unprecedented levels of income for
FIFA, and went on to apply the same principles to the raising of global awareness of

the Olympic brand; The *Olympic Programme (TOP) revolutionized Olympic finances and infrastructure in turn. Broadcasting rights were also acquired by ISL.

Overreaching itself into sports beyond football and the Olympics, the company went bankrupt in 2001, though some of its top executives had already left to start their own businesses, including Hempel and Lenz, who established TEAM and implemented the marketing strategy underlying the reformatted European Cup/ *UEFA Champions League. FIFA established its own in-house marketing group to take the place of ISL; the International Olympic Committee had already done so. ISL was implicated in dubious financial payments to its clients, administered by Dassler's former aide Jean-Marie Weber, some of which have been the focus of proceedings in the Swiss courts. ISL represented the deal-making practices of Dassler in a climate of negligible transparency, and this has tarnished the reputation of a company whose pioneering vision established sport marketing on an unprecedentedly worldwide level.

international trade   Trade in goods and/or services that involves the movement of goods and people across national boundaries, which, in expansionist and anti-protectionist times, increased exchange between societies of different kinds. Sport contributes to such forms of trade in several ways, two of which are *sport tourism and image-enhancement of a location, and the operations of transnational corporations (TNCs). Large-scale international sport events such as the Olympics can without doubt prompt new international trade relations, as any executive from a South Korean enterprise entering the global economy after the Seoul 1988 Olympics will testify. The staging and transmission of the Games transformed worldwide perceptions of the effectiveness of the Korean economy, and provided a focus for reworking relationships with the Soviet Union and Eastern European states. Tourism benefits might have been negligible and short-lived, but trade relations were not. China's emergence as a world economic superpower was linked to its desperation to secure the Olympic Games, and during the run-up to Beijing 2008 it joined the World Trade Organization. The operation of transnational corporations also contributes to international trade: *Adidas launches new models of its football in the context of high-profile *UEFA Champions League matches.

But the scale of internationalism of the operations of the most prominent TNCs remains, to economists, unclear and under-researched. It seems that developed countries (from the North Atlantic Free Trade Association, NAFTA; and the European Union, EU) develop mutual trade in sports goods together:

> About two-thirds of the NAFTA sports goods trade is with other NAFTA and EU countries; nearly two-thirds of the EU sports goods trade is with other EU and NAFTA countries. Thus, the trade displays a geographical concentration on developed countries just like most manufactured products whose global trade concentrates (approximately 66 per cent), on North–North trade. (Wladimir Andreff, 'International Trade in Sports Goods', in Wladimir Andreff and Stefan Szymanski, eds, *Handbook on the Economics of Sport*, 2006).

The founder of the modern Olympic Games, de *Coubertin, called sport and his Olympic model of sport the 'free trade' of the future. He hardly foresaw the extent to which this has proved true, attractive as the appropriate sporting event, brand, and product have been to national governments, major cities, and transnational corporations. *See also* SPONSORSHIP.

internet A system of global communication (World Wide Web), invented (1989–90) but not patented by Englishman Tim Berners-Lee, professor at Massachusetts Institute of Technology, and founded on a principle and culture of free use. The downturn in the advertising market during the collapse of the dot.com boom in the late 1990s meant that the internet has not 'become a direct source of financing for sport by paying fees in compensation for exclusive rights, as is the case with television' (Frédéric Bolotny and Jean-François Bourg, 'The Demand for Media Coverage', in Wladimir Andreff and Stefan Szymanski, eds, *Handbook on the Economics of Sport*, 2009). Nevertheless, clubs and sports organizers see in the internet 'a particularly dynamic vehicle for images and communications', and it operates as an outlet for ticket distributions and sport-associated products. As a source of information—update on match scores, gossip on sporting celebrities—the internet has become a form as well as a source of *sports chatter, providing a serious threat to the viability of the traditional written press; print sport journalists have had to adapt to writing for the web as well as the mainstream newspaper. Sport is a major reason for connecting to the internet; in France in 2001, 67 per cent of netsurfers already reported that they had looked for sports information on the web. The internet has generated interactive forms of participation during sport events, so that fans can engage with experts and participate in schemes linked to the teams or individuals that they are following. Unpoliceable, the internet also makes available live sporting action on pirate sites from major sporting events across the world.

interpretivism The approach in social science, and particularly sociology, that places the question of interpretation and understanding at the centre of the investigation. Interpretation is built into any observation or statement about a phenomenon: a rugby scrum can be seen as a harmless physical activity allowing people to let off steam in a competitive context, as a subtle and strategic game-play, or (in the context of men's *Rugby Union in England) as an expression of the perpetuation of class-based culture. This example shows that interpretations are wide-ranging and the challenge in studying the meaning of social action is to place the action in its context, including consideration of the meanings of the actions to the social actors themselves. Interpretivism is contrasted with *positivism, which attempts to apply the procedures of natural science to the study of the social world. Rather than seeking general explanations and identifying laws that apply to all social situations and all human behaviour, the interpretivist social scientist recognizes the differences that characterize cultures and societies, and interpretivism has provided the basis for empathetic, focused, and comparative understanding of disparate cultures. Research methods closely associated with interpretivism include *ethnography and *participant observation. *See also* HERMENEUTICS; PHENOMENOLOGY; VERSTEHEN.

interval training The combination of different forms and intensities of exercise and training to increase performance capacity by combining sustained effort with explosive performance. At the 1952 Helsinki Olympics, the levels of performance achieved by athletes from the USSR (at its first Olympics) and Eastern Europe (such as Czech Emil *Zátopek) were associated with the benefits of interval training, and its techniques became widely adopted. *See also* FARTLEK; FOUR-MINUTE MILE; STAMPFL, FRANZ.

interview A fundamental and indispensable research technique in the social sciences, for the collection of data at the level of the individual subject or respondent in particular. Interviews can be used in large-scale surveys, guaranteeing higher response rates to questionnaires than, for instance, in postal questionnaires requiring self-completion. Used in this context, interviewer bias may be a problem if large numbers of responses are completed by teams of different interviewers. For particular kinds of qualitative research, interviews are essential, to allow in-depth exploration of themes that emerge in the face-to-face interview. Life histories, or oral histories of athletes' sporting careers, have provided invaluable data on the context, meaning, and significance of sporting lives. The researcher must always decide clearly in advance of the interview whether it is to be structured or semi-structured, and any interview raises questions of an ethical kind concerning the interviewer–interviewee relation, and the use of the data generated in the interview. As many commentators have noted, particularly in relation to well-known interviewees, the interviewer must pay the subject the respect of finding out all that can be known about the individual before the interview itself. To interview a famous athlete knowing nothing about his or her biography would be unprofessional and in all likelihood ineffective.

investigative research Research aimed at revealing the underlying power relations between subjects and those over whom they have influence or control, or illuminating the often undeclared interests of individuals in powerful organizations and institutions. Investigative research in social science shares features with investigative journalism. A pioneering rationale for investigative research in sociology was provided by Californian sociologist Jack Douglas. The frontispiece to Douglas's book on investigative research (Douglas, 1976) is a quote from Thucydides' *The Peloponnesian War*: 'Not that even so the truth was easy to discover: different eye witnesses give different accounts of the same events, speaking out of partiality for one side or the other or else from imperfect memories.' Here Douglas turns to classical literature to reaffirm an ancient interpretive principle—and the important word in the quotation is not so much 'different' or 'imperfect', but 'partiality'. For Douglas:

> using basic ideas of truth, we find that the social world in which we live, especially American society, is a complex, conflictual, and problematic world in which people, both unintentionally and purposefully, often (but not always) construct complex ways of hiding important parts of their lives from the outside public, especially researchers. Social research methods must always be constructed in accord with the basic ideas of truth and the basic goal of achieving truth in this kind of social world. (1976: 3).

Within Douglas's investigative framework, then, there is no absolute truth, rather a 'multiperspectival conception of truth'. And it is not to scientific methods and replicatable techniques that the investigative Douglas turns in his quest for such truths:

Only a tiny fraction of the information collected and social research done in our society is collected or done by sociologists or by people who have seriously studied sociology. Most social research information is discovered by social research done by people of practical affairs, such as journalists collecting information through interviews, writers doing life stories by taping long talks with the subjects, retired politicians writing memoirs or publishing diaries, businessmen trying to determine the profitability of a new housing development or a new toothpaste, government officials trying to determine public response to a new schedule of bus fares or the amount of crime, and so on almost endlessly. (1976: 14).

This is not a programme for systematic research methods training in graduate schools of social science (Sugden and Tomlinson, 1999). It is, though, a realistic appraisal of the nature of knowledge generation in advanced liberal democratic consumerist societies. And Douglas's arguments lie within a well-established critical tradition in North American cultural criticism, journalism, and campaigning sociology (and comparable streams of critical oppositional and investigative traditions in other countries). The roots of the investigative tradition lie within the muckraking tradition of journalistic writing in the USA in the first decade of the 20th century, when 'investigation and exposure, watchdog functions of a democratic press' (Kaplan, 1975: 151) characterized the investigations and writings of a generation of journalists—and novelists such as Upton Sinclair—who prompted reform and intervention by the federal government in the ruthless and exploitative practices of giant industries. Insurance companies, railroads, the liquor business, and the medicine and meat industries were all exposed, and opened up to the reforming regulatory zeal of the US president, Theodore Roosevelt. Lincoln Steffens, from 1901 editing the *McClure's Magazine* (monthly circulation 360,000), was the most prominent of such journalists, 'the publicly recognized leader of a movement that was at the peak of its influence at the beginning of 1906' (Kaplan, 1975: 146). The investigative muckraking tradition was later complemented by a radical strain of critical writing best embodied in the figure of Randolph Bourne. Bourne's essays for the *New Republic* from 1914 included 'The Undergraduate', in which he bemoaned the fraternity-dominated college life based on a 'sporting attitude' which is anathema to an intellectual, enquiring life (Bourne, 1977: 212–15).

The muckraking metaphor, cited by Roosevelt in 1906 when turning against the critical tide of those investigative and radical writers who had fuelled his political agenda, is from English radical Parliamentarian, religious thinker, and writer John Bunyan. In his spiritual allegory *Pilgrim's Progress* Bunyan wrote of the Man with a Muckrake, digging up all before him in selfish fashion. Roosevelt used the muckraking metaphor in a way that has been challenged, as noted by Jensen (2004: 431–2): the muckraker of Bunyan's allegory was the wealthy greedy figure raking the earth for more riches. Calling those who exposed the wealthy and the unaccountable muckrakers was a misinterpretation of the Bunyan text—it got things the wrong way round: 'John D. Rockefeller was king of the muckrakers, not Lincoln Steffens' (Jensen, 2004: 432). But the term has come to refer to the investigative missions of the successors of Steffens: the process of searching out and revealing scandal, particularly in relation to the famous and the privileged and powerful. Steffens himself felt badly let down by the President, seeing

Roosevelt's speeches on the theme as an attack 'on a group of writers who helped make him a reform hero' (Kaplan, 1975: 149).

Within the academy and academic research departments in the universities—and the Chicago School sociologists of the University of Chicago became the most pre-eminent example—this tradition of investigative work became recognized as a significant element of the sociological project (Marx, 1972), however marginalized in cycles of methodological fashion and orthodoxy. In a world of sport dominated by the ruthless competitiveness of ambitious individuals in both performance and administration, investigative research is essential as a means of adequately analysing the ideologies, interests, and motivations underpinning high-level sport and high-profile sports events, as in the case of Sugden and Tomlinson's (2003) study of world football's governing body FIFA (*Fédération Internationale de Football Association).

References

Bourne, R. (1977) *The Radical Will: Selected Writings, 1911–1918*, preface by Christopher Lasch, selection and introductions by Olaf Hansen; New York: Urizen Books; Douglas, J. D. (1976) *Investigative Social Research: Individual and Team Field Research*, Beverly Hills/London: Sage Publications; Jensen, C. (2004) 'What Happened to Good Old-Fashioned Muck-Raking?', in K. Borjesson (ed.), *Into the Buzzsaw: Leading Journalists Expose the Myth of a Free Press* (revised and expanded), Amherst, New York: Prometheus Books, pp. 417–34; Kaplan, J. (1975) *Lincoln Steffens: A Biography*, London: Jonathan Cape; Marx, G. T. (ed.) (1972) *Muckraking Sociology: Research as Social Criticism*, New Brunswick, New Jersey: Transaction Books; Sugden, J., and Tomlinson, A. (1999) 'Digging the Dirt and Staying Clean: Retrieving the Investigative Tradition for a Critical Sociology of Sport', *International Review for the Sociology of Sport*, 34 /4: 385–97; Sugden, J., and Tomlinson, A. (2003) *Badfellas: FIFA Family at war*, Edinburgh and London: Mainstream.

((⊕)) SEE WEB LINKS

• The website of leading investigative journalist and writer Andrew Jennings, focusing on organizational corruption in sport administration.

IOC *See* INTERNATIONAL OLYMPIC COMMITTEE.

ISL *See* INTERNATIONAL SPORT AND LEISURE.

isokinetic dynamometer An electromechanical device for assessing muscle torque throughout the full range of a joint movement and at a set speed of movement. The advantage of an isokinetic dynamometer is that the controlled speed of movement allows the exertion of muscle force throughout the entire range of movement, more closely replicating real-life body movements than a typical weight-lifting exercise. The dynamometer unit comprises a rotating arm with a speed-controlling mechanism and associated microprocessor-controlled data collection, analysis, and display equipment. Specialized attachments allow the unit to be placed alongside a chair or bench in order to measure muscle performance during a wide range of movements of the ankle, knee, hip, back, shoulder, and elbow. The rotation speed of the unit's main axle can be preset and when the athlete attempts to rotate the device a servomechanism imposes a resistance so however much force the athlete imposes the rate of rotation is constant. Isokinetic dynamometry is particularly useful in the assessment and rehabilitation of athletes after joint injury or surgery such as cruciate ligament repair in the knee. *See also* DYNAMOMETER; RESISTANCE TRAINING.

Jahn, Friedrich Ludwig (1778–1852) A German Prussian gymnastics educator, the inventor of *Turnen, who allied a belief in the benefits of physical exercise to a creed of collective nationalism. Widely known as *Turnvater* ('father of gymastics'), Jahn had studied theology and philology (language and literature) at ten universities, a restless romantic and liberal reformer who never completed his studies, and was expelled from the University of Halle in 1803, before serving the Prussian state as an agent for the 'nationalisation of the masses': 'Jahn's job was to agitate among the lower middle class, particularly among the younger generation' (Christiane Eisenberg, 'Charismatic Nationalist Leader: *Turnvater* Jahn', in Richard Holt, J. A. Mangan and Pierre Lanfranchi, eds, *European Heroes: Myth, Identity, Sport*, 1996). *Turnen*, as a paramilitary form and method of physical exercise, was part of this brief, prompted by Prussia's experience of defeat by Napoleon Bonaparte's France: a nation could be restored and revived by forms of gymnastics designed to transmit a collective morality as well as beneficial effects upon health and strength. Jahn inaugurated the open-air gymnasium, the *Turnplatz*, in Berlin in 1811, after beginning teaching classes at a school in 1810; gymnastics associations (*Turnverein*) became established swiftly throughout the country, and Jahn was well remunerated by the state. His appeal was strongest among the rising, young middle classes, particularly students and skilled artisans. His innovations included a vaulting horse, and bars and beams, for exercise. Nationalistic pride and national restoration were emphasized as the context of and predominant themes for the physical exercisers. His associations perpetuated the motto 'Hardy, Pious, Cheerful, Free', and Jahn combined his liberal reformism with a nationalist political vision that anticipated German unification; for his time, he was perceived as a liberal, but a change of political climate with the ascendancy of an aristocratic regime led to his exercise groups, seen as threatening to the status quo, being closed down (or relocated indoors) by the state authorities, and he himself imprisoned for six years in 1819. An adapted model of *Turnen* became a core element of the popular culture and associational life of 19th-century Germany, but in forms increasingly void of Jahn's vision, based in indoor facilities and absorbing elements of military drill.

James, C. L. R. (1901–89) A political radical, literary critic, and cricket writer, James was raised in the country of his birth, Trinidad and Tobago, but spent long periods of his life living in the United Kingdom and the USA. He was educated at the Queen's Royal College in Port of Spain, Trinidad, where his passion for cricket was cultivated in the *fair play spirit of the English public school. In 1932 he spent some time living in Nelson, in the north of England, drawn there by his cricket-playing compatriot Sir Learie *Constantine, who played as a professional for the town's team in the Lancashire League. James's lasting legacy to sports studies is his book *Beyond a Boundary* (first published 1963), written in the years after he returned to Trinidad in 1958. Autobiographical and polemical, simultaneously personal and political, the book shows the power of sport to shape character, reproduce privilege and inequality, and also stimulate cultural and political change.

jarai A form of standing-target *archery performed at the Japanese imperial court, possibly from as early as AD 483, though the earliest identified documentation of it dates from AD 647, when a unified Japanese state was in the making. *Jarai* was a ritual of status, deference, and fealty (Allen Guttmann and Lee Thompson, *Japanese Sports: A History*, 2001). It was a court ritual held in the middle of the first lunar month, in which twenty noblemen (including imperial princes) competed against twenty archers selected from among the palace guards. Officials of the state gathered in the presence of the emperor to demonstrate their allegiance, and nobles who did not attend the ceremony were punished. Members of the imperial family had targets 20 per cent larger than those of the other contestants. Rank, rather than performance, usually determined the prizes; and after the middle of the 9th century, when the emperor began not to attend the ceremony, it lost its ceremonial and ritualistic significance.

Jeffries, James Jackson (Jim) (1875–1953) A US heavyweight boxing champion of the world, who was born in Ohio and moved to Los Angeles in 1891, where he boxed as an amateur for several years, turning professional at 20, and winning the world title in 1899, in a championship bout in Brooklyn, New York. He retired undefeated but his record was blemished by a comeback fight, for which he was flagged by racists and promoters as the 'Great White Hope', against black champion Jack *Johnson.

jeu de paume A ball game in which the ball was propelled by the palm ('paume') of the hand against a wall, the predecessor of a racket-based variant in France; its English counterpart was *real tennis, and what was developed as *lawn tennis; its Spanish equivalent is *pelota. Historical legend attributes the death of France's Louis X to exertions at *paume*; playing 'with his last ounce of strength' in the woods at Vincennes in 1316, he rested in a cave where he drank so much water that he 'took a chill', and died of a consequent fever. The sport remained popular among the clergy and the nobility despite royal proclamations blaming it, among other games, for contributing to the neglect of cultivation of 'manly arms'. *Paume* was included in the catalogue of sports compiled by *Rabelais, and his hero Pantagruel included 'a ball in one's breeches' and 'a racket in one's hand' as one of the sought-after skills—along with dancing and a law degree—that was looked for in the professional ('doctor') of the day. At the time (the early 16th century), Orléans, where Pantagruel was making such a hit, had forty *paume* courts; Paris had well over a thousand; and by the mid 16th century, the game was increasingly often played with the racket rather than the palm of the hand.

Imported to Scotland and England, *jeu de paume* became not just adopted but renamed, as 'tennis'. In the 17th and 18th centuries in France, *paume* often shared the same premises and programme as theatrical comedy. The sport never revived to its mid-16th-century level of popularity, and in 1789 the covered courts at Versailles were transformed into the headquarters of the Revolution's National Assembly. French *paume* masters crossed *La Manche* to find work in teaching the sport among the English leisured classes, and laid the basis for the boosting of the profile of real tennis, and the late-19th-century development of lawn tennis. A lavishly illustrated account of *jeu de paume* is provided in chapters 3–6 of Gianni Clerici's *Tennis* (1976).

jogging Recreational running for health and/or fun. Initially a warming-up exercise, jogging became part of standard routines of training and preparation from the later 19th century, and in the later 1970s became increasingly popular as a sporting activity in its own right, linked to both enhanced sensitivity towards health issues such as excess weight, and the perceived benefits of exercise and fitness in the sculpturing of the physical self. The guru of jogging was James F. *Fixx, and the endurance of jogging in the public spaces of communities and neighbourhoods testifies to his long-term legacy, proving patronizing commentators on the allegedly faddish nature of the jogging boom to be seriously out of touch with a major trend in participatory sporting culture.

Johansson, Ingemar (1932–2009) A Swedish boxer who fought the black US fighter Floyd *Patterson three times for the world heavyweight championship in 1959–61. He won the title in the first of these bouts, at the Yankee Stadium in New York, becoming one of the few non-US champions, but lost the two consequent contests. Retiring in 1963, he operated successful businesses and acted as a boxing analyst for television. Johansson's significance lay in his white European identity in the emergent age of live television coverage of sport, offering as it did a focus and a narrative for the media in which Europe could be seen to be challenging the USA, in the context too of a symbolic confrontation of black and white cultures in the ring.

John Hancock A US financial company that, as an established sponsor of the Olympic Games, was a major influence upon the internal reforms of the International Olympic Committee after the revelations of bribery and corruption in the late 1990s. In 2003, the company was acquired by Canada's Manulife Financial Corporation and the Olympic sponsorship terminated in 2008. *See also* OLYMPIC PROGRAMME, THE.

Johnson, John Arthur (Jack) (1878–1946) The first black heavyweight boxing champion of the world, defeating Canadian Tommy *Burns in Sydney in the fourteenth round of the fight. Johnson was born in Galveston, Texas, the son of former slaves. His boxing talent was prodigious, but his opportunities were initially limited by racist slurs, alleging that his style was devious and cunning (when in fact it was studied and calculated). His accession to the title sparked a racist reaction as whites called out for a 'Great White Hope' to win back the championship. Undefeated former champion Jim *Jeffries came out of retirement, declaring that 'a white man is better than a negro', to challenge Johnson in Reno, Nevada, on 4 July 1910. An all-white crowd was stirred on by the band playing 'All coons look alike to me', but Johnson outboxed Jeffries, who withdrew after fifteen rounds. That night, blacks celebrated and whites rioted in public as the USA's Independence Day celebrations unravelled into an expression of the racially divided culture of the nation. Johnson lost his title to Jess Willard in 1915, knocked out in the twenty-sixth round in Havana, Cuba, watched by more than 25,000. His personal life kept him in the public eye, particularly his relationships with and marriages to white women and his business interests (the club he began in 1920 in Harlem was renamed when he sold it three years later, and became the famous black cultural centre the Cotton Club). Johnson was jailed on trumped-up sexual misconduct charges, and a posthumous pardon has been called for, led most recently by Republican politician and presidential candidate John McCain. Muhammad Ali has acknowledged Johnson as an inspiration, and his name and exploits have featured in popular music, including black blues (Leadbelly).

jouissance A French word for enjoyment, or bliss (which can be of a sexual kind). The term has been used by several French cultural and social theorists, including Roland Barthes (1915–80) in his *Le plaisir du texte* (1973) addressing the nature of readership; *jouissance* is exciting, unsettling, unlike mere 'pleasure' which is familiar, known, and comforting. This Barthesian perspective can be applied to the spectator experience in sport, much of which is familiar, routine, and unremarkable; but some elements of which are arousing, and destabilizing. The sporting encounter is not just one or other of these forms of response and experience. The dynamic of the contest and the unknownness of the outcome can combine the comforting 'pleasure' with the unanticipated *jouissance*.

jousting 1. A form of armed combat between two mounted knights, prominent in the later Middle Ages among the privileged elites of northern European kingdoms, where rulers developed *tournaments as a vehicle for the display of their power and status. The term derives from the Old French *juster*, meaning to unite and bring together on horseback. 2. Jousting on water, known in south-east France as *joutes lyonnaises*, is a form of contest between combatants armed with wooden lances and wooden shields who, from their standing positions on platforms (or *tintaines*) on boats, aim to knock their opponent on the other boat into the water by thrusting their own lance against their shield. Sète, on the Mediterranean coast, is famous for its own variant, *joutes languedociennes*, presented by the town's tourist department as 'an important component of the local heritage'. The jousting contests take place in the Canal Royal from April to September, and top jousters are given nicknames, such as the 'Terrible', the 'Hundred Wins Man', and the 'Unmovable'. The Sète water joust has combined heritage with tourism, regional pride with history, and the town has established a jousting school for children and a museum of the history of water jousting in the Languedoc region. Water jousting was initially a work-based diversion, a form of amusement and competition among fishermen and dockers. Charles Pigeassou and Jérôme Pruneau have studied the jousting societies of Sète, identifying their contribution to forms of sociability and deep interpersonal networks that have proved attractive to local participants and supporters in the context of the relative emptiness of modernity.

judo In Japanese, literally 'the easy way' or 'the way of gentleness', referring to an unarmed combat sport in which individuals seek to disable the opponent by throwing, armlocking, neck lock, or holding down. Its origins lie in ancient schools of *ju-jitsu, from which educator Dr Kano Jigoro (1860–1938) evolved the simple and modern style of the modern judo form. He was also active in international sporting politics, the first Asian member of the International Olympic Committee, from 1909 until his death. The sport gradually gained an international profile, the first men's world championship taking place in Tokyo in 1956. The International Judo Federation had been founded in 1951, with Kano's son as its second president, though a women's world championship was not staged until 1980, in New York City. A men's event was first staged at the Olympics in Tokyo in 1964, a women's at Barcelona's Games in 1992. Japan, and latterly China, have dominated Olympic titles, though Cuban women have featured as medal winners in the early years of the women's events, taking gold in the middleweight category at Barcelona (1992) and Sydney (2000).

ju-jitsu In Japanese, 'the soft art', though this was a far from soft form of unarmed combat in which the original aim was to disable, cripple, or even kill the opponent. It developed as a variant of the barehanded fighting traditionally practised by Japanese samurai (warriors), and in the 17th and 18th centuries ju-jitsu schools developed widely in the country, with distinctive and varied styles. It was from these that the modern form of judo was evolved. An International Ju-Jitsu Federation (based in Belgium) continues to oversee the worldwide profile of the sport.

Juvenal (*c.*AD 60–*c.*130) A Roman poet and writer, widely recognized as the greatest satirist of Imperial Rome, and also as the last significant Roman poet. Born Decimus Junius Juvenalis in the reign of the Emperor *Nero, he grew up during the reign of those emperors establishing the *Colosseum, and began writing in his fifties. His literary output began when the tyrannical years of the Emperor Domitian were succeeded by a more tolerant imperial regime, but one in which public spectacles and ostentatious displays of status and power were still hugely visible in the everyday cultural life of Rome. Juvenal could therefore comment on the prospects of ex-slaves as well as the downfall of powerful dynasties, on the position of wealthy freedmen and the condition of the politics of the day. His satires have provided what specialist classical scholars agree are 'two of the best known Latin tags, *panem et circenses* ("bread and races", 10.81) and *mens sana in corpore sano* ("a healthy mind in a healthy body", 10.356)' (William Barr, 'Introduction' to *Juvenal: The Satires*, Oxford, Oxford University Press, 1992, p. ix). Both of these phrases refer to the Roman ethos of sport and physical culture, in its public and more private forms respectively. The first has been variously translated as 'bread and the big match' or, in its usually quoted form, 'bread and circuses'. The second phrase was adopted by physical educationists in the modern Western tradition favouring the integration of the physical and the mental or spiritual in new forms of character-building pedagogy. Both phrases feature in Juvenal's tenth satire, entitled *The Futility of Aspirations* and published just five years before his death. The work addresses the futility of praying for political power, military prowess, or good looks. 'Bread and races' refers to the way in which public entertainment or spectacle had become the focus of the populace at a time of the decline of the political spirit; 'a healthy mind in a healthy body' is said to be something worth praying for, and sums up the formula that can guarantee a 'tranquil life . . . reached through the path of goodness'.

kabaddi A traditional team game played in its main form between two sides of twelve players, though only seven are in the playing area at any one time; the three traditional variants, of which the modern form is a synthesis, are *surjeevani*, *gaminee*, and *amar*. It is a contest based on pursuit, with no equipment, and in which touch and movement are the basis of scoring, points being gained by putting opponents out of play. It is known as the 'game of the masses' in India, and other prominent bodily practices such as *yoga are connected to it, as the individual raiding the defensive zone of the opposing team must make the move holding a single breath, while chanting the word 'kabaddi'. Cultural historians and sociologists have linked the sport to the notion of *Ahimsa*, which represents the separation of the self from injurious or violent acts, and material possessions.

The sport was organized and standardized into its modern form in Baroda, India, in the early 1920s, and it has been claimed that it featured as a demonstration sport at the 1936 Berlin Olympics (the official report of the 1936 Games mentions only baseball and gliding as demonstration sports). It was amended into a nationally accepted form across the subcontinent in the mid 1940s, when a standard mode of playing was accepted by the Indian Olympic Association. In 1950, an All India Kabaddi Federation was established, as the governing authority for the sport; university and school professional associations promoted the sport in the early 1960s, and men's and women's national championships were staged in the early 1970s after the Amateur Kabaddi Federation of India took over authority for the sport in 1972, and the National Institute of Sports began training and certificating coaches in 1971. The sport was promoted as an indigenous cultural practice and as a form of resistance to colonial culture from 1915, and it has been linked to militant Hindu politics (Allen Guttmann, *Sports: The First Five Millennia*, 2004). The growth in recognition and popularity of the sport has been marked, though, and along with running it has provided Indian women with a route towards sport stardom in the later 1980s and the 1990s.

kalarippayattu An indigenous, traditional form of martial art practised in the state of Kerala in South India, in which, in Ian McDonald's words: 'Self-realization is sought through prolonged immersion in this arduous practice, culminating in an optimal state of body-mind consciousness such that "the body becomes all eyes"' ('Hindu Nationalism, Cultural Spaces, and Bodily Practices in India', *American Behavioral Scientist*, 46, 2003). With military roots in its 11th-century origins, the practice was revitalized by a 1920s nationalist reaction against colonial domination. It incorporates a range of styles, with core elements stressing the importance of meditative exercises based on breathing techniques, designed to prepare both body and mind for forms of combat including hand-based techniques, fighting with short and long sticks, and with sword and shield. The *kalari* is the roofed pit dugout in which *payattu* (exercise) takes place—constituting a kind of 'exercise temple'. *Kalarippayattu* has contributed to the perpetuation of Kerala's heroic self-image, while also accommodating new modes of globally popular martial arts, such as *karate and street fighting. As a regional cultural legacy surviving in an internationally prominent tourist region, it is a revealing case of how the culturally specific also lends itself to new forms of display in the global marketplace.

kangding A form of *weightlifting that was a popular demonstration of strength (lifting a tripod) in ancient China. Its popularity was established in the Spring and Autumn Period (770–476 BC) and the Warring States Period (475–221 BC). During the Western Han dynasty, during periods of economic development and in a relatively stable political situation, *kangding* became a source of status and social mobility, when an official at court was appointed to run competitions, and victors were given honorary titles and sometimes positions of high office. Professional weightlifters thrived in the period, excelling in feats of strength with objects other than tripods, including large wheels and heavy stones (Michael Speak, 'Recreation and Sport in Ancient China: Primitive Society to AD 960', in J. Riordan and R. Jones, eds, *Sport and Physical Education in China*, 1999).

karate From the Japanese meaning 'empty hand', karate is a martial art and form of unarmed combat. Though it dates in its organized form from the 1930s, its origins can be traced to practices in India in the 5th century BC, and physical practices based on breathing exercises, such as *yoga, in China even earlier. Drawing on principles derived from the philosophy of Zen Buddhism, karate gives great emphasis to silent meditation, in controlling any factors that might divert from the full focus upon the achievement of serenity and calmness. These elements were fused together in the teachings of Funakoshi *Gichin, who wrote in 1922 that the practitioner must 'render his mind empty of selfishness and wickedness' (*Ryukyu Kempo: Karate*, reissued as *Rentan Goshin Karate-jitsu* ('Strengthening of Willpower and Self-defense through Techniques of Karate')). Karate is practised in a *dojo*, literally a 'way place' that can show the practitioner the 'way' towards enlightenment. Punching and kicking are the core skills, and these are employed for both defence and attack, and can be delivered at breathtaking speed. Novices achieving the black belt progress to the status of *dan*, and practitioners can rise to the status of ninth or tenth *dan*.

A World Karate Federation (WKF) emerged out of European networks that were developed by the influence of Japanese masters in Europe from the 1950s and the 1960s, and has organized world championships after it was confirmed that karate could not be reconciled with judo. The WKF was formally established in 1970, superseding a previous network or union of karate organizations. With over 170 member countries, the WKF has gained recognition from the International Olympic Committee (IOC), lobbying with some success for inclusion in the Olympic programme: at an IOC meeting in 2009, it was one of five sports short-listed by the IOC for inclusion in the summer Olympics. Unsurprisingly, Japanese teams have dominated world championships, though France has been very successful, and the UK, Italy, and Spain have also been champions. In England in 2005, it was the forty-second most popular participation sport, a minority sport in terms of profile, but one demanding extreme commitment and embodying an ethics and philosophy of existence that makes of the art a *lifestyle as much as a sport.

kayaking *See* CANOEING.

Kellerman, Annette (1887–1975) An Australian professional swimmer who popularized women's swimming attire and worked too in vaudeville/music hall and Hollywood feature films. In 1907 in the New York Hippodrome, performing a water ballet in a glass tank, she introduced what was to become *synchronized swimming. As a child, a weakness in her legs meant that Kellerman had to wear steel leg braces, and she took up swimming to strengthen these limbs. As a schoolgirl in Melbourne, she began performing swimming and diving, including swimming with fish in tanks; and swimming beckoned as a career, though her three attempts to swim the English Channel (1905), from England to France, were unsuccessful. Kellerman had dramatic success in Hollywood, displaying a strong female physicality in films with swimming themes, diving stunts, and (for their time) sexual overtones; she was the first actress to appear nude in a Hollywood film (*A Daughter of the Gods*, 1916), and her earlier films featured her as a mermaid in costumes of her own design. Kellerman had innovated the one-piece swimming costume for women, even being arrested for indecency when wearing it on a Boston beach (1907). Her 1910 film *The Perfectly Formed Woman* echoed the judgement of Harvard's Dr Dudley A. Sargent in 1908 when he called Kellerman 'the Perfect Woman', comparing her body to that of the Venus de Milo, the ancient Greek statue of Aphrodite of Milos.

Kellerman's impact was worldwide, as Jennifer Hargreaves confirms when explaining the popularity of sports events as forms of spectacular entertainment at London's Wembley Stadium in the 1930s:

> there were female professionals in several of the "sporting" entertainments such as ice-pantomimes and water carnivals. The American influence was apparent in the aquatic shows which were modelled on the swimming and diving spectaculars of Annette Kellerman, and American performers like Gloria Nord, the ice-ballerina, were employed. These entertainments were new and exciting, and they produced an alluring world of fantasy, fun and spectacle. For women in particular, sports spectacles were suggestive of a much freer, more provocative use of the body than ever before, quite in contrast to the traditional attitudes to the sporting female institutionalized in clubs, schools and colleges. (*Sporting Females: Critical Issues in the History and Sociology of Women's Sports*, 1994).

Kellerman was portrayed by swimmer-turned-movie-star Esther Williams in *Million Dollar Mermaid* (1952; UK title *The One Piece Bathing Suit*); her life and career demonstrated the potential of the sporting body for both breaking stereotypes of female physicality, and extending the boundaries of the public erotic in the sporting—and entertainment—realm.

kemari An outdoor ball game played for exercise, practised by courtiers at the Japanese imperial court in the Heian-kyo (794–1185) period. Eight players stationed in pairs at a tree endeavoured to keep a deerskin ball off the ground, by kicking it. Successful manoeuvres were not measured, but judged in relation to strategic acumen, speed and skill with the ball, and position and posture. 'From the twelfth century to the nineteenth, *kemari* was a popular aristocratic pastime' (Allen Guttmann, *Sports: The First Five Millennia*, 2004).

kendo In Japanese, 'the way of the sword', referring to the warrior or the samurai's arts of swordsmanship and archery as they were blended into a philosophy and an ethics, making of the practices a combination of sporting competition and spiritual exercise rather than a means of mortal combat and professional military skills. In the early 18th century, protective gear and innovative equipment (such as the bamboo swords commoners were allowed to use) were made available to a wider range of social groups, meaning that *kendo* moved further away from its militaristic genre, and towards a more egalitarian participation base. *Kendo*'s more modern forms have sustained the blend of body and mind, the sense of harmony between physical fitness and spiritual well-being. In targeting 'the four poisons of *kendo*'—fear, doubt, surprise, and confusion—the 'way of the sword' aspires to a state of calmness in the mind, as well as competence and expertise in the context of combat. The International Kendo Federation, established in 1970, had 47 affiliated national associations by 2006, across its continental regions—the Americas, Africa, Europe, Asia, and Oceania. The world championships for both men and women have been dominated by Japan, although in the latter years Koreans have won world titles. *See also* HERRIGEL, EUGEN.

Kentucky Derby *See* HORSE RACING.

Killanin, Lord *See* MORRIS, MICHAEL, THIRD BARON KILLANIN.

kinanthropometry *See* ANTHROPOMETRY.

King's Book of Sports, The Declarations by James I, and Charles I, kings of England, relating to the permissibility of sports on Sundays. James I issued a royal proclamation in 1618, reissued by Charles I in 1633, authorizing the practice of some sports on Sundays, after evening church service. The declaration, issued in response to the pleas of Catholics in Lancashire whose activities were being curtailed by zealous Puritan reformers during the Protestant ascendancy, stated that 'our good people's lawfull Recreation' should not be discouraged or undermined. Dancing (for both men and women), leaping and vaulting ('or any other such harmlesse Recreation'), May Days, Whitsun ales, morris dances, and maypole were encouraged, as long as people had attended church service. Prohibited were 'unlawfull games': bear- and bull-baiting, and, 'in the meaner sort of people, Bowling'. At stake here was more than people's sporting preferences: the intervention represented by the declaration demonstrated the significance of sport in the wider context of *social control and in relation to the dynamics of church and state of the time, just decades before the success of the Puritans under Oliver *Cromwell and the establishment of the Commonwealth.

Kingsley, Charles (1819–75) A 19th-century English novelist, social reformer, and Church of England clergyman, who also held professorial positions in literature at London University and in history at Cambridge, and was active in the Christian socialist movement in the 1840s. He studied classics at Magdalene College, Cambridge, from 1838, where he countered his 'lonely, intensely shy, and physically restless' disposition by finding 'companionship through rowing and riding to hounds' (Norman Vance, *Oxford Dictionary of National Biography*, 2004). His sporting interests—fishing and boxing—provided diversion and focus while he decided on his future direction in the Church on leaving Cambridge in 1842. The social condition of the 1840s stimulated Kingsley's social conscience, and, along with others such as Thomas *Hughes, he wrote and campaigned for democratic and social reform that would alleviate poverty and inequality. Religion and politics became intermeshed for Kingsley—his *Alton Locke* (1850) was a classic condition-of-England novel—and he wrote political pamphlets and set up Christian socialist publications. His historical and literary writings—some for children—featured rugged heroes, from early English history and ancient Greece: as Vance writes,

> T. C. Sandars, reviewing *Two Years Ago* in the *Saturday Review* (February 1857), insisted that he preached a gospel of "muscular Christianity" (February 1857, 176), a gibe taken up by other critics, but Kingsley preferred to call it "Christian manliness", exemplified by biblical heroes such as David, on whom he delivered a series of sermons published in 1865.

Weak as a child, and recurrently in frail health as an adult, his own experience of sport's rehabilitative capacity was central to the influential ethos of *muscular Christianity.

knur-and-spell A game played in the north of England, with a continuous popularity from the mid 1700s to the 1930s, surviving into the later 20th century in some forms as an element of heritage culture. The sport is based upon the striking of a pot knur—a small spherical ball, suspended on a string from a gallows-like contraption known as the spell—with a long stick, rather like a golf club. The sport was popular in particular in regions of north-east Lancashire and south Yorkshire, areas which produced some of the most notable 'world champions' of the sport. Matches, or challenges, could be played on common land, often across the fields and moors outside built-up areas and under the patronage of entrepreneurial publicans. Matches were decided in two ways: the shortest number of 'knocks' (hits, or strikes) with which a player proceeded between two set points; or the single longest knock or hit, from a set number of attempts. The second of these was the more common mode of competitive play. Also known as 'poor man's golf', or 'tipping', the sport's popularity declined with the emergence of wider options in the changing *leisure economy and *consumer culture of the later 20th century.

Kodak *See* Olympic Programme, The.

korfball A twelve-a-side ball-handling field game of Dutch origins invented for mixed teams of males and females, who directly encounter in play only opponents of the same sex. The game is lauded by its enthusiasts as the world's only genuinely mixed team sport, based too on the fairness of the direct competition between the players. It was invented by an Amsterdam educator, Nico Broekhuysen

(1876–1958) in 1901–2. The International Korfball Federation was established in 1933 (from a predecessor organisation dating from 1923), and the sport, with 37 affiliated national associations (Asian and North and South American as well as European), has gained recognition from the International Olympic Committee. The game is played on both outdoor and indoor pitches.

Krebs cycle A cycle of biochemical transformations which are integral to the aerobic metabolism of fuels to release energy for muscular contraction. The cycle is named after Sir Hans Krebs, whose detailed investigations developed the idea; it is also known as the tricarboxylic acid cycle or the citric acid cycle. The cycle acts only under aerobic conditions and, in effect, each time a circuit is completed a six-carbon unit is dissimilated to a four-carbon unit with the release of two molecules of carbon dioxide and eight atoms of hydrogen, which are passed along the respiratory chain to form four molecules of water, and energy is released.

kyūdō The Japanese art of *archery, meaning, literally, 'the way of the bow'. Archery in Japan, when weapons equipment and design superseded the bow as an effective military weapon by the end of the 18th century, provided a basis for the expression of physical skill with the bow as both an aesthetic practice and a source of spiritual values. Technique and self-discipline are more important than are hits on the particular target. The International Kyūdō Federation, founded in 2006, built on the work and international impact of the Japanese All Nippon Kyūdō Federation (established in 1949). European and American federations had been formed in the 1980s and 1990s, based on the work of All Nippon delegations in establishing 'a proper appreciation of kyūdō, which understands that kyūdō is not simply about hitting a target, but a practice to train the whole person—both body and mind'. *See also* HERRIGEL, EUGEN.

LA84 Foundation A private, non-profit institution on three sites in Los Angeles, USA, dedicated to the promotion of youth sport, and teaching and understanding sport and its qualities and benefits. It was established with the surplus funds of the 1984 Los Angeles Olympic Games. Previously known as the Amateur Athletic Foundation of Los Angeles, it has, in the Paul Ziffren Sport Resource Centre, one of the foremost collections of sport literature and sport data in the world. In its first 25 years of operation, the Foundation reported, it had dispensed over $185 million, benefiting directly more than two million boys and girls and over one thousand youth sports organizations in Southern California.

(())) SEE WEB LINKS
- A site with invaluable bibliographic detail, downloadable digital resources (official Olympic reports), and other sources such as oral histories of athletes.

labelling theory Labelling theory emerged within an alternative, radical sociology of deviance in the 1950s and 1960s, a leading proponent of which was US sociologist Howard Becker, whose *Outsiders* (1963) asserted that deviance is not an act of the pathological individual, but is a process and an act created by society. It is social groups that create rules which when broken generate deviance, so marking the rule-breakers as outsiders. So, as Becker wrote: 'deviant behaviour is behaviour that people so label'. Related theory also identified the process whereby the labelling can generate an amplification—often perceived rather than demonstrable—of deviance. A particular interpretation is made—predominantly in the *mass media—of a social act or social actor, and that interpretation is amplified in an often spiralling process of confirmation and reaffirmation of that interpretation, and often the associated misrepresentation of the nature of the phenomenon: the antisocial behaviour of a few sport spectators can lead to the labelling of the sports crowd as a whole; the wild antics of a single sport star can lead to the labelling of a whole category of sportsmen or -women as morally inadequate. Labelling theory has been criticized as portraying deviants as victims, and selecting particular cases to fit the theory. It has remained a hugely influential approach despite such criticisms, and continues to have much to offer the study of sport-related phenomena, from transgressive acts in sport performance to the distinctive character of particular sport *subcultures. *See also* DEVIANCE; DEVIANCE AMPLIFICATION; MORAL PANICS; ROLE MODEL.

labour migration The movement of sportworkers, both within countries, and across national and continental boundaries, to play at professional levels in sport. On the international level, this refers not to the international match between

individuals (as in say boxing) or in travelling tournaments (as in say tennis), but to
the membership of a club or a team in a country not of the player's birth. Irish and
Scottish players in English football; Canadian players in English ice hockey in the
1930s; Australian players in English Rugby League; Cuban players in USA baseball;
African players in French and English football. The migration of players has been a
source of economic mobility for individuals, and often an influence on improved
standards in and standing of the sport. Or in the global media age—Japan's Hiteka
Nakamura in his years playing for Glasgow Celtic in Scotland—it has boosted the
television audience, and sales of club merchandise, in the player's home country.
Labour migration in sport has therefore done much to internationalize sport
cultures, and to establish multicultural profiles in some sports. There is also a
negative approach to labour migration, which appeals to the nationalist sentiments
of the receiving country, and argues that labour migration can stunt the growth
potential of its home-grown sport performers. Some nations also exploit migratory
aspirations and patterns, by offering rapid routes to national citizenship for
individuals from, say, South America, who can then play in the national football
team of a European country. Labour migration in sport is therefore a positive
influence, generating an international dimension to a national sport, but also a
target for ethnocentric and racist reactionaries who claim that migrant players are
diluting the national sporting resource. It has also been shown, by David Runciman
(*New Statesman*, 29 May 2006), that the recruitment practices of clubs in wealthy
countries can have a deleterious effect on the football culture of the African player's
home nation.

lacrosse A field game played with a ball and a stick with a net on the end, by
teams of ten-a-side (men) and twelve-a-side (women), in an expansive outdoor
space. The word 'lacrosse' derives from the French word for a bishop's crook (*la
crosse*), which was said by a French Jesuit missionary in 1636 to resemble the stick
used by Huron Indians playing their traditional game of *baggataway* in the region of
what is now Ontario, Canada. For North American Indians, matches could last three
days, the goals marked by trees. The modern codified form of the game developed
in Montreal in the mid 19th century, and was then established in Britain and the
USA. The visit of a Montreal club side and a Caughnawaga Indian team to England,
Ireland, and Scotland in 1876 stimulated the game in Britain, and the English
Lacrosse Union was formed later in the decade. The sport was also introduced into
Australia and New Zealand. Women's lacrosse in England dates from the 1880s, and
it was swiftly adopted in leading girls' schools of the time. The headmistress of a
Manchester preparatory school, Ladyburn House, imported sticks from Canada.
One enthusiast, Dame Frances Dove, writing in 1898, saw the sport as character-
building for the girls, requiring not just skill and perseverance but 'good temper
under trying circumstances, courage and determination . . . rapidity of thought and
action, judgement and above all things unselfishness'. Historian Gillian Avery
juxtaposed this view with her own: 'Lacrosse—that game of unparalleled ferocity
which English schoolgirls play with the minimum of protective clothing while in
Canada . . . men appear in armour'.

The game has established and retained strong bases in independent schools and
universities in Britain and North America. In England, the national association of

the sport has sponsors (or 'commercial partners') that include specialist equipment and kit providers, as well as the country's most conservative broadsheet newspaper, *The Daily Telegraph*; participants numbered fewer than 0.1 per cent of England's adult population in Sport England's participation survey of 2005–6. In the USA, the sport remains firmly established as one of the 23 sports of the *National Collegiate Athletic Association (NCCA).

lactic acid An end product of the breakdown of glucose. Lactic acid is mainly produced during high-intensity exercise under *anaerobic conditions. The lactic acid molecule dissociates into a lactate ion and a hydrogen ion, resulting in metabolic acidosis and compromised muscular function. Sensory nerve fibres within muscle allow the perception of these conditions in the muscles concerned and terms such as 'muscle burn' are loosely but aptly in common use. Lactate can pass across the muscle membrane into the bloodstream and be distributed around the body. Lactate is removed by oxidation or by conversion back into glucose. Lactic acid is produced at all intensities of exercise, but during low and moderate intensities the rate of production is low and is balanced by the rate of removal from the blood, resulting in a blood level of 2 mM or lower. As the intensity of exercise increases the lactate levels rise but a steady state can still be maintained, i.e. the rate of removal balances the rate of production. But above the 'lactate threshold', typically around 4 millimoles, levels rise and may reach in excess of 12 millimoles following exhaustive high-intensity exercise. The development of micro-sample blood lactate analysers in the 1980s led to a considerable advance in the use of blood lactate measurement. These analysers require around 10 microlitres or less of capillary blood which can easily be obtained from a prick to the fingertip or earlobe. Analysis takes less than one minute and can provide the coach with valuable information to guide the intensity of training.

Lardner, Ring (1885–1933) An American sport and short-story writer. Born in Michigan, Lardner began his professional writing life reporting on major-league professional baseball for the *Chicago Tribune* (1908–13). In his daily column for the *Tribune* from 1913 to 1919, baseball remained one of his most frequently discussed topics. Lardner also covered baseball's annual World Series up until the mid 1920s. He began writing fiction in 1914, on a baseball theme, and his baseball stories were published as *You Know Me Al*. Of the book's protagonist Jack Keefe, experimental English writer Virginia *Woolf was to observe, in the magazine *Dial* in 1925, that Mr Lardner's 'mind is on the story. Hence all our minds are on the story. Hence, incidentally, he writes the best prose that has come our way. Hence we feel at last freely admitted to the society of our fellows.' Lardner's prose style and American idiom confirmed sport as a credible and illuminating topic for the literary practitioner.

lawn tennis A court-based racket and ball game played between individuals or pairs on a variety of surfaces including the original one of grass, cement, clay, tarmac, and wood. Its modern internationally-established form was developed in England in the 1870s, in part adapted from *real tennis and other forms of tennis that had been modelled on the French *jeu de paume*. At the Manor House Hotel in Leamington Spa the first lawn tennis club in the world was founded in 1872, and the following year Major Walter Wingfield (1833–1912) introduced clearer rules, and rackets, to entertain guests at a country house Christmas party, calling his game *spharistiké* (Greek for 'ball games'). The All England Croquet Club (founded 1868) introduced the new game of lawn tennis to its members in 1877, as a fund-raising initiative, formalized the rules, and staged the first Wimbledon lawn tennis championships that year. The middle and upper classes took to the new sport swiftly, and it was also seen as a sport suitable for women as well as men. Women first competed at Wimbledon in 1884, and the University of Oxford staged the first men's doubles championship in 1879. Tennis courts, clubs, and tournaments were also established in Ireland, Scotland, and Wales; and the tennis court or club became a key feature of suburban culture, and a site for courtship in respectable public space. A variant of *spharistiké* was introduced to Australia in the 1870s, and in New York City at the Staten Island Cricket and Baseball Club in 1880. The following year the United States Lawn Tennis Association was formed, standardizing rules and organizing national championships.

Tennis featured in the Olympic Games from 1896 (1900 for women) to 1924, and was then omitted from the programme until 1988; German Steffi Graf had won the Olympic demonstration tournament at the Los Angeles 1984 Games, at the age of 15. Until 1968, the big tennis championships of the world—Wimbledon, and the Australian, French, and US Opens—were open only to amateurs, but the rise of television and the more ambitious organization of the professional circuit made the end of amateurism in the game inevitable. 'Big Bill' *Tilden and others had established professional circuits and exhibitions in the 1930s; French star Henri Cochet, one of the all-conquering 'Four Musketeers' that dominated the *Davis Cup, was offered 200,000 francs a year and a share of the receipts at the Roland Garros stadium. By the 1950s most outstanding players turned professional and the great tournaments were becoming devalued. Professional initiatives included a National Tennis League in the USA from 1965 to 1967, and a World Championship Tennis event during the same years, following on from competitions organized by the Association of Tennis Professionals; in April 1968 the ruling bodies voted to accept professionals into the big tournaments, and the commercial potential of the professional game began to be fully realized. The first Olympic tennis champion, John Pius Boland (1870–1958), was a graduating Oxford student visiting a Greek friend, and entered on speculation to emerge with two Olympic titles; when US protégé John McEnroe entered Stanford University his career trajectory was already mapped out in a new commercial landscape for the initially genteel pastime of the suburban middle classes. *See also* ASHE, ARTHUR; DOD, LOTTIE; GIBSON, ALTHEA; GRAND SLAM (TENNIS); LENGLEN, SUZANNE; PERRY, FRED; WILLS MOODY, HELEN NEWINGTON.

leadership The capacity to influence behaviours and actions. In sport, there is much talk of the qualities of the 'leader': the capacity of the captain on the pitch to inspire the other players; the ability of the decision-making coach or manager to affect the outcome of the contest. There remains, though, little systematic study of or analytical consensus on the basis of effective leadership in sport, whether this be of the team, the group, or the overarching sporting organization. If the elements of the successful or effective leader were more reliably known, there would be fewer examples of crises of succession in roles of responsibility. The study of leadership, as opposed to institutionalized forms of authority, could gain much from a fuller application of leadership models as developed in business and management studies and specialist forms of applied psychology.

leap-frog A children's game that has been documented in literary sources since the 16th century, and has changed little in format, as Joseph Strutt's 1801 account in *The Sports and Pastimes of the People of England* shows: 'One boy stoops down with his hands upon his knees and others leap over him, every one of them running forward and stooping in his turn. The game consists in a continued succession of stooping and leaping.' Strutt also cites Shakespeare's reference to the game in *King Henry V*: 'If I could win a lady at leap-frog, I should quickly leap into a wife', probably with more than athletic innocence in mind. Girls and boys have for centuries played the game, though, as an inexpensive and fun-based activity, that also cultivates athletic competence and physical flexibility. In France its equivalent has been called *saute-mouton* (sheep-leaping).

leisure The word derives from the Latin verb *licere*, meaning 'to allow'. A sense of the permissible is therefore built in to the term, though in much analytical work on leisure the word has been understood as coupled with the notion of labour or work; as was the case in Greek thought, Aristotle seeing leisure as a serious business: 'We conduct business in order to have leisure,' he wrote. Leisure in this sense is not merely what is permissible, but is an ideal state to which the citizen can aspire, in which to live a life of leisure is a primary goal of human existence, and is premised on ensuring that as much time as possible is free. In modern English usage, the term came to mean 'opportunity for free time' by the 14th century, in contrast to working time that was becoming increasingly perceived as measured and remunerated time; leisure-time activities were those sorts of activities one could engage in away from work.

Peter Burke has written of 'The Invention of Leisure in Early Modern Europe' (*Past and Present: A Journal of Historical Studies*, 1995), pointing out that to claim a fundamental discontinuity between the early modern and the more modern industrialized contexts does not account for things that were there that then made the modern concept of leisure possible. Four influential discourses in early modern Europe (medical, legal/political, religious/moral, educational) shaped and reframed perceptions of spare time to make the modern concept of leisure possible, Burke argues; it was not a matter of moving in any simple linear way from a pre-modern 'festival' culture to a modern 'leisure' culture. Seven processes identified by Burke show this transformation underway, though, and highlight the trends that underlie the emergence of a modern conception of leisure and its concomitant forms such as organized sport. First, guides to conduct began to emphasize the importance of recreation; second, 'how to do it' books multiplied in the early modern period, and historians began to take note of Greek gymnastics and games, and Roman circuses; third, fine art and paintings gave more visibility to leisure activities; fourth, the upper classes began to cultivate leisure and outdoor country activities with the establishing of the summer 'season'; fifth, urban and city environments provided for and catalogued organized pastimes, in gardens and playing courts as well as theatres; sixth, expressing a sharper distinction between work and leisure, there was a gradual rise in the sense of free time being available to ordinary people beyond the male elites who had dominated the emergent leisure spaces—'a shift from an annual turning of the world upside-down at Carnival to small but regular doses of daily or weekly recreation', including a growing commercialization of leisure presaging a *consumer society; and seventh, reformers did not oppose leisure, indeed welcomed it, if nevertheless seeking to impose their preferred models of what the mass of the population should do with its spare time.

Burke detects, drawing upon Norbert Elias's theory of the *civilizing process and Michel *Foucault's identification of the disciplinary society, a trend of increasing regulation over several centuries, proposing that leisure, as a recognizable concept, emerges as a reaction to this trend. In the key transitional period towards the new industrial society and culture, leisure was a sphere of social, cultural, and political struggle; in sports, the tension between *amateurism and professionalism showed starkly the depth of cultural meanings that characterized debates over leisure and spare-time activities. The truly 'leisured' were those who had no need to work, those with the means for *conspicuous consumption, in the phrase of Thorstein *Veblen. A 'problem' of leisure has also been regularly rediscovered, at times of widespread unemployment or downturns in the economy; and in relation to arguments about deterring *delinquency, whether this was street fighting in 1920s cities or drug-taking in late 19th-century inner-city areas. Sport has been widely claimed as one means of channelling young people's energies into alternative and less antisocial forms of activity.

Leisure has, then, had a rising prominence in social sciences and social history, as its centrality to the nature of societies has been more widely acknowledged. The contemporary consumer is seen to have a choice of leisure *lifestyles; the leisure and cultural industries have huge influences on everyday life, prompting reworked conceptions of older models of the production–consumption dynamic. Sport is an element in this leisure economy and culture; without the leisure choices of sporting audiences (at the contest itself, or in front of the screen), or the discerning consumer choices of fans, the high-profile sporting event would be grey and colourless, or simply non-existent. In this sense, sports studies needs to be related to the broader field of leisure studies, to avoid inflated or at least decontextualized readings of the place, scale, and significance of sport in its historical and social settings.

((⊕)) SEE WEB LINKS

• The site of the UK's Leisure Studies Association, detailing extensive publications available from the association's list from the mid 1970s to the present.

Le Mans A motor-racing circuit in France, which established a 24-hour event for sports cars in 1923, held annually in June. Races had been held at the Le Mans track since before World War I, but the all-day and all-night model captured the public imagination. It was promoted by the newspaper *L'Auto* (later *L'Équipe*) as a novel combination of speed and endurance. This is still the core element of its appeal, brand, and marketing package, with 250,000 spectators attending the motor-race event, and other Le Mans products developed for motorcyclists, karters, and even truck-drivers.

Lenglen, Suzanne (1899–1938) A French lawn tennis player who won 15 (6 singles and 9 doubles) titles at the *Wimbledon Championships, and 2 Olympic gold medals at the Antwerp Games in 1920. Unbeaten at Wimbledon throughout six years, she lost only once in her amateur career, when retiring through illness related to her asthma, in the US Championships. Lenglen turned professional in 1926 after a dispute with the Wimbledon authorities, and defaulting from the tournament having kept Queen Mary waiting for half an hour for a match that never took place. Her sponsor in her professional career was American promoter C. C. ('Cash and Carry') Pyle, and in her home country she founded the Lenglen School of Tennis in Paris.

Lenglen's competitive and physical style changed the approach to the women's game: a frail child, her father encouraged her to play tennis to gain strength, and she practised her strokes by aiming for a pocket handkerchief as a target, and also cultivated what were seen as unladylike overhead shots. Her impact transcended the tennis court, as her competitive philosophy and aggressive physical style challenged conventional notions of genteel *femininity. Her designer tennis dresses and groomed bobbed hair radiated fashion style and sexuality across and beyond the sporting world. Allen Guttmann (*Sports: The First Five Millennia*, 2004) has called Lenglen the 'first sportswoman to become an international celebrity', famed as she was for her 'exotic attire and flamboyant behaviour as well as for athletic skill'. Jennifer Hargreaves emphasizes her importance as a symbol of alternative sexuality. Her playing attire 'made possible an image of the "real" body underneath . . . and allowed her to move energetically so that people caught glimpses of parts that "respectable" ladies never made visible in public' (*Sporting Females: Critical Issues in the History and Sociology of Women's Sports*, 1994). Spectators at Wimbledon were divided: some enjoyed her radical presence; some saw this as indecent, and walked out in protest. This combination of impacts confirmed Lenglen's status as one of the first modern women superstars of the sporting world.

Leotard, Julian (1838–70) A French circus artist specializing in aerial acts, who died young from smallpox or cholera, while in Spain, but whose name is immortalized in his invention of the leotard as a practical clothing for his art. Born in Toulouse, where his father taught gymnastics, he forsook a training in law to develop his gymnastic art. Using three trapezes and a routine involving elaborate somersaults and physical dexterity, Leotard was a performance celebrity in Paris, London, and New York. Jules Verne cross-referenced him in his *Around the World in 80 Days* (1873); Leotard cravats, brooches, and walking-sticks became fashionable and popular; and George Leybourne's song (1867) celebrated him: 'He flies through the air with the greatest of ease, That daring young man on the flying trapeze'. Leotard is an early case study in the cross-over between physical and body culture, spectator sport, commercial spin-offs, and fashion.

L'Équipe See ÉQUIPE, L'.

Liddell, Eric (1902–45) A Scottish athlete, born in Tianjin, China, raised in Scotland from the age of 5, and educated initially in a village school before attending the School for the Sons of Missionaries in London. At school and at Edinburgh

University (where he studied pure science) Liddell was an outstanding athlete, at 100, 200, and 440 yards. He also played rugby union for Scotland. At the 1924 Paris Olympics, he refused to run in the 100 metres, as the heats were scheduled for a Sunday and to run on the Sabbath was contrary to his sabbatarian principles. Liddell nevertheless won a bronze medal in the 200 metres, and a gold medal in the 400 metres. His story is dramatized in the film *Chariots of Fire*, which also features his strong athletics rivalry with English runner Harold *Abrahams. Graduating from Edinburgh just days after his Olympic triumph, Liddell then studied divinity for a year, and began his missionary career in earnest, speaking at evangelical meetings across the country at weekends. His last athletics appearance in Scotland—at which he won three national Scottish titles—was in 1925, and he dedicated the rest of his life to missionary work and writing, posted to China as a missionary teacher. Liddell developed athletics at the college where he taught, and continued to run at athletics meetings, using sport as an element of his evangelical mission. Interned by the Japanese after their invasion of China in 1941, Liddell died of a brain tumour in the camp in 1945, remembered by camp survivors for his Christian principles and forbearance of the difficult circumstances, and—flouting the principles of his athletic prime, but in the name of the greater good—for refereeing Sunday hockey matches for young internees.

life chances Max *Weber associated 'differences in chances in life' with the 'distribution of property' and/or the 'structure of the concrete economic order'. This notion of 'chances in life' has come to have wider application in consideration of the opportunities or chances available to different groups in society; studies of *sport participation continue to show how influences such as the distribution of wealth shape a society's sporting culture. Ralf Dahrendorf (*Life Chances: Approaches to Social and Political Theory*, 1979) sees life chances as 'a function of two elements, *options* and *ligatures*'. Options are the possibilities of choice, while ligatures are allegiance, linkages, or bonds that, as the medical metaphor stresses, restrain or hold back the individual. Sport may offer opportunities such as *social mobility, for some individuals; for many, though, the ligatures continue to be a bigger influence on their sporting lives than any options.

life course A term referring to an individual's passage through life, understood in the light of significant markers in the personal life narrative. For many, this will chart a life from early socialization to education, employment, adulthood, phases of work, family and personal relations, and retirement. The life course of many sportsmen and -women will often focus in disproportionate detail upon youth and early adulthood, when sporting potential and performance are at their peak. Analysis of the life course has much to offer our understanding of individual sporting biographies, in charting the factors affecting success and decline in any individual sporting life.

life history A detailed, highly focused account of an individual life, based upon intensive interviewing and associated documentation of a personal type (ephemera, diaries, memoirs, photographs). Biographies and autobiographies of sportsmen and -women are in essence life histories, though the selective account of the life of a sporting *celebrity often lacks the objectivity to illuminate wider social contexts; such accounts can nevertheless be interpreted as indicators of the nature of the very celebrity culture that spawns them. Full, intensely detailed life histories carefully gathered and accumulated retain a vast potential for understanding the cultural significance of sport, and share this potential with *oral history. For some revealing life histories of selected US Olympic athletes and participants, see the website of the *LA84 Foundation.

(((●))) SEE WEB LINKS

- Obituaries produced in the UK national paper the *Daily Telegraph* on well-known sportsmen and -women.

lifesaving The combination of techniques and skills developed, in the words of the Royal Lifesaving Society UK, 'to safeguard lives in, on and near water'. The Society aims to inform 'everyone' on techniques of resuscitation and principles of water safety, and reported in early 2009 that a million people in the UK were trained annually by ten thousand volunteers. The skills have also been developed into competitive formats, and lifesavers compete in their own organized lifesaving sports in teams and as individuals, in particular techniques in the water and in skills such as line-throwing. In the USA, a Lifeguard Games was held in Carpenteria, California, in 1967, concentrating on swimming, rowing, paddling through surf, and sprinting on sand; and in 2008, sponsored by American Red Cross, a Lifeguard Games continued to attract teams and individuals to an event at Carlsbad, Southern California.

lifestyle A concept referring to a variety of ways of living, often in relation to choices about leisure and other forms of consumption, from holidays to eating. The concept has been attributed to Max *Weber, for whom the concept of *status was connected to observable styles of life. In his 1922 essay 'Classes, Status Groups and Parties', in *Economy and Society*, Weber wrote that 'social status is normally expressed above all in the imputation of a specifically regulated style of life to everyone who wishes to belong to the circle'. In its more contemporary usage in relation to 'lifestyle sport', the term refers to a range of sporting activities, often taking place in spaces lacking regulation and control, and expressing fun, creativity, and performance. The most traditional of sports can provide a basis for a particular lifestyle, but lifestyle sports are the newer sporting forms variously labelled action sports, new sports, whiz sports, and extreme sports. Belinda Wheaton's *Understanding Lifestyle Sports: Consumption, Identity and Difference* (2004) collects together essays on skateboarding, rock climbing, surfing, windsurfing, adventure racing, and ultimate frisbee. Sports such as these challenge traditional approaches to sport, and the rise of lifestyle sports has contributed to the generation of new forms of social identity based, as David Chaney observes (*Lifestyles*, 1996), upon increased choices explicitly made by people, a consumption or leisure base to those choices, and affiliations and sensibilities characterizing those personal choices. Lifestyle sports can in this sense be seen not merely as interesting aspects of the consumer landscape, but as harbingers of cultural change.

liminality A concept, in the works of cultural anthropologist Victor Turner (1920–83), referring to a phase—often transitional or transitory—'betwixt and between' positions or states. Turner writes of 'the liminal community or comity of comrades' as set apart from any 'structure of hierarchically arranged positions'. The phase of the liminal has spatial dimensions, so that in certain ritualistic elements of the sport spectacle or event new meanings and relationships can emerge. John MacAloon's brilliant study of the first modern Summer Olympic Games of Athens 1896 locates the athletes entering Olympia in the Games's opening ceremony as making a 'journey through liminal space'. He also describes the École des Sciences Politiques (attended by Baron Pierre de *Coubertin in Paris in the mid 1880s) as a 'liminal institution, standing betwixt and between the academic and aristocratic establishments and the workaday world of bourgeois place-getting'; and so allowing the founder of the modern Olympic Games the space in which to evolve his distinctive vision and mission. (See John J. MacAloon, *This Great Symbol—Pierre de Coubertin and the Origins of the Modern Olympic Games*, 1981.)

Ling, Per Henrik (1776–1839) A Swedish gymnastics pioneer and paramedical thinker whose training in physical activity and then theology blended with an increasing preoccupation with Chinese-influenced theories of the philosophy of health and exercise also incorporating disciplined forms of contest and fighting and principles of *martial arts. Ling was especially interested in fencing and was employed as the University of Uppsala's fencing master in 1805. He linked his eclectic ideas to the emergent medical curriculum of *anatomy and *physiology, and gained support from the Swedish government to establish the Royal Gymnastic Central Institute (1813) in Stockholm. Ling was the principal, and the Institute trained gymnastic instructors in his own pedagogical, medical, military, and aesthetic syllabus. Opposed by more scientific practitioners, Ling nevertheless attained the title of professor and was elected to the Swedish General Medical Association. His creed of gymnastics has been explained as a romantic celebration of northern European ethnicity, and as a model that provided new forms of masculinity that were a response to emergent forms of feminism in the later 19th century (Jens Ljunggren, 'The Masculine Road through Modernity: Ling Gymnastics and Male Socialisation in Nineteenth-Century Sweden', in J. A. Mangan, ed., *Making European Masculinities: Sport, Europe, Gender*, 2000). Ling's model contrasted with the competitive team games of British *athleticism, and the model of exercise established by Germans Johann *Guts-Muths and Friedrich Ludwig *Jahn, and had extensive influence across Europe, including on the thinking and pedagogical innovations of Lingian disciples such as Martina Bergman *Österberg, a graduate of his Stockholm institute who introduced Ling gymnastics into the English education system and its system of physical education training in women's colleges.

lipids Organic compounds of carbon, hydrogen, and oxygen, such as fats, oils, and waxes. About 90 per cent of the body's lipid is in the form of fat in adipose tissue, which functions as an energy store, insulation, and protection. The remainder plays essential roles in many body structures and functions such as cell membranes, nerves, hormones, and the carriage of vitamins. Fat and oils in food provide a significant source of energy in the diet, amounting to around 40 per cent of the average daily calorie intake. The metabolism of stored fat provides the majority of energy for mild and moderate intensities of exercise, with the balance provided

by *carbohydrates and a small amount by *proteins. The limited rate at which fat
can be metabolized restricts the extent to which it can provide energy for higher-
intensity exercise and carbohydrate is the predominant fuel. Fat becomes the
predominant fuel during lengthy periods (more than about 90 minutes) of exercise
and the extremely large energy store in adipose tissue (over 100,000 kilocalories)
is never depleted. Regular exercise training impacts on fat metabolism to the
benefit of both sports performance and health. It increases the use of fat as a fuel
(thus sparing limited stores of *glycogen and reducing excess weight), improves
mobilization of fats from adipose tissue, and has positive effects on coronary
heart disease risk factors.

Liston, Charles L. ('Sonny') (1932?–70) A US boxer born in Arkansas, and
physically abused as a child, who became heavyweight boxing champion of the
world when defeating Floyd *Patterson in 1962, knocking him out in the first round.
Liston had a background of petty crime and hoodlum behaviour, and served time in
prison for robbery, before being directed towards boxing by a Roman Catholic
priest. His raw power, and his criminal connections, made him a fearsome figure in
the sport and the wider media; though his refusal to fight on in a title defence
against Cassius Clay in 1964 generated allegations about betting scandals. These
were scarcely abated the following year when Liston fell to defeat from a whiplash,
but relatively light-looking, punch from the renamed champion, Muhammad Ali, in
the first two minutes of the bout. Liston died in mysterious circumstances, found
dead at home by his wife. The official, police account claimed that he had
overdosed on heroin; many speculated that he was murdered by his connections in
the criminal underworld. It was unclear how long he had lain dead alone, just as
his actual age was uncertain (Liston himself claimed to have been born in 1932,
though his mother claimed his birthdate as 1928).

locker-room culture Forms of behaviour that are characteristic of sportsmen
within the confines of the changing room or the locker room. This culture is
associated with male-dominated humour and prejudice, sexist, racist, and
homophobic so-called banter. Such male preserves treat the locker room as a form
of off-limits territory, a *backstage sphere in which views might be expressed and
behaviours condoned that would never be accepted in more public spaces.
Comparable backstage spheres are the club room or the private dinner. In April
1991 *Boston Herald* sportswriter Lisa Olson took legal action in Massachusetts
(Suffolk County Superior Court) against the New England Patriots of the National
Football League (NFL). She alleged that a locker-room incident involving three
players in September 1990 violated her civil rights, and constituted sexual
harassment. The legal suit stated that Olson had been 'held up to public ridicule,
scorn and derision' because of 'the disparaging and demeaning statements and
actions' of the players and team officials. Compensatory damages were sought for
medical treatment following the incident, and for continued 'emotional distress'.
The NFL mounted an investigation and offending players were punished. Olson
was, however, vilified and persecuted by Patriots' fans, and moved to Australia to
work for several years, before moving back to the USA in 1997. What Olson herself
called her experience of 'mind-rape' certainly altered the conditions in which

women journalists could go about their business in the world of male sports, reducing the acceptability and incidence of ritual *hazing, but any participant in or observer of male sporting cultures knows that the locker-room culture remains in large part a bastion of atavistic male prejudice.

logrolling A form of what Allen Guttmann (*Sports: The First Five Millennia*, 2004) calls 'workplace competitions', logrolling derives from the lumberjack trade in Canada and the north-eastern USA. Lumberjacks who rolled their logs downriver would compete to see who could balance longest on a log while the log was still floating or rolling in the water. One lumberjack would stand on each end of the log, and one would start walking on or 'rolling' the log, while the other sought to keep his balance. The successful contestant was the one who stayed on the log while the other fell into the water. Contests were first held in Canadian lumbercamps around 1840. A variant, 'log birling', was a race over a measured course, with lumberjacks using a pole to steer their way downriver: the first known contest was held in 1888, and a world championship was held in Nebraska, USA, in 1898, though the sport became more a performative item at exhibitions and riverside fairs. Logrolling has had some popularity among the wider public as a general recreation and sporting event. For six years up until 2006 US sport-based cable television channel ESPN featured it in its Great Outdoor Games. But it proved more of a novelty than a cultural magnet, and the sport's overarching association, Lumberjack Water Sports, has described the sport, since the end of the ESPN deal, as 'diminishing', not least because of the attempt by some to introduce carpeted logs:

> Rolling on regular logs requires a greater amount of skill and athleticism than is required by carpeted logs. The goal of Lumberjack Water Sports is to make the sport bigger and better, not degrade sport . . . Lumberjack Water Sports does not support the move to carpeted professional logs, as it threatens the sport of log rolling's integrity and future.

Lombardi, Vincent Thomas (1913–70) A US American football coach, born in Brooklyn, New York, and raised as a Roman Catholic, who attended the Jesuit-based Fordham University in New York. Lombardi graduated in business but his prowess on the football field steered him towards a career in coaching. His hugely successful career included unprecedented runs of success coaching the New York Giants, the Green Bay Packers, and the Washington Redskins. At the Giants, he transformed the career of Frank Gifford, making him one of the biggest names in the history of the gridiron game. Renowned for his highly quotable comments on personal sacrifice and self-belief, Lombardi is widely misunderstood to have coined the saying 'Winning isn't everything, it's the only thing'. James A. Michener (*Sports in America*, 1976) called this Lombardi's 'summation of the competitor's creed'. Equally quotable from the Lombardi stock is the observation: 'Football isn't a contact sport, it's a collision sport. Dancing is a contact sport.'

longitudinal analysis The study of a sample of a population over time. The longitudinal approach contrasts with cross-sectional analysis, which analyses the sample at one single point in time. Examples include *life histories, *panel studies, and *time-series analysis, all of which assume different lengths of time for a credible or valid study. Longitudinal analysis is essential for some forms of study of social or behavioural change, and has been employed effectively in studies of exercise interventions, elite performance, and rehabilitation processes related to sports injury. Strictly speaking, longitudinal analysis is based upon a tracking of the same population, but regular sampling of a population's *sport participation, for instance, as in the UK's General Household Survey, can produce valuable and comparable data over time. Longitudinal analysis is not to be undertaken lightly, as it is a long-term commitment and requires guarantees of access and resources that a lone researcher, for instance, may not be in a position to secure.

long jumping An established field event in modern athletic championships and the Olympic Games, with origins in the ancient Olympic Games in Greece; it is in many respects one of the most fundamental of sports, needing no equipment and having a fundamentally simplistic competitive character. In less organized formats, long-jumping challenges have characterized everyday sporting cultures—the challenge of rural workers to leap the longest distance in the fields, of industrial workers to leap the breadth of a canal. This basic appeal of the body in motion and flight, unaided by artificial aids (weights, once allowed to enhance momentum, were banned in the modern mode), has sustained the popularity of the event. It is also an event that has been combined with other events by individual athletes, thus increasing medal tallies: Jesse *Owens at the 1936 Berlin Olympic Games; Carl Lewis at the 1984 Los Angeles Olympic Games. The most famous individual achievement in the history of the long jump was, however, US athlete Bob Beaman's leap of 29 feet 2.5 inches (8.90 metres) at the 1968 Mexico City Olympics, which improved the world record by 21.5 inches (55 centimetres), more than had been achieved accumulatively over the previous forty years of record-breaking. Beaman's Olympic record still stood forty years later after the Beijing 2008 Olympics, though the US's Mike Powell had achieved a world-record jump of 8.95 metres in Tokyo in 1991. The Olympic men's event has been dominated by the USA, winning 22 out of 27 of the gold medals at the modern Games. The women's long jump was not held until the London 1948 Olympics: no single nation has dominated the event, and South America produced its first women's Olympic champion in an individual event, Brazil's Maurren Higa Maggi (Beijing 2008).

looking-glass self A concept developed by the US sociologist Charles Cooley (1864–1929). For Cooley (*Human Nature and the Social Order*, 1902), individual and society were not separate entities but related dimensions of the same phenomenon, and his main interest was in what constitutes social subjectivity. Drawing upon the metaphor of the mirror, Cooley proposed that in social life the individual imagines how he or she 'appears in a particular mind', and this produces a 'self-feeling' framed by how that other mind is felt to perceive the individual; so our own reflection in the mirror stimulates responses to how we look, and Cooley transfers this to interpersonal relations. The other person is like the mirror, and we imagine what we look like to that person, and respond accordingly. The concept captures the subtleties and uncertainties of interpersonal relations; and ways in which strutting boxers pose prior to the fight, or direct opponents in team games seek to assert a one-to-one dominance in combinations of *body language and demeanour, are examples of the relevance of Cooley's 'self idea'. See also GOFFMAN, ERVING.

Loues, Spiridon (1873–1940) Winner of the first marathon race in the Athens Olympics of 1896. Loues was what John J. MacAloon has called the 'epic hero' of the first modern Games (*This Great Symbol: Pierre de Coubertin and the Origins of the Modern Olympic Games*, 1981). A modest peasant and water-carrier by occupation, from Maroussi, Loues's victory for the host nation stimulated wild scenes of nationalist celebration that observers of the time and those who were at the stadium itself called 'unforgettable' and 'incredible'. In 1936, Carl *Diem, primary organizer of the Berlin Olympics, brought a slim 63-year-old Loues to Germany, to present a bouquet of flowers to Adolf *Hitler during the opening ceremonies. Dressed in fustanella (the traditional Greek white kilt), Loues was used there as an echo of the symbol that he had been during his run forty years earlier, in a powerful and politically repugnant example of the invention of *tradition in sport. Loues's name was tarnished when he was accused, but acquitted, of falsifying military documents in 1926, though he had to endure a year in prison. His story is also told, and his symbolic significance evaluated, in James P. Verinis, 'Spiridon Loues, the Modern *Foustanéla*, and the Symbolic Power of *Pallikariá* at the 1896 Olympic Games', *Journal of Modern Greek Studies*, 23 (2005). Loues's name has become a folk-heroic legend in Greece, and was the basis of the naming of the modern Olympic stadium constructed for the Athens Olympics of 2004.

Louis, Joe (Joseph Louis Barrow) (1914–81) Born Joseph Louis Barrow, an African American from Alabama who became heavyweight boxing champion of the world in the 1930s and the 1940s, successfully defending his title 25 times from 1937 until 1949. Nicknamed the 'Brown Bomber', he was a national patriot in World War II—a poster had Private Joe Louis, bayonet at the ready, saying to the nation 'We're going to do our part and we'll win because we're on God's side'—and a popular, though impecunious, celebrity after retirement from the boxing ring. His most famous fight is the second fight that he had with German Max *Schmeling, which not only made Louis champion but assumed a political significance with a black American fighting someone presented as the embodiment of Aryan racial superiority. In the early 1960s Gay Talese reported some Philadelphians recalling that 'There was a time when nothing was more important to coloured people than God and Joe Louis' ('Joe Louis: The King as a Middle-Aged Man', *Fame and Obscurity*, 1981). Having lost to Schmeling in 1936, Louis prepared for the second fight with commitment and intensity. Bob Considine's report for the International News Service, 22 June 1938, conveyed the scene and the Louis power: 'He was a big, lean copper spring, tightened and retightened through weeks of training until he was one pregnant package of coiled venom . . . Louis—his nostrils like the mouth of a double-barrelled shotgun—took a quiet lead and let him have both barrels'.

ludic activity From the Latin *ludus* (play, or game), a term referring to forms of activity at different levels of seriousness and on varied scales of organization, but that have in common some form of play or sport element. A typical usage is found in Allen Guttmann's *Games and Empires: Modern Sports and Cultural*

Imperialism (1994), where he observes that most modern sports originated in Britain and the United States, accompanied by 'the process of ludic diffusion that distributed these sports across the entire globe'. It is a useful term in that it is flexible and all-embracing enough to capture a wide range of contexts and sport forms, though that very quality can also limit its analytical depth.

luge A form of *tobogganing for two-person crews or single riders, in which the riders sit in a backward-leaning position on the ice sled. The first organized international competition was held in Davos, Switzerland, in 1883. British tourists had developed sled racing on snowed-up Alpine roads from the mid 19th century: luge was one of these, along with (Cresta Run) tobogganing, and *bobsleigh. Ernest *Hemingway, writing for the *Toronto Star Weekly*, observed the British and the Swiss at play on their luges in March 1922: 'Luge . . . is a short, stout sled of hickory built on the pattern of little girls' sleds in Canada', he wrote, and reported that 'all of Switzerland, from old grandmothers to street children', would flock to the mountains on a Sunday to make mountain descents on their 'little elevated pancakes'. A particularly steep and dangerous run between Chamby and Montreux attracted daring Britons and Hemingway captured the 'wonderful sight' of the former military governor of Khartoum speeding into Montreux, 'cherubic smile on his face', and welcomed by the cheers of the town's children. Hemingway concluded his piece: 'It is easy to understand how the British have such a great Empire after you have seen them luge.'

A first European championships had been held in Austria in 1914, but the competitive profile of the sport really took off in the 1930s, with the invention of the flexible sled. At its 1954 meeting in Athens, the International Olympic Committee granted formal recognition to luge, identifying it as the successor to skeleton/Cresta Run tobogganing on the Olympic programme. A world championship was inaugurated in Oslo in 1955, and the International Luge Federation formed in 1957 (luge had previously shared an international federation with bobsleigh). In 1964, at Innsbruck, luge made its debut at the Olympics, where the dominant competitive nations have been Austria, Germany (both the German Democratic Republic and the Federal Republic of Germany), Italy, and the former USSR.

Lunn, Arnold Henry Moore (1888–1974) Born in Madras, a skier and religious polemicist, the son of travel agent and medical missionary Sir Henry Simpson Lunn (1859–1939). The elder Lunn, terminating his ministerial career in 1895, developed a travel agency specializing in winter sports, opening up the Swiss Alps to the English public through bodies such as his Alpine Sport Limited, and the Hellenic Travellers' Club (the company was successful into the 20th century as *Lunn Poly). The young Lunn attended Harrow Scool, and Balliol College, Oxford (1907–11), where he took no degree but, following his father's enthusiasms, founded the Oxford University mountaineering club and the Alpine Ski Club. He was also secretary of the Oxford Union and edited the university magazine *The Isis*.

Mürren, Switzerland, had been made accessible and developed by his father in 1910, and was the base for Arnold Lunn's skiing achievements and innovations. He invented the modern slalom in 1922 and went on to gain recognition for the sport, and for downhill racing, at international level—staging world championships at

Mürren in 1931 and 1935—and in the 1936 Olympics at Garmisch-Partenkirchen, Germany. Lunn had made adventurous skiing expeditions in the Alps, and a serious fall in Wales when climbing lost him three inches from one leg; this did not stop him becoming the first man to make a ski ascent of the Eiger in 1924. Lunn produced 23 books on mountaineering and skiing, and, echoing his father's dual interest, numerous further books on religious polemics. He himself converted from Methodism to Roman Catholicism in 1933. Lunn's combination of upper-class privilege and adventurism, blended with the international business initiatives of his father, created an influential early case of amateur sport working in tandem with the emerging, lucrative *sport tourism market.

Lunn Poly A travel agency, incorporated into the Thomson self-acclaimed 'powerbrand' of travel agencies in the UK in 2004, that had been the largest chain of travel agents in the United Kingdom. The name Lunn Poly derived from the combination of the Polytechnic Touring Association with Sir Henry Simpson Lunn's travel businesses. Lunn (1859–1939) was a religious reformer as well as a travel agent, and from 1895 organized tours abroad to venues such as Switzerand (for winter sports), and Italy and Israel (religious tours and cruises). His integrated packages of travel and activity revolutionized the leisure travel industry, and also offered early forms of theming to the business—Hellenic Travel, and Alpine Tours, for instance. His son, Arnold *Lunn, was a pioneer of winter sports, and their expansion as forms of *sport tourism, in the Alps.

luxury tax A scheme in which teams or clubs in a league pool a percentage of net local income (after local expenses are deducted), a proportion of which is then redistributed to the less financially well-off clubs or teams in the lower half of the league. The luxury tax is a modern innovation, operated only in the USA, conceived as a form of *revenue sharing. It was first operated by Major League Baseball (MLB) in a 1996 agreement, implemented for season 1997–9, dropped, and then reinstated in 2002. The National Basketball Association initiated a luxury tax under the name of a 'team tax' in a 1999 agreement, which was implemented in the 2002–3 season, and revised in 2005. In such a Collective Bargaining Agreement (CBA), the monies from the luxury tax are owned, allocated, and distributed by the league itself.

Lyotard, Jacques (1924–98) A French philosopher and social theorist, and proponent of postmodern theory. Lyotard questioned the traditional scientific preoccupation with facts, noting that 'interpretations' are what the intellectual should be concerned with. He generated scepticism towards any notion of the 'great' works of a period or era (the 'canon'), and called for what he called an 'incredulity towards meta-narratives', identifying instead a much more fluid and flexible human state of affairs that might be labelled 'the postmodern condition'. Lyotard's thinking has influenced sport theorists who are questioning of any overarching theory of sport or sport development, but to wholly accept such a postmodern perspective is to sacrifice any attempt at locating the determining influence upon the making of sport or any other cultural form; and along with that, to abandon any attempt at explaining how a dominant sporting culture has come into its position of dominance.

McCormack, Mark Hume (1930-2003) A US lawyer, marketing pioneer, and sport entrepreneur, who founded the international management and marketing organization *International Management Group (IMG). McCormack's breakthrough idea was to introduce the notion of the management of a sporting star or celebrity's commercial affairs by a specialist agency, and to link this to the cross-media potential of the star's sporting profile and celebrity in the new television era. He graduated from Yale Law School, was at almost national level as a competitive golfer in his youth, and worked in law for several years before, alert to the unexploited commercial potential of top sporting stars, he signed the golfer Arnold Palmer as IMG's first client. IMG made McCormack one of the most powerful people in world sport, and his later clients included tennis player Pete Sampras, Formula One driver Michael Schumacher, golfer Tiger Woods, and the English supermodel Kate Moss; he was also involved in special projects for political and religious figures.

McCormack's wealth was based too on his high-selling motivational writings, headed up by the brilliantly opportunistic—and tongue-in-cheek, for a Yale alumnus—*What They Don't Teach You at Harvard Business School: Notes from a Street-Smart Executive* (1984), occupant of the coveted and lucrative Number 1 spot on the *New York Times* bestseller list for 21 consecutive weeks. McCormack's impact and profile were influential, his timing impeccable: the book's success coincided with the success of the 1984 Los Angeles Olympics, and the remaking of the international sporting economy as sport bodies and organizations sought new relations with corporate sponsors. In 1990, *Sports Illustrated* called him the most powerful man in world sport. He also introduced annual golf publication *The World of Professional Golf* (1967 onwards) and, with his wife, founded a tennis centre. McCormack's marketing vision and corporate know-how changed the financial basis and cultural profile of modern professional sport. His early success prompted influential bodies—such as the *International Olympic Committee (IOC) and the *Fédération Internationale de Football Association (FIFA)—to review their financial operations, and move into a new economic order consonant with the media demands in a period of *globalization.

McDonaldization A term coined by sociologist George Ritzer to refer to a wide-ranging process 'by which the principles of the fast-food restaurant are coming to dominate more and more sectors of American society as well as of the rest of the world' (*The McDonaldization of Society*, 1993). There are four dimensions to the McDonald's model: efficiency; quantified and calculated service; predictability; and control of both employees and customers, through substituting non-human for human technology. Ritzer instances the 24-hour clock in basketball as one advantage in the sporting sphere of the McDonaldization process: it has enabled exceptional athletes such as Michael Jordan to exhibit to their full potential their exceptional talents. But he sees the process as also depriving sport of some of the dramatic appeal of the unpredictability of the contest. Tie-breakers in tennis and the rationalization of racehorse training are two examples provided by Ritzer of the increasing predictability of sport. The manipulation of baseball to ensure high-scoring matches is for him an example of calculability applied to performance; and the 'run and shoot' modern style of baseball is said to be comparable to McDonald's 'eat and move' world of drive-through dining. In health clubs people use exercise machines that embody a fusion of technology and calculability. Modern athletic stadiums shut out the weather, and move large numbers of people around with great efficiency; and sports are played on artificial turf to defy the natural elements of the weather.

(⊕) SEE WEB LINKS

• The website of George Ritzer, theorist of McDonaldization, conveying his evolving thinking on this aspect of globalization.

Machiavelli, Niccolò (1469–1527) An Italian statesman and writer on politics whose works are among the foundation texts of political science. His most famous work, *The Prince* (1513/14), comprises a series of statements and commentaries on the nature of statecraft as required for survival in the ruthless and calculating world of politics among the Borgias. The term 'Machiavellian' has become a byword for brutal and decisive use and disposal of individuals and colleagues in political and organizational contexts lacking in representative structures and processes, and principles of accountability. It is a term that can be illuminatingly applied to individuals holding positions of influence and power, and to their use of this power to protect their personal position regardless of the consequences for others or the wider declared interests of the organization. International organizations such as the *International Olympic Committee (IOC) and the *Fédération Internationale de Football Association (FIFA) can certainly be said to have exhibited Machiavellian forms of leadership at various points in their history. Machiavelli wrote: 'It is much safer for a prince to be feared than loved', and that any 'wise prince must devise ways by which his citizens are always and in all circumstances dependent on him and on his authority; and then they will always be faithful to him'. Individuals gaining and holding on to power in such organizations can rule quite as much by fear and patronage as by respect, or on the basis of any normal model of organizational accountability.

McLuhan, (Herbert) Marshall (1911–80) A Canadian academic, literary scholar, and media theorist who, in the second half of the 20th century, achieved stellar celebrity status in an expanding globalizing media world, for his commentaries on the nature and significance of the contemporary media. McLuhan studied for a BA in literature and took a doctorate in literary-historical studies at the University of Cambridge, England, but his greatest impact came in his reflections on the mass media in the contemporary world. McLuhan's ideas about hot and cool media, his dictum that the medium is the *message, and his term 'the global village' inspired some early adaptations in the emergent sociology of sport.

macrosociological approaches In contrast to *microsociological approaches, the study of large-scale social phenomena and entities, from institutions to societies. Typical of such approaches are studies of sport's place in a particular social, political, and economic system, such as *capitalism, or *communism. *Comparative studies of the place of a particular sporting institution in selected different societies are also based on macrosociological approaches.

mad money A term coined by the political economist Susan Strange to describe the nature of international money markets at the end of the 20th century. Following the dictionary, Strange defines 'mad' as 'wildly foolish', which is what she considers it to be to allow financial markets to be so far beyond the control of state and international authorities. In a world of mad money, Strange points out, there is a widening of long-established gaps in power and wealth, and a widening gap between big business and small business. The social consequences of such gaps include the emergence of an underclass and an increase in dropouts:

> The alienation of what the French aptly call *les exclus* is made greater by the increasing concentration of wealth at the other end of the social scale. Flagrant *conspicuous consumption by the very rich—pop stars, tycoons, financiers, sports stars—is not in itself the problem. But it can become one when growth slows, jobs disappear and times for ordinary people suddenly become very hard. (*Mad Money*, 1998).

The super-rich sports star could in such a context symbolize the gross inequalities at the heart of what Strange, in an arresting metaphor, labels *casino capitalism.

magnificent trivia Large-scale sporting events—*mega-events, or *media events—have combined performative spectacle with the sporting action or endeavour itself. Typical of such phenomena are the opening and closing ceremonies of the Olympic Games (*see* OLYMPIC CEREMONY), particularly in the broadcasting age when global audiences in the billions can be claimed and reported. Such spectacles have what is known as the 'wow' factor, and can hold huge audiences spellbound and speechless in what has been described as a form of 'magnificent trivia' (Alan Tomlinson, *Sport and Leisure Cultures*, 2005, following his use of the term in 2000). The term, or terms close to it, have been variously attributed in other contexts. Kevin Mitchell of *The Observer* wrote, in the wake of the 2001 destruction of Manhattan's World Trade Center, that 'sport is our magnificent triviality'. Phil Bull (1910–89), founder of horse-race betting publication business Timeform in 1948, is credited with coining the term 'the great triviality', as a description for sport (*The Oxford Pocket Thesaurus of Current English*, 2008). The power of the term 'magnificent trivia', though, lies in its truly oxymoronic impact; the Bull term uses 'great' as a mere qualifier, while 'magnificent trivia' evokes dimensions of splendour, human accomplishment, and irresistible appeal in the sport-related spectacle alongside an infantilization of the onlooker.

Mallory, George Herbert Leigh (1886–1924) An English mountaineer whose early death in the Alps generated a national debate on the ethics of mountaineering. Mallory was a student at Winchester school, where he was cultivated as a gymnast, and then Magdalene College, Cambridge, where he leaned towards the left in politics, engaged in dramatics, and captained his college boat. He also frequented the salons of a university librarian that were designed to attract, as Peter J. Hansen puts it (*Oxford Dictionary of National Biography*, 2004), the 'bright and beautiful'. Mallory's physical beauty was widely commented upon, and Hansen's article is accompanied by a painting of Mallory by Duncan Grant, an artist of the bohemian and sexually unorthodox Bloomsbury set within which Mallory moved: Mallory is portrayed as naked from the waist up, his chest and profile conveying an epicene beauty. His bisexuality, physical beauty, daredevil and mystical approach to the mountains, and early death combined to make him a controversial and contested figure in English cultural history.

managerialism 1. In relation to sport organizations, the preponderance of the influence of the professional manager or executive officer rather than the sport-based professional. In an everyday sense, this produces the tension between the workings of the boardroom and the ethos of the training-ground; in some high-profile professional sports, such as association football, the separation of the functions of the general manager and the team coach has exacerbated this tension. 2. A term in urban sociology referring to the influence of local managers of public resources and facilities upon the infrastructural provision for education, housing, or leisure in a locality or region; such urban managerialism largely affects the social and spatial characteristics of a population, and in turn access to particular facilities and so sporting activities.

marathon *See* Loues, Spiridon; Phidippides.

Marciano, Rocky (Rocco Francis Marchegiano) (1923–69) Born as Rocco Francis Marchegiano, a US boxer who was world heavyweight champion from 1952 to 1956, when he retired undefeated, after six successful title defences and 49 fights as a professional. His aggressive style made him dominant for his time, with only five opponents lasting the distance to the end of the bout, and Marciano defeated distinguished veteran Joe *Louis so fully that it marked the end of the veteran's career.

market The sphere in which goods, products, and services are exchanged or traded, with producers, workers, and consumers contributing to this recurring cycle of the economic process. The market operates differently in relation to, say, recreational golfers and occasional skiers than in relation to the production of professional team sports or large-scale international competition. But—and whatever the emerging levels of mediation of markets, such as the internet—all markets are based on a production process, variously regulated from case to case, and the (potentially discriminating) response of consumers.

martial arts A generic term referring to forms of physical combat between individuals, in which the object is to defeat the other by a combination of self-defence strategies and attacking measures. Some martial arts are particularly linked to wider existentialist beliefs or philosophies, and have often had both a military and a sporting rationale. The term has come to have such a wide application that it has begun to lack precision, though it can be a useful embracing category for particular activities and practices within established traditions or countries, such as when talking of *judo or *ju-jitsu in the context of Japan.

Marx, Karl (1818–83) A German philosopher, economist, and polemicist whose works, often in collaboration with Friedrich Engels (1820–95), also provided the basis for communist theory and revolutionary movements. Marx wrote nothing about sport, and was interested in leisure and recreation only insofar as they fuelled the worker for his or her re-entry into the world of work and, especially, capitalist production. But Marx's thought has had substantial influence in the sphere of critical sports studies, and his concepts of *alienation and *commodity fetishism have been adapted to the analysis of sport in the workplace and the economy. Ben Carrington and Ian McDonald's edited collection *Marxism, Cultural Studies and Sport* (2009) reviews both classic and neo-Marxist perspectives as they have been brought to bear on the place of sport in capitalist society, and on the production of the sporting spectacle. *See also* COMMUNISM, SPORT IN.

masculinity The characteristics of the male sex, as socially constructed. Much that is studied on masculinity was previously taken for granted in studies of males by other males, and *feminist theory challenged this position and stimulated a more reflective approach to researching male roles and identities (indeed, masculinities, in the plural). In sport, feminist studies challenged assumptions about the natural nature of gender differences in sport, by building on 'a framework developed by feminist analyses of women and sport to demonstrate the fundamental importance of gender in men's sports' (Jim McKay, Michael A. Messner, and Don Sabo, *Masculinities, Gender Relations, and Sport*, 2000). Roger Connell's work and influence were also extensive (*Gender and Power*, 1987; *Masculinities*, 1995), and did much to reframe the approach to gender relations in sport. Messner and Sabo's *Sport, Men and the Gender Order* (1990) put gender at the heart of research into men's experiences of sport. With McKay, they also laid out three questions that should be pursued in this recognition of the centrality of gender analysis to sports studies: first, how could work on masculinities be integrated with critical feminist studies? Second, how should researchers respond to critical sport sociology's overemphasis on how dominant sport institutions produce negative outcomes for men? And third, how might studies of masculinity and gender relations in sport be connected to analyses of ethnicity and race, social class, and sexual orientation? As these three questions show, the innovative work on masculinity and masculinities in sport has sought to make some ambitious connections, including the aspiration for men (male scholars) to generate feminist insights for themselves and their feminist counterparts.

mass culture A term used, often pejoratively, to refer to the products manufactured and produced for large markets of consumers, and constituting the culture, therefore, of the mass of the population. Sport, with its staged events, expanding media schedules, and accompanying fashion and style products, made significant contributions to the evolution of a mass culture. Critics, from C. Wright *Mills to Theodor *Adorno and others working in *critical theory, have condemned mass culture for lacking taste and discrimination, or for producing models of the homogeneous consumer—*one-dimensional man—at the expense of the discriminating and active citizen, or the reflective participant in more elevated cultural and artistic activities. Although the term has less obvious currency in a culture and economy characterized by niche marketing and targeted branding, the scale of operations of production and consumption of sporting events and goods in the global marketplace shares much in common with the processes underlying the mass culture model.

massivity A term used within the sport administration of the Castro regime in Cuba, referring to grass roots participation in sport, or claims relating to the involvement of the mass of the population in physical culture.

mass media The techniques and institutions of communication in print, broadcasting, and the expanded multimedia outlets of the digital age. The term mass media also assumes a wide dissemination to and impact upon a large number of heterogeneous and widely dispersed readers, listeners, and/or viewers. Prior to this form of far-reaching impact, communication was essentially a face-to-face phenomenon. Denis McQuail observes that in face-to-face communication feedback of some sort is guaranteed (*Sociology of Mass Communications*, 1972). But in a modern era of 'entertainment rituals', mass marketing, advertising, and the manipulation of customers, 'direct feedback is shrunken to the small volume of fan mail'. For McQuail, technology has created more tightly integrated forms of social organization capable of building authority into the organizational system; media, essentially, become ways of wielding authority and manipulating the mass population.

These large-scale constituencies of reception began to emerge in the 19th century, with the development of communicative technologies and the growth of commercial entertainment; photography, film/cinema, cable telegraphy, the gramophone, telephone, wireless, and television were invented in the 70 years from 1860 onwards. Sport, as an outdoor public practice, was prominent in these developments. It generated in numerous countries a national, specialist sporting press; it featured in Britain in *Mitchell and Kenyon's revolutionary film-making in the first years of the 20th century; it was prominent in the diet provided by the mass circulation newspapers at the same time; it spawned a distinctive brand of creative sport-based writing in the USA, crossing journalism and fiction; it generated international markets for events broadcast on the new radio technologies, such as the first men's football World Cup Final in Montevideo, Uruguay, and USA–Europe clashes in the boxing ring like Germany's Max *Schmeling against 'Brown Bomber' Joe *Louis in New York in 1938 (the latter providing the opportunity for International News Service's Bob Considine's legendary wire report describing Joe Louis's look, 'his nostrils like the mouth of a double-barrelled shotgun').

As broadcasting possibilities expanded, sport remained at the forefront of developments. In June 1962 AT&T (American Telephone and Telegraph Company) used the artificial satellite Telstar to relay a television signal between North America (the state of Maine, USA) and Western Europe (the county of Cornwall, UK, and the region of Brittany, France). A little over two years of experimentation later, the first public use of satellite television relayed the opening ceremonies of the

Tokyo Olympic Games from Japan to North America. From that point on, in knowledge of the global audiences to be won, sport has been increasingly interwoven with the growth of communications technologies, and the interests of cultural entrepreneurs, broadcasting executives, and corporate sponsors.

C. Wright *Mills noted that mass media were based on two premises. First, they allowed the few to communicate to the many; second, they allowed no effective way of the recipients making a response. More niched, interactive forms of the media have challenged this one-way model, but responses from the public in the sport media are often little more than tokenistic one-liners or predictable fan gossip, or inane and trivial *sports chatter. The form whereby the communication is made might have altered dramatically, but the content may be little changed. As Raymond Williams put it, we must remember that 'the technology will not [necessarily] determine the effects', and a 'sub-culture of sporting gossip' on television, he observes, was well established in the print media (*Television: Technology and Cultural Form*, 1974). But Williams also noted that 'new international commercial and sponsoring interests' were having 'mixed effects', both creating new kinds of interest among spectators in expanded media coverage, and establishing marketing niches for the particular sponsor. The term 'mass media' itself has been seen by some critics as too deterministic a model, implying a passivity and powerlessness in the media audience(s); and there is undeniably a greater choice for consumers concerning where and when and how to view the media sport event. But as giant media corporations continue to dominate ownership, *vortextuality characterizes the media landscape, and much of media interactivity is sporting gossip or sports chatter, it is too early to consign the 'mass media' model to the waste bin of sport-media theory.

mass production The production of standardized goods through means of industrial and technological techniques on a scale that makes those goods accessible to extensive constituencies of consumer, or mass markets. Mass production brings prices down, expands markets, and makes products less exclusive: generally, the production of standardized sports goods has been an equalizing and democratizing influence upon sport. The possession of a set of golf clubs as good as the next man or woman's, though, will not guarantee access to or acceptance in the private golf club, for whom the profession, sex, or social status of the potential member remains a core consideration of the recruitment committee.

MasterCard A US-based financial services company specializing in payment systems, the processing of credit card and debit card payments between the banks of suppliers and the banks of consumers; it was founded in 1966, and has used sport as a way of building its brand in a highly competitive market. 'Master Charge: The Interbank Card' became simply 'MasterCard' in 1979, and the company bought up the UK's Access Card and the Eurocard brand: under its more globally embracing new name 'MasterCard Worldwide', the company became a publicly traded company in 2006. In that forty years of success and growth, MasterCard has successfully used sport as a way of building and consolidating its brand. Its overlapping two-sphere logo on the card resonates with sporting imagery,

particularly of ball games such as football, and, though unstated, its expanded
logo in 2000 with a third overlapping circle increasingly evokes the internationalism
of the five rings of the International Olympic Committee (MasterCard is not, though,
one of its sponsoring partners); it can be read as embracing the company's three
primary markets of the Americas, Europe, and Asia. Its 'Priceless' advertising
campaign with the line 'There are some things money can't buy. For everything else,
there's MasterCard' was launched during the (baseball) World Series in 1997. It
has targeted sponsorship deals with the major football bodies and tournaments: the
European football confederations' Euro competition for national sides, the *UEFA
Champions League, and the men's World Cup (though *Visa, in ethically
contentious behind-the-scenes negotiations with the *Fédération Internationale
de Football Association, replaced MasterCard as World Cup sponsor in 2007). Other
sponsorship deals embodying MasterCard's global reach have included contracts
with the Indian Premier League (IPL) team Mumbai Indians, the Australian
national cricket team, and Canadian ice hockey.

match analysis The analysis of patterns of play and player performance and
effectiveness in matches and contests, increasingly aided by forms of computer
software such as Prozone, as applied in professional soccer in England. Match
analysis has long informed commentary and punditry in sport journalism and
sport broadcasting, and in its more analytical and statistical forms underpins tactics
and planning in sport coaching.

Matthews, Sir Stanley (1915–2000) An English professional footballer who
played at the highest levels from 1932, when he first played for Stoke City, to 1965,
when he retired, and was awarded the knighthood that made him 'Sir Stanley'.
He had played for Blackpool after World War II, and the first FA Cup Final to be
televised became known as the 'Matthews Final' after he orchestrated a dramatic
comeback to defeat Lancashire rivals Bolton Wanderers by the score 4–3.
Matthews later returned to his first club, Stoke, where he finished his career at the
age of 50. He first played for the national England team in 1934, and played his
last international game in 1957 at the age of 42. This longevity and loyalty account
for the widespread respect that Matthews engendered in sports fans and the
general public. His brilliant playing style with the ball at his feet attracted the tag the
'Wizard of Dribble', and Matthews was famously Spartan in habit and diet,
sustaining regular and rigorous training schedules and programmes that gave
him the basis of such a protracted career at the top level of the game. Garry
Whannel has listed the traits that characterize media representations of the
Matthews persona and career: ordinariness; working-class context; thrift; sobriety;
respect for paternal authority; modesty; shunning of the limelight; dedication;
invisibility of family. This is contrasted with the football player who is more
a product of the forces of *celebrity, such as David Beckham. Matthews was
a national icon, prominent in the illustrations on the back of cigarette cards,
glimpsed on the new television sets in his Cup Final glory, and on Pathé news
clips of him in action at the cinema. But his image remains one of a disciplined,
modest player representing traditional values on the eve of a seismic change in
the political economy and accompanying culture of the professional game. Reports

of financial indiscretions in Matthews's brief managerial career, and revelations in the sensationalist media about his post-playing private life, did little to change this image.

maximum wage The imposition, by the employing club, of a limit on the earnings of a professional player. In professional football in England, the maximum wage had fixed the upper limit of a player's wage, for the winter playing season, and for the summer 'close' season. In 1961, the Professional Footballers' Association challenged the English Football League on this issue, as a matter of employment rights. National government (the Ministry of Labour) was involved in the conciliation process, and the players' threats of strikes were withdrawn when the maximum wage restriction was abolished. Soon, Johnny Haynes (1934–2005) of Fulham became England's first '£100-a-week' professional footballer. Some people in the game—such as the chairmen of smaller clubs in the provinces—predicted that the abolition of the maximum wage, combined with the reform of the *retain and transfer system, would play into the hands of the rich, metropolitan clubs. Burnley had won the English Football League championship in the 1959–60 season; Ipswich Town won the title in the 1961–2 season. Blackburn Rovers became champions of the newly formatted Premiership in 1993, after local businessman Jack Walker (1929–2000) invested heavily in the club. But, generally, the critics have been proven right; constraining and restraining as such controls might have been for the geographical and financial careers of players, their abolition has strengthened the resource base of metropolitan elites. *See also* SALARY CAP.

Mead, George Herbert (1863–1931) A US philosopher and social scientist who spent the bulk of his career at the University of Chicago, Mead was concerned with the nature of communication in the social order, and argued that the mind, self, and society should be understood in interrelated fashion. His thinking stimulated *symbolic interactionism, and is a reminder that over-specialization—as in the treatment, say, of the athlete as a self-contained machine—is to lose sight of the whole. He observed the 'conversation of gestures' in a dog fight, to show how social reality is a product of accumulative interactions and responses; and distinguished between the 'me', the social self, and the 'I', the creative response to the 'me'.

media events A term defining the core elements of a category of special events in the broadcasting media. Daniel Dayan and Elihu Katz (*Media Events: The Live Broadcasting of History*, 1992) listed six such elements. Media events must be pre-planned and publicized; be live; take space from the normal rhythms of television and everyday schedules; be organized by non-broadcasting bodies; hold audience attention; and draw upon narrative forms resonant of the heroic. Large-scale sporting events such as the Olympic Games and the FIFA men's football World Cup clearly meet these criteria and have proved irresistible media events for the broadcasting industry.

Mediterranean Games A multi-sport games held every four years, for countries from Europe, Asia, and Africa bordering the Mediterranean Sea (excepting Israel), and three other European countries (Andorra, San Marino, and Serbia). The Games were first held in Alexandria, Egypt, in 1951, and the Greek

Olympian legacy is invoked in the International Mediterranean Games Committee's rationale to strengthen cultural bonds between young people. The Committee is permanently located in Athens, Greece, and its general secretary must be a Greek national. The Games are authorized by the International Olympic Committee and the Hellenic (Greek) Olympic Committee. The logo of the Games, dating from 1979, comprises three white overlapping circles (for its three participating continents) on a sea-blue background, with the circles dissolving in their lower part in an image evoking the immersion of the rings in the common waters of the Mediterranean. Italy, France, and Spain have dominated the medal counts, with Egypt the top African nation and Syria the top Asian one. The geographic criteria of the Games are interesting, allowing a French region—Languedoc and Roussillon—to host the 1993 Games, rather than a city.

mega-events   A term for large-scale cultural events that have usually at least a national profile and impact, and often an international one, and that are organized on a larger scale than routine fixtures in the sporting calendar. In sport, the Olympic Games are the epitome of the mega-event (*see* OLYMPIC GAMES, MODERN (AS GLOBAL CULTURAL EVENT)). According to Maurice Roche (*Mega-Events and Modernity: Olympics and Expos in the Growth of Global Culture*, 2000), mega-events are modern and seen as progressive; they can be national and international (this latter divided into multinational, cosmopolitan, supernational, and global); and they have a capacity to reposition cities and places. Roche also identifies three levels of analysis of the mega-event: the 'event core' zone, focusing upon the event as performance or drama; the 'intermediate' event zone, looking at political and economic uses, functions, aims, and impacts of the event; and the 'event horizon', past and present and pitched towards an understanding of the implications of the event and what have also widely been discussed as mega-event legacies. *See also* MEDIA EVENTS; SPECTACLE.

Meisl, Hugo (1881–1937)   A Football coach, administrator, and referee, who coached the Austrian *Wunderteam* of the late 1920s and the early 1930s. Meisl was born in Maleschau, Bohemia, and moved to Vienna as a boy. He became the general secretary of the Austrian Football Association, and refereed international and Olympics (1912) matches. An internationalist, Meisl spoke several European languages and inaugurated the Mitropa Cup and a central European international cup. He communicated with other progressive European coaches and managers— Vittorio *Pozzo in Italy, and Herbert *Chapman in England. Another English coach who worked in Vienna, Jimmy Hogan, influenced Meisl's approach to playing the ball along the ground in a fluent passing style. Meisl was national coach from 1919, and his Austrian side dominated European competition though never winning either the Olympic title (1936) or the World Cup (Italy, 1934); and by 1938 Austria had been annexed by the Third Reich, and Meisl's wonder-team was, the year after his death, suddenly German.

memory   1. The psychological function that preserves information, with the capacity to select, store, and retrieve. Memory is also divided into short-term, long-term, and sensory memory (this latter drawing upon visual materials for short periods of storage). Another division has also been made between episodic memory, which focuses upon individuals' experiences and significant events in their lives, and semantic memory, relating to more factual information about the external world. Clearly, psychologists of sporting performance and practical applied psychologists such as informed and analytical coaches develop the athlete's capacity to utilize and mobilize particular memory functions, often focusing upon the here and now of the competitive action and moment, or manipulating memory to erase negative influences. Some of these forms and functions of memory could also be further developed and applied in the analysis of sport fans' selective remembering. 2. A more sociological and cultural concept of memory refers to the ways in which social institutions or collectivities remember the past and use this in the understanding of the present (an influential text here is Paul Connerton's *How Societies Remember*, 1989, with its memorable opening line, 'All beginnings contain an element of recollection'); in sport, past performers are memorialized in memoirs, institutional histories, and sometimes in public art forms such as statues.

mental practice and preparation *See* IMAGERY; RELAXATION.

mesomorph *See* SOMATOTYPE.

message In Marshall *McLuhan's analysis of modern communications, 'the medium is the message' is one of his most widely cited aphorisms. It is the title of the opening chapter of his *Understanding Media: The Extensions of Man* (1964). His thesis is that our personal and social lives are shaped by the medium itself, regardless of what the medium produces, as either content or product. The medium creates an environment:

> the "message" of any medium or technology is the change of scale or pace or pattern that it introduced into human affairs. The railway did not introduce movement or transportation or wheel or road into human society, but it accelerated and enlarged the scale of previous human functions, creating totally new kinds of cities and new kinds of work and leisure . . . quite independent of the freight or content of the railway medium.

Media sport as a medium, then, is not best understood in terms of the minutiae of the content of programming, but in terms of the conventions of the medium and its consequences for people's ways of living, for 'it is the medium that shapes and controls the scale and form of human association and action'. As the sport viewer watches the scheduled weekly game in the domestic, club, or sports bar setting almost half a century on from McLuhan's polemic, his observations have a prescient resonance.

metaphor A figure of speech in which a term or a name is used to refer to an object to which the term does not literally belong. Examples abound in sport writing and sport journalism, in attempts to lighten up or add colour to literal accounts of sporting action. The tennis player *coaxes* the ball into the corner of the court; the spin bowler in cricket bowls a *magical* delivery; the *God* of the water Michael Phelps *smashes* previous Olympic records. A variant of the metaphor is the trope; sport is conducive to recollection and discussion on the basis of tropes. Roger Bannister's *four-minute mile in 1954 is a trope evoking images of the apogee of British amateurism; the phrase 'Roy of the Rovers' is a trope known to generations of

British male readers of football comics, and sport commentators, using the comic-strip hero Roy Race of Melchester Rovers as a convenient shorthand for moments of memorable individual sporting achievement, particularly victory against the odds or the most unlikely of comebacks.

methodology Often confused with the particular experimental research methods or fieldwork techniques employed in a study, in sociocultural studies this term actually means the theory of or rationale for the methods and analytical techniques that are chosen for a study, including consideration of the wider questions generated by the philosophy of science. How is evidence gathered? What is the relationship of the researcher to, say, the sport subculture under study? What is the role of the researcher in the fieldwork setting? Is a value-free, neutral sociocultural analysis possible? What is the status of the knowledge generated in the study? How do the experiences and views of the researcher—as, say, an experienced and knowledgeable sports performer or enthusiast—relate to the sport subculture he or she is studying? Should sociocultural studies be verifiable? Such questions are also within the territory of *epistemology, the theory of knowledge, and *ontology, the theory of being or existence.

metric system An international system of measurement based on fundamental physical units such as the metre, second, litre, and gram. The system is a decimal one, with changes to the power of 10 indicated by successive prefixes such as 'kilo-' (one thousand) and 'micro-' (one millionth). The metric system is also known as the SI system from the French *Système International*. The primary units relevant to sport and exercise science are as follows: amount (moles) of a chemical substance as the quantity equal to the molecular weight; energy (joules) as a measure of the amount of work done or heat generated or contained within a food; force (newtons) as a measure of that which changes the state of rest or motion of a mass; mass (kilograms) as a measure of the amount of matter; power (watts) as a measure of exercise intensity to describe the work done or the energy expended per second; speed (metres per second) as a measure of the distance travelled per unit of time; torque (newton metres) as force producing rotation; volume (litres) as the space occupied by a liquid or a gas; work (joules) as the force (newtons) displaced by a distance (metres). Not all measurements are routinely expressed in pure metric units, the two notable exceptions being pressure (e.g. blood pressure in mmHg rather than pascals) and energy (eg. food energy in kilocalories rather than kilojoules).

microlight flying The flying of microlight or ultralight aviation machines that can look like tiny conventional aicraft, or like a go-kart with wings, or might be the powered paraglider or hang glider. As a recreational sport and competitive activity it became established in the 1980s and 1990s as an affordable form of flying in affluent countries, and is best understood as a form of lifestyle sport, combining thrill with display. In the USA the sport is called 'light-sport aircraft' flying. There is little international consistency of regulations or rules, as national regulations regarding safety and technical criteria vary widely. *See also* AIRSPORTS.

microsociogical approaches In contrast to *macrosociological approaches, the study of social phenomena and social institutions that is based on a concentrated focus upon the smaller group, or a particular facet of the everyday life of the group, or the workings and practices of an institution. Typical of such approaches are studies of selected sport *subcultures or detailed consideration and analysis of the *life courses of individual sportsmen and -women.

military preparedness A widely influential but often neglected contributor to the profile of sport in some societies. When the fighting soldiers of Britain's army were found to be lacking in fitness and strength in the second Boer War (1899–1902) in the former Transvaal Republic (later, South Africa), measures were introduced to improve the physical fitness of the (male) population. In landlocked Switzerland, competence if not prowess in archery and shooting has been demanded of all of the (male) population since the formation of the Swiss Confederation, linked to the sense that a fit and skilled armed force would be ready to repel any invader. The ideology of *athleticism in Britain's public schools fostered an *esprit de corps* that was directly transferable to the fighting ranks of troops in World War I, as shown in some actual and corroborated, and numerous apocryphal, accounts of kicking footballs ahead of trench advances.

Mill, John Stuart (1806–73) An English philosopher and political economist, and champion of women's rights. Mill was at various times also a Liberal Member of Parliament and a business administrator. His wide-ranging ideas addressed fundamental problems such as the nature of scientific thinking, the nature of liberty, historical change and continuity, and the relation of the individual to society. One of his most famous works (1861/3) was *Utilitarianism*, one of his most famous epithets the declaration that, through the action of the state/government, one could aspire to 'the greatest happiness of the greatest number'. The most prominent application of Mill's ideas to the analysis of sport is in Lincoln Allison's work (see, for instance, *Amateurism in Sport: An Analysis and a Defence*, 2001), in what he calls his 'liberal utilitarian point of view' concerning 'the possibility of good living' that sport might or might not offer. Allison's utilitarianism is liberal, he states, in two senses: first, individual autonomy and choice should be favoured when there is doubt; second, following Mill, any simple concept of pleasure or happiness should be rejected 'in favour of an acceptance of the complexity of ideas of human well-being'. A Mill-inspired approach to understanding sport is thus a reminder to sport policy bodies and the more messianic end of sport organizations that there is no single, indisputable model of the benefits and positive outcomes of sport.

Mill knew little of the pleasures or benefits of sport, as he noted in *Autobiography of John Stuart Mill* (1853/6, final version published 1873). His education—learning Greek at the age of 3, Latin at 7, logic five years later and political economy the following year—hardly provided the all-round model for mind–body development and harmony. He did, though, grow up 'healthy and hardy', if not 'muscular', satisfying the 'animal need of physical activity . . . by walking', filling his 'ample leisure' with bookish pursuits rather than play (lacking, he recalled, boy companions with whom to engage in play); but always remaining 'inexpert in anything requiring manual dexterity'. Such a life of the mind has nevertheless generated conceptual and theoretical issues that cannot be ignored in thinking about sport's place in society, its cultural significance, and its human meaning and potential.

Mills, Charles Wright (1916–62) An influential US sociologist whose work on the nature of the class system and on the influence of the power elite in society countered the functionalist consensus of other sociologists of the mid 20th century. Mills also wrote on the *sociological imagination, arguing for the integrated study of self and society, history and biography, and on the importance of understanding how participatory forms of public culture are jeopardized by the development of mass media owned by elites (he might have added 'such as sport businesses or media sport' here). A particular strand in the sociology of sport—variously categorized as critical sociology or a cultural studies approach to sport—has acknowledged the deep influence of Mills's work.

Mitchell and Kenyon Sagar Mitchell and James Kenyon were two English film-makers who established their film company in 1897, and whose early filming of people in everyday public life captured the range of sports and games played by groups and communities in the first decade of the 20th century in Britain (mainly in England). Their films, fortuitously saved when demolitionists were working on a building in Blackburn, Lancashire, showed cricket professionals at training; rugby and football (soccer) matches between professional sides such as Manchester United (known then as Newton Heath) and Burnley, the top clubs and teams of the time; national athletic meets between the English association and teams from the USA; as well as community games and contests on traditional holiday schedules, and racing events mixing athletic prowess with novelty features.

mixed martial arts (MMA) *See* TOTAL FIGHTING.

MLB (Major League Baseball) *See* BASEBALL.

modernity Krishan Kumar writes: 'Modernity is a "contrast concept". It takes its meaning as much from what it denies as what it affirms' (W. Outhwaite, ed., *The Blackwell Dictionary of Modern Social Thought*, 2nd edn, 2003). The term therefore has had 'widely varied meanings', and Kumar gives revealing historical examples, such as the Enlightenment's insertion of the category of 'medieval' between 'ancient' and 'modern'. This gave the term a resonance of the here-and-now, and modernity as a world view and a system evokes images of the new, the modern, and the future. Modern sports, as depicted in the ideal type central to the work of Allen Guttmann—secularism, equality, specialization, rationalization, bureaucracy, quantification, records (*From Ritual to Record: The Nature of Modern Sports*, 1978) —are, from this point of view, typical products, and indeed cultural manifestations of, modernity. But modernity never comprised a stable set of absolute certainties, and classical social scientific theorists pointed to the contradictions and tensions within modernity. Sports can embody the modernity of their here-and-nowness in a variety of ways—the *parkour performance in the urban spectacle, the windsurfer and the paraglider on coast and mountainside. As Kumar warns, any effort to pin down modernity is likely to be undermined by the complex trajectories of a society and culture—including its sporting cultures. *See also* POSTMODERNISM AND POSTMODERNITY.

modern pentathlon A multi-discipline competitive sport, comprising five elements: shooting, fencing, swimming, horse-riding, and cross-country running. The sport was introduced in the Olympic Games programme in 1912, and its military pedigree ensured that it was not until 1952 that the event was won by a competitor without any military background: Lars Hall, a Swedish carpenter, broke that monopoly. The Olympic event was also dominated by men, until women first competed at the 2000 Sydney Games. East European countries (Hungary, the former Soviet Union, Poland, and Russia) have been dominant medal winners, with Sweden a close second to Hungary in the overall Olympic medal table. UK journalist Kevin Mitchell captures the cultural quirkiness of the event: 'It is quintessentially exotic, peopled by enthusiasts who toil anonymously in five disciplines that are not remotely related to each other yet demand utter dedication.' In fact, the disciplines were of course interrelated in the event's historical origins, being the skills that could be required of a cavalry courier. Bronze medallist in the event at Montreal in 1976, Czech Jan Bartu, performance director of the UK modern pentathlon team in 2008, highlighted the virtues of the sport:

> it is the most versatile sport in the Olympics—and it takes tremendous dedication to get to this level. It is a massive undertaking to train across five different sports. Not many can do it. There are maybe 80 or 90 competing at this World Cup level, 70 or so in the women's. They are all tremendous athletes.

molecular biology The study of biological processes at the molecular level. It concerns how biological function is affected by the organization and activity of chromosomes, nucleic acids, and subcellular organelles. Molecular biologists are particularly interested in gene expression—how the information coded in a gene (a segment of DNA) is transcribed (copied) into mRNA and then translated by ribosomes (organelles within a cell) to form *proteins. Molecular biology is in effect the detailed mechanistic explanation of the broad theories of genetics and inheritance introduced by Darwin and Mendel and developed through Watson and Crick's explanation of the basic structure of DNA. Sequencing of the human genome has provided fruitful ground for the development of molecular biology, aided by computational advances (bioinformatics) to deal with the large volume and complexity of data.

Proteomics, the detailed analysis of protein expression, is of major importance in the study of sport and exercise due to protein's key role in structure (e.g. muscle) and regulation (e.g. hormones and enzymes). It is likely that research will lead to an improved understanding of how training improves fitness and therefore of how to optimize training to promote the greatest change in sports performance. In the medical arena a greater understanding of disease will lead to an improved understanding of how exercise can promote health, or how injured tissues can be repaired. In parallel with these advances, concerns are coming to be expressed about the ethical implications and the potential to cheat. For example, gene therapy offers the opportunity for improved treatment of injuries such as a muscle tear but the same knowledge also offers the potential to increase muscle mass in an uninjured athlete.

monetarism An economic doctrine favouring the autonomy and the free play of the market and market forces, and inherently unsympathetic to and in large part opposed to public sector expenditure. A monetarist sport policy may be a contradiction in terms, in that from a monetarist perspective sport as culture should be left to the initiatives of the *voluntary sector or *civil society, and the sport industry should be a part of the market economy. English prime minister Margaret Thatcher (in office from 1979 to 1990) was a confirmed monetarist who had no interest in the place of sport in society, apart from when it manifested a particular social problem: Soviet foreign policy in Afghanistan, and the USA-led boycott that she so unsuccessfully sought to emulate in Britain; football hooliganism and crowd problems that were manifest in stadium tragedies of the 1980s. The laissez-faire policies of the monetarist have had an enervating effect on parts of the sporting infrastructure of Britain, with the selling off of school playing fields in the Thatcher years the prime example.

monopoly The dominance within a *market of a single supplier. A case often cited from the USA is the control that Major League Baseball (MLB) has had over competitive baseball in the USA. Establishing a monopoly situation by merger with or absorption of rivals, and recognized in the Supreme Court as exempt from antitrust law, it was free from competitive challenge throughout the 20th century, expanding through competition for new markets, rather than any competition within the market. Preserving its monopoly, MLB expanded from its sixteen franchises in set locations, which stood from 1903 to 1953, and moved into new markets in the west and the south, enhancing its reach into a product space of its own making. Governance at national level in sport, and at the global level in international federations, creates conditions of potential monopoly, as established organizations have the regulatory and quasi-legal capacity to administer a sport with no threat of competitive challenge.

Monte Carlo Rally A motor-car rally held in the European principality of Monte Carlo in midwinter, when driving conditions are at their worst and potentially most dangerous. It was first held in 1911, and used as a means of testing new technologies in and designs of vehicles. The combination of glamour in the Mediterranean location with toughness and endurance in the driving made the Monte Carlo rally a symbol of early and mid 20th-century glamour, and for car manufacturers the rally was an important forum for exhibiting their products.

morality As a prescription for how to live, the considerations and principles guiding the way of living of a particular individual or collectivity. Some conceptions of sport are implicitly moral, in this sense: *amateurism, for instance. Some codes of living, such as *communitarianism, also purvey visions of what it is to abide by a particular morality. When particular ideals are claimed for the meaning and significance of sport, such claims are statements of adherence to specific moral beliefs, expressions of sport's potential for and contribution to morality, its impact as an essentially worthwhile activity and enterprise, a 'good thing'. *See also* MORAL LABORATORY.

moral laboratory A term used by Graham McFee referring to sport's concern with fairness (*Sport, Rules and Values: Philosophical Investigations into the Nature of Sport*, 2004). Rules, McFee notes, are sometimes changed to encourage if not ensure *fair play, or what in a more philosophical terminology he calls 'just performance'. Sport as a moral laboratory is about learning to play within the rules, and this is based upon learned principles. Three intrinsic characteristics of sport give it its 'possibilities as a moral laboratory': it is rule-governed; human interactions in sport can generate and express fairness and harm; and the risk to human participants is (usually) not too excessive. Provocatively, McFee develops his arguments to propose that some sports—his examples are boxing, synchronized swimming, and basketball—have little moral worth or potential to contribute to moral education.

moral panic A reaction—fuelled by the media—to forms of *deviance or social disturbance that, with no or negligible evidence, escalates concern about the issue to make of it a prominent and often major social concern. Stanley Cohen's *Folk Devils and Moral Panics: The Creation of the Mods and Rockers* (1972) traced this process on the basis of his study of the 1964 responses to the scooter- and motorbike-riding youth groups. First, 'a condition, episode, person or group of persons' is seen and defined as a threat to general social values. Second, the nature of this threat is communicated in the mass media, in 'stylized and stereotypical fashion'. Third, the 'moral barricades are manned' by prominent establishment figures. Fourth, 'socially accredited experts' comment on the issue and possible responses and solutions. Fifth, 'ways of coping' are identified. Sixth, the condition goes away, fades from the limelight, or 'deteriorates and becomes more visible'.

Numerous such panics have related to youth culture, and the most high-profile case in sport has been *football hooliganism. On lesser levels, though, moral concerns about drug use in sport, alcoholic consumption and obesity among the wider population, and gambling in relation to sporting integrity have provided foci for the emergence and cultivation of moral panics. Chas Critcher has examined 'Moral Panics and Newspaper Coverage of Binge Drinking' (in Bob Franklin, ed. *Pulling Newspapers Apart: Analysing Print Journalism*, 2008), demonstrating the continuing usefulness of Cohen's *ideal type of, or classification of the characteristics of, the moral panic. Critcher concludes that binge drinking is a 'fairly mild moral panic . . . It has a new name but lacks a folk devil'. This is a very interesting observation, and in high-performance sport at least, individuals flouting the moral expectations of the respectable public are easily available potential folk devils. *See also* DEVIANCE AMPLIFICATION; LABELLING.

mores A term introduced by William Graham Sumner (1840–1910) in his 1906 book *Folkways*, referring to the morally prescribed and generally accepted forms of behaviour characteristic of a community or society. Sport is based upon sets of shared principles that in Sumner's sense are mores, without which the structure of competition, or the informal contract between spectator and player, would be jeopardized. Mores were contrasted by Sumner with folkways, the more everyday customs that, if transgressed, are less threatening to the social order.

Morris, Michael, third Baron Killanin (1914–99) An Irish-born journalist, film producer, and sport administrator, who became the sixth president of the International Olympic Committee (IOC). Morris inherited the title of Baron Killanin at the age of 13. He attended Eton College, the Sorbonne, and Magdalene College, Cambridge. At Cambridge he was president of the Footlights, the light entertainment association of the university, edited the literary magazine *Varsity*, and participated in a range of sports, boxing, rowing, and playing rugby. He was also a great follower of horse racing. After acting as president of the Olympic Council of Ireland, he joined the International Olympic Committee in 1952 and succeeded Avery *Brundage as president in 1972. He introduced new levels of funding to the organization, through the sale of television rights, and was left to deal with the consequences of the tragic events of Munich 1972, officially presided over by Brundage at the time, but haunting the subsequent decade. *Boycotts (by African nations of the 1976 Montreal Games, and by the USA and other non-communist nations at Moscow 1980, after the USSR's invasion of Afghanistan) dominated the difficult years of Killanin's presidency.

motivation The direction and intensity of an individual's effort towards a goal. Some motives, such as thirst and hunger, are biologically based and are driven by homeostatic mechanisms, but can become disordered by behavioural factors leading, for example, to *obesity. In sport, motivation is usually considered as an interaction between the characteristics of the participant (personality, needs, interests, etc.) and the situation (type of sport, *coaching style, team, etc.). Vallerand and Losier's integrated theory proposes that social factors are mediated by the individual's psychological perceptions of competence, autonomy, and relatedness to determine motivation, which is described as a self-determination continuum. At one end lies amotivation. Next lies extrinsic motivation, which arises from an external source such as the winning of a medal, prize money, social approval, or punishment. At the far end of the continuum lies intrinsic motivation, which is internal and involves the athlete participating because they really want to take part and gain personal satisfaction from doing so. Intrinsic motivation is considered desirable and sports coaching techniques to encourage it include the use of praise rather than punishment, involvement of athletes in decision making, *goal setting, and rewards contingent on performance not results. *See also* NEEDS, HIERARCHY OF.

motocross Also known as 'scrambling', this is a specialized form of racing on motorcycles, over closed-circuit courses across rough cross-country terrain. Organization of the sport dates from the late 1920s, when English motorcycle clubmen in the south of the country developed more of a 'scramble'-type race as an alternative to observed time trials on roads. In 1945, a more organized format was developed on the outskirts of Paris, and two years later, the Moto-Cross des Nations was inaugurated. Britain, Belgium, and Sweden were dominant in the early years of the sport: in more recent years, Italy and France have produced the World Champion team, but the USA took the World Championship from 2005 to 2008.

motor control The structure, organization, and functioning of the nervous system which leads to the stimulation of muscles to produce purposeful movement. The movement functions of the nervous system may be considered in two divisions—the central and the peripheral. The central division comprises the brain and spinal cord. The peripheral comprises the motor neurons running from the spine to the muscles and various forms of sensory nerves. Commands are initiated and programmed in the brain with the cerebellum providing a specialist area to integrate and adjust neural commands in tune with feedback from sensory neurons. The spinal cord includes tracts of neurons to transmit signals down the body.

The functional unit of motor control is the motor unit. This consists of a motor neuron running from the spinal cord into a muscle and thence to a group of muscle fibres. There are over 200 million muscle fibres in the human body and each motor neuron innervates a number. The number varies according to the function of the muscle, ranging from just a few fibres per motor neuron where low force and precise movement are required (e.g. in the muscles of the eye), to many thousand fibres per motor neuron where high force and only coarse control are needed (e.g. in the muscles of the buttocks). The firing of the motor unit causes all the fibres in that group to contract; there is no gradation of contraction, a muscle fibre either contracts or does not. Graduation of force in the muscle as a whole is achieved by either increasing the number of motor units stimulated (recruitment) or increasing the frequency of neural discharge (rate coding). A muscle may have several hundred motor units and a combination of their selective recruitment and rate coding allows a fine gradation of force production.

The control of movement is aided by feedback from visual and vestibulatory sources and from proprioceptors which provide a perception of movement and position of the body parts, usually at a subconscious level. These specialist receptors reside in the muscles, tendon, joints, and skin and include the muscle spindles, Golgi tendon organs, joint receptors, and Pacinian corpuscles. While some elements of movement are initiated consciously, a great deal takes place subconsciously as a result of learned patterns of muscle activity (*see* MOTOR LEARNING). A proportion of control also takes place at a reflex level in the spinal cord.

motorcycle racing Forms of competitive racing between individuals or teams of motorcyclists. These include the cross-country version, *motocross, and *speedway, on dirt tracks of shale or cinder. Early forms of racing were on normal roads between European cities, with all the accompanying dangers for riders and spectators alike. Racing was therefore moved on to closed-circuit tracks, and forms of Grand Prix racing established. Technological development of competitive machines and success on the track became attractive indices of modernity and progress for national governments, and Germany and Italy rivalled the British for dominance in the 1930s. The 1950s saw growth and the peak in the profile of this form of the sport, Italian firms withdrawing their support after 1957. Some categories of racing then became dominated by Japanese machines in the 1960s, though the Japanese manufacturers switched their focus from Europe to the USA at the end of that decade. In 1971 the Fédération Internationale Motocycliste, founded in Paris in 1904, collaborated with the American Motorcycle Association, founded in 1924, to innovate a new racing category to accommodate glamorous large-capacity superbikes. The history of motorcycle racing is one of product

development, consumer branding, and global marketing as well as the thrill of the
speed and the excitement of the race.

motor learning The acquiring of new or more skilled patterns of movement as
a result of instruction or experience. Many of the fundamental skills of human
movement, such as walking, running, and throwing, are gained as part of the normal
maturation of the human from birth. Motor learning in sport is concerned with how
'normal' human movement is adapted and refined to allow the very specific actions
involved in the techniques of individual sports. A refined sports skill allows the athlete
to effect an appropriate combination of efficient movement, powerful force production,
and adaptability to various circumstances. Fitts and Posner in 1967 described three
stages that can be applied to learning a sports skill. The first, or cognitive stage involves
developing an understanding of the skill and a mental picture of the technique. This
stage is characterized by gross errors, poor timing, and truncated action as the
component parts of the skill are thought through separately. Knowledge of results
(such as whether a ball is hit and how far) and knowledge of performance (such as a
coach's comment) lead to gradual improvement and learning moves into the second or
associative stage. Here the component parts are linked together more smoothly and
errors are reduced. There is a greater reliance on internal feedback from
proprioceptors—the 'feel' of the technique—and how that relates to good or poor
performance based on knowledge of results. The third, or autonomous stage of learning
is characterized by a highly consistent and smooth technique. To the athlete much
of the movement is automatic, allowing them to concentrate on subtler or more
peripheral internal and external cues. The technique is refined but responsive to
variations in the external environment, leading to enhanced performance.

motor racing A competition between land vehicles that are mechanically
propelled and driven over closed-circuit tracks or on specified point-to-point
routes. Separate timings are made in competitions where drivers race singly; where
competitors race together, the winner is the first to finish the allocated distance,
or number of laps of the circuit. Competition began almost as soon as the first
petrol-driven car was invented, with timed trials in France in the later 1880s and the
1890s, and organized automobile races in Chicago and the East Coast of the USA
in the 1890s. Speed was the great attraction to competitor and spectator alike. In the
USA, perhaps the most prominent single motor-racing event has been the
Indianapolis 500-mile race, first held in 1911. In Europe, the first Grand Prix race
was held in 1906 at Le Mans, France, won by the Renault company's vehicle, driven
by its chief mechanic. Germany and Italy developed competitive vehicles and
high profiles in the sport in the 1920s and 1930s, though British competitiveness was
held back by its amateur ethos. The European Grand Prix cycle of events was
superseded by the Formula One competition in 1950, and consolidation and
expansion of the sport in the television age guaranteed worldwide exposure,
attracting competitors from Brazil and Argentina as well as the traditional European
constituencies. The Fédération Internationale de l'Automobile (FIA), founded in
1904 in Paris, now with its administration in Geneva, Switzerland, oversees the
sport. (As it stated on its website in 2009, it 'brings together 221 national

motoring and sporting organisations from 132 countries on five continents. Its member clubs represent over 100 million motorists and their families.')

In 2008, a worldwide television viewing audience of 600 million was reported for Formula One, and despite the volatility of the global economy, the sport continues to attract manufacturers and sponsors. The sport has been rife, in the early 20th century, with controversy concerning the business interests of FIA personnel and their partners, and the unethical and even corrupt practices that have been revealed in the racing events themselves: these have included industrial espionage between rival teams, and ploys such as deliberately crashing to hamper or disrupt the racing progress of other drivers. Despite such dubious morals on the track and in the boardroom, Formula One's winning formula of speed, glamour, celebrity, and cosmopolitanism sustains the sport's global profile. *See also* HOT ROD; LE MANS; NASCAR; SENNA (DA SILVA), AYRTON.

mountaineering The ascent of mountains for the purpose of recreation or exploration. In some definitional arguments, it is not a sport at all, with no specified contest or tournament schedule, and the danger to human lives that is constant. But any adequate overview of sporting and body culture in the modern period must recognize the significance of mountaineering. The attraction of scaling summits, defying danger, stretching the limits of human attainment—elements central to the competitive sporting ethos—is fundamental to mountaineering and associated activities such as climbing. It is also pivotal in the Western Romantic and post-Romantic imagination. *See also* HARGREAVES, ALISON; HILLARY, SIR EDMUND PERCIVAL; MALLORY, GEORGE HERBERT LEIGH; STEPHEN, LESLIE; TENZING NORGAY.

multidisciplinarity The application of more than one discipline to an object of study. A runner, for instance, may be studied by the exercise physiologist, the biomechanist, and the psychologist so that a full performance profile is generated from a number of perspectives; or the International Olympic Committee could be analysed by a sociologist specializing in large-scale organizations, an economist, and a political scientist with expertise in *governance. These analyses may be complementary, but not necessarily integrated, as would be the case in a study based upon the principle of *interdisciplinarity.

muscle action The activation of a muscle generates tension, and the resulting change in muscle length and movement around a joint is described by four terms. In a concentric action the muscle tension is greater than the external resistance and the muscle shortens, as for example the biceps in the upward phase of a weightlifting curl. In an eccentric action the muscle tension is less than the external resistance and the muscle lengthens, as for example the biceps in the downward phase of a weightlifting curl. In an isometric action the muscle tension is the same as the external resistance and no change in muscle length occurs, such as when a barbell is held in a stationary position. In an isokinetic action the muscle tension is greater than the external resistance and the rate of shortening maintains a constant angular velocity at the joint concerned. These forms of action are utilized in weight-training exercises. Free weightlifting techniques and a variety of rigs can be used to mimic human movements while focusing the load on to particular muscles to stimulate their development.

muscle fibre type The classification of muscle fibres according to their contractile and metabolic characteristics. The simplest classification is into slow-twitch (or type I) and fast-twitch (or type II) fibres although some classifications subdivide these two types further. Slow-twitch fibres generate energy mainly aerobically, shorten slowly, and are able to produce lesser force, but are fatigue-resistant. Fast-twitch fibres generate energy mainly anaerobically, shorten more quickly, and are able to produce greater force, but fatigue more rapidly. Muscles are composed of both types of fibre but the proportion varies between muscles and between individuals. The average adult has about an equal proportion of each type of fibre. Elite endurance runners typically have 70 per cent or more slow-twitch fibres in the leg muscles while sprinters have a predominance of fast-twitch fibres. Differences between individuals are mainly genetically driven.

muscular Christianity The association of sporting prowess and *athleticism with the religious and spiritual values of Christianity. This was cultivated strongly in 19th-century Britain, and found expression in preachings and popular writings, including the novel *Tom Brown's School Days* by Thomas *Hughes. It was a form of mind–body theory, a version of what the Roman writer *Juvenal referred to as "a healthy mind in a healthy body". Muscular Christianity pervaded the British public-school system, and became prominent in many other societies, including the USA, where the Young Men's Christian Association (*YMCA) espoused the values of sport within its general teachings. *See also* KINGSLEY, CHARLES.

Mussolini, Benito Amilcare Andrea (1883–1945) An Italian politician who is credited with establishing *fascism as a dominant political force in early to mid 20th-century Western Europe, influencing the political thinking and ambitions of Adolf *Hitler as an emerging politician in Germany. Mussolini saw sport as a powerful political tool through which the youth of the nation could be indoctrinated into fascist thinking, and the prowess of the nation could be expressed in sporting competition such as the men's football World Cup and the Olympic Games. As Robert S. C. Gordon and John London (2006: 43) put it:

> Although Fascism as an ideology has proved notoriously hard to define, certain persistent elements in its makeup drew it ineluctably toward sport from the outset, even if on occasion from contradictory directions. These elements include its nationalism; its militarism, anti-individualism, and pedagogical totalitarianism; its aesthetics and culture of consent; and the myth of Mussolini.

A 1933 booklet on the 'International University Games' (Tomlinson, 2005: 54–5) celebrated the youthful sporting body in an intriguing mix of universal idealism and fascist indoctrination. Ten years of sporting success—at the Los Angeles Olympic Games, and in international competition in horse racing, football, swimming, fencing, and motor racing—were cited as evidence of

> wonderful progress made by Italy in this field of human activity . . . the result of ten years of the Fascist Regime which places in the front rank the health and physical improvement of the Italian race . . . and successful efforts made to give a sporting education to young men which will strengthen their muscles today and mould their character in the future.

Fascist University Groups had been initiated in 1920, their 'sporting education' a priority. The Yearly Littoriali Sporting Competition provided a platform for these fascist uses of the sporting body, and in the first ten years of the fascist regime, Gordon and London (2006) report, over 2,000 new stadiums or tracks were built or created (500 new stadiums inaugurated at the same time on a single day in 1929); 3,500 sporting associations were also organized. The Forum of Mussolini, an exercise venue in Rome, could hold 20,000 spectators and was designed to recall Graeco-Roman buildings of classical antiquity. Mussolini had been elected to power in 1922, and in 1925 he seized dictatorial powers as Head of Government, or *Il Duce* (The Leader). The Italian national football team won the first European-based World Cup in 1934, and Gordon and London observe the echo of the key characteristics of the fascist New Man project in the hailed method of the Italian football coach Vittorio *Pozzo: an embracing of risk and danger, a pledge and sacrifice to the national cause, and pride in the nation and the race. FIFA president Jules *Rimet responded to the Italian 1934 victory with a recognition of fascism as 'a faith able to perform such miracles'. Mussolini himself was regularly depicted as a sporting figure, as runner, swimmer, fencer, skier, rider, and pilot.

Italy was second behind the USA in the medal table at the Los Angeles 1932 Olympics, and came fourth at the Berlin Olympics in 1936. Mussolini looked to an Olympics in Rome to both express the Italian fascist ideal and immortalize his own image. For this, he planned the construction of a huge sporting complex upstream by the Tiber, which would include a 25-foot-high statue of himself, semi-nude and dressed as Hercules. The area of the complex was named Foro Mussolini, though its name was changed to Foro Italica after World War II. Still visible at the entrance to the complex are the letters 'MUSSOLINI DUX' on a 55-foot obelisk, behind which the paving of the Forum featured tiled mosaics of athletic heroes. Next to the Forum, the Marble Stadium was planned as the site of the Olympics, with 60 gigantic stone statues of athletes placed on top of the oval. Swimming and fencing complexes were also constructed by Mussolini in his ill-fated plans to emulate Hitler's propagandistic use of the Olympic Games.

References

Gordon, R. S. C and London, J. (2006) 'Italy 1934: Football and Fascism', in A. Tomlinson and C. Young (eds), *National Identity and Global Sports Events: Culture, Politics, and Spectacle in the Olympics and the Football World Cup*, Albany: State University of New York Press, pp. 41–63; Tomlinson, A. (2005), 'Olympic Survivals: The Olympic Games as a Global Phenomenon', in L. Allison (ed.), *The Global Politics of Sport: The Role of Global Institutions in Sport*, London: Routledge, pp. 46–62.

myth An account of a figure or an event that is sustained through time in a particular society or culture, and that resonates with meanings related to the morality of human conduct. Sociologists and anthropologists have studied the nature of myth in particular cultural settings, and some have sought to identify the underlying patterns of myth across societies (their universal structures). Roland Barthes, though, writes that 'one can conceive of very ancient myths, but there are no eternal ones' (*Mythologies*, 1957, English edition 1972), and in his approach to the study of mythologies he emphasized the process of *signification and the analytical approach of *semiology for understanding the generation of myths. A historical approach by Philip Carter ('Myth, Legend, and Mystery in the *Oxford DNB*', 2004) retrieves some of the general significance of the mythical in his observation that 'common to all types' of mythical figures 'are names and deeds that have generated popular perceptions, or misconceptions, of British history', and that 'common to all is the power afforded to a generic cause' such as 'national rivalry . . . when expressed and interpreted through the medium of biography'. Stories of individual sporting lives can in this sense be seen as the stuff of national myth, where the individual sporting accomplishment stands for so much more than the life trajectory of the single individual. This serious level of analysis of sport's contribution to cultural meanings is not to be confused with the everyday sense of myth as something untrue, or not real.

m

narcissism Narcisssus was, in ancient Greek mythology, a Thespian with a 'stubborn pride in his own beauty', pursued by countless 'lovers of both sexes' (Robert Graves, *The Greek Myths,* 1960). Told as a child that he would 'live to a ripe old age, provided that he never knows himself', Narcissus's undoing came when one rejected lover killed himself with a sword sent to him by Narcissus, calling, in his death throes, on the gods to avenge him. The god Artemis obliged, arranging for Narcissus to drink from a spring 'clear as silver', whereupon he fell in love with his own reflection; unable to consummate this love, he stabbed himself in the breast, uttering the melodramatic and solipsistic words 'Ah youth, beloved in vain, farewell!', his words repeated by one of his rejected suitors, the faithful nymph Echo. This myth was used by Sigmund *Freud in developing a theory of homosexuality within his analysis of psychosexual stages of development. More generally, narcissism has come to refer to the idea of self-love, and a preoccupation with image, beauty, and attractiveness.

The cultural critic and commentator Christopher Lasch (1932–94) contrasted a particular traditional model of sport (as a form of delight-inducing escape) with a burgeoning preoccupation with individual and self, the 'production and consumption of images', 'the emergence of *spectacle as a dominant form of cultural expression', all amounting to 'the assimilation of sport to show business' (*The Culture of Narcissism: American Life in an Age of Diminishing Expectations*, 1979). Lasch wrote of a 'pathological narcissism' framed as a kind of deficiency of selfhood, or personality disorder, giving a twist to the established sense of narcissism as just *hedonism or pleasure-seeking; the pleasures of the body and the thrill of sports would increasingly, from this perspective, be 'kindly' forms of provision for the masses. Jennifer Maguire Smith, in an illuminating article in the *International Review for the Sociology of Sport* (2002), analysed a selection of fitness publishing texts, concluding: 'Through the fitness field, our bodies are reflected back to us through the lens of products and services, and consumption is promoted as the primary arena in which we make and remake our bodies.' There has long been a strutting physical self-promotion in sporting figures, from Regency boxers to amateur Olympians, from Denis Compton's hair oil to David Beckham's underwear, but this has escalated in the age of *celebrity. At the level of the spectacular sporting event, the individual exercising body, and the promotion of the celebrity sport star, the echo of Narcissus remains audible.

narrative Initially rooted in literary theory, and adapted in media studies and sociology, narrative as an analytical framework has had an immense influence upon the study of cultural forms, practices, the individual *life course, and collectivities such as societies and their institutions. In a general sense, narrative is an identifiable sequence of meaning-conveying images and/or words, comprising a coherent way of understanding the world or some particular aspect of the world. Garry Whannel has applied narrative to the study of media sport, arguing that 'television narrativizes events, turning them into stories with narrative structures that correspond in some ways to the conventions of literary narrative' (John Horne, Alan Tomlinson, and Garry Whannel, *Understanding Sport: An Introduction to the Sociological and Cultural Analysis of Sport*, 1999). As such, television sport coverage can be subject to analysis on the basis of the *hermeneutic code, which,

> poses the initial enigma of a narrative, and gives the text its forward progression towards the resolution of the enigma. So as not to answer the question too soon, a number of strategies are adopted . . . constant reformulation of the question, the promise that there will be an answer, and the provision of a partial answer. (Whannel, *Fields in Vision: Television Sport and Cultural Transformation*, 1992).

Whannel provides a classic case study of this process in his analysis of how British television narrativized the rivalry between English runners Sebastian Coe and Steve Ovett, showing how the coverage of the runners' contests at the 1980 Moscow Olympics comprised the posing of the question, a partial answer based in Ovett's surprise victory in their first encounter in the 800-metre race, a periodic organization of the story elements, an answer revealed when Coe avenged his earlier defeat by winning the 1,500 metres, and a second phase of periodic organization resolving much of the narrative but not completing it. Each had won, Britain had two gold medals, the good guy won the second race, the bad guy turned out to be not so bad after all, and television sport had irresistible questions to re-pose in the runners' continuing rivalry in subsequent contests.

Narrative has been applied to individual lives, and the representation of those lives in *biography and *autobiography as well as sociological initiatives in drawing upon life accounts as forms of documents. Andrew C. Sparkes (*Talking Bodies: Men's Narratives of the Body and Sport*, with B. Smith, 1999) has championed work on the narrative reconstruction of self in sport-related fields, and the production of sporting biographies and autobiographies. Work in this area has provided powerful testimony on the actual experience of sport and its core meaning to the individual him- or herself, and has challenged some of the *idealist conceptions of the nature and benefits of sporting experience. Richard Pringle, for instance, drawing upon his own sporting life in New Zealand in a piece of *autoethnography, rereads the meaning of Rugby Union, emphasizing its threatening and destructive violence in its stress on the 'ability to inflict and take pain' ('Competing Discourses: Narratives of a Fragmented Self, Manliness and Rugby Union', *International Review for the Sociology of Sport*, 1991).

While, by definition, the autoethnographer may have a limited number of stories to tell or experiences to relate, the gathering of a wide variety of accounts of sporting lives and analysis of their narrative structure is a well-tried and revealing method in qualitative sports studies. The who-will-win, what's-the-result-based, constantly recurring enigma intrinsic to the sporting event guarantees its appeal as narrative both in the representational outlets of a media culture and the everyday life and conversations of sport fans. The significance of such narratives can lie way beyond the field of play too: Michael Sandel (*Democracy's Discontent*, 1998) comments that if societies and communities slip into a 'fragmented, storyless condition' this could generate a loss of humans' capacity for narrative, amounting to a disempowerment of the human subject. We are 'bound to rebel', Sandel says, 'against the drift to storylessness'. Sporting narratives based on shared experiences are one bulwark against such disempowerment.

NASCAR (National Association for Stock Car Auto Racing) The origins of this US association lay in Florida in the 1920s and 1930s, where attempts were made on land-speed records at Dayton Beach. Its most famous meeting remains the Daytona 500, whose sixtieth anniversary was celebrated in 2009. The cars used in the races are customized versions of everyday vehicles, and at most of the tracks the races are run on ovals, drivers frequently reaching speeds of 200 miles per hour. Seventy-five million fans—mostly blue-collar/working-class—are claimed for the sport, and sociologists have linked its growing popularity in the first decade of the 21st century with a reactionary populist and nationalist response to the 11 September 2001 destruction of New York's World Trade Center (the Twin Towers): 'these weekly races held throughout North America are transformed from benign sites of automative adoration to grandiose affirmations of "*Dubya*"-era political discourses and cultural economies' (Joshua L. Newman, 'A Detour through "Nascar Nation": Ethnographic Articulations of a Neoliberal Sporting Spectacle', *International Review for the Sociology of Sport*, 42, 2007). The scale and profile of the sport were threatened by the global economic circumstances of 2008–9, with the withdrawal of corporate sponsors and a dramatic reduction in ticket sales; and at the same time the political discourses of the years in power of George W. Bush that it celebrated were challenged by the victory of Barack Obama and his accession to the White House. Former Formula One drivers have competed on the NASCAR circuit, broadening its sponsorship base during economically buoyant periods, and raising its profile outside the USA. *See also* MOTOR RACING.

National Basketball Association (NBA) One of the four major North American sports leagues, founded in 1946 as the Basketball Association of North America, becoming the NBA in 1949 after merging with the National Basketball League. The NBA is a member of the USA's national governing body of basketball as well as the hub of an extensive media and entertainment business in its own right. *See also* BASKETBALL.

National Collegiate Athletic Association (NCAA) The overarching body that administers college sport in the USA, founded in 1906. It introduced a national basketball championship in 1939, based on geographical qualifying competitions ('conferences' or leagues), play-offs, and a final to decide the national champion. This became a model for the structure and administration of national college/ university competition across the USA. The NCAA's most dominant competitions are college basketball and college (American) football, and it was estimated in 2000 that 75 per cent of US colleges made profits from these sports, enabling the subsidization of other sport-activity programmes. NCAA conferences can also sign their own contracts with media providers, and in 1996–2000 the total value of those contracts for college football (for the Atlantic Coast and Big East conferences, the Southern Conference and Notre Dame, and the Big Ten/Pac10, with broadcasters ABC, CBS, NBC, and ESPN) was US$373 million per year (Wladimir Andreff, 'Sport and Financing', in Wladimir Andreff and Stefan Szymanski, eds, *Handbook on the Economics of Sport*, 2009). Conference championships have also been sponsored for millions of dollars, and stadium and arena naming rights sold in lucrative long-term deals. Alumni subscriptions and ticket sales have also boosted the income of NCAA members.

The NCAA acts, essentially, as the overarching authority of a multi-billion dollar industry that also provides a source of recruitment, via the *draft system, into professional sports. This has created controversy over the scale and direction of college sports, and in 2003 Senator Orrin G. Hatch wrote of his, and many others', concern 'that all this college football money is turning college sports into nothing more than a minor league for pro football rather than a legitimate educational activity for student athletes' (Senate Committee on the Judiciary Hearing, Wednesday, 29 October). The NCAA therefore represents a central tension in the history of modern sport: the ideal of amateur, non-profit participation, threatened by the commercialization of the activity that it administers. It is a non-profit organization, pledged to its educational mission and the retention of 'a clear line of demarcation between intercollegiate athletics and professional sports' (as stated in a 2003–4 manual), but with an annual revenue the previous year of US$354 million. Economists have also observed that in imposing rules on non-payment for student athletes, the NCAA operates a form of control over its labour force that creates a non-market situation to the benefit of itself and its members.

(⊕) SEE WEB LINKS

- The official site of the USA's association for college athletics and sports, providing background history and news.

national identity The attribution of certain characteristics to an individual, group, or whole population on the basis of the nation state to which it belongs. In some ways, the term is a modern variant of the now deeply unfashionable and discredited notion of 'national character'. In sport, nation-state-based achievements at high-profile international sporting events can be claimed as expressions of national identity and targeted as sources of national pride. At the Beijing Olympic Games of 2008, for instance, organizers—and some partisan commentators—could claim that the world's perceptions of the Chinese were altered, that Chinese national identity was confirmed as courteous, welcoming, and modern, alongside the national pride that was reaffirmed in the host nation's topping of the gold medal table. Sport has made innumerable contributions to the articulation of national identity: rugby union in the newly industrialized south Wales in the UK at the end of the 19th century and the beginning of the 20th; cricket in the Caribbean, the pan-Caribbean West Indian cricketing formation of the mid 20th century also fuelling national pride and bolstering national identity in the individual and emergently autonomous separate nation-states of the region; football (soccer) as an expression of a national culture, in countless cases and markedly in the case of Brazil, the record-breaking five-time (up to 2009) winner of the FIFA men's World Cup.

Examples of national identity can sometimes look like the perpetuation of stereotypes or a form of cultural caricaturing. But the concept points to an important aspect of sport's social—and political—importance. As Ernest Gellner (*Nations and Nationalism*, 1983, p. 49) noted: 'nationalism is not the awakening and assertion of . . . mythical, supposedly natural and given units. It is, on the contrary, the crystallization of new units, suitable for the conditions now prevailing, though admittedly using as their raw material the cultural, historical and other inheritances from the pre-nationalist world.' Sport at the national level, or in nationalist forms, has shaped and given form, voice, and expression to such crystallizations, not merely reflected them. In Benedict Anderson's widely cited and influential work (*Imagined Communities: Reflections on the Origins and Spread of Nationalism*, 1983), it is stressed that in the formation of nations, national identity is imagined into being, on three levels: as limited, as having boundaries; as free, under the sovereign state; and as a community, 'conceived as deep, horizontal comradeship'. International sport can be seen to articulate emergent national identity on, especially, the first and third of these levels. National identity is also, in some circumstances, generated and reproduced on the basis of three (overlapping) types of 'invented traditions' (Eric Hobsbawm, 'The Invention of Tradition', in his co-edited book of the same name, 1983): those establishing social cohesion or group membership; those establishing 'institutions, status or relations of authority'; and those 'whose main purpose was socialization, the inculcation of beliefs, value systems and conventions of behaviour'. Sport, at numerous levels, can be seen to contribute to those invented traditions that are necessary to the project of the making and articulation of national identity. *See also* NATIONALISM.

National Institute for Health and Clinical Excellence (NICE) A publicly funded body in the UK, an element in the National Health Service (NHS), that is dedicated to the promotion of health and health-enhancing policies, programmes, and technologies. NICE has recognized the importance of sport and exercise as a preventative measure, and has produced strong scientifically supported reviews and analysis of the benefits of physical activity for children and young people in particular.

SEE WEB LINKS

• The official site of NICE, the National Health Service-based institute providing evidence and research on health and well-being.

nationalism The sense of belonging to a people on the basis of shared ties—which can be historical, linguistic, ethnic, or any combination of these—that have a geographical or territorial basis, and that are the foundation of a nation state or provide the aspirations to form a nation state. Sport has both contributed to and underpinned such expressions of belonging. The national organization of sports and sports teams, and the prominence of the national (in individual performance as well as team performance) in international competition, show the strong relationship between nationalism and sport. Politicians have also used national and international sporting occasions to identify themselves with the wider population:

examples include Nelson Mandela when South Africa triumphed in the rugby union World Cup, and France's president Jacques Chirac identifying himself with the national side's victory at Paris's Stade de France in the final of the 1998 World Cup. Nationalism is not always smoothly coterminous with the nation state, however, as numerous sporting examples testify: the United Kingdom of Great Britain and Northern Ireland includes fiercely nationalist fans of Scottish football and Welsh rugby, and Northern Irish rugby players who can play in an all-Ireland team; Basque football in the north of Spain symbolizes nationalist aspirations for the region. While sport continues to have a strong nationalist foundation, and to act as a powerful source of statement of nationalist aspirations (as in the case of Gaelic games), the nationalist base has been challenged by the increasing influence of global media and forces of *globalization, for whom nation states are little more than segments of a single, integrated market. Unbridled forms of nationalism can also fuel politically extreme views and movements. *See also* NATIONAL IDENTITY.

nature–nurture debate The debate concerning the influences that create the person or the individual, in terms of both physical characteristics and a person's outlook on the world. Hereditary forces (nature) are given, while influences of *socialization and learning (nurture) are varied across social and cultural environments. It is a mistake to seek to establish the primacy of one or the other, as natural and environmental influences interact so extensively, and some environmental contexts—take the example of Kenyan athletes running to and from school at high altitude in their childhood and youth—are a mix of the natural and the nurtured. The debate continues to have resonance in the study of gender influences, and persisting arguments about boys' and girls' different approaches to sporting competition; or in controversial assertions that there are few top-level black swimmers, due to anatomical and physiological characteristics. Overall, though, there is a consensus that the given (nature) produces raw materials for human performance that are then subject to formation and development on the basis of learned processes (nurture).

Nazism, sport in Sport featured in the political strategies of the German National Socialist (Nazi) Party in several ways: as a way of building physical strength in the country's citizens ('strength through joy' was a slogan of the party); as a means of asserting the physical superiority of the white Aryan race (foiled by various successful black achievements in the boxing ring and in the athletics stadium, for instance); and as a statement of the organizational and technical prowess and modernity of the German Reich (in the appropriation of the Berlin 1936 Olympics). Nazism, with its ideologies of the body and physical culture, was a particularly extreme form of fascism, in which the supremacist evils of Aryanism shaped the conception of the sports culture and the views of the social values and benefits of sport to both the society and the individual. J. A. Mangan's edited volume *Shaping the Superman* (1999) provides analysis and commentary on these issues. *See also* HITLER, ADOLF; OWENS, JESSE; OLYMPIA; RIEFENSTAHL, LENI; SCHMELING, MAXIMILIAN ADOLPH OTTO SIEGFRIED.

NBA *See* BASKETBALL; NATIONAL BASKETBALL ASSOCIATION.

NBC TV *See* ABC TV.

NCAA *See* NATIONAL COLLEGIATE ATHLETIC ASSOCIATION.

Nebiolo, Primo (1923–99) A long jumper as a youth, born in Torino, Italy, who studied law before entering the construction industry and moving into sport administration. He built his power base in world sport as president of the International University Sports Federation (1961), the organization that stages the World Student Games; and then as president of Italy's athletics federation (1969–89). Joining the council of the International Amateur Athletics Federation (*see* INTERNATIONAL ASSOCIATION OF ATHLETICS FEDERATIONS) in 1972, he won the presidency in 1981, and took the word 'amateur' out of its name while introducing a World Championships for professional athletes. He had also become president of the Association of Summer Olympic Federations in 1983. He was elected on to the International Olympic Committee (IOC) in 1991. Dying of a heart attack while still IAAF president, he was called 'one of the greatest leading sportsmen of this century' by the president of the IOC, Juan Antonio Samaranch. Both Samaranch and Nebiolo were actually leading 'Lords of the Rings', as Vyv Simson and Andrew Jennings dubbed them (*Lords of the Rings: Money, Power and Drugs at the Olympics*, 1992). Nebiolo even changed the measurements in one jumping event, to ensure that his home-nation competitor would win. The Nebiolo formula of law–business–sport was symptomatic of the changing organizational and economic basis of international sporting events and competition during the last quarter of the 20th century.

needs, hierarchy of A classification of needs by the US psychologist Abraham H. Maslow (1908–70), prioritizing basic physiological needs for food, water, oxygen, and sex, and then safety; psychological needs of love and belonging, and then esteem, follow. A final need—should the preconditions of the physiological and the psychological be met—was identified as self-actualization (*Motivation and Personality*, 1954; *Toward a Psychology of Being*, 1962). It is clear that, if sport is to be credibly described as a need of any sort, then it belongs to the categories of the psychological and the self-actualizing. For followers of sport, their identification with a club, team, or performer is undeniably felt as an expression or articulation of belonging; for the aspiring high-performance athlete, self-actualization can be conceived as a form of *peaking, or peak performance.

negative dialectic The process, in the work of Theodor *Adorno, whereby a structure of domination characteristic of a society can be critiqued, and potentially opposed. If sport, then, is part of that structure of domination, serving the interests of the powerful few and placating and diverting the population, other cultural forms are needed to provide an alternative lens on the world. For Adorno, these were more available in the cultural artefacts of the mind (and particularly experimental versions of these in music, art, and literature) than the bodily arts of *mass culture such as sport or popular music. Dialectics is defined by Adorno as 'the quest to see the new in the old' (*Against Epistemology*, 1956, English translation 1962); but if the structure of domination is as entrenched as he saw it to be in modern consumer capitalism, then there is little or no scope for the identification or articulation of the 'new'. Therefore, critique and condemnation of the system of domination, its authoritarian character, and its cultural products were essential to Adorno's 'negative dialectics'. As Susan Buck-Morss puts it: 'The whole point of his relentless insistence on negativity was to resist repeating in thought the structures of domination and reification that existed in society, so that instead of reproducing reality, consciousness could be critical' (*The Origin of Negative Dialectics: Theodor W. Adorno, Walter Benjamin, and the Frankfurt Institute*, 1977).

Adorno's negative dialectics provide an impressive intellectual apparatus for the critique of mass sports, or sport serving the interests of those in power, but it remains hard to see just how this 'relentless negativity' could have much if any effect upon the producers, owners, and players at the heart of the sport industry. David Inglis, in his 'Theodor Adorno on Sport' (Richard Giulianotti, *Sport and Modern Social Theorists*, 2004), finds in some of Adorno's work a sense that within sport itself there may be a utopian moment challenging the grip of domination—'contemporary sports . . . is found to contain seeds of hope within a shell of despair'. This glimmer of hope is linked by Inglis to the prospect of students of sport conceiving of 'freer and liberating ways' of organizing and playing sport. But there are less intellectually dense routes towards such prospects than the dialectical negativity of Adorno's method.

neo-Marxism Adaptations to, or developed versions of, the actual writings of Karl *Marx; 'neo' is from the Greek for 'new', and this term can be adapted to any thinker or theorist whose work is used in new situations. A neo-Marxist approach to sport, therefore, as in the work of Jean-Marie Brohm in *Sport: A Prison of Measured Time* (1978), might cite little of Marx's original work, but is an application of the neo-Marxist insights of Louis *Althusser (1918–90), whose writings on the power of institutions such as education (as elements of the ideological state apparatus (ISA) rather than the repressive state apparatus (RSA), such as the police or the military) have relevance to the contribution of sport in both the education and the high-performance systems of a society. Important concepts that sustain a neo-Marxist momentum in sports studies include *commodity and *alienation.

neo-tribes A term coined by French sociologist Michel Maffesoli, in his 1985 study *The Time of the Tribes: The Decline of Individualism in Mass Society*. This was a clever inversion of a common sociological theme concerning the prominence of individualism in a time of the decline of community. Maffesoli identified neo-tribes, primarily in urban contexts, as sources of informal, often emotionally driven, cultural expression. The term is a relatively modern variant on the classic term *subculture, and the notion of 'tribal' has appealed to new generations of sociologists and has found currency in work on *lifestyle sports and research into informal cultures of sporting commitment, such as *parkour.

Nero, Claudius Caesar Augustus Germanicus (AD 37–68) Roman emperor from AD 54 to 68, Nero was one of the emperor-charioteers, along with Caligula and Commodus, for whom the attraction of the sporting spectacle was not only in the watching, but in the participation. Nero wore the helmet and dress of charioteers when he drove a chariot, and even, when needing to don chains, ensured that these were golden ones. As a populist, tax-cutting emperor, Nero saw sport as a means of affirming his status and connecting with the populace, and he lavished large sums of public expenditure on entertainment. In AD 60 he established a new festival in his own name, the Neronia, comprising games, poetry, and theatre, though this only occurred twice before Nero's suicide, and did not outlast his death. At the *Colosseum, his reign encouraged excess and ostentation: on one single occasion, 400 bears and 300 lions are said to have been killed; on another, the floor of the arena opened to reveal a magic forest, sporting aromatic fountains and golden bushes, and inhabited by exotic animals that then set upon each other. Sport could be rationalized as a form of diplomacy too, justifying Nero's entry in the Olympic Games of AD 67: although he fell from his chariot, and did not complete the course, he was nevertheless declared the winner and received the victor's wreath. His entry was justified in relation to the display of Roman qualities, and to potentially improved relations with Greece: the outcome merited neither justification. Nero's vainglorious equation of spectacle, sport, and self-image also stimulated the construction of the 35-metre-high bronze statue of himself, inspired by the Colossus of Rhodes of the 3rd century BC (and after which the Colosseum was later named). But Nero's commitment to sport for the people, including the building of gymnasia, has been considered the main reason for his persisting popularity after his death.

nervous system A network of neurons that perceive information, process information, and effect control. The nervous system is organized into two major divisions. The central nervous system (CNS) comprises the brain and spinal cord, and acts with integrating and command functions. The peripheral nervous system (PNS) consists of all other nerves, and comprises afferent sensory nerves which carry impulses to the CNS and efferent motor nerves which carry impulses from the CNS to muscles (the voluntary division) and to organs and glands (the autonomic division). In turn the autonomic system is divided into the sympathetic and parasympathetic systems, with the former responsible for stimulating effector systems to mobilize the body (in what is commonly called the 'fight or flight response', involving for example increases in heart rate and blood glucose level) and the latter responsible for the opposite effect. The functional unit of the nervous system is a neuron, which comprises a cell body, an axon to carry information from the cell body to the target tissue, and dendrites projecting from the cell body to receive information from the axon terminals of other neurons. Transfer of information between nerves occurs at the synapse by the release of transmitter substances such as acetylcholine. The operation of the nervous system is seen in every aspect of sport, from the *motor control of muscles to the cognitive and somatic impact of *anxiety.

netball A seven-a-side court game played mostly by women and girls. The game was created in Britain in 1901 when the organization based upon the philosophy of the Swedish pioneer of gymnastics, Per Henrik *Ling, adapted the rules of *basketball, the latter having been introduced to Britain in 1895. The seven players are designated particular positions, and their movement on the court is prescribed by those positions. Goals can be scored by only two players from the team, and running with the ball is not permitted. The sport developed a strong institutional base in the new women's physical education colleges, and a global presence in Australia, New Zealand, Canada, South Africa, and northern Europe. Its popularity has ensured that in some countries women continue to play long beyond their school years. The parks of Australian suburbia are dominated on weekend mornings by netball matches and contests, and the world rankings have a cultural continuity based on historical pedigree: in 2008, Australia, New Zealand, and England were first, second, and third in the rankings of the International Federation of Netball Associations (IFNA), which claimed more than 70 million netball players across 70 countries. IFNA had been founded in 1960, in Colombo, Ceylon, and the first World Championship was held at Eastbourne, England, in 1963. Educational networks have generated a strong presence of the developing world in netball: four West Indian countries featured in the top twelve in the world in 2008 (Jamaica, Trinidad and Tobago, Barbados, and St Vincent and the Grenadines), as well as the Pacific Islanders of Fiji and Samoa. Netball is a well-established part of the Commonwealth Games, and IFNA's 60 members are organized into five regional confederations.

The game has been controlled by women, and this degree of autonomy has been preserved throughout its history, but has in turn been seen as stifling. Jennifer Hargreaves has shown how a working-class and predominantly black club called the Queens of the Castle, based in south-east London, England, has challenged the mainstream image of netball, which the Queens saw as strait-laced, socially restricting, and having a schoolgirl image. The Queens dressed flamboyantly, and cultivated a philosophy of collective teamwork and a caring ethos. Netball policy-makers, Hargreaves concluded, have not understood 'the specific needs of young, urban, working-class women' (Jennifer Hargreaves, *Sporting Females: Critical Issues in the History and Sociology of Women's Sports*, 1994).

new economy The doctrine, increasingly popular among economists and business commentators throughout the 1990s, that the globalization of business (in part stimulated by widespread lifting of trade restrictions) and the revolution in information technology were creating a 'new economy'. It was believed, or at least implied, that this new economy could combine continual growth with negligible or no inflation, and that the new market for this economy was without limit. A commentary in *Business Week* in November 1997 claimed that this new economy was at the very least 'transforming Corporate America'. It seemed that the leisure nirvana had really arrived, that the global sport tourist was a figure not just of the here-and-now but for the foreseeable future, and that the new companies sprouting in Southern California's Silicon Valley at eleven per week would help make the world just one extended marketplace. The *sports goods industry made its own contribution to the buoyant optimism of this new economy, but the crash of the dot.com boom, followed a few years later by the sub-prime mortgage crisis in the USA in 2007, revealed the fragility of the new economic framework. Nevertheless, cities and national governments continue to invest in sport events and sport achievements in the confident—or desperate—belief that the rest of the world will join in and that the economic benefits will flow.

new international division of cultural labour (NICL) A variant of the new international division of labour (NIDL), in which forms of cultural production such as sport operate in global labour markets in an international context in a climate of fragmented production. Emerging in the 1970s as the global economic order was responding to widespread inflation, and production was distributed across continents, the NIDL was identified by theorists of first- and third-world industrialization and labour markets. Toby Miller, in a 1990 article, 'Mission Impossible and the New International Division of Labour' (*Metro*, no. 82), adapted the NIDL to the cultural industries, so coining the acronym NICL. In the NICL, markets transcend national boundaries, and the sporting body (of both the player and the spectator) is trained and commodified for global consumption, 'honed by the human sciences, the media, capital, and government to perform and to be interpreted' (Toby Miller, Geoffrey Lawrence, Jim McKay, and David Rowe, *Globalization and Sport: Playing the World*, 2001). In soccer, for instance, the NICL has escalated the exploitation of the human resources of poorer countries (in the recruitment of players to top-level soccer in Europe), and the expansion of media markets (in Asian and African territories in particular).

new journalism A form of writing in which the techniques of fiction writing were applied to journalistic reportage. American writer and novelist Tom Wolfe identifies four devices that were characteristic of the new journalism of the 1960s, as journalists learned the techniques of literary realism: scene-by-scene construction; full recording of dialogue; third-person point of view, presenting scenes to the reader through a particular character's eyes, conveying the sense of 'being inside the character's mind'; and the recording of the 'symbolic details . . . of people's *status life*, using that term in the broad sense of the entire pattern of behaviour and possessions through which people express their position in the world or what they think it is or what they hope it to be' (Tom Wolfe, *The New Journalism*, 1975). Wolfe notes that the new journalists 'somehow had the moxie to talk their way inside of any milieu, even closed societies, and hang on for dear life' (p. 41), a capacity for empathy that was central to the impact of the genre. He singles out George *Plimpton's 'extraordinary sporting feats with the sports world' (p. 67) as an example of how a writer could become part of the milieu of the reportage. Sport events and personalities offered attractive subjects to the new journalists, and it was Gay Talese's 1962 *Esquire* feature on boxer Joe *Louis that first alerted Wolfe to this style of writing. Talese also produced pieces on boxer Floyd *Patterson and baseball legend Joe *DiMaggio. Hunter S. Thompson was another new journalism writer to focus upon the subculture of sports.

Nice declaration on sport The recognition by the European Council, in a declaration made at Nice, France, in 2000, of the special characteristics of European sport. This followed on from a full consultation paper by the European Commission's Directorate General X, in 1998, in which the fivefold (educational, health-related, social, cultural, and recreational) functions of sport were recognized, and in particular the pyramid model of European sport (from the apex, the European, down to the broad base of the grass-roots, via the national and the regional). The declaration is as follows:

The European Council has noted the report on sport submitted to it by the European Commission in Helsinki in December 1999 with a view to safeguarding current sports structures and maintaining the social function of sport within the European Union. Sporting organisations and the Member States have a primary responsibility in the conduct of sporting affairs. Even though not having any direct powers in this area, the Community must, in its action under the various Treaty provisions, take account of the social, educational and cultural functions inherent in sport and making it special, in order that the code of ethics and the solidarity essential to the preservation of its social role may be respected and nurtured.

There had been an emotive commitment to amateur participation in debate, the European Commission's sport representative Marcelino Oreja arguing that, in Europe, sporting amateurs displayed a 'genuine, disinterested love in taking part in sport'. These arguments and formulations developed over the decade and culminated in the European Council's 'Declaration on Sport' published in December 2008, with four clauses: 'The European Council recognises the importance of the values attached to sport, which are essential to European society. It stresses the need to take account of the specific characteristics of sport, over and above its economic dimension.' The third clause talked of the continuing promotion of dialogue through the European Sport Forum. And finally: 'It calls for the strengthening of . . . dialogue with the International Olympic Committee and representatives of the world of sport, in particular on the question of combined sports training and education for young people.' This, the culmination of a decade of debate, lobbying, and campaigning, was the fifth appendix in this document, following appendices on defence, the Middle East, and Zimbabwe. In such pan-European policy-making, the journey from the grandiose to the bland is not unusual: the key words in the 2008 appendix/declaration are 'essential' and 'specific characteristics'— but what these words really refer to remains as elusive, and contestable, as ever.

Nike   The leading manufacturer and retailer of athletics sports shoes, or trainers, in the world, with a workforce of more than thirty thousand and a revenue exceeding $US18.6 billion in the fiscal year ending in March 2008. Originally called Blue Ribbon Sports, the company was established in 1964 in Oregon, USA, by athletics coach Bill Bowerman, and University of Oregon athlete Phil Knight. Initially a small-scale retail operation, and a distributor for manufacturers, the company moved into manufacture and design in the early 1970s, launching a football/soccer boot with the name of 'Nike' in 1971, named after the Greek god of victory, and running shoes with the name and the Swoosh logo the following year. The Swoosh logo, a cross between florid signature and giant tick, branded a product that became increasingly popular in the Californian running market. Their experiments in running shoe design produced, in 1974, what became known as The Waffle, a trainer/shoe with an outsole that could better grip the running track; Bowerman reports that this evolved from him pouring liquid urethane into his wife's waffle iron, in their kitchen one Sunday morning.

In 1978 the company renamed itself Nike, Inc. and by 1980 it had captured half of the USA's market for athletics shoes. Bill Bowerman had established jogging classes in the later 1960s, and Nike capitalized on the running and jogging boom of the 1970s. It quickly moved into other sports, signing histrionic Romanian tennis player Ilie Nastase in 1972 on a US$5,000 contract, for which he wore Nike shoes emblazoned with 'Nasty' on the heel; his doubles partner, USA's Jimmy Connors, sported his nickname 'Jimbo' on his heels for no fee at all. Nastase was signed by Adidas the following year, but Nike continued to expand by contracting—and in some cases creating—global superstars, most notably, in the 1980s, basketball player Michael Jordan, and, in the 1990s, golfer Tiger Woods.

German giant *Adidas was dismissive of what was brushed aside as a Californian gimmick, but its own erratic supply lines to US distributors allowed Nike to establish deals with retailers that allowed reinvestment in Asian manufacturing suppliers at little risk. In 1978 Adidas's Horst Dassler, alerted by senior colleagues to the growing threat from Nike, met Nike's Phil Knight and other Nike executives at a trade show in Houston, USA. Dassler revealed to his rivals that a good sale for an Adidas shoe was 100,000 pairs per year in the USA; Blue Ribbon Sports, on the verge of its renaming, was selling as many pairs of its Waffle trainers each month. Nike's growth continued unabated. Adidas saw its US share collapse, and Nike—adding advertising (the first national ones during the 1982 New York Marathon) and the award-winning slogan 'Just do it' (1988) to its 'word-of-foot' marketing strategy—and the other emerging market leader, Reebok, became the new giants of the sports-shoe business.

Nike has sustained its global profile by acquiring other businesses such as Converse, Inc., specialized US basketball brand (2003), and Umbro, manufacturers of the England football team's kit (2008). It has been accused of the violation of human rights in its commissioning practices with contract factories in poorer countries in Asia, but denies malpractice, and where abuses have been identified, has pledged to take corrective action. The Nike brand has been constantly refreshed by staying in touch with emerging and new markets such as *skateboarding, or established markets with new levels of exposure. Nike, paying US$43 million, outbid Adidas and Puma to sponsor India's national cricketing side from 2006 to 2010. The company has teamed with Apple Inc. to devise ways of combining iPod software with in-shoe radio technology, as a means of monitoring a runner's performance. It has continued to contract leading world sport stars—cyclist Lance Armstrong, tennis player Roger Federer—as a means of consolidating its global profile. The company's flagship stores, Niketown, in the world's major cities, show the fusion of fashion, sport, and branding in its most advanced consumerist form.

((⊕)) SEE WEB LINKS

- The site of the sport shoes and clothing company, with specialist pitches to the world's major participation sports, basketball and football, and to constituencies such as women.

Noel-Baker, Philip John (1889–1982) The son of a Canadian-born Quaker industrialist, born Philip John Baker, adopting his wife's surname, 'Noel', on their marriage in 1915, and hyphenating his surname in the 1940s. Noel-Baker was born in London, England, educated at the Quaker institutions of Bootham School, York, England, and Haverford College, Pennsylvania. He then entered King's College, University of Cambridge, in 1908, studying economics and law, also acting as president of the debating society and, from 1910 to 1912, as president of the university's Athletic Club. He represented Great Britain in the 1912 Stockholm Olympics, and captained the British athletics team at the Games of 1920 (Antwerp) and 1924 (Paris).

Noel-Baker was awarded the Nobel Peace Prize in 1959, for his tireless work in international diplomacy, and his pacifist writings that included condemnation of the international arms race; he had worked in ambulance units during World War I. Noel-Baker was involved in the setting up of the League of Nations (its covenant drafted during 1918–19, at the Paris peace conference) and the United Nations (drafting its charter at San Francisco in 1945). Throughout a career also embracing productive academic positions, and a political career (elected as Member of Parliament for Coventry 1929–31, and for Derby 1936–70), he sustained his commitment to high-level performance sport, championing its positive internationalism. He was commandant of the 1952 Olympic team in Helsinki in 1952, and in 1960 founded and became the inaugural president of the International Council of Sport and Physical Education (later called the *International Council of Sport Science and Physical Education), the sport-based body established by UNESCO (the United Nations Educational, Scientific and Cultural Organization).

non-verbal communication Communication that is based on means of conveying meaning that are not language-based. In everyday life, we talk of eye-contact, or the look or *gaze, or the gesture of the hand. In the organs of the mass communication media, the telling photograph can convey atmosphere and glamour and a host of meanings, as the analytical method of *semiotics has shown. There is a tradition of the study of non-verbal communication in branches of social psychology, and forms of such communication are clearly important in sporting competition and encounters. The snooker player tapping the edge of the table to acknowledge the skill of the opponent; the footballer raising his arm, or arms, at whatever angle, to indicate to his team-mates the intention of his corner kick; the gestures of the athlete or the player to the crowd, in celebration or hostility; the hand-wringing and arm-waving of the team coach or manager from the edge of the playing area—these varied forms of bodily communication are an integral part of the sporting contest, and remain ripe for sustained and systematic analysis of their effects. *See also* BODY LANGUAGE.

Nordic sport *See* SKIING.

norms Standards or rules—formal or informal—determining how people behave in a particular social or cultural context or setting. They need to be learned, or could be observed, so that one understands that it is acceptable—indeed expected—that one behaves differently in the boardroom of the basketball or football club than on the bleachers or the terraces. If norms are not understood or accepted, breakdown in a social situation is likely. In Lindsay Anderson's 1963 film of David Storey's 1960 novel *This Sporting Life*, the protagonist Frank Machin's story is a typical one of sporting rags-to-riches, and inevitable tragic downfall. A central tension in the film is between the acceptable face of Machin, the rough, tough, and violent rugby league player, and the boorish socially crude working-class outsider. As his playing counterparts accept their middle-class opportunities and act in accordance with their socially superior mentors, Machin fails to adapt to the norms of different situations. In one particularly revealing scene, Machin and his landlady-cum-lover visit a restaurant and his braggart manner confirms his ignorance of the norms of the middle-class culture. His mentor, the rugby club owner Slomer, refuses to acknowledge Machin as he leaves the restaurant. Machin has refused to abide by the norms of the particular social milieu, and is branded as a social and cultural outcast.

North Dallas Forty A 1979 film adapting Peter Gent's novel, in which he drew upon his own experience as a professional football player for the Dallas Cowboys. The film's chief character, Phillip Elliott, is ageing and reliant upon painkillers to keep his ailing body going. The film evokes the hedonism of the male football culture, the brutish demeanour of the coach, and the desperation behind the fragile status of the sporting superstar. Garry Whannel has summarized the 'grotesque world' of the culture of 'gridiron masculinity' evoked in the film, listing its components: the close relationship of power and violence; the robotic nature of the players' lives, in that they are treated as automata; the interplay of Christian morality and the work ethic; the role of sex as a substitute for human relationships; and pain as 'confirmation of a job well done' ('No Room for Uncertainty: Gridiron Masculinity in *North Dallas Forty*', in Pat Kirkham and Janet Thumim, eds, *You Tarzan: Masculinities, Movies and Men*, 1993).

Nurmi, Paavo Johannes (1897–1973) A Finnish middle- and long-distance runner whose dedicated, disciplined approach to competitive running— introducing new levels of endurance training—was a modernizing influence on the sport. In the three Olympic Games of the 1920s, Nurmi won nine gold and three silver Olympic medals. His profile helped Finland, a relatively new independent nation, enhance its profile in the international world, and was instrumental in gaining the 1952 Olympic Games for Finland's capital, Helsinki. Nurmi is commemorated not just in his home country, but in bronze splendour at the front of the Olympic Museum in Lausanne, Switzerland.

nursery In relation to the production of high-level athletes and sportsmen and -women, a source of development and recruitment. A prominent top-level club, for instance, might secure a contractual relationship with a lower-league club, sometimes in another country, at which young players will be developed and identified for the potential to transfer through to the higher levels. *See also* FARM SYSTEM.

nutrition The study of the nature and effects of diet upon health and performance. The six components of a diet are *carbohydrates, fats, *protein, vitamins, minerals, and water. Sport places nutritional demands on the body beyond those associated with normal health, including the need for a higher calorie intake to provide the fuel required to energize muscular contraction, an increased protein intake to provide for an increased muscle mass, and an increased fluid intake to provide for sweating. From the time of the ancient Olympics there has been a belief that an athlete's diet needed special preparation and that certain foods, especially proteinaceous ones, were essential. The wrestler Milon of Croton who won competitions at six ancient Olympics was reputed to 'eat 20 pounds of meat'. The 19th-century pedestrians continued this approach; Captain *Barclay, who famously covered 1 mile every hour for 1,000 hours, ate a diet predominantly of meat with dairy products and vegetables avoided. At the 1936 Olympics athletes are reported as consuming an average of nearly 500 grams of meat a day, and right through until almost the end of the 20th century a pre-event meal based on meat was thought essential for many sports. By the 1970s research into carbohydrate storage and utilization was beginning to demonstrate *glycogen's critical role in energy supply, and the athletic diet shifted in emphasis from protein to carbohydrate. This emphasis was confirmed as research into *protein metabolism showed that only a modest additional consumption was necessary.

Vitamin and mineral supplementation has not been demonstrated to improve sports performance, except in selected cases where an athlete has a deficient diet and a supplement is needed to bring the intake up to normal levels. The most common example is the need for iron supplementation in female athletes, where three factors combine to provide a particular challenge to achieving an adequate intake of iron from diet alone. Iron is a constituent part of haemoglobin and thus critical to oxygen carriage in the blood, so any deficiency will affect *aerobic performance; menstrual blood flow will increase iron loss; and a diet high in carbohydrate and low in red meat will limit iron intake. For other vitamins and minerals the adequacy of diet is predicated on that diet being varied. However, food tastes, preferences, and fads are legion and any particular individual may have a diet deficient in one or more of these substances. It is common therefore for athletes to take a multi-vitamin and mineral supplement as a type of 'insurance policy' against deficiency. *Vegetarianism need not disadvantage the sports performer. Many other substances are promoted for their ergogenic effect, such as single amino acids, carnitine, and coenzyme Q10, but with little evidence of any effectiveness. An exception is creatine, where a dose of several times normal daily intake for several days has been demonstrated to increase *anaerobic power output.

The general pattern for the optimal athletic diet matches closely the pattern of the diet recommended for health, with a slightly greater emphasis on carbohydrate intake: that is, nutrients providing energy in the proportion of about 60 per cent carbohydrate, 25 per cent fat, and 15 per cent protein. If foodstuffs are drawn from a varied range, then other dietary needs such as those for vitamins are met. Since an athlete is expending greater amounts of energy compared to a sedentary person the food intake is greater and the diet therefore automatically provides an increased intake of minerals, vitamins, and protein. While the overall athletic diet may not need to be particularly different from the average healthy diet, the timing of intake can be challenging. To supplement a normal diet, special sports nutrition drinks can be used before exercise to ensure fuel stores are complete, during exercise to sustain energy output, and after exercise to aid recovery. Exercising for health or recreational purposes requires no adjustment if the normal diet is varied. Businesses promote numerous foods, diets, and supplements as enhancements to health or weight loss. The majority rely on the (false) logic that if a particular substance is involved in metabolism then a surplus of that substance will promote that aspect of metabolism. *See also* WEIGHT CONTROL.

obesity A medical condition characterized by excessive body fat. The generally accepted measure is a body mass index above 30. Obesity is associated with a range of health disorders including an increased risk of coronary heart disease, type II diabetes, hypertension, some cancers, and osteoarthritis. The prevalence of obesity in the UK in 2006 was 21 per cent in both adult males and females; 6 per cent of UK deaths are attributed to obesity and these deaths shortened life by an average of 9 years. Obesity also carries a range of psychosocial burdens including low self-esteem, reduced mobility, and a general lower level of *wellness. The prevalence of obesity is increasing rapidly in both adults and children. It has tripled in the UK in 20 years (Department of Health surveys) and global prevalence is projected by the World Health Organization to increase from 400 million adults (2005) to 700 million adults (2015). The causes of obesity include a genetic predisposition, but the rapid rise in its occurrence, particularly in middle- and high-income countries and urban settings, lends support to the contention that the primary cause is a combination of energy-dense convenience foods or meals along with decreased physical activity due to mechanization in employment, the home, and transport. *See also* WEIGHT CONTROL.

objectivity The capacity to analyse a given phenomenon without bias, on the basis of evidence and arguments supported by that evidence, regardless of any interests or personal or political principles that the researcher might hold. If a researcher interested in the community significance of the LA Lakers has been a lifelong fan of that basketball team, he or she must be especially vigilant to ensure that personal interests or enthusiasms do not distort the research design, fieldwork, analysis, or conclusions of the study. Similarly, if a political activist adhering to socialist beliefs studies the earning levels of top sports performers, the analysis must be based upon rigorous economic analysis and not political commitment or the simplistic application of, say, Marxist concepts to the empirical object of study.

Objectivity, however, is not always so straightforward, as influential intellectual currents such as *feminism have shown; or as Karl *Marx, in the eleventh of his *Theses on Feuerbach* (1845) stated: 'The philosophers have only *interpreted* the world, in various ways; the point, however, is to *change* it.' If a social cause such as egalitarianism or a concern with a principle such as social justice is adhered to by the researcher, then the basic concept of objectivity seems naive and misplaced; thus feminist scholarship can be drawn upon in reformist campaigns and to inform policy, as in the case of Title IX in the USA. Max *Weber recognized the methodological complexity of arguments concerning objectivity—in relation to the humanities and the social sciences—in his essay '"Objectivity" in Social Science and

Social Policy', noting that 'personal value-judgements have tended to influence scientific arguments without being explicitly admitted'. Alvin Gouldner's article 'The Sociologist as Partisan' (*American Sociologist*, 1968) made a positive virtue out of the difficulty of objectivity in any critically engaged and potentially interventionist social science. Some aspects of this debate have been developed by Ian McDonald and applied to research on cricket, in 'Critical Social Research and Political Intervention: Moralistic versus Radical Approaches' (in Alan Tomlinson and John Sugden's *Power Games: A Critical Sociology of Sport*, 2002).

observation A central principle and method in scientific enquiry. Rigorous observation is fundamental to systematic experimental work in laboratory sciences. In the sociocultural study of sport, observation is essential for the understanding of smaller-scale human collectivities such as sport subcultures and for capturing the minutiae of sporting practices in everyday life. Observational fieldwork strategies are critical to the credibility of much qualitative social science. Does the researcher want to be the proverbial 'fly on the wall' unbeknown to those being observed, or be introduced to the group and accept that this known presence might alter the behaviour and activities of the members of the group? Carefully employed, observation is also valuable for the generation of accounts of events. The observational 'I saw it, I was there' criterion is a central one identified by John Carey as defining top reportage (*The Faber Book of Reportage*, 1987). In a time of increasing control of knowledge and information by a professional public relations industry, observation is a threatened quality of the sport media professional. *See also* COVERT OBSERVATION; HAWTHORNE EFFECT; PARTICIPANT OBSERVATION.

obsolescence A condition arising when an object or service is no longer deemed useable even though the object or service still functions efficiently. Rule changes, or technological breakthroughs, in sports can render perfectly serviceable objects obsolete: when Swedish tennis player Björn Borg attempted a comeback wielding his cherished wooden Dunlop Maxply racket, he warmed many a traditionalist's heart, but lost in all of his comeback matches to run-of-the-mill opponents playing with the new large aluminium rackets. Ideally, from the perspective of the *sports goods industry, many forms of equipment or attire would be rendered similarly obsolete, but for the sportsman or -woman, irrational attachments often develop to familiar items of equipment.

occupational mobility The process whereby, on the basis of an occupation and its concomitant rewards in both remuneration and *status, an individual moves to a perceived higher level of the hierarchy of a society, often perceived in terms of *social class position. This is widely identified as inter-generational mobility; a talented athlete from a working-class background might, through sporting success and prestige, move to a different level of the *social stratification system. This is by no means a smooth process, though, as the volatile professional and post-competition lives of many figures, from US boxer Mike Tyson to Northern Ireland's football star George *Best, tragically testify.

Oceania Football Confederation (OFC) Formed in 1966 (with founder
members Australia, Fiji, New Zealand, and Papua New Guinea), the Oceania
Football Confederation was initially recognized by the *Fédération Internationale
de Football Association (FIFA) as an independent geographical entity that could
represent the interests of football development in the South Pacific, and to which
the executive committee of FIFA could grant some of the rights conferred to the five
other fully recognized continental confederations. At its Congress in 1996, FIFA
conferred full confederational status upon Oceania, and incorporated this decision
into its statutes. Oceania emerged from the ambitions of Australian and New
Zealand football administrators to gain some geopolitical recognition from FIFA.
Early presidents were Australians Sir William Walkley and Vic Tutting. Australia was
soon lobbying to join the Asian confederation, and pulled out of Oceania in 1972.
New Zealander Jack Cowie took over the vacant presidential position until Australia,
snubbed by the Asian confederation, rejoined with Australian Sir Arthur George as
president, in 1977. In 1982 Charles Dempsey, Oceania secretary, made a successful
challenge for the presidency. Dempsey resigned in 2000, after controversially
abstaining from the FIFA executive committee vote that awarded the 2006 (men's)
World Cup Finals to Germany rather than South Africa. Though Oceania has had up
to twelve members, and for fourteen years accommodated Chinese Taipei so that
the Republic of China would not withdraw from the Asian confederation, Australian
and New Zealand rivalries have dominated confederation politics; and on 1 January
2006 Australia again withdrew to join the Asian confederation, in which a
guaranteed place for the World Cup Finals could be allocated through the
confederation's qualifying competition. The OFC continued to be based at its
headquarters in Auckland, New Zealand, with eleven members.

(🌐) SEE WEB LINKS

• The official site of the federation, including news, features, publications, and contacts.

OFC *See* OCEANIA FOOTBALL CONFEDERATION.

Olympia A documentary film of the 1936 Berlin Olympic Games made by Leni
*Riefenstahl under the patronage of the Nazi propaganda chief Joseph Goebbels
(1897–1945) and Adolf *Hitler himself. The film is in two parts—*Festival of Nations*
and *Festival of Beauty*—and it is widely agreed that it constitutes an innovative,
pioneering piece of film-making, capturing the human body in action and athletic
performance from angles and in close-ups that few if any film-makers had
previously achieved. The film's opening sequence is a memorable one, depicting
the torch relay—an innovation of the 1936 Games—following the metamorphosis
of Myron's statue of a discus-thrower (Discobulus) into a living human being; the
classical is thus fused with the modern, the individual with the purportedly universal.
The English version of the film comprises 218 minutes of coverage of more than
thirty events, and also shots of athletes swimming naked in forest-bordered lakes.

Riefenstahl, with an earlier history of acting in romantic mountain films, and a
later history of filming sealife and the Nuba of Sudan, consistently sought to depict
her subjects as examples of a pure untainted community or natural order. In
Olympia this is certainly the case, with the notion of physical excellence and beauty
framed so as to all but transcend the political, historical, and moral order in which it

is exercised and expressed. The Riefenstahl *oeuvre* has almost routinely abstracted the human body from its social, cultural, and political context; and this allows some to argue that *Olympia* should be read as an autonomous piece of aesthetic brilliance. But two years after the Berlin Games a Nazi film journalist could observe that the work is 'filled with a spirit which we sense not only as the spirit of *Olympia* but also as the spirit of the German reality of today'. The film is a multi-layered text, articulating Riefenstahl's artistic genius and her romantic and primitivist philosophy and aesthetic (particularly in her focus upon US black athlete Jesse *Owens), and upholding the corporeal and athleticist ideals of the Olympics; but, intended or not, the film is also a visual hymn to the Nazi principles of pure physicality and physical might, celebratory of a particular and extreme political variant of the celebration of the corporeal.

Olympic ceremony High-profile public occasions provide opportunities to celebrate particular values and achievements, as coronations have shown in relation to monarchies, and parliamentary rituals have demonstrated in relation to political democratic systems. Such events are rooted in forms of ceremony that are linked to established or invented traditions, recognizable symbols, and ritual performances. Eric Hobsbawm and Terence Ranger's edited volume *The Invention of Tradition* (1992) conveys the strong political impact that such invented, and mass-produced, traditions can have, in creating collective bonds and, at the national level, boosting a sense of national belonging. The Olympic Games has provided the most prominent international sporting platform for such national traditions, but in a context of global international cooperation. The Olympics has sustained this profile in an uninterrupted fashion since 1896, and this has been made possible by the rituals and traditions on the basis of which it has conveyed the claimed meanings of Olympism to an expanding constituency of nations in a changing world. Among the most prominent of these objects and practices are the five-ring logo, the flame, the torch relay, the opening and closing ceremonies, the motto, and the truce.

The *Olympic rings*—in blue, yellow, black, green, and red—are said to symbolize the reach of the Games across the (main) five continents. They first appeared on the letterhead of Pierre de *Coubertin, the founder of the Games, in 1913. He took the idea from the symbol of two interlocking rings which had been used by the French sporting federation when it was formed from the merger of two organizations in 1892, and which was sported by French international athletes on their running jerseys from 1896 through to the 1920s (when replaced by the French Olympic Committee's fighting cock symbol). De Coubertin's 20th-anniversary Paris Congress of June 1914 featured the new symbol on a white background on the Olympic flags on display, and de Coubertin associated the five interlocked rings with the 'five parts of the world won over to Olympism', and claimed too that at least one of the five colours was in the national flag of each of the nations that had competed at the 1912 Stockholm Games. The Olympic flag was first flown at the 1920 Antwerp Games. It was not until 1929 that de Coubertin replaced 'parts of the world' with 'continents' (meaning Asia, Africa, Oceania, Europe, and the Americas), and since then the Olympic Charter has associated the rings with the continents. The five rings had first appeared on official

Olympic posters in 1928, for the Winter Games at St Moritz and the Summer Games at Amsterdam. In the later history of the Games, the five rings have become one of the most lucrative marketing images, or branding logos, in the history of sport.

The *Olympic flame* was an initiative of the main organizer of the 1936 Berlin Olympics, Dr Carl *Diem. This theme of the *torch relay* carrying the flame from the site of the ancient Olympics to the stadium of the host city where it would then light the stadium flame has become a combination of community celebration, commercialization, and political posturing and protest. There was much controversy when the torch relay was first sponsored for the 1984 Los Angeles Olympics, the Greek National Olympic Committee protesting at what it saw as a soiling of the purity of Olympic ritual (even though the ritual dated only from the 1936 Games that became widely known as Hitler's 'Nazi' Games). In April 2008, protests against China's treatment of Tibet disrupted the Beijing Games' torch relay in London, Paris, and San Francisco, exposing the fragility of Olympic claims to bring nations together.

But the persisting attraction, as media event, of forms of ceremony such as the *opening and closing ceremonies* keeps the rhetoric of Olympism alive. Such ceremonies combine established Olympic protocol—Olympic oath, hymn, and fanfare, and in the opening ceremony the parade of the athletes—with spectacular presentations of selective histories and cultural representations of the host city and nation. Many of them have combined a notion of the birth narrative of the city or nation with a recognition of the universalizing spirit and internationalism of Olympism. These ceremonies are reported—albeit by the International Olympic Committee itself—to attract the biggest worldwide media audiences in history. The *Olympic motto*—'Citius, Altius, Fortius' ('Faster, Higher, Stronger')—is also prominent in Olympic ceremony, ritual, and—it has to be said, on a less idealistic but more realistic note—marketing. The motto is said to have been coined for de Coubertin by his friend Henri Didon, a French Dominican preacher and educator.

Not all invented traditions took hold of the public's imagination; the giant bell, also inaugurated for the 1936 Berlin Games, tolled only the once. And though much is made, drawing upon a reading of the peace-making rationale of the ancient Greek Games, of the notion of the *Olympic truce*, the armed conflict between Russia and Georgia during the 2008 Beijing Games was just one instance of the ineffectiveness of this claimed tradition. It is, nevertheless, undeniable that the Olympic Games has contributed a global cultural legacy, and how this has been achieved and sustained within a complex mix of political and economic power relations continues to be a central question for sport scholars; the continuing appeal of forms of Olympic ceremony to the popular consciousness and to the media and marketing conglomerates alike provides one way of answering this question.

Olympic flame *See* OLYMPIC CEREMONY.

Olympic Games, ancient The ancient Olympics had an extraordinarily long history, from their origins in ancient Greece to the fifth century AD, over a thousand years of sustained organized athletic competition surviving the collapse and rise of empires and cultures. On their inauguration in 776 BC, the games at Olympia in ancient Greece were comparatively modest and local; crucial for their expansion was the Mediterranean-based, and especially western, spread of Greek colonization. Donald Kyle notes that the 'Colonies cherished the games as ties to the motherland, Olympia was an attractive place of assembly, and Olympia's programme and crowds grew accordingly' (*Sport and Spectacle in the Ancient World*, 2007). Gymnastic games were instantly successful, and equestrian events were added; aristocrats and tyrants patronized them; emerging states rivalled each other, giving rewards to or for victory. 'Olympia became a prime locus for competitive display among aristocrats and city-states. Athletic and extra-athletic performances turned Olympia into a Panhellenic center of spectacles.'

The programme was relatively simple. But for equestrian events, everything took place in the stadium, a simple running track with a grassy embankment, and, by 325 BC, there was a Hippodrome running parallel to it. For several centuries there was no seating, though elsewhere stone seating was provided. Runners early on were flogged for false starts at their stone starting grooves, and horses and chariots raced in intense and dangerous fashion. This mixture of festival, sanctuary, and games lasted over 1,000 years. Administration and preparations at nearby Elis were thorough and extensive; the event began with a procession of officials, athletes, trainers, and gift-bearers, with up to 100,000 in attendance, and at Olympia athletes swore oaths at the statue of Zeus. The programme of contests (based on Kyle's listing) at Olympia was established by the first five and a half centuries of the games (compare that scale with the little over a century of the modern Olympics):

776	*stadion* (sprint of 200 m)
724	*diaulos* (double race of 400 m, down and back)
720	*dolichos* (long race of around 20–24 laps)
708	pentathlon (comprising broad jump, discus, javelin, running, wrestling) and wrestling (*pale*)
688	boxing (*pyx*)
680	*tethrippon* (four-horse chariot race of 12 laps)
648	*pankration* (all-in wrestling) and *keles* (horseback race of around 2–6 laps)
632	boys' *stadion* and boys' wrestling
628	boys' pentathlon (held just the once)
616	boys' boxing
520	*hoplitodromos* (race in armour down and back)
500	*apene* (mule-cart race)
496	*kalpe* or *anabetes* (a dismounting race with mares)—dropped by 444
408	*synoris* (two-horse chariot race of 8 laps)
396	contests for heralds and trumpeters
384	four-colt (*poloi*) chariot race
268	two-colt chariot race
256	*keles* for colts
200	boys' *pankration*

There was no marathon or torch relay, and no formal inclusion of art, music, or drama (apart from when the Roman emperor *Nero customized the event for his own ego and glory in the first century AD). Once the custom was introduced, nudity was the costume, and only chariot drivers and jockeys could be clothed. Pausanius, visiting Greece in the middle of the 2nd century after Christ, wrote a form of guidebook on Greece, drawing upon monuments and the illustrations and inscriptions that he observed on them. At the cemetery of Megara, he observed that near the tomb of Koroibus,

> is buried Orsippos, who won the *stadion* at Olympia [720 BC]. While the other athletes in the competition wore *perizomata* in accordance with the ancient practice, he ran naked... I think that the *perizoma* slipped off deliberately at Olympia, for he recognized that a nude man can run more easily than one who is girt. (Stephen G. Miller, *Arete: Greek Sports from Ancient Sources*, 2nd and expanded edn, 1991).

Pausanius did not record any speculations on whether the gathered spectators approved the slippage or not, but the unconventional soon became the norm after this early innovation in the history of the Olympics; as did the oiling of the naked athletic body before competition. It was at that same games as Orsippos's ditching of the loincloth that the long-distance foot race, the *dolichos*, was also introduced (around 5,000 metres), and so the innovations were not merely in the display of the body, but also related to its capacity for endurance. Once established, the programme was for, in Kyle's witty wordplay, 'the oily trinity of free, Greek, and male'.

> The five-day festival was established by the mid 5th century BC and might go as follows: Day 1—oath ceremony, boys' events, prayers, sacrifices; Day 2—procession of competitors and contestants in equestrian events and pentathlon, and also a night-time sacrifice (to Pelops) of a black ram; Day 3 (full moon, midpoint)—central rituals: parade of judges, ambassadors, and athletes, and a main sacrifice of 100 oxen to Zeus; foot races; and a public feast; Day 4—combat events and hoplite (armour-clad) race; Day 5—procession and crowning of victors, feasting and celebration.

Stories abounded of the feats and fates of competitors. *Pankratist* Arrachion of Phigaleia is reported to have, as dying in a stranglehold, dislocated the ankle of his opponent so much that the latter submitted to what then had become a victorious corpse. *Pankration* (literal translation, 'all-powerful') was, in Kyle's words, 'a brutal free-for-all combining wrestling, boxing and kicking', ending in either capitulation or incapacitation. Punching, kicking, choking, and assault on the genitals were allowed, though not biting or gouging; in the mid 4th century BC, Sostratos of Sikyon won three times, often breaking fingers of opponents. Equestrian events, introduced in 680, were forms of *conspicuous consumption and assertion of *status of the Greek leisure class. Athletes trained hard, were highly motivated, and saw Olympic victory as their primary goal as competitors. With no team events, there were only first-place finishes: winning was the main thing, losers were shamed and humiliated. The ancient Greek Olympics were not some ideal world of pure innocence; athletes cheated, fouled, hedged, were bribed, and officials could be fraudulent. Entrepreneurs hustled commercially (selling 'votives, victuals,

victory odes' as Kyle puts it), poets sought commissions, and spectators preened.
Herodotus read his *Histories* at the Temple of Zeus; Plato may have mingled
anonymously in the crowds.

The remarkable longevity of the Olympics was aided by the essential
simplicity and continuity of their programme, and the objectivity of the process by
which the winner was decided. That longevity also included their revival in the
Roman period, and, despite opposition to them as pagan events after the rise
of Christianity, they were not ended even by Theodosius I's ban on pagan cults in
AD 393. Theodosius II destroyed the Temple of Zeus in 426, but the stadium
stayed open and evidence suggests that some Games were staged in the
5th century, before Olympia finally became the victim of human invasion
and natural disaster, after around thirteen centuries of athletic endeavour and
sporting myth-making.

Olympic Games, modern (as global cultural event) Sociologists and social
historians of sport have long recognized the centrality of the Olympics in any
historical narrative of the rise and spread of international sport. Miller et al. (2001)
observe how, as forms of television-based popular culture, events such as the
Olympics provide 'a crucial site where populations are targeted by different forms of
governmental and commercial knowledge/power' (p. 2). They ask us to attempt
to imagine such an event stripped of all the familiar cultural and political symbols
that have become so familiar to worldwide audiences: 'No comprehensive media
coverage, no national flags flying, no playing of national anthems, no politicians
involved in the ceremonies, no military displays, no tables comparing national
standings, and athletes competing in whatever clothing they desired instead of
national uniforms' (ibid.). It is of course difficult to achieve this act of the
imagination. A deeply entrenched and historically claimed symbolism of coexisting
national rivalries, perpetuated alongside the commercially branded later cases of
the corporatized Games, pervades the taken-for-granted mediated mega-events of
contemporary global culture. Maurice Roche locates this merging of the
commercial and the political on the level of global consumer culture, linked to what
he calls 'touristic consumerism', and the depiction of 'one world' through the
appeal to notions of a universalized ideal and shared meanings (Roche, 2000: 26).
Mega-events such as the Olympics are, for Roche, quintessential phenomena of
global modernity, 'intrinsically complex processes' which combine the interests of
political and economic elites and professionals from the increasingly supranational
cultural industries. These interlocking elites operate on a number of levels,
Roche goes on: 'within and between urban, national and international
levels . . . working together in a medium-term time-horizon both to produce the
events and to manage their effects' (Roche, 2000: 233).

The Olympics are, of course, more than mere reflections of social processes and
trends. They are formative as well as formed, pointing the way towards new cultural
formations, and as such important indices of change and cultural transformation.
Maguire identifies the last quarter of the 19th century as a major phase in 'the
international spread of sport, the establishment of international sports
organizations, the growth of competition between national teams, the worldwide
acceptance of rules governing specific sport forms and the establishment of

global competitions such as the Olympic Games' (Maguire, 1999: 88). In this list, it is the Olympics and the very grandeur of the scale of the conception of de *Coubertin (the *Rénovateur*) that constitutes a project of seriously globalizing proportion and potential, ridden with contradictions (Tomlinson, 1984) stemming from de Coubertin's aristocratic, imperialist, patriarchal roots, but nevertheless premised on a vision of an increasingly networked, compressed, and orchestrated global culture. As Maguire also notes, the Olympic Games continue to provide a stage on which can be played out some of the recurring tensions of global politics. The West 'still has hegemonic control in the global sport figuration' but for non-Westerners a 'main source of potential dispute may well be the Olympic Games' (p. 92). Miller et al. (2001: 12) note the strong opposition of the Third World to the 'undemocratic ways' of the International Olympic Committee's international Court of Arbitration for Sport. And the Games have provided, case after case through their history, an opportunity for the expression of national identity. Bairner (2001) has reaffirmed how, on the level of the national, different statements can be made to a world audience, in the context of the Olympics, about what it is to be American or Canadian.

The Olympics operate therefore as a focus for the articulation of serious national and global political dynamics, and as a giant billboard for the elite crop of multinational corporations that are the preferred sponsorship partners of the International Olympic Committee. These political and economic dimensions are interconnected and serve the interests of what Miller et al. (2001: 40) call the *new international division of cultural labour, which operates in the context of 'five simultaneous, uneven, interconnected processes which characterize the present moment in sport: Globalization, Governmentalization, Americanization, Televisualization, and Commodification (GGATaC)'. The economic, the political, and the cultural combine in their influence on the modern Olympics. Studying the global reach of events such as this requires an analytical approach sensitive to the ways in which these dimensions intermesh.

Sklair's analysis of the macro-level of the workings and reach of transnational companies (TNCs) and capital casts light upon the Olympic phenomenon: 'No social movement appears even remotely likely to overthrow the three fundamental institutional supports of global capitalism that have been identified, namely the TNCs, the transnational capitalist class, and the culture-ideology of consumerism' (Sklair, 2001: 296). The Olympics is in some senses, from this macro perspective, just one example of the operationalization of the practices and ideologies of global capital and the transnational companies that dominate the centres of international capital. Anthony Giddens writes of time–space distanciation, and its implications for people's experience of place, as a core element of globalization, referring to the 'phantasmagoric' nature of modern places (Giddens, 1990: 19). Olympic villages and stadiums, Olympic parks and sites could usefully be viewed as illuminating cases of such places. Such approaches to the Olympic Games as a prominent cultural event in the modern increasingly globalized world order locate critical analyses of the Olympic phenomenon within the context of debates concerning the nature of international cultural politics, the operation of the interests of transnational companies and international capital, and the nature of international sport's relation to global consumer culture and international markets.

References

Bairner, A. (2001) *Sport, Nationalism and Globalization: European and North American Perspectives,* Albany, NY: State University of New York Press; Giddens, A. (1990) *The Consequences of Modernity,* Cambridge: Polity Press; Maguire, J. A. (1999) *Global Sport: Identities, Societies, Civilizations,* Cambridge: Polity Press; Miller, T., Lawrence, G., McKay, J., and Rowe, D. (2001) *Globalization and Sport: Playing the World,* London: Sage; Roche, M. (2000) *Mega-Events and Modernity: Olympics and Expos in the Growth of Global Culture,* London: Routledge; Sklair, L. (2001) *The Transnational Capitalist Class,* Oxford: Blackwell; Tomlinson, A. (1984) 'De Coubertin and the Modern Olympics', in A. Tomlinson and G. Whannel (eds), *Five-Ring Circus: Money, Power and Politics at the Olympic Games,* London: Pluto Press, pp. 84–97.

Olympic Games, modern (history of the Summer Games, 1896–2008) The simple facts of the growth of the Olympic Games are widely established, in an expanding line-up of events, participants, media personnel, media coverage, and worldwide spectators and television viewers. But the story of the survival and eventual expansion into everyday global consciousness of the Games was not an even one. Early Games after the inaugural success in Athens in 1896 were linked to expos (Roche, 2000). In Paris in 1900 and in St Louis in 1904, events with few spectators were marginal, peripheral aspects of great trades shows that were celebrations of expanding international trade markets. As high-profile cultural events they were insignificant flops. London in 1908 recaptured some of the revivalist momentum of the founder de *Coubertin's project. The British Olympic Association (BOA) had been created in 1905, allocated a seat on the *International Olympic Committee (IOC), and with its well-established athletics organization in the form of the *Amateur Athletics Association it could respond to a desperate IOC, looking for a replacement host city in 1906 when Rome had withdrawn just two years before the event. The Franco-British Exhibition of 1908 became the saviour of the Olympic idea. Though by the final day 90,000 turned out to witness the marathon race, spurred on by a media picking up on British–American athletic rivalries, the Games was again a marginal appendage to a bigger event. It did show, though, the power of the Olympics to foster *nationalism: the British Olympic Committee stated its desire 'that the celebration should be worthy of the Motherland of International Sport' (British Olympic Committee, 1908). These London Games sustained the Olympic initiative, but also confirmed the fragile cultural and economic basis of the Olympics. They nevertheless provided some basis for the consolidation of the project in Stockholm in 1912. The Games after World War I (Antwerp 1920, Paris 1924, Amsterdam 1928) remained on a relatively modest scale, though the US presence was becoming increasingly dominant, and included powerful statements of athletic prowess by women athletes. The media profile of the Olympic Games was also expanding: telegraph technology at Amsterdam in 1928 increased the speed of international communications, though the (radio) broadcasting of results was resisted, to protect the exclusivity of coverage of the written press. At Amsterdam, a mere 317 journalists were present during the first period of the Games (van Rossem, 1928); for Los Angeles 1932, the organizers put in place a Press Department to serve as a 'bureau of information to

Olympic Groups as well as a news disseminating agency for the World Press' (Tomlinson, 2006: 172).

If the first eight Summer Olympic Games were relatively low-profile, politically and commercially, the Games of the 1930s were more overtly political and expressive of national interests. In this sense, the Games from 1932 to 1984 can be seen as more explicitly political projects, in the 1920s and 1930s matched by the Soviet experiments in the use of sport for display and propaganda. At the twelve Summer games in that period the political stakes became higher and higher. This included the exploitation of the 1936 Games in the cause of fascism and Nazism, and after World War II the use of the Games to fuel Cold War rivalries, once the Soviet Union was allowed to participate. The Olympics also offered nations the possibility of rehabilitation into the world community (Italy, Japan, and Germany) after the conflict of World War II. Across this phase of the Olympic story, the explicit political motivation of intensely national interests catapulted the Games to a new level. The Games represented the wider sport cultures of the nations that participated in them. In 1929 Benito *Mussolini sought to win the 1936 Games for Rome, and at Berlin in 1936 failed again in a bid to stage the 1940 Games. For all of Jesse *Owens's gold medals and dignity at Berlin in 1936, it made no difference whatsoever to the momentum of the Nazi project. In such cultural moments and spaces the body is an instrument of the ideology on the basis of which the sporting practice has been planned and produced. The Olympics inscribe wider cultural projects and ideologies. All the Olympic hyperbole in the world does not alter this. In the explicitly nationalist second phase in the history of the Olympic Games, they prospered primarily on the basis of their usefulness as a vehicle for the articulation of political meanings and national rivalries. But as the Olympic project veered from crisis to crisis in the 'M' years from 1968 to 1980 (Mexico 1968, Munich 1972, Montreal 1976, and Moscow 1980), rocked by political protest, terrorist incursions, unprecedented losses, and major boycotts, it was its combined commercial potential and political use as shown in the 1984 Games that secured its future as a mega-event of the televisual age.

Based on restoration of facilities as much as new provision, and the use of an army of volunteer labour, LA 1984 reported a US$225 million profit. The event celebrated the values of the free Western world after the US-led boycott of Moscow in 1980, and produced opening and closing ceremonies based on sheer Hollywood razzmatazz. The LA Games marked a point of transformation in the cultural staging and underpinning *political economy of world sport. It was the first Games held under the presidency of Juan Antonio *Samaranch, and launched the Games into a new phase of development hand-in-hand with television companies willing to pay unheard-of sums to cover the events, and economic partners paying huge sums for their exclusive sponsorship status and rights in the TOP (The *Olympic Programme) scheme. From that point on, the Games were guaranteed a future as one of the most high-profile global commodities. The Seoul Games (1988) carried on the political mission of host cities, but the cultural–commercial–economic rebalancing of interests was best encapsulated in the cases of Barcelona (1992) and Sydney (2000), sandwiched by the attempt of Atlanta (1996) to reconfigure the worldwide audience's perception of US geography. The Games of this third phase, including Athens (2004) and Beijing (2008), were immersed in a developmental cultural logic of economic regeneration and global self-promotion of cities and states, justified widely and recurrently on the basis of some amorphous spiritual value of benefit to all of humankind. This logic continues to fuel the scramble to win the right to host the Games, with seven cities (Baku, Chicago, Doha, Madrid, Prague, Rio de Janeiro, and Tokyo) lining up in 2008 to do battle to win the 2016 Games. Chicago, Madrid, Rio, and Tokyo contested a final vote in October 2009, won by the Brazilian city and so taking the Games to South America for the first time.

References
British Olympic Committee, *Programme for 1908 Olympic Games*, consulted in John Johnson Collection of Ephemera, Bodleian Library, Oxford; Roche, M. (2000) *Mega-Events and Modernity: Olympics and Expos in the Growth of Global Culture*, London: Routledge; Tomlinson. A. (2006) 'Los Angeles 1984 and 1932: Commercializing the American Dream', in A. Tomlinson and C. Young (eds), *National Identity and Global Sports Events: Culture, Politics, and Spectacle in the Olympics and the Football World Cup*, Albany, NY: State University of New York Press, pp. 163–76; Van Rossem, G. (ed.) *The Ninth Olympiad, being the Official Report of the Olympic Games of 1928 celebrated at Amsterdam, issued by the Netherlands Olympic Committee*, translated by Sydney W. Fleming and J. H. De Bussy, Amsterdam.

Olympic Games, Winter A multi-sport event for winter sports, held every four years under the auspices of the International Olympic Committee (IOC). The first Winter Games was held in Chamonix, France, in 1924, with fourteen events and just sixteen participating nations. Some figure skating events had been held in London in 1908, but international competition in winter sports had been mostly organized within the Swedish Nordic Games, held each four years from 1901. Separate Winter Olympics were lobbied for within the IOC during the early 1920s, and an 'International Sports Week' organized for Chamonix, which was retrospectively recognized as the inaugural Winter Olympics. The first sixteen Games shared the year of their staging with the Summer Olympics, but, to spread the events across the media schedules and to give more sustained exposure to sponsors, the Winter Games were moved on to a different cycle from 1994 (Lillehammer, Norway) onwards. Scandinavian and Alpine countries, along with the former Soviet Union, the USA, and Germany, have headed national medal tables. The post-unification Germany headed the table at both Albertville, France, in 1992, and Torino, Italy, in 2006. At the 2010 Winter Olympics in Vancouver, seven main sports were to be contested: *skiing (with the six specialist disciplines of snowboard, ski jumping, Alpine skiing, freestyle skiing, Nordic combined, and cross-country skiing); skating (figure skating, speed skating, and short-track speed skating); *bobsleigh (skeleton and bobsleigh); *biathlon; *curling; *ice hockey; and *luge. The Torino Games had 2,508 athletes competing from 80 National Olympic Committees, with 9,408 media in attendance. The organizing body, torino2006.org, reported 700 million page views on its internet site. Although criticized by environmentalists, and smaller in scale and less globally representative than its Summer counterpart, the Winter Olympics continues to attract bidding cities: its mix of modernity (the introduction of snowboard in 2006) and glamour and thrill (the beauty and excitement of the visual coverage of most of its events) ensures its persisting prominence in the international sporting calendar. *See also* Henie, Sonja; ice skating.

Olympic Museum A museum established by the International Olympic Committee (IOC) and dedicated to the preservation of the legacy of the Olympic movement. It was opened in 1993, a long-term project of the IOC eventually realized on the basis of the increase in revenue enabled by the television and sponsorship deals (such as The *Olympic Programme) achieved in the 1980s and 1990s. The museum was originally housed in the Villa Mon Repos in central Lausanne, Switzerland, a location used by Pierre de *Coubertin, and was moved to its location in Ouchy, beside Lac Léman (Lake Geneva), in 1993. The cost of its construction was around US$68.6 million, 56.4 million of which was funded from donations or sponsorship. The museum's building and fittings are owned by the Olympic Museum Foundation, its collections, artefacts, and archives on loan, at no cost, from the IOC. The museum incorporates an Olympic Studies Centre, where the archives of the IOC can be consulted, subject to rules of confidentiality and access.

(⊕) SEE WEB LINKS

• The official website of the International Olympic Committee's museum in Lausanne, Switzerland, including the Olympic Studies Centre which holds files and archives on the Olympics and the IOC.

Olympic Programme, The (TOP) A programme of sponsorship established by the International Olympic Committee (IOC) in the 1980s, put in place by the incoming IOC president Juan Antonio *Samaranch, with the assistance of the Adidas entrepreneur Horst *Dassler, and known within the business as the TOP initiative. Following the model of the football World Cup, in seeking major corporate sponsors who would be granted exclusive sponsorship profiles worldwide, the IOC attracted nine select companies into its TOP I programme from 1985 to 1988 (covering Calgary and Seoul), generating US$106 million. This scheme proved so successful that by TOP IV, from 1997 to 2000, eleven TOP sponsors generated US$579 million, and had a profile in 199 countries. For TOP VI (Turin and Beijing) the eleven sponsors generated approximately $US866 million to IOC revenues over 2006–8. Such levels of penetration prove highly attractive to global brands, so *Coca-Cola has signed up as a TOP partner with the IOC through to and including the 2020 Summer Games. Coca-Cola was one of just four of the TOP I partners—along with Kodak, Panasonic, and Visa—remaining in TOP VI, and Kodak did not renew its deal with the IOC from 2008 onwards. Also withdrawing from Olympic sponsorship in 2008 were insurance giant Manulife/John Hancock, a partner from TOP III (1993–6) onwards, and Johnson & Johnson/Athos-Origin after just one Olympiad of TOP status. IBM had been in TOP III (1993–6, covering Lillehammer and Atlanta) and TOP IV (1997–2000, Nagano and Sydney), SchlumbergerSema in TOP V (2001–4). Sports Illustrated/Time had been a founding partner, but did not renew after TOP V. Samsung was a sponsor from TOP IV to TOP VI. The TOP programme, along with dramatically increased revenues for the sale of broadcasting rights from the early 1980s onwards, transformed the finance, aspirations, and objectives of the Olympic organization.

Olympic rings *See* OLYMPIC CEREMONY.

Olympic torch relay *See* AT&T CORPORATION; OLYMPIA; OLYMPIC CEREMONY.

Olympic truce *See* OLYMPIC GAMES, ANCIENT.

One Day in September A documentary film (1999) of the Palestinian terrorist attack on, and murder of, eleven Israeli athletes at the 1972 Munich Olympics. Directed by Kevin Macdonald, it won an Oscar (Academy Award for Best Documentary Feature 2000). The film was a landmark in the investigative sport documentary, including an interview with Jamal Al-Gashey, believed to be the only surviving terrorist (and in hiding in Africa). The film also implies that the German security service was inadequate, in marked contrast to the security systems that underpin the staging of large-scale sporting events in the 21st century.

one-dimensional man The subject of a highly influential study by the Marxist philosopher and sociologist Herbert Marcuse (1898–1979). *One-Dimensional Man* (1964) argued that modern capitalist society suppressed the human potential of individuals and produced one-dimensional people who would inevitably be unquestioning and without the capacity to challenge authorities and rulers: 'the irresistible output of the entertainment and information industry' creates attitudes that 'bind the consumers more or less pleasantly to the producers and, through the latter, to the whole.' 'A good way of life . . . militates against qualitative change' and from this condition emerges 'a pattern of *one-dimensional thought and behaviour*' in which any oppositional or potentially transcendent ideas are either 'repelled', or reduced to the terms of the dominant system. Politicians and information professionals collude in the systematic promotion of the one-dimensionality of existence.

Marcuse's radical stance was a combination of Marxism and Freudianism, and, despite the snappy title and Marcuse's claim to base his critical theory on 'empirical grounds', the book was actually a dense text of philosophical speculation. Nevertheless, Marcuse without doubt captured the spirit of a radicalized age and the book's title became one form of shorthand for the oppressed and repressed mass of the population controlled by the dominant few. Some radical analyses of sport, such as Paul *Hoch's *Rip Off the Big Game: The Exploitation of Sports by the Power Elite* (1972), captured the one-dimensionality of the increasingly commercialized elite sport model, in which the human impulse to play is perverted by 'the increasingly anti-human society around us'. Ian McDonald (2007) has claimed that, though the one-dimensionality theory falls short of accounting for the nature of capitalist society as a whole, it continues to have some relevance to the understanding of 'one-dimensional sport' (http://www.idrottsforum.org/articles/mcdonald071212.html).

ontology The theory, in philosophical terms, of the existence of things, posing fundamental questions concerning the very nature of being itself. In relation to understanding the place of sport in society, the ontological questions are: is sport simply a reflection of whatever society is said to be? Or does—or can—sport create the social anew, or at least elements of the wider society? These are versions of the structure–agency debate that has dominated sociocultural studies, and particularly sociological approaches such as the British sociologist Anthony Giddens's *structuration theory. Ontological issues are therefore relevant not just to the more arcane areas of the philosophical investigation of sport, but also to any analysis purporting to locate sport in its social context.

oral history A method in social and cultural history based upon the collection of the life history of a living person, in the form of extensive interviews stimulating recollection of the individual's life and experience. Paul Thompson (*The Voice of the Past: Oral History*, 1978) reminded historians that oral history might be a new term, but that oral history as a practice was 'as old as history itself. It was the *first* kind of history'. Its re-emergence in the 1970s was boosted in part by the excitement of new technologies such as the tape recorder, in part by the excitement of giving voice to ordinary people. Oral history has also been undertaken by pioneering journalists such as the veteran US writer Studs Terkel (1912–2008), whose book *Working* (1977) includes moving commentary by Canadian ice-hockey player Eric Nesterenko on what it feels like to be owned: 'You know you're just a piece of property . . . It becomes a job, just a shitty job.' The *LA84 Foundation (the former Amateur Athletic Foundation of Los Angeles) has transcribed numerous oral histories of US Olympians, and these are available on its website. Oral history can generate understanding, of both individual experience and contextual detail, that is not available in documented form. The accounts need to be interpreted with care, checked alongside other accounts and complementary sources, but respected; it is not always the literal accuracy of an account that is of most interest or importance, though, but the interpretation of an event, time, or place that the method brings to the surface.

( ) SEE WEB LINKS

- The official site of the Oral History Society (of Britain and Northern Ireland).
- A section, within the website 'Making history: the changing face of the profession in Britain', concerned with 'The making of oral history'.

orienteering A sport in which runners compete in completing navigated routes based upon control points in natural countryside, each point to be reached in a stated sequence. The winner is the runner to complete the full circuit in the fastest time, and this form of the sport is known as cross-country orienteering. There are other types: line orienteering, route orienteering, and score orienteering demand varying levels of skill in map-reading. Orienteering has its origins in Norway and Sweden. In 1918 a youth leader adapted established military training exercises to attract young men to competitive running. The International Orienteering Federation (IOF) was founded in 1961, comprising Scandinavian and East European national members. In Britain, the sport was introduced into Scotland and northern and southern parts of England in the 1960s. The IOF oversees foot, mountain-bike, ski, and trail orienteering and by the first decade of the 21st century had 70 affiliated national associations.

Orwell, George (pseudonym of Eric Arthur Blair) (1903–50) An English journalist, cultural critic, political commentator, and novelist whose extended essays offered some commentary upon the nature of English people's daily life and leisure and some of their sports, and in whose fictional work sport has been seen as a nostalgic metaphor for a lost and simpler life. In his autobiographical memoir of preparatory school life (*Such, Such Were the Joys*, written in 1947), Orwell recalled the hierarchical and bullying dimension of organized school sports, calling football— at which I was a funk'—a 'species of fighting. The lovers of football are large, boisterous, knobbly boys who are good at knocking down and trampling on slightly smaller boys.' His essay on *The Sporting Spirit* (1945), published in the socialist magazine/newspaper *Tribune*, was prompted by a visit to Britain of the Moscow Dynamo football team from the USSR. In this piece, Orwell argued that 'sport is an unfailing cause of ill-will', contributing to 'orgies of hatred' and so the worsening of international relations rather than their improvement. Orwell called international sport 'mimic warfare' and described serious sport as 'war minus the shooting'. He instanced boxing, as well as football, as 'bound up with the rise of nationalism'. In the novel *Coming Up for Air* (1939) George 'Fatty' Bowling disappears from his everyday life of domestic misery to revisit childhood settings redolent of a time before Hitler, aeroplanes, radio, aspirins, or the cinema and the concentration camp: sport for Fatty is 'sitting all day under a willow tree beside a quiet pool', a source of peacefulness available even in the solid English names of coarse fish. Orwell was of course no systematic social scientist, and the assertion that 'nearly all modern-minded people dislike' cricket (*Raffles and Miss Blandish*, 1944) has no substance. But his perceptions that sport could be used as a form of control in institutional schooling, as a vehicle for intensifying forms of *nationalism, and in its more individualized and non-competitive forms as a source of yearning for the pre-modern, are convincing and powerfully expressed.

osteoporosis A condition of the bones causing them to become less dense and weaker. Bone mass increases up until middle age, when it begins to decline. The decline is greater in women after the menopause when oestrogen levels fall and by the sixth decade of life around 20 per cent of women will be affected. Osteoporosis increases the risk of fractures, particularly of the wrists, hips, and spine. Regular exercise helps maintain bone mass throughout life through the stimulation of mechanical stress. In young sportswomen excessive exercise can paradoxically lead to, rather than prevent, osteoporosis through the syndrome known as the female athlete triad. The combination of intense training and associated *eating disorders promote osteoporosis through a combination of an insufficient energy and calcium intake, along with a reduction in body fat leading to amenorrhoea and a lowering of oestrogen's protective effect.

Österberg, Martina Sofia Helena Bergman (1849–1915) Born in Sweden, Martina Bergman (later, after her marriage, known as Madame Bergman Österberg) worked initially as a governess and librarian before entering the Royal Central Gymnastics Institute, established by Per Hendrick *Ling, at which the therapeutic benefit of exercise was prioritized. Moving to England as a specialist in this novel Swedish system of exercise, she became an important contributor to the provision of physical training, championing the Ling system in the London school board and, in 1885, inaugurating the Hampstead Physical Education College, and then establishing the Dartford College in Kent in 1887. The pioneering course was based on Swedish gymnastics, physiology, anatomy, and English team games. As Sheila Fletcher puts it: 'Amid the apprehensions of national decline which prevailed around the turn of the century, she convinced the heads of countless high schools for girls that the gymnastics and games mistress—the specialist in health—had become essential' (*Oxford Dictionary of National Biography*, 2004). Bergman Österberg's contribution to the professions and science of the body also indirectly generated the emergence of physiotherapy.

outdoor recreation A generic term for sporting activities and physical practices undertaken outdoors, but with particular resonance in relation to non-urban settings and activities in the natural environment, from climbing to hiking, from camping to fishing. In historical settings, and particularly in the context of urban and industrial environments, outdoor recreation was also seen as an antidote to the health-threatening effects of unregulated and polluting industrial practices, so in 1898 New York's Outdoor Recreation League founded parks in which were organized sporting competitions and team games.

overtraining A state where excessive physical training leads to feelings of fatigue and poor sports performance. Sometimes known as staleness, overtraining is associated with a wide range of symptoms. These include chronic fatigue, poor sleep or appetite, susceptibility to infection, and mood disturbances such as depression and anxiety. Overtraining syndrome is not well understood. It appears to result from disturbance to nervous and hormonal control mechanisms and depletion or imbalance in nutrients. The symptoms of overtraining vary between individuals. The syndrome is not easily monitored or diagnosed. Recovery takes the form of decreased training or complete rest.

Owens, Jesse (James Cleveland) (1913–80) A US athlete, born in Alabama, the son of sharecroppers, who displayed a precocious athletic talent, culminating in his astonishing achievements at the 1936 Olympic Games in Berlin, where he won three individual gold medals, for the 100 metres, 200 metres, and long jump. Owens became a pawn in—though arguably in effect a counterpoint to—the nationalist and racist ideologies of the German fascist state, by which the Games were seen as a vehicle for the assertion of Aryan superiority. Owens's victories undermined these aspirations and claims, and the filmed version of his triumphs—in the film *Olympia* directed by Leni *Riefenstahl—gave warranted attention to his achievements. It is arguable that, alongside the 1936 and 1938 boxing matches between the USA's Joe *Louis and Germany's Max *Schmeling, Owens's performances at the Berlin Olympics were the most publicized cultural forum in which fascist and racist ideologies such as Nazism could be publicly challenged. After his Olympic victories, Owens became a professional, running in exhibition events, even racing against thoroughbred racehorses. Mundane jobs followed, but in his later life Owens acted as a US goodwill ambassador in the international sporting field. He was, though, resented and even hated by some blacks for his anti-civil rights perspectives in the 1960s.

Oxford–Cambridge Boat Race First rowed, and won by Oxford, at Henley-on-Thames in 1829, the Boat Race, as it has become known worldwide, is contested annually between teams of eight rowers from the two ancient English universities. It was held again in London in 1836, and became an annual event in 1839. In 1845 the race was held over the stretch of river from

Putney to Mortlake, four and a quarter miles of the River Thames. At three times the length of a regular Summer Olympic course, the race is 'one of the world's great endurance tests, and it takes its participants to the brink of total collapse and sometimes beyond . . . It demands courage, strength, skill, superb fitness and dedication' (Daniel Topolski with Patrick Robinson, *True Blue: The Oxford Boat Race Mutiny*, 1989). Xchanging, the event's sponsor for 2009 and 2010, describes the race as 'a winner-takes-all battle of gladiatorial proportions'. In the 1980s, women coxes began to be used. Although staunchly amateur, the event attracts effectively full-time rowers, the universities often recruiting international athletes on to postgraduate courses. The highest UK television audience for the race was 8.9 million for the BBC coverage of the 2004 event, and the race is broadcast to 113 countries. From 2010 the BBC resumed coverage of the event. *See also* BLUES, OXFORD AND CAMBRIDGE; ROWING.

Oxford University, sport at Sporting pursuits at the University of Oxford have been built into its more modern culture and image from the 18th century onwards, from the recreational pursuits of an aristocratic elite to the aspirations of competitive amateurs in the 19th century and well into the 20th. The college system fostered intra-university rivalries, some the direct continuation of public school encounters, and the rivalry on the river and the athletics track fostered inter-university rivalry with the University of Cambridge. The professionalization and commercialization of sports, particularly in the last quarter of the 20th century, meant that the university base for amateur excellence was increasingly adrift from the circumstances and conditions conducive to the production of top-level sporting performance. With the increase in Britain of lottery funding for athletes targeting Olympic achievements, however, university students and graduates have been able to aspire again to the highest level of achievement, particularly in sports within the university tradition such as rowing, or all-round sports such as the modern pentathlon. The University of Oxford's student sports federation supports a wide range of activities, and some sports such as rowing, rugby, and men's cricket benefit from considerable external sponsorship; this can be fragile though, as the collapse of the rugby club sponsor Lehman Brothers demonstrated during the economic crisis of 2008. Those high-profile sports have also been the focus of some controversy in relation to student recruitment, with specialist sport competitors with established international (and professional) backgrounds accepted on to postgraduate courses of dubious academic standing. *See also* BLUES, OXFORD AND CAMBRIDGE; CAMBRIDGE UNIVERSITY, SPORT AT; FOUR-MINUTE MILE; LAWN TENNIS; OXFORD-CAMBRIDGE BOAT RACE.

Packer, Kerry (1937–2005) Born Kerry Francis Bullmore Packer, the son of a rich Australian business magnate, a media tycoon who inherited his father's business portfolio of media stations, magazine publishing, and property in 1972. He expanded the dynasty's business and media empire to become at the time Australia's wealthiest individual, said to be worth more than £3 billion. He challenged the traditional hierarchy of world cricket in 1977 by establishing World Series Cricket, to which he attracted the world's top players to play in matches in teams of his own making, in a format featuring bright playing outfits, and associated showbiz razzmatazz. This initiative was also a means of restructuring television rights and media coverage of the traditional international game. Packer had been a boxer as a schoolboy, after a childhood in which he suffered poliomyelitis at the age of 8, which compensated for his lack of academic prowess (he was diagnosed as dyslexic). His business practice exhibited a parallel pugnacious style throughout his life. *The Times* (London, 28 December 2005) commemorated him as the 'uncompromising media proprietor who became Australia's richest man and dragged cricket into the television age'.

pageantry A form of splendid display, often seen as without substance. The term pageant dates from late medieval English, referring specifically to scenes acted out on a stage, or a single scene or act of a medieval mystery play; and to public and royal processions. At the end of such processions, spectacles of competition and physical contest and performance were sometimes arranged. In sporting competition, pageants and pageantry came to be associated with *jousting and *tournaments, and the public display of status and wealth could take over from the competitive events themselves. In 15th-century France, as Allen Guttmann (*Sport: The First Five Millennia*, 2004) notes, chivalric combat was certainly relegated to the sidelines in favour of the ceremony and costume of sumptuous festivals. Pageant cars became a bigger spectacle than the tournament, forms of *conspicuous consumption of the day as well as fantastical representation and performative display. More modern forms of sporting pageantry—such as *Olympic ceremony—also introduce the spectacle as a framing of the sporting competition, and also claim the larger audiences for the far from peripheral, and in fact often deeply ideological, sideshow.

paintball A sport or team game in which players shoot pellets containing paint at each other, using specifically designed paintball guns (also called 'markers'). In the USA, according to estimates by the *Sporting Goods Manufacturers Association, more than 5.4 million people played the game in 2007, over one and a half million of these playing fifteen times or more. In England, according to a

*Sport England 2005–6 survey, only 20,731 people in the adult population played the sport, though this was enough to place it seventy-fourth in the list of popular recreational sports. Paintball can be played indoors or outdoors, in woods with natural obstacles and barriers (woodsball), or on open fields with artificial obstacles (speedball). Participants wear paramilitary attire, and though enthusiasts hail the essential safety of the game, the pellets can be painful when striking the body, and leave bruising on the player. The most common form of the game is for opposing teams to aim to capture the other team's flag and relocate it in its starting position, reducing the ranks of the opposition in the process by landing direct shots of paint on individuals. Other variants include eliminating all of the other team, or introducing varied forms of attack or defence. The game became established in the 1980s and escalated in popularity in the 1990s, with an expanding number of tournaments and leagues; in the 2000s, some professional players began to make a living from the sport. To downplay the military connections (it has been used in some military training programmes), some players wear colourful athletic costumes rather than camouflage. But its paramilitary format is the essence of the sport, and it provides outlets for male combat fantasies in regular paintball contests, as well as more innocent fun for young people in one-off party-based outings.

Pan-American Games A multi-sport event staged every four years, featuring national teams of athletes from the Americas and the Caribbean.

panel studies Studies investigating change over time based on the continuing study of the opinions or views of a sample of people, called the 'panel'. They are in a broad sense *longitudinal studies, and are based on the questioning or interviewing of the same people at regular intervals in a specified period. Panel studies have great potential for the study of sporting *careers and of groups of sporting fans, and in their most sustained form for rigorous work on factors affecting sport performance.

pankration See OLYMPIC GAMES, ANCIENT.

panopticon A term first used by 18th-century English philosopher Jeremy *Bentham in his notion of an 'inspection house' model for institutions in which surveillance was an essential function: these included asylums, prisons, and workhouses. In the panopticon an inspection tower was at the centre of a circle of single, open cells. The inmates were therefore under constant surveillance, though not always aware of by whom, and when, they were being watched. Bentham conceived of a situation in which the dynamic of surveillance itself pervaded the panopticon, so that in its most developed form the surveillance might not need the actual presence of an inspector: seeing the inspection tower itself could effect the necessary control. Bentham's notion was taken up and developed by Michel *Foucault, and used to describe the workings of power in institutional and impersonal ways, linked to increasing forms of control and regulation in modern society. At first sight, the modern all-seated sport stadium, with its electronic security systems and its sophisticated technological forms of crowd control, might seem to be a further version of the panoptic process, though the stadium is more loosely structured than the panopticon ideal, and the licence granted to sport crowds more open-ended than that to the inmates of the panopticon. Nevertheless, Foucault's emphasis on increasing (and often invisible yet all-pervading) controls of the spaces of modern life has some resonance at sport events, particularly large-scale and high-profile ones at which security has become a major consideration.

parachuting The act of returning to the ground from an aircraft, suspended from the parachute that is opened after jumping from the aircraft: the parachute, made of a fabric such as silk, is designed to create drag and so slow the motion of the falling human body. The term derives from Latin *parare* ('to defend from') and French *chute* ('fall'). Competitive forms include 'accuracy jumping', aiming to land in a target area, and 'style jumping', in which predetermined manoeuvres are performed in freefall prior to opening the parachute. Parachuting as display and performance predated military or life-saving uses: jumps were made from towers in European cities in the 17th and 18th centuries; in 1797 André-Jacques Garnerin jumped from a balloon and descended over Paris; and in the USA circus-style touring exhibitions of jumpers drew large crowds from the 1880s. Contests began in the USA in the 1920s, and the Soviet Union also promoted the activity for both sporting and military purposes. Parachuting is also known as 'skydiving'. World championships are overseen by the Fédération Aéronautique Internationale, founded in 1905, and include a range of individual and team events for both men and women. Participants are mostly from the affluent countries of the world, comprising either a cosmopolitan hedonist clientele with adequate disposable income, or members of the military. *See also* AIRSPORTS.

paradigm From the Greek for 'example', the general sense of paradigm is of a pattern or an exemplar. In social science it has come to mean a particular way of going about the analysis of the topic being researched. In the work of US philosopher Thomas Kuhn (1922–96) the paradigm, as an exemplary way of conducting scientific puzzle-solving, produces a basis for normal science based upon a consensus view; this is the foundation of the perceived procedures of a mature science (*The Structure of Scientific Revolutions*, 1962). Science proceeds in this generally agreed-upon fashion, though still retaining the capacity to pose questions or puzzles that find no easy solution, so proving disruptive to the exemplar and ushering in a more volatile phase of potential scientific revolution. An immature science remains immature because it cannot find a paradigm providing such a foundation. Social scientists, and sociologists in particular, have argued that social science, not conducive to the shared practices and conventions of natural or laboratory sciences, is inherently pre-paradigmatic (in Kuhn's terms, therefore, forever immature). All scientific and social scientific researchers need to locate themselves in relation to the state of their discipline, and understand the nature of their scientific and research practice with reference to debates concerning the nature of paradigms and exemplars. A far too loose use of the term in sports studies, though, has led to talk of 'paradigm wars' between *qualitative and *quantitative approaches in social scientific work, or between opposing

theoretical approaches that are not really so different when identifying the
parameters of the discipline and the underlying principles on which it is based.

paragliding *See* AIRSPORTS.

Paralympics Competitive sport for athletes in *disability sports. The
International Paralympic Committee (IPC) stages the Winter and Summer
Paralympic Games, which has grown into a high-profile partner of the Olympic
Games. Sporting competition for people with disabilities had been organized by
Sir Ludwig Guttmann at Stoke Mandeville hospital in England in 1948, for war
veterans with spinal cord injuries, and in 1952 competitors from the Netherlands
joined the games. Four hundred athletes with disability (from 23 countries)
competed in some events alongside the 1960 Rome Olympics, and by the Athens
2004 Summer Olympics, Paralympic Games athletes numbered 3,806 (from
136 countries). From the Seoul 1988 Summer Games, and the Albertville 1992
Winter Games, the Paralympic Games have been staged at the same venues as
the Olympics. In 2001, the International Olympic Committee and the IPC signed an
agreement to establish this principle for the foreseeable future. The twenty sports
at the Summer Paralympics include *boccia*, a ball and target game that was
developed specifically for wheelchair-based players.

   The Paralympics has had an important influence upon the public perception of
disability, challenging stereotypes of able-bodied and disabled in the sphere of
athletic achievement and physical performance. It has also generated controversies
and ethical debates concerning the definition of disability, and the notion of
eligibility for the able-bodied Games—this latter in the case of the aspirations of
South African Oscar Pistorius, 200-metre gold medal winner at the Athens 2004
Paralympics, to run at the Olympics. Pistorius was born with no bones below
the knee, and competed with false lower legs that some commentators
considered to be artificial aids, giving potentially unfair advantage.

parkour From French *parcour* meaning 'trail or route', and sometimes called
'free running', this is an urban sport combining athletic and gymnastic skills in
using the built environment as a kind of obstacle course. It took some
established forms of military training techniques in Switzerland, adapted them
to an aesthetics of movement, and has claimed some counter-cultural youthful
adherents.

Parsons, Talcott (1902–79) In the mid 20th century, the dominant figure in
US sociology, and in all likelihood world sociology. His lifetime work was
dedicated to the development of a general sociological theory that could account for
modern society as exemplified in the affluent liberal democracy of the USA
itself, where at the time it was assumed that most social conflicts were
resolved or soluble: the framework for this theory became widely known as
structural-functionalism, as Parsons sought a general framework to account for
the whole of *The Social System* (1951). The core proposition of this framework
was that societies held together on the basis of pattern variables, and so every
aspect of society had its place that contributed to the equilibrium of the whole.
From such a perspective, sport could be seen as having an essentially

integrating role in the wider society, embodying widely held values and cementing consensus. Given the prominence of Parsons in general sociology, it is surprising that his elaborate framework has been relatively underdeveloped in the sociology of sport. Two reasons account for this: first, his work was subjected to widespread critique at the time of the 1960s cultural revolution and the Vietnam war (when it became unambiguously clear that US society was hardly the integrated harmonious whole depicted in Parsonian theory)—and this was a time of the emergence of the sociology of sport in the USA; and second, sociologists of sport of a functionalist persuasion could refer to classic functionalist theorists such as Émile *Durkheim, with no need to tackle the grand theoretical schemas, as C. Wright *Mills called them, of Parsons.

participant observation A social scientific method whereby the researcher adopts a position or role in a group, community, or organization, and as such is part of the ongoing everyday life and evolving social relations of those whom he or she is studying. A classic statement on the evolution of the participant observer's role is made by William Foot Whyte in his study *Street Corner Society: The Social Structure of an Italian Slum* (1943), in his Appendix on the evolution of the research study. Whyte studied his selected community of corner-boys and racketeers in 'Cornerville' from 1937 to 1940. To facilitate access to settings and subjects, he had found a gatekeeper, Doc, recommended by a community worker in a local settlement house, and moved into the community from his university base (Harvard) to live among the group that he was studying. He hung out with them, joined in social and club activities, including racketeering, and so developed from being a non-participant observer—'accepted into the community . . . becoming almost a nonobserving participant'—to having a more active, participatory role among the corner-boys: 'I was dealing with particular individuals and with particular groups . . . I was taking a moving picture instead of a still photograph.' To get such a dynamic picture of a selected group Whyte needed to be more than the proverbial 'fly on the wall', and this participant observer role might obviously affect the setting under observation. Doc actually recognized this, telling Whyte: 'You've slowed me up plenty since you've been down here. Now, when I do something, I have to think what Bill Whyte would want to know about it and how I can explain it. Before, I used to do things by instinct.'

Participant observation has its pitfalls and limitations then, but these are counterbalanced by the depth of data that the method can generate. In his 'Ethnographic Notes' appended to his 1993 study *Little Big Men: Bodybuilding Subculture and Gender Construction*, Alan Klein recalls the seven-year period during which he undertook 'field stints lasting from one month to one year at four locations on the West Coast' of the USA. These locations were elite gyms, and Klein trained for some of the time with the bodybuilders whom he was observing, and some of whom he was to interview, after introductions establishing him as a 'quasi-insider'; but not for all of his time there. Participant observation is not, therefore, an all-or-nothing position, and dovetails with other research methods that fit into a selected—and sometimes pragmatically developing—fieldwork strategy. Some illuminating accounts of the participant observer role, including considerations and reflections on the adoption of *covert and overt roles, can be found in Alan Tomlinson and Graham McFee's edited collection *Ethics, Sport and Leisure: Crises and Critiques* (1997). These include Belinda Wheaton on windsurfing subculture, Scott Fleming on Asian British schoolchildren, Ilkay Yorganci on sexual harassment of young athletes, and John Sugden on boxing subcultures. *See also* ETHNOGRAPHY; HAWTHORNE EFFECT; OBJECTIVITY.

paternalism A relationship between parties in which the dominant party views the subordinate groups and individuals as in need of—and potentially benefiting from—caring forms of provision. In his *Principles of Political Economy*, John Stuart *Mill commented of the relationship between the rich and the poor that it should be both authoritative and amiable: 'affectionate tutelage on the one side, respectful and grateful deference on the other. The rich should be in *loco parentis* to the poor, guiding and restraining them like children.' In the history of sport, employers and industrialists have often provided sport facilities and activities for their employees, in paternalist strategies to provide balance in the lives of those workers. Paul Gilchrist's 'Sport in the Shadow of Industry: Paternalism at Alfred Herbert Ltd' (in Alan Tomlinson and Jonathan Woodham, eds, *Image, Power and Space: Studies in Consumption and Identity*, 2007) looks at a particular case in Coventry, England, and also reviews the literature on enlightened and benevolent industrialists such as the Quaker families Rowntree and Cadbury. Gilchrist concludes his case study with the observation that such employers can generate vibrant sporting cultures, in which workers are aware that the playing conditions are not of their own choosing, but they are willing nevertheless to 'play the system to their own advantages'.

pato A sporting contest played on horseback by two teams of four, combining aspects of polo and basketball. Players dispute possession of a ball throughout six eight-minute periods; the ball has handles, players tug at it in the outstretched grip of rivals while both standing in their stirrups, and to score it must be thrown through a vertically positioned ring. Early forms were particularly popular among the gauchos of Argentina, dating in recognizable form from the end of the 18th century, but with a live duck rather than a ball: 'the game has been described as cruel and accident-prone, provoking the death of horses, local disorders, drunkenness and knife-duels among the participants' (Eduardo P. Archetti, *Masculinities: Football, Polo and the Tango in Argentina*, 1999). A playing area might then have been all of the land (with few if any declared boundaries) between neighbouring ranches, the victorious team being the one to reach its own ranch-house with the duck (*pato* is Spanish for duck) inside a basket. Such violent pre-modern forms generated moral disapproval, and religious and governmental interventions sought to ban the activity; General Rosa, governor of the province of Buenos Aires, outlawed the game in 1822. It has survived in a regulated, modified form established in the 1930s (in 1937, 10 November was declared the Day of Tradition by the national government), drawing upon the rules of modern *polo, and with a federation established in 1947. In the 1950s the country's president, Juan Perón, pronounced it to be the country's national game, though with its organized basis in the province of Buenos Aires it remains more a regional than a national game. The sport is played in organized competitive forms, and also features in festivals and fairs, perpetuating the macho values of a traditional, even primitivist sport of Argentina.

patriarchy 1. Literally, 'rule of the father', linked in English political science to the rationale for the divine right of kings. In a wider sense, patriarchy also generates associated value systems such as *paternalism. 2. In feminist theory, the system of power relations on the basis of which women are dominated by men. Locating the patriarchal roots of sport, and the capacity of a patriarchal system and culture to reproduce itself, has been an immense contribution to sports studies by feminist scholars. *See also* FEMININITY, CULTURE OF; FEMINISM; GENDER RELATIONS; MASCULINITY.

Patterson, Floyd (1935–2006) An African American boxer born in Waco, North Carolina, and raised in Brooklyn, New York, where boxing redirected him from a youth of street life and petty crime. Patterson became the youngest world heavyweight champion to date when defeating Archie Moore in 1956. Patterson had won the gold medal at middleweight in the Helsinki Olympics of 1952, and was the first Olympic gold medallist to go on to become a professional world champion. He lost his title to Swede Ingemar *Johansson in 1959, regaining it in 1961, but then losing it to Sonny *Liston in a first-round knockout in 1962. A rematch with Liston produced another first-round knockout. Patterson's experience of these defeats is often focused upon more than is his decade of achievement. Gay Talese, one of the architects of the *new journalism, captured the depression into which Patterson fell after his second defeat by Liston: 'At the foot of a mountain in upstate New York, about sixty miles from Manhattan . . . Patterson lives alone in a two-room apartment in the rear of the house and has remained there in almost complete seclusion since getting knocked out a second time by Sonny Liston' ('The Loser', in *Fame and Obscurity*, 1981). Talese also wrote of how Patterson, haunted by the prospect and consequences of failure, had carried with him a set of false whiskers and moustache ever since his defeat to Johansson in 1959, for disguise and escape. Patterson recovered from his depression to relaunch his fighting career and live a dignified and respected life, but Talese's close-up profile of the still young 29-year-old fighter demonstrates the vicissitudes and personal costs of sporting celebrity and fame. To some, though, his respectability on his re-emergence in public life confirmed his reactionary cultural and political position: from such a perspective his role as New York City boxing commissioner confirmed his status as the 'house negro' of the Republicans.

PB *See* PERSONAL BEST.

peaking A reduction in the volume and/or intensity of training in the period leading up to a competition in order to achieve a peak performance. This adjustment to the training regime is also known as tapering. Peaking is based on the theory that while an athlete's intense training is promoting physiological adaptation, its daily basis never gives the body adequate time to recuperate fully, leaving the athlete in a state of chronic, mild, relative weakness and under-performance. A period of 3 to 7 days of reduced training allows physiological systems to recover, resulting in maximal levels of *glycogen stores, blood volume, and muscle enzymes. Further, minor injuries can heal and the athlete is psychologically refreshed. A reduction in the volume of training while retaining some high-intensity work appears optimal.

pedestrianism A term referring to competitive walking or running contests, popular and prominent from the late 17th to the early 19th century in Britain. Individuals were professionals, competing for prize money or as representatives of gentlemen who were wagering sums on the outcome of the race. Prominent pedestrians included Foster Powell and Captain *Barclay. Pedestrianism was also associated with the manipulation of the outcome of the race, and as such was morally disapproved of by the proponents of *amateurism and *athleticism. Pedestrian contests were predominantly between males, but also took place between females. Pedestrianism was the most popular sport in the USA from the 1830s up to the 1860s (when the Civil War began), and attracted top professional runners from England. Local sports entrepreneurs would offer prize monies for set challenges, some, in the 1840s, for as much as a thousand dollars, attracting forty thousand spectators. Allen Guttmann observes that the standardization of equipment and the design of 'measured tracks' undermined pedestrianism's model of 'challenge matches for high stakes', and pedestrianism in the USA was superseded by 'an American equivalent of the Oxford-Cambridge athletics meets' (*Sports: The First Five Millennia*, 2001).

pelota The generic name for a variety of ball games, played using hand, glove, racquet, or bat, that are said to have derived from the French *jeu de paume*, and which were developed in the Basque regions of France and Spain. Its variants have flourished in all of the South American countries, North America, and parts of Asia. A national French association was formed for the sport in 1921, standardizing rules and practices, and The International Federation of Basque Pelota was formed at the end of that decade, classifying forms and modalities of the sport. The sport was included in early Olympics and then as a demonstration sport at Hispanic-based Games in Mexico in 1968 and Barcelona in 1992.

pentathlon, modern *See* MODERN PENTATHLON.

performativity A 'carry-home concept', James Loxley (*Performativity*, 2007), citing a colleague, called this term. It is carry-home and convenient in its apparent capacity to give focus to an important idea, to be used without too much difficulty out of the context of its original formulation, and in its applicability to numerous contexts and intellectual challenges. The term has a clear appeal to the sport scholar, in a range of sport contexts: the strutting individual bodybuilder at the gymnasium; the expensively attired fun runner on the streets or in the park; the arrival of the high-performance team in the atmospheric stadium—in all of these cases, the sport is a form of performance, and the concept of performativity, understood as the theorization of performance and the impact of a performance on an audience or onlooker, appears to have much potential for the analysis of sport.

The conceptual origins of the term lie in the work of the English philosopher J. L. Austin (1911–60), who understood the 'speech act' as a form of performance, its performative impact demonstrating that words themselves are performed actions like any other action; and they make a difference to the world, even make a world themselves. Clearly, the application of such a perspective to sporting actions and practices might highlight the meaning-making significance of a sporting encounter or event. Performativity has also been used by feminist scholars, most notably Judith Butler (for instance, *Gender Trouble: Feminism and the Subversion of Identity*, 1999), to aid the critical analysis of gendered identities, thus combining the conceptual stance of deconstruction with a cultural politics of intervention and change; 'Is "the Body" itself shaped by particular forces with strategic interests in keeping that body bounded and constituted by the markers of sex?', Butler asked. Within sports studies, *queer theory has provided a vehicle for the exploration of the performative dimensions of the sporting body.

periodization The dividing up of longer historical processes into phases or periods, allowing the historian to identify distinctive patterns or features of a sport or leisure culture, or a particular sporting practice or institution. On a general level, Peter Borsay (*A History of Leisure: The British Experience since 1500*, 2006) has identified 'six phases of change between 1500 and 2000': 1350–1530, a late medieval period of communal customs; 1530–1660, stimulated by the Reformation and leading to a Protestant suppression of some games and sports, and the increasing recognition of the importance of 'hard work'; 1660–1780, following the Restoration of Charles II, and in the context of the Enlightenment, an increase in the commercialization of leisure, including *horse racing; 1780–1870, a quickening of industrial growth, in the context of the Industrial Revolution and urban expansion, including critiques of popular recreations and the structuring of new ways of playing; 1870–1960, with the growth of communications and technology underpinning a transformation of the leisure and sporting culture of the country; and 1960 to the present day, 'comprising the internationalization and globalization of leisure through developments in the media, communications and transport.' John Bale (*Sports Geography*, 1989) has provided a useful periodization of sporting institutions, identifying five stages through which, in the transition from folk game to the modern form, a sport has typically developed: folk game; club formation; establishment of rule-making national bureaucracy; diffusion of sport to, and adoption in, other countries; and formation of an international bureaucracy. Approaching the historical narrative of any sport's development, it is useful to draw on such models of periodization as a means of identifying patterns and commonalities in the more general history of sporting developments.

Perry, Fred (Frederick John) (1909–95) An English-born tennis player who won the men's Wimbledon championship in three consecutive years (1934–6), among his eight *Grand Slam victories. He was the first player to win all four Grand Slam championships, after which he turned professional and lived in the USA. Perry had been world-champion table-tennis player at the age of 20, and trained at tennis with great commitment and ambition, making him a fearsome competitor for Britain in *Davis Cup matches, as well as an outstanding individual tournament player. He combined his professional playing career with successful businesses in the sportswear industry and personal coaching. Perry was from modest social origins though his father, a cotton spinner, became a Labour Member of Parliament in the national UK government. Perry had felt snubbed by the Wimbledon establishment when winning its championship in 1934, the first Englishman to triumph there in twenty years. He wrote in his autobiography of how he felt shunned and often related the words that he overheard spoken by a member of the All England Club (Wimbledon) committee to the defending, but defeated Australian champion Jack Crawford: 'Congratulations. This was one day when the best man didn't win.'

Perry saw the USA as a far more open and accepting society for the ambitious sports professional, touring successfully, gaining sponsorship from Slazenger, buying a share of the Beverly Hills Tennis Club, founding Fred Perry Sportswear in 1950, and also serving in the US airforce in World War II and adopting US citizenship. He commentated for the BBC—proving itself a less rigid British institution than the tennis establishment—at Wimbledon from 1948. In 1984, though, commemorating the half-century that had passed since Perry's first Wimbledon victory, the All England Club commissioned a statue of him by David Wynne (in the rose garden opposite the members' enclosure), and renamed the entrance to the grounds in Somerset Road the 'Fred Perry Gates'. Perry's life and career illuminated the changing ethos of the sporting establishment and the changing status of the sporting celebrity: 'with the abolition of the old amateur–professional distinctions, the British tennis establishment began to look more fondly on their erstwhile rebel son', as Tony Mason writes (*Oxford Dictionary of National Biography*, 2004). Mason adds that 'in a typical Perry mixture of pride and wit he pointed out that whenever he turned up at Wimbledon without a pass', he just pointed at the statue and said to the gateman 'That's me'.

personal best A term that, abbreviated to PB, has passed into everyday use and is used by sporting participants in individual activities to measure and gauge their developing levels of performance. Although the PB might have connotations of elite performance and therefore unattainability for the majority, it is equally appropriate for participants at any level, as a guide to personal achievement and aspirations.

Personal Best A 1982 film focusing upon the relationships among women aspiring to qualify for the US Olympics track-and-field team. It provided an exploration of athlete–coach dynamics, but more unusually of the sexual identities of its protagonists, including an older lesbian athlete.

pétanque A French form of *bowls, or boules (a variant of the latter is also known as *boules Lyonnaise*, based in the Lyons region of France). Standing with the feet together at a specified mark, the player aims metal balls at a small wooden ball, on a gravel or dirt surface. The game is widely played in France, where every small town or village will have enthusiasts and dedicated public areas for play; the game can also be played on grass surfaces. It originated in the first decade of the 20th century in Provence, whose dialect gave the sport its name, *pétanque* meaning 'feet closed', referring to how the thrower must keep the feet together when launching the ball. The Fédération Française de Pétanque & de Jeu Provençal has reported 375,000 registered players, though millions of French people play the game casually, on vacations and on feast-days. The federation abides by the national Ministry of Youth and Sport's conditions, and so declares its support for the fight against doping/drugs, an absurd necessity for an accessible, inexpensive sport rooted in tradition, community, and recreational leisure.

phenomenology A branch of philosophy that has generated a position in social theory that prioritizes the study of consciousness. It is premised on the view that the world that we inhabit is a product of our actions and our (often intentional) conscious projections; and that the only phenomenon about which we can have any certainty is consciousness itself. Categories such as lived experience, and subjective experience, are central in the phenomenologist's conceptual armoury. To achieve this sort of analysis, the phenomenologist argued that belief in the existence of the 'outer world' should be suspended, as Alfred *Schutz wrote, in the attempt 'to disclose the pure field of consciousness'. One could imagine some branches of sport psychology adopting such a position, and in general psychology the phenomenological approach has come to mean a concentration on mental acts as opposed to behaviour. But the application of the approach in sports studies has been limited, as is the case in established sociology. Phenomenology was nevertheless an important corrective to accounts of the social world that left little scope for the recognition of human agency. An accessible, lucid, and persuasive critique of the phenomenological stance is available in Part III of Richard J. Bernstein's *The Restructuring of Social and Political Theory* (1976).

phersu The Etruscan word for a mask; murals in an Etruscan tomb depicting a masked man disguised as an animal, confronting a dog, and a man fleeing, have been taken by some as evidence of an Etruscan sport that may have influenced Roman games; though as Allen Guttmann observes, if this was at all the case, 'it was probably upon the *venations*, in which men were matched against wild animals' (*Sports: The First Five Millennia*, 2004).

Phidippides Phidippides was a soldier/messenger sent by the Athenians to other Greek city-states to raise troops to resist the invasion of the Persians, reported as running the 140 miles to Sparta in 36 hours—and back. A messenger—widely, but possibly apocryphally, reported as Phidippides—ran from the Battle of Marathon (490 BC) to Athens, a distance of 26 miles, to relay news of the Athenian triumph over the more numerous and powerful Persians; and, his mission accomplished, collapsed and died of exhaustion. In commemoration of this historical legend, the Greek hosts included the marathon event in the first modern Olympic Games at Athens in 1896, when the victory of Spiridon *Loues was a highlight of the proceedings.

physical activity A term relating to the recreational and sporting practices of individuals or groups. Many surveys of sport include informal physical activities such as walking, or individual forms of exercise, alongside more organized collective forms of activity, and so the general term has some currency. It has some uses as a synonym for fitness programmes but is too loose a term to be of real analytical use.

physical education A generic term referring to the institutionalization of exercise, games, and sports in the educational institution, particularly the school. It has become a widely accepted term for the school-based curriculum covering what has sometimes been called movement education. Curricula vary widely across different societies and cultures, and there has been long-standing debate on the relationship between organized sport outside the curriculum and the activities within the curriculum itself. The term can also be used to refer to general philosophies of the body or of physical well-being, or to exercise activities organized by voluntary bodies or non-educational organizations. *See also* GALEN; JAHN, FRIEDRICH LUDWIG; LING, PER HENRIK; ÖSTERBERG, MARTINA SOFIA HELENA BERGMAN; SPENCER, HERBERT; WILKIE, DORETTE.

pigeon racing A sport in which the (predominantly male) enthusiast (or 'fancier') combines the roles of owner, breeder, trainer, and gambler, in preparing to release 'homing' pigeons from a specified racepoint from which they then fly back to the owner, who presents the verifiable pigeon at the agreed reporting centre. The winner is the bird covering the journey—which can be hundreds of miles—from the point of release or 'liberation' at the highest average speed. The sport became popular in Belgium and the United Kingdom: the Royal Fédération Colombophile Belge was formed in the 1890s, and the (British) National Homing Union in 1896, in Leeds and Manchester in the north of England (this later became the Royal Pigeon Racing Association or RPRA). The emergence of the railways in the 19th century allowed working-class people access to points from which races could start, and in the late 1950s the Midland region of British railways reported that it carried over three million pigeons to races every week. Ron Bisset (*Pigeon Racing and Fancying*, 1963) observed that 'pigeon racing is the only sport in which a man can compete in his own home and in which his family can take part', in a 'wonderful competitive yet cooperative spirit' with husband and wife racing pigeons against each other.

Homing pigeons have been vital means of communication in wartime in the 20th century, and the British monarch Edward VII (1841–1910) raced pigeons, a tradition maintained by Queen Elizabeth II's Royal Lofts at her Sandringham residence. The RPRA estimates that in the late 1980s it had 60,000 members, since when the membership has been 'declining steadily', though the sport stays faithful to its northern English roots with an annual show at the coastal resort of Blackpool. One of the attractions of the sport is the lack of firm knowledge about what actually enables the pigeon to fly 'home': in this sense, the appeal of the sport can be seen to combine instinct with analysis, empowering the working man and woman with a sense of creative cultural accomplishment of their own making.

pig-sticking The 'running down and spearing of a boar from horseback' (Richard Holt, *Sport and the British: A Modern History*, 1989). This was a practice popular among the officer class of the British military in India in the 19th century. The boars were strong, dangerous, and mature, and the activity was popular among officers as a substitute for fox hunting. The Meeret Tent Club established the Kadir Cup in 1874, awarded to outstanding individual riders, and a Muttra Cup was inaugurated for team events based upon how much 'pig' teams of three could kill.

Justified as a means of sustaining the 'fitness and morale of officers', as Holt observes, pig-sticking, with its inherently barbaric nature, remained the indulgence of the imperious and cruel British officer class.

pilates A form of exercise designed to develop body awareness and cultivate flexibility, sound posture, and ease of movement, in part based upon breathing techniques. It is based upon the movement theory of Joseph Hubertus *Pilates, German-born movement theorist with a childhood background of sickliness and bullying by other boys. Pilates spent time during his twenties in England in boxing and circus performance. In the 1920s, he moved to New York and opened a studio focused upon his method, and included among his clients the dancer Martha Graham and her pupils. The Pilates Method spread after Pilates' lifetime, as converts and followers of the method opened venues in London, and disseminated the method in the new technological form of the video, linked to celebrity endorsements of the approach. Pilates adherents claim a holistic approach to physical well-being, and in the UK it has one of the most expanding profiles for physical activity or *sport participation in the early 21st century. Its expanding profile and increasing popularity are explained in part by both its widespread use in rehabilitation after injury (as recommended by physiotherapists), and the recognition of its value as an element in sports training for numerous sports.

Pilates, Joseph Hubertus (1880–1967) German inventor of *pilates, a method of physical fitness. Pilates' father was an elite gymnast, his mother a naturopath. Taunted as a child for the similarity of the family name to the killer of Jesus Christ, Pilates was also asthmatic and in ill health. He found in physical exercise and strength-development programmes the means to establish self-esteem, and from his study of gymnastics, yoga, and bodybuilding he devised the Pilates system, which he piloted among inmates in an internment camp on the Isle of Man during World War I, having moved to England in 1912. It was his move to New York City (c.1925) that established a base for the recognition and popularity of his system, particularly among performing artists, and his clients included dancer Martha Graham. Pilates and his wife Clara had initially called the system 'contrology', and one of his co-authored, main books, *Return to Life through Contrology* (1945), captured in its title the system's promise of personal, individual restoration.

pistol shooting *See* SHOOTING.

player migration The flow of professional sportspeople across national borders. There is a long history of player migration—black US boxers to England in the early 19th century, Indian cricketers to England in the late Victorian age, South American footballers to Europe in the mid 20th century, and black African footballers to European leagues in the later 20th century are just some examples. While player migration represents a principle of open opportunities and global markets in sport, it also leads to controversies concerning the national balance of sport teams, the rapidity of changed citizenship status, and the exploitative dynamic of advanced nations' recruitment of players from underdeveloped nations.

plc In the United Kingdom, the acronym for a public limited company, which means a limited company that can offer shares for sale to the public. Numerous

British football clubs transformed themselves into plcs in the 1990s, though only
Manchester United and Arsenal were reporting rises in share prices by 2004/5.
The debate within the football world set the notion of the club as a community
asset against that of the club as a money-making corporation. In 2004 Alex Flitcroft,
head of sport at accounting and consultancy firm Ernst & Young, commented
that: 'Football clubs are not suited to PLC status . . . promotion and relegation create
too much uncertainty', fans are inherently anti-corporate, and falling revenues
are a 'poor bet' for investors. A club like Manchester United, with its profile and
business plan, was perhaps an exception, he conceded. But by any economic
criteria, football clubs below the very top levels of the game are widely recognized
as non-profitable financial risks.

pleasure   Sport is plainly a source of pleasure, and associated elements of
experience such as fun and joy; Norbert Elias included sport as one contributory
area to the neglected sociology of the emotions. Michel Novak's *The Joy of Sports*
(1976) recognized this emotional side of sport: 'Sports are bursts of dust, squeaky
wood, infield grass, collisions at second base, an explosive tackle—they are vivid,
concrete, swift and fun.' But the 'joy' that Novak was really interested in, as a
theologian, was religious joy, and he saw sports as 'natural religions' which in
pushing humanness to extremes provide a kind of testing-ground for faith and
religious virtues: 'Sports tutor us in the basic lived experiences of the humanist
tradition.'

    There are other ways of accounting for the pleasures expressed in sport, though,
including approaches in cultural and film studies, drawing upon theorists such as
dramatist Bertolt Brecht (1898–1956) and semiotician Roland Barthes (1915–80).
Brecht, as a revolutionary Marxist intellectual, opposed the forms of theatre in
which audiences simply accepted what was represented on stage, in a form of
passive watching rather than active engagement; he sought to develop an epic
theatre in which the simple pleasures of such watching were disrupted by the
questioning of orthodoxies, and for which new relations between audience and
performance might be devised. Barthes's work developed categories related to
the process of reading, and in *The Pleasure of the Text* (1975) he distinguished
between the text of pleasure and the text of bliss: in the former, reading is comfortable,
it 'contents, fills' and 'grants euphoria' to the reader; in the latter, the text discomforts,
unsettling the readers' cultural, psychological, and historical assumptions, and his
or her 'tastes, values, memories'. Sporting contests clearly rest for the most part in
the category of Brecht's passive watching, and Barthes's text of pleasure; the
abandonment of memory, history, culture, of comfortable identification with the
team, would jeopardize the supporter–team, or fan–player, dynamic.

    Yet there is also something in the sporting contest that rises above the
comfortable, the suspense attained by the built-in *narrative of the contest; an
ecstasy of identification with the execution of the supreme athletic skill or sporting
performance. Hans-Ulrich Gumbrecht captures this at the end of his *In Praise
of Athletic Beauty* (2006), quoting his friend Martin Seel: 'By watching sports we
can enjoy, in our imagination, certain lives that we have neither the talent nor the
time to live.' Perhaps this is where the secret of the pleasures of sport spectating at
least lies; in the vicarious pleasure that sport grants us of being part of a special

moment, on the edge of a state of bliss, or in Barthes's own word **jouissance*. And
this is far from a comfortable state, or a mere condition of *bread and races, so
demonstrating that the pleasures of sports transcend the divisions of the Brechtian
and Barthesian categorizations. *See also* ONE-DIMENSIONAL MAN.

Plimpton, George Ames (1927–2003) A US writer whose forays into the world
of competitive sports generated several best-selling books in which the culture of
the professional sports world was laid bare. These included *Out of My League*
(1960), on baseball; *Paper Lion* (1964), on American football; and *The Bogey Man*
(1967), on golf. Combining diaries and observation, and appropriate commissions
and projects for *Sports Illustrated, in the mode of the *new journalism, Plimpton
crafted a distinctive mode of sports reporting that is of value as well to social
scientists interested in the inner culture of the professional sports world. His
knack was also to live the amateur's dream of contact with the stars, including
sparring with world champion boxers for one of his journalistic assignments.
Training pre-season with the Detroit Lions, he insisted that he should be 'thought of
as just another rookie, an odd one maybe, but no special favors or anything because
I'm a writer. The point is to write about it first hand.' In the more individual sport
of golf, he wrote, almost all can aspire to a single moment of playing like the
champion:

> High performance in the great spectator sports for the average man exists
> only in his daydreams; but the Olympian glory of a hole played in par, or a
> birdie, is always a possibility, even in the game of the direst duffer; all he
> must do (he keeps telling himself) is to put three or four shots together.

This combination of bravado, experience, observation, and high-quality writing
blended humorous reportage with serious commentary on the culture and
practices of the sporting elite.

ploughing One of what Allen Guttmann calls 'workplace competitions'
(*Sports: The First Five Millennia*, 2004), in which ploughers have a set time in which
to plough a number of rows as straight as they can, and as cleanly as
possible. Competitions continue in local agrarian and rural districts, such as parts
of south-west Ireland, and according to categorizations of machine or tractor,
or horse and plough.

plyometrics A form of resistance training designed to improve explosive power.
Plyometrics is based on the proposition that stimulating a muscle's stretch reflex
can lead to a more powerful contraction and thus a greater training effect.
Plyometrics consists of a variety of jumping and bounding exercises, using the body
mass as resistance. An example exercise is jumping down from a box to the floor
and then immediately jumping explosively upwards in the air. The rapid
lengthening of the muscle as the athlete lands on the ground initiates a contraction
of the leg muscles (a reflex reaction to prevent damage from over-stretching),
leading to a more forceful subsequent upward jump. Since plyometric exercises
can closely replicate the type of movement often seen in sport, such as a sprint
start or a basketball dunk, this form of exercise may also improve neuromuscular

coordination. Plyometrics is an effective means to improve muscle power but the high-impact forces involved carry a risk of injury, which limits its value.

pole vault An established event in athletic programmes, in which the vaulter uses a pole to lever his or her body over a horizontal bar that is raised until a single competitor has cleared the greatest height. Precursors of the modern form are said to be forms of vaulting in marshy terrain, but as a formalized athletic activity the pole vault was not established until the 19th century, in forms of German gymnastics and in athletic competition in the USA. It has been a staple of the Olympic programme (for men) since the first modern Games in Athens in 1896, and US men won every Olympic competition from then until 1968, recognized as the longest winning streak by a nation in Olympic history. A German Democratic Republic athlete ended this streak at the Munich Games in 1972, amid controversy and farce concerning the rules whereby particular types of pole could be used. Women's pole vaulting entered the Olympics only in Sydney in 2000, showing the remarkable longevity of the persistence of the prejudices that restricted women's participation in the full range of sporting competition. The inaugural women's champion, Stacy Dragila of the USA, had posed naked for a calendar before the event; the silver medallist, Russian-born Australian Tatiana Grigorieva, had modelled for a magazine. The contradictions of breakthroughs in women's sport were captured in Dragila's comment that athletics organizers now wanted women vaulters: 'Back when I started . . . [they] thought we were boring. Now that there's hot chicks out there clearing fifteen feet, they want us.'

policy The adopted and stated course of action, including intentions, aspirations, and objectives, of an administration or government. Sport policies of governments have usually related to issues such as the health of the population and sport's potential benefits to healthier living; and to increased and widening participation in sport and the national prestige that might accrue from success in sport (this latter dubbed, more recently, 'podium policy'). In numerous cases, a so-called *pyramid model of sport involvement has been said to underpin both increased involvement and national success. The French *politique* refers to both policy and politics, a recognition that these spheres of operation are interdependent.

policy community A set of interrelated actors (individuals and organizations) with a common interest in an issue or a problem that could be furthered on the basis of governmental policy. An effective policy community is usually a relatively small group with shared views, values, and interests, and good access to influential figures in the policy-making process. Barrie Houlihan's 'The Politics of Sports Policy in Britain: The Example of Drug Abuse' (in *Leisure Studies*, 9/1, 1990) adapts M. Laffin's writings, on professional and policy communities, to the sport context. He shows that, though some of the conditions of the policy community are met by those concerned with drug abuse in sport, the vital ingredient of value consensus 'seems to be missing', so rendering this particular policy community less influential and effective.

policy cycle The process, from agenda-setting through decision-making and potential implementation and evaluation, whereby policy emerges, is or is not adopted and implemented, and, if implemented, is then sustained (see Brian Hogwood and Lewis Gunn, *Policy Analysis for the Real World*, 1985). In liberal democracies, sporting interest groups are so varied and dispersed, and potentially in opposition to one another, that the stages necessary for the genesis of sport policy within the political system are complicated and hazardous.

policy network The linked organizations and individuals for which and whom a particular issue or policy is a potentially common and binding concern. Policy networks exist as informal pressure groups with the potential to set the policy agenda, or contribute to debate concerning the policy-making process. Organizing bodies of sport; local authority sport and leisure professionals; physical educationists and sport development officers; government policy-makers in sport and education—all of these might be recognized as parts of a national policy network. Such networks may, though, lack the unity and coherent vision to seriously affect the policy process, and so are less obviously influential than are *policy communities of fewer, but like-minded, actors.

polo A four-a-side stick-and-ball game in which players mounted on ponies or horses use long sticks with mallet heads to strike a wooden ball towards the opposing side's goal. Records exist of variants of the sport being played in ancient cultures, including Persia, Arabia, Byzantine Greece, Japan, and China. Its modern form was established by British army officers who discovered the sport in Assam, India, in the 1850s. The first polo club was established in Calcutta in 1862, and the game spread beyond the British cavalry to become a source of status among Indian princes. Hounslow Heath, west London, was the venue for Britain's first polo match between the Tenth Hussars and the Ninth Lancers. British teams dominated the polo event at the Olympic Games of 1900, 1908, and 1920, but at Paris in 1924 Argentina took the title. Polo's final appearance at the Olympics was at Berlin in 1936, when Argentina defeated Great Britain 11–0.

  Polo remains a sport of the privileged few, and any observer at one of its remaining sites, such as Cowdray Park Polo Club ('the home of English polo') in West Sussex, England, can confirm its continuing cultural exclusivity, and its place—alongside pony riding for young females in the Pony Club—in the minority culture of an affluent elite: the club's annual Gold Cup championship is sponsored by Veuve Clicquot champagne house (of Reims, France, founded in 1722). In Argentina, a British Polo Association of the River Plate was replaced by the Asociación de Polo de Argentina in 1923, and the British imperial game was essentially 'nationalized' (Eduardo Archetti, *Masculinities: Football, Polo and the Tango in Argentina*, 1999). Argentina's Polo Open championship became the leading international tournament.

pool A cue-and-ball game played recreationally in clubs and public venues, such as bars and poolrooms in the USA and, in England, the public house; and with a long tradition of wagering, betting, and hustling in the USA. 'Toward the middle of the nineteenth century, hard upon the great waves of Irish and German immigration, the American poolroom began to emerge as the major physical locus of the rising bachelor sub-culture' (Ned Polsky, *Hustlers, Beats and Others*, 1967). There are variants of the game (English pool has smaller pockets than

American pool, for instance), and the American version has gained most popularity among young players. A World Confederation of Billiards Sports, formed in 1992 and based in Belgium, reports 148 nationally affiliated associations and has lobbied, with negligible impact, for the inclusion of billiard sports as a discipline in the Olympic programme (though the International Olympic Committee has included the generic category on its lists of recognized sports). In North America, the United States Professional Poolplayers Association promotes championships and touring events, and there is also a women's professional tour.

positivism   A term derived from the work of French social theorist Auguste Comte (1798–1857). Comte coined the term 'sociology' in the context of the development of what he called a 'positive philosophy', with the stress on the positive nature of the endeavour. He took the natural sciences as the model for the development of a new science of social physics, later renamed sociology. Positivism in the social sciences has come to be associated with several core tenets: that the social world can be understood on the basis of the same procedures as are employed in the natural sciences; that knowledge is based on experience, and the kind of facts that are generated by close observation; that reliably generated knowledge can achieve lawlike generalizations about the social world; and that scientific knowledge is neutral. Although in modern social science positivism has been widely denigrated, and *interpretivism recognized as a more suitable framework for understanding sociocultural phenomena, a knowledge of the nature of the positivist debate remains important as a dimension of the philosophy of science. Within sports studies this remains especially important, so that neither sport science research nor sociocultural studies are undertaken in ignorance of such fundamental debates about the nature of science.

postcolonialism   A term used to refer both to a historical phase in which cultures, societies, and nations emerged from periods of colonial domination, and to perspectives developed to speak on behalf of colonized peoples as opposed to writing the history of the colonizers. Postcolonial theory has generated important concepts such as *alterity and *hybridity. John Bale and Mike Cronin (*Sport and Postcolonialism*, 2003) have identified 'seven types of postcolonial sports or sportoid forms'. First, pre-colonial body cultures that were never reshaped into modern forms, surviving colonialism and preserving their own cultural character: their example is Rwandan high jumping. Second, indigenous forms, such as lacrosse, that were transformed into modern sports. Third, sport forms created by former colonies, such as baseball and basketball in the USA, to assert a sense of cultural autonomy. Fourth, colonial sports modified into national ones, as in the case of Australian Rules football and Gaelic football. Fifth, sports established by imperialists and adopted with no changes in the colonized countries, such as association football and cricket. Sixth, sports established within the colonizing process, but adapted in particular ways to develop distinctive styles: Kenyan running and Brazilian football, for instance. And seventh, 'hybrid sportoids' such as *Trobriand cricket.

   Postcolonial sport has been widely seen as a form of resistance, by colonies, to the dominant colonial powers or authorities, and for Bale and Cronin a postcolonial method applied to sports and body cultures can not just highlight the colonial relations between colonized and colonizer, but could provide 'alternative readings of conventional colonial wisdoms and dominant meanings', and generate new understandings, or rewritings, of colonial texts, practices, and discourses. The core idea of the postcolonial framework is the notion that culture can be analysed, history reinterpreted, from a subaltern (from below) perspective, disputing the accounts and the histories of the dominant colonial voices. Revitalized understandings of sport and associated conceptions of the body in the colonial context can be generated from such a perspective.

postmodernism and postmodernity 'The postmodern is many things to many people', writes Toby Miller (*Technologies of Truth: Cultural Citizenship and the Popular Media*, 1998). These many things include: the aesthetic style that draws upon a range of sources to create new cultural mixes; a historical framework in which an economic internationalism changes the global balance of service and manufacturing industries; a philosophical approach deconstructing established forms of knowledge; an identity politics going beyond class-based or constitutional criteria in defining political action; a decline of large-scale theories or grand narratives seeking to explain the whole of human and social complexity in one framework; and an array of conceptual approaches deriving from these five trends. If the term modern conjures up—albeit in exaggerated form—associations of certainty, the postmodern concern is with the sources of uncertainty and constant renewal and innovation in cultural life. Chris Rojek (*Decentring Leisure: Rethinking Leisure Theory*, 1998) identifies three social formations: capitalism, modernity, and postmodernity, the latter widely recognized as emerging in the later 20th century, driven by new communication technologies and processes of globalization.

Some new forms of sport might be described as postmodern, in their break with the conventions, structures, and assumptions of mainstream dominant sports. Lincoln Allison (*The Changing Politics of Sport*, 1993), warning against the use of the term postmodernism ('a promiscuous and mystical term which is high on fashionability and low on clarity'), nevertheless outlined how sport at the end of the 20th century could be seen as postmodern: 'there is the breakdown of a unified, rationalised pattern and a return to aspects of the pre-modern; no longer is there consensus on the direction of progress; developments are very diffused'. With the fuller emergence of *extreme sports and the mediatization of traditional sports creating new modes of consumption, the sporting landscape cannot be conceived on the basis of any single, all-embracing analytical model. The *cultural turn in history, sociology, and areas such as sports studies recognizes this. An emphasis on the postmodern characteristics of some sports, though, should not lead to the complete jettisoning of concepts such as class and power. The 'very diffused' developments of which Allison rightly talks may well remain in the interests of particular sets of entrepreneurs and business concerns. *See also* MODERNITY.

post-structuralism An intellectual movement based initially in French social theory and philosophy in the 1960s and the 1970s, and emanating in great part from the works of French social theorist Jacques Derrida (1930–2004). The movement prioritized the study of language within its own meaning-making terms, with no need for reference to a world beyond language itself (the structured and structuring world which the post-structuralist was aspiring to transcend). In relation to sport, post-structuralist interventions have been part of the wider *cultural turn in the field, and have brought to the fore analyses of the sporting body and its ideological significance, and—particularly in feminist applications of post-structuralist approaches—of the place and power of sport-based discourses and practices.

power Thinking about and researching power is fundamental to the study of the place of sport in society. Anthony Giddens (*The Constitution of Society: Outline of a Theory of Structuration*, 1984) developed *structuration theory as a departure from the dichotomous agency–structure debates, to synthesize elements of classical sociological positions and rework them in an integrated and interpretative sociology centred around power relations. For Giddens power is the central dynamic of all human societies, at all levels of institutional life, interpersonal relations, and everyday practice. It is not merely a matter of having power or not having power; rather, power relations are inherent in and integral to all social life: 'The use of power characterizes not specific types of conduct but all action.' It is the omnipresent transformative capacity of power that is important, its place in the relations between all parties in the power relation, and Giddens draws our attention to what he calls the 'dialectic of control'.

This notion involves two key elements: the first centres on the idea that all human beings possess some power in the form of their ability to transform, to some extent, the circumstances in which they find themselves; the second element follows from this and points to the fact that, although it is usually one person or a group that dominates in a power relationship, the subordinate individual or group always has some power. Philosophy, particularly in the writings of Bertrand Russell, provided an early and powerful rationale for this position. Writing in the context of Nazi and Stalinist totalitarianism, Russell (*Power: A New Social Analysis*, 1940) saw 'love of power' as the critical determinant of social affairs, and power as the 'fundamental concept in social science', just as energy is 'the fundamental concept in physics'. Forms of power might include 'wealth, armaments, civil authority, influence on opinion', but none of these 'can be regarded as subordinate to any other, and there is no one form from which the others are derived'. Russell defined power as the 'production of intended effects . . . ; it is easy to say, roughly, that A has more power than B, if A achieves many intended effects and B only a few'. Clearly this does not mean that B is powerless, but simply that B is less powerful than A. For Russell, power over human beings involves the influencing of individuals by (a) direct physical power, typically exercised by organizations such as the army and the police; (b) inducements on the basis of rewards and punishments, typically used by employers or economic organizations; and (c) the influencing of opinion, or propaganda, including the cultivation of 'desired habits in others', such as military drill, by organizations such as schools, churches, and political parties. Russell, taking a leaf out of Max *Weber's book, also distinguished between traditional, naked, and revolutionary power, and explored different forms of the power of individuals: the business executive, the politician, and the wire-puller behind the scenes.

Social scientists should recognize and seek to understand and explain when, why, and how power transforms from one of its dimensions, or balance of dimensions, to another. Too often, treatments of power have lacked Russell's detail and subtlety, by locating power in only one source or another, or confusing the consequences of power (for instance domination) with power per se. Some key works on the sociology of sport have tended to fall into this trap. George Sage (*Power and Ideology in American Sport*, 1990) presents sport as 'one of various cultural settings in which the hegemonic structure of power and privilege in capitalist society is continually fortified', but a picture is painted of a monolithic and systemic power structure in sports that does not adequately capture the dynamics of power within sports cultures and practices. In *Sport, Power and Culture: A Social and Historical Analysis of Popular Sports in Britain* (1986), John Hargreaves offers a concise, flexible, and accessible definition of power: 'When we use the term power, we are referring . . . to a relationship between agents, the outcome of which is determined by agents' access to relevant resources and their use of appropriate strategies in specific conditions of struggle with other agents.'

Critical here is the recognition that power is a relationship, a dynamic, and that the relationship involves human agents struggling over resources and outcomes. There are various forms in which power relations are manifest, and Hargreaves outlines four such forms by which the compliance of subordinate groups may be obtained: physical force or its threatened use; economic sanctions; the assertion of authority or prestige; and persuasion. Rather than working with the couplet power/resistance, it is surely important to see resistance as a form of power itself, as a response to say, domination, or in Russell's terms, to a particular form of power, say naked or traditional power. For if actors have some capacity to affect outcomes, they are exercising some degree of power. Lukes (*Power: A Radical View*, 1974) has problematized simplistic formulations of the exercise of power and urged that a deeper study of power must recognize how, in complex and subtle ways, the inactivity of leaders and sheer weight of institutions is a form of power. Doing nothing can have great impact on events as surely as can doing something. More generally he stresses the relational dimensions of power:

> Power is the capacity to produce, or contribute to, outcomes—to make a difference to the world. In social life, we may say, power is the capacity to do this through social relationships: it is the capacity to produce, or contribute to, outcomes by significantly affecting another or others. (in William Outhwaite, *The Blackwell Dictionary of Modern Social Thought*, 2nd edn, 2003).

Lukes formulates five key questions: Who or what possesses power? What outcomes count as the effects of power? What distinguishes power relationships? How is the capacity of power to be conceived, by agents or actors? How is power to be identified? These remain key questions for understanding the significance of sport in the making and remaking of cultures and societies. *See also* CAPILLARY POWER; CHARISMA; DOMINATION; FOUCAULT, MICHEL; RESISTANCE.

powerboat racing Races between boats propelled by outboard or inboard motors, on either inland waters (such as large lakes or wide rivers) or offshore waters, and sometimes over routes (such as London to Monte Carlo) combining the two Classes are determined by the power and length of the boat. Obviously an activity for a wealthy and leisured elite, the sport became popular off the coasts of Europe, the USA, Australia, South Africa, and parts of the South Americas; it continues to take place in such privileged contexts and circumstances, with a Formula One World Championship featuring teams sponsored by the likes of the Gulf emirates Abu Dhabi and Qatar, and multiple world champion Guido Capellini testing his boat on the waters of Lake Como, Italy. The excitement of the combination of speed, technology, and glamour attracted sponsors to the sport in earlier periods, Britain's *Daily Express* and *Daily Telegraph* promoting annual offshore races and round-Britain races in the 1960s.

Pozzo, Vittorio (1886–1968) An Italian football player and coach/manager who achieved unprecedented international success leading Italy's national side to World Cup titles in 1934 and 1938, the Olympic title in 1936, and two victories in the same decade in what was then the central European championships for national sides. From a middle-class Italian background, Pozzo was well travelled and had played football in Switzerland and followed football in England. He is notable for his tactical acumen, evolving the *metodo* defensive formation, and for his open-minded internationalism towards *oriundi* ('nationals', or players from other countries with some Italian ancestry, in particular Argentines). The wider context, with obviously determining influences, was that his major achievements came during the fascist dictatorship of Benito *Mussolini, when state-sponsored sport received great priority, and all the national side's players could be registered as full-time students. Referees made suspiciously dubious decisions in key World Cup matches, and controversy was generated by Pozzo's insistence that his players make the fascist salute at matches and ceremonies, arguing disingenuously that the action was merely the national symbol of the moment. Some speculation has linked his name to the blind, privileged, disrupting, and aristocratic character Pozzo in Samuel Beckett's *Waiting for Godot*.

practice 1. A noun referring to the general category of human activity, so that to speak of cultural and/or social practices is to refer to the myriad of human actions and activities that comprise a culture and a society; conceptually, it is a version of the everyday term defined as 'the action of doing something'. To talk therefore of 'sporting practices' is to refer to the activities that human subjects undertake in the specifically sporting sphere.

2. The noun 'practice' and verb 'practise' also refer to the habitual and repetitive experience of an activity or skill undertaken to achieve proficiency in the performance of that skill. In his 2008 book, *Outliers*, the Canadian writer Malcolm Gladwell argued that notions such as genius, or the view that people are biologically endowed as achievers, are misplaced. Rather, as John Willman of the *Financial Times* (17 November 2008) put it, Gladwell's argument 'boils down to three propositions: first, success is made possible by an accumulation of advantages; second, taking advantage of those circumstances requires hard work; and third, people from backgrounds that espouse hard work are more likely to work hard.' Gladwell has cited hard work and practice as the key components in the make-up of prominent sport champions such as golfer Tiger Woods. Woods may have started

with some social advantages such as a supportive family, but as Gladwell asserts: 'No one, not rock stars, not professional athletes, not software billionaires, and not even geniuses—ever makes it alone.' Gladwell even postulates the amount of hours needed to achieve competence: 10,000 concentrated hours, undertaken at an early age, will make you an outlier and potentially a champion. Gladwell's populist synthesizing lacks any rigorous scientific or experimental basis, but his accessible insights are a reminder of the importance of the essential process of practising in the development of sporting competence.

More systematically, psychologists have explored the notion of 'deliberate practice'. In their 1993 paper 'The Role of Deliberate Practice in the Acquisition of Expert Performance' (*Psychological Review*, vol. 100), K. Anders Ericsson, Ralf Th. Krampe, and Clemens Tesch-Römer claimed that: 'The commitment to deliberate practice distinguished the expert performer from the vast majority of children and adults who seem to have remarkable difficulty meeting the much lower demands on practice in schools, adult education, and in physical exercise programs.' They state that 'a decade or more of maximal effort' in a domain is a precondition for elite performance. Their study was empirically focused upon young violinists, but also cited historical improvements in typing, and in Olympic performance.

practise *See* PRACTICE.

Preemont Stakes *See* HORSE RACING.

prejudice An attitude or opinion unjustified by evidence or facts, concerning a person or a thing; this can be in favour of or against that person or thing, but usage of the term often has a negative connotation, and its more common application is towards that of which the critic of the prejudice disapproves. A source of prejudice—and this could be expressed by fan, coach, or co-player—might be ingrained bias or sheer ignorance concerning the qualities of a player, as judged by his or her ethnicity or race, or physical characteristics, or sexual identity. Sport both perpetuates prejudice, in that it can encourage the persistence of *stereotypes, and has the capacity to challenge it, by revealing the unsound basis upon which prejudices are held.

price and pricing *See* SPORTS PRICING.

primary socialization Early forms of influence in the social and psychological formation and development of the child, usually associated, in orthodox Western societies, with the family unit into which the child is born. The relevance of primary socialization into sport lies in the influence of early forms of play and of gender dynamic to which the child is exposed. *See also* TENCULTURATION; SOCIALIZATION.

prisoners' base A territorial game between two teams demanding agility and skill in running, noted by Joseph Strutt as a 'rustic game . . . much practised in former times', and still extant at the beginning of the 19th century (*The Sports and Pastimes of the People of England*, 1801). It was prohibited on the avenues in the vicinity of the palace at Westminster in the reign of Edward III (1312–77), but survived as a chasing and touching game between equally matched sides.

profit

Strutt himself recalled a '**grand** match at base' in the fields behind what is now the British Museum (in London) around 1770, with twelve-a-side teams of men from Cheshire and Derbyshire, much wagering, and a large and entertained crowd.

process sociology A term associated with the work of Norbert *Elias, and studies by Eric Dunning, who worked closely with Elias on groundbreaking scholarship and research in the sociology of sport. In *The Court Society* (1983), Elias opposed what he called 'the retreat of sociology into the present', and proposed, both there and throughout his life's work, that sociologists should be centrally concerned with historical or long-term processes. Dunning's own work—for example, on sport as a sphere serving the interests of *masculinity; on the socio-historical roots of *football hooliganism; or on the battle between the sexes in the changing gender relations in the sporting sphere—has sustained a sensitivity to the impact in the here and now of long-term and formative historical processes. As Dunning writes (*Sport Matters: Sociological Studies of Sport, Violence and Civilization*, 1999), Elias suggested that 'the dynamics of long-term social processes derive from the interweaving of aggregates of individual acts'. The history of a sport, therefore, must recognize the formative moments when such combinations of acts were genuinely developmental, as in, say, the making of modern sporting forms. *See also* ELIASIAN.

production Generally referring to the process whereby resources are transformed into goods or services, production is more specifically widely contrasted with *consumption, and refers to the making of the product. A sports event is an act of consumption for the audience or the fan, but it is made—or produced—by teams of specialist workers, including the sport contestants themselves, for whom the occasion is an example of their productive capacity within the particular polity, economy, and society.

productivity The output of an organization or an individual in a particular sphere of work or performance. Industrial organizations have sometimes reported a rise in productivity after its workforce has experienced a trophy win by its favourite sports team: some surveys (including in France and Canada) have identified lower absenteeism and higher productivity in enterprises where the organization offers a physical activity or a sports programme. In professional sport, individual players can be minutely analysed in relation to their performance, by means of computer analysis schemes such as Prozone, and their performance matched against cost in an evaluation of productivity (number of goals scored, for instance, by a footballer on a particular pay level). There are real problems of comparability here, between the 'productive' goal-scorer and the apparently less productive lynchpin of the team's midfield: but the tendency towards productivity analysis and evaluation is an example of the increasing professionalism of team sports business.

profit The margin by which income exceeds expenditure and creates a surplus. In pure terms, any enterprise in the market economy that does not operate at a profit is threatened with extinction, as financially it makes no sense to continue in a loss-making spiral. But in sport, there is great variance in the profit-making profiles of sports institutions, from sport to sport, and country to country.

protein Any of a class of chemical compounds which have a structural and regulatory role in the body. An average adult body has around 10 kilograms of protein with about 70 per cent of this in the form of muscle. Proteins are formed of chains of amino acids. There are 20 different types of amino acid. Each type is based on a common structure of an amino group (NH_2) and an organic acid group (COOH) each attached to a central carbon atom. The remaining atoms of each type of amino acid form a side chain which provides the distinguishing feature. The chains of amino acids may range in length from about 20 amino acid units to many thousands of units. Chains may be linear or branched and can form complex three-dimensional arrangements. This variety in length and shape of the amino acid chain, plus the numerous permutations of the constituent amino acid units, give rise to the wide diversity of proteins in the body. The regulatory functions of protein are displayed in such forms as hormones, enzymes, antibodies, and transport receptors. The structural functions of proteins are displayed in muscles, connective tissues, and numerous specialist cells. Protein can also be used as a fuel to generate energy but this is subsidiary to the use of carbohydrate and fat, with protein providing only around 5 per cent of the energy on average.

Historically, a high-protein diet was considered essential for sport, and the athletic diet sought two or three times the normal intake of protein through the copious consumption of meat, fish, eggs, and dairy products. Coaches and athletes made the (fallacious) assumption that, since muscles were made of protein and muscular contraction propelled the body, physical exertion would break down the muscles and it would be necessary to consume extra protein for repair and to cause muscle growth (*see also* VEGETARIANISM). Contemporary understanding of the dynamics of protein metabolism demonstrates that the needs of athletes are met by an intake of 50 per cent above the normal recommended daily consumption of 0.8 grams of protein per kilogram of body mass per day.

Protestantism, sport in See CATHOLIC CHURCH, ATTITUDE TOWARDS SPORT IN THE; ELECTIVE AFFINITY; CROMWELL, OLIVER; KING'S BOOK OF SPORTS, THE.

psychoanalysis A theory deriving from the work of Sigmund *Freud, and linked to the treatment of psychological disorders. At the heart of the Freudian approach is the theory of the unconscious, and the model of the psyche comprising the interrelated elements of the *id, *ego, and *superego. Andrew Blake (*The Body Language: The Meaning of Sport*, 1996) notes three aspects of cultural studies that have borrowed from psychoanalysis: memory as far from all-inclusive; the receding of much that is not kept at the forefront of the memory into the unconscious or subconscious mind; and the prominence of fantasy and desire—core dimensions of sport participation and spectatorship—as formative influences upon identity. Psychoanalysis has had little impact upon mainstream sport psychology, though one prominent sporting figure to claim its relevance to the sporting world is Michael Brearley, former England cricket captain and, in 2009, president of the British Psychoanalytical Society.

public sphere A term widely associated with the work of the German political scientist and philosopher Jürgen Habermas (b. 1929). In his *The Structural Transformation of the Public Sphere: An Inquiry into a Category of Bourgeois Society*

(German edition 1962, English version 1989), Habermas provided an account, on a historico-sociological basis, of the emergence and disintegration of what he called the (liberal) public sphere—a space, between *civil society and the state, that provided the basis for public discussion of matters of general interest, a space that was also the product of a developing market economy. Such a space—emerging, historically, with the loss of power of traditional authority systems, and generated by new means of communication that were not yet specifically regulated by the emergent state—was undermined by, for instance, 'the integration of mass entertainment with advertising', which puts in place a form of address treating 'citizens like consumers', by even the state itself.

The importance of this Habermasian framework for sports studies lies in the suggestion that a commercial market in the history of sport—in Western democratizing and industrializing societies at least—allowed the debate for the evolution of particular forms of association. Victoria de Grazia (*The Sex of Things: Gender and Consumption in Historical Perspective*, edited by Victoria de Grazia, with Ellen Furlough, 1996) has described this general process and context of 'the development of the modern public sphere'. It

> was associated with the spaces, inventions and sociability of the commercial revolution. Printing houses, markets and bourses, salons, and cafes had as their common characteristic that they arose outside of the rule of absolutism and acted more or less independently of the canons of courtly taste and religious authority. Accordingly, the public sphere comprised the societal institutions in which modern public opinion was formed, as distinct and separate from the sites of private activity, namely, the household and the workplace. Expanding with industrialization and democratization in the nineteenth century, the public sphere, according to some theorists, offered the space in which citizens could mount a critique of the social system. It was this capacity, originally generated by commercial culture, that was then destined to be occluded in the twentieth century as the public sphere was overrun by highly manipulated mass commodity and mass communication systems.

One might be describing here a process encompassing the growth of sports on a relatively autonomous associational basis, and their appropriation by the mass communications and consumerist market, alongside what Habermas identified as the interventions of mass welfare-state democracies. According to this process, sport—as a public sphere—becomes squeezed by both the market and the state.

Puma *See* ADIDAS.

pumping iron A term referring to the activities of bodybuilders or weight specialists whose concern is with the cultivation of a carefully sculpted physique, and not merely the health-inducing effects of the exercise. The 1977 film documentary *Pumping Iron*, featuring Arnold Schwarzenegger, popularized the term if not the activity.

punting A form of *boating in a flat-bottomed rectangular boat, in which a pole is used to propel and direct the vessel on the river. Although it was a work-based competitive activity among watermen of the River Thames in London in the late

18th century, it became popular as a sport among amateurs of the elite classes from the mid 19th century. Punting in the 20th century is a lucrative form of tourism in the English university cities of Oxford and Cambridge, where leisurely punts along the river afford views of the architecture of the colleges of the ancient universities, and evoke bucolic pastimes redolent of a privileged past.

Puskàs, Ferenc (1927-2006) A Hungarian footballer, born in Budapest, dying there at the age of 79, whose football career reflected the politics and culture of 20th-century international sport. He was the star of the legendary Hungarian team of the 1950s, seen by many as the best side never to win the World Cup, when losing 3-2 to Germany in 1954 in Berne, Switzerland; and the talisman of a multi-talented Real Madrid team assembled under the patronage of fascist dictator General Franco in Spain in the later 1950s. The Hungary side had won the 1952 Olympic football tournament with its socialist state-sponsored blend of speed, fitness, and discipline, then defeating the England side at Wembley in London in 1953 by 6-3, and in the return in Budapest the following summer by 7-1. This was a pivotal moment in the internationalization and modernization of the game. In one of Real Madrid's most memorable European Cup triumphs, when Eintracht Frankfurt was defeated by 7-3 in Glasgow, Scotland, in 1960, Puskàs scored four of the goals. A product of the communist system in his early career, and a beneficiary of the far right at his peak, Puskàs's career illustrates vividly the political uses to which sport and international sporting encounters can be put.

pyramid model of sport involvement A model, in the form of a pyramid, indicating (claimed or projected) connections between a broad base of participation in sport (at the bottom of the pyramid) and a narrow focused population of top-class performers (at the apex of the pyramid). Some models have included layers of developmental levels from foundation through different levels of performance to the elite or high-performance level. Such models have also been used to justify elite programmes alongside *'sport for all' policies, implying—but with patchy supportive evidence—that the base is a necessary precondition for the apex.

qualitative research Research employing methods such as interviewing or forms of *observation that rely upon the application of the cultivated skills of the researcher—including *empathy—in the study context or setting. This can include, in for instance semi-structured interviews or *oral history, responses of the researcher to the respondent, so that interviews become forms of dialogue or even conversations. In *participant observation or *ethnography, the qualitative researcher typically combines a range of qualitative methods, in order to generate in-depth data on a unique cultural or social context, such as the sporting subculture or the sporting event. There is long-standing debate concerning the relationship of qualitative methods to approaches towards and methods used in *quantitative research.

quango A quasi-non-governmental organization, operationally independent but funded by and accountable to government. In Britain, *Sport England is such a body.

quantification In the work of Allen Guttmann, one of seven formal-structural characteristics defining modern sports. In sports, he says, just as in most aspects of daily life, 'we live in a world of numbers'. Ancient Greeks measured neither times run in races at their Panhellenic athletic festivals, nor distances attained by throwers (*Sports: The First Five Millennia*, 2004). In modern sports, performance is timed and measured, documented and recorded. It is a criterion that has pervaded sporting activity from the highest levels to grass-roots participation, increased too by the availability of self-generated forms of communication—such as the *internet—that can classify and reproduce performance data regularly, reliably, and swiftly. Whether the jogger at the municipal park looking to set a *personal best, or the world-record-chasing athlete with an eye on a lucrative cash bonus, the modern sportsman or -woman is unprecedentedly interested in the quantification of the performance.

quantitative research Research based upon the generation of numerical and statistical data. In social science it is largely associated with social surveys based upon large and representative samples of an identified population—*sport participation surveys, for instance, or attitude surveys as to one's reasons for doing sports (or for not participating). In experimental sciences, numbers may not need to be large, but the measurement procedures must be rigorous, and the data generated in the experimental or field test must be what is often called robust—controlled experiments of runners on the treadmill must have tight and replicable parameters for the findings to have scientific credibility. While some see the qualitative and quantitative approaches as paradigmatically distinct, in sociocultural studies of sport the two are often employed together: the large-scale survey might generate broad findings and detailed data sets, and then be followed by a number of in-depth interviews with individual subjects on themes and issues identified in the large-scale questionnaire survey. An example might be research into sexual harassment or abuse in sport, in which the survey identifies the incidence of the phenomenon, and the relationship of different variables to the harassment and/or abuse, and targeted in-depth interviews explore the individual's experience of the harassment and/or abuse.

queer theory An approach to the study of gender relations and sexual identity premised upon the proposition that theorization of these areas has been dominated by a deep-rooted and entrenched set of assumptions concerning heterosexuality and a male/female gender divide as the norm. Heather Sykes ('Queering Theories of Sexuality in Sport Studies', in Jayne Caudwell, ed., *Sport, Sexualities and Queer/Theory*, 2006) identifies four primary areas that 'queer theorists have etched a space to think about': the construction of heterosexuality; a dominant heteronormativity that has aligned the dominance of whiteness and late capitalism with heterosexuality; hetero-Other relations; and theories and practices seeing queerness as a catalyst for transforming 'homosexual, gay, lesbian theory into a general social theory'. This is a huge agenda, a manifesto for the reorientation of social theory, no mere list of research questions relating to any particular cultural sphere or domain. The implications for studying sport are parallel to the implications of the stance for the study of any other popular cultural sphere, though the prominence of the body in sport, and of discourses of the body in critical analysis of sport, may lend a particular prominence to queer theoretical challenges to the established sociology of sport; queer theory's concentration on textual analyses is certainly conducive to its application in sports studies, and careful analysis and deconstruction of discourses of the body in banter or subcultural literature or songs can reaffirm the heteronormative nature of much of sporting practice and culture.

Sykes concludes, in her overview, that 'queering sport studies'—the play on verb and adjective here is deliberate—'has the potential to alter how we think about sexualities, desires and bodies'. It is in this rendition an interdisciplinary, deconstructionist, and self-reflexive theoretical approach, that should not 'become commodified as identity politics'. This latter comment posits a continuing openness in the approach, and also signals a tension in that other approaches, such as radical lesbian feminism, see queer theory as unanchored, and threatening to the gains made by forms of feminism in specifying the roots of male domination and women's subordination to men. As in any other version of *critical theory, queer theory must remain alert to the minutiae of the purported object of its scholarly focus—in this case sport—or it will be considered as either peripheral to the mainstream concerns of sports studies, or fuelled primarily by an overarching social theory rather than by careful study of the sporting world.

quoits An outdoor game in which a ring, usually made of iron, is aimed at a target stuck in the ground, commonly a pin or a peg. It was played in England in the 14th century, and branded as illegal by a statute of 1388. It was considered that the game undermined archery practice and other forms of martial preparation at a time of elongated war with the French. The game's popularity persisted, despite the legislation, and it was one of the activities common to the festivities of holiday times such as Easter in the later 18th century. In the early 1800s, as Robert Malcolmson documents, drawing on a source describing the 'agriculture of Derbyshire', 'Quoits seemed a very prevalent amusement of the lower and more idle part of the manufacturing People, at the Ale-house Doors, in the north of the county, about Sheffield in particular' (*Popular Recreations in English Society, 1700–1850*, 1973). At the same time, the tin miners of Cornwall in south-west England were observed to practise quoits among their 'idle exercises'. In the north and eastern regions of England, often in mining communities, and in Scotland, the sport remained visible into the modern industrial period as far as the 1930s. Part of its popularity lay in its flexibility: it could be played between pairs, teams, or individuals, the scoring system could be decided between participants, and it could be played in and among what historians have called 'casual social gatherings' outside or in the vicinity of public or communal spaces such as alehouses or taverns.

quota systems Schemes whereby the composition of a sporting team or squad is made up of proportions or allocations of individuals having particular characteristics. There has been long-standing debate in national and international football about the number of non-national players in national leagues (complicated, in Europe, by the cross-border citizen rights consequent upon the stances adopted by the European Commission). Most controversially, quota systems in post-apartheid South Africa in sports such as Rugby Union and cricket have required the presence of specified numbers of non-white players in selected national squads; this has generated heated debate concerning the basis of selection, in the form of—from the point of view of opponents of the quota system—allegations that the meritocratic basis of sport is jeopardized by non-sporting considerations. Such allegations, of course, conveniently ignore the forms of *inequality and the rootedness of the *cultural capital upon which the so-called meritocratic system is based.

q

R

Rabbit Run A 1960 novel by US writer John Updike (1932–2009) in which small-town protagonist Harry 'Rabbit' Angstrom never fulfils his boyhood potential as a basketball player, and this failure fixes his identity as he meanders through a life of underachievement. The powerful use of sport as a metaphor for an unrealized life is carried through into three further 'Rabbit' novels, and related fiction.

Rabelais, François (1483/94–1553) A French writer of the early Renaissance period, whose training in the Catholic priesthood and in early systematic forms of Western medicine equipped him with a sense of both the spiritual and the secular in relation to the philosophical, religious, and political issues of the day. His controversial writings raised critical questions about the human condition, as manifest in particular in the human body, its functions and its composition. A major theme in these writings was the nature of excess, and in the first book of his *Gargantua and Pantagruel* (1532–52) he included a chapter (chap. 22) on games and sports, in which he listed—on the basis initially of reportage and then of a fiery imagination—216 or 217 games/sports. These included, in an expanded final list added to over the years of republication of the work: *tobogganing; lawn billiards; the dart; *quoits; *tug-of-war; short bowls; the small bowl; nine-pins; shuttlecock; hamstool; bowman's shot; and *jeu de paume*. These activities were listed as examples of time-wasting activity engaged in by Rabelais's protagonist Gargantua (whose character is the etymological source of the adjective 'gargantuan'). Such activities were indulged in between bouts of drinking, eating, wench-seeking, and sleeping. In the two chapters following this listing, Rabelais described an alternative view of sports and games—including the arts of chivalry—in which physical activities and sport-based contest have more character-building dimensions and purportedly positive social value. In posing this duality of meaning of sports and games, Rabelais reiterated the long-term theme of the question of the morality of sports: waste versus worth; hedonism versus self-denial; the papacy versus the puritan. In emphasizing the secular and the physical as a source of cultural radicalism, his work inspired the writings of Mikhail Bakhtin in the USSR in the 1920s, and the numerous Bakhtin-inspired applications of the notion of the *carnivalesque to particular sport and popular cultural contexts and situations.

race-walking Walking either solo or in competition over agreed lengths or times, initially in the 18th and 19th centuries, in Britain, for agreed financial reward for the successful soloist or the winner in a contest, and as a focus for wagers for the betting public. This early form of race-walking was also known as *pedestrianism. Race-walking also flourished in Germany, France, Sweden, and

Italy, and was promoted in the Soviet Union once it became an Olympic discipline. Within that more formalized context, race-walking has been defined more tightly: in the Olympics, there are 20 kilometre walking races for men and women (from Melbourne 1956 and Sydney 2000 respectively), and a 50 kilometre walk for men (introduced at the 1932 Los Angeles Games). Race-walking has also spawned novelty acts bordering on freakshows, such as Plennie L. Wingo (1895–1993), who in 1931–2 (a period of the Great Depression and diversions such as dance marathons) walked backwards from Santa Monica, California, to Istanbul, Turkey, around 8,000 miles.

racism The process whereby people's social relations are determined by the attribution of particular biological and/or cultural characteristics, with the consequence that social groups are differentiated according to those attributions. Racism generates claims that such differentiated groups have a natural or unchanging character, and perpetuates discriminatory and prejudiced beliefs and practices. Ben Carrington and Ian McDonald, in their edited volume *'Race', Sport and British Society* (2001), state that the 'discourse of racism' has shifted since the end of World War II, from a crude biological model identifying biologically discrete races, to a 'cultural racism' positing that discrete groups have 'their own incompatible lifestyles, customs and ways of seeing the world'. In reality, they say, the biological and the cultural forms of racism 'co-exist and often inter-penetrate'. Examples of persisting racisms in sport—and among some sport scientists—include the views that 'white men can't jump' or 'black people are poor swimmers'. Sport has offered an irresistible vehicle for some looking to perpetuate views concerning the superiority of particular racial categories or races, most infamously in Adolf *Hitler's use of the 1936 Berlin Olympics as a stage for the expression of Aryan superiority: the triumphs of black US athlete Jesse *Owens were a magnificent counterweight to such a racist-based ideology and programme.

Important campaigns have been mounted by sport bodies and national sport associations to counter and eradicate racism in sport, particularly among spectators at sporting venues. Racist behaviours have certainly been reduced, though this is not necessarily evidence of the elimination of racist views; non-racist behaviours at the stadium are not automatically matched by non-racist views and attitudes held and expressed in other settings. In some countries, racist abuse has continued to have a high profile, as some black English footballers, and 2008 Formula One world champion racing driver Lewis Hamilton, have learned when playing and competing in Spain. The question of whether institutionalized racism continues to characterize sport institutions and cultures remains an important one: why do so few black players continue into management and coaching in their sport? Are positions and roles in teams to some degree determined by race-based stereotypes? *See also* STACKING.

rackets A court game played with a racket and ball, played in its early forms in France and Italy in open spaces in towns, such as courtyards and piazzas, often with gloved hands or a primitive kind of bat. In England it was initially played in the yards of taverns, or where high walls were available. An early rackets venue in London (late 18th and early 19th centuries) was the Fleet Prison, but it was the

schoolboys of the elite public school of Harrow who established regular
contests, also developing the variant of *squash rackets. Enclosed courts
in exclusive clubs made the game an expensive, and minority, sport, rooted in
the networks of the public schools and the ancient universities, Oxford and
Cambridge first competing against each other in the sport in 1858, and the public
schools inaugurating a national championship in 1868. The British armed forces
exported the game and from a base in Canada it also developed a profile on the
east coast of the USA. Amateur championships were established in 1888
(singles) and 1890 (doubles), and the Tennis & Rackets Association (T&RA)
formed as the English governing body in 1907. Men's singles and double events
were held at the Olympic Games just once, in London in 1908, when all medallists
were British.

During its 'centenary season' of 2007–8 the T&RA could still champion the
principles of *amateurism, and uphold rules of amateur status, stating that the
'spirit of the Rules' involved 'playing for the love of doing so and for no financial
gain'. At the same time it could boast a high-profile list of sponsors: lead
sponsors British Land (real estate) and Lacoste (fashion); Square Mile Sourcing
(information technology specialists); Pol Roger Champagne; Neptune (investment
management); The Jester's Club/Cos d'Estournel (connoisseur wine outlet); Hiscox
(insurance); Grays (sports clothing and equipment, particularly rackets);
Cambridge Tele.com (communications); and Spring Law (business law, including
sport litigation). The schools' racket results listed on the T&RA website confirmed
the continuing exclusive base of the sport, and a link to T&RA sponsor Spring
Law showed the firm to be winner of the Law Society Rugby 7s in 2007, further
reaffirming the buoyancy of old public school values in networks of elite British
business and sport. At the centenary ball (£115 per ticket for those over
28 years old) in April 2008, a Brazilian samba band and dancers provided the
floor show, Pol Roger the champagne reception.

Ranjitsinhji, Vibhaji (1872–1933) An Indian cricketer who gained great fame in
late Victorian and Edwardian England. Ranjitsinhji was a claimant (eventually
successful) to a Rajput princehood, who was schooled in the English style in his
home country, and then attended Trinity College, Cambridge, where he won a
*blue for cricket. In his published works he used the style 'K.S. Ranjitsinhji'; at
Cambridge he went by the title 'Smith'. In the mid 1980s he played—though not yet
strictly eligible—as an amateur for the county club Sussex. Most of his club-mates,
and the cricket-fan public, knew him as 'Ranji'. Along with C. B. *Fry, he typified
what many cricket writers have labelled cricket's Golden Age, playing with
flamboyant brilliance and unusual elegance. He wore silk shirts, and endorsed a
range of products from hair-restorer to sandwiches. In his *Jubilee Book of Cricket* he
described the sport as one of the 'most powerful links which keep our Empire
together'. Richard Holt has called Ranjitsinhji 'an icon of Edwardian England, a
symbol of how the spirit of the gentleman amateur could transcend racial if not
social barriers'. Ranji renamed himself with the princely prefix, as Simon Wilde
puts it, of K. S.—Kumar Shri—soon after arriving in England. When succeeding
to the throne of Navanagar after the (untimely and even suspicious) death of
the first in line to the title, he went on to persuade the Indian government to

grant him the title of 'Maharaja Jam Sahib of Nawanagar'. Wilde (*Oxford Dictionary of National Biography*, 2004) gets at both the cricketer and the politician in his comment that, in this fascinating life of the first Indian to gain a cricket blue, 'a steely resolve was wrapped in clothes of charm'.

rating of perceived exertion (RPE) A scale to provide a subjective measure of the perceived physical effort associated with any given intensity of exercise. Originally developed by Gunnar Borg in the 1960s, RPE derives from a general psychophysical law whereby the perceived intensity of a stimulus is equal to a constant multiplied by the stimulus intensity raised to the power n. This relationship holds for most forms of human perception, such as brightness, loudness, smell, temperature, force, and vibration. Borg demonstrated that this psychophysical power law is also valid for physical effort and he described how the perceived effort could be scored on a 6-to-20 scale. The odd digits on the scale have written descriptors to aid judgement (e.g. 11 = fairly light, 19 = very, very hard). The Borg scale is widely used since it provides a simple and quantitative means of assessing an individual's feelings of effort. It can be used in conjunction with other measures of physiological strain (e.g. heart rate) and physical work (e.g. running speed) to provide a rounded view of the stress of exercise from psychological, physiological, and performance perspectives. Alternatives to Borg's 6-to-20 scale have been developed, including scales with visual cues for children, and ratio scales felt to be more fitting to the fundamental stimulus/perception power relationship. The perception of physical exertion does not rely on a single cue such as the heart rate; rather it is a multi-layered perception wherein multiple cues arising from the physiological perturbations of muscular, metabolic, and cardio-respiratory systems are integrated and then interpreted cognitively according to the psychological state and traits of the individual.

rationalization At the heart of Max *Weber's sociological *oeuvre* is a concern with the process of rationalization, and its effects on people's lives. For Weber, modern society and its administration stripped society of its mystery, tradition, and customs, and people of their affects, or emotions; at the end of his *Protestant Ethic and the Spirit of Capitalism* he used the phrase 'the iron cage of rationality' as a metaphor for the stifling consequences of the modernizing process of rationalization. The formalization and standardization of modern sports have been interpreted within this Weberian framework by Allen Guttmann, for whom, in a range of works across a third of a century, rationalization has been a core characteristic of his model of 'modern sports': 'the rules of modern sports are constantly scrutinized and undergo frequent revision from a means-ends point of view; athletes train scientifically, employ technologically advanced equipment, and strive for the most efficient employment of their skills' (*Games and Empires: Modern Sports and Cultural Imperialism*, 1994).

rational recreation The view, common to the dominant classes and established elites in a variety of modernizing societies, that participation in certain sports could create a disciplined and healthy labour force and general populace. Rational recreation in mid and late 19th-century Britain was a reforming and moral project, in which professional groups such as priests, schoolteachers, or industrialists saw particular physical activities as more conducive to an acceptable, respectable social order than the traditional popular recreations and pastimes of the pre-industrial type, or less improving leisure activities that might be conducted in the local public house or in an unregulated way in local public space. As J. M. Golby and A. W. Purdue put it, rational recreation was used as a method, by reformers, 'of providing "improving" and "rational" pastimes in place of debasing and degrading ones', and so ensuring that 'the lower orders could be weaned away from drinking and gambling and other excesses and could develop as members of a culturally harmonious society' (*The Civilisation of the Crowd: Popular Culture in England, 1750–1900*, 1984). The influence of the rational recreationists was widespread, but not long-lasting: the popular classes, as in the case of football clubs initially formed by local priests or religious institutions, proved very capable of accepting the facilities and the opportunity to play organized sport, while rejecting the moral message that the rational recreationists hoped to convey.

Reagan, Ronald (1911–2004) The fortieth president of the USA (1981–9), and the oldest incumbent ever to achieve the position, Reagan was a radio sport broadcaster for WOC Radio in Davenport, Ia. from 1932–7, before moving into film acting and then regional politics, as governor of California. In the 1940 film *Knute Rockne: All American* Reagan played George Gipp, star player of the Notre Dame football side coached by Rockne in the 1920s. A line in the film turns back-to-the-wall football tactics into homespun philosophy: 'sometime when the team is up against it and the breaks are beating the boys, tell them to go out there with all they've got and win just one for the Gipper'. Reagan was nicknamed The Gipper after this film, and used the sobriquet in his campaigning for the presidency. Reagan used sport both as high-profile international relations—the 1984 Los Angeles Olympics opening and closing ceremonies were an apogee of Cold War triumphalism—and as a folksy appeal to all-American values and local identity, when addressing local communities. In an example of the latter, a year before the Los Angeles Olympics, Reagan hailed the nation's can-do spirit in a speech to the United States Olympic Committee. He cited the volunteers and donors who had made possible the Ronald Reagan Sports Park in Temecula, California:

> The folks in a rather small town, Temecula . . . got together and built themselves a sports park, held fund-raising barbecues and dinners. And those that didn't have money, volunteered the time and energy. And now the young people of that community have baseball diamonds for Little League and other sports events, just due to what's traditional Americanism.

real tennis A racket-and-ball sport played in an indoor court. It is the sport from which *lawn tennis was derived, the word 'real' being a claim to pedigree and history, and a derogatory riposte to those in lawn tennis who abbreviated their sport to just 'tennis'. In the USA real tennis is known as 'court tennis'; in France *jeu de paume*; and in Australia it was formerly known as 'royal tennis'. In England, the universities of Oxford and Cambridge were traditional strongholds of the game: Oxford had operational courts in 1595, and there is evidence of the

game being played at Cambridge in 1637. The game still has a presence at
Oxbridge, with two functional courts in Cambridge, and 250 members of Oxford's
club in 2008; and in exclusive clubs, which offer a basis for a limited number
of professionals to both compete and coach. Several sponsors of the International
Real Tennis Professionals Association, including Pol Roger Champagne, have
also sponsored the governing body of *rackets, the Tennis & Rackets
Association. Australians, Britons, and Americans comprised the line-up of
seven at the 2008 US Open.

recession A downturn in the economy, identified in economic factors such as
decrease in production, reduction in borrowing and consumer spending, and
rising unemployment. This has serious implications for leisure choices and
consumer expenditure in the sports goods industry. If the circumstances of a
recession persist, this can create the conditions of a *depression.

reciprocity A relationship of mutuality between two parties—individuals or
groups—based upon the notion that there is give and take between the parties, and
often expressed in the giving and receiving of a gift. Anthropologist Marcel Mauss
(*The Gift*, 1954) argued that the gift is both obligatory (in some cultures the visiting
relative must slip the unbeknown but expected cash gift to the youngest member
of the family) and reciprocal (the recipient is expected to reciprocate on any parallel
occasion). In sport, rival teams and individuals, and sporting diplomats, exchange
pennants and related objects, symbolizing in reciprocal gifts their sporting
understanding and cooperative premises. Indeed, the very notions of
*sportsmanship and *fair play rest on the social acceptability of a principle of
reciprocity; and much of sport at its grass-roots levels relies on the volunteer
and unpaid labour of officials and administrators whose motivations are not fuelled
by the prospect of remuneration (comparable to blood-donation as studied in
Richard Titmuss's *The Gift Relationship* of 1970).

records Beyond the widest sense of the logging of sport performance and
results and the general statistical recording of types and levels of performance, the
notion of the record refers to the highest level of achievement attained in a
particular sport: the highest jump, the fastest run, the perfect score, the longest
innings, the greatest number of home runs or touchdowns. Although a certain
model of Olympism emphasized participation over winning, the idea of the
record has been enshrined in the Olympic Games in its motto *Citius, Altius, Fortius*
(Swifter, Higher, Stronger). Winners, but not performance times, heights, or
distances, were documented in the ancient Olympic Games, and Allen Guttman
identified the record as one of the seven defining features of modern sport:
'Combine the impulse to quantification with the desire to win, to excel, to be the
best—and the result is the concept of the record' (*From Ritual to Record: The Nature
of Modern Sports*, 1978). The record attracts extensive public attention, becoming
what Guttman calls 'a psychological presence in the mind of everyone involved in
the event', and drawing in—particularly in an age of the mass and multi-media—
vast audiences. There is controversy over explicit record-breaking attempts, in that
the chase for and obsession with the record, by competitor, broadcaster, and
spectator alike, has been seen to disrupt—some might say corrupt—genuine

competition. Also, the pursuit of records, and the rewards available to record-breakers, have without doubt fuelled the use of performance-enhancing drugs and dubious preparatory biomedical procedures.

recovery *See* REHABILITATION.

Reebok *See* ADIDAS.

reference group Introduced by the psychologist Herbert Hyman (1918–85) in his 1942 monograph *The Psychology of Status*, the concept of reference group is based on the recognition that people judge situations and other people, and arrive at self-assessments, on the basis of their psychological identifications with others, rather than any formal membership of a group; on the basis of such identification processes, individuals are said to assign themselves to social categories—member of youth group, or political community, or sport group or subculture, for instance. The concept has had enduring currency among social psychologists and sociologists interested in group dynamics and inter-cultural relations and formations, and continues to offer potential for the illumination of the construction, composition, and perpetuation of athlete/competitor or fan-based sport subcultures. *See also* SYMBOLIC INTERACTIONISM.

rehabilitation A programme of exercise to aid recovery from illness. Programmes are most commonly seen in cardiac rehabilitation and in weight training for the recovery of muscle strength and mobility following a sports injury or joint operation in athletes. For many other illnesses, bed rest and medical treatment lower the body's muscle mass and functional capacity, and even once the illness is cured lifestyle and independence may be compromised; a programme of progressive rehabilitation exercises is used to help restore a patient's normal lifestyle. *See also* CORONARY HEART DISEASE.

relaxation A state of parasympathetic dominance characterized by a slowing of heart rate and breathing rate, and a lowered muscle tension. Relaxation is used in sport to reduce *anxiety before competition, in the form of techniques of mental practice and preparation as well as physical techniques. There are several common relaxation techniques that are used by athletes. Jacobson's progressive relaxation involves the contraction and relaxation of muscle groups in a systematic order from one group to the next. Autogenic training relies on suggesting feelings of warmth and heaviness followed by visualization of calm environments such as a sandy beach. Meditation, breath control, and *biofeedback are further techniques used to promote relaxation.

relay races Races—in running or swimming, most commonly—in which the team involves a number of individuals (customarily four) who undertake the same distance in sequence. In running, the individual runner must carry a baton for the stage that he or she runs; in swimming, the swimmer must touch the pool edge before the next swimmer launches him- or herself into the water. The appeal of the relay event is that the individuals are balanced on the basis of their varied talents, and errors can be made at points of changeover. The relay therefore introduoos an inci cased element of chance into the event, thus proving popular with the casual and expert spectator alike.

research methods Not to be confused with the more overarching term *methodology, research methods are those investigative methods or techniques whereby data are generated and analysed, whether this be in controlled experiments relating to human performance, observational studies of sport fan behaviour, or the operations of sport bureaucracies. Research methods will be selected within a research design, on the principle of the proven effectiveness of the method or technique in relation to the stated research question or problem. In scientific studies of performance and exercise, researchers must demonstrate that their methods can be reliably replicated by other researchers. In sociocultural studies of sport and leisure, as in sociology and the social sciences more generally, there is extensive debate on the relative merits of *quantitative research and *qualitative research. Each approach has its proven strengths and it would be unwise, indeed erroneous, to champion the alleged superiority of the quantitative over the qualitative or vice versa. If there is the need to know trends in sport participation, there is no substitute for *survey methods; to understand the meanings of that participation requires more qualitative approaches such as the *interview, *observation of various kinds, or *ethnography. Messianic commitment to just one framework with its established and rigidly applied research methods can produce rigorous findings, but of sometimes limited application. The sport researcher needs a rounded awareness of the research methods available, in order to make an informed choice of the application of methods in relation to the specific research question or problem. Sometimes several methods are used, in seeking to strengthen findings, a process sometimes claimed as *triangulation.

reserve clause A clause in a professional player's contract that binds the player to a team for the length of the contract plus an additional year. During that extra year, owners would not play players unless and until the player signed a new contract. Such overlapping commitments and contracts meant that the player was bound to the team for as long as the owner/employer wanted that player. It created a form of monopsony ('one buyer') power over players, whose wages could then be kept substantially lower than they would be in a free market. The National Football League in the USA adopted the reserve clause from baseball's model that had been created in 1887, but a series of legal challenges and modifications to the clause, from the late 1950s and throughout the rest of the century into the 1990s, eventually saw the nullification of the clause. This generated the implementation of the *salary cap as a means of controlling the finances of professional sports.

resistance In general terms, resistance in relation to human relations is the act of resisting, opposing, or withstanding, or the power or capacity so to do; and in relation to forces or material things it is the opposition of one phenomenon to another. It is therefore worth distinguishing between the meanings of resistance in applied sport science, psychoanalysis, and sociocultural studies of sport.

 1. 'Energy is the fundamental concept in physics', wrote Bertrand Russell (1872–1970) in his 1940 book *Power*, and the principle of resistance is central to an understanding of the dynamics of energy, referring to the capacity of a substance

to prevent or resist the flow of energy: in electricity, copper resists less than plastic or glass, for instance, and so is a conductor rather than an insulator. But the collision that occurs as a manifestation of the resistance can convert the energy, and is transformative. In *biomechanics, the principle of resistance is central to the analysis of effective performance in particular sports, and in the applied practical domain to the design of strength and resistance training programmes.

2. In *psychoanalysis, resistance refers to the refusal to allow repressed feelings to be transferred from the unconscious to the conscious. This has scarcely been studied in relation to sport: 'Resistance is a concept with a long history in psychoanalysis and almost no history at all in sport psychology', D. E. Lindner, D. R. Pillow, and R. R. Reno wrote in the 1989 volume of the *Journal of Sport and Exercise Psychology*. Those seeking to remedy this have noted that athletes themselves often recognize that defeat stems from their incapacity to manage forms of anxiety or fear, and that athletes are often diagnosed with personality disorders. Such commentaries have also noted that coaches remain ill-equipped to respond to such cases of repression in their individual charges.

3. Resistance as a concept in the social sciences should be seen as a variant of power, a response to, say, domination. For if actors have some capacity to affect outcomes, they are exercising some degree of power. Steven Lukes (*Power: A Radical View*, 1974) has problematized simplistic formulations of the exercise of power and urged that a deeper study of power must recognize how, in complex and subtle ways, the inactivity of leaders and sheer weight of institutions are a form of power. Doing nothing can have great impact on events as surely as can doing something. More generally, he stresses the relational dimensions of power:

> Power is the capacity to produce, or contribute to, outcomes—to make a difference to the world. In social life, we may say, power is the capacity to do this through social relationships: it is the capacity to produce, or contribute to, outcomes by significantly affecting another or others.
> (in William Outhwaite, *The Blackwell Dictionary of Modern Social Thought*, 2nd edn, 2003).

By such a definition, resistance to domination—as in the refusal to comply—must itself be seen as a form of power. Indeed, in a note on historical method, Friedrich Nietzsche (1854–1900) specified resistance as a central process. In *The Genealogy of Morals* (1887), he talked of how 'the whole history of a thing', such as a custom, constitutes a 'chain of reinterpretations and rearrangements'. Such a history

is a sequence of more or less profound, more or less independent processes of appropriation, including the resistances used in each instance, the attempted transformations for purposes of defence or reaction, as well as the results of successful counterattacks. While forms are fluid, their 'meaning' is even more so.

Echoes of Nietzsche inform Michel *Foucault's writings on power and resistance, particularly his section on method in *The History of Sexuality* (1976). Foucault disputes that any 'over-all unity of domination' is 'given at the outset'. He argues that power must be understood as 'the multiplicity of force relations immanent in the sphere in which they operate and which constitute their own organisation', and furthermore, involving struggles and confrontation that affect the power relations by transforming, strengthening, or reversing them. These force relations might also form a chain or a system, or be isolated from one another, and they take effect as strategies. According to Foucault, power is not an institution, and not a structure; yet neither is it a certain strength we are endowed with; it is the name one attributes to a complex strategic situation of struggle in a particular society. With, not apart from, these very power relations, resides the potential for resistance, not a sporadic, dramatic, revolutionary intervention, but something more internal to the power dynamic itself. 'Where there is power there is resistance, and yet, or rather consequently, this resistance is never in a position of exteriority in relation to power.' Foucault goes on to emphasize the relational character of power relations, arguing that:

> Their existence depends on a multiplicity of points of resistance: these play the role of adversary, target, support, or handle in power relations. These points of resistance are present everywhere in the power network . . . There is a plurality of resistances, each of them a special case: resistances that are possible, necessary, improbable; others that are spontaneous, savage, solitary, concerted, rampant, or violent: still others that are quick to compromise, interested, or sacrificial; by definition, they can only exist in the field of power relations.

Foucault's abstract account at least implies that nobody is excluded from the power game and that individuals can operate in a myriad of ways at points of resistance while playing it. In processes of appropriation and resistance, it is human agents who make a difference to the world. Thus, the question of agency has to be located within any adequate conceptualization of power. Anthony Giddens recognizes this when he says: 'Action depends upon the capacity of the individual to "make a difference" to a pre-existing state of affairs or course of events. An agent ceases to be such if he or she loses the capacity to "make a difference", that is, to exercise some sort of power' (*The Constitution of Society: Outline of a Theory of Structuration*, 1984).

Sport is of course just one cultural form in which these agency/power dynamics can be studied. In the work of Michel de Certeau (1925–86) on *The Practice of Everyday Life* (1988), culture is viewed as the product of the tension inherent in the political dynamics of power relations at every level of society. John Fiske (*Understanding Popular Culture*, 1989) draws upon de Certeau's theory in his argument for the recognition of everyday life as a significant sphere in which 'the people' undermine the 'strategies of the powerful, make poaching raids upon their texts or structures, and play constant tricks upon the system'. Fiske uses this approach to illustrate the progressive, rather than radical, nature of popular culture, and highlights the interpretative and creative capacity of human agents to employ such tactics. Although such an approach can be criticized for an over-celebration of the everyday and the popular, it is nevertheless a reminder that there is no everyday practice without interpretation. It also points to the fact that the interpretative act itself is a form of human agency, an act of appropriation and a potential form of resistance. Within popular culture, there is what Stuart Hall, in his 'Notes on Deconstructing the Popular', calls 'the double stake . . . the double movement of containment and resistance, which is always inevitably inside it' (R. Samuel, ed., *People's History and Socialist Theory*, 1981). The study of particular sport cultures can demonstrate this, showing how power relations themselves involve an ebb and flow of influences, illustrative of the reflexive and generative capacity of human actors to confirm, adapt, negotiate, and at times, through these various levels and degrees of resistance, remake their institutions and cultures. *See also* CULTURAL CONTESTATION; POWER.

resistance training A form of physical training designed to develop muscle strength by the imposition of a resistance to a muscle's contraction. The simplest forms of resistance training use the athlete's own body weight to provide the resistance, e.g. a press-up. The most common form of resistance training is weightlifting. Barbells or specialist weight machines allow an exercise to be focused on a particular muscle or group of muscles and altering the weight allows the overload (*see* TRAINING) to be optimized. Weightlifting may involve static exercise where the muscle contracts isometrically, or dynamic exercise involving movement. Weight training exercises are usually organized in terms of repeated movements broken down into sets to allow rest (e.g. 3 sets of 10 repetitions of biceps curl). Particular exercises, sets, repetitions, and resistances are organized and progressed in a complex manner to optimize strength or power gains. Resistance training improves muscle function through two main mechanisms: an improved neurological ability to activate and control muscle fibres, and hypertrophy (growth) of the muscle.

restraint of trade Processes whereby the free flow of market forces is, by intervention or manipulation, constrained. In professional football, for instance, the maximum wage that players could earn up to 1961 acted as a constraint on the trade of players whom some clubs saw as warranting much higher levels of remuneration. Abolition of the maximum wage opened up the market for top players. In 1995, the European Court of Justice in Luxembourg abolished the transfer system (for free agents) in European sports, and also the 3 + 2 rule that restricted the number of foreign players (3) and semi-foreign players (2) that could play in any club football team. Greeted by national, European, and world football bodies as a ruling that would ruin the game, this removal of constraint upon the trade of players opened up the possibilities in the football labour market that allowed sportsworkers to move with new levels of employer freedom. One consequence of the removal of such constraints has been the monopolization of available talent by the richest clubs.

retain and transfer system A form of player contract management used in English professional football from 1891 to 1963, that operated as a restriction on the mobility of players, and therefore of their labour rights. The English Football League (FL) adopted what the *Football Association (FA) had required from 1885: the annual registration of players on one-year contracts. Clubs in the FL could employ and play only those players who had registered for the club, and a player could not transfer to any other club without the consent of his employing club, and the approval of the regulatory bodies. A club could therefore retain a player indefinitely, until the player's services were no longer required, or an agreement was made to transfer the player's registration to another club. At the end of contracts, players had no negotiating powers, and even if a contract was not renewed or renegotiated, the player's registration could be retained by the club while he was placed on the 'transfer' list.

In 1963 Newcastle United's George Eastham took court action against the club, the FL, and the FA, disputing a retain and transfer system that was preventing him from joining the London club Arsenal as the employer of his choice at the end of his contract. The High Court in London ruled the system to be an 'unreasonable restraint of trade', though it was not deemed illegal: Eastham's successful challenge, with the Professional Footballers' Association, was the beginning of the reform of this feudal form of control by clubs of its workforce. The subsequent changes increased player power as well as mobility, and the capacity of the richest clubs to harness the best talent.

revenue sharing The principle whereby revenue is shared between teams in a league, by allocating, for instance, a specified percentage of stadium income to the visiting team. In the USA, baseball's National League, from its foundation in 1876, shared the gate revenues equally. By the mid 1990s, though, visiting teams received only 5 per cent of the gate money, and other sources of revenue sharing, in particular the *luxury tax, have picked up some of the redistributive slack. In England, football's Premier League/Premiership has operated a redistributive model for television income based on profile and achievement: 50 per cent shared equally between the clubs, 25 per cent allocated on the basis of league performance, and 25 per cent in relation to the number of appearances in televised matches. Such schemes are of particular interest to economists for their potential impact upon the distribution of talent in a league, and the latter's profitability. Restrictions in the labour market such as the *reserve clause and the *salary cap are also analysed in relation to these potential outcomes. *See also* COLLECTIVE SELLING.

Richmond, Bill (1763–1829) A slave born in Staten Island, New York, USA, who beame a self-taught boxer. Richmond had been a servant to the English Duke of Northumberland during the American Revolutionary War, and was brought to England by the duke. In England, though he worked as a hangman and trained as a cabinet-maker, Richmond made his living as a boxer, fighting Englishman Tom *Cribb, and befriending another freed slave, Tom Molineaux. Richmond was famous for his elusive dancing style, which enabled him to defeat much stronger and bigger opponents up to seventy pounds heavier than him. Known as 'The Black Terror', Richmond retired into respectability, running the Horse and Dolphin pub in central London, and operating a boxing academy where his pupils included English writer William Hazlitt. Richmond is featured in Alan Hollinghurst's gay novel *The Swimming-Pool Library* (1988) in a historical echo of his prominence and celebrity, and as a kind of ancestral exemplar for the celebration of the beautiful male body.

Riefenstahl, Leni (1902–2003) A German dancer, film actress, and documentary film-maker. Riefenstahl was the young star of several films in a genre romanticizing the mountains and the expressive human body. Her lasting fame came when she moved into documentary film-making and directed *Triumph of the Will* (1934) and *Olympia* (1936), the first focusing upon the Nazi regime's mass rally at Nuremberg, the second upon the 1936 Berlin Olympics. Riefenstahl was supported in these projects by the hierarchy of the Nazi Party, particularly the propaganda chief Josef Goebbels. After World War II she concentrated on films of pre-modern cultures and animal life, and refused to be drawn upon the question of the precise nature of her close working relationship with the Nazi Party. There is widespread agreement that her films were brilliant in technological innovation and cinematic quality, but the question of her political leanings—if these were at all significant—and their relationship to her artistic intent has never been settled. *See also* OWENS, JESSE.

rifle shooting *See* SHOOTING.

Riggs, Bobby (Robert Larimore) (1918–95) A US tennis player who competed on the national tennis circuit in the USA in the 1940s and was ranked as world number one for three years. Riggs remarked, at the age of 55: 'Even an old man like me, with one foot in the grave, could beat any woman player.' Australia's Margaret Court, the world's top player, played him and lost by 6–2, 6–1. The US world number two, Billie Jean King, then played him, in 1973 in an exhibition match of razzmatazz proportions, and won 6–4, 6–3, 6–3. His provocative showmanship had the effect of publicizing and popularizing the women's game, and despite his real competitive talent as a player, he is remembered, as in his obituary in *The Economist*, as a 'braggart male chauvinist'.

Rimet, Jules (1873–1956) The creator of the football World Cup, Frenchman Jules Rimet was president of world football's governing body the *Fédération Internationale de Football Association (FIFA) from 1921 to 1954. It was this self-made professional man and religious believer who dominated the growth of international football. He was trained in law, and as an older man, the bearded, bowler-hatted, and bourgeois Rimet was an established figure among Parisian polite society. But he came from humble origins, born in 1873 into a modest family in rural France, and from an early age helped his father in the family's grocer's shop. From the age of 11, though, he was raised in Paris where his father had moved in search of work. He lived in the heart of the city, learning to survive in the tough urban setting, in part by playing football on the street. A conscientious and able schoolboy, he worked his way towards a full legal qualification, as well as encouraging football among the poorer children of the city. He was one of a philanthropic breed of sport administrators who saw sport as a means of building good character. Christian and patriotic, his love of God and France came together in his passion for football. He believed in the universality of the church and saw in football the chance to create a worldwide 'football family' wedded to Christian principles. Like his countryman, Baron Pierre de *Coubertin, the founder of the modern Olympics, Rimet believed that sport could be a force for national and international good. Sport and football could bring people and nations together in a healthy competitiveness, he thought. Sport could be a powerful means of both physical and moral progress, providing healthy pleasure and fun, and promoting friendship between races. He resisted, though, the development of continental confederations and the empowerment of football confederations in Africa and in Asia, arguing that decentralization would destroy FIFA, and that 'only direct membership will retain FIFA as one family'.

Heading FIFA during its formative years, Rimet gave it a clear mission: to produce a global football family. But he found it difficult to escape Europe's imperiousness. Europeans still adopted supercilious approaches to South American members of the international football community. For example, at the first World Cup in Uruguay in 1930 only four of the fifteen competing teams—Rimet's own France, Belgium, Yugoslavia, and Romania—were from Europe. Uruguay's victories in the 1924 and 1928 Olympic football tournaments had encouraged the country's diplomats to lobby for the inaugural world football championships, and Rimet agreed to this prospect of spreading the FIFA gospel on the other side of the world. But although the World Cup was to be staged in Brazil in 1950, Rimet still resisted the formation of worldwide confederations, preferring to deal solely with the South American confederation, *CONMEBOL, established in 1916. It was not until the end of and after his extended presidency that confederations were established for Europe, Africa, Asia, Oceania, North and Central Americas and the Caribbean. Rimet's vision was rooted in what he called, speaking at the FIFA Congress in Rio de Janeiro in 1950, the 'finest human qualities' that football and sport could impart: loyalty to the spirit of the game; moderation in competition and sporting rivalry; and solidarity in clubs. But his philosophy of commonality of values—'world unity of football, the essential goal of FIFA, has been an accomplished fact: unity both moral and material', he claimed—was to be overtaken by the burgeoning ambitions of new nations in the postcolonial world. Rimet lent his name to the first World Cup trophy, which was won outright by Brazil on its third World Cup victory in 1970.

risk A term with a strong sense of everyday meaning and some specific conceptual and analytical variants in sports studies, widely derived from psychology, social psychology, and sociology. In a combination of its prevailing sense in sports studies and the everyday understanding of the term, risk sports are hazardous or dangerous activities—sometimes called *adventure or *extreme sports, and recognized as a subcategory of *lifestyle sports—that are undertaken in contexts or environments in which there are conditions beyond the control of the participant or any other involved person: these conditions have the capacity to generate injury or, in the ultimate case of loss, death. If an ice-hockey or rugby match breaks out in violence, the referee or official can cancel the event; in risk sports the influences of weather or environment exacerbate the inherent risk of the physical activity itself.

Most activities do not result in serious injury or death, though, and the psychological concept of *risk aversion* recognizes this: most people calculate that they will not be seriously injured or killed, anticipating eventualities and outcomes, probabilities and possibilities, and so estimating likelihood and levels of risk (another everyday variant, risk assessment, has become a commonplace principle of organizational life). Aversion to risk was identified by the Swiss scientist Daniel Bernoulli (1700–82), writing as early as 1738, confirming the cross-temporal and cross-societal significance of the concept of risk, and its empirical significance, in social life. In psychology, risk has also been studied in the context of gambling, with wagering on the outcome of a race or contest a widely popular form of *risk seeking*; and a tendency for people to take riskier, more threatening or potentially hazardous, decisions when they are in groups than when they are alone has been labelled the *risky-shift effect* (consider here the number of cases of death on the mountains of groups, in circumstances and conditions in which it is hugely likely—though one can never know—that an individual on his or her own would have turned back or gone no further).

In sociology, the principle of risk has been placed at the centre of a theory of society by the German sociologist Ulrich Beck, whose *Risk Society: Towards a New Modernity* (1986) contrasted earlier pre-industrial values such as fate with an approach to risk assessment characteristic of the rational values of modern industrial society; and located, in the second half of the 20th century, a further form of risk, recognizing the global scale of uncontrollable—environmental, meteorological, financial—risk underpinning much of social life. The search for adventurous physical activity, the expansion in the participant and spectator base of extreme or risk sports, are interesting examples in sport of a cultural trend to seek risks and associated thrills, in contexts and environments on the edge of the uncontrollable, and often way beyond the insurable.

rites of passage The processes identified by the Belgian anthropologist Arnold van Gennep, referring to the stages or *rituals through which an individual must pass in order to achieve full acceptance into a society or a culture (*The Rites of Passage*, 1909). There were three such stages: first, separation from a former status; second, a state of limbo, or *liminality, between the old and the new status; third, the symbolic consummation of the new status, linked to the reincorporation of the individual into the group, culture, or society. Sport cultures, from fan groups to college sport teams, mobilize such rites of passage in the maintenance of their subcultural identities. Peter Marsh's research on football-terrace cultures highlighted rituals, and ritual insults, 'related to the age-old problem of proving that one is better at being a man than one's rival' (Peter Marsh, Elizabeth Rosser, and Rom Harré, *The Rules of Disorder*, 1978: 133). Such affirmations of masculinity allowed the fan to progress through, and be accepted by, different levels of the football-terrace culture's hierarchy. In numerous sporting cultures, *hazing has been a form of ritual initiation into the group, a necessary rite of passage.

ritual A term referring to recurring activities or behaviours, in predominantly collective settings, that highlight activities and/or feelings that have the effect of reinforcing how one lives or what one believes. Rituals have been fundamental to forms of religious practice, in highly symbolic forms in the institutional setting of the particular doctrine or belief-system. Ritual symbols have the power to express values claimed to be of widely collective significance: in Victor Turner's formulation, they can unite a multitude of sources of meaning into a single expression of thought and feeling. Anthropologists have recognized the widespread significance of forms of secular ritual, in activities and institutional settings such as politics, health, music, tourism, and sport. Rituals might be reinforcing, confirming the stability of a culture, the nature of a group, and the sources of its identity. But a ritual might also be a *rite of passage for an individual, confirming entry to another status within the group. Ritual has been studied at the level of the local culture and a sport's contribution to traditional values; at the level of institutions such as schools in which conceptions of the preferred curriculum construct particular understandings of the body; and at the level of mediated sport, in which ritual may give way to *ceremony or *spectacle. At all these levels 'sports are extremely rich in symbolization and undoubtedly possess the capacity to represent social relationships in a particularly striking, preferred way [and] can function to symbolize or encode preferred views of the social order and thus legitimize power relations' (John Hargreaves, *Sport, Power and Culture: A Social and Historical Analysis of Popular Sports in Britain*, 1986).

road walking *See* RACE-WALKING; PEDESTRIANISM.

Robinson, Jackie (Jack Roosevelt) (1919–72) A US baseball player, born in Georgia, whose debut for the Brooklyn Dodgers in 1947 was the first case of a black player competing in the modern competitive game, breaking sixty years of prejudice and discrimination in professional baseball's segregation system. In 1949 Robinson was the first black player to be awarded the Most Valuable Player (MVP) title for the season, and was top of the National League's batting figures. After retirement Robinson went on to successful business ventures, in sport commentary, and banking (an enterprise based entirely in Harlem). He had also acted as himself in the film *The Jackie Robinson Story* (1950). Dying suddenly of a heart attack, Robinson was posthumously awarded the Presidential Medal of Freedom and the Congressional Gold Medal. A half century on from his debut for the Dodgers, the MLB (Major League Baseball) withdrew its number 42 shirt/jersey number from all its teams, at a ceremony in the Dodgers' home venue, the Shea Stadium, in tribute to Robinson's achievements and symbolic status as an influential and pioneering African American *role model.

rodeo A competitive exhibition of the skills of individual cowboys (or cattle-punchers), particularly in riding, that is established as a popular spectacle in North America. The term 'rodeo' is from the Spanish *rodear* ('to go round'). In its organized form, it originated in the southern and south-west states of the USA in the 1860s and 1870s, established with paying spectators in the 1880s. Its six classic events are *calf roping, bull riding, team roping, saddle bronco riding, bareback bronco riding, and steer wrestling. A seventh event, barrel racing, was introduced initially for women riders. Animal rights activists have opposed rodeo, seeing it as a form of cruelty, and professional rodeo organizations have responded by introducing measures to protect the animals. Rodeo has remained popular in the western states of the USA, and in Canada where the showcase event is the *Calgary Stampede.

role Role is a long-established core concept in social psychological and sociological theory. Hans Gerth and C. Wright Mills wrote, in their *Character and Social Structure* (1953), that, as a historical creation, a person 'can most readily be understood in terms of the roles which he enacts and incorporates', and 'one person may play many different roles'. In sport culture this is instanced in the different roles that the same individual can adopt as performer, competitor, fan, critic, and the like. Roles also have varying levels of influence or authority attached to them—coach, captain, trainer, manager, for instance—and confusion over the specific nature of those roles can lead to the breakdown of social coherence or social organization, in forms of *role-conflict. Roles in sociological approaches are seen as the positions occupied by people within the social structure; in social psychology they are seen as elements manifest in the interactions that make up social life (for this perspective, see the work of Erving *Goffman). The sum of a number of roles has been referred to as the *role-set*: I might be the parent at home, the departmental boss at work, and the cricket captain at weekends. Juggling the obligations of, and expectations of others towards, that role-set makes up much of what constitutes a person's social identity and individuality. In looking at roles in sport cultures, therefore, the most illuminating approach is to see roles as both imposed and self-generated, in an integrated sociological and social psychological framework.

role-conflict The experience of tensions in handling the obligations of different and sometimes incompatible roles. In a sport team, for instance, if a captain assumes too much personal authority this may produce a clash with the coach; a manager may find the economic responsibilities of the chief executive spilling over into playing matters. In professional team sports, such role-conflicts frequently lead to the dismissal of individuals from those key roles. Role-conflict can also be generated in professional contexts such as the teaching of physical education, and in the pressures on individuals to conform with role expectations associated with a dominant sense of sporting values. Leo Hendry's 'Survival in a Marginal Role: The Professional Identity of the Physical Education Teacher' (*British Journal of Sociology*, 1975) showed how the relatively low status of the physical education (PE) teacher in the school hierarchy produced tensions in the teacher's relationships with teachers of other subjects, and difficulties of career progression; this, exacerbated by the ageing process, meant that for many PE teachers, professional advancement was dependent upon a move into other spheres, such as pastoral work or management. Doing sport, for some groups, has also involved tensions and role conflict, as widely researched and reported in the case of girls' experiences of sport and physical education in schools. Claudia Cockburn and Gill Clarke's '"Everybody's looking at you!" Girls negotiating the "femininity deficit" they incur in physical education' (*Women's Studies International Forum*, vol. 25, 2002) identified the persistingly polarized images of tomboy and girlie that young women have to negotiate. To cope with this, the subjects in the study adopted double identities and lived split lives.

role model A term that has been adopted in everyday language and life to refer to the (usually positive) attributes of a prominent individual, whose behaviour and conduct is assumed to have an effect upon the attitudes and actions of groups and individuals. 'Oh, s/he's a great role model' has become a form of shorthand in evaluating positively the impact of an influential or prominent individual. In social psychology, the role model is a *significant other whose behaviour in a particular *role provides a pattern for other individuals: a great sportsman or -woman might restrict public knowledge of himself or herself to the sphere of the sporting contest, so the role model effect then refers only to the approach to the playing of the sport. But role models in sport have been seen in an increasing number of roles—advertisement for a particular commercial product, ambassador for the political ambitions of a nation, for instance—and the terms of the role model debate have, as a consequence, widened. The term was popularized in sociology by Robert K. Merton (1910–2003): 'The term "role model" first appeared in a Columbia study of the socialization of medical students, and was to become wildly popular', observed Gerald Holton in his biographical memoir of Merton (*Proceedings of the American Philosophical Society*, vol. 148, 2004). For Merton, the role model was one of the available exemplars within a *reference group of potentially available roles. The term role model has been criticized as 'outdated', based in a 'discredited functionalist model of socialisation' (Garry Whannel, *Media Sport Stars: Masculinities and Moralities*, 2002). But the term continues to have a prominent profile in everyday parlance, a powerful presence in media and cultural industries, and a place in sport policy development. It is important to critique the underlying flaws of the concept as a sociocultural process, but equally important to recognize its currency in the popular consciousness and the cultural industries. *See also* REFERENCE GROUP.

role theory A sociological approach concerned with the identification and analysis of roles and role-taking in social relations, and the significance of roles in the construction and reproduction of social relations and social organization. *See also* ROLE; ROLE-CONFLICT; ROLE MODEL.

roller hockey A five-a-side stick-and-ball game combining elements of *ice hockey and *field hockey. It is played on *roller-skating rinks and also known, in Europe, as rink-hockey. Introduced in London in the later 1870s, its first international fixture was between British and French teams at the Paris Hippodrome in 1910, won by the Crystal Palace Engineers club. An Amateur Rink Hockey Association had been formed in the UK in 1908. A European championship was inaugurated at Herne Bay, Kent, England, in 1926, and Britain won the first world championship ten years later. After World War II, the main base of the game was in Portugal, and across southern Europe, with strong teams emerging in Spain, Switzerland, and Italy. The Fédération Internationale de Patinage à Roulettes was established in Montreux, Switzerland, in 1924, becoming the Fédération Internationale de Roller Skating in the mid 1960s, and the Fédération Internationale de Roller Sports in 2000. Roller hockey was a demonstration sport at the 1992 Barcelona Olympic Games, and roller sports are a recognized sport of the International Olympic Committee. Roller hockey has remained a relatively low-profile sport, though it still generates national and international competition among its enthusiasts.

roller skating A competitive sport that has taken three forms, as in *ice skating: speed roller skating; figure roller skating; and roller dancing. The four-wheel roller skate was invented by James L. Plimpton (1828–1911), who opened the first rink in Newport, Rhode Island, USA, in 1866, initially for ice skaters to practise off-ice. Technological advances such as the ball-bearing skate (1884) gave the activity a momentum of its own, and its combination of speed, performance, and display attracted large numbers of participants in the USA and Britain in the years preceding World War I. Speed skating and figure skating world championships were held (in Italy and Germany) in 1937, and roller dancing championships in the USA in 1947. The competitive dimension of roller skating has been undermined by further technological and design-led changes, the more individualized and performative activity of roller booting superseding the more old-fashioned look and style of the roller skater. *See also* ROLLER HOCKEY.

Roman baths Public facilities developed in ancient Rome, based upon customs imported from Campania, also known as *thermae*. The first such facility constructed in the Republic was the Baths of Agrippa, situated behind the Pantheon in Rome. Public baths became an established feature of all Roman cities. The largest examples in Rome were the Baths of Caracalla and Diocletian (AD 298), made possible in part by the use of concrete that could facilitate expansive architectural design on unprecedented scale. The Baths of Diocletian occupied around 27 acres of land, and could accommodate 3,000 bathers, twice as many as those of Caracalla. The baths comprised a range of facilities: hot, warm, and cold rooms; changing rooms where slaves would guard the bathers' garments in the niches in the wall that acted as lockers; rooms for getting rubbed down with oil; the Greek-style *palaestra* where exercisers could work out, wrestle, fence, or box, but mostly played ball games; gardens and an outdoor running track; corners and colonnades for rest and contemplation. The ball games were mostly played before bathing, and mostly involved groups: one group would try to grab, or rob, the coloured (stuffed, or air-filled leather) ball from another group. There were also Greek and Latin libraries in the complex. Classicist Norma Goldman notes that: 'Baths were not just for bathing, they were social centers where Romans spent entire afternoons' (Robert Kahn, ed., *City Secrets: Rome*, New York, The Little Bookroom, p. 35). Conversation as well as callisthenics was certainly on the agenda at complexes such as these. The Roman baths showed the persisting influence of Greek physical culture in at least one element of Roman cultural and physical life, offering a means of combining a healthy mind with a healthy body, as recommended by *Juvenal as a way of countering excess.

Rome, ancient, sport in The histories of the Roman Republic (established in 509 BC, though Rome's Forum and the *Circus Maximus were laid out in the later years of the seventh century BC) and of the Roman Empire (the last emperor of the western empire relinquished power in AD 475 when Byzantium became the new seat of the empire, in the east) include the recognition of the cultural, social, and political significance of sport. Sport had particular ceremonial uses and meanings at various points of Roman history, sometimes linked to religion, but always and increasingly linked to networks of political power and social status. Political figures such as the military leader and political dictator Julius *Caesar and the Emperor *Nero used sport to boost personal reputations and bolster political power; and sport and the provision of sporting facilities affected much prominent architecture, such as the *Colosseum, at which *gladiatorial games were staged; or the *Roman baths, where a more genteel form of physical culture and sporting endeavour was manifest.

Given the longevity of Roman civilization it would serve no purpose to provided an overview of sport in ancient Rome. It is more productive to focus upon particular sport-related institutions of ancient Rome, such as those cross-referenced here, and to point to some general features characterizing sport's place in that culture. Sport was more violent in ancient Rome than in classical Greek culture, and developed as politically motivated forms of spectacle. The increasing influence of Christianity undermined the cultural and cognitive basis of combat sports, if not *chariot racing, and leaves one with the question: what were the sources of and influences upon the sporting morality of a culture in which the sporting spectacle was of a kind that many cultures and societies, both before and since, have considered as cruel and inhuman? One answer might be to look closely at the cultural commentators of the time, such as poet and satirist *Juvenal.

Roosevelt, Theodore (1858–1919) The twenty-ninth president of the USA (1901–9), who was educated privately and attended Harvard. Born and raised into a wealthy family in New York City, Roosevelt was asthmatic and relatively weakly as a child and came to believe in the value of physical activity and strenuous exercise and sports as both a means of recuperation or strengthening, and an expression of moral worth. In his mid twenties, his mother and his first wife died on the same day and he coped with this by staying at his ranch in Dakota Territory, riding, cattle-driving, and big-game hunting. In his early thirties he published an article in the *The North American Review* (vol. 405, issue 151) extolling the virtues of an athletic life:

> There is a certain tendency in the civilization of our time to underestimate or overlook the need of the virile, masterful qualities of the heart and mind which have built up and alone can maintain and defend this very civilization, and which generally go hand in hand with good health and the capacity to get the utmost possible use out of the body. There is no better way of counteracting this tendency than by encouraging bodily exercise, and especially the sports which develop such qualities as courage, resolution, and endurance.

During the Spanish-American War (April–August 1898) Roosevelt was a lieutenant-colonel in the Rough Rider Regiment, achieving heroic status after leading a cavalry charge at the Battle of San Juan. Persuaded, as this heroic figure, to enter politics, he won the governorship of New York that same year. Winning the presidency, at 43 years of age the youngest ever incumbent, he had no hesitation in mobilizing the power of government in reforming corporate practices and the easily corruptible economic system, conceding that 'I did greatly broaden the use of executive power'. As the White House potted biography notes (2009), throughout his presidency Roosevelt continued to advocate 'the life of strenuous endeavor', which 'was a must for those around him, as he romped with his five younger children and led ambassadors on hikes through Rock Creek Park in Washington, D.C.'. Roosevelt's enthusiasm for the benefits of the sporting life and what his 1890 essay called 'healthy muscular amusements' was shared with his contemporary, the British prime minister A. J. *Balfour, with whom he conducted a correspondence on such issues: 'In college and in most of the schools which are preparatory for college rowing, foot-ball, base-ball, running, jumping, sparring, and the like have assumed a constantly increasing prominence. Nor is this in any way a matter for regret.' His essay entitled 'Professionalism in Sports' condemned the rise of paid performance in a number of sports (he excluded baseball):

aside from this one pastime, professionalism is the curse of many an athletic sport, and the chief obstacle to its healthy development. Professional rowing is under a dark cloud of suspicion because of the crooked practices which have disgraced it. Horse-racing is certainly not in an ideal condition. A prize-fight is simply brutal and degrading.

rounders A nine-a-side outdoor bat-and-ball game, originating in Britain and called 'base-ball' in *A Little Pretty Pocket Book* (1744). The game is seen as an early form of what was developed into *baseball. Rules were formalized in the early 20th century, with a version published by the *Ling Association in 1931. A National Rounders Association was founded in 1943. Played by both boys and girls, it is a sport still conducive to spontaneous forms of organization.

Rous, Sir Stanley (1895–1986) An influential football administrator who was secretary of the English Football Association (FA) and went on to be president of world football's governing body, the *Fédération Internationale de Football Association (FIFA). Although not assuming the FIFA presidency until 1961, Sir Stanley Rous was an influential force in the game of association football after World War II, holding the post of secretary of the (English) Football Association from 1934 to 1961. Rous took over at FIFA in his mid sixties, the age at which most people retired, and he grasped this new challenge with typical energy and commitment. Walter Winterbottom, the first man to be appointed as manager of the England team, says that 'in our own country he took us out of being an insular Association Football League and got us back into world football and this was tremendous'. Winterbottom also praised Rous's exceptional charm and diplomatic skills.

A son of the middle classes, Rous's father had planned for him to go to Emmanuel College, Cambridge. But, after service in Africa during World War I, Rous studied at St. Luke's College, Exeter, and then taught at Watford Grammar School. He was not born into the establishment but through football he became an establishment figure. For him, teaching and football were acts of public service. He played football at college, then in the Army during the War. Though he may have been good enough to play the game professionally, his commitment to amateur ideals denied him the chance to be paid for playing. Instead, in 1927 Rous became a referee of international repute. This is where he made his first impact on world football. His rewriting of the rules of the game in 1938 was immensely influential. In administration, he went on to modernize the English game, establishing a more efficient bureaucratic base, introducing teaching schemes for all levels of the game —coaching, playing, refereeing.

The FA had left FIFA in 1928 and Rous believed that it was time for Britain to be reintegrated with world football. In a paper which he presented to the Football Association, first drafted in May 1943, he claimed that the activities of the FA's War Emergency Committee had boosted football's international profile by fostering relations with government departments and by establishing links with influential people through cooperation with the armed forces. Recognizing that Britain's formal political empire was about to shrink dramatically, he saw in football a chance to retain some influence over world culture: 'The unparalleled opportunity which the war years have given the Association of being of service to countries other than our own', he wrote, 'has laid an excellent foundation for post-war international development.' A modernizer on the world stage, he remained nevertheless trapped in an anachronistic set of values. 'We used to look upon it as a sport, as a recreation,' he said in a BBC interview in the early 1980s. 'We had little regard of points and league position and cup competitions. We used to play friendly matches, mostly. There was always such a sporting attitude and the winners always clapped the others off the field and so on.' Ruefully he added, 'That's all changed of course.'

Despite such a nostalgic sentiment Rous transformed the profile of England in the international sporting world. He was knighted for his contribution to the London 1948 Olympic Games, and was instrumental in getting the 1966 World Cup located in England. He was, however, concerned at the economic practices and interpersonal pressures which surrounded the bids of Argentina and Mexico to host the 1970 finals. To curb this, as FIFA president, he developed a planning cycle for the event, calling this 'the long look ahead', designed to give adequate notice to those committing themselves to such a major event. He wanted to give hosts the advantage of a twelve-year lead-in, and at FIFA's 1963 Congress in Tokyo, a future list for post-England 1966 was confirmed: Mexico 1970; West Germany 1974; Argentina 1978; Spain 1982. Colombia received the same twelve years of notice, at the end of Rous's presidency, for the 1986 finals (but ended up having to pull out). Rous foresaw the co-hosting role, and proposed that FIFA's long-term plan should envisage zoning the finals, suggesting that the event could be split up between three or four countries.

As the media profile of the modern game expanded, Rous was increasingly uncomfortable with the intrusiveness of the broadcast media, and the politics of the world game, and was defeated by the Brazilian Dr João Havelange in a vote for the presidency at the FIFA Congress of 1974. When he stood for re-election, claiming that he wanted 'just a couple of years to push through some important schemes', Rous either had a confidence which was misplaced, or he had miscalculated the institutional politics of FIFA. Ten years on he put his defeat down to the limitless ambitions of his rival: 'I know what activity was being practised by my successor, the appeals that he'd made to countries'. The countries to which Havelange had appealed included the newly independent nations of Africa and Asia, some of whom Rous had offended in what were perceived as neocolonial positions on issues such as the South African question. For all Rous's forward thinking, his defeat by Havelange was a barometer of a changing international sporting politics, in which the aspirations of emerging and developing countries and the ambitions of new players in the international sporting economy combined to oust him.

rowing The act of propelling a boat by the use of oars, practised on inland rivers, lakes, and canals, and sometimes in coastal waters. Rowers in what are called sweep events use a single oar each and so the coordination of their strokes in eight- and four-person crews is the key to competitive success. In sculling events, the rower pulls two oars. Oarsmen were described by the Roman poet Virgil in his *Aeneid*, on the occasion of some funeral games staged by Aeneas to honour his father: 'crowned with poplar wreaths', the crews' 'naked shoulders glisten, moist with oil' as their arms and oars 'churn the water into foam'. Practised by watermen on the

River Thames in England in the later 18th century, competitive rowing was established in British public schools at around the same time, from where participants and competitors went on to establish the sport at the universities of Oxford and Cambridge in the early 19th century: the first boat race between the two universities took place at Henley in 1829. Henley instituted its regatta (from the Italian *regatta*, the term for Venice's Grand Canal boat races) ten years later. In the USA, professional watermen raced in New York waters in the early 19th century, and amateur clubs formed in New York in the 1830s. Harvard and Yale raced each other in the country's first inter-collegiate boat race in 1852. Rowing in Australia dates from the 1830s, when whaling boat crews competed with crews from stations on the shore in Tasmania, and the Royal Hobart Regatta was founded in 1838. Sydney and Melbourne universities raced each other for the first time on the Paramatta River in Sydney in 1863.

Professional rowing and sculling, combining outdoor spectacle and the excitement of the wager, was widely popular in the 19th century, with a sculling world championship from 1831 to 1875, but amateur/professional crises in rowing and the place of the sport in the Olympic programme cemented the amateurist hegemony. The Fédération Internationale des Sociétés d'Aviron (FISA) was founded in 1892 by federations of the Adriatic, Belgium, France, Italy, and Switzerland: Britain remained insular and haughtily aloof, only joining FISA in 1947. The first European Rowing Championship was held (for men) in 1894, a women's equivalent in 1954. Modern Olympic rowing has established eight men's events (from 1900 onwards) and six women's events (from 1972 onwards), and there have been numerous discontinued specialist events in Olympic history. The spectator appeal of rowing lies in the utter intensity of the physical effort of the rower, and the machine-like efficiency that underlies the rower's contribution to the collective effort, while also illuminating the human pain and vulnerability of the contestant in the moment of maximum effort and physical and psychological demands. *See also* OXFORD-CAMBRIDGE BOAT RACE.

Royal & Ancient (R&A) A golf club based at St Andrews, Scotland, where golfing enthusiasts played a competition based on written rules in 1754. The St Andrews golfers played eleven holes along the shoreline, and the same holes in reverse direction. In 1764, the club converted the first four holes into two, thus constituting a round of eighteen holes. As it came to be recognized as the primary authority on golf in the UK, eighteen holes became the standard round; though it was not until 1919 that the R&A became officially recognized as the overarching authority for the game in the UK, much later than its opposite number in the USA, the United States Golf Association, formed in 1891. *See also* GOLF.

Rudolph, Wilma Glodean (1940–94) A black US athlete whose three winner's medals in athletics (100 metres, 200 metres, and 4 × 100 metres) at the 1960 Rome Summer Olympic Games constituted the first three-gold haul by a US woman at an Olympics. These triumphs attracted her the nickname 'The Tornado', though in France she was known as 'The Black Pearl' and in Italy 'The Black Gazelle'. A talented basketball player as a schoolgirl, Rudolph had overcome crippling forms of polio as a young child, and was the twentieth of 22 children in a poor family in

Clarksville, Tennessee. Her athletic potential was seen by Ed Temple, coach of the Tennessee State University's Tigerbelles women's athletics team, and she received a scholarship to the university. She saw her athletic talent as an important statement about the status and abilities of African Americans, and paid tribute to Jesse *Owens as an example and an inspiration; on returning from Rome, she insisted that her homecoming parade be integrated, and not racially segregated. Retiring from the still-amateur athletics world, she completed her degree and qualified as a schoolteacher, though she went on to hold university coaching appointments and combined this with some sport commentating and public speaking, before dying of cancer at the age of 54. After her Olympic triumphs she was also asked by the US State Department to act as a goodwill ambassador at the Games of Friendship in Dakar, Senegal (1963). She is commemorated in the US Women's Sports Foundation's award for outstanding courage and achievement:

> The Wilma Rudolph Courage Award is presented to a female athlete who exhibits extraordinary courage in her athletic performance, demonstrates the ability to overcome adversity, makes significant contributions to sports and serves as an inspiration and role model to those who face challenges, overcomes them and strives for success at all levels.

Rugby League football A thirteen-a-side game played with an oval ball, in which players run with the ball, pass it from hand to hand, and kick it towards an opponent's goalposts in order to score points by way of goal-kicking and achieving tries (these latter being the placing of the ball by hand in the space behind the opposition's goalposts). The game derived from *Rugby Union, in what Tony Collins has called *Rugby's great split*, when 21 clubs formed the Northern Union in England, at a meeting in Huddersfield, Yorkshire, in 1895. This group of northern clubs favoured compensation and incentive payments to players, accepted professionalism three years later, and pioneered a form of the game in which running and fluency could be emphasized to appeal to a paying public. In challenging the amateur hegemony of the Rugby Union, the northern breakaway (which went from fifteen to thirteen players per side in 1906, and changed its name to the Rugby Football League in 1922) was therefore also a cultural formation of a particular social-class dynamic, with a commercial class blending with the working class to develop a professionalized form of the sport that might have more of the spectator appeal of the professional and widely popular association code (soccer).

Within Britain, the sport remained predominantly regional, its heartlands the northern counties of Lancashire and Yorkshire; initiatives to establish it in Wales and in London and the south of England were short-lived and unsuccessful. The game has been associated with a local cultural base in the particular community, though it has also had a more global dimension in the number of non-British players who came to England to play the game professionally. In 1949, an 'Other Nationalities' team was allowed to compete in Britain's international championship, and fielded players from Australia, Scotland, South Africa, and New Zealand: it won the title in 1953 and 1955. Internationally, the game has flourished in parts of Australia, France, and New Zealand. Catalans Dragons versus Wakefield Wildcats became a regular fixture in the first decade of the 21st century; the sight of a Yorkshire club side playing a transnational side among a modest but sell-out crowd at the foot of the Pyrenees is testimony to sport's capacity to transcend cultural barriers and bolster the local tourist economy.

Rugby Union football A fifteen-a-side game based on handling, passing, and kicking an oval ball, and aiming to accumulate points by kicking goals or scoring tries (these latter being the placing of the ball by hand in the space behind the opposition's goalposts). With origins in the football played at Rugby School, England, the game was one of two evolving codes or forms of play in the mid 19th century: the dribbling code, and the handling code. This latter was favoured by the pupils and old boys (alumni) of Rugby, Marlborough, and Cheltenham, while the dribblers came from Eton, Harrow, Westminster, and Charterhouse. At the University of Cambridge, a football club had been founded by Old Rugbeians as early as 1839, and undergraduates who had come from Eton were infuriated when the Rugbeians picked up the ball in the middle of play. At a meeting in 1846 (in the same year that a set of rules was published at Rugby School), the Old Etonians formulated the *Cambridge Rules that were the basis of the code adopted by the Football Association on its formation in 1863: the code of association *football, or soccer. The Rugby Football Union (RFU) organization was founded in 1871, and codified the rugby game in the context of an extended debate about hacking (the kicking of opponents). A meeting at Cambridge in 1863 had banned hacking, but those clubs that continued to accept hacking played the game that the 1871 governing body then oversaw. Games at Rugby School might sometimes have involved three hundred boys, and teams of twenty-five and more often took the field up to the last quarter of the 19th century. Fifteen-a-side teams were introduced in the fourth Oxford versus Cambridge match of 1875, and at international level when England played Ireland in 1877.

The RFU's membership rose from 31 clubs in 1872 to 481 in 1893, but this growth also spread and popularized the game among non-traditionalists in working-class, industrial areas in the country, where a competitive sport played for money had much appeal. The breakaway that led to *Rugby League occurred in 1895. The RFU had reaffirmed its naming rights in 1893, when specifying that its membership be 'composed entirely of amateurs . . . and its headquarters . . . in London where all general meetings shall be held'. Within a decade, the RFU lost 237 member clubs to the rival codes of Rugby League and association football, and its avowed amateur stance consolidated Rugby Union's status in England as a recreation of the established classes. The Rugby game was established in Scotland and in Ireland, in Edinburgh and Dublin respectively, in the mid 1850s. The game came later to Wales, introduced in its codified form by Oxford and Cambridge graduates, and enthusiastically embraced by male players of both the professional and the working classes. In the first decade of the 20th century, Wales was the dominant international side in Great Britain, also inflicting the only defeat on the touring New Zealand side (the All Blacks) at Cardiff in 1905.

Rugby had been adopted in the British Commonwealth in New Zealand, South Africa, and Australia in the 1870s, and in Canada in the 1880s. Cambridge graduates introduced the game in Japan in 1899, and, encouraged by New Zealand's support, it took hold in Tonga and Fiji in the early 20th century. In

South America, British railway engineers and builders working in Buenos Aires introduced the game to Argentina, where the national Rugby Union was founded in 1899. In France, the game was introduced into the northern regions and Paris by British businessmen and residents, and prospered in Bordeaux in the first decade of the 20th century, while in the south-east a Welsh immigrant established a strong institutional club base for the game in Perpignan in 1912.

The RFU and the International Rugby Board adhered to the amateur ethos for decades, throughout notorious cases of *shamateurism and underhand sponsorship payments, but recognized the power of the international marketplace in the mid 1990s when professionalism was accepted, and domestic leagues and world tournaments were repackaged in return for unprecedented levels of income from television and sponsors. The Rugby World Cup staged in France in 2007 was heralded as an all-round success, with early games characterized by a party atmosphere among spectators, in which entertaining stylists and ambitious outsiders brought colour and drama to the 'manly' game evolved by the privileged schoolboys and undergraduates of Victorian Britain.

running One of the most fundamental of human sporting practices, running has appealed to participants and spectators for its combination of speed and endurance in performance, the visibly dramatic element of competition, and its health-promoting qualities. Regardless of advances in training and equipment, the essential simplicity of the sport—first past the post or to the finishing line—continues to place running at the core of sporting traditions and events. Sprinting generates interest in the fastest man or woman on earth; the marathon rewards endurance and toughness. This elemental dimension of running has kept running events at the heart of the athletics and track-and-field agenda, a major draw in the core location of the stadium at the Olympics. Running has also been a pivotal activity in the expansion of leisure sports, linked to fitness and fashion but also to health-promotion drives by policy-makers and providers. On the more individual, experiential level running also offers a source of aesthetic experience, what English runner Roger Bannister recalled as a 'unity with nature . . . a new source of power and beauty', as well as 'a joy, freedom and challenge which cannot be found elsewhere' (*First Four Minutes*, 1955). The widespread appeal of running—or 'foot-racing'—was recognized by Joseph Strutt (*Sports and Pastimes of the People of England*, 1801): 'There is no kind of exercise that has more uniformly met the approbation of authors than running. In the middle ages, foot-racing was considered as an essential part of a young man's education, especially if he was the son of a man of rank, and brought up to a military profession.' The development of different and specialized forms of running—middle-distance, long-distance—has fed the hunger for records in modern professional sports, as well as the attraction of the 'personal best' to runners at all levels of achievement. *See also* CROSS-COUNTRY RUNNING; JOGGING; LOUES, SPIRIDON; OLYMPIC GAMES, ANCIENT; PHIDIPPIDES; RACE-WALKING; SPRINTING.

Runyon, Damon (1884–1946) Born in Kansas, raised in Colorado, Runyon was an innovative sports writer for the *New York American* and other publications. He was particularly interested in the character and context of the baseball or boxing match. His short stories also highlighted gambling and the theatrical world. Runyon was, as Jonathan Yardley has observed, 'the most prominent and financially successful *Lardner imitator in journalism, transposing Ring's use of Middle Western vernacular to the Broadway world of showbiz people and small-time punks he himself knew well' (*Ring: A Biography of Ring Lardner*, 1977). Runyon is included in the writers' wing of the Baseball Hall of Fame.

Ruth, George Herman (Babe) (1895–1948) A US-born American baseball player whose combination of record-breaking performances (as a power-hitter and a pitcher) and commercial and celebrity profile symbolized the emergence of baseball in its modernized and professionalized form. Born in Baltimore, Maryland, Ruth was raised for twelve years in St Mary's Industrial School for Boys, a reformatory and orphanage to which his parents, who ran a waterfront bar, consigned him at the age of 7. Xaverian brothers (Catholic missionaries) at St Mary's instilled in the young Ruth a commitment to baseball, as a way of curbing his indiscipline and rebelliousness. Ruth was signed to play for the local International League side, Baltimore Orioles, in 1914, and within five months his contract was purchased by the American League's Boston Red Sox, for whom he played for six years before moving to the New York Yankees for an unprecedentedly high fee of $125,000 plus a loan of $350,000. He played in New York until 1934, and then from the following year for Boston Braves for two seasons.

Generations after Ruth finished playing, the Yankee Stadium was still referred to as 'the House that Ruth built'. His popularity and performance—he set 76 batting and pitching records—attracted capacity crowds that helped fund the new Yankee Stadium that opened in 1923, and he was sponsored by manufacturers of breakfast cereal as well as baseball bats and balls. Marrying his second wife—an actress and model—in 1929, the next day Ruth hit a ball out of the stadium in the Yankees' opening game of the new season, claiming to have planned this in celebration of the marriage. In 1932, he struck what has been claimed as the longest home run ever hit, at the Chicago Cubs' ground, in the direction in which he had pointed before striking the ball. These forms of showmanship and repeated winning performances cemented Ruth's place in the pantheon of American sport stars. Mindful of his unhappy childhood, and at the same time his debt to those who raised him, Ruth in his retirement made frequent appearances at hospitals and orphanages, and established the Babe Ruth Foundation for Underprivileged Children, to which he left most of his estate on his death.

Rwandan high jumping A form of jumping over a horizontal bar, practised by Rwandan males in Africa, and documented by European travellers and imperialists through the first third of the 20th century. John Bale (*Imagined Olympians: Body Culture and Colonial Representation in Rwanda*, 2002) has explored the activity in the context of *postcolonialism, in a project of what he calls 'imaginative sports geography', in which 'the colonial textual creation of sports out of regionally specific body cultures' is as much the focus of study as is the precise nature of the practice itself. Rwandan high jumping was several things at once: manly training, including in the context of warrior education; courtly performance or celebration; a focus for popular amusement and recreational gatherings in the community; a source, for the jumpers themselves, of communal fame; and, possibly, an element in wider *ritual. But what it was not was a type of formal, documented achievement sport: it remained a 'folk-like activity that never became sportized', as Bale puts it; and one that excited the European imagination through the elastic and arresting physical feats of the Rwandans. The study of such a sporting practice or dimension of a body culture is a reminder of the specificity of Western conceptions of the sporting body, and close study of the visual and written representations of the jumper, in deconstructing photographic and written texts as Bale does, demonstrates the specificity of some body cultures at the time of the ascendancy of dominant models of modern sport. *See also* HIGH JUMPING.

Ryder Cup A golf tournament played in alternate years, initially between male professional golfers in teams representing the USA and Great Britain. It began in 1927, following an exhibition match in 1926 at the Wentworth Course, Virginia Water, Surrey, England. Samuel Ryder, a seed merchant from Hertfordshire, England, had watched the exhibition match (overwhelmingly won by the British side), and donated a trophy that then bore his name. The US teams performed more successfully in the early regular events, but the evenness of early matches was not sustained as the USA recurrently outplayed the British/Irish teams (players from the Republic of Ireland became eligible from 1973 to 1977). In 1979, therefore, the USA's opponent was broadened to accommodate continental Europe. Severiano Ballesteros of Spain played in the event in 1979. This pan-European side has introduced a more competitive element to the event.

r

S

sack racing A traditional form of racing at fairs and on sports days, in which the contestant races in a sack, often jumping to make the most effective progress. Joseph Strutt's *Sports and Pastimes of the People of England* (1801) identified sack running as a popular rustic pastime: 'that is, men tied up in sacks, every part of them being enclosed except their heads', and racing over a set distance. Sack racing has long been seen as a harmless and enjoyable family game, and a fun item for young children at schools. In July 2008, though, at the John F. Kennedy School in Washington, north-east England, the activity (along with the three-legged race) was banned from the school sports day, on safety grounds.

sailing Races between yachts or dinghies (categories of small sailing craft) over designated (commonly coastal) waters; or endurance events, such as crossing the Atlantic or sailing around the world. The term 'yacht' derives from the Dutch *jacht*, the word for a small pleasure craft. The English monarch Charles II, exiled in the Netherlands for a decade until his restoration to the throne in 1660, was a keen yachtsman, and sailing developed unevenly over the next two centuries, but with connotations of privilege, exclusivity, and *conspicuous consumption: to sail was to display status as well as seek pleasure. In the Olympics, sailing was included at London's 1908 Games, where the British dominated (more disputedly, it featured at the Paris 1900 Games, where the yachting regatta staged no separate finals for the different classes: Olympic historians therefore exclude these from the official Olympic record). Ocean-based yacht racing also has a long pre-Olympic history, the *America's Cup dating from 1851. Changing technology has affected aspirations and practices in sailing, and accumulative skills of individuals and teams can establish longevity of performance in the sport. Women participated in men's events at the Olympics as crew members in 1908, 1920, and 1928, but women's sailing events were not held until 1988 in Seoul (in the category of the 470, a two-person fibreglass craft), and then in an expanded programme (including *windsurfing) at Barcelona in 1992. On the recreational side, small categories of dinghy, cheaper and relatively accessible, have been the basis of some widening of participation. *See also* BOATING; PUNTING: YACHTING.

salary cap The placing of limits on team payrolls, usually set at a fixed percentage of league revenues, and so constraining each team within the league to spend between a specified minimum and maximum on player salaries. The salary cap was a response to the successful legal challenge in the USA to Major League Baseball's and the National Football League's *reserve clauses, the effect of which was to spiral player earnings upwards as players negotiated terms from team to team. The big professional sports in the USA responded with the implementation of salary caps: the National Basketball Association for the 1984–5 season, the National Football League in 1994. In practice, employers could undermine the principles of the cap. Re-signed free agents were exempted from the cap in basketball (what was known as the 'Larry Bird exception'), and in 1997–8 Michael Jordan received more than $33 million from the Chicago Bulls, when its salary cap for the team payroll was $26.9 million. The efficacy of the salary cap depends upon the integrity of the employers, in their intra-league networks, and the credibility of the capping process itself (whether it is a 'soft', as in baseball, or a 'hard', as in American football, version of the principle). Overall, though, debates about the salary cap and efforts to implement it demonstrate the recognition by sport organizations that a free-for-all in the market threatens the equilibrium of sporting finances, and the *competitive balance of sporting encounters. *See also* MAXIMUM WAGE.

Samsung *See* OLYMPIC PROGRAMME, THE.

Sandow, Eugen (1867–1925) A pioneering bodybuilder who, from the unpromising circumstances of a weakly childhood, resculptured his own physique along the lines of classical Greek and Roman statues and gained many admirers and followers in the late Victorian period. Born Friedrich Wilhelm Müller in eastern Europe, Sandow first appeared on stage in London, England, but became internationally famous when he joined Florenz Ziegfeld's Trocadero Company at the 1893 World's Columbian Exhibition in Chicago. He toured the North American continent for several years, and a Harvard physical educator, examining Sandow, proclaimed him the finest specimen of manhood that he had ever seen. Sandow increasingly concentrated on the display of the body and his muscles, rather than feats of lifting, and left the USA as a national celebrity, and a rich man. He established a lucrative business in publications, ushering in an age of narcissistic body cultures linked to notions of self-improvement, and catering too for an increasingly public voyeuristic dimension to physical performance and the consumption of the performing body. Sandow influenced others such as Charles *Atlas, and is widely recognized as the 'father of modern bodybuilding'.

Sartre, Jean-Paul (1905–80) A French philosopher, intellectual, and playwright famed for his existentialist perspectives on the nature of human existence, and in particular his exploration of subjective experience and the conditions of individuality, freedom, and morality. In his book *Being and Nothingness: An Essay on Phenomenological Ontology* (French edition 1953, English translation 1969), described by philosopher Mary Warnock as 'a textbook of existentialism itself', Sartre refers to the activity of play, and any drives associated with it, as 'entirely gratuitous', and as in contrast to the realm of the serious in the material world. Play, writes Sartre, 'releases subjectivity', and can help an individual 'attain himself as a certain being': 'the fact remains that the desire to play is fundamentally the desire to be' (p. 581). From Sartre's perspective, sport is creative like art. His example is skiing, which from this existentialist or phenomenological perspective is more than a technique or a skill, or a playful dynamic with the course: to ski is to change, to 'possess' the field of snow, to change 'the matter and meaning of the snow'. Scarcely substantiated in any empirical terms, this Sartrean perspective remains speculative but intriguing, offering a way of accounting for the attraction of the sporting experience to the individual consciousness.

SchlumbergerSema *See* OLYMPIC PROGRAMME, THE.

Schmeling, Maximillian Adolph Otto Siegfried (Max) (1905–2005) German world heavyweight boxing champion from 1930 to 1932, a paratrooper in World War II, and a successful businessman after the war, holder of Coca-Cola's German franchise. Schmeling is most famous for his two fights with black fighter Joe *Louis of the USA, in 1936 and 1938. His surprise victory in the first fight with Louis was exploited by Nazi propagandists, and, when a rematch was arranged in 1938, by which time Louis had become world champion, the fight took on worldwide symbolic significance: political and racist claims of Nazism were challenged and destroyed in Louis's clinical victory. Implicated in the propagandistic momentum of the time, Schmeling proved in later life that he was not a Nazi, fascist, or racist: it was revealed that he had helped Jews escape from pre-war Germany; and he befriended Louis and supported him in his financial difficulties, acting as a pallbearer at and helping pay for his old rival's funeral. The Louis–Schmeling fights were pivotal international sporting events, linking national politics and media interests to attract worldwide attention. Schmeling, married to film actress Anny Ondra for 54 years, also represented the emerging media profile and celebrity glamour that could be generated in the sporting sphere.

Schutz, Alfred (1899–1959) A social philosopher and sociologist, born in Austria, who developed ideas and concepts designed to frame 'the phenomenology of the social world', the title of his 1932 book. In this *phenomenology, he tackled complex philosophical and epistemological problems, but demonstrated the importance of a series of themes and concepts in interpretive sociology. These include 'stock of knowledge', referring to the knowledge that social actors bring to their involvement in and understanding of any social situation; 'context of experience' and 'lived experience'; and 'face-to-face' situation. In explicating these categories he was consistently concerned with the nature of the individual's experience and consciousness, and the ways in which meaning is conveyed, generated, and reproduced in everyday life. A Schutzian, or phenomenological, approach to the meaning of sport can be illuminating of the subjective dimensions of the sporting experience, for competitors and onlookers, players and spectators, alike. A brilliant evocation of a phenomenological approach to sport, rooted in personal experience but simultaneously anchored in wide-ranging scholarship, can be found in Hans Ulrich Gumbrecht's *In Praise of Athletic Beauty* (2006).

scientific management An approach to the management of the workplace and the specific work task pioneered by Frederick Winslow Taylor (1856–1915) in the last two decades of the 19th century in the rapidly industrializing USA. Taylor was particularly interested in the 'one best way' of doing each task, and in his *The Principles Of Scientific Management* (1911) he depersonalized the task—in this case, pig-iron handling—to its crudest parameters: 'This work is so crude and elementary in its nature that the writer firmly believes it would be possible to train an intelligent gorilla so as to become a more efficient pig-iron handler than any man could be'; and, he added, any person engaging regularly in such an occupation 'shall be so stupid and phlegmatic that he more nearly resembles the ox than any other type'. Also known as Taylorism, this approach was formalized in systematic analyses of work performance such as time and motion studies.

Early applications of Taylorism in sport were developed by Walter Camp, legendary football coach at *Yale University; and the growth of sport science itself can be seen as an advanced version of scientific management, when Olympic or world championship victories rest on the tiniest fraction of a second that might be gained in the minutiae of the preparatory process. In professional football, software-based modes of analysis such as the Prozone system have provided ongoing analysis of and instant feedback on individual performance by team members, and can be called upon in changing a team formation or making a tactical change. Marxist critics in particular (see, for instance, Bero Rigauer's *Sport and Work*, 1969) have detected a Taylorist approach to sport performance in some versions of sport science and movement studies that have sought to optimize the scientific analysis of athletic practice in the pursuit of the perfect outcome, whatever the cost to the individual athlete.

scuba-diving   Underwater swimming, aided by a form of aqualung, developed in 1942–3 by French navy diver Jacques-Yves Cousteau and engineer Émile Gagnan. SCUBA is an acronym for 'self-contained underwater breathing apparatus'. *See also* SWIMMING.

Seabiscuit (1933–47) A champion thoroughbred racehorse in the USA, Seabiscuit became a legendary all-time money winner and has been seen as a symbol of hope for the ordinary individual during the period of the Great Depression in the 1930s. Sold on by a top breeder and trainer when seemingly underachieving, the horse was bought by the automobile businessman Charles S. Howard, who found an Irish-Canadian jockey, Red Pollard, and an experienced yet all but washed-up trainer, Tom Smith, and forged a story of three men and a horse that has entered US folklore. Seabiscuit was seen not just as a symbol of hope for the people, but as an expression of the character of the newer, West Coast Californian culture. The horse's victorious challenge race against War Admiral in 1938 has been claimed as the most eagerly anticipated sporting event to have occurred in the USA up to that date. Laura Hillenbrand's *Seabiscuit: The True Story of Three Men and a Racehorse* (2001) captures the outcome: 'Seabiscuit's wake seemed to create an irresistible vacuum, sucking the fans in behind him. Police dashed over the track, but the fans simply ran past them, leaping and clapping.' Underachieving in his early career, recovering from injuries, and adapting to a different rider when Pollard was injured, the Seabiscuit story has produced an irresistible narrative of hope, recovery, and family—losers becoming winners—that has been immortalized in film as well as literature, including the 2003 film *Seabiscuit*.

secularization   The process in modern societies whereby religious ideas and institutions come to have less influence upon the overall society, and less impact upon the nature of everyday life. Sport is not necessarily a secular practice, as sport institutions have often been established by religious bodies and organizations; but the rise of modern forms of sport, played and watched at any time regardless of religious schedules or traditions, can be widely seen to represent the increasing dominance of secular culture in many modern societies.

securitization The identification of future income against lack of income in the here and now, as a means of demonstrating the long-term viability and solvency of an organization. When the governing body of world football, the Fédération Internationale de Football Association (FIFA), suffered the loss of its marketing partner *International Sport and Leisure (ISL) in 2001, the organization looked financially over-committed and vulnerable in terms of its level of identifiable revenues. But, the organization argued, its primary product of the (men's) football World Cup was so desirable a global product that reworked and reaffirmed contracts for sponsorship and broadcasting rights would more than balance the books: this accounting against future income proved successful for the organization, which reported record annual surplus for 2007.

Seeldrayers, Rodolphe William (1876–1955) The fourth president of world football governing body the *Fédération Internationale de Football Association (FIFA), Seeldrayers was a lawyer from Brussels, Belgium. He was an accomplished football player as a young man, playing for Belgian champions Racing Club Brussels, where he was later the president. He was a FIFA vice-president for 27 years before succeeding Jules *Rimet in 1954, but was president for only a short period, dying in office the following year. Seeldrayers had also served on the *International Olympic Committee, and in his youth had been a hockey international and a national champion in the 110-metre hurdles. His all-round sporting qualities, and a declared enthusiasm for British *athleticism, made him a symbol of a traditional model of sporting prowess and sporting administration that was to be radically changed in the emerging media age.

self-actualization The development to their full potential of the human and psychological capacities of any single individual. *See also* INNER GAME; NEEDS, HIERARCHY OF.

self-concept The notion that an individual has of all of his or her characteristics and dispositions that make up the totality of the self. Any self-concept is therefore also bound up with the interactions and social relationships experienced by the individual: the aggressive champion might be the shyest person in a different cultural and social setting; the confident team player might be tongue-tied at a social gathering. Self-concept is an important notion that highlights the complex make-up of the individual in his or her sociocultural environment; but its very general and all-inclusive scope is its flaw, making it difficult to specify its determinants and its effects.

self-esteem The respect that an individual has for him- or herself on the basis of the perceived values and qualities that characterize the individual. It is often seen as a product of the process of *socialization, and if a person has emerged from childhood with a low sense of self-esteem, sport is sometimes seen as a way of increasing that person's level of self-esteem: classic examples include getting the ghetto kid into the boxing ring, or the academic underachiever into the school sport team.

semiology Also known as semiotics, semiology is the science of *signs*, these latter being words (spoken or written), gestures, media images, or cultural artefacts more generally, and their generated meanings. Much semiotic analysis of sport and the sport media has illuminated the cultural meanings of sport, and its tendency to reaffirm dominant values such as *patriarchy or *nationalism. The approach stems from linguistic theory pioneered by the Swiss theorist Ferdinand de Saussure (1857–1913), and developed in its most influential form by the French academic Roland Barthes (1915–80). In his 1957 book *Mythologies*, Barthes commented on a range of phenomena in everyday life, including wrestling, in what he called an attempt 'to reflect regularly on some myths of French daily life' of the time. Wrestling is said to be a spectacle intelligible to its audience on the basis of its iconography, its set of images, including the moral image constructed in wrestling of 'the perfect "bastard"': 'A wrestler can irritate or disgust, he never disappoints, for he always accomplishes completely, by a progressive solidification of signs, what the public expects of him.' More analytically, the process of *signification involves recognizing the *signifier* (a tangible cultural object, in the form of images or words) and the *signified* (the meaning or meanings of that object): the *sign* is the association that can be established between these. Barthes called doodling 'the signifier without the signified' (*Roland Barthes on Roland Barthes*, 1975). Take the image of a player of *American football, giant physical frame in padded attire and features hidden in helmeted anonymity. To rise above the mere description of this figure, semiology identifies it as a *sign* representing physicality, toughness, and machismo. The key insight of the semiological approach is to highlight the complexity of levels and layers of meaning characteristic of what at first might seem to be simple representational forms.

Senna (da Silva), Ayrton (1960–94) A Brazilian Formula One Grand Prix motor-racing champion, son of a wealthy businessman and rancher. Born in a suburb of São Paulo, he began driving motorized go-karts on the family farm or grounds from the age of 4, in part to help him with what were thought to be physical disabilities. Leaving university (business school) at the age of 19, he went on to become three-times world champion. His greatness as a racing driver in a Europe-dominated sport was important to his nation's self-image, complementing as it did the traditional style and image of its all-conquering yet recently underachieving football side. Senna represented glamour as well as discipline, technology not tradition. After his death in an accident at the Imola track in north-central Italy, three-mile-long queues formed to file past his coffin in his home city, and three days of national mourning were declared. Richard Williams notes that most of those in the queues were under 25:

> Senna was young and beautiful in a country where those assets have often seemed to represent the only stable currency, and the naked distress of the young mourners—university students and McDonald's workers alike—showed very starkly what he meant to them. 'He was our hero,' said eighteen-year-old Silvia Barros, 'our only one.' (*The Death of Ayrton Senna*, 1995).

At all of its matches at the men's soccer World Cup in the USA several months after Senna's death, Brazilian football fans carried banners saluting the driver; Brazil's goalkeeper Claudio Taffarel said that the team dedicated its 'victory to our friend Ayrton Senna. He too was heading for his fourth title.' Senna gave large sums to charity—$100 million to a children's hospital, $75 million for the health care of rubber plantation workers and Indians—personifying his claim that 'the wealthy can no longer continue to live on an island in a sea of poverty'. His glamour, skill, and daring (seen as a kind of dodgem attacking style), and his philanthropy, transcended his competitive egotism and arrogance in a powerful blend that— further enhanced by his tragic early death—constituted a case of the sporting heroic on national and international levels alike.

sepak raga *See* SEPAK TAKRAW.

sepak takraw A hybrid term derived from the Malay word for 'kick', *sepak*, and the Thai word for 'ball', **takraw*, to describe a three-a-side sport played on a *badminton court. In Malaysia the game is known as *sepak raga*. It has also been compared to *volleyball, though no part of the hand can be used in keeping the ball up and propelling it over the net. Men and women play the game, and it is an established event in the *Asian Games.

sexism Any practice or set of attitudes that takes sexual status as a basis for discriminating between men and women, in terms of language, policies, institutions, and social relationships. Sexism in sport has been deeply entrenched, comprising the stereotyping of men and women's physical capacity and potential, and the language or discourse in which sport is discussed, understood, and reported. *See also* PATRIARCHY.

sexual abuse The sexual exploitation, frequently of young people and minors, by figures in positions of authority. Coach–athlete relationship\s, intense and often authoritarian, have sometimes been shown to provide access to female victims for older male coaches. It is a sensitive area and a potentially sensationalist sphere of debate and study, not least due to the fear that victims feel concerning the consequences of revelations of abuse. Celia Brackenridge warned, in a 1994 article, 'Fair Play or Fair Game? Child Sexual Abuse in Sport Organisations' (*International Review for the Sociology of Sport*, 29), that the structural context of child sexual abuse (CSA) in sports remained, and continues widely to remain, unexplored while the issue was explained in terms of psychology. Voluntary sport organizations would in those circumstances continue to 'evade accountability' for the problem. The work of Brackenridge and others has provided a basis for recognition of the issue, for intervention in risk situations, and for the production of codes of practice that change the structural basis of the problem. *See also* SEXUAL HARASSMENT.

sexual harassment Forms of unsolicited, unwelcome, and unreciprocated behaviour, including comments, approaches, physical contact or touch, or even ways of looking at an individual. These would usually emanate from an individual in a position of authority or power, such as the sport coach or the team manager. Research on relationships between female athletes and male coaches has established that young female athletes, dedicated to training at the expense of a more balanced social life, lack experience of negotiating relationships, and are consequently vulnerable to the overtures of, for instance, coaches or veteran athletes. Sport institutions and organizations have been slow to acknowledge the vulnerability of young participants in their charge, but have come increasingly to recognize the necessity for codes of ethics explicitly countering the circumstances in which sexual harassment continues unchecked. *See also* HAZING; LOCKER-ROOM CULTURE.

shakha The location of, and the name for, a form of bodily practice undertaken by members of the Rashtriya Swayamsevak Sangh (RSS), an organization promoting extreme Hindu nationalism. It is a combination of indigenous games and exercises, and Western-style military *drill, designed to develop in young males an all-embracing commitment to a particular model of the Indian nation state. In this case, the RSS uses bodily practices and sporting activity as a form of indoctrination into a wider cultural and political project.

shamateurism The pretence that the athlete has the status of an amateur, when he or she is in fact a full-time and/or professional sportsman or -woman. This pretence was at its height in the later 1970s and the early 1980s when the International Olympic Committee was moving towards the acceptance of the principle of professionalism, and some athletes—nominally amateur—could divert all their income into trust funds, for use on international travel or anything at all that could be linked to their training needs. In some sports, amateurs also accepted under-the-table payments to wear particular apparel or use specific brands of equipment. State socialist societies had also supported the shamateur quite blatantly, in giving individuals positions in, say, the military, while they led the life of the full-time elite competitor.

shinty A stick-and-ball field game played between teams of twelve. Played in the Scottish Highlands, it derives from the Irish sport of *hurling. The word 'shinty' comes from the Gaelic word for 'a leap', *sinteag*. The early form of the game, brought into Scotland by Irish Gaels in the Middle Ages, was expressive of local parish or clan rivalries, and rooted in numerous Scottish counties. Land reformers and nationalists supported the development and organization of the game: rules were drawn up in 1879–80, and the Camanachd Association formed in 1893 (the Highlands word for the stick with the hooked top was *caman*). Shinty in this more organized form, though, retained its prominence only in the eastern Highlands, and among Glasgow's Gaelic community and within the universities. In its surviving form shinty symbolizes the capacity of indigenous sports to represent traditional cultural values, yet they can, as Grant Jarvie has commented, become 'overlooked or marginalized and discriminated against because they don't neatly fit with a global or Olympic strategy designed to win medals' (*Sport, Culture and Society: An Introduction*, 2006). The Camanachd Association, based in Inverness, continues to represent shinty and to support its potential development in England and parts of the USA beyond its Highlands base.

shooting The firing of air-weapons, pistols, or rifles with the aim of placing the bullets in the centre (or bull's eye) of a target. Competitive shooting emerged with improvements in gun and rifle technology throughout the 19th century, with strong links to military skills and practice of those skills (military-trained Swiss marksmen dominated early world championships), and pistol shooting was included in the first modern Olympic Games at Athens in 1896. Rifle shooting was first included at the 1908 London Games, where the top eight small-bore rifle shooters were all British. Shooting in its traditional recreational form among the elite was also interwined with some forms of *hunting, and the rifle remains a recreational resource for the (predominantly male) wild-boar (*sanglier*) hunters of France's mountainous regions of the Languedoc, and other equivalent organized groups in Europe, North America, and Africa. Whether such playful pursuit of the relatively powerless prey is a sport remains open to moral and ethical debate: it is a matter of historical record, though, that such forms of shooting were synonymous with conceptions of sporting prowess. To be a good shot was to be a good sport. The profile of shooting in the modern Olympic programme has at least redefined the objective of the practice. At the 1968 Mexico Olympics, men and women competed against each other in an integrated event, though some categories were separated again at the 1984 LA Olympics. Twelve years later, at Atlanta, men's and women's competitions were reintegrated. *See also* CLAY-PIGEON SHOOTING.

significant other A concept that emerged in the middle of the 20th century, referring to each of those people and individuals who influenced the internalization of norms for other individuals, and so potentially shaped the individual self. Tamotsu Shibutani's 'Reference Groups as Perspectives' (*American Journal of Sociology*, vol. LX, 1955) reported the use of the term by psychiatrist Harry Stack Sullivan (1892–1949) as early as 1947, and talked of how social groups related to each other on the basis of 'personal loyalty to significant others of that social world'. Sport and its cultures and traditions have generated multitudinous and varied forms of such loyalty and affiliation, in sporting clubs and formations to which individuals have sustained strong and loyal connections throughout a life that in other spheres (the family, the workplace or profession) may have developed very varied and separate trajectories. In this sense sport and its cultural formations and meanings provide a source for the continuing reaffirmation of self in relationships with significant others. *See also* REFERENCE GROUPS.

signification The process, in the making and transmission of cultural meanings, in which cultural objects or signs come to have particular meanings to specific recipients, or in relation to media forms, audiences and readerships. In sport, the culture of the fan group may be based upon a mix of colours, symbols, gestural rituals, and language, all of which contribute to the meaning-making at the heart of the signification process. *See also* SEMIOLOGY.

silat An umbrella term for diverse forms of *martial arts in south-east Asia, particularly in the Malaysian archipelago. It fuses into forms of folk dance and its proponents also attribute a spiritual dimension to the practice. In Indonesia, the term *pencak silat* was adopted in 1948 as a unifying term for the different martial arts traditions. *Silat* features in the South-East Asian Games, and its survival has contributed to expressions of cultural nationalism as well as regional identity.

Simmel, Georg (1858–1918) A German sociologist whose recognition of the different levels at which sociocultural analysis can be conducted was a sophisticated early contribution to social scientific method and theorization. His threefold classification of approaches to sociological analysis identified general sociology as an approach to studying the whole of historical life, formal sociology as a study of societal forms, and philosophical sociology as concerned with issues of method. Simmel's essayist style and his observations across a range of topics from money to skiing led him to work most fully in the second of these sociological approaches: his 'formal' sociology was a sociology of societal forms, far from formal in implementation and focus, and concentrated upon the minutiae of social life and the forms whereby they are given some shape. In his essay on the European Alps (*Qualitative Sociology*, 16/2, 1993), his sociological observations betray a judgemental elitism, or, as some might have it, display a prescient environmentalism.

simulacrum A concept with a philosophical lineage—the concept was employed by Plato—rooted in the notion of reproduction, and concerned with the nature of image-making. It was developed influentially in the social and cultural theory of Jean *Baudrillard (1929–2007). Baudrillard recognized different types or levels of reproduction of an object: basic reflection of the reality of an object; perversion of the object; pretence that there is an object of reflection; and recognition that there is no relation whatsoever to any reality. In contemporary culture, for Baudrillard, the media-generated simulacra are their own reality rather than the representation of any other reality. Debates have considered the relevance of the concept to mediated sport; for the most part sports covered on live television have their roots in a pre-mediated reality, but the increasingly packaged and spectacularized form of after-the-event programming could certainly be seen as a form of cultural reality in itself. *See also* SIMULATION.

simulation 1. In sport science, the reproduction of conditions of performance in, for instance, an environmental chamber, enabling the analysis of the influence of different variables upon physical performance. 2. In cultural theory, in the writings of Jean *Baudrillard, a central feature of contemporary culture in which culture is produced via 'the generation by models of a real without origin or reality: a hyperreal' (*Simulations*, 1983). Culture, from this perspective, is a product of the media consumed by mass markets interested in the constant flow of mediated events and spectacle. The increase in made-for-media sport contests, particularly ones glamorizing physical prowess and display, can be seen as a case of 'the implosion of the social in the media' that Baudrillard sees as the consequence of the intensification of simulation. *See also* SIMULACRUM.

skateboarding An individual sport in which the boarder balances on a board that is attached to wheels, and performs a range of physical manoeuvres of, at a competitive level, increasingly acrobatic and sophisticated complexity. Skateboards were first produced in the 1960s, in California, when the activity was known as sidewalk or concrete surfing. The introduction of polyurethane wheels in 1970 expanded its market, and it was a popular fad among the young in the 1970s in the UK as well as the USA, though health and safety issues eroded its profile in the 1980s. It re-emerged in popularity, based on a more streamlined and advanced product in the 1990s; and has become so popular that, given its appeal to new global youth markets, its possible inclusion in the Olympic Games (within the cycling category) has been debated. By no means all have supported this possibility, as a condition of acceptance would be that skateboarding comes under the control of the International Cycling Federation. To the governing body of the sport, the International Skateboarding Federation, it has been more important to uphold its mission principles, fostering 'freedom of self-expression and authenticity', and maintaining the 'integrity and authenticity of skateboarding as a sport, a passion, and a lifestyle'. As a *lifestyle sport, with star practitioner Tony Hawk (born San Diego, California, 1968) its figurehead and his video games a legendary success in the electronic games industry, and its high profile in the X Games (Extreme Games), skateboarding is branded and marketed for a limitless youth consumer market. It has less need of the Olympics than has the Olympics for this quintessential youth activity.

Skateboarders also continue to celebrate the anti-establishment ethos of the practice. Justin Hanna, of Canadian company FIGJAM Apparel, is unequivocal on this point:

> we need to make sure that the culture of skateboarding is respected. Skateboarding has its roots in pushing the limits, being anti-establishment and anti-authoritative—setting its own style through creativity that harnesses the individual spirit. To mold exactly into what the IOC has in store for skateboarding would be a denial of its very roots...

Skateboarding has also been an illuminating example of the tensions that can characterize the growth and commercial development of an alternative or lifestyle sport; and of the persisting dominance of 'traditional masculinity' in the core values of a purportedly progressive sport (Becky Beal and Charlene Wilson, '"Chicks Dig Scars": Commercialisation and the Transformations of Skateboarders' Identities', in Belinda Wheaton, ed., *Understanding Lifestyle Sports: Consumption, Identity and Difference*, 2004).

skiing The sport of moving across snow-based terrain with the feet clad in purpose-made boots that clip on to long, thinly-shaped wooden, metal, or synthetic-fibre runners (skis). For recreation, the dominant forms of skiing are Alpine or downhill (descents of varying steepness), and Nordic or cross-country (across more level, often wooded, terrain). Forms of competitive skiing also include slalom (within the Alpine category), in which racers swerve between upright poles in the snow, and jumping (within the Nordic category), in which skiers launch themselves from high up a hillside and seek to land as far as possible down the hill or slope, and in which points are awarded for style as well as distance. The Fédération Internationale de Ski has overseen the competitive form of the sport, and the sport has been a central one in the expanding profile of the Winter Olympics from 1928 onwards. A further discipline on skis, combining cross-country and target-shooting, is the *biathlon, administered by the International Modern Pentathlon and Biathlon Union.

Skiing of sorts was a form of subsistence and survival in cold northern European areas (such as modern Finland) and the furthest east of European countries (such as Turkey). Norwegian breakthroughs in the design of the boot and the ski, so holding the foot in place, in the mid 19th century created the basis for competitions in jumping and racing, and clubs soon formed in Norway, and in California. The British became active in the Swiss Alps, and the English novelist Arthur Conan Doyle wrote in the *Strand Magazine* of his ski journey from Davos to Arosa in 1894. Skiing soon became one of the daredevil yet fashionable winter sports of the cosmopolitan European elite, encouraged by entrepreneurs such as Henry Lunn, father of Arnold *Lunn. The Public Schools Alpine Sports Club, which opened in 1902–3 in Switzerland, announced the new sport to a wealthy and socially conscious constituency, for which how-to manuals and ski-analysis booklets began to be produced. Competitions began to be staged, and cups awarded.

Skiing's wider markets were opened up in the second half of the 20th century, with breakthroughs in mass (and cheap) tourism and travel, advances in the technology for being lifted up the slopes, and the popularization of the sport through its profile at the Olympics and the advent of colour television. Into the 1970s, top-level competitive skiers were purportedly amateur while the International Olympic Committee continued to oppose professionalism, though after their performance peaks some skiers could use their profile and celebrity to make lucrative livings, or lead initiatives that expanded the burgeoning recreational ski-resort industry; in the French Alps, for instance, Olympic champion and local boy Jean Vuarnet returned from his gold-medal downhill triumph at the 1960 Squaw Valley (USA) Olympics to lead the development of the model, architecturally modernist, carless resort Avoriaz at the heart of Portes du Soleil, the largest ski area in the world. By the mid 1990s, analysts reported a global ski market of 65–70 million skiers (55 million downhill, the rest cross-country); in these estimates, the USA with 15 million and Japan with 14 million were by far the biggest sub-markets, though *pro rata* Scandinavian and Alpine countries had much higher proportions of active skiers in their populations. Skiing remains the cultural preserve of affluent groups and individuals, though its trend-setting image has been challenged by the emergence of the more youthful, stylish, and free-styling activity of *snowboarding.

skipping A traditional form of physical exercise, comprising a single individual or small groups using a rope that is swung or twirled so that the individual 'skips' over the rope in an even rhythm as the rope swings over his or her head and under the feet. As a recreational pastime it has a long history, and Joseph Strutt (*Sports and Pastimes of the People of England*, 1801) wrote that it was 'probably very ancient' as a children's game and amusement. Strutt noted too, in an observation showing the adaptability of the environment to the recreational inclinations of rural populations, that during the hop season, a hop stem stripped of its leaves could be used in the place of a rope. Skipping has been used by some competitors in sports such as boxing, as a form of *aerobic exercise or training. Skipping still features in informal programmes in some schools, and inter-school competitions have continued to be held. *Rope-skipping* as a form of intensive cardiovascular exercise and competition has been promoted in a number of countries in south-east Asia, and in North America. The Fédération Internationale de Saute à la Corde (the International Rope Skipping Federation) promotes international meetings, and was based in Canada in the early 2000s, when 1,200 competitive skippers were reported in the country. World championships were staged from 1997, and team displays of rope-skipping can combine elements of dance, acrobatics, and hip-hop. *See also* STREET GAMES.

skittles A target game in which a projectile such as a ball or bowl—sometimes called a 'cheese'—is launched at a set of wooden pins. It was a popular recreation in Germany, France, and Britain during the Middle Ages in France the game was known as *quilles*. Joseph Strutt (*Sports and Pastimes of the People of England*, 1801) noted that the kayle (from *quille*) pins became known as kittle-pins and then skittle-pins. Strutt described both nine-pins and skittles, with varying modes of play: but what they had in common was the bowling at the pins, with the basic aim 'to beat them all down with the fewest throws'. In earlier periods, kittle-pins were made with animal bones, and he quotes an author of the *Merry Milk-Maid of Islington* (1680) who gave the following words to one of his characters: 'I'll cleave you from the skull to the twist, and make nine skittles of thy bones'. Skittles, on which wagers were often made, was banned in royal edicts, and in the early 19th century still forbidden in the City of London. But its popularity reflected its simplicity, edicts were widely ignored, and English monarch *Henry VIII became an enthusiast, even having a skittle alley built for his personal use.

The game has retained some popularity in local settings across many regions of Europe, though taking differing forms even in the one country: Old English Skittles in the London area, Western Skittles in Wessex, and Long Alley Skittles in the north Midlands are variants of the game that have been popular in England. In Ireland, an Irish Skittles Association has endeavoured to keep the game alive by including it in Community Games. In any genealogy of the game itself, its most thriving legacy is *(tenpin) bowling, which Dutch colonists are said to have introduced to the USA. The language of skittles has entered the idiom or lexicon of sporting achievement, so that a bowler in cricket is often said, on taking a number of wickets of the opposition, to have 'skittled' out the opposing batsmen.

skydiving *See* PARACHUTING.

Sky Television The popular name for British Sky Broadcasting (BSkyB), a media provider that has dominated the coverage of top-level club football in its rise to a position of dominance in the international sport-media market. Sky Television merged with British Satellite Broadcasting in 1990, forming BSkyB, and Sky went on to compete with great success for sports rights, particularly for the newly-formed (1992) Premier League launched by England's Football Association; and, later, a growing share of European club soccer in the *UEFA Champions League. The Sky model of satellite provision, based on monthly charges, achieved consistently expanding subscriber numbers throughout the 1990s and into the 21st century. Sky, part of Rupert Murdoch's News Corporation, has sustained its dominant position in the market, outbidding rivals such as the ill-fated Setanta, the latter failing to achieve its projected subscription numbers and going into administration in 2009. Sky has dominated the 24/7 sports news agenda, and its magazine format on soccer match days has displaced traditional coverage on rival broadcast providers such as the BBC. Sky also attempted to buy soccer club Manchester United in 1998, but this was blocked by the UK's Monopolies and Merger Commission, one objection being that there would be a conflict of interest in both owning and potentially reporting on the club. It nevertheless pursued an alternative strategy, buying into several leading clubs within Premier League rules (no more than ten per cent investment permitted in any one club). Sky has also secured rights for the coverage in the UK of rugby league, rugby union, and the Australian, French, and US Open tennis championships. Backed by the power of News Corporation, the world's leading news conglomerate, Sky has been able to consolidate and reinvest in its sport-based portfolio in ways unmatched by any other provider.

slamdunk The act of scoring in basketball by placing rather than throwing the ball into the basket, with one hand at least over the basket rim so making the art of scoring look certain, and at the same time relatively effortless. The term is said to have been coined by an LA Lakers announcer and has come to refer to a near-certainty, or the high probability of success, in other spheres of life, and also to a particularly stylish way of achieving a task. In the USA, sponsors—the soft drinks company Sprite, for instance—have promoted 'Rising Stars' competitions for slamdunking, in which style—the leap, the swivel, the 720 degrees dunk—is all.

sliding filament theory A theory to explain how muscles contract. Until the 1950s it was not known how muscles contracted to produce force, with vague propositions about spring or pump mechanisms gathering little support. The availability of electron microscopy and X-ray diffraction analysis led A. F. Huxley and R. Niedergerke (1954) and H. E. Huxley and J. Hanson (1954) to hypothesize that muscles contracted through filaments sliding over one another. The sliding filament theory is of great historical importance since it links biological structure, biochemical pathways of energy metabolism, and physical force production. Although still always called a theory, it is well supported by extensive experimental evidence.

A muscle comprises many thousands of long individual fibres. Each single fibre is composed of thousands of thread-like myofibrils formed of contracting units (sarcomeres) aligned end to end. Each sarcomere is composed of thick filaments of myosin which interdigitate with thin filaments of actin. A muscle shortens by a paddle-like myosin cross-bridge cyclically attaching to a thin filament, rotating at the neck, and detaching. The thin and thick filaments therefore slide past each other and do not change in length like a spring. There are millions of filaments in a muscle and cross-bridge formation occurs extremely rapidly but asynchronously so the resulting muscle action is smooth.

snooker A table game played with a *cue with which a ball is struck with the aim of 'potting' 22 balls in a particular sequence according to their colours into any of six pockets on the table. The game was developed as an alternative to the *billiards table, by British military officers in India, adding further coloured balls to the table: people who missed a shot were branded 'snookers', 'snooker' being army slang for 'novice'. The game became very popular in men's clubs across the social classes, in the gentleman's clubs of London, and in the working-men's clubs of industrial districts across Britain. As Richard Holt observed in the late 1980s: 'It is one of the minor ironies of history that what is now the most popular televised indoor sport had its origins amongst pig-sticking and polo-playing army officers' (*Sport and the British: A Modern History*). World champions were weaned on the tables of miners' clubs and working-men's institutes; and on UK television, the climax of the world championship final between Dennis Taylor and Steve Davis in 1985 set a record for a post-midnight live television audience. But that was snooker's peak in popularity, and in 1988 Adrian Metcalfe, Channel 4's commissioning editor for sport, described snooker as a sedative not a stimulant: 'You just sort of nod off . . . It's Mogadon.' More have come to see the sport as a stale media product in the years since, with the multimedia alternatives available to viewers via an expanded range of screen and media outlets rendering the drawn-out snooker match dull and limited viewing to the channel-zapping satellite surfer. The snooker authorities and the television producers, showing awareness of this, talked of fresh formats and novel events, and in 2009 the world championship final was refereed for the first time by a woman.

snowboarding A sport based upon descents down snow-covered slopes, in which the boarder's feet are attached to a snowboard using a boot mounted on the board. The sport was developed in the region of Michigan, USA, in the 1960s and 1970s. Organized national and international competitions were staged in the early 1980s. In 1985, the first World Cup was held in Austria, and the International Snowboard Federation (ISF) was founded in 1989, with the objective of standardizing competition criteria and regulations but also seeking to sustain the fun in competition. In 1998, at Nagano, Japan, the sport made its Olympic debut. The increasing popularity of the sport and the alternative style of the snowboarders (in both physical dexterity and clothing image) initially created tensions on the slopes of *skiing resorts, but as the sophistication of the boarders increased, they were permitted to use almost all ski slopes. Jake Burton, an early innovator of the snowboard, who went on to found a leading equipment provider for the sport, commented in a radio interview in the USA in 2002 on the cultural distinctiveness of snowboarding:

> It doesn't have to be an *extreme sport at all. There's a lot of people that, you know, snowboard in a conservative manner. But I think that what's a better moniker is maybe that it's a *lifestyle sport*, and a lot of the kids and people that are doing it are just completely living it all the time, and that's what distinguishes snowboarding from a lot of other sports. (cited in Belinda Wheaton, ed., *Understanding Lifestyle Sports: Consumption, Identity and Difference*, London, Routledge, 2004, p. 4).

Burton also stressed the sheer fun of board sports.

With Olympic recognition, snowboarding came under the control of the International Ski Federation, and the ISF folded in 2002, losing its sponsors while still seeking to speak on behalf of 'the kids in baggy pants and backward hats'.

The ISF had declared itself to be more than just a sports federation, also 'a lifestyle/ peace movement and philosophy'. As the sport's popularity continued to grow worldwide, the sport's culture was changing under the media spotlight and in the marketplace: the first snowboarding magazine, produced in 1985, was named *Absolutely Radical*, but later renamed more prosaically the *International Snowboarding Magazine*. Inspired by *motocross, Snowboard Cross was a new event introduced at the 2006 Olympics in Torino, Italy.

sociability Social activity and interaction existing for its own sake, called by the German sociologist Georg *Simmel the 'play-form' of interaction that has no necessary outcome or results. Pure play-forms of sociability abound in sport, where talk about the last game and the forthcoming match provides a never-ending agenda for sociable exchanges. Such sociable encounters, exchanges, and interactions can also have serious constitutive dimensions, as they confirm opinions, attitudes, and values, as well as providing opportunities for leisure and recreation.

social capital A concept describing forms of relationships between individuals, in communities and families in particular. The concept gained extended currency in the work of political scientist Robert Putnam. His book *Bowling Alone: The Collapse and Survival of American Community* (New York, 2000) depicts a society of decreasing social bonds amid increasing individualist activity. People are not doing less, but they are doing fewer things in the setting of a group. Putnam's book opens with reference to the closure (in one case in Pennsylvania) and decline (in another case in Arkansas) of community bridge (cards) clubs. He goes on to catalogue the decline of community associations concerning civil rights, charity, and alumni fund-raising, showing that their demise has arisen as committed members age and no (or not enough) younger participants emerge to revitalize the groups and their activities. It is a situation of crisis for the 'civic and social life in American communities', explicable in terms of 'social capital theory', whose central idea is 'that social networks have value. Just as a screwdriver (physical capital) or a college education (human capital) can increase productivity (both individual and collective), so too social contacts affect the productivity of individuals and groups'.

The notion of social capital, Putnam goes on, is about the connections between and among individuals, their social networks and elements of trust and reciprocity that are generated by those networks. The 'dense network of reciprocal social relations' is critical to social capital: for Putnam, the community bonds must flow from face-to-face contacts in community activities in sport, leisure, the arts, and voluntary organizations of just about any kind. His remedy for the 'civic malaise' of disengagement that he diagnoses is social interaction at the level of people, not top-down initiatives from institutions—people themselves must 'become reconnected with' their 'friends and neighbours'. For Putnam, social capital is not about spending time with people just like yourself, and 'this is why team sports provide good venues for social-capital creation'. Playing, singing, or bowling together do not 'require shared ideology or shared social or ethnic provenance'. People can 'build bridging social capital' by transcending their 'social and political identities and connecting with people unlike' themselves. Putnam considers sports, in his most sustained way, in his chapter on informal social connections. Several trends are identified, particularly in participation rates in sport activities. Increases in sport spectating are also discussed by Putnam, and noted as 'not a dead loss from the point of view of social capital', though he sees spectatorship as a lesser form of social capital than participation—'watching a team play is not the same thing as playing on a team'. Putnam's work has provided a framework, applicable across a range of societal types, for making sense of statistical trends in sporting participation and practice.

social class A term with many variations and nuances, most of which can be subsumed by two main senses of the term. 1. A general category of people or groups in society, whatever the source of the distinctiveness of the class grouping. 2. Distinctions of a hierarchical kind that exist between groups, often understood, on the basis of Marxist thinking for instance, in terms of economic influences and the conflictual struggles that flow from economic inequalities. Sport, though theoretically a sphere of open meritocratic competitions, can be seen to embody many of the tensions of relationships of social class. *See also* CLASS; CLASS CONSCIOUSNESS; CLASS DIVISIONS; CLASS HABITUS; CLASS MOBILITY; CLASS STRUGGLE.

social control A term encompassing the processes and practices that may be mobilized and used by a—usually powerful—social group to achieve compliance or conformity of other groups. Forms of sport and leisure have often been seen—for instance, in the *bread and circuses argument—as ways of diverting people from engagement with more explicitly political matters. The concept has been criticized by Gareth Stedman Jones as too general and all-encompassing. In his 'Class Expression versus Social Control?' (*History Workshop: A Journal of Socialist Historians*, issue 4, 1977), Stedman Jones asserted that casual references to or uses of the term are vacuous, unclear as to who the agents of control are, or how control is enforced: 'It is not difficult to demonstrate that a casual usage of "social control" metaphors leads to non-explanation and incoherence. There is no political or ideological institution which could not in some way be interpreted as an agency of social control.' While this criticism is without doubt a substantial one, the use of sport and leisure forms by particular political and ideological institutions for the purposes of entertaining or reforming a population or a populace is well established, and it is the specific means and strategies whereby such social control is exerted or imposed that need to be identified. Lazy or casual uses of the term do not exhaust its analytical usefulness, power, and continuing potential.

socialization The process whereby individuals become members of groups or society, sharing common understanding and experiences and learning the values that are considered central to that group or society. Social scientists have distinguished between the phases of primary socialization, experienced by the infant and the child in the home and the family, and then institutions such as the school and the mass media; and secondary socialization, when the influence of adult peers and institutions also contributes to the making of the individual. Sport may feature within either of these phases (as of course do the media), though widespread surveys across many societies and cultures have shown the important and long-lasting effect of early and formative phases of socialization into sport there are many cases of people who have participated in sport early in their lives returning to sport at a later phase, fewer cases of people taking up sport later in life when they had not participated in it earlier. Socialization is a central sociological category, but it must be understood alongside the analysis of socially determining influences such as *social class, *gender, and *ethnicity. *See also* ENCULTURATION.

social mobility The movement of social groups and/or individuals between different levels or hierarchies of a society. Social mobility—widely analysed and measured in terms of occupational mobility between generations—can be *upward* or *downward*. In sport, a professional career can catapult an individual up the status hierarchy, but in many biographical cases the higher status is not sustained after the peak of a playing or competitive career. In recreational sport, acceptance into an exclusive sporting setting—such as a private golf club—might be sought and granted as a recognition of achieved social mobility. *See also* CONTEST AND SPONSORED MOBILITY; SOCIAL STRATIFICATION.

social problem The sociologist C. Wright *Mills argued that the *sociological imagination should distinguish between 'personal troubles of milieu' and 'public issues of social structure', with issues being public matters and often involving 'a crisis in institutional organization'. Take drugs in the sport of cycling. If only one of the population of competitive cyclists takes performance-enhancing and life-endangering drugs, then that individual can be helped personally to deal with a personal trouble; if one in three or four of that population takes drugs, there arises a public issue or what can be identified as a social problem. In this latter case, the structure of fair competition has been destroyed, and any solution must be wide-ranging and structural. Social problems in sport—drugs, homophobia, racism—need to be tackled in ways that address the wider structural question of how the problems or issues arose in the first place.

social stratification The term stratification derives from the geological word for the different layers of the earth's crust. In sociology, it has come to refer to the way in which a society comprises layered groupings, separate yet interconnected within a totality. It was applied specifically to society by the second half of the 19th century. H. M. Hodges (*Social Stratification: Class in America*, 1964) wrote: 'Complex societies are everywhere and always *stratified* societies: this is inescapable fact. It is a fact as true of today's United States . . . and of contemporary Japan or the Soviet Union or Thailand or Paraguay—as it was of medieval Europe, classical Greece, or ancient Mesopotamia.' Sport can offer dramatic possibilities for *social mobility, but also often echoes the stratified nature of the wider society. Sport can challenge such stratified entities—women contesting male hegemony in sport, gay footballers questioning deep-rooted homophobia in men's football—but in general it has confirmed the stratified patterns of the society and culture of which it is a part.

sociological imagination A term widely associated with the US sociologist C. Wright *Mills, who in his book *The Sociological Imagination* (1959) formulated the task of sociology: 'The sociological imagination enables us to grasp history and biography and the relations between the two within society. This is its task and its promise.' Mills pointed to three fundamental 'sorts of questions': What is the structure of a society as a whole? Where does a society 'stand in human history', and in relation to the mechanics of change? What 'varieties of men and women' characterize a society and a period? All of these questions can be applied to a subset of a society, such as sport, but merely replacing 'society' with the word 'sport' in the questions runs the risk of reducing sport to a realm of pseudo-autonomy, for it is as a part of the overall society that sport institutions and sport cultures must be properly understood. For Mills, adequate grasp of the sociological imagination meant that people's 'capacity for astonishment is made lively again'. This is a vital insight, a reminder that the study of sport must beware any apologetic over-familiar and unquestioning reproduction of sport's dominant values and ideologies. Anthony Giddens's *Sociology: A Brief but Critical Introduction* (1986) echoed these principles, in calling for critical, historical, and comparative (countering *ethnocentrism) dimensions of the sociological project. Grasping the sociological imagination in this way, there can be no separation of history and sociology in terms of their fundamental preoccupations: as Philip Abrams put it in his *Historical Sociology* (1980), in terms of

their fundamental preoccupations, history and sociology are and always have been the same thing. Both seek to understand the puzzle of human agency and both seek to do so in terms of the process of social structuring. It is the task that commands the attention, and not the disciplines.

From these perspectives, the history of sport should avoid antiquarian excesses in which the sport is studied in isolation from wider social processes; and the sociology and politics of sport should be alert and sensitive to historical legacies, cultural traditions, and social change.

softball A bat-and-ball game played by teams of nine, originating in the USA, popular too throughout Latin America, and in Australia, New Zealand, Japan, the Philippines, and Canada. It needs less space to play than its parent sport, *baseball, and is played at a faster pace, with comparatively inexpensive equipment. Invented in Illinois as a form of indoor baseball, it was played in many versions until standardized rules were formed in 1933, establishing a basis that saw the sport develop into what has been claimed as the largest participation sport of the mid-20th-century USA. Its international profile expanded in the 1950s, and world championships for men and for women were inaugurated in 1965 and 1966 respectively, Australia winning the women's title and the USA the men's. The Japanese team won the second women's world championship in 1970. Softball, in the form of the fast-pitched women's game, featured in the Olympics for the first time at Atlanta in 1996, where the US team defeated China for the gold medal, going on to win the next two Olympics at Sydney and Athens, beating Japan and Australia respectively. At softball's final Olympics in Beijing in 2008, the USA had been ranked number one in the world from 1986. Softball was discontinued from the Olympics programme after the 2008 Games. In a secret vote in Singapore in 2005, the International Olympic Committee eliminated softball (and baseball) from the schedule of the Summer Games, reputedly due to the innate Americanism of the two sports. These were the first events to be discontinued since *polo's last appearance in 1936. Reapplication is allowed, but softball cannot reappear at the Olympics until 2016 at the earliest.

Sokol A collective form of physical exercise and gymnastics established in 19th-century Czech and Slavic society, founded in Prague in 1862 by Miroslav Tyrš (1832–84) and Jindřich Fügner (1822–65). Tyrš had an academic background in aesthetics and enthused about ancient Greek physical culture and education, also writing a book entitled *Olympic Homage* before Pierre de Coubertin had established his Olympic project in the 1890s. Sokol is the term for both the place at which exercises were practised, and the associated teachings that were promulgated in journals, discussions, lectures, excursions, and performances, and the movement was influenced by the *Turnen* movement initiated by German Prussian *Jahn. Although the Sokol was proclaimed as an apolitical institution of *civil society, it expressed nationalist values and aspirations in training programmes and events that included young people from all social backgrounds, and, from the 1890s, women as well as men. 'Sokol' derives from the Czech word for 'falcon', and the periodic large-scale mass gatherings of the many Sokol (first staged in 1882) were called 'Slets', the Czech word for a flock of birds; this complementary imagery captured the strong individual creature's immersion in a bigger collective whole taking flight. In this way, the mass gatherings of Sokol contributed to the soaring development of Czech nationalism, and also assumed a militaristic dimension. Uniformed young people were trained in marching, fencing, and weightlifting; the uniforms combined revolutionary motifs from various countries, as well as a red shirt inspired by Italian revolutionary leader Giuseppe Garibaldi (1807–82).

A union of Sokol clubs was permitted by the authorities of the ruling Habsburg Empire in 1887. In 1889, in defiance of these authorities, some members of the Prague Sokol participated in the World's Fair in Paris, establishing relations with other gymnastic movements. Internal disputes pitted working-class interests against established middle-class influence, and participatory modes of performance against competition; extreme forms of ethnic purity were also claimed by some Sokols in the early 20th century, when opposing the Workers' Gymnastic Club established by Social Democrats—these latter were vilified as 'Jews' or 'Germans' threatening the true national Czech cause. The Sokols were disbanded at the onset of World War I, though members performed paramilitary functions during the formation of the Czechoslovak nation at the end of the war. Two Slets were held in the inter-war period, and 350,000 Sokols attended the last one in 1938, but then Nazi occupation suppressed the movement. Suppression was also the policy of the communist regime after World War II, which aimed to replace the Slet with the Soviet model of the *Spartakiad. Slets have, though, survived but on a much smaller scale than in their earlier history, being revived periodically at distinctive political moments, such as the Prague Spring in 1968, and the mid 1990s after the fall of *communism.

somatotype The classification of a human body according to its physical shape in terms of fatness, thinness, and muscularity. Throughout history the shape of the human body has been thought to reflect health and psychological character. Hippocrates, around 400 BC, recognized two main body forms, *status phthisicus* and *status epilepticus*. The former was of linear shape and liable to respiratory diseases while the latter was more rotund and liable to cardiovascular disease. Shakespeare's Cassius, with a 'lean and hungry look', is seen by Caesar as a dangerous man who thinks too much. The modern somatotype derives from the work of Kretschmer (1929), who identified three types of physique and classified all humans into one of three groups—pyknic (rotund and fat), leptosome (linear and thin), and athletic (broad and muscular).

Sheldon, Stevens, and Tucker (1940), and then Heath and Carter (1967), developed this three-way classification from the fixed classes of Kretschmer to the concept that each individual has all three characteristics, but in individual proportions. Three numbers are used to represent the proportions of endomorphy, mesomorphy, and ectomorphy. The endomorphy component represents the relative fatness or roundness of the body and is assessed by skinfold measurements of subcutaneous fat. The mesomorphy component represents the muscularity and compactness of the body and is assessed using bone widths and limb girths. The ectomorphy component represents the linearity of the body and is assessed by the height/weight ratio. An average adult might have a somatotype of 3-3-4, demonstrating a middling level of each component. A weightlifter might be scored as 4-8-3 to reflect a much higher than average level of mesomorphy due to muscle hypertrophy and a lower than average linearity due to a squatter body shape. A considerable volume of research in the second half of the 20th century explored the somatotype of athletes in numerous sports but yielded little useful information beyond a detailed description of the typical profile and how this differed between sports. Some exceptions apply, such as the waist-to-hip ratio, which has diagnostic value when considering the health of overweight and obese people. But in the main, simply describing the external appearance of the body has proved of limited value either psychologically or physiologically.

References
Heath, B. H. and Carter, J. E. L. (1967) 'A Modified Somatotype Method', *American Journal of Physical Anthropology*, 27: 57–74; Kretschmer, E. (1929) *Körperbau und Charakter*, Berlin: Julius Springer; Sheldon, W. H., Stevens, S. S. and Tucker, W. B. (1940) *The Varieties of Human Physique*, New York: Harper and Brothers.

spaceball trampoline A recreational activity in which are combined the skills of *trampolining, *basketball, and *volleyball. The object of the game is to propel the ball through a suspended basket, endeavouring to get the opponent to drop, or fail to catch, the ball. Evolved by George Nissen in the USA in the 1960s, the game is based on training techniques adopted by NASA (National Aeronautics and Space Administration) astronauts. The activity is said to increase physical endurance and enhance coordination and balance.

Spalding, Albert Goodwill (1850–1915) A US baseball player, a successful and specialist pitcher during the early years of the professional game, who established a company that produced baseball equipment for the national league. He was the first player to be hired as a professional by the Chicago Excelsiors, and on the formation of the first professional association in 1871, joined the Boston

Redstockings, for whom he played for five years. He led the Chicago White
Stockings to the first ever national title, retiring in 1876 before managing the team
to national victories and gaining the rights to produce the official National
League baseball. With his brother, Spalding opened the Chicago-based sporting
goods business, A. G. Spalding & Bros, which, with its slogan 'Quality first', had
fourteen stores by 1901 and a national network of companies that used the Spalding
catalogue as a basis for their trade, Spalding having moved into manufacturing as
well as retail. While running his business, Spalding promoted the Chicago White
Stockings, and initiated reforms within the game, countering gambling,
condemning drinking, and eliminating player collusion. He also confirmed the rules
of the game, and international promotional tours were organized to exhibit the
USA's cleaned-up national game. Spalding was US commissioner at the 1900
Olympic Games in Paris, at the bequest of the US President William McKinley.
His international exhibition tour climaxed on returning to the USA in a
grand parade and banquet in New York City, attended by popular war hero and
soon-to-be president Theodore *Roosevelt. In 1905 Spalding established a
commission to investigate the origins of baseball, which in 1907 declared the
game to have been invented by Abner Doubleday, a claim that has never been
corroborated but came to act as a powerful foundational myth relating to the
distinctive national game. His *America's National Game* was published in 1911,
perpetuating this myth.

   Spalding is more than an outstanding pitcher in the early history of baseball, or an
opportunistic entrepreneur in the expanding sport and leisure markets of the USA;
he is a figure who embodied the cultural and economic aspirations of an emergent
nation as expressed in the cultivation of its distinctive sporting forms. It is figures
such as Spalding who ensured that baseball, and not, say, cricket, became the
national game of the USA:

> Though baseball and cricket both began as relatively informal leisure games
> in the United States, baseball was later blessed by a cadre of brilliant
> entrepreneurs determined to make it the "nation's pastime." One such
> person was A. G. Spalding, star player, manager, league organizer, and sports
> manufacturer. To call Spalding an impresario or a marketing genius would
> be a bit of an understatement. He engaged in every part of the game, from
> promoting star players and intercity rivalries to squelching nascent efforts
> at labor organization among players'. (Jason Kaufman and Orlando
> Patterson, 'Cross-National Cultural Diffusion: The Global Spread of Cricket',
> *American Sociological Review*, vol. 70, 2005).

Spartakiads Forms of mass activity that were promoted in the Soviet Union in the
1920s and 1930s, combining competitive athletics and gymnastics and public
pageants in cultural spectacles driven by particular political principles and goals.
The multi-sport event enabled messages and slogans embracing the new
revolutionary values to be conveyed to large gatherings of young people, and
combined forms of sport and political parade and display were held from 1919.
By the 1930s there were All-Union Spartakiads complemented by Spartakiads for
different work-based groupings, including trade unions, collective farms, medical
workers, the police, and the army. The first such event was held in 1928, named after

Spartacus, the rebel slave of ancient Rome. Seven thousand male and female athletes from throughout the USSR competed, along with six hundred foreign guests. Organized by the communist Red Sport International, they were intended as a direct challenge to the Amsterdam—seen by the USSR as the bourgeois—Olympics of the same year, and to complement the *Workers' Olympics held in Frankfurt in 1925. The emphasis on mass participation included non-competitive hikes, and reproductions of historical revolutionary events. But it also included military-based events such as tossing the grenade, and swimming underwater clothed in full battle dress. Less than half the participants were from the working class, and virtually no peasants participated. The majority of participants were from the category of employee/white-collar worker. This first Spartakiad was staged in 1928, the key year in the consolidation of Stalin's power, and served important internal ideological purposes in legitimating and profiling the new regime.

By the mid to late 1930s, the Red Sport International was urging communists in capitalist countries to join National Olympic Committees. Robert Edelman notes that though the Spartakiad arose as a direct alternative to the Olympic Games, its success within the USSR provided a basis for the Soviet impact at the country's first Olympics at Helsinki in 1952: 'the "system" that emerged so surprisingly' in Helsinki 'had first been put into place much earlier. It developed through the 1930s as an elitist and a statist version of competitive but non-commercial sport' ('Moscow 1980: Stalinism or Good, Clean Fun?' in Alan Tomlinson and Christopher Young, eds, *National Identity and Global Sports Events: Culture, Politics, and Spectacle in the Olympics and the Football World Cup*, 2006).

specialization The process whereby activities and tasks are broken down into component parts of an increasingly specialized nature. In modern sports, positions or roles in teams have called for specialist skills that constitute one of what Eric Dunning and Kenneth Sheard called the structural properties of a sport: in contrast to folk games in which several 'game elements' might be 'rolled into one', modern sports called for 'increased specialization around kicking, carrying and throwing, the use of sticks, etc.' (*Barbarians, Gentlemen and Players: A Sociological Study of the Development of Rugby Football*, 1979). Specialization is also a primary characteristic of modern sports for Allen Guttmann, who identifies specialized elements in Greek and Roman sports, but especially high degrees of specialization in modern sports, both 'upon the modern field of play' and in an 'intricate system of supportive personnel' (*From Ritual to Record: The Nature of Modern Sports*, 1978). Sport performance has become so specialized that there is almost novelty value in any multi-activity contest calling for a range of skills, such as *Gaelic football or the *modern pentathlon.

spectacle In her 'Sports Spectacular: The Social Ritual of Power' (*Quest*, 1968), Alyce Taylor Cheska noted that any secular activity has the capacity to be shaped into a dramatic performance and exhibit the features of a *ritual:

> The concept of power is often objectified in the sports spectacular, and elaborately colorful ritual ceremony... the New Year's Day football Rose Bowl and the Basketball tournament 'March Madness' in the United States; the South American national soccer matches; the southeastern Asian

colorful sepak takraw contests; the eastern European elaborate sports Spartakiads; and the crowning international grandeur of the modern Olympics.

Concentrating on the successor to the Rose Bowl event, the *Super Bowl (first staged in 1967), Michael R. Real called the event a diverting spectacle, celebrating the dominant aspects of a society—male-dominated, violent, technological, corporate, nationalistic—but providing most of all a cultural space away from the demands of everyday life at work, in the community, or in the home ('Super Bowl: Mythic Spectacle', *Journal of Communication*, 1975). These adaptations of the term spectacle placed the sporting event in the interpretive frameworks of ritual, and myth/ideology respectively; and both recognized that the spectacle embodies expressions of social and cultural power.

Guy Debord (1931–94) published his *The Society of the Spectacle* in 1967, bringing a revolutionary Marxist dimension to the theorization of the spectacular: 'The SPECTACLE is *capital* accumulated to the point where it becomes image'. This can become a kind of shorthand for referring to the economic framework and context of the sporting spectacle, and a sole reliance on the Debord definition can overlook the less imposed, more negotiated meanings of a spectacle as experienced by the participants in the event. David Harvey's *The Condition of Postmodernity* (1989) recognized both the 'sensationalism of the spectacle' and a revolutionary potential, in a spectacle form that is capable of forging consciousness. Analysis of the sporting spectacle should therefore employ a *depth hermeneutic, acknowledging the circumstances of production of the event, its expressed meanings, and the cycles of interpretation by which the spectacle is both experienced and made intelligible. *See also* MEDIA EVENTS; MEGA-EVENTS; OLYMPIC CEREMONY.

spectator A person who watches the sporting event as it unfolds, either through live attendance at the event itself, or through a visual medium by which the live action is conveyed. The core dictionary definitions (*Oxford English Dictionary*, Compact edition, 1971) place presence (being there) and seeing (the word derives from the Latin word for gazing at or looking) at the heart of the condition of spectatorship or spectatordom. Work on the context and conditions of spectating has identified political effects, and a wide range of cultural meanings associated with watching the sports event: from the positive articulation of *community to the display of status, from atavistic tribalism to the relatively repressed sexual and voyeuristic motivation of some spectators fixated on particular sporting bodies. Allen Guttmann has written of this latter aspect of spectating with reference to the tournaments of the Middle Ages, which were characterized by 'strong erotic undercurrents', being places for 'spectators to conduct "affairs of the heart"' (*Sports Spectators*, 1986). The increasing mediatization of the sporting experience means that any contemporary study of the spectator must also include consideration of the nature of the media and the ways in which the spectator consumes the sporting event and associated cultural forms. *See also* FANDOM.

speedway Racing on motorcycles on oval dirt tracks, by (male) professional riders in organized leagues, on single-gear motorcycles with no brakes. Speedway grew rapidly in the 1920s and the 1930s, and a World Championship was organized in 1936. Australia, the USA, and the UK provided champion riders. In the mid 1970s, speedway was claimed as the second most popular spectator sport in the UK. It had been established in 1928, when the British Auto-Cycle Union licensed meetings at 34 tracks (generally, adapted from greyhound tracks), though only ten tracks remained in 1932, when two professional leagues merged to form the National League. Speedway could attract large crowds, such as the 93,000 who watched the World Championship Final at Wembley, London, in 1938, when Bluey Wilkinson of Australia beat Jack Milne of the USA. Other European countries, beyond the UK, where speedway has established a presence are Sweden, Denmark, and Poland. From 1912 to 1959, the Fédération Internationale de Motocyclisme (which had joined with Britain's AutoCycle Union when the international body, initially founded in 1904 in Paris, was revived) was based in London, before moving to Geneva, Switzerland. *See also* MOTORCYCLE RACING.

Spencer, Herbert (1820–1903) A philosopher and pioneer of sociology, Spencer became a professional writer without formal academic training or study. Born in Derby, England, in a spirit of 'very vibrant radical, scientific, and nonconformist culture' (José Harris, *Oxford Dictionary of National Biography*, 2004), and son of the honorary secretary of the town's Philosophical Society, Spencer pursued for much of his life an exceptionally successful and lucrative writing career. His books explored new levels of synthesis and appealed to expanding audiences in Europe and North America as well as Britain: *The Study of Sociology* (1873) went into 21 editions by 1894. Eschewing the formal academic route of the universities, Spencer initially became a civil engineer in the new railway industry, and taught himself the philosophy and the theory of society by voracious but maverick reading, the classic Victorian autodidact.

As part of his project to establish an integrated and overarching *synthetic philosophy* Spencer expressed an interest in the physical education of the person. In his *Education: Intellectual, Moral, and Physical* (1859–61, and called 'the author's most popular work' when reissued in the Thinker's Library in 1929), Spencer railed against the 'improper scantiness' of clothing, food habits, and the difference in the exercise made available to boys and girls in schools. Spencer criticized the lack of provision of vigorous exercise for girls, but also condemned the functional artificiality of gymnastics as inferior to play. Analysing the daily routine of a male training college, Spencer observed that the imbalance of the mental and the physical activities was such that 'the bodily injury inflicted must be great'. Spencer found the physical education of children to be 'seriously faulty':

> Instead of respecting the body and ignoring the mind, we now respect the mind and ignore the body. Both these attitudes are wrong. We do not yet realize the truth that as, in this life of ours, the physical underlies the mental, the mental must not be developed at the expense of the physical. The ancient and modern conceptions must be combined.

Spencer sought to integrate the insights, Harris reminds us, of 'theology, epistemology, thermodynamics, astronomy, biology, psychology, ethics, and political thought'. To this extraordinarily ambitious list might be added 'nutrition' and 'exercise science': his observations on physical education make Spencer a significant, and relatively neglected, voice in the history of the rising awareness of the importance of the healthy body.

sponsored mobility *See* CONTEST AND SPONSORED MOBILITY.

sponsorship The association of a company name, brand, or associated activity with a particular sport organization or sport event, for which the sponsor pays for the rights of association for a specified period or cycle of events. Sports marketing specialists claim that sponsorship is not mere advertising, and usually seeks to achieve outcomes or benefits that would not occur without the sponsorship and its generated activities and effects. This is an easier argument to sustain for ancillary activities at high-profile events—sponsors funding children, for instance, to attend international matches at month-long tournaments—than for shirt sponsorship by alcohol manufacturers of individual teams in national leagues. Sponsorship has had an immense effect on the economics of modern sporting competition, reshaping the finances of mega-events such as the Olympic Games (*see* OLYMPIC GAMES, MODERN (AS GLOBAL CULTURAL EVENT)), the FIFA (men's soccer) World Cup and *UEFA Champions League, *Grand Slam events in golf and tennis, and almost every sport that has sustained or established its profile in the marketplace, particularly in association with television and multi-media contracts and schedules. *See also* ADIDAS; COCA-COLA; COMMERCIALISM; COMMERCIALIZATION; CORPORATE SPONSORSHIP.

sport A human activity, usually associated with a degree of physical exertion, in which a skill is accomplished in performance or contest, and for which there is either a competitive outcome (winner, loser, or position), a measurable achievement (logged by the rowing-machine or the timer's stopwatch), or some other or further perceived benefit (health, fitness, pleasure/fun). Etymologically, the word derives from the medieval 'disport', meaning 'to show or display', and became associated with forms of fun and diversion in which the hunting and shooting sports of the leisured classes were particularly prominent. Philosophers, sociologists, and historians, among others, have addressed the definitional challenge of specifying the precise nature of sport. Ken Roberts (*The Leisure Industries*, 2004) finds it 'unsatisfactory to sidestep the definitional problem', and lists four characteristics of sport: it is separate from the rest of life, in its rules, place, and times; it is based on skill that is improvable by practice and preparation; it is based on energy that requires stamina and exertion; and it is competitive, geared to winning. Allen Guttmann's works—spanning *From Ritual to Record: The Nature of Modern Sports* (1978) to *Sport: The First Five Millennia* (2004)—have consistently defined sport as 'autotelic physical contests'. For Guttmann, people 'work because they have to; they play because they want to. The pleasures of *play* are intrinsic rather than extrinsic to the activity. In a word, play is autotelic (from *auto*, "its own," and *telos*, "goal, end, or purpose").' The International Olympic Committee, though, includes *chess on its list of 'recognized sports', and in this *Dictionary of Sports Studies* this broader conception of sport is adopted, embracing exercise as well as elite sport performance and contest, leisure and recreational sporting activity as well as formal participation or organized competition. As the inclusion of sport and games of many kinds demonstrates, sport and sporting activity have had many forms and meanings, as the products of societies and cultures of varying kinds in past and present time.

sport and exercise psychology A specialist branch of psychology—the study of people, the mind, and human behaviour—in the particular setting of sport and exercise. Sport and exercise psychology is both a theoretical and an applied subject. In sport its practitioners undertake research to increase understanding and to develop theories about how and why athletes behave as they do. Its practitioners are also involved in direct work with athletes and coaches to develop strategies and techniques to improve performance. In exercise contexts the psychologist seeks to understand why people exercise, why they stop, and how people can be helped to establish and maintain an active lifestyle. Some of the primary areas of work in sport and exercise psychology are *arousal, *anxiety, group dynamics and *team building, communication, competition, motivation, concentration, and *goal setting. The psychologist would apply theoretical knowledge and understanding of these topics by, for example, helping an athlete reach an optimal level of arousal during competition; working with a sports team to improve communication between players; or advising organizations about how to structure exercise programmes to improve adherence. Sport and exercise psychology also deals with illness-related matters such as the psychological factors involved in injury and rehabilitation, *burnout, *eating disorders, and the beneficial role of exercise in smoking cessation and the treatment of substance abuse. A branch of sport and exercise psychology is concerned with the neuromuscular control of movement and *motor learning.

sport development An approach to sport based upon the premise that sport is a good thing and a worthy activity, warranting the attention of a profession for the promotion and development of positive models of sport. The term was used in the 1960 Wolfenden Report in the UK, *Sport in the Community*, which proposed the formation of a Sports Development Council, to aid 'coherent policy-making', advise government, and allocate public funding in order to meet 'the proper claims of recreative physical activity, as an integral part of the nation's life'. The report anticipated that such a council would be made up of 'a small body of six to ten persons', and those reporting would have been shocked at the explosion of sport development as a profession at local community, regional, and national levels. Sport development experts are concerned with the making of policy, issues such as *equity and *equality in relation to sport and participation in sport, and ways of minimizing, through intervention and facilitation, social exclusion in sport.

Sport England A *quango (quasi non-governmental organization) dedicated to the promotion and development of sport in England. Formerly the Sports Council (England), it has campaigned to raise the awareness of the benefits of sport at all levels from the recreational to the world-beating competitive performance. If a body such as Sport England achieved all its goals, it would no longer need to exist. Unfortunately, as experienced members of the body have recognized, despite decades of research, initiatives, and promotional policies, *sport participation rates have remained 'stubbornly static'. The successful bid by London to stage the 2012 Olympic Games has diverted attention—and resources—away from the broader mission of Sport England, and more towards the 'podium policies' that support selected medal hopefuls in a limited number of sports.

(⊕) SEE WEB LINKS

• The former Sports Council (England) site with a section on research that is based in a commitment to generating 'evidence, insight and understanding' on sport participation and performance.

sport for all A slogan, principle, and then widely adopted policy that was taken up by many countries and nations, particularly in Europe, from the 1960s and 1970s onwards. The Council of Europe stimulated sport ministers from member countries to adopt a Sport for All charter in 1975, committed to making sport more widely available to all people in the population, for its health and educational benefits, and its potential contribution to social integration. This was a cross-national rallying call to sports administrators and the new leisure professionals in the public sector that sporting opportunities should be made available to all individuals regardless of social background or status. It was an important reminder that much of sport wasn't 'for all': male membership committees of golf clubs; aristocratic dominance of some governing bodies; all-white skins as well as playing outfits at tennis clubs; upper-class raucousness of Rugby Union fans at Twickenham—the list could go on, referring to many other societies as well as Britain, to show how *class, *patriarchy, and race (*see* RACISM) erected barriers to participation. So the policy accomplished important interventionist work in raising awareness of the policy work that lay ahead to make 'sport for all' more than a slogan. For any sport analyst fifty years later, the appositeness of the term persists, but the optimism of the early practitioners has not been matched by the effects of well-intentioned interventions. *See also* SPORT PARTICIPATION.

Sporting Goods Manufacturers Association A US-based trade association of sport retailers and fitness brands whose monitoring of trends in the sports goods business provides data on participation in and expenditure upon sport. It was founded in New York, USA, in 1906 by sports businessmen, and has promoted partnerships with the federal government on schemes such as PE4life (2001). Its Sports and Fitness Participation Report, analysing participation patterns in over a hundred sports and physical activities, has become an essential source of data and market intelligence for the sector, though it does not come cheap: a full report for one year can cost up to US$500.

(⊕) SEE WEB LINKS

• The site of this US trade organization, which provides, at a charge, reports on trends in sport participation and patterns of sport markets.

sportization A term coined by Norbert Elias to describe the process whereby popular cultural activities or folk games were changed by the development of codes of conduct and rules, and by changing conceptions of the acceptable limits of violence. Elias referred to the '"sportization" of pastimes . . . as a shorthand for their transformation in English society into sports and the export of some of them on an almost global scale' (*Quest for Excitement: Sport and Leisure in the Civilizing Process*, with Eric Dunning, 1986). *See also* CIVILIZING PROCESS.

sport participation A measure, or at least indication, of the proportion of a population or a group engaging in a particular activity, usually on the basis of a stated frequency of participation in that activity. In contemporary affluent societies, late 20th-century trends in sport participation have exhibited a decline in participation in traditional team sports, and a rise in the popularity of individual and lifestyle sports (from skateboarding and snowboarding, t'ai chi and aerobics, to surfing and windsurfing). These latter activities constitute conspicuous forms of display, in heightened forms of individualism combining display and dexterity: very different from traditional forms of physicality and bodily expression rooted in sports such as classic team games. Lifestyle sports are, for participants, 'very much an expression of their identities and lifestyles rather than existing as institutional forms in their own rights' (Tomlinson et al., 2005: 4). 'New social practices', as Ravenscroft puts it, underlie contemporary forms of participation: 'It seems to be increasingly accepted that people are becoming more reluctant to join clubs and societies' (2004, p. 129).

In the UK, statistics from the 2002/3 General Household Survey (GHS) for the UK population aged 16 and over (Fox and Rickards, 2004, Figure B, p. 7) identified the top ten activities for men and women, based on participation in the four weeks before interview, with seasonality considered:

Men	%	Women	%
Walking	36	Walking	34
Snooker, etc.	15	Keep fit/yoga	16
Cycling	12	Swimming	15
Swimming	12	Cycling	6
Soccer	10	Snooker, etc.	4
Golf	9	Weights	3
Weights	9	Running	3
Keep fit/yoga	7	10-pin bowling	3
Running	7	Horse riding	2
10-pin bowling	4	Tennis	2

Note the absentees from the respective lists: soccer and golf do not feature in the women's list; horse riding and tennis are not in the men's list. Some figures of the most general kind are reported, suggesting that a majority of the population is physically active—75% of adults have participated in a 'sport, game or physical activity' in the last 12 months, 59% in the previous four weeks (though these are reduced to 66% and 43% respectively when walking is excluded).

National participation figures are notoriously difficult to unravel in completely reliable ways, but Sport England's Head of Strategy Research and Planning Nick Rowe acknowledged in April 2004 that 'participation rates have remained stubbornly static and inequities in participation between different social groups have continued largely unchanged over the last 30 years or so with perhaps the exception of more women taking part in fitness related activities' (Rowe, 2004: 2–3).

This observation was borne out by data in Sport England's Active People Survey (Sport England, 2006), described by the organization as 'the largest sport and recreation survey ever undertaken'. A total of 363,724 people was interviewed by telephone between mid October 2005 and mid October 2006, representative of the adult population of England. Excluding recreational walking and swimming, which 20% and 13.8% of the population took part in at least once a month, the top sports and recreational activities of the population were as follows: gym (including exercise bikes and rowing machines), 7.8%; all forms of football, 7.1%; running/jogging, 4.6%; golf/pitch and putt/putting, 3.6%; badminton, 2.2% (and at 900,332 people—the participation figure projected on the basis of the sample interviewed—the first in the top ten to be under one million); tennis, 2.1%; and, in tenth position, aerobics, 1.5%. Yoga, squash, and keep-fit/sit-ups filled the next three places. Fishing, widely but falsely hailed as a top-participation sport, was eighteenth, one place behind cricket. A new entry to the top 20 confirmed the challenge of individualized forms of self-enhancing physical activity to traditional team games: 270,071 adults in England regularly participated in pilates. Activities such as the individual and lifestyle activities mentioned above were confirmed as niche markets in the expanding landscape of physical and sporting activities: skateboarding, snowboarding, surfing, and windsurfing each attracted 0.1% of the adult population; t'ai chi 0.3%.

References
Fox, K. and Rickards, L. (2004) *Sport and Leisure: Results from the Sport and Leisure Module of the 2002 General Household Survey*, London: TSO; Ravenscroft, N. (2004) 'Sport and Local Delivery', in Sport England, *Driving Up Participation: The Challenge for Sport* (academic review papers commissioned by Sport England as contextual analysis to inform the preparation of the Framework for Sport in England), London: Sport England, pp. 123–34; Rowe, N. (2004) Introduction to Sport England, *Driving up Participation: The Challenge for Sport*, London: Sport England; Sport England (2006) *Active People Survey Headline Results: Sport by Sport Fact Sheet*, published 7 December 2006, London: Sport England; Tomlinson, A., Ravenscroft, N., Wheaton, B., and Gilchrist, P. (2005) *Lifestyle Sports and National Sport Policy: An Agenda for Research*, London: Sport England.

(((·))) SEE WEB LINKS

• Data and profiles on sport participation (in England) from the biggest-ever running survey of its kind.

sports bars   A site for public sports viewing where matches and events can be collectively consumed, in the sociable group context of the public space. Institutionalized widely in the USA, the sports bar and parallel forms of public viewing have been developed worldwide. Susan Tyler Eastman and Arthur M. Land, in 'The Best of Both Worlds: Sports Fans Find Good Seats at the Bar' (*Journal of Sport & Social Issues*, 1997), identified four aspects of sports bar viewing: 'participation in a membership community, opportunity for social interaction, access to otherwise unobtainable events, and diversionary activity'. This range of social experiences illustrates the attraction of the sports bar as a regular forum for viewing sport, as well as a catalyst and a focus for fans for one-off high-profile sport events.

sportscape   Historians and geographers of sport recognize the emergence of the sportscape as a distinctly modernizing dimension of sport. While many sports may initially have been played on open and unconfined—or at least unmarked—spaces, existing as part of an existing landscape, the modern sporting form became increasingly 'refined and ordered in both time and space', as John Bale puts it (*Sports Geography*, 2nd edn, 2003). A trend towards specifically designed sportscapes began in the 19th century, and in the 20th century 'sportscapes—monocultural sites given over solely to sport, rather than multifunctional landscapes—have increasingly tended to characterize the sports environment'.

sports chatter A term coined by Italian academic Umberto Eco in a magazine/newspaper essay written in 1969. Eco sees sports activity as a form of 'waste', labels 'the athlete as monster' when forms of 'play' become 'spectacle for others', and claims that the boundaries between doing sport and merely talking about it have become blurred: 'since chatter about sport gives the illusion of interest in sport, the notion of *practicing sport* becomes confused with that of *talking sport*; the chatterer thinks himself an athlete and is no longer aware that he doesn't engage in sport'. Eco is no fan of sport, and calls his essays in this genre his 'invectives against sport'. And if sport equals 'Waste', for Eco, 'sports chatter is the glorification of Waste, and therefore the maximum point of Consumption' ('Sports Chatter', in *Travels in Hyper Reality: Essays*, 1986).

sports goods industry The sphere of production creating goods for purchase and consumption relating to the practice of or an interest in a sport: this can be any of a myriad of economic goods or products, from the tennis racket to the computer game. The scale of the industry's subsector will be related to the number of participants (the potential market) in a particular sport: demand for cricket goods, for instance, in England, will far exceed demand for *mountaineering or *snowboarding equipment. The biggest demand is for goods that can be used in multiple contexts—the crossover trainer in gymnasium and in hillwalking, the T-shirt in cycling and general leisure activity, what are called 'trite' sports goods. More specialist sports goods restricted to one sporting practice are called 'equipment-intensive' goods. Trite sports goods operate in macro-markets, equipment-intensive goods in micro-markets (but with the potential for high levels of profit).

The sports goods industry exhibited high growth in the final quarter of the 20th century, with the emergence of a more sophisticated media image for sport, the emphasis on leisure and lifestyle markets, and a loosening of constraints on clothing styles and conventions. But in the final years of the century the boom growth looked over, with slowed growth and lower profitability. A decade on from then, in the global economic downturn in which discriminating consumers began to look for durability rather than the new or the novel, the sports goods industry's future looked less certain than it had seemed in the expansive years of the later 1980s and the early 1990s. *See also* DEMAND; SUPPLY.

Sports Illustrated A weekly magazine in the USA, dedicated to sports, and selling 3 million copies to subscribers, reaching a readership claimed at over 23 million adults, mostly men. *Sports Illustrated* (*SI*) was first published on 16 August 1954, and its atmospheric full-colour cover featured a night-time baseball game between the Milwaukee Braves and the New York Giants, a clever pitch to the national market, embracing the Midwest as well as the metropolitan east coast, and combining the tradition of the national game with the modernity of its depiction. It was more than a decade before Time Warner's new title became profitable; when it did, though, it was spectacularly successful, part of a consumer boom and the integration of a new broadcast television market and complementary print media.

From the beginning, *SI* set out to be more than just a sports magazine, but to be '*the* sports magazine'. Defying the intellectual and cultural superciliousness of other writers in the company, *SI* promoted talented writers to research in-depth sport stories, attracted established names to contribute features, and combined creative illustration with innovative photography. In 1964 it launched—this was to become a matter of controversy among liberals, progressives, and feminists—its swimsuit issue. Time Warner used the *Sports Illustrated* brand for its sponsorship of several Olympic Games, in The *Olympic Programme (TOP) that remade the financial basis of the Olympics. In 1983, the magazine became the USA's first full-colour weekly. Critics argue that *SI* has lost its sharpness at the cutting edge of sport writing and sport journalism, but despite the competition of the multimedia market and 24-hour sports news and broadcasting, it has sustained its profile in the marketplace, and retains the capacity to spark debate and controversy within the widespread constituency of sports fans; much of its success lies in its consistent pitch to the male-dominated and still loyal national readership.

(⊕) SEE WEB LINKS

• The archive of the magazine, including access to all magazine covers and stories.

sportsmanship The quality of playing a sporting competition or match by the rules, with respect for the opponent(s) and in the spirit of *fair play. It is contrasted with *gamesmanship, and was seen as a core value of the amateur ethos in sport, threatened by the monetary motivations of sporting professionals. In reality, a degree of sportsmanship is necessary for the possibility of a balanced encounter in sporting competition and the continuing evenness of competitive encounters.

sports medicine The treatment and study of medical problems arising from participation in sport and exercise. The roots of sports medicine lie in the treatment of acute sports injuries and the *rehabilitation of the athlete back to fitness. Sports injuries may be traumatic or overuse injuries. Traumatic injuries mainly occur in contact sports like football and rugby, and typically involve injury to the joints, fractures, cuts, and bruising. Overuse injuries mainly occur in individual sports with a repetitive nature, such as tennis or running, and include such complaints as tennis elbow, Achilles tendonitis, and shin splints. A typical sports medicine clinic will include not only clinical and physiotherapy services but often also allied treatments such as acupuncture, osteopathy, and massage. From these roots in the treatment of injury, sports medicine has expanded considerably and is now more concerned with the broad interface between exercise and health. The discipline therefore includes consideration of heart disease, diabetes, neurology, rheumatology, and disability, as well as support for the less athletic segments of the population who are trying to increase their habitual activity.

sport space A concept referring to the profile of sports in any particular society, and the capacity of sport cultures and institutions to occupy the cultural space available. The concept refers to what is culturally constructed, not merely physically determined. Sport space is about the cultural resonances of a sport form throughout a culture: the folklore of the game; the debates on outcomes in the bars and workplaces of the nation; the way in which the sport is featured in the press and broadcast in burgeoning forms of new media. Andrei S. Markovits (*Offside: Soccer and American Exceptionalism*, with S. L. Hellman, 2001) has used the concept to account for the persisting marginality of soccer in US sport space, where the Big Four sports of American football, baseball, basketball, and ice hockey dominate the available cultural space of the society. Sport space should not be reduced to simplicities of the spatio-physical, but should be analysed in relation to the culture and power relations of both sporting institutions and the society of which they are a part.

sports physiology *See* EXERCISE PHYSIOLOGY.

sports pricing The setting of a cost for the consumption of a sporting event, whether watched on a broadcast transmission or in live attendance at the event itself. It is not easy to unravel the actual pricing of a transmitted event, as in an outlet like *Sky Television the sport event is usually part of a wider package of channels, though for some events pay-per-view (for, say, boxing) has a clearer one-off cost. In ticket pricing, sports teams are seen as local monopolists, in that they usually sell to a captive, loyal, and returning spectator base. Fans of football clubs in Europe would rarely switch from one club to another, particularly in the same locality—though they may adopt a second- or third-favourite club, based on their own social and geographical mobility or some family history or connection. Spectators of team sports are seen to be unresponsive to changes in admission price (in technical economic language, 'demand is price inelastic'), and tickets have therefore been priced based on the loyalty of the established fan base.

Market size obviously affects pricing, though, and if demand exceeds supply, a *black economy in touting or, in the US term scalping, will find different levels of pricing, particularly for big games or special matches, such as finals or derby games against local rivals. With established fan bases, pricing can be lowered by block deals such as season tickets, where the supporter buys a seat for all of the team's home fixtures (nominally non-transferable, but widely offered to friends and relatives in practice for some fixtures, as such tickets are often bought before the fixtures for the season have been released or confirmed). When such discounted ticketing is available, fans have proved willing to pay higher prices for one-off games, such as an attractive title decider or cup tie. But if the accumulative cost of the ticket price and the associated expenditure on complementary goods in the stadium rises too much, even the most loyal and committed of fans will reconsider the scale of financial commitment to the club. Sport pricing therefore remains a delicate balancing act, combining hard-nosed economics and sensitivity towards the emotional commitment of traditional supporters.

sport tourism Sport participation or spectatorship based upon travel, by either the high-performance competitor or team (as in the use of the term 'tourists' for visiting sport teams, particularly in cricket and rugby, a legacy of the early amateur-based international fixture list); the committed sporting practitioner at whatever level of accomplishment, attainment, or aspiration; or the travelling fan or spectator. For the sport participant, sport tourism has been stimulated by the expanding global holiday industry, with an emphasis on outdoor adventure holidays as well as focused individual activity: sport tourism covers a multitude of possible activities, destinations, and sites, from white-water rafting to skiing and snowboarding; from golf courses to tennis training camps and self-organized cycling breaks; from the Olympics and football World Cups to city-based marathons.

Sport tourism establishes new markets for the tourism industry, often targeting what has been called 'skilled consumption', the 'search by many consumers for more challenging and stimulating forms of leisure experience', as sport economists Chris Gratton and Peter Taylor, drawing upon economist Tibor Scitovsky's (1981) study *The Joyless Economy: An Enquiry into Human Satisfaction and Consumer Dissatisfaction* (1990), expressed it; the skilled consumer looks for repeated experiences, aspires to rising skill levels and constant new challenges, and comprises a lucrative niche market for the sport tourist provider and entrepreneur. The jogger aspiring to complete a four-hour marathon 'simply needs to understand the process by which enjoyment is generated . . . needs to be a skilled consumer, not necessarily a skilled sportsman' (Gratton and Taylor, *Government and the Economics of Sport*, 1991).

Sport tourism has frequently been seen as a form of revitalization and regeneration of a local or regional economy, such as the introduction of outdoor sports—particularly ski-resorts—in mountainous areas where the traditional and agrarian subsistence economy could no longer be sustained. Sport tourism has also targeted spectator audiences for high-profile international sporting competitions, most visibly at events such as Olympic Games and football World Cups, where fan zones and public screenings have encouraged international visitors to attend the venue or the site, regardless of whether they have tickets for the actual stadium. The knock-on effects of such strategies are of course beneficial for the hospitality industries of any host nation. Analysis of the impact of sport tourism requires consideration of not just economic but also environmental factors.

sprinting A form of intense running at speed over a short distance. Sprinting carries with it an aura of glamour, attracting labels such as 'the fastest in the world', bringing into the athletics arena the showbusiness dazzle of the circus or the spectacle. The build-up to the sub-ten-second explosive event combines expectation with focused concentration, for both participant and spectator. Sprints also feature in multi-activity disciplines such as the *decathlon, and are integral to other track-and-field events such as pole vault, long jump, and triple jump. The 100-metre sprint—also, historically, known as the 'dash'—bestows great status on its champions, such as Beijing 2008 triple Olympic champion and world record breaker Usain Bolt, from Jamaica. Sponsored since the age of 16 by Puma AG, Bolt's 'media value' for the company after Beijing was said by chief executive Jochen Zeitz to be around US$358 million. Breaking the world record again at the World Championships in Berlin the following year, Bolt stimulated a complete sell-out of all of Puma's merchandise and products developed for the World Championships. *See too* ABRAHAMS, HAROLD MAURICE; OWENS, JESSE; THORPE, JIM.

squash rackets A bat-and-ball game for two players, played inside a four-walled rectangular court. It originated in the English boys' public school of Harrow towards the end of the first half of the 19th century. The hollow ball, traditionally black but now often white, is made of rubber or butyl, and the traditional variant was squashable in the hand, thus lending the sport its distinctive name that distinguished it from *rackets: the younger Harrow boys, unable to claim regular court time on the established rackets courts, improvised a slower game with the softer ball. The sport became a country-house enthusiasm of the English upper classes, courts being constructed in the elite public schools and the exclusive social clubs of London: 'In 1883 the first private court was built by Vernon Harcourt, [sc. Augustus G. Vernon-Harcourt], Harrow class of 1855, at his home along the Cherwell in Oxford' (James Zug, *The History of Squash in 8.5 Chapters*, http://www.worldsquash.org.uk/history1.html, accessed 1 April 2008).

Rules were formulated only in 1907 in Great Britain, and the Squash Rackets Association (SRA), founded in 1929, sought to standardize the different ways of playing, and established consistency in tournament organization, the British Open having been staged earlier in the decade, and international competition having been inaugurated in the USA and Canada's match for the Lapham Cup in 1922. The universities of Oxford and Cambridge began their annual encounters in 1925. The Women's SRA was founded in 1934. Between the two World Wars, squash retained its elite profile, with suburban clubs established in the London region, squash courts constructed in hotels, and even five ocean liners constructing courts for the leisured classes. Military institutions, particularly the UK's Royal Air Force (RAF) and its Army, also recognized the benefits of the sport for the fitness of its personnel: courts were provided at Army bases in India and Egypt, and at many of the RAF's stations. During World War II, then, the diffusion of the game attained a genuinely international level.

In 1967, the International Squash Rackets Federation, from 1992 the World Squash Federation (WSF), was established: founding members, displaying the British imperial legacy, were Great Britain, Australia, India, New Zealand, Pakistan, Southern Africa, and the United Arab Republic. The USA and Canada were initially excluded, due to competing claims and contested interpretations of rules and regulations, the USA having established the first SRA in 1907, and Canada one in 1911. The two countries were later added to the list of founder members when a compromise was reached. Squash became a boom sport in the 1960s, shedding some degree of its exclusivity, though its expansion was among the more affluent and privileged social groupings. In Australia, public courts were constructed, and the country emerged, alongside Pakistan, as the most powerful presence in the sport in both individual and team events. For some time, the sport had both its established and amateur-based infrastructure, and a professional touring circuit based upon contests between former amateur champions. The international federation opened its championships to professionals in

1980, and in 1985 the women's international body (founded in 1976) merged with the federation.

United, and increasingly international, squash nevertheless experienced difficulty in fitting the mould of sport's new financial and media landscape: the pace of the ball, and the concentrated built-in location of the sport, made it a marginal spectator sport and a far from televisual attraction to sponsors and media entrepreneurs. This did not deter the WSF from pursuing ambitious developmental options, and the universal acceptance of the soft ball and development of portable glass-walled courts have fuelled those ambitions. Tournaments have been staged beneath Egypt's Giza Pyramids, and in New York's Grand Central (railway) Terminal. The biggest ambition of all was to establish squash as an Olympic event, and the WSF formulated a seven-point manifesto in pursuing this: outstanding athleticism, reported by *Forbes* magazine to be the 'healthiest' sport of all; 'best-player guarantee', meaning that all the world's top players would appear at the Olympics; 'iconic locations', with matches staged at metropolitan centres and next to globally known landmarks; top-quality sport broadcast at low cost; universality, WSF having 125 member nations; growing popularity, with squash played in a further 25 countries beyond its formal membership; and 'rich history and tradition', combined with a forward-looking vision. The International Olympic Committee (IOC) granted the sport 'recognised status' in 1986, but more than twenty years on the sport had still not been accepted into the Olympic programme, failing in 2009 to claim one of the slots in the programme vacated by the dropped sports of baseball and softball. With the IOC allocating those slots to golf and rugby 7s, the WSF was unsuccessful in its Olympic aspirations.

Stack, Mary Meta (Mollie) Bagot (1883–1935) Born and educated in Dublin, Bagot Stack took a course at Mrs Josef Conn's Institute of Physical Training in London, and trained there as a teacher, moving to Manchester in 1910 and opening her own centre, also teaching groups of factory girls. In 1912, marrying her third cousin who was serving in the Indian army, she moved to India, returning to England after her husband was killed early in World War I. She established the Bagot Stack Health School in 1926, and, most famously, the *Women's League of Health and Beauty in 1930. Her *Building the Body Beautiful* was published in 1931. The League prospered in the 1930s, benefiting from Bagot Stack's entrepreneurial flair and canny targeting of particular groups of women, and her cultivation of the image of her daughter Prunella as a model of physical perfection. Prunella Stack's own autobiography took the league's motto—'Movement for life'—as its title; and her mother's legacy provided her with her own personal mission. The Stack-inspired philosophy of fitness was also enmeshed with upper-class and far-right conservative racist convictions and values. Some of these views are expressed in an interview with Prunella Stack in Adele Carroll's (1999) documentary *This is the League that Jane Joined!: The Early Years of the Women's League of Health and Beauty*.

stacking The allocation of players to playing positions and team roles on the basis of the perceived attributes—both physical and psychological—of the individual athlete, leading to the under- or over-representation of particular ethnic or racial groups in particular positions and roles. The most commented-on context is American football, in which black players are said to have been assigned to roles based on brute strength or speed, rather than roles, such as the quarterback, based on guile, decision-making, and tactical acumen. Jay J. Coakley documents other sports in which stacking has been observed: baseball, ice hockey, and women's volleyball in the USA and Canada, rugby in Australia, and cricket and soccer in the United Kingdom (*Sport in Society: Issues and Controversies*, 5th edn, 1994). Where stacking is demonstrated to exist, it amounts to the manifestation of prejudice and discrimination, and the mobilization and reproduction—in processes of recruitment, development, and selection—of deeply ingrained *stereotypes.

stade In French, the word for stadium, deriving from the name—*stadion*—for the basic running race that was held at the ancient Olympic Games. The distance of the race was a single length of the stadium, and the name of the race was derived from the word for stadium. From that quintessential athletic event, the word has come to refer to sites of and facilities for performative events of many types, in worldwide settings. *See also* OLYMPIC GAMES, ANCIENT.

Stampfl, Franz (1913–95) An Austrian athletics coach whose systematic, all-round approach to training was one of the modernizing influences upon the sport. Stampfl claimed to have introduced 'scientific' methods of coaching in Britain in 1938; though this has been disputed, there is no doubt that Stampfl was an important influence upon coaching and training. Leaving Germany after experiencing the military politicization of the Olympics in Berlin in 1936, Stampfl went to England and was given coaching opportunities by Harold *Abrahams. As a German citizen, he endured the war years as an intern in Canada and Australia, surviving the torpedoing of a ship in the Atlantic. Returning to England after the war, with no formal coaching qualifications, Stampfl nevertheless achieved influence over English runners such as Chris *Brasher, Chris Chataway, and Roger Bannister. Chataway recalls how Stampfl, an 'ebullient mid-European', could invest athletic ambitions and the mundanities of training with 'glamour and magic'. His focus on *interval training reshaped the coaching manuals, and he ran open-access training sessions at an army barracks in Chelsea, London. Stampfl also coached at the University of Oxford in the early 1950s. His approach to athletes was based on the mind as well as the body, including getting to know the personality of each athlete in a confidential coach–client relationship.

Raised in Vienna, Stampfl was a javelin thrower, trained as an artist, and mixed in poetry and philosophy circles. For him, coaching was a vocation, not a mere job. The coach has 'the same sort of compulsion as drives some to write, some to paint, some to build bridges'; emerging from the city of Sigmund *Freud, Stampfl stressed psychological and mental preparation as much as physical training, and was the lynchpin in the backroom planning (with a strong emphasis on pacemaking) for Bannister's successful campaign to break the four-minute mile barrier. Bannister acknowledged Stampfl as 'an adviser, not a coach'. It was the holistic approach to the coaching role that marked Stampfl's distinctive impact:

'Guide, philosopher and friend, counsellor and confessor, a prop at times of mental tension' were the key components of the role as envisaged and lived by this Austrian pioneer.

Stasi Perhaps the most notorious surveillance organization of its kind, in the former German Democratic Republic. At the sports club, the movies, or the match, if you were not careful what you said, you could have been incarcerated in the Stasi interrogation centre in the former East Berlin, then interrogated expertly and brutally on your loyalty to the state by the highly educated recruits to the state's secret service.

status *See* ASCRIBED AND ACHIEVED STATUS; STATUS PASSAGE; STATUS SYMBOL.

status passage The transitional phase or turning point through which the individual passes as he or she acquires new attributes and/or social positions. In a sport *subculture, moving from newcomer to core member will entail a number of status passages, often in what Anselm Strauss (*Mirrors and Masks*, 1959) calls 'an orderly line of development'. Strauss observes that membership of any enduring group 'inevitably involves passage from status to status'. Accounts of professional sporting lives, particularly in group contexts such as team games, confirm this: the veteran captain was the less mature and impulsive rookie earlier in his or her sporting *career, and a series of turning points have developed the player as both person and performer. Studying status passages in sporting careers is a way of analysing the conditions and circumstances of sporting achievement.

status symbol A cultural object acquired in order to express an individual or collectivity's sense of its own place in the publicly perceived hierarchy of status. The term has currency in both everyday parlance and academic social science. Vance Packard's *The Status Seekers* (1959) popularized the notion, and more theoretically the work of Pierre *Bourdieu has demonstrated how sport and related bodily practices operate in modern societies as forms of status symbol, or what he called distinction.

steeplechase 1. Steeplechasing is a an established form of *horse racing. 2. In athletics, the 3,000-metre steeplechase is an established event in the Summer Olympics, and is run over a course of 28 hurdles and 8 water jumps. It was first run at the second modern Olympic Games in Paris in 1900, though the 3,000-metre course was not standardized until 1920. British, US, and Finnish runners dominated early events, and East European and other Scandinavian nations produced gold medallists. But from the 1968 Games, Kenyan athletes have been astonishingly successful, winning eight of the eleven gold medals. The 3,000-metre steeplechase for women was not introduced into the Olympic programme until the 2008 Beijing Summer Olympic Games, where three of the first four were Russians, third place being taken by a Kenyan. The first documented steeplechase in England was run over a two-mile cross-country course in Oxford over 24 obstacles, at a university sports event in the mid 1800s. The term is derived from the tradition of racing between the steeples of churches (or at least the churches) in different localities, and traversing any natural objects that were encountered along the way.

Stephen, Leslie (1832–1904) An author, literary critic, publisher, the first editor of the *Dictionary of National Biography*, and a sporting enthusiast with passions for rowing, long-distance running and walking, and Alpine climbing. A weakly child, born in London and then raised for a short time in Brighton, Stephen attended Eton College, Windsor, and then studied mathematics at Trinity Hall, Cambridge, his father's old college (the latter, Sir James Stephen, was by now regius professor of modern history and in residence at Trinity College, Cambridge). Belying—and superseding—his sickly childhood, he engaged in athletic pursuits in the boats and clubs of his college, and was elected to a bye-fellowship (which carried clerical duties) at his college in 1854. He continued his commitment to the sporting culture of the college. In one famous feat of endurance, he walked the fifty miles from Cambridge to London in twelve hours, in summer heat, to dine with fellow enthusiasts at the Alpine Club. Stephens's earliest publications were on mountaineering, and he joined the Alpine Club the year after its formation in 1857. In the 1860s he ascended many of the most demanding Alpine peaks. From 1865 he was president of the Alpine Club for three years, also editing its journal. In 1871 his collection of writings on the Alps was published as *The Playground of Europe*; he had left Cambridge in 1864 to concentrate on a literary career, and eventually renounced Anglican orders in 1875.

Stephen fathered four children in his second marriage, the younger of the two daughters, experimental novelist Virginia *Woolf, inheriting her father's zest for long walks cultivated on family holidays in Cornwall; Virginia was famous for striding across the Sussex Downs from her home in Rodmell, to visit sister Vanessa Bell and others at the bohemian Charleston Farmhouse that served as the country retreat of the Bloomsbury group. In 1879, Stephen and several friends established the 'Sunday Tramps' for serious country walkers, sixty of whom over the next decade and a half might join these outings of ten or so at any one time, and would cover twenty miles in six hours on a route within a comfortable railway journey from London. It is clear, in retrospect, that athleticism and sporting achievement provided a counterbalance for Stephen to the life of the mind, and an unthreatening form of sociability without the sustained and at times onerous responsibilities of, for instance, domestic and household life.

S

stereotype A view, or understanding, of a group or a category of people based on the generalization of some perceived or alleged characteristic or distinctive feature. The term has an established pedigree in psychology, and was employed in studies of prejudice, showing in mid-20th-century research in the USA how stereotyping of particular ethnic groups was deeply rooted, and stubbornly resistant to correction by evidence and proof. Stereotypes of sportsmen and -women have contributed significantly to the reproduction of inequality and discrimination in sport. The *stacking debate about the inherent qualities (and associated positioning) of black players in team sports is one such case; as is the commonly asserted assumption that black athletes are inherently less accomplished in water sports than are white athletes (the stereotypical generalization is made without reference to any rigorous scientific evidence). Stereotyping of sportspeople according to cultural assumptions, physical features, or purported psychological characteristics is harmful, undermining the potential of individuals and groups to develop their sporting abilities to the full.

stickball A stick-and-ball game acknowledged as the predecessor of *lacrosse. It was played by the Native American communities of the south-east of North America, most prominently the Choctaws and the Cherokees. Teams might comprise nine or ten, or several hundred, male players, and playing areas could be huge and unlimited; women onlookers could perform ceremonial dances. The sport was in some of its forms bound up with rituals and ceremonies, sometimes concerning fertility rites. Sticks could be made of hickory or pecan, balls of deerskin, stuffed with squirrel hair. Artistic representations of tribal versions documented in the late 1800s show striking similarities of equipment and technique between stickball and lacrosse.

stoolball A bat-and-ball game with a rich and sustained history and cultural presence in England. Joseph Strutt's *The Sports and Pastimes of the People of England* noted the frequent mention of stoolball by writers throughout the 16th, 17th, and 18th centuries, and cited reports of its popularity 'to this [1801] day in the northern parts of England'. The egalitarian basis of the sport lay in the elementary nature of the equipment: a stool, a ball, and the human hand with which to defend the stool from contact with the opponent's thrown ball. Strutt's description implied a one-a-side contest, but the more modern formalized version has replaced the hand with the bat, involves two teams of eleven players, and shares numerous features with cricket, some even claiming stoolball as cricket's predecessor. Critically, though, its surviving format has been prominent in southern counties of England, where it was played predominantly by women, from the working and labouring classes as well as the middle classes and the gentry, from the second half of the 19th century. It was this gender profile that particularly attracted anthropologist Shirley Prendergast to the sport in her fieldwork. In 1917 the sport was introduced to wounded World War I servicemen, as a gentler form of sport than tennis or cricket for their physical rehabilitation; the Stoolball Association for Great Britain was founded in 1923. (See M. S. Russell-Goggs, 'Stoolball in Sussex', *The Sussex County Magazine*, 11/7, July 1928).

In the counties of East and West Sussex in England the sport continued to be dominated by women: in the farming village studied by Prendergast in 1977 regular matches occurred between village teams, and these teams 'acted as a focus for many women's activities over the Summer months and into Autumn' ('Stoolball: The Pursuit of Vertigo?', *Women's Studies International Quarterly*, 1, 1978). Much physical display, jokiness, laughter, and distraction were expressed at regular practices, the emphasis being on this kind of sociability rather than performance improvement. Male responses sexualized the sporting women, and young male villagers would disrupt the women's games, riding motorbikes across playing areas. Male talk in the village pub alleged that stoolball players were 'up for the tup'—a shepherding term implying ripe for sexual exploitation—as well as being neglectful parents, selfish spouses, and greedy for money. Talk of (men's) football and cricket was, on the contrary, suitably serious. Here, the physical—and in this case confidently vigorous—presence of sporting women in public was seen as threatening to the established male-dominated order. Despite such instances of male opposition, over the last third of the 20th century women's leagues prospered, more men have been drawn to the sport, and the sport could claim three or four thousand regular players, of both sexes, in 2008. In March of 2008 the national policy/developmental body, Sport England, recognized stoolball as a sport in a formal declaration that included recognition of its suitability for inclusion in school sport curricula.

street games A term referring to games and sports played on the streets, usually in relatively informal fashion. From hopscotch to blind man's buff, street racing to chanting and playing with hoops and tops, children in particular would use the street as a playground. Modern urban conditions and the growth of traffic on the streets, as well as domestic-based modes of media consumption and the provision of municipal parks, have made street games a thing of the past. Street life and games were an important element of a culture in dense urban settings, and were also undermined by liberal reformists, as described in Cary Goodman's *Choosing Sides: Playground and Streetlife on the Lower East Side* (1979), in relation to the German Jewish immigrant communities of 1890–1914 New York city: 'our grandparents lived and laughed and loved and grew to adulthood in the streets. The streets provided opportunities for community, kibitzing, and recreation.' A National Amateur Athletic Federation survey showed that participation in 'sandlot baseball' fell by 50 per cent from 1923 to 1925, the years cementing what has been labelled the USA's Goden Age of sport, when stadiums, multimillion-dollar sports, radio, and newpapers transformed the base of the sporting culture and began to sell the new forms back to the people. Stanley Aronowitz, in his preface to Goodman's study, argues that the study of street culture and its erosion is a confirmation of how 'time and space are categories of power'.

stress A term used in two contrasting ways in the study of sport and exercise. 1. It is used in a physical sense where stress is neither good nor bad but simply the physical quantity of force applied to the body, such as in biomechanics when determining the stress (measured as Newtons per unit area) on the sole of the foot when landing from a jump, or in physiology where the exercise stress might be the running speed on a treadmill. 2. It is used in a psychological sense where stress is an imbalance between the demand placed on an individual and his or her capability to respond. The perception of an imbalance leads to a stress response with both cognitive and somatic components and behavioural consequences which diminish sports performance.

stretching Exercises used to maintain or improve the range of motion around a joint, also known as flexibility exercises. The range of motion of a joint is determined by its bony structure, the ligaments surrounding the joint, and the associated connective tissue, tendons, and muscles. In some sports (e.g. hurdling) stretching is used to permanently increase the range of motion around a joint (such as the hip) in order to allow proper technique. In all sports, stretching is used in response to the tightening felt due to training.

There are three main forms of stretching exercise. Passive or static stretching involves stretching to a point where some discomfort is felt and then holding this stretch for 10 to 60 seconds. When the stretch is first imposed a reflex protective contraction of the muscle takes place to resist the stretch but this declines over time allowing the stretch to be effective. Ballistic stretching involves dynamic movements of a limb where contraction of a muscle stretches the antagonistic (opposite) muscle (e.g. leg and arm swings). Ballistic stretching used to be common in sport but is now recognized as exposing the athlete to risk of injury since the swinging movements elicit forceful reflex muscle contractions. Proprioceptive neuromuscular facilitation (PNF) stretching involves repeated contraction and relaxation while a partner moves a limb further. The contraction–relaxation cycle moderates reflex muscle contractions and allows greater stretching of connective tissues.

The primary effect of stretching is not on the muscles themselves but on connective tissue. Stretching exercise might be performed to achieve short-term or long-term changes. In the short term, stretching exercises are included as part of preparatory exercises before training or competition wherein the direct physical increase in tissue temperature (hence '*warm-up') allows greater temporary extensibility of the elastic components of the connective tissue. Additional and more extreme stretching can cause permanent lengthening of these elastic components.

structuration theory A general framework for the analysis of society developed by Anthony Giddens, with 'the focus upon the understanding of human agency and social institutions' (*The Constitution of Society: Outline of a Theory of Structuration*, 1984). Giddens identified three core issues underlying structuration theory: human conduct has a reflexive character, and human behaviour is the result of forces that human actors can comprehend and control; language use partly constitutes the 'concrete activities of day-to-day life'; and the interpretation of meaning is central to the social sciences. For Giddens, the central feature of the idea of structuration is 'the theorem of the duality of structure': 'The constitution of agents and structures are not two independently given sets of phenomena, a dualism, but represent a duality.'

The integrated nature of structuration theory means that sport organizations and institutions can be understood as the outcome of individuals' actions and interactions in relation to institutional roles and resources. What Giddens calls the 'dialectic of control' refers to the relative power of different actors in the institutional context, and his theoretical synthesis seeks to avoid granting primacy to either agency or structure in social scientific explanation. A sports club or team must, from this perspective, be understood as the product of the interrelationship of agency and structure. A trophy-winning club's success is achieved on the basis of, for instance, the outstanding insights and methods of the coach or manager, the talent and motivations of the team members themselves, and the history, tradition, and organizational principles of the club. The constitution of sport must be recognized as an outcome of the interconnected dynamics of all of these dimensions.

style The ways in which a cultural identity is expressed or a cultural practice performed. Style can refer both to the classification of objects or artefacts (clothes, fashion accessories, sport fan insignia) and to the ways in which things are done (the element of display in lifestyle sports, for instance). Stuart Ewen, in 'Marketing Dreams: The Political Elements of Style' (1990, in Alan Tomlinson, ed., *Consumption, Identity and Style: Marketing, Meaning and the Packaging of Pleasure*), sees three dimensions of the notion of style: its contribution to definitions of the self; the institutional images through which society is understood; and the way in which information is constructed and transmitted in society. The first of these, style as self, has generated an intensifying connectedness of sport and style in an expanding culture of consumerism, in which the sporting body is foregrounded in fashion retailing and the advertising and branding industries. Institutional images, the second dimension, are widely visible in sponsorship logos and trademark identities of companies. The third dimension, style as information, has reshaped the available discourse of sport, in multimedia forms that have challenged the dominance of traditional print and broadcast forms. Instantaneity and a degree of interactivity have become the hallmarks of this new informational style.

subculture Any social grouping comprising a recognizable minority of the overall culture or wider society based upon shared beliefs and attitudes and common practices and activities. Sport generates a multitude of such subcultures, and Peter Donnelly listed the core characteristics of an *achieved* subculture (in contrast to *ascribed* cultural groupings based on inherited characteristics). Such a subculture is identifiable as a group, can be seen to be structured or composed in a particular way, exhibits distinct cultural characteristics, has a distinctive and often exclusive identity, shows scope and potential for development, fulfils the individual needs of its members, provides sources of interaction and communication, and expresses a lifestyle at various levels of member commitment (these latter can be core, auxiliary, associate, marginal, or occasional) ('Toward a Definition of Subcultures', in Marie Hart and Susan Birrell, eds, *Sport in the Socio-Cultural Process*, 3rd edn, 1981). Donnelly added that individual needs of subcultural members could be catered for through psychological, social, and material rewards. Feminist critiques of subcultural research have identified a neglect of girls' and women's experiences of sport, and have widened the research agenda in the field; and subcultural definitions have been seen as too dislocated from wider theoretical questions concerning power and inequality. Notions such as *neo-tribe have provided alternative conceptualizations. But the core concept of subculture has endured and continues to provide a useful and illuminating framework for understanding the nature and appeal of specific and distinctive sport-based cultural formations. *See also* CONTRA-CULTURE; ETHNOGRAPHY.

sublime A philosophical concept referring to the elevated levels of perception and experience related to particular objects or events. In relation to sport, the sublime is an underexplored sphere, though in sport journalism the close-to-perfect performance is frequently described as sublime, implying a sense of not-of-this-world. The perfect execution of a tennis stroke; the effortless and graceful volley by the soccer player—these moments, often recalled as suspended in time in the retrospective consciousness of the onlooker, are potential sources of the experience of the sublime for the sport practitioner and spectator alike.

Sullivan, John Lawrence (1858–1918) An Irish-American born in Boston who is acknowledged as the last bare-knuckle heavyweight champion (under London Prize Ring rules), and the first champion of gloved boxing. Sullivan's career was a reflection of the expansion of the transport system and the urge for spectator entertainments—with betting providing the economic basis. He was a big draw on exhibition tours and won many hundreds of fights in hundreds of US cities in this context, when there were no formal titles. Sullivan was recognized as the first world heavyweight champion, in 1888 or 1889, though one of these decisive fights, in France, was still scheduled as an 80-round bout. Sullivan was featured on cigarette cards in the 1880s, and launched boxing as a source of celebrity and wealth, becoming the first US sportsman to earn a million dollars. He lost his title to Gentleman *Jim Corbett in 1892 under the new Queensberry Rules, engaging in celebrity baseball umpiring, sport reporting, stage acting, and running a bar after retiring from the ring. His distinctive attire in the ring has been said to have given the name 'Long Johns' to men's long underpants or nightwear, though these undoubtedly existed before Sullivan donned them in public.

sumo wrestling A form of Japanese wrestling that is one of the oldest martial arts, accounts of which, from the 8th century AD, have dated the sport as far back as 23 BC: in the 8th century, annual matches were staged at the imperial court (Nara); and over these earlier centuries sumo acted also as a form of *ritual linked to religion and seasonal festivals. The foundation for sumo as a professional competitive sport was laid in the later 16th and early 17th centuries, during the Tokugawa shogunate, and in the newly developing urban centres of Japan. The ring ceremony that is the basis of the modern contest, and its associated bow-dance ceremony, were introduced at the end of the 1790s for contests staged for the shogun (the general). Patricia L. Cuyler (*Sumo: From Rite to Sport*, 1979) writes that this 'lifted the sport out of the vulgar world of entertainment', giving it 'a sense of ritual that later became its major characteristic'. In the early Meiji period in the later 1800s, as a Japanese preoccupation with modernity marginalized traditional practices such as sumo, the sport was rejuvenated in what Allen Guttmann and Lee Thompson have called a simultaneous modernization and retraditionalization of the sport (*Japanese Sports*, 2001). In 1909 the first covered hall was constructed for the sport, and referees were required to dress in traditional 11th-century costume and headgear. In 1926 a national federation was established which, among other reforms, evolved a coherent national championship system, in which individual victors could be identified in tournaments. Radio broadcasting also began in 1928, and increased interest in the live event. Television in the 1950s and the 1960s consolidated the sport's place in the national culture.

Attempts have been made to transplant the sport into other sporting and media contexts, and potential new audiences have been intrigued by the combination of preparatory ritual—in the crouching pre-combat *shikiri* of the oversized figures of the combatants—and the explosively short physical contest in the actual confrontation. In the UK, for instance, Channel 4 Television sought to popularize the sport, and scientist Dr Lyall Watson was commissioned to educate this potential new public in his book *Sumo* (1988), featuring pictures of the typical 26-stone mid-20s wrestler: 'It is a spectacle with colour and texture, a ceremony of style and beauty, and a conflict filled with drama and suspense. But perhaps most important of all, it is a matter of dignity. And that today is rare.' After some initial interest in the transmissions, there was little established or growing market share: the novelty of the event, and its visual distinctiveness, were an insufficient basis for the sport to flourish in a context where it had no basis in the sporting culture or the national tradition or history. Nevertheless, a quarter of a century after its formation in 1992, the International Sumo Federation had gained recognition for the sport on the Recognised Sports List of the International Olympic Committee, and had 87 affiliated national associations.

Super Bowl The final match in the USA's American football season, the winner of which is the national champion for that season. Established in 1967, it generated unprecedented levels of television viewing in the USA; in the Super Bowl game of 1972, 65 million people in 27.5 million homes watched the game, the highest figure for a regularly scheduled television event yet recorded in the country. In 2004, the Super Bowl was broadcast in 21 languages to 229 countries; its coverage on CBS captured the partial or total attention of 143.6 million viewers within the USA. It claims almost half of the 50 highest audiences in the history of US broadcasting. In its patriotic pageantry and patriarchal celebration of tough masculine values, the Super Bowl is both global *spectacle and national *myth. *See also* ECONOMIC IMPACT.

superego In the work of Sigmund *Freud, the part of the personality operating as the conscience, developed as an internalization of the standards of influential others, such as parents. Coaches and managers have extensive influence upon the superego of athletes and sport performers in their charge.

supply The production of goods and/or services for purchase in the marketplace. In sport, this can include anything from the seat in the stadium or an annual season ticket, to the drinks on offer in the stadium, from the latest swimsuit style to the most scientifically corroborated cross-trainer for the all-round athlete. In relation to sports goods, the industry is an oligopoly (domination by the few) comprising a small number of transnational corporations (TNCs) that dominate the global market: on the periphery, a few small firms operate in domestic markets, often stressing budget considerations rather than style, cheapness over cool. Supply will also be determined by the exclusivity of the product: there need not be a mass market in sailing boats when profits can be made by selling such luxury items to a tiny minority of the population. Products whose equipment rate is high (with large proportions of the population owning one or more of them, such as sports shoes) are targeted and marketed not merely on the basis of price, but in relation to the specific image of the product, and claims about innovation. Michael Jordan was used in this way to demarcate the *Nike product of his time. Overall, the supply in the global sports goods industry is in the hands of a few firms; at the end of the 1990s, Nike, *Adidas, and Reebok held almost two-thirds of the global market for sports footwear. As the most prominent players in this lucrative global industry, these firms consider more than mere price as the primary determinant for the retention of their market share: 'In an oligopoly, a price war might have a disastrous outcome, such as a number of bankruptcies ... Oligopolistic competition is fought more on product quality, cost reduction and innovation than on pricing' (Wladimir Andreff, 'The Sports Goods Industry', in Wladimir Andreff and Stefan Szymanski, eds, *Handbook on the Economics of Sport*, 2006). *See also* SPORTS PRICING.

surfing The art of 'planing', without or with a board, on the forward portion of a wave as it moves towards the shore and breaks into a white cascade of foam and water (known as 'the soup'). Surfing as both a recreation and competitive sport became popular in the 1950s and the 1960s, particularly along the west coast of the USA and in Australia. It is the forerunner and in many respects the quintessential form of what French sociologist Pierre *Bourdieu (*Distinction: A Social Critique of the Judgement of Taste*, 1979) called 'Californian sports ... the new sporting activities' characterized by 'the dream of social weightlessness' but high in the participant's investment of *cultural capital, knowledge, and use of equipment, and the verbalization of the experiences of doing the sport. Surfing became, in the 1960s, a symbol of cool modernity and the almost unbounded limitlessness of individual and subcultural hedonism, embodied in the Beach Boys' 1962 song *Surfin' Safari*, an invitation to an affluent generation to combine sporting display and thrill with lifestyle and liberating consumption.

The International Surfing Federation was founded in 1962, in Peru, and world championships were inaugurated two years later in Sydney, Australia; though it is the International Surfing Association, founded in 1976 and with 51 affiliated national associations 30 years later, that has gained recognition from the International Olympic Committee (IOC) for the sport. In surfing, there is an inbuilt tension between its spontaneous and informal cultural appeal, and its organization, administration, and regulation as a sport—what Douglas Booth has called 'ambiguities in pleasure and discipline'. Despite the pressures towards institutionalization, though, Booth sees three factors as sustaining the irreverence and extreme nature of surfing culture: the pure hedonism of the surfers, for whom their sport has no element of social utility; the lack of constraining institutional structures in relation to irreverent or antisocial conduct; and the consistently declared intent of (mostly male) surfers to be different ('Surfing: From One (Cultural) Extreme to Another', in Belinda Wheaton, ed., *Understanding Lifestyle Sports: Consumption, Identity and Difference*, 2004). Despite women's presence and visibility in surfing, and a thriving women's professional circuit, males remain dominant in the surfing culture.

survey method A form of empirical study based upon questionnaires completed by selected samples of a population. The survey method is an efficient and, at least on the smaller scale, relatively inexpensive way of generating *quantitative analysis of data on specific aspects of the population, and indispensable for investigating matters such as sport participation rates, or sport media viewing. Conducted on a regular basis, implemented in consistent fashion, the survey method can also generate *longitudinal data. The survey method is very reliant upon the veracity of what respondents state or write in response to the questions put to them, and so preparation and piloting (trying out the research instrument in a pre- or mock study) are essential to the credibility and quality of the method.

swimming The skill of propelling oneself through water, either recreationally and for fitness and health benefits, or in competition. In the latter, four techniques are recognized: freestyle (effectively, the front crawl stroke); breaststroke; backstroke; and butterfly. The four strokes can be combined by the one swimmer in the individual medley, and teams compete in relays in the freestyle and in the medley. Swimming—lauded and respected in ancient Greece, but not part of the Olympic programme—was introduced, for men, at the first modern Olympic Games in Athens in 1896. The first women's event, the 100-metre freestyle at the 1912 Stockholm Games, was won by Australia's Sarah 'Fanny' Durack, who was forced to pay her own way to the event, and at one point was world record holder at all swimming distances from 100 yards to a mile.

Swimming races have been a prominent and glamorous element of the programme ever since. Some of this glamour is due to the display of the relatively unclad human body that the sport permitted, at least in the build-up to the contest and after. Swimming stars of the Olympic pool could follow lucrative careers as models and showmen and -women. The glamour is also due to the memorable feats that dominant swimmers can achieve in concentrated spells: the USA's Mark Spitz won seven gold medals at the Munich Olympics in 1972, to add to his two in Mexico in 1968; at Beijing 2008, the USA's Michael Phelps exceeded this record for a single games, winning eight gold medals, breaking world records in all but one of these events (at Athens 2004 Phelps took six golds). Australia has, especially from the second half of the 20th century, produced world-beating swimmers (Dawn Fraser, 100-metre freestyle champion in 1956, 1960, and 1964; Ian Thorpe, in 2000 and 2004) to challenge US dominance; and China's women have had a formidable impact, though the international body's liberal policy on doping has left many questions lingering about Chinese preparatory techniques. European swimming championships were organized in 1926, and the sport was prominent in the British Empire Games, first held in Hamilton, Ontario, Canada, in 1930. Long-distance and endurance swimming has also captured the modern imagination, the swimmer seeming to defy the laws of nature in dedication to superhuman tasks. *See also* CHANNEL SWIMMING; SYNCHRONIZED SWIMMING; WEISMULLER, JOHNNY.

Swiss Timing A Swiss-based company specializing in the manufacture of watches and timing devices, and the constantly developing technologies underlying the products; sport has been an important focus for the marketing of its products, and the company has also served as a training ground for ambitious sport administrators and entrepreneurs. The president of the Fédération Internationale de Football Association (FIFA), Joseph 'Sepp' Blatter, is a 'graduate' of the company.

symbolic interactionism An approach to the study of the individual and society concerned with both the nature of small-scale human interactions and communicative behaviours, and the social consequence of those behaviours, interactions, and meanings. As Jerome G. Manis and Bernard M. Melzer put it: 'Symbolic interactionists stress the primacy of society. Yet, they are also inclined to consider the individual as an active, creative source of behaviour' (*Symbolic Interaction: A Reader in Social Psychology*, 1967). It was a hugely popular approach in the mid 20th century, though much criticized by more scientifically oriented psychologists and sociologists more concerned with structures and systems. But symbolic interactionism had widespread influence upon approaches to the study of group cultures, and its attempt to synthesize the social and the individual levels of human life stimulated important work on subcultures and groups, and the sociology and social psychology of everyday life. Such attempts at merging these levels of analysis are important for understanding how sport has particular meanings for specific groups and cultures, contributing to the making and expression of a culture, while simultaneously expressing the wider values and ideologies of a society. Herbert Blumer, who first used the expression 'symbolic interaction' in 1937, reaffirmed in a 1962 essay entitled 'Society as Symbolic Interaction' the interpretive dimension of human interaction. People do not, from this perspective, merely respond to others; they define and interpret each others' actions, 'based on the meaning which they attach to such actions' (in Arnold Rose, ed., *Human Behaviour and Social Processes*). Prominent proponents of approaches informing of or complementary to symbolic interactionism include G. H. *Mead, Charles *Cooley, and Erving *Goffman.

synchronized swimming A form of physical performance in water seen as a form of stunt swimming, popular in the USA in the 1930s, but developing competitive formats in the 1950s, after national championships were staged in the USA. It was recognized as an international sport in 1952, by the international swimming federation, and featured (with a solo event and a duet event) for the first time in the Summer Olympics at Los Angeles 1984. These were both won by the USA, and both were dropped after the 1992 Games, replaced by a team event in 1996 and a reinstated duet event in 2000. A US team won Olympic gold at Atlanta in 1996 but since then all Olympic gold medals have been won by Russian swimmers. The sport provides an interesting case of the exclusion of males from a particular sporting practice.

systems theory 1. In general sociocultural terms, an approach seeing society as a set of interrelated elements, with a capacity to sustain its purpose and its structure, often in relation to an external environment. From such a perspective, sport could be seen as contributing to the overall goals of the society or system, and it has been criticized as an innately conservative approach to the analysis of society and culture. 2. In sport and exercise science, the branch of *biomechanics, in which the human body's functioning as both organism and machine is analysed on the basis of the interrelated functions and forces of its various parts.

table tennis A game, usually played indoors but sometimes outdoors for fun or recreation, in which two individuals, or two pairs, use bats or small rackets to strike a ball so that it clears a net that is hung across the centre of a rectangular table. The game was developed in the last two decades of the 19th century in England as a form of miniature *lawn tennis at the same time as the latter became established within middle-class and upper-class culture. The sound of a celluloid ball bouncing on the table led to the onomatopoeic label 'ping-pong', a term that was quickly patented. Improvised forms of the game were played by undergraduates and army officers, and in the early 20th century the game became a popular craze for children and families.

Attempts to organize competitive forms were hampered by a lack of standardization of the rules, and limited equipment, until more sophisticated rubber coverings were developed for the rubber bats, and an English Table Tennis Association was founded in 1922, an international federation being founded four years later at what was retrospectively acknowledged as the first world championship, held in Berlin. The sport was taken up in youth organizations and youth clubs in the UK, and for players from less privileged backgrounds, such as Fred *Perry, became a form of introduction to lawn tennis. The sport became hugely popular in Asian countries, particularly China, and was cultivated as both a recreational and high-performance activity in communist regimes. On the sport's introduction to the Olympics at Seoul in 1988, the host nation won the men's individual gold and the women's doubles; but from 1992 to 2008, China took eight of the ten men's gold medals, and nine of the ten golds for women.

tae kwon do A form of individual combat sport in the martial arts tradition, rooted in ancient Korean practices, etymologically meaning 'to kick with the foot' (*tae*), 'to destroy with the fist' (*kwon*), in the context of 'the way or art of' (*do*). It was formalized into its modern version in 1957, and a world championship was held in 1973. Presented as a demonstration sport at the Seoul Olympics (1988), the sport was introduced at several weights, for both men and women, to the Olympic programme in 2000, at the Sydney Games.

takraw A seven-a-side ball game popular in south-east Asia. *Takraw* means 'ball', and in no variant of the game can the ball (made of woven rattan) touch the hand or the ground. One version, long established in Thailand, is played with hoops, and has generated comparisons with *basketball. The ball is propelled by any part of the body bar the hands, and requires highly developed physical skills, agility, and bodily flexibility.

talent identification The process of identifying potential in young people, as part of the recruitment process of elite performers. This can involve moving talented young sportsmen and -women across regions within countries (young male footballers attached to professional clubs), or across national boundaries to reside and train near or at specialist facilities (young Russian tennis players at a Florida academy). Such processes can also involve *somatotyping, matching physical characteristics to specialist sport skills, and can lead to serious ethical debates, issues, and questions, such as whether treating young talent in this way is a form of child cruelty.

tapering *See* PEAKING.

taste In his *Distinction: A Social Critique of the Judgement of Taste* (1986), Pierre *Bourdieu called 'taste' the 'practical operator' that transmutes things into particular and distinctive signs, and it is in and through taste that a social class's condition is turned into a symbolic expression of a class position. Abstract as this may sound, it is often in identifiable choices of what sports to play, and of how the body is approached and displayed in such sports, that social groups confirm their identity. Taste—'the taste of necessity or the taste of luxury'—affects how human agents make their choices, in relation to what they like, and how much they like what they have.

team building The process of increasing cohesiveness in a sports team. Team cohesion in sport is seen when the performance of a team is greater than the sum of the individual skills of the members of the team. It is determined by a range of factors such as the individual characteristics of the team members, communication, leadership, a common goal, organizational structures, and the size of the team. Team cohesion may be reflected in task cohesion (the extent to which team members work together to achieve a specific goal, usually seen in a sport competition) and social cohesion (the extent to which team members like each other and gain satisfaction from being a member of the team). These two characteristics may be independent of one another and it is task cohesion that is most strongly related to sports performance, particularly in sports where the team members play together (e.g. football, netball) rather than separately (e.g. athletics and swimming). Intervention programmes to build team cohesiveness use education and activities to develop factors such as players' understanding of others in the team, clarity in individual roles, common goals, identity and pride, avoidance of cliques, and cooperation. These principles have also been applied to exercise settings. The dropout rate from exercise classes is typically over 50 per cent in the first few weeks but this is reduced in clubs and classes where the members show high levels of group cohesion. The strong cohesiveness of a sports team has led to interest from business and it is common for corporate team building programmes to include sporting analogies, sports activities, and the involvement of coaches and champion athletes.

teleology Derived from the Greek word *telos*, meaning 'purpose', the term initially—in 19th-century philosophy—referred to the approach attributing a goal or a purpose to human history, so that teleological explanations were seen as the unwinding of, say, the rational potential in humankind. The weakness of teleological thinking lies in the inbuilt connection between the designated purpose of a process and identified intentions and outcomes of human actions. In some versions of sport or play theory and analysis, for instance, this can lead to flawed theories of sport for sport's sake, insensitive to the specific conditions and circumstances of time and place, or history and society.

televisualization The process whereby sport becomes increasingly prominent in television coverage and associated screen-based multimedia forms. According to Miller, Lawrence, McKay, and Rowe, televisualization is one of five processes characterizing sport in the late 20th and early 21st centuries, the others being *globalization, governmentalization, Americanization, and commodification (*Globalization and Sport: Playing the World*, 2001). Television has been the key transforming influence upon the sporting world, leading the professionalization, rationalization, and commercialization of sporting contests in the modern world, and generating a 'televisualization of sport and a sportification of television'. Audiences become increasingly targeted as consumers, and new technologies within the media use sport as the vanguard for the promotion of expanding markets. Sport has proved conducive to televisualization due to its innate *narrative drama, its relative cheapness for basic transmission, and its supra-linguistic appeal to global media markets.

tennis *See* JEU DE PAUME; LAWN TENNIS; REAL TENNIS; TABLE TENNIS.

tenpin bowling An indoor game played between individuals or teams, in which a ball is bowled down a smooth wooden 'lane' towards a set of 'pins' arranged in a triangular fashion, with the aim of knocking all of them down. It is most widely popular in the USA, where it was developed as an adaptation of a European variant called 'ninepins', and played informally on the east coast of the country in the early 19th century. The American Bowling Congress (ABC) was formed in 1895, and by the last quarter of the 20th century the sport could claim to be one of the world's most popular participant sports. Its success in the USA combined modern technology with family entertainment. The Fédération Internationale des Quilleurs (FIQ), founded in 1952, invited the ABC to become affiliated in 1961. The FIQ was recognized by the International Olympic Committee in 1979, as representing both tenpin and ninepin variants of the sport, which it claimed, twenty years later, to be 'one of the largest and best organized sports in the world', with 100 million participants, 10 million competitors, and 250,000 bowling lanes. Despite such claims, the collective base of the sport in the USA has been in decline, and has acted as a metaphor in the work of political scientist Robert Putnam for the move away from collective participation, in leagues, to individual participation, 'bowling alone'—an example, for Putnam, of diminishing *social capital in communities.

Tenzing Norgay (Sherpa Tenzing) (1914–86) A Nepalese-Tibetan mountaineer who with Edmund *Hillary achieved the first known ascent of Everest (29 May 1953), the world's highest mountain peak; he is often referred to as 'Sherpa Tenzing'. Tenzing was the eleventh of thirteen children; his father was a yak herder. After a restless childhood, Tenzing settled in Darjeeling, India; he gained experience of the mountains as a high-altitude porter on British climbing expeditions in the 1930s, and ascended a record height on Everest with a Swiss expedition in 1952. The ice pick that Tenzing stuck into the peak of Everest had the flags of India, Nepal, the UK, and the UN flying from it, and academic and journalistic debates have flourished since as to who was the first man to reach the top, and what the meaning of the achievement was in terms of a changing, postcolonial world. (See for instance Peter H. Hansen and Gordon T. Stewart, 'Debate—Tenzing's Two Wrist Watches: The Conquest of Everest and Late Imperial Culture in Britain 1921–1953', *Past and Present*, 157, 1997.) Tenzing was awarded the George Medal by Queen Elizabeth II in 1953, and established a successful mountaineering school, though his later life also included a losing battle with alcoholism.

testosterone A hormone produced mainly by the Leydig cells of the testes and to a much smaller extent by the adrenal cortex. Testosterone is usually regarded as the male hormone since its primary effects are to promote spermatogenesis and the secondary male characteristics, such as hair growth, along with anabolic or tissue-building functions such as increasing bone and muscle mass. The average plasma concentration of testosterone in young men is 10 to 40 nmol.L^{-1}, decreasing to half by the age of 50. The level in women is around 1 to 3 nmol.L^{-1}. Exercise increases testosterone levels temporarily providing a favourable environment for adaptive growth of muscle. The potent effect of testosterone on muscle strength and power has led to the widespread abuse of testosterone and close hormone analogues, usually referred to as *anabolic steroids. One side effect of steroid use is the inhibition of normal testosterone production, leading to a low sperm count and testicular atrophy. Normal function will return several months after steroid use is halted, although long-term use may cause permanent infertility.

textual analysis The study of written or visual texts—documents, print media, images—to ascertain their cultural meanings, or the ways in which the texts operate. Textual analysis, involving the unravelling of discourse as articulated in texts, is a core method in *semiology, and research into the nature of such discourse is central to an understanding of the place of sport in contemporary, multimedia culture. *See also* DISCOURSE ANALYSIS.

theocracy, sport in A theocracy is a society in which the ruling and religious powers are one and the same, and in which power is passed on by dynastic means with no serious commitment to the democratic process (the word is a combination of the Greek words for 'god' and 'power'). Sport in a theocracy is a tool of the religious state. In the United Arab Emirates, for instance, the ministry of youth and sport is placed in the hands of a relation of the ruler, and sport teams (such as football teams) are elements of the state apparatus. Questions arise concerning the ethics of theocratic states' participation in world sport because women, for instance, are barely represented in their Olympic teams. If sport is about *fair play, opportunity for all, and all that a body such as the International Olympic Committee claims to stand for under its slogan '*celebrate humanity', then the very eligibility of theocratic states to participate is in need of review.

The Olympic Programme (TOP) *See* OLYMPIC PROGRAMME, THE.

thick description A term taken by anthropologist Clifford *Geertz from philosopher Gilbert Ryle's example of distinguishing between the meanings of contracting eyelids in the cases of three boys: one twitching, one winking, and a third parodying the boy who winks. Ryle distinguished between the 'thin description' of the act that the three cases have in common—the rapid contraction of the eyelid—and the 'thick description' of what (at least) two of the boys are actually doing, as what we might call self-conscious human agents competent in communication and interaction. Geertz, in *The Interpretation of Cultures* (1973), cites some of his own field notes to show that cultural anthropology, and the *ethnography that a particular piece of work aims to produce, has four characteristics. First, it is interpretive, geared to the understanding of meaning; second, these interpretations focus upon 'the flow of social discourse'; third, interpretation is a matter of seeking to rescue what is said in such discourse from its innate transience and to 'fix it in perusable terms'; and fourth, it is microscopic, it should generate 'a collection of ethnographic miniatures'. What this means is that the thick description of the sporting event must comprise full and detailed accounts of the context and dimensions of the event, and of the participants in that event and their interrelationships. This does not mean, for Geertz, that thick description has no wider application: for 'small facts' can 'speak to large issues', and cultural analysis can grow 'in spurts', based upon thick descriptions subtly interpreted. Too often 'thick description' has been used as a shorthand to justify *participant observation or *case-study approaches, reduced to a tag for lazy designs for qualitative studies. In the study of sport, and particularly observable sporting cultures and institutions in which the researcher can achieve genuine immersion, Geertz's adaptation of Ryle continues to have much methodological potential, and epistemological validity.

This Sporting Life A film (1961) based on David Storey's 1960 novel of the same name. It focuses upon the rise to local stardom of a young working-class man in an industrial town in Yorkshire, England, for whom the tough, macho world of rugby league offers the possibility of the good life: cars; well-cut clothes; the admiration of women; the high-class restaurant. But his fame is short-lived, his landlady cum lover dies tragically, and his boorish behaviour alienates him from his once adulatory public. The film, following the book, is a parable on the transitory nature of sporting fame. *See also* NORMS.

Thomas Cook An English company which pioneered the travel industry. Its eponymous founder (1808–92) was an English Baptist minister whose organized excursions for temperance campaigners developed into national operations, to Britain's Great Exhibition of 1851 and then to exhibitions across Europe and beyond. Innovations included the packaging of the travel experience, the issue of hotel coupons, and in 1874 the introduction of 'circular notes', forms of the travellers' cheques later issued by *American Express.

Thorpe, Jim (Jacobus Franciscus) (1888–1953) A multi-talented US sportsman, and winner of the Olympic gold medals for pentathlon and *decathlon at the Stockholm Olympic Games in 1912. Thorpe, a Native American raised in the Sac and Fox nation in Oklahoma, was also of French and Irish descent. His Native American name was Wa-Tho-Huk (or, in brief, 'Bright Path'). After a turbulent childhood, Thorpe's bright path towards sporting fame lay in his natural athletic talent. Dwight Eisenhower, later president of the USA, and an opponent of Thorpe on the American football field in their youth, hailed him as the most naturally gifted sportsman in the country's history. Thorpe played basketball and baseball as well as football, playing collegiate football before a professional career in leagues and also on exhibition tours, often in teams made up wholly of Native Americans, and branded as 'all-Indian'. In 1911 his college team, Carlisle, defeated Harvard and reportage of this dubbed the victory one for 'Indians' against 'Harvard'. Thorpe was stripped of his Olympic medals by the International Olympic Committee (IOC) after it was learned that he had played as a professional in minor league baseball before the 1912 Games, thus breaking the IOC's strict rules on amateurism. Thorpe never sought to deny this, professing—to no avail—ignorance of the rules. In 1982, the IOC reinstated him as an Olympic champion, almost thirty years after his death. Thorpe died penniless and an alcoholic, his athletic, performance, and exhibition career having come to an end during the economic depression of the 1930s.

Tilden, William Tatem (1893–1953) A US lawn tennis player, known as 'Big Bill' Tilden, the first player from the USA to win the Wimbledon title (1920), and winner of seven US national championships. Tilden was born into a privileged elite in a rich family, and raised in the family mansion in the wealthy Germantown section of Philadelphia, spending the summer at Onteora, a Catskill resort, where he learned tennis at the end of the 1890s. A competent all-round athlete, and dancer, Tilden attended the University of Pennsylvania; while he was there, a Yale boxing coach, seeing him on the tennis court, tried to get him to take up fighting, commenting that Tilden had 'the most amazing footwork I've ever seen'. Frank Deford expands: 'Playing, he moved with a grace that compared itself naturally to the dance, which he also had a talent for. He was a superb ice-skater as well. Slim, double-jointed, with long arms and legs, Tilden had the perfect athletic build' (*Big Bill Tilden: The Triumphs and the Tragedy*, 1977). He transformed himself into a champion at the relatively late age of 27, on the basis of technical analysis of the game and a grasp of the psychology of competition. Living the cosmopolitan life of a mobile elite, in the international world of amateur tennis, he was an inveterate snob, calling the hoi polloi 'brainless', 'hopeless', and seeing ordinary people as having an 'ingrown stupidity'. He also acted and wrote fiction and an autobiography.

He turned professional in 1931, touring extensively as the lynchpin of the professional tour, and associating with film celebrities and actors such as Charlie Chaplin; he established the Professional Tennis Players' Association after World War II, still competing successfully into his early fifties. But his career and reputation hit a downward spiral when in 1946 he was criminally convicted for sexual acts with a 14-year-old boy in a car on Sunset Boulevard on a Saturday night. Tilden's long-established homosexual practices had been an open secret in his sporting and social circles, in which he was known for 'fooling around' with young boys at tennis clubs; he also mentored (as a coach) a series of young male protégés. Tilden never really recovered from his jail sentence of a year (serving seven and a half months), experiencing a kind of social ostracism. He had been banned from coaching minors, and so sustained himself for a while by writing; but, excluded from sporting circles, began picking up young men off the street, to be jailed again in 1949, released at the end of the year a few days before the Associated Press half-century poll voted him the greatest athlete of all time in his sport. His final years were depressing and increasingly miserable. Dunlop dropped its sponsorship, clubs were closed to him, and, as Deford put it, 'fewer students would dare go to the old queer for lessons'. Tilden scratched out a living on the public courts of Los Angeles for a few more years, supported by some faithful friends and still with access to the tennis court on Chaplin's property, but at his death left nothing but a few unpawned trophies, $142.11 in cash, and $140 of American Express travellers' cheques.

time series Data sets based on substantial samples or clearly specified quantities that are recorded over time and if at all possible at equally spaced points in time in a specified period. Such research data are expensive and time-consuming to generate, though in the UK the General Household Survey has provided a consistent source over many years for the analysis of levels of sport participation among the adult population. Where such time series exist, questions of social and cultural change and continuity can be examined on an empirically verifiable basis. *See also* LONGITUDINAL ANALYSIS; SPORT PARTICIPATION.

tobogganing In its modern form, the sport of riding down a snow-covered or ice-covered track or slope on a sled. The word derives from a French Canadian term and the toboggan was a basic form of sled used by Native Americans. The sport was developed in Canada, the USA, and Europe in the later 19th century. In the Alps, tracks laid out at Davos, Switzerland, in 1879 provided the foundation for wider participation and experimentation in technique and performance. Three forms of tobogganing evolved from this: *luge, skeleton *tobogganing, and *bobsleigh.

tobogganing, skeleton The sport of descending down a constructed ice-covered track or channel, on a sled with metal runners (known as the skeleton). A famous track is the Cresta Run (St Moritz, Switzerland), constructed anew annually, and presided over by the St Moritz Tobogganing Club (SMTC), a private members' club founded in 1887. The skeleton toboggan's sliding seat, introduced in 1901–2, on which the rider lies chest down and head first, popularized the activity. Contemporary toboggans no longer have a sliding seat, but riders do wear special boots with rakes on the end of them to enable braking and steering. Riding face forward and 'on the tummy' had been innovated in the later 1880s, and the skeleton introduced in 1892, providing an alternative to the *luge. Events were held in the January–February Cresta winter season that attracted the British upper classes, both men and women, for whom the Alps had become a mecca of sociability and *conspicuous consumption. The last competitive run by a woman was in 1925, and, as the SMTC website has pedantically documented, women were banned on 6 January 1929. Other nations to provide prominent participants have included the Alpine nations and the USA. Skeleton tobogganing was included in the two Winter

Olympic Games to have been held at St Moritz, in 1928 and 1948, providing champions from the USA and Italy respectively.

The SMTC claims to represent 'one of the last truly amateur sports', has approximately 1,300 members, and allows limited pay-as-you-go access for riders who can buy forms of supplementary membership. The club announces that 'the home of the Cresta outside riding hours is the Sunny Bar of the Kulm Hotel'; the club's website cites the first Lord Brabazon's observation that 'the Cresta is like a woman with this cynical difference—to love her once is to love her always'; its sponsors or donors in 2008 were Krug (champagne), Vertical Vision (information technology), Ciber (business solutions), W. & H. Graham's Port (port), Hicks & Don ('all your every day, party and cellar requirements'), Omega (timing/boarding), and Julius Bar (asset management). In its concentration on sociability as well as derring-do sporting thrills, its male exclusivity, and its success at gaining elite donors and sponsors, the SMTC perpetuates a particular model of privileged leisure in which sport is a marker of distinction (in Pierre *Bourdieu's sense) and *inequality. In the mid 1960s writer Howard Bass asked Lord Brabazon of Tara, then president of the SMTC, a position previously held by his father, whether there were any prospects of his 'favourite pastime regaining Olympic recognition': 'Most unlikely I should imagine', he replied. 'Because there is only one Cresta Run the sport cannot hope to be so internationally representative as lugeing.' But despite Lord Brabazon of Tara's bullish parochialism, skeleton tobogganing regained its slot in the Olympic programme for the Salt Lake City Games in 2002, where both the men's and women's gold medals were taken by US riders. At Torino in 2006, the champions were from Canada and Switzerland.

TOP *See* Olympic Programme, The.

topophilia Deriving from the Greek words for 'place' and 'love', topophilia is a term used by geographers to describe the powerful emotional attachments that people can have to a place, location, or site. Attachment to and affection for sport places, particularly those imbued with traditional meanings, are evidence compiled by John Bale (*Sports Geography*, 2nd edn, 2003) of the topophilic dimension of sport. The term derives from the work of geographer Yi-Fu Tuan (*Topophilia*, 1974) and has had a particular influence on how the impact of stadium moves upon established spectator communities has been interpreted.

total fighting A combat sport in which individual opponents can punch, kick, or choke their opponents into submission. It is little regulated, and inherently violent: any form of assault is permitted apart from eye-gouging, striking the throat or the groin, biting, or bending back fingers. The sport was cleverly marketed to audiences of young males in the USA (where it is also known as 'ultimate fighting') and Japan in the 1990s. Promoters have developed it in other national markets including the UK, where at the end of the 1990s there were 30 professional fighters. Medical advisers warned of brain damage, and noted that the sport was not independently regulated, its rules framed by promoters or participants alone. Enthusiasts express an almost atavistic commitment to the sport as a spectacle of male violence. In the USA, the Republican presidential candidate of 2009, John McCain, has condemned the sport: 'It is a commentary on the sickness at the heart of American life', he has said, calling it 'human cockfighting', and campaigning successfully for the cancellation of numerous bouts.

total institution A concept developed by Erving *Goffman to describe institutions with extremely developed 'encompassing tendencies'. Institutions with an encompassing or a total character are symbolized by barriers to social intercourse with the outside, and controlling features that prevent departure from these institutions (in the case of prisons, for instance, locked doors and high walls). Goffman identified five 'rough groupings' of total institutions (*Asylums: Essays on the Social Situation of Mental Patients and Other Inmates*, 1961): first, institutions catering for those considered to be both harmless and incapable, such as the blind or the aged or the orphaned; second, places established to care for people who cannot look after themselves but, usually though physical or mental ill health, are seen as a threat to others; third, places protecting the wider public, such as prisons or concentration camps; fourth, institutions devoted to work-like tasks, including army barracks and boarding schools; fifth, retreats, often religious. It is the fourth type that can be observed in particular sport cultures: for example, the boarding schools of the 19th century in Britain, in which organized games in the form of *athleticism played such a prominent part in the school's everyday life but also discipline-enforcing culture; or the specialist sport schools of communist states, from the former East Germany to Cuba, in which children selected according to *somatotype were prepared for international sporting competition.

touhou A courtly game in imperial China in which the player threw an arrow into a vase. Such were the subtleties of the contest that a two-person match might be overseen by up to nine officials, though *touhou* represented 'the tradition of gentle sports practiced in a spirit of harmony' rather than the tradition of unarmed or armed martial arts collectively known as *wushu* (Allen Guttmann, *Sports: The First Five Millennia*, 2004).

Tour de France The most famous cycling race in the world, which began in 1903, organized by the sport-based publication *L'Auto* that later became *L'Équipe* (*see* ÉQUIPE, L'). It was an instant success with the public on its launch, and gained in popularity when mountain stages were introduced in 1905. Much of its popularity was based on the way in which a major national sporting event was brought into the neighbourhoods and communities of a dispersed population in an expansive and still largely rural country, and on the character of the riders, mostly from peasant or modest working-class backgrounds, yet making careers in heroic exploits on machines resonant of modern production and technology. Christopher S. Thompson illustrates (*The Tour de France: A Cultural History*, 2006) the recurrent motif or narrative of suffering and survival that has characterized riders' careers and performances, throughout periods of changed formats (from a points system to an accumulated time system; from sponsored teams to national teams in the 1930s; and the introduction of derailleur gears, and of timed sprints).

The Tour also developed a strong economic base: in 1924, Produits Gibbs soap company provided 45,000 francs for distribution among stage winners and the top two in the final standings; in 1930, *L'Auto* created the race's enduring feature, the *caravane publicitaire*. Thompson captures the impact and continuing popularity of this initiative, in,

> exploiting previously untapped commercial interests for whom the race's greatest selling point was its itinerary; each sponsor paid a fee to enter one or more vehicles in a noisy, colorful procession that preceded the racers along the route. From these vehicles sponsors broadcast their advertising jingles and slogans and distributed flyers, samples, and gifts to millions of spectators patiently awaiting the racers. The *caravane publicitaire* quickly became one of the Tour's main attractions, both along the itinerary and in host communities, where it provided an evening of entertainment.

Any roadside observer of the Tour at the end of the first decade of the 21st century can testify to the continuing popularity of the *caravane*.

Radio in the 1930s, and then television in the 1950s (in communal viewings in cafes and bars for many who did not yet own a set), complemented the coverage of the Tour in *L'Équipe* and its rivals in the print media. Branding initiatives continued to be successful, with the introduction in 1948 of the yellow jersey for the race leader, sponsored by a wool company, at the forefront of these branding initiatives. Forty years of drug-testing from 1966 onwards, including the 1998 police raid on the Festina team's van that exposed the extent of the use of performance-enhancing drugs, have not undermined the popularity of the event. The death of Englishman Tom Simpson (1937–67) while ascending Mont Ventoux in south-east France, and dosed up on amphetamine and methamphetamine with further doses stocked in his jersey pocket, led to realistic appraisals of the toughness of the Tour and the sufferings of the riders, rather than to moral condemnation; on that thirteenth stage on 13 July, the temperature was 45 degrees Celsius in the shade. The debate concerning the price to be paid for tackling and enduring the demands of the Tour has resurfaced throughout the successive decades.

Apparently cleaned of the dopers after the 1998 Festina affair, the Tour has gone on to set new time records, and US rider Lance Armstrong, recovered from cancer, set a new time record for the Tour on his seventh victory in 2005. Immediately after that victory, controversy raged over a *L'Équipe* report of urine samples of Armstrong's from six stages of his first victory, in 1999, tested in France in 2004, and found positive for the banned substance EPO (erythropoietin). Four years later Armstrong was back in the saddle on the Tour, having denied the validity of the tests and, to explain the matter, even talked of an anti-USA conspiracy. The continuing popularity of the Tour with its audiences in France and contiguous countries that have hosted stages of the Tour, and with the viewing public worldwide for what has been claimed as the focus of the largest television audience in the world of any annual sporting event, suggests that the combination of suffering and survival is a recipe for a form of sporting accomplishment and heroism that transcends the controversies and polemics of the day. *See also* ANQUETIL, JACQUES; CYCLING.

tournaments 1. In the most general sense, a tournament is a contest in any game or sport in which a number of competitors plays a series of competitive games, and in the later 18th century the term was used in Western societies to refer to competitions in activities ranging from tennis to chess. 2. A more specific meaning of the term refers to exercises of martial arts of the Middle Ages, in which two mounted horsemen attired in armour fought, with blunted instruments, for honour or prestige (in what became known as jousts). In the 12th century, numerous knights might be fighting at one time at tournaments held in France, Germany, and England, or other parts of northern Europe, and hostage-taking and ransoms were also associated risks or spoils. Rather than ban tournaments, Richard I of England regulated them, as Allen Guttmann puts it, to 'minimize the mayhem' (*Sports: The First Five Millennia*, 2004). Early forms of the tournament were not staged for spectators and it was between the 12th and the 16th centuries that the more organized form, based on the organized joust, and dramatic performance and pageantry, evolved. Monarchs and rulers, such as *Henry VIII of England and his daughter Elizabeth I, used tournaments as an expression of their political power. Tournaments across medieval Europe also functioned as sites of courtship and erotic as well as exotic display, though this may have been exaggerated in literary and artistic representations of the event.

tradition A set of social activities and events appealing to a group, community, or society's sense of its own past, largely in relation to perceived or claimed values and beliefs that have had some expression in cultural practices and forms or public *ritual. Sporting contests and events have been prominent and significant purveyors of such senses of tradition, imagined, invented, or otherwise. Sport is recognized as a mass-producing tradition by Eric Hobsbawm. It produced invented traditions for the middle classes in Europe, at the end of the 19th century and in the early 20th century, and could also 'combine the invention of political and social traditions . . . by providing a medium for national identification and factitious community', in German *Turnen*, Czech *Sokols, rifle shooting in Switzerland, Welsh rugby, or Gaelic football in Ireland. 'Invented tradition' (Eric Hobsbawm and Terence Ranger, *The Invention of Tradition*, 1983) is 'a set of practices, normally governed by overtly or tacitly accepted rules and of a ritual and symbolic nature, which seek to inculcate certain values and norms of behaviour by repetition, which automatically implies continuity with the past'. A form of such invented tradition instanced by Hobsbawm, emerging in just a few years and becoming rapidly established, was the set of practices associated with the English Football Association's FA Cup Final in Britain. Such invented traditions have been rooted in, and more lately potentially undermined by, the *televisualization of sport.

training A regimen of exercises designed to stimulate structural and functional changes in the body that improve performance; also known as conditioning. The fundamental principle of training is that of overload, illustrated by the classical Greek tale of Milo, an Olympic wrestler who performed his morning exercises with a calf draped over his shoulders. As the calf grew in weight, the overload increased, as did Milo's strength, so that eventually he could complete his exercises with a full-grown bull on his shoulders. When the body is challenged by the imposition of a physical stress greater than normal, a variety of adaptations result, such as increased muscle bulk, increased cardiac output, and increases in the enzymes involved in the biochemical processes of energy release. The overload is characterized by the intensity of physical work, by the duration (number of minutes), and by the frequency (number of times per week). Training is specific to the biological systems which are challenged—so, for example, distance running will improve *aerobic function but not muscle strength. The adaptive changes are reversible and are gradually lost if training is stopped.

As a general principle, the greater the total overload the greater the adaptive response, but in practice the design of a training programme is complex since it must stimulate a range of adaptive responses appropriate to the sport, allow recovery, and also account for the athlete's need to develop skills and tactics. The concept of periodization, first fully developed by Matveyev in the 1960s, provided a structured set of training cycles (macro-, meso-, and microcycles of approximately one year, twelve weeks, and one week respectively) in which the volume and intensity of training were varied to promote optimal improvement in fitness. Athletes in all sports continue to seek the best way to structure training that maximizes the benefit without *overtraining. Training is most commonly applied to the physical aspects of sports performance but can be applied to the development of technique (*motor learning) or psychological skills. In the context of general exercise for health the same fundamental principle of overload applies but participants are not seeking the level of adaptation necessary to the competitive athlete. The subtleties of how training is programmed are therefore largely irrelevant. Although any degree of overload will cause adaptive changes it is generally recognized that a minimum of 30 minutes of moderate exercise at least five times a week is the threshold to yield health benefits.

trampolining An acrobatic sport comprising aerial manoeuvres based on balancing upon and jumping on a springy mat in a piece of apparatus known as the trampoline, from the Spanish *trampolin*, meaning 'diving board'. The sport became popular initially in the USA, and then in Western European countries, after forms of equipment aiding jumping and tumbling were devised for acrobats. It was first known in England, when introduced in the 1960s, as 'rebound tumbling'. An international federation was formed in 1964, and the sport aspired to be accepted into the Olympics for the 1976 Montreal Games, but was not accepted into the programme until Sydney 2000. It is a sport that has a buoyant profile at its recreational levels, in family gardens, as well as at organized and competitive levels, from local institutions such as clubs and schools, to the Olympic levels, in which Chinese men and women won China's first trampolining gold medals at the Beijing 2008 Olympics.

triangulation The use of a number of *research methods in the belief that if their findings are complementary, the overall validity of the analysis will be enhanced. Often used quite loosely as a synonym for multi-methods, triangulation as a procedure emerged in mathematics, surveying, and navigation, referring to the location of a point via diverse starting points. In sociocultural studies, triangulation is most convincingly achieved when these starting points are independent of each other. To ask an athlete to complete a questionnaire on motivation, and then interview him or her equipped with the knowledge of the questionnaire responses, is not in a strict sense triangulation, rather an example of the sequential application of accumulative research techniques. Triangulated results in the strongest sense require that the same findings be arrived at independently by each of the employed methods or techniques.

triathlon A trilogy of sporting activities undertaken as one timed race, comprising a 1,500-metre open-water swim, a 40-kilometre cycle ride, and a 10,000-metre run. The triathlon was first staged in San Diego, California, in 1974; the first world championship took place in Avignon, France, in 1989; and the event was included in the programme of the Olympic Games, for both men and women, from the Sydney 2000 Summer Games. In the first six of these events, gold medallists came from six different nations.

Triumph of the Will A documentary film of the Nazi Party's Nuremberg Congress in 1934. Leni *Riefenstahl directed the film and it exudes a strong sense of her preoccupation with the human body, which achieved its fullest expression in *Olympia*. Both films blended contemporary events—political spectacle in the case of *Triumph of the Will*, sporting spectacle in the case of *Olympia*—with images of traditional history and classical cultural legacies. In the film of the Nuremberg congress and rally, mass marches demonstrating unstoppable political power dovetail with shots of semi-naked male Aryan bodies being groomed for display, and innocent-looking but swastika-bedecked young males piggy-back-wrestling in the sun. The individual human bodies, the smiling faces of the young wrestlers, personalize the supra-human political machine in a sinister use of physical culture to simultaneously lighten and bolster the political message.

Trobriand cricket A version of cricket played in the Trobriand Islands, in the South Pacific, off the coast of Papua New Guinea. Cricket was introduced to the islanders by a British missionary in 1903, as a means to pacify the relations between rival groups. The game was then adapted in ways that incorporated some of the islanders' own cultural traditions such as dancing and singing, and its ritual practices. Numbers of players were multiplied, and scoring systems developed in response to the playing environment. The Trobriand case is a famous example of the appropriation of a sporting form in ways that were far from intended by the cultural imperialist, but which had some of the intended effects of the intervention, in that the cricket matches became symbols of earlier forms of warlike encounter. Trobriand cricket remains a classic example of a hybrid cultural form.

trope 'A figure of speech which consists in the use of a word or phrase in a sense other than that which is proper to it' (*Oxford English Dictionary*, Compact edition, 1971). William Gladstone (1809–98), in his writings on classical Greek literature, wrote of the need to 'treat as a poetical trope this idea of kings as god-born or god-reared'. Tropes, then, can perpetuate interpretations, and contribute to the understanding of cultural meaning. The concept of the trope has been widely, though not always clearly, adopted in literary theory, to refer to forms of figures of speech or metaphor. Sporting moments, and their associated interpretations and understandings, can be understood as tropes, as cultural constructions, replete with meanings, significant for how they express complex and at times contested values. They provide clues as to the ideological make-up of a particular culture and time. They can—as acts or feats, moments or names—become, in the classic definitional sense of the term, tropes.

To look at Englishman Roger Bannister's achievement in becoming the first person to run a mile in under four minutes on 6 May 1954, and how that feat has been reported, recollected, and recalled, is to engage in the study of a powerful trope. Brian Glanville, writing about the post-war years in his essay 'Britain against the Rest', stated that 'athletics—until Olympic year—is no more than a minor sport, watched and supported by the few' (*Age of Austerity, 1945–51*, 1964, ed. Michael Sissons and Philip French). But if the few include the privileged few of the educated and upper classes, and their activities are regularly covered by the most influential organs of the media, the achievements of the few will be magnified, celebrated, and commemorated. Within two days of his run, Bannister could read in *The Times* that while 'the hero himself was resting quietly in London yesterday the athletics world continued to ring out its congratulations' on his 'great achievement', which was already producing 'echoes' around the world. The fact of the achievement was matched by the interpretations of the 'four-minute mile' breaker's act: the four-minute mile motif became the stuff of *myth.

Bannister is not mythical in the sense of fictitious figures from the past: Oxford student, London medical school trainee (on his famous May day in 1954), successful surgeon, head of an Oxford college, first chairman of the UK's Sports Council. But Philip Carter, writing on myth, legend, and history, argues that 'common to all types' of mythical figures 'are names and deeds that have generated popular perceptions, or misconceptions, of British history', and that 'common to all is the power afforded to a generic cause' such as 'national rivalry . . . when expressed and interpreted through the medium of biography' (*Oxford Dictionary of National Biography*, 2004). In these senses the Bannister name and deed can be understood as myth: he beat tough new world rivals in American Wes Santee and Australian John Landy, having recovered from the shock of defeat at the Helsinki Olympics in 1952; and was widely reported as an Oxford University student athlete (in fact, on that record-breaking day Bannister was running in the vest of the Amateur Athletic Association). The interpretive tradition underlying the Bannister trope places at the centre of the four-minute mile myth a set of values that fuels a particular model of British character: determination, fighting back against the odds, *esprit de corps*, honour and national pride, fair play, decency, amateurism, grit in the face of adversity, golden moments in the greyness of the time. The Bannister, or four-minute mile, trope illustrates the way in which dominant cultures can make their own history, and contribute in turn to history's examination of their own historical worth.

trotting *See* HORSE RACING.

trust funds Forms of income specified for particular purposes and therefore not susceptible to orthodox or mainstream accounting procedures. In sport, before the International Olympic Committee recognized that the era of the amateur code had ended, a compromise position adopted by sporting organizations was to recognize that athletes might secure large levels of funding—from a sponsor, or in advertising or endorsement deals—but that this should be perceived as separate from earned income. Such monies could be placed in a trust fund, and the athlete's 'amateur' status remained secure. Athletes could then expend large sums on training camps in appropriate parts of the world, without explicitly earning as a professional, which would have jeopardized their eligibility for Olympics competition.

tsan A traditional bat-and-ball game played in the Alpine valley of Aosta. The batter from one team hits the ball as far as possible, to where the opposing team waits to catch it. Played predominantly by men in its traditional form, women and young girls have played the game since the 1990s. It was also one of the sports comprising a planned (1988) First Spring of South European games, designed to 'show off...indigenous traditional games and sports', to demonstrate the cultural distinctiveness of regions or territories not allied in any simple or even harmonious way with a national state (Henning Eichberg, *Essays on Sport, Space and Identity*, 1998).

Tudor, Henry *See* HENRY VIII.

tug-of-war A contest between two teams, with an agreed number of participants (most often male) on each side, which pull against each other from the end of a thick rope in a trial of strength. Reputedly rooted in rural recreational calendars, the sport was recognized in Britain by the Amateur Athletic Association in 1880, and included in the Olympic Games from 1900 to 1920. Swedish, German, US, and British teams were prominent at those events, the team from the USA withdrawing in 1908 in London in protest at the footwear worn by the Liverpool Police team that was representing Great Britain. The Liverpool policemen, protesting innocence and continuing to wear steel-reinforced boots, went on to take the silver medal behind London's own City Police. The sport has featured at Scotland's *Highland Games meetings, and by the 2000s the Tug of War International Federation could list 53 countries as member associations, referring to itself as 'a still young and dynamic sport in the global scene of sport', overseeing world championships for women's as well as men's teams, and developing a focus on youth and the introduction of the sport at school level.

Turnen A form of gymnastics pioneered by German 'Turnvater' *Jahn in the early 19th century, intended to develop both individual physique and strength of character. The organized gymnastic groups going by the collective name of *Turnen* came to represent not just a form of exercise training but a political philosophy stressing collective homogenization and nationalist aspirations, and so influencing conceptions of sport in the united Germany of the later 19th century and beyond.

typology Any conceptual scheme of classification that identifies the types of phenomenon that exist within the more general overarching category. Sport, for instance, can be undertaken at recreational, seriously participatory, or high-performance levels. Types of sport can be individual or team-based. The International Olympic Committee recognizes its approved number of sporting disciplines, and specialist disciplines within disciplines. Sports experience can be participatory (in terms of activity) or spectator-based. Typologies are thus widely and continually generated in the course of research, based on the empirical evidence that is the basis of the conceptualization of the subcategories of the phenomenon. *See also* IDEAL TYPE.

U

UEFA (Union des Associations Européennes de Football; European Football Union) The governing body of European football. The acronym has come to be pronounced in two syllables—as in the English word 'wafer'—in continental Europe, and worldwide, though in English the first letter is often stressed as a single syllable in a three-syllable pronunciation. Formed in 1954, UEFA initially comprised the established football associations of Europe: 25 of the continent's 31 associations attended the inaugural meeting in Basle in 1954. Fifty years later the association had 52 members. UEFA's earliest aspirations were to organize cross-continent club competitions and a Europe-based tournament for national teams. It established the Inter-Cities Industrial Fairs' Cup (to become the UEFA Cup in 1971–2), and embraced the European Champion Clubs' Cup (widely known as the European Cup), which had been stimulated by the French sports publication *L'Équipe* (*See* ÉQUIPE, L'), and was first competed for in season 1955–6. The European Nations' Cup, or European Championship, was first staged over a 22-month period between 1958 and 1960. In 1960–61 the European Cup Winners' Cup became UEFA's third club competition. The union, brainchild of the Belgian, Italian, and French football associations, was stimulated by the united front in *Fédération Internationale de Football Association (FIFA) matters and business shown by the long-established South American federation.

Based for its early years at the headquarters of the French Football Federation in Paris, it transferred to Berne in Switzerland in 1960, with Swiss Hans Bangerter as general secretary and Ebbe Schwartz of Denmark as president. In the late 1990s UEFA relocated to Nyon, near Geneva, opening its futuristic and lush headquarters on the shore of Lac Léman in 1999. UEFA president for seventeen years was Swede Lennart Johansson, who championed principles of accountability and democracy, alongside the restructuring and rebranding of the old European Cup into the *UEFA Champions League in 1992 (allowing the participation of two, three, or four teams from the strongest and most influential member nations). UEFA's constituency expanded after 1990, with the collapse of the USSR and the establishment and formation of new independent states with their own football associations. Drawing support from some of these, on a platform and manifesto seeking greater rewards for small nations from the Champions League, French former football star and FIFA executive member Michel Platini (aged 51) won the UEFA presidency, ousting the 77-year-old Johansson by 27 votes to 23. From 1954 to 2007 UEFA had six presidents: Schwartz from 1954 to 1962; Gustav Wiederkeher of Switzerland from 1962 to 1972; Artemio Franchi of Italy from 1973 to 1983; Jacques Georges of France from 1983 to 1990; Johansson from 1990 to 2007; and Platini, elected in January 2007.

🌐 SEE WEB LINKS

- The official site of the federation of national football associations in Europe, offering descriptions of its organization and European competition, and features.

UEFA Champions League Formerly the European Champion Clubs' Cup, popularly known as the European Cup, the UEFA Champions League is a club-based European tournament for the national champions and other top clubs in major national leagues of European football (soccer) associations. It started as the European Champion Clubs' Cup when French newspaperman Gabriel *Hanot was provoked by the response of English tabloid newspapers to Wolverhampton Wanderers' defeat of the Hungarian side Honved (of Budapest) in December 1954. Wolverhampton had beaten the Soviet side Moscow Spartak the previous month, and the English team was hailed in the press as champions of the world. Hanot was at the game and wrote that this was an unjustified claim, and called for the launching of a European-wide competition, less episodic than the mid-European initiative the Mitropa Cup, and embracing Milan in Italy and Real Madrid in Spain. The French Football Federation supported the principle of the idea, but offered no formal leadership. World governing body the *Fédération Internationale de Football Association (FIFA) said it was not competent to do it, but the president Rodolphe *Seeldrayers offered encouraging words, saying that FIFA dealt only with contests between national associations, but that if match dates could be balanced with the proposed tournament, then the latter 'would be extremely interesting and would be a great success'.

Hanot turned to the new European association, *UEFA, and presented his brainchild to its first General Assembly, in Vienna on 2 March 1955. UEFA said initially through its president Ebbe Schwartz that UEFA was concerned with inter-national competitions, not inter-club tournaments. Nevertheless, a Belgian, José Crahay, picked up the challenge, and on 2 April 1955 at the Ambassador de Paris Hotel, Boulevard d'Haussmann, the cup was born. After this meeting in Paris, FIFA's Emergency Committee met in London and decided to authorize the competition on three conditions: the clubs must be authorized by their federations; the tournament must be organized under the authority and responsibility of the European (football) Union; and the name Europe must be used only for competition between national teams. UEFA then had little choice but to support the initiative and on 21 May decided to organize the competition itself. In response to the third condition, the new competition was called 'Coupe des Clubs Champions Européens'. For most people this became the European Cup.

Initially, sixteen clubs were invited, not necessarily all champions as the launch needed big names, though in two cases (Holland and Denmark) the actual champions replaced the nominated club. The FA (England) refused to authorize its champion, Chelsea, to participate; and so Gwardia Varsovie (Warsaw, Poland) stepped in to take its place. Real Madrid dominated the first five years of the tournament, which, revamped in 1992, prospered as one of the most lucrative media sport commodities in the world. Fifty years after the launch, UEFA and its partner TEAM (originally 'The Event Agency & Marketing AG', and then 'Television Event & Media Marketing AG') could describe what was now called the UEFA Champions League (UCL) as a 'unique property', and the best football competition in the world, quoting *Gazetto dello Sport* on the event's contribution to European identity: 'at these times of European Union expansion, nothing unites the people of Europe like the UEFA Champions League'. By now, the UCL included several clubs—not just champions—from the dominant football nations, and also dominated midweek television schedules—both free-to-air and pay-per-view— throughout Europe and beyond. The UCL global audience reflected 'the exceptional demand for the product from fans, not only in Europe, but also increasingly in Asia, Africa, Oceania and the Americas'.

The cumulative audiences for the major markets for UCL finals from 2000 to 2007 were as follows: 2000, Real Madrid v. Valencia, 39.5 million; 2001, Bayern Munich v. Valencia, 47.8 million; 2002, Bayer Leverkusen v. Real Madrid, 46.8 million; 2003, Juventus v. AC Milan, 45.5 million; 2004, Monaco v. Porto 33.7 million; 2005, AC Milan v. Liverpool, 44.2 million; 2006, Barcelona v. Arsenal, 51.4 million; 2007, AC Milan v. Liverpool, 43.1 million. Apart from the 2004 final between two clubs from the smaller European leagues, in France and Portugal, these figures can be sustained; the sponsors secured into long-term contracts even in volatile economic circumstances; the broadcasters provided with unusually reliable large markets in a turbulent media context; and the elite clubs in the top countries guaranteed high levels of income based on qualification for the UCL, and the progress made in it throughout the season. Coverage reaches 220 or more territories, the cumulative worldwide audience in 2006–7 was 3.95 billion, and more than 25,000 hours of match coverage were broadcast. In a UCL match week, the global television audience was more than 300 million.

UEFA and its partners have changed the format several times since 1992, to increase the number of matches, to ensure a competitive dimension in the different stages, to increase—from season 2009–10 onwards—the representation of less powerful football nations, and to move the final from midweek to a Saturday (from 2010). The success of the UCL format also led to the UEFA Cup's makeover into the Europa League, from 2009. Much work has gone into sustaining the brand: UEFA points to the 'Excellence' of the players, the 'Inspiring' values that motivate both players and fans, and the 'Passion' that they display; and the 'Proud' aspect of being part of a European and world elite. The slogan for the event boasts 'The Best of the Best on the Ultimate Stage'. 'UCL viewing improves in a declining market', UEFA could report in 2008, and with huge and reliable audiences in countries such as Vietnam, it could continue to promise its sponsors unprecedented global exposure.

The UCL became such a critical source of income to European clubs—the winning champion grossing around £25 million in a single successful season in the early 2000s—that top clubs in respective countries began to prioritize the event over other national events or competitions. In some countries—such as Greece, for instance, where by 2009 the Olympiakos club had secured its twelfth national championship in thirteen seasons—the prominence of the UCL, the imperative of qualification for the event, has even generated corruption and match-fixing. The UCL is therefore a revealing case study of the creation of a global sporting brand that has exploited a sense of emerging European identity within the wider context of expanding global media markets. Without doubt it has enraptured fans, but it has also been a major strand in the global strategies of broadcasters—especially Sky Television—and sponsors. From 2006 to 2009, the same select sponsors—Heineken (beer), Ford (automotive), Playstation/Sony (consoles), MasterCard (financial), and Vodaphone (wireless communications)— and the single select supplier, *Adidas, were the basis of the UCL marketing programme. With such a powerful hold on the global viewing market, UEFA could be confident that the UCL would sustain its profile even in the global economic crisis that plunged consumer industries and national finances into crisis in 2009. With its musical anthem, its (Adidas) starball product and logo, its place in peak-time top-market broadcasting schedules, the event represented both a pan-European consumerism (albeit based in national rivalries) and the triumph of a model of commercialization of the sporting product.

ulmaliztil A ritual-linked and myth-based ball game played by the Aztecs and other peoples of the ancient Americas, geographically established from modern Guatemala in the south to modern Arizona in the north. The game's object was to propel the ball through a stone ring, and the players moved the ball with the aid of padded elbows, knees, hips, and buttocks. As Allen Guttmann observes, the actual meaning of the game is not definitively established: cult; fertility rite; political symbol? (*Sports: The First Five Millennia*, 2004). The missionaries among the invading Spanish in the 16th century perceived the game as blasphemous, and banned the activity.

unemployment The inability of those seeking paid work to find *employment, so that—in any society where such accounting is feasible—that inability can be measured as the unemployment rate, a percentage of the job-seeking population that is registered as unemployed. A rising unemployment rate can have various outcomes for the sporting sphere. It can reduce the number of active consumers in a sector, as disposable income declines for individuals and households with dramatically decreased incomes. Theoretically, it can increase certain levels of participation, though this is historically and socially contingent: in northern England in the 1920s and 1930s, declining textile production and then the Great Depression were the basis of the revival of the traditional sport of *knur-and-spell; in England in the 1970s and 1980s, schemes to grant cheap-rate access to public facilities (swimming pools, leisure centres) to the unemployed at off-peak times were far from successful, associated as they were in the minds of many individuals with the stigma of worklessness. In a number of northern European countries, sports organizations have brought in unemployed people as temporary, short-term contract, or voluntary workers, in joint-funding partnerships between the state and the voluntary sport sector. Worthwhile as these schemes may be, they can only make small dents in the problems that a rising unemployment rate generates.

Union des Associations Européennes de Football (European Football Union) *See* UEFA.

United Nations An international agency—essentially, a voluntary association— established after World War II to create a forum for harmonious and peaceful global development and to monitor and protect human rights, a successor to the League of Nations that was established after World War I. Its membership stands at around 190 national states, and its headquarters is in Manhattan, New York City. Its cultural arm has been UNESCO (United Nations Educational, Scientific, and Cultural Organization), which has given some consideration to sport and its contribution to the fostering of intercultural understanding and international relations: it supported the creation of the International Council for Sport and Physical Education in 1958; it intervened on doping tests (in particular in relation to cycling) in the mid and later 1960s; and the apartheid-linked boycotts of the 1970s Olympics led it to consider superseding the International Olympic Committee (IOC) by framing an International Charter of Physical Education and Sport in 1978, at the member states' first meeting of Ministers and Senior Officials Responsible for Physical Education and Sport (Jean-Loup Chappelet and Brenda Kübler-Mabbott, *The International Olympic Committee and the Olympic System: The Governance of World Sport*, 2008).

More modestly, in 1989 UNESCO's General Conference adopted three sport-related resolutions, concerning the battle against drug use, the universality of the Olympic Games, and the need for cooperation between sport organizations and public authorities. In 1993, resolutions concerning the Olympic Truce—connected to both the end of the Cold War and the aspiration of IOC president Juan-Antonio Samaranch to receive a Nobel peace prize nomination—also reached the United Nations, and 1994 was recognized as the International Year of Sport and the Olympic Ideal. But the United Nations itself and UNESCO did not approach sport in any complementary and evenly committed fashion, and it took the appointment in 2001 of a special adviser on sport and development by the UN Secretary-General Kofi Annan to reignite the sporting theme within the organization. An associated outcome was the designation of 2005 as the International Year of Sport, and related conferences on sport and development.

upward mobility *See* SOCIAL MOBILITY.

US Open Tennis Championship *See* GRAND SLAM (TENNIS).

utopia From the Greek for 'not-place', utopia as a term was invented by Sir Thomas More in his *Utopia*, first published in 1516. More's Utopians considered sports such as hunting as 'below the dignity of free men', as 'the vilest department of butchery'. Hundreds of so-called pleasures, for Utopians, actually have nothing to do with real pleasure, or enjoyment; they are 'stupid pleasures', far removed from the 'real pleasures' of a mental and physical kind. Utopia is used by More as a satirical device whereby the customs of his own day might be ridiculed. In more modern social thinking, utopia has also referred to projected future conditions—such as a society of leisure—in which a kind of scientific utopia might relieve all people of the chores and mundanities of everyday living and survival.

The power of the idea of utopia, though, lies in the inevitability that the utopia will not be attained. In some critical thinking such as that of Theodor *Adorno, the utopian motif is posited as a counter-force to the negative forces of domination in the modern rational consumer society: 'Adorno excoriates the guises sport takes today in order to think about what forms it might take in the future . . . The core of

Adorno's approach is that there is always a potential, redemptive element in a cultural object that looks towards a utopian future', writes David Inglis, in his 'Theodor Adorno on Sport' (in Richard Giulianotti, ed., *Sport and Modern Social Theorists*, 2004). The term also has currency—in a realistic sense—in the institutional politics of sport, where the International Olympic Committee president Jacques Rogge can proclaim (to the BBC in 2008) that the ideal of a drug-free, doping-cleansed sporting world will never be achieved: 'Drug-free sport in general is a Utopia.'

value added The notion that an action, a product, or a purchase has more actual value—or potential impact—than the concrete tangible features, or measurable impacts. Take the arguments often touted for the benefits of staging a sporting mega-event. Besides the stated *economic impact of the event, backers of the event might talk up the value-added dimensions of the event as a positive further benefit or outcome. It is a slippery concept, in whatever its formulation, and has little to offer the systematic analysis of sport, though it remains a focus for analysis of the rhetoric and hyperbole of sport promoters and mega-event organizers.

value freedom The notion that the object under study can be understood in a value-free or value-neutral way, through a combination of conceptual and empirical analysis, regardless of the personal views or values of the researcher or analyst. Thus the male domination of, say, team games at national and international level can be demonstrated and evidenced, but this is not to say, within the analysis offered, that this is a bad or an undesirable thing. The quest for a value-free sociocultural analysis has been questioned by theorists arguing that social science is concerned with change as well as analysis, with intervention as well as illumination. Feminist theories in particular have challenged purportedly value-free accounts of male domination. Commissioned works—on, say, the contribution of sport to a healthy and worthy social and cultural life, or on government policy concerning sport's regenerative capacity—can also often be compromised by claims to value freedom, when the apparently open but in reality restricted agenda of the commissioning client overrides the evidence of the study. The debate over value freedom and neutrality remains central to epistemological debates in the social sciences, and particularly to the sort of applied studies that are widely sought and commissioned on sport-related policy and aspects of sport performance.

values 1. In statistical analysis, values are quantified amounts, the scores in quantitative data sets that are attributed to variables; they are the measures fundamental to the analysis of sport performance, or the benefits of exercise. 2. In more general sociocultural terms, values are the sum of the beliefs and the ideals of a group, community, or society. Much talk of sporting values is rooted in commitment to particular models of sport, such as *amateurism, or linked to values as articulated in associated spheres, such as *nationalism. Values have been central analytical categories for some prescriptive, conservative analytical frameworks such as *functionalism, but this should not deter the researcher from the study of the influential and often formative values that shape and reproduce particular sporting cultures and institutions.

vegetarianism A diet which avoids the consumption of meat. Vegetarians choose such a diet for a variety of religious, ethical, health, and environmental reasons. A variety of subcategories of vegetarian are identified, such as ovo-lacto-vegetarians (who will eat eggs and dairy products) and pisco-vegetarians (who will eat fish). Vegetarians who avoid all animal foods (i.e. milk, eggs, fish, etc. as well as meat) are known as vegans. In recent years a hybrid, ethically-based semi-vegetarian diet has become more common wherein a person will shun red meat but will occasionally eat white meat such as chicken breast. The vegetarian diet may be more healthy than the omnivorous one since it is likely to contain less fat, more fibre, a greater proportion of carbohydrate, and a greater range of foods leading to a better profile of vitamin and mineral intake.

For sport and exercise a vegetarian diet is fundamentally sound but may be limited in certain respects. In terms of *protein a mixture of sources is required to provide the full spectrum of amino acids. The vegetarian cook's staple recipes, which combine cereals and grains with pulses, nuts, and seeds, ensure the full spectrum of amino acids is obtained. Vitamin B12 is not found in higher plants and a supplement may be needed, particularly for vegans. Iron is a particular challenge. Although iron is widespread in vegetable foods, it is in the form of non-haem iron whose rate of absorption by the human gut is about 5 per cent, compared with the haem iron in meat of which 20 per cent is absorbed. Mild anaemia is common in vegetarians, particularly women in whom menstrual blood loss increases the need for iron. While mild anaemia may not be an issue in daily life, in sport the direct relationship between iron, haemoglobin, and oxygen-carrying capacity of the blood means that even mild anaemia will compromise performance.

Verstehen The German word for 'understanding', referring in particular to how human actions and social and cultural phenomena might be understood in ways comparable to the interpretation of texts, comparable in many ways to the approach of *hermeneutics. The philosopher Wilhelm Dilthey (1833–1911) placed *Verstehen* at the centre of his method, linking the analysis of understanding to the culture or language of the wider system as well as a concern with the subjectively intended meaning of the individual actor. A *Verstehen*-led approach to the analysis of sport requires a version of these two levels of concern. What the sportsman or -woman, or the club official, sees as the meaning and significance of their sporting culture (the subjectively intended meaning) may be very different from what journalists, investigative sociologists, sport psychologists, or sport scientists offer in the way of interpretations or explanations of the sporting culture. Georg *Simmel and Max *Weber are prominent and influential thinkers whose work contributed to a form of *interpretivism that places the understanding of meaning at the centre of the analytical agenda.

vertigo The core characteristic of a particular form of game—games of disorientation, in the classification of games by French philosopher Roger *Caillois. Vertigo is the element that provides the disorienting risk or thrill, that can 'momentarily destroy the stability of perception and inflict a kind of voluptuous panic upon an otherwise lucid mind'. It undermines the everyday, normal reality, and its appeal can be seen in fairgrounds and theme parks, and also in some categories of risky and extreme sports, though the discipline required in the application of physical competence in many of those sports is deliberately focused upon the control of the boundaries at which vertigo comes into play.

Vikelas, Demetrius (1805–1908) The Greek first president of the *International Olympic Committee (IOC), holding the position because early IOC rules specified the president should be a representative of the country at which the forthcoming Games was to be held. Vikelas was a general educationalist with no specific sporting background, though he attended de *Coubertin's 1894 Congress in Paris as a representative of the Pan-Hellenic Gymnastics Club. After the 1896 inaugural event, de Coubertin became president and the revolving principle was abolished. Early IOC minutes are written in Vikelas's meticulous longhand, a testimony to the small-scale origins of what was to become an extraordinary global and modern phenomenon.

Visa A financial services company specializing in credit and debit cards, and with a history of sport sponsorship, having been a founder and constant member of the TOP (The *Olympic Programme) selective sponsor model put in place in 1985 by the International Olympic Committee. It also became a sponsor of the men's football/soccer World Cup in 2007, replacing MasterCard after some far from ethical negotiations with the *Fédération Internationale de Football Association (FIFA). Jerome Valcke of FIFA, who negotiated that deal, told a New York court that in relation to financial services sponsors, if 'you have to think about various companies potentially who could have an interest or are already in the world of sport, you're thinking about MasterCard and Visa' (United States District Court, Southern District of New York, MasterCard International Incorporated [plaintiff] versus Fédération Internationale de Football Association [defendant], 06 Civ. 3036 (LAP), 'Amended Findings of Fact and Conclusions of Law'). MasterCard's negotiating team believed that a FIFA financial services package was being presented exclusively to MasterCard, as incumbent partner with a clause for first claim on a new deal. The deception underlying the FIFA–MasterCard negotiations was seen by Chuck Blazer, FIFA Executive Committee member and also on FIFA's Marketing & TV AG Board, as perfectly normal; the New York court wrote that 'Mr Blazer's testimony was generally without credibility based on his attitude and demeanor and on his evasive answers on cross-examination'. There is no indication that Visa acted in any corrupt fashion in gaining status as World Cup sponsor, but the *c.*$US100 million sponsoring partnership was gained in full knowledge of the incumbent status of MasterCard. Such select sponsoring partnerships certainly repay the investment (*see also* HYUNDAI); but the ethics and morality of the processes by which they are achieved warrant fuller scrutiny.

Visions of 8 A film of the 1972 Munich Olympics based upon ten- to twelve-minute mini-films made by eight directors from different countries, and spliced together into a single feature by the man who had the idea, Hollywood

documentary producer David Wolper. The eight were Milos Forman from
Czechoslovakia; Kon Ichikawa from Japan; Claude Lelouch from France; Juri
Ozerov from the Soviet Union; Arthur Penn from the USA; Michael Pfleghar from
Germany; John Schlesinger from the UK; and Mai Zetterling from Sweden.
Wolper had planned for *Visions of 10*, but Italian Franco Zefferelli withdrew in
objection to Rhodesia's expulsion from the Games, and Senegalese Ousman
Sembene got so immersed in the fortunes of his topic, his home country's basketball
team, that he never delivered his contribution. The directors toyed with many
ideas for their individual contributions, Milos Forman finally focusing upon the
drama of the decathlon competition, and those former athletes who now acted as
officials carrying their fold-up chairs officiously and in orderly marching fashion
across the field: 'They seemed like such drones', noted Forman, adding that 'it is
sad to see how they have gone from being athletes to functionaries'. The resulting
film was a highly original departure from the usual model of official Olympic
documentary, assembling distinctive interpretive angles on the meaning and the
drama of the Games. It was a necessary innovation, too, in that advances in
television technology in the 1960s meant that broadcasters could capture on an
everyday, routine basis the drama of athletic performance and sporting
competition; an official documentary needed to offer something discrete and
different, and this is what Wolper's vision produced. Writer George
*Plimpton provided an illuminating review of the film in 'Olympic Visions of
Eight' (*Sports Illustrated*, 27 August 1973).

visualization *See* IMAGERY; RELAXATION.

volleyball A team game between two teams of six players, based upon
keeping the ball in the air and aiming to send the ball over the opposing team's
net so that it strikes the floor on the opponent's side of the court, or to provoke the
opposing side to strike the ball out of the boundaries of the court. Volleyball
became an Olympic event for men and women at the 1964 Tokyo Olympics,
where the host nation provided the gold medal-winning team in the women's event,
and the bronze medallists in the men's event, the Soviet Union triumphing in the
men's event, and taking the silver medal in the women's event. Wallechinsky
(*The Complete Book of the Olympics*, 1996) describes the draconian method of
the coach of the Japanese women's team, Hirofumi Daimatsu. Ten of the twelve
members of his squad were drawn from a spinning mill near Osaka, where he was
a departmental manager. He enforced a brutal regime, the players training and
playing for a minimum of six hours a day every day of the week throughout the
year, and the Japanese team was never remotely challenged. At two successive
Olympics after Tokyo, the Soviet Union secured the gold medal, Japan reclaiming
it in 1976. Other outstanding teams thereafter, in the women's event, emerged
from China and Cuba. The latter won the Olympic title three times in succession
from 1992 to 2000, though finishing in bronze position behind Russia and
champions China in 2004. These achievements in women's volleyball confirm
the commitment of communist and former communist states to the cultivation
of high-level and physically powerful sport performance in women's sports.
Men's champions have included Brazil, the Netherlands, the USA, and

Yugoslavia as well as the Soviet Union. The accessibility of the sport, and its familiarity to players from all levels, have spawned the associated sport of *beach volleyball.

voluntarism A term referring in a general way to the view that individual choices and decisions are the basis of society and culture, premised on the claim that individuals can exert control over what they do. It is, in the social sciences, contrasted with the view that individual experiences are determined by forces out of the control of the individual. In reality, as a knowledge of sporting subcultures and sporting biographies confirms, social life and human activity are a combination of what is determined and what is chosen. Philosophical approaches to voluntarism raise further, age-old questions concerning the nature and possibility of free will. Certainly sport provides some outlets for the individual expression of personal choices, aspirations, and experiences, more in the individualized sports of personal display than in more traditional team sports. Sporting cultures therefore provide a lively context for the exploration of voluntarism in everyday life.

voluntary sector A sphere of social action and human organization that is based upon neither the market (the private sector) nor the government (the state), but upon the self-organized activities and institutions of individuals, groups, and communities. Membership of such organizations or institutions is a matter of personal choice (within, of course, the terms laid down by the voluntary organization itself). Sport at the grass-roots level is dependent upon the buoyancy of the voluntary sector, *clubs, and the availability of the willing *volunteer. Voluntary organizations have been widely seen as vital for the effective functioning of participatory democracy, particularly in the USA, where debates about *social capital have used the decline in community-based sport as a powerful metaphor for the process of disengagement from a public life and the weakening of *civil society.

volunteer An individual who provides support or services at no financial cost to an organization or association, such as a charity, a political association, or a sports club. Volunteers are vital to the running of such associations, at levels of involvement from catering to cleaning, and administration to accounting. Volunteers also provide mass labour forces for some large-scale sporting events, such as the Olympic Games. Armies of volunteers at the Olympics are trained to welcome visitors to host cities and venues, and mask the real costs of staging such events: a 1999 international symposium at Lausanne's Olympic Museum reported 60,000 for the Atlanta 1996 Summer Games, and 30,000 at Nagano's 1998 Winter Games. John MacAloon has argued that volunteers are not driven by any commercial logic, or to support the private enjoyment of elites; rather, he claims, 'volunteers are people seeking to be and being touched by the Olympic Movement . . . the **real** Olympic Movement' (IOC, *Volunteers, Global Society and the Olympic Movement*, 2000).

vortextuality A term used to refer to the whirlpool effect of the media in relation to a particular major issue or event. In the age of multimedia and rapid electronic and digital communication within a knowledge economy, some such event can dominate the range of media forms and outlets for extended periods. In such circumstances, non-specialists are drawn into the vortextual effect, commenting on and writing about issues on which they have little knowledge and, usually, no informed opinion. Olympic Games and football World Cups, Superbowl and Formula One, are among the sporting events that can generate this vortextual effect. Garry Whannel has developed the concept: 'The vortextual effect produces a short-term compression of the media agenda in which other topics either disappear or have to be connected to the vortextual event' (*Media Sport Stars: Masculinities and Moralities*, 2002).

WADA *See* World Anti-Doping Agency.

Walton, Izaak (1593–1683) An English author born in Stafford, largely self-taught, who on moving to London at the age of 15 worked in the linen trade, selling and making cloth products, and mixed in the literary circles of the capital. His output included a life of the metaphysical poet and cleric John Donne (a friend and neighbour), and other biographies, but his most famous book was *The Compleat Angler* (1653), a fishing manual that has been published in more than four hundred editions, five of them by Walton himself (the final one, in 1676, published along with complementary texts by other authors, under the title *The Universal Angler*). In his first version of this text Walton constructed a dialogue between two men travelling on foot, Piscator, representing the sport of angling/ fishing, and Viator, speaking for the activity of travelling. The dialogue—expanded to three conversationalists in a second edition—concerned the art of fishing, its techniques and principles, in an extended metaphor for a good life. Early on in this dialogue, Piscator responds to Viator's observation that many serious and grave men have pitied, and many pleasant men scoffed at, 'Anglers'. Piscator takes this as a cue to lambast the 'serious grave men' as:

> men of sowre complexions; money-getting men, that spend all their time
> first in getting, and next in anxious care to keep it: men that are condemn'd
> to be rich, and always discontented, or busie. For these poor-rich-men,
> wee Anglers pitie them . . . we enjoy a contentednesse above the reach of
> such dispositions.

The 'scoffers' are also peremptorily dismissed by Piscator.

   This is a not-so-veiled attack on the Protestant ascendancy and its associated values; Walton was a royalist in the tempestuous time of the civil war, interregnum, and the ascendancy of Oliver *Cromwell, and his angling book (written in self-imposed exile from London, in the year in which Cromwell assumed the position of lord protector) can also be read as a coded call for a peaceful harmonious order of things and way of life, rooted in a traditional and conservative model of society. The extraordinary longevity of the popularity of *The Compleat Angler* shows how sport (and its representation in literary form) can contribute to, not merely reflect, the crucial social, political, and cultural debates of an age; and be interpreted anew by future readers and enthusiasts equally interested in Walton's own faith in the sporting life and the natural world as a source of tranquillity.

warm-up Preliminary exercise to prepare the body for subsequent more vigorous exercise. Traditionally a warm-up comprises two components: (a) mild exercise to, literally, raise tissue temperature along with *stretching exercises to reduce the risk of muscle and joint injury, and (b) specific movements to rehearse the skills involved in the movement and to prepare the athlete psychologically. Physiologically the increase in body temperature increases the rate of metabolic processes and primes the body for exercise by redistributing the cardiac output towards the active musculature. Whether warm-up is beneficial has not been subject to much research. The theory that the body requires time to warm up in the same way as might a machine is not well founded; the body is able to switch from rest to maximal *anaerobic power within a few seconds, or from rest to maximal *aerobic power in less than two minutes, yet the time lapse between warm-up and actual competition can be many minutes. Nevertheless, the fear of injury and the benefit of psychological preparation make a warm-up an indispensable part of sport.

water jousting *See* JOUSTING.

water polo A ball game played by teams of seven players in the water, called—rather curiously, as the ball is propelled by hand—'football in the water' in late 19th-century Britain as the sport was being developed. The comparison with football (on mainland Europe, its comparable name would have been 'handball in the water', and its origins in Britain were really as a form of aquatic rugby) says much about the hegemony of association football at the time, though the common features are that they are both passing games, and the aim is to propel the ball into a goal-framed net guarded by a goalkeeper at the end of the playing area. In the USA, softball in the water was a variant played at the end of the 19th century. The sport, for men, has featured in all major swimming competitions. It was recognized by the official swimming governing body in Britain in 1885, and Britain (represented by the Osborne Club from Manchester) won the first gold medal in the event at an Olympics (Paris 1900), going on to win the event in 1908, 1912, and 1920. The USA had won the 1904 event in St Louis (USA), where the British did not enter. After a French victory on home territory in 1924, the Olympic event was dominated by Hungary, taking the silver medal in 1928 and then five of the next seven Olympic titles. The USSR, Yugoslavia, and East Germany then dominated the sport at its competitive level, the communist states dedicating extensive resources to the sport at the height of the sporting Cold War. Hungary reasserted its dominance in the early 21st century with three (2000, 2004, 2008) Olympic gold medals in succession. Women's water polo was introduced into the Olympics for Sydney 2000, after protests and successful lobbying by Australian sport authorities and women sport activists. Australia won that inaugural event, Italy and the Netherlands the 2004 and 2008 titles respectively.

waterskiing The act of moving along, or planing on, the surface of water standing on two flat skis, or boards, attached to the feet, and pulled along by a line attached to the rear of a powerboat. Variants of the sport have included trick or figure skiing, slalom skiing, jumping, racing, and show skiing. Early experimental waterskiers included inventors in the USA in the early 1900s, individual pioneers (both men and women) in the USA in the 1920s, and French army officers on Lake Annecy. The first organized competitions included events organized on

Long Island, USA, in 1935, and within four years a national championship was staged by a governing body. With parallel initiatives taking place in the Mediterranean area of Europe, the World Water Ski Union was formed in 1946. The International Water Ski Federation, based in Switzerland, has continued to support championships and competitions for men and women, and the sport also has a strong profile in the coastal contexts of its origins, as a leisure sport among visitors and holidaymakers.

Webb, Matthew (Captain Webb) (1848–83) *See* CHANNEL SWIMMING.

Weber, Max (1864–1920) A German pioneer of the discipline of sociology. Weber's major studies were ambitiously comparative and historically wide-ranging in scope, and philosophically reflective in the area of methodology. His contributions to sociology included the conceptual clarification of the nature of authority. One form of authority Weber saw as linked to *charisma. He also provided a framework for the study of *bureaucracy and *rationalization, and for considering how different forces in society might reciprocally inform and confirm each other in what he called *elective affinity. Much of Weber's own work exemplified his notion of the *ideal type in sociological thinking and analysis. Allen Guttmann's analysis of modern sport (*From Ritual to Record: The Nature of Modern Sports*, 1977) has been referred to as Weberian in spirit, given its emphasis upon characteristics such as rationalization, quantification, and bureaucratization. Guttmann also saw secularization and some other features as core characteristics, but the rationalization process is his main focus. Although Weber linked the process of rationalization to the loss of mystery and the 'disenchantment' of the world, referring in a powerful metaphor to the 'iron cage' of rationalization, Guttmann's understanding of modern sport has little sense of this critical pessimism; nor, indeed, much explicit reference to the writings and works of Weber. Weber's lasting contribution lies in part in his recognition that sociological analysis involves an interpretive act, a consequence of the recognition of the subjective basis of much of social life and interaction. In this, he can continue to act as a source of inspiration for *interpretivist work in the sociology of sport.

weight control Techniques, processes, and strategies for monitoring and determining the weight of individuals. Body weight depends on the balance between calorie consumption and calorie expenditure. The control of appetite is precise, and once adulthood is reached body weight normally only fluctuates by a kilogram or two over a year, despite an annual food intake of about 900 kilograms. The sense of appetite depends on a number of factors, including physical ones such as the volume of food eaten or its palatability and biochemical ones such as the levels of glucose and fat. The *body composition describes how the overall weight is distributed between lean tissue and fat tissue; one measure used is the body mass index (BMI), the mass (kg) divided by the height squared (m). Distortion of weight control may take two forms, underweight and overweight. Underweight is by far the less frequent and usually only associated with disease or *eating disorders and has a prevalence of less than 5 per cent of the population. Overweight in the form of excess of muscle mass is only seen in certain sportsmen such as weightlifters, rugby players, and the like, since muscle will not accumulate by simply eating but only as a result of intensive physical training. The overwhelming manifestation of overweight is an excess accumulation of body fat. Overweight (a BMI above 25) and obesity (a BMI above 30) have shown a steadily increasing prevalence over the last 40 years, and in 2009 over half of women and over two-thirds of men were overweight or obese in the UK.

Obesity is associated with a wide range of health problems leading to increased morbidity and mortality, including type II diabetes, hypertension, stroke, impaired cardiac function, and joint problems. Obesity is the result of a progressive accumulation of excess body weight over many years, usually at the rate of a kilogram or two per year. Several hypotheses are presented to explain the rise in the prevalence of obesity across most countries in the developed world. These include an evolutionary hypothesis wherein the feast and famine of the hunter-gatherer led to biological adaptations that are ill-fitted to modern lifestyles; an appetite hypothesis wherein calorie-dense and readily available meals inadequately stimulate a sense of satiety; and a habitual activity hypothesis wherein the decline of physical labour in farming, industry, and the home has significantly reduced energy expenditure below energy intake. Furthermore, genetic factors appear to determine about a quarter of the variation between people in obesity and there may be a genetic predisposition to energy imbalance.

In a very small percentage of people excess weight is associated with a medical condition. In the vast majority excess weight is associated with an imbalance between energy intake and energy expenditure. Weight-loss diets predominantly work by altering sensations of appetite (e.g. stomach fullness with high-fibre diets), shifting control from the individual to an external prescription (e.g. replacement meals), or education and social support (e.g. slimming clubs); in all cases the desired effect is the same—a reduction in calorie intake by altering the biological or psychological control of satiety. Exercise is seen as a preferential method of weight management since it results in additional energy expenditure, promotes the development of lean body mass, and yields subsidiary benefits such as reduced risk of *coronary heart disease or *eating disorders.

weightlifting A competitive sport in which contestants in variously defined categories of body-weight aim to lift a bigger weight than any other contestant. The weights are attached to a barbell that the lifter must lift to his or her shoulders ('clean and jerk') or above the head ('snatch'). Forms of weightlifting have existed in many informal contexts in which individuals might challenge other individuals to contests of strength, lifting stones, rocks, or boulders (such as stone-lifting in Basque regions of France and Spain, linked to wagers and prizes), and in routinized display forms such as *kangding*. The popularity of weightlifting was established in 19th-century strongman acts in circuses and music-halls, and it developed its own particular professional trajectory in the careers of the likes of Eugen *Sandow. The formalized procedures of modern weightlifting were defined and developed when the International Olympic Committee stimulated the formation of the Fédération Haltérophile Internationale (International Weightlifting Federation, IWF) in Paris in 1920, to standardize the rules of the discipline. World championships were established in 1922, changed to the

European Championships in 1924 and then back to the World Championships in 1937, when the USA won the title, soon to be overtaken by the lifters from the USSR and other East European communist societies at world and Olympic events.

While weightlifting can claim a long, strong Olympic pedigree, its credibility has long been threatened by the obvious use by successful competitors of performance-enhancing drugs and stimulants. After the Barcelona 1992 Olympics, though, the IWF changed all of the weight categories, also introducing new ones after the 1996 Atlanta Games: this was designed so as to start afresh in relation to world and Olympic records, and so cleanse the sport of its tainted reputation from decades of drug abuse. Women's weightlifting was introduced at the Sydney 2000 Games, where Chinese lifters took four gold medals of the seven available; at Athens in 2004, they took three golds, but not in the heavyweight division, after world-record-holder Shang Shichun was stripped of her record and 2003 world title and suspended for two years after testing positive for drugs. This obviously tarnished the achievements of her countrywomen, and raised questions concerning the ethics of China's relentless assault on the Olympic medals table. In men's wrestling, Russia dominated at Beijing 2008.

Weismuller, Johnny (Johann) (1904–84) A US champion swimmer at the 1924 and 1928 Olympic Games, who acted in Hollywood films in the role of Tarzan. Weismuller's switch of professions represented the rise of the celebrity sport star in the expansive age of the mass media (cf. swimmer turned Hollywood star Esther Williams, b. 1921), and the exploitation of the (all but) naked athletic body; the athlete turned actor had little to do in the Tarzan movies beyond swing among trees, beat his chest, and emit jungle-like sounds and cries. An obituary in the UK's *Daily Telegraph* evokes a poignant image of Weismuller's past glories in his elder years in a home for retired actors in Hollywood: afflicted by a stroke, he would howl out his Tarzan call in the middle of the night, lost in the memory of his sporting and filmic celebrity; upsetting the other patients, he was committed to a mental hospital. Later, friends recalled him pacing his garden trying, without success, to emit his trademark Tarzan cry. Born in Austro-Hungary, Weismuller was the son of immigrants to the USA. A sickly child, swimming from the age of 12 on the advice of a doctor, he grew to 6 feet 4 inches, was educated at the University of Chicago, and won three gold medals at the 1924 Paris Olympics, and two more at Amsterdam in 1928. He broke 67 swimming records and never lost in competition. He made nineteen Tarzan films between 1932 and 1949, at around $100,000 a performance ('I blew it on boats and good living', he later recalled), and in his early seventies worked as a celebrity greeter for Caesar's Palace in Las Vegas.

wellness An optimal state of health. Wellness as a concept became commonly used towards the end of the 20th century and maintains that health is not simply the absence of illness and disease but is a continuum from death at one end, through absence of illness, to an optimal state of being at the other end. The World Health Organization defines wellness through two foci: 'the realization of the fullest potential of an individual physically, psychologically, socially, spiritually and economically, and the fulfillment of one's role expectations in the family, community, workplace, place of worship and other settings'.

wheelbarrow race In pre-industrial settings such as fairs and carnivals, the wheelbarrow race took place on an open green or in a field, and blindfolded contestants raced each other in driving the wheelbarrow from a starting point to an agreed mark (Joseph Strutt, *Sport and Pastimes of the People of England*, 1801). It was more an entertainment than a contest, though, with most racers losing their way in 'windings and wanderings' that generated 'much merriment'. As with other simple popular recreations, the wheelbarrow race resurfaced in the informal curriculum of schools in the 19th and 20th centuries, with one participant playing the wheelbarrow, walking on his or her hands as the legs are held by the barrow driver. The activity has also featured in novelty events as a cross between a knockabout entertainment and an endurance test.

whiz sports A term coined by French sociologist Nancy Midol to describe the kind of sports whose appeal is based on the cultivation of particular skills and thrills, in which display of individual prowess is more significant than teamwork or rules. They are sports that also prioritize speed and apparent spontaneity in execution and performance. *See also* CALIFORNIAN SPORTS; EXTREME SPORTS; LIFESTYLE.

Wilkie, Dorette (1867–1930) An influential physical educator who was one of the shapers of women's physical education in late 19th-century England. Born in Magdeburg, Prussia, as Dorette Wilke, and arriving in England as a weakly young woman in 1885, her spinal defect was cured by training at the Adolf A. Stempel gymnasium in London, and she began teaching the benefits of exercise and physical education. Appointed to the staff of Battersea Polytechnic in 1891, she moved in 1896 to the South Western Polytechnic, Chelsea, London, and in 1898 started a gymnastic teachers' training department: as headmistress, Wilkie reigned over what was to become the Chelsea College of Physical Education for 31 years. Naturalized as a British subject in 1908, she also changed her surname to Wilkie, and became known as 'Domina'; bolstering this British identity, a close association with Cecil Sharp included joint provision of morris dancing teaching (1909), and support for his English Folk Dance Society (1911), including demonstrations on national tours by Chelsea students of dances discovered by Sharp. The curriculum was broadened into the science of movement—physiology, anatomy, psychology—in that first expansive decade, and Wilkie insisted upon a strict dress code. Wilkie combined philanthropic activity within her vision: 'In 1902 she instituted Saturday games in Battersea Park for deprived children, and Chelsea students taught at London working girls' clubs' (Gill Clarke and Ida M. Webb, *Oxford Dictionary Of National Biography*, 2004). After evacuation to West Wales during World War II, the 'Founder' Wilkie's Chelsea College was relocated at Eastbourne and survives there as the Chelsea School in the University of Brighton's Faculty of Education and Sport.

Wills Moody, Helen Newington (1905–98) A US tennis player who, following the dominance of the international circuit by Frenchwoman Suzanne *Lenglen and then Lenglen's decision to turn professional, was the world's top woman player for much of a fifteen-year period from 1923 to 1938. Wills Moody attended the University of California, Berkeley, though she did not graduate, and was famous for her concentration and strength: her nickname Little Miss Poker Face embodied the first of these qualities, her strategy of training with male players consolidated the second. She won nineteen *Grand Slam singles titles: the Wimbledon title eight times, a record until Martina Navratilova's ninth title in 1990; and seven successive US Open titles in which she competed (1923–31, not participating in 1926 and 1930). She took the singles and the doubles titles at the 1924 Paris Olympics (the last Olympics to include tennis until 1988). Wills Moody appeared on the cover of *Time* magazine in 1926 and 1929, making her the first US sportswoman to achieve such a level of national and international profile and celebrity.

Wimbledon *See* GRAND SLAM (TENNIS); LAWN TENNIS; PERRY, FRED.

windsurfing A water-based activity practised in coastal settings and on lakes, in which the individual stands on and sails a board fitted with a sail and a mast. Initially known also as board sailing or sailboarding, the sport emerged in the late 1960s in the USA, its popularity then spreading to Britain and Europe (in particular, France and Germany) in the 1970s. The sport's emergence and growth was linked to the *counter-cultures of those decades, and it has been said to have 'evolved in opposition to dominant sporting cultures, and in particular the institutionalisation of sport in late modernity' (Belinda Wheaton, *Understanding Lifestyle Sports: Consumption, Identity and Difference*, 2004). Its oppositional features have also included a reduction of the concern with rules, and the cultivation of an ethos of participation. Nevertheless, the institutionalization of the sport has included the establishing of a global regulatory body, the recognition of official World Championships, and acceptance into the (men's) yachting category of the Olympics at the 1984 Los Angeles Games under the older name of 'boardsailing' and using a longer board than that used by most participants. Wheaton has noted a persisting tension between the Olympic discipline and the more expressive variant of the sport: 'the pinnacle of sporting success tends to be associated with the wave acrobatics, slalom racing, and freestyle tricks promoted and administered by the Professional World Windsurfing Association'.

Wirth, Louis (1897–1952) A US urban sociologist whose work at the University of Chicago had widespread worldwide impact. His article 'Urbanism as a Way of Life' (first published in the *American Journal of Sociology*, XLIV, 1938) identified size, density, and heterogeneity as the core features of contemporary urban living, affirming 'the growth of great cities' as a critical index of 'what is distinctly modern in our civilization'. In cities, sport and leisure interests are among the forms of collective behaviour that Wirth considered to be vital forms of social organization. So cities prompted 'the enormous multiplication of voluntary organizations': 'It is largely through the activities of the voluntary groups, be their objectives economic, political, educational, religious, recreational, or cultural, that the urbanite expresses and develops his personality, acquires status, and is able to carry on the round of activities that constitute his life career.' The recognition that voluntary associations could generate status was an insight that was pivotal for the study of the social and cultural significance of leisure and sport organizations.

women's cricket An eleven-a-side bat-and-ball game played under the auspices of the International Cricket Council. Women played the game recreationally as early as 1677 in England, when the wife of the Earl of Sussex registered that she was growing tired of the amusement, as played in the village of Dicker, near Hurstmonceaux. Women played inter-village matches in the counties of Sussex and Surrey in south-east England: the *Reading Mercury* published an account of a match that took place on 26 July 1745, between 'eleven maids of Bramley and eleven maids of Hambleton, dressed all in white . . . The girls bowled, batted, ran and catched as well as most men could do in that game.' Such matches generated boisterous crowds and significant stakes with accompanying betting. Women also played, in more genteel settings, in the grounds of the landed gentry and aristocracy. Organized forms of the game in the later 19th century included the foundation of England's first women's cricket club, the White Heather, in 1887, at Nun Appleton, Yorkshire: six of its eight founding members bore the prefix 'Hon.' or 'Lady'. A commercial initiative of 1890, 'The Original English Lady Cricketers', recruited two teams that toured the country playing each other under the watchful eye of a 'matron', and giving the players pseudonyms: a crowd of 15,000 attended the first event, at Liverpool's Police Athletic ground, but the venture lasted only two years.

Cricket prospered, nevertheless, in the elite girls' public schools in the early years of the 20th century: the Women's Cricket Association (WCA) was formed in 1926, and the foundations of the organized women's game were established in the 1930s, seen as the 'Golden Age' of women's cricket. In 1934, an English side defeated Australia in Brisbane, Queensland, in the first women's Test Match. Women also played the game in parts of India in the 1890s, though initially in mixed-sex teams, and the nationalist drive in that country in the 1930s further boosted the game. The International Women's Cricket Council (IWCC), formed in 1958, comprised Australia, England, New Zealand, Pakistan, South Africa, Sri Lanka, and the West Indies. A first World Cup Cricket competition was held in England in 1973, a one-off sponsored event based on invitation: Australia, New Zealand, Jamaica, and Trinidad and Tobago were invited, and England topped the table to finish as champions. Women's cricket continued to bear the stamp of Britain and its empire and dominions.

The IWCC merged with the International Cricket Council (ICC) in 2005—in England, the WCA had merged with the England and Wales Cricket Board in 1998—and, at the ICC's World Twenty20 in England in 2009, it was the English team, reigning world champions, that took the title in a final against New Zealand. While the history of the women's game has received welcome attention (see Rachael Heyhoe Flint and Netta Rheinberg's *Fair Play: The Story of Women's Cricket*, 1976, for a pioneering contribution), and the organization of the game has been brought within a coherent overall infrastructure for the sport, women's cricket remains comparatively marginal in the consciousness of a wider sporting public and almost invisible in a sport media preoccupied with the dominant male-based forms of the game.

women's football The game of association football (soccer) as played by girls and women. There is uneven evidence of women's involvement in early forms of football, beyond a spectating role on the periphery of the action or the enthusiasm of the occasional middle-class or privileged individual, such as English feminist Nettie Honeyball, who formed a British Ladies Football Club and organized a match between the North and South of England Ladies at Crouch End, London, in 1895; and Lady Florence Dixie, who became the club/association's president and managed a women's football team on a tour of Scotland. But when working-class women organized football more extensively and regularly, in England during World War I, for instance, while working as munitions workers, the effect was explosive. In 1916–17 male footballers were drafted, and organized leagues were all but suspended, in the heartlands of the professional men's game in the north of England in particular. Saturday afternoons offered little substitute until welfare workers and others encouraged the women workers in the north of England to organize into competitive teams, also motivated by charity and fund-raising to support rehabilitation and emergency centres for returning soldiers.

The most prominent of these women's factory teams, named after the Preston-based factory, was Dick, Kerr's Ladies, which became a football legend. John Kerr, younger partner to Scot W. B. Dick, had opened the factory for the Dick, Kerr's company in Preston in 1899, manufacturing trams. During the war, the company switched to war transport and munitions. Alfred Frankland, a tailor turned administrator at the factory, organized a charity game for Christmas Day 1917 and staged it at the iconic Deepdale Ground, home of the all-conquering Preston North End men's team of the early days of the professional game in England. Ten thousand people attended the game. Dick, Kerr's Ladies went on to play further fixtures against town teams, and played a series of four international games—widely recognized as the first women's internationals—against France in 1920: at Deepdale, the English won 2–0, at Stockport 5–2; the third game, at Manchester, was a 1–1 draw; and in the last game the French won 2–1, at Stamford Bridge in London. This was followed by a tour of four games undefeated in France; and back in England at Goodison Park, Liverpool, on Boxing Day 1920, a match against St Helen's Ladies drew a crowd of 50,000.

The team and the women's game were becoming a national institution, with extensive—if initially patronizing—press coverage, and coverage in the cinema in Pathé newsreels. The men's game's authorities, as the professional game resumed after the end of the war, became nervous, and the (English) Football Association (FA) banned women's football at its members' grounds at a meeting on 5 December 1921, stating in its minute that 'the game of football is quite unsuitable for females and should not be encouraged'. The team continued, on smaller grounds beyond the bureaucratic control of the FA, and also toured the USA, playing men's teams and winning three, drawing three, and losing three matches. But the pre-war order was reimposing itself, and the team received no official welcome home from either Preston dignitary or club official, just a speech by the ex-mayor of Burnley. It was not until 1971 that the English FA officially recognized the women's game.

In Germany and other countries too development of the women's game was curtailed or held back. Germany's national association used old anatomical and pseudo-medical arguments about the unsuitability of the female physique for the game (women were 'knock-kneed'; football would create a 'diminished ability to reproduce'). A Dutch philosopher cum anthropologist, F. J. J. Buytendijk, wrote that football was in part produced by a 'hormonal irritation' specific to men: 'Kicking is thus presumably a male activity'. In Germany, the national football federation's negative attitude to the women's game meant that 'women were only able to play football "unofficially" in recreational teams throughout the 1950s and well into the 1960s' (Gertude Pfister, 'Women's Football in Germany', in A. Tomlinson and C. Young, eds, *German Football: History, Culture, Society*, 2006). Responding to the pressures of the women's movement and the revolutionary cultural upheaval of the time, though, the German federation was forced to change its policies, and in 1970 'ladies' football' was finally officially recognized. In that same year, the first unofficial World Cup tournament for women was held in Italy, attracting crowds of up to 35,000. German journalists wrote more about 'giggling team mates' and 'hairdressers' appointments' than about the play, even writing of one encounter that, 'Unfortunately the prettiest team lost'. It was not until 1979 that recognized organized, competitive women's football began, in East Germany.

Italy pioneered women's professional leagues, and in the 1990s the women's international game took off, the first women's football Olympic Games event taking place at the 1996 Atlanta Games. The USA has won three of those four competitions, Norway having taken the title at the 2000 Sydney Games. Continental confederations introduced championships for women before FIFA's World Cup. Asia was the pioneer in 1975, followed by Oceania in 1983, Europe in 1984, and the central/north Americas and Caribbean, South Americans, and Africa all in 1991. In the women's World Cup, inaugurated in China in 1991, and played every four years, the champions have been the USA; Norway (in Sweden, 1995); the USA (also the host nation, in 1999); Germany (in the USA, 2003); and Germany again (in China, in 2007, defeating the 'flair' side Brazil).

FIFA, the world governing body, projected that by 2008, more than 40 million women and girls would be playing the game worldwide. Yet double world champion and triple Olympian champion the USA continued to have difficulty sustaining a full-time professional league, and securing the sponsorship and backing needed for consolidation and further development of the women's game. Women's bodies and traditional feminine sexualized physicality still captured the headlines—even for Brazilian star Marta—as much as teamwork and athleticism. This had not been helped by the comments of FIFA president Joseph Blatter in 2004:

> Let the women play in more feminine clothes like they do in volleyball . . . They could, for example, have tighter shorts. Female players are pretty, if you excuse me for saying so, and they already have some different rules to men—such as playing with a lighter ball. That decision was taken to create a more female aesthetic, so why not do it in fashion?

Women's League of Health and Beauty A mass fitness movement established in the 1930s by Mary Bagot *Stack. The league's motto, 'Movement is life', expressed its evangelical message, though its first stated aim of cultivating 'racial health' indicated its imperialist, elite premises and racist overtones. The league's membership rose to 60,000, 'based on its judicious appeal to an older, class-bound, service-motivated, maternal femininity, while having a modern, mass-market, commercial style' (Jill Julius Matthews, *Oxford Dictionary of National Biography*, 2004; see too her '"They had such a lot of fun": The Women's

League of Health and Beauty between the Wars', *History Workshop Journal*, 30, 1990). The league staged high-profile demonstrations of its mass exercise programmes in Hyde Park, London, and at the Albert Hall and Wembley Stadium (in 1950, for instance), and marketed recordings of exercise instructions on the new gramophone technology. Bagot Stack's daughter Prunella remained a staunch defendant of the league's values throughout her life.

Woolf, Virginia (1882–1941) An English experimental novelist whose interest in sport was minimal but for whom a typical English sport like cricket could symbolize stability and longevity. Her character Peter Walsh, in *Mrs Dalloway* (1925), as he reflects on the 'interminable' nature of the voyage of life, reaches for a coin to buy a paper to see how the county cricket side Surrey is faring against Yorkshire, an act that he had done 'millions of times'. Walsh turns to cricket as a kind of solid reassurance of the familiar, a state that is nevertheless enriching: 'But cricket was no mere game. Cricket was important. He could never help reading about cricket. He read the scores in the stop press first, then how it was a hot day; then about a murder case.' Far from trivializing sport, Woolf here acknowledges the potentially deep significance of the routine that can be found in sporting matters and detail. She also praised the vernacular style of US sport writing in the work of Ring *Lardner.

Woolfall, Daniel Burley (1852–1918) An English civil servant and contributor to Blackburn Rovers' domination of the English FA Cup competition in the 1880s, who became the second president of world football's governing body the *Fédération Internationale de Football Association (FIFA), from 1906 to his death in 1918. Initially, when FIFA was founded in 1904, the British associations had turned down overtures from the founding nations. Woolfall attended a meeting in Berne in 1905, in negotiation with those founding members after the British had accepted FIFA's objectives and agreed to cooperate, but reported back to the Football Association in England: 'it is important to the FA and other European Associations that a properly constituted Federation should be established and the Football Association should use its influence to regulate football on the Continent as a pure sport and give all Continental associations the full benefit of the many years experience of the FA'. The language is telling: the FIFA initiative was seen by the English as not 'properly constituted', the FA as the guardian of the purity of the game.

When, the following year, Robert Guérin resigned after his attempts to organize an inaugural international competition came to nothing, a four-man British delegation arrived at the third FIFA Congress in Berne in 1906. Woolfall was one of these and was duly elected president, though the football associations of Ireland, Scotland, and Wales were denied membership for several years, mainly as a result of the objections from Germany and Austria on the basis that all of those associations were actually in the one country or nation, the United Kingdom. Woolfall's board eventually granted separate membership to all four British associations in 1912, though this was clearly still against the statutes. Woolfall also stubbornly persisted in keeping the laws of the game in the hands of the British body, the International Board, that had set the rules of the game.

His legacy was therefore to establish, whatever the succeeding volatility of the FIFA–British relationship, an unrepresentative presence for British football in the international context, and an extraordinary—and long-lasting—influence of the British over the rules and laws of the sport.

Workers' Olympics Internationalist competitive sport events organized by the Socialist International movement in Europe in the 1920s and 1930s. The label 'internationalist' is a precise one, as the Workers' Olympics were conceived in ideological opposition to the modern Olympic Games, in which the competition is organized on the basis of the nation state, and whose amateur ethos privileged the well-off and the upper classes. The workers' sports movement opposed elite participation, and 'invited all-comers, putting the accent on mass participation, as well as extending events to include poetry and song, drama, artistic displays, political lectures and pageantry' (James Riordan, 'The Workers' Olympics', in Alan Tomlinson and Garry Whannel, eds, *Five-Ring Circus: Money, Power and Politics at the Olympic Games*, 1984). Three such events were held, in Frankfurt, Germany (1925), Vienna, Austria (1931), and Antwerp, Belgium, in 1937. The third event had been planned for Barcelona in 1936, but on the morning of the scheduled opening ceremony the Spanish Civil War was started by the fascist military putsch. A fourth event, planned for Helsinki, Finland, in 1943, was a victim of World War II. The first two events were organized by Lucerne Sport International (LSI), a branch of the Bureau of the Socialist International; for the third one, this socialist body cooperated with Moscow's communist Red Sport International, a branch of the Communist International (Comintern). The 1931 Vienna event attracted 80,000 worker-athletes from 23 countries, and the socialist Viennese government constructed a new stadium. For a brief period, the Workers' Olympics represented an effective mix of sport and political cultures.

work ethic The set of values whereby work, with its associated values and demands such as diligence and commitment, is the central activity of human life. Too full a dedication to the work ethic leads to questions such as 'Do we work to live or live to work?', and raises important issues concerning the role of leisure in people's lives, and the social significance of sport in the broader context of a work-based culture. The popular articulation of the dilemma for many of establishing a work–life balance has fuelled arguments and provision for recreational and health-based sporting participation and facilities in affluent societies. For people for whom sport performance becomes a job of work, what initially absorbed them as a sporting pastime and pleasurable form of leisure becomes transformed into a manifestation of the work ethic, as eloquently testified by hockey player Eric Nesterenko in the *oral history of Studs Terkel.

work–life balance *See* WORK ETHIC.

workout A term that, initially referring to the schedules of gymnasium exercisers, has become common in everyday language for a period of planned exercise usually combining *aerobic and *anaerobic elements, and linked to personal body image as well as health and strength. 'Workouts' have also become commodities in themselves, the *Jane Fonda Workout* video (1982) selling more than 17 million copies and, in popularizing the video cassette recorder, becoming a world record-breaking technological and cultural landmark; it enabled individuals to replicate the practices and aspirations of the like of former model and film actress Fonda in the privacy of their own homes, as well as in the facilities of the burgeoning health and exercise industry. A quarter of a century on, Tracy Anderson, personal trainer to actress Gwyneth Paltrow and singer Madonna (her only clients), demanded two-hour workouts on six days of the week. Releasing her *The Tracy Anderson Method: Dance Cardio Workout* in 2009, Anderson promised transformations to the common woman willing to commit to the six-days-a-week schedule: 'Nothing less is going to work if you want to become the perfect version of you'. Here the workout becomes the embodiment of the fusion of body culture and *narcissism, and everyday aesthetics of the body the source of limitless commodification. Another interpretation, shared by feminists and marketing professionals, is that the workout is an index of women's emancipation and empowerment, in using challenging and progressive body cultures to question stereotypes of physicality and the status quo of a male-dominated physical and sport culture.

World Anti-Doping Agency (WADA) A Swiss private law foundation established in 1999, in Lausanne, Swirtzerland, in line with articles of the Swiss Civil Code, created by the International Olympic Committee (IOC), which paid its operating costs of 20 million Swiss francs for its first two years of operation in 2000 and 2001. It was under the control of the Swiss Federal Authority for Supervision of Foundations in Switzerland's Federal Department of Home Affairs. WADA's presidency alternates, according to its statutes, between the Olympic movement and public authorities, and John Fahey, former finance minister of Australia and premier of New South Wales during the Sydney 2000 Olympics, replaced Canadian veteran Olympic administrator Richard Pound in 2007. Its eight objectives focus upon 'the fight against doping in sport in all its forms', prioritizing ethical and healthy sporting competition, encouraging and supporting out-of-competition testing of athletes, and promoting scientific sampling and analytical procedures and research. Much lobbying characterized the bidding to become the WADA headquarters, and Lausanne (Switzerland), Montreal (Canada), and Vienna (Austria) emerged as the favourites, ahead of Stockholm (Sweden) and Bonn (Germany). Montreal won a tight vote against Lausanne to become the headquarters, and continental regional offices have been established in Johannesburg (South Africa), Tokyo (Japan), and Montevideo (Uruguay), for Africa, the Asia–Pacific region, and Latin America respectively. Lausanne, having done all it could to keep WADA, became the agency's European office.

WADA's main goal in its first years was to establish a World Anti-Doping Code, officially adopted in 2003, and applied at the 2004 Athens Olympic Games. Its revised objectives concentrated on the implementation of the code, the adoption of that code in international associations and national Olympic committees, and the recognition and acceptance of suspension periods for athletes who have 'tested positive' (Jean-Loup Chappelet and Brenda Kübler-Mabbott, *The International Olympic Committee and the Olympic System: The Governance of World*

Sport, 2008). The impact of WADA has been strong, and its role is widely recognized as crucial in any 'fight against doping'. Yet its own evaluation of the compliancy of countries and federations has confirmed that its principles are far from universally accepted—evidence itself of the necessity of its work and interventions. One reason for this might be the inbuilt reluctance of some sporting institutions to expose drug use, as this could deprive the sport of stars (through suspension and disqualification) and reduce the credibility of sport in the eyes of the paying public. WADA's move away from Lausanne, the home of the International Olympic Committee, and its funding by national governments rather than the IOC, have established a fuller sense of independence of the institution, and this can only strengthen its impact and status.

(⊕) SEE WEB LINKS

• The source for the anti-doping code of practice in world sport, and the list of banned substances.

World Games A multi-sports competition planned in 1980 by twelve international sports federations whose sports were not on the Olympic programme. They were organized by a Council for the World Games, which became the International World Games Association. The first event was held in Santa Clara, USA, in 1981, and it has offered a forum for less established sports to profile themselves in the global consciousness; badminton, tae kwon do, triathlon, and softball were featured at World Games before gaining their places in the Olympic programme (though softball has since been omitted from the programme). In the early 1990s, *ESPN provided daily coverage, and in the later 1990s marketing company *International Management Group (IMG) took the Games on as a client. It has been a modest growth for an event staged in Taiwan in 2009, but has served to boost the image of the non-Olympic sports, and the ambitions of federation administrators who seek to gain entry for their sport to the Olympic programme.

World Student Games A multi-sport event organized by the Fédération Internationale du Sport Universitaire (founded in 1949), and drawing upon a tradition of world student games first held in Paris, France, in 1923. The Summer Games have been staged since 1959, the Winter Games since 1960. The Games are officially known as the Universidade, a compound of 'university' and 'Olympiad'.

Worrell, Sir Frank Mortimer Maglinne (1924–67) The first black player to captain the West Indies cricket team. Worrell was born in Barbados but raised for much of his childhood in Jamaica. The successful campaign for him to have the captaincy was led by writer, journalist, and activist C. L. R. *James, and Worrell led the West Indies from 1960–61 to 1963. His captaincy was a major stimulus to the development of black Caribbean political consciousness and he also acted as a senator in Jamaica, and was knighted in 1964; after his tragically early death from leukaemia, a memorial service was held in Westminster Abbey, the first time that such an event had occurred for a sporting figure.

wrestling An individual combat activity in which strength and skill are combined to achieve a specified manoeuvre or the accumulation of points, or to enforce the submission of the opponent. Ancient cultures usually promoted some form of wrestling for either the amusement of the privileged social elite, or the entertainment of the wider public. In the modern Olympics two types of wrestling have been recognized: freestyle and Graeco-Roman. Men's freestyle dates from the 1904 St Louis Games, and Irini Merleni of Ukraine became the first women's Olympic wrestling champion (flyweight) at the 2004 Athens Games. The Graeco-Roman form (invented in France in the 19th century, in tribute to the sporting cultures of Greece and Rome) dates from the 1924 Paris Games. British and US wrestlers were prominent in early Olympics (on their own territory), and later Greece, the Scandinavian countries, Turkey, the USSR, and Japan produced dominant fighters in world championships and Olympics. The international federation (Fédération Internationale des Luttes Amateurs) was founded in 1921.

As a commercialized form of entertainment, wrestling has also had waves of popularity as televised spectacle: the World Wrestling Federation (WWF) in the USA combined staged pantomime with sadomasochistic physical performances that attracted young male viewers and fans less interested in the minutiae of wrestling technique than the theatrical demeanour of the protagonists. It created larger-than-life stars such as Hulk Hogan, and when a 'Summerslam' was staged at Wembley, London, in 1992, a capacity crowd of 81,000 cheered Hogan and his co-stars. The Federation changed its name to World Wrestling Entertainment after losing a court case to the World Wildlife Fund over the rights to the acronym. This kind of theatrical wrestling had also been popular in Britain in the 1960s and 1970s, on Independent Television's *World of Sport*, on Saturday afternoons, and Frank Sinatra is said to have told Martin Ruane, also known as Giant Haystacks, that British wrestlers were world-leading entertainers. In 1988, however, the commercial network axed wrestling from its schedules, chasing a more lucrative demographic.

The wrestling dream lives on in some community settings, though: Andy Baker, also known as Scouse Lover, started his Runcorn Wrestling Academy in north-west England in 2005 ('Wrestlers', *Granta*, 104, 2008), and Kevin Cummins's photoessay of the range of the male and female characters at the academy fuels the stuff of fantasy and dreams, the monikers of the members of the academy transcending the mundanities of everyday life. 'Runcorn's not one of the poshest towns in Cheshire', observed Baker, 'but this gives people the chance to get fit, have fun and to live their dreams. As soon as you come through that curtain you have to be a totally transformed person.' *See also* Cornish wrestling; Cumberland and Westmorland wrestling; Graeco-Roman wrestling; Olympic Games, ancient; sumo wrestling; total fighting.

wushu A term referring to sporting practices and disciplines based on traditional Chinese martial arts. It was established in its modern form by the state policy of the People's Republic of China, in the mid 20th century. An International Wushu Federation was founded in Beijing in 1990, and *wushu* has become a recognized sport of the International Olympic Committee.

xenophobia A term referring to hostility as felt or expressed towards foreigners. A xenophobic outlook fuels a fear of others unlike you. The potential of sport to bring people together in collective ways in forms of inter-cultural understanding can be offset by its capacity to mark difference and intensify these differences in sporting competition and rivalry. Thus xenophobic tendencies can be exacerbated by sport, particularly in international sporting competition. A xenophobic element connected to a racist disposition—a not uncommon cocktail in international sporting rivalries—can threaten the values of a civilized society and a culturally tolerant international community.

yabusame A sport practised by courtiers at the Japanese imperial court, prominent from the 12th to 15th centuries, combining the skills of the archer with those of the equestrian. 'The contestants drew their bows and loosed their arrows while galloping down a straight track some 220 to 270 meters long' (Allen Guttmann, *Sports: The First Five Millennia*, 2004). The sport combined entertainment for the court with the exhibition of military skills.

yachting The use of small sailing and power craft for pleasure or for competition. The term 'yacht' derives from the Dutch *jacht*, the name given to small passenger or cargo carriers that used Holland's waterways in the 17th century. Crafts fitting the modern definition might be dinghies, catamarans, trimarans, or yachts (larger craft incorporating living accommodation). Competitions are organized at national level, having begun as individual challenges between yacht owners, and the most famous international tournament, the *America's Cup, began in 1857. Yachting at the Olympics began at the 1908 London Games, where Britons took four gold medals in races on the Solent (southern England) and the Clyde (Scotland), with negligible overseas opposition. Successful nations at the Olympics have not infrequently been the nation of the host city, as in the Barcelona Olympics in 1992, when Spain triumphed with little tradition of accomplishment in the sport, but much opportunity to learn and practise on the waters on which the Olympic races would be run. Other contributing factors to such success in competitive *sailing include state-of-the-art technology and a historical and cultural legacy—as in Britain—that embedded the activity within the (albeit relatively affluent and better-off) sport and leisure culture of the country.

Yale University A private, Ivy League university on the east coast of the USA, at which sports were given a high profile. The annual rowing competition with *Harvard University began in 1852, and is the oldest inter-university sporting event in the USA. Yale has provided Olympic champions in rowing, and did much to establish *American football in its modern form, under the influence of Walter Camp (1859–1925), a player at Yale for five years from 1876, and coach from 1888 to 1892. Camp employed the principles of F. W. Taylor's *scientific management in training and performance, and is recognized as one of the most innovative figures in the growth of the college game. Up to 1900 Yale had a run of thirteen unbeaten seasons, and won or shared fourteen national championships. Camp wrote his *Book of College Sports* in 1893 and went on to publish numerous further books and more than 250 magazine articles. 'Manly toughness', as Rupert Wilkinson calls it, underlay the cultivation of the Yale sport culture: 'exponents of manliness like Walter Camp and Theodore Roosevelt used ideas of

gentlemanly fair play to distinguish controlled virility from viciously tough
behaviour and goody-good sissiness' (*American Tough: The Tough-Guy
Tradition and American Character*, 1984).

yellow-dog contract A contract, or a clause in a contract, constituting an
agreement between an employer and an employee in which the latter agrees not to
join a labour union. The price of breaking the agreement was loss of employment.
The contract/clause was introduced after a failed strike in the saddlery industry in
the USA in 1910, and labour representatives dubbed it as a 'yellow-dog' measure,
reducing the dignity of human labour in treating workers as little more than
slaves of the employer. Although the form of contract was outlawed in the USA in
1932 legislation, professional sportworkers, subject to the *reserve clause in US
professional sports (and the comparable *retain and transfer system in English
professional football), were long subject to binding agreements of the yellow-dog
kind. Welsh soccer player Billy Meredith (1874–1958), the activist for football
players' rights in England who chaired the first meeting of the players' union in
1907, played for Manchester City and Manchester United before World War I, and
suffered discrimination from employers akin to that form of control exerted over
employees bound to the yellow-dog clause. Athletes' and players' rights have been
fought for and widely achieved in the century since then, but rapacious and
ruthless employers and entrepreneurs in sport are perfectly capable of
reintroducing such controlling measures, by backdoor means if necessary, and
vigilance is needed to ensure the protection of sportworkers' hard-won rights in
the employment sphere.

YMCA (Young Men's Christian Association) A worldwide organization
based upon the fostering of a healthy mind, body, and spirit through the worthy
activities of young people. Founded in the 1840s in industrializing England, the
organization—which became known as the 'Y'—spread rapidly in international
contexts, especially the USA. The 'Y' has provided swimming pools, gymnasia,
and activity rooms at modest rates for generations of young people, shedding its
religious rationale and promoting intercultural exchange and understanding
through travel and sport.

yoga A form of physical exercise which seeks to blend physical dexterity with
mental relaxation. It derives from conceptions of the harmony of body and mind in
India, and became popular in Western societies in the second half of the 20th
century. Particularly popular among professional and middle-class women in those
societies, it made important inroads into the established patriarchal sports
culture, showing that physical culture and sporting participation need not always be
a matter of competitive outcomes and aggressive rivalry. The popularity of
yoga, often dismissed as fad, has had an important influence upon conceptions and
interpretations of body culture, presaging the emergence of other comparable
practices such as *pilates.

y

Z

Zátopek, Emil (1922–2000) A Czech middle- and long-distance runner who revolutionized his sport. Born in Moravia, soon after the formation of the Czechoslovakian state, Zátopek began running at the age of 18. Adopting the method of *interval training, running 15 miles a day in army boots, he achieved levels that broke the dominance of generations of Finnish distance runners, winning the 10,000 metres gold medal at the 1948 London Olympics ahead of the favourites from Finland. He broke 18 world records, his first one in 1949. At the 1952 Helsinki Olympics, Zátopek won the 5,000 metres, the 10,000 metres, and—in his debut at the distance—the marathon, 2.5 minutes clear of the silver medallist. He held the status of colonel in the army, and was a member of the Communist Party until being expelled when he expressed support for the democratic wing of the Party in the Prague Spring of 1968. Zátopek was stripped of his army status and sent to work in a uranium mine for six years, though he was given a post in the country's Ministry of Sport in 1982; he died in a Prague military hospital. Zátopek's career and his phenomenal achievements embodied the importance granted by communist states to sporting achievement on the international stage.

zeitgeist A German word combining the terms *Geist* (spirit) and *Zeit* (time or historical period or era) and so referring to the spirit of an age. In the philosophy of history of Georg Hegel (1770–1831) it is an encompassing concept, implying that any cultural practice is expressive of the age in which it is produced: Beethoven's symphonies are of the age of revolutionary romanticism, for instance. It is a seductive shorthand to talk of the spirit of the age in this way, and so locate sport in its social context at different points of its sociocultural and historical development. But the term tends towards the homogenization of the cultural, in that the abiding spirit imbues all cultural pursuits. A less philosophized and more popular variant of the term has been applied to particular periods or conditions—the Jazz Age, the Age of Austerity, to take some early and mid 20th-century cases—with more journalistic buoyancy than analytic rigour; but cultural historical and qualitative social scientific work have identified sport's contribution to fashion and *celebrity, and a burgeoning individualism of sporting culture, in interesting ways that suggest sport's centrality in the constitution of an emergent and identifiable zeitgeist.

zero-sum game A game in which the participants determine the distribution of a fixed total of costs or benefits between them. The zero-sum game is anathema to the central principle of sport, and the uncertainty of outcome (or at least score) that is the fundamental attraction of a sporting encounter. Yet cases of such games can be found in sport, when little is at stake in terms of competitive outcomes (such as in 'dead rubbers', when a match has to occur even though the main outcome is already resolved), and when contestants engage in match-fixing or collusion: notorious drawn games have occurred in soccer in collusive performances that suited both sides at that stage of the tournament (both would progress to the next phase); the tennis player who suddenly collapses, in a way that has already engendered multiple wagers at bookmakers, has clearly determined the outcome with the opponent, and corrupt figures from betting syndicates; the boxer who makes no objection to a decision going against him, when he has outfought a reigning champion who has a continuing television channel deal for a series of defences, might already have been tempted by a fixed distribution of benefits. In all such cases, the essence of the sporting endeavour and contest is abused: when sport is reduced to a zero-sum game, it at the very least borders on, and is usually mired in, the murky waters of *corruption.

zone A lay term referring to an athlete's psychological space linked to a particular physical performance, particularly associated with the achievement of peak experience. *See also* COMFORT ZONE; FLOW; FOCUSED INTENSITY; NEEDS, HIERARCHY OF; PEAKING.

zûrkhânah 'Houses of strength' attended by male members of wrestling guilds in the Ottoman realm of the Turks in the 16th century. In these houses, wrestlers would call upon the support of Allah to secure victory, and poets wrote celebratory and commemorative accounts of victories. Such houses, Allen Guttmann writes (*Sports: The First Five Millennia*, 2004), 'are still an important part of Iranian culture, where they continue to emphasize the ideals of traditional masculinity'. They are open only to Muslims, and combine worship with sports. Philippe Rochard's 'The Identities of the Iranian *Zûrkhânah*' (*Iranian Studies*, vol. 35, 2002) evokes the atmosphere of past and present that the houses of strength represent; during the wrestler's preparation, chants and drum rolls celebrate the heroic combatants and chroniclers of earlier centuries.

z

Appendix 1
Principal Sources, and Further Reading

Humanities and Social Sciences

Andreff, Wladimir and Szymanski, Stefan (eds.) (2009) *Handbook on the Economics of Sport*, London: Edward Elgar.

Cashmore, Ellis (2002) *Sports Psychology: The Key Concepts*, London: Routledge.

Guttmann, Allen (2004) *Sports: The First Five Millennia*, Amherst: University of Massachusetts Press.

Wallechinsky, David and Loucky, Jaime (2008) *The Complete Book of the Olympics*, London: Aurum Press.

International Journal of the History of Sport.

International Review for the Sociology of Sport.

Journal of Sport and Social Issues

Journal of Sport History

Sociology of Sport Journal

Sport in History (formerly *The Sport Historian*)

Sport Science/Psychology

Armstrong, N. (2006) *Paediatric Exercise Physiology*, Edinburgh: Churchill Livingstone.

Bartlett, R. (1999) *Sports Biomechanics: Reducing Injury and Improving Performance*, London: E. & F. N. Spon.

Biddle, S. J. H., Fox, K. R. and Boutcher, S. (2000) *Physical Activity and Psychological Well-Being*, London: Routledge.

Cox, R. H. (2006) *Sport Psychology: Concepts and Applications* (6th edn), New York: McGraw-Hill.

Department of Health (2009) *Health improvement*, http://www.dh.gov.uk/en/Publichealth/Healthimprovement/index.htm

Eston, R. and Reilly, T. (2001) *Kinanthropometry and Exercise Physiology Laboratory Manual: Tests, Procedures and Data*, 2 vols (2nd edn), London: Routledge.

Hardman, A. and Stensel, D. (2003) *Physical Activity and Health: The Evidence Explained*, London: Routledge.

McArdle, W., Katch, F. and Katch, V. (2006) *Exercise Physiology: Energy, Nutrition and Human Performance* (6th edn), Baltimore: Lippincott Williams and Wilkins.

Weinburg, R. and Gould, D. (2007) *Foundations of Sport and Exercise Psychology* (4th edn), Champaign IL: Human Kinetics.

Winter, E. M., Jones, A. M., Davison, R., Bromley, P. D., Mercer, T. H. (2007) *Sport and Exercise Physiology Testing Guidelines*, vol. 1, *Sport Testing*, London: Routledge.

World Health Organization (2009) http://www.who.int/topics

General Web Resources

( ) SEE WEB LINKS

- A web link, entitled *Scholarly Sport Sites: A Subject Directory*, providing hundreds of web addresses and links to professional organizations, sport organizations, and academic and research resources. http://sportinfo.ning.com/
- The website of the International Association for Sports Information, which 'promotes the collection and dissemination of sports information to physical educators, sports scientists, documentalists and sports researchers'.

Appendix 2
Summer Olympic Medal Tables

The following table of the top four Summer Olympic Medal winners by nationality is based on the tables compiled in David Wallechinsky and Jaime Loucky, *The Complete Book of the Olympics* (London: Aurum Press, 2008), along with additional detail on Beijing 2008. We have reproduced the top four nations for each Summer Olympics since 1896, including the out-of-sequence event in Athens in 1906. The Games are altogether on a different scale in the thirtieth Olympiad leading up to London 2012: at Athens in 1896 only around 245 competitors participated, from 14 nations; in Beijing in 2008, 10,560 athletes from 201 nations were represented at the event. Actual medals began to be awarded from 1904, so the tables allocate them retrospectively to those who finished first, second, or third at the 1896 and 1900 Games.

In the first four Games, competitors entered as individuals, not as selected members of national teams, and Wallechinsky and Loucky note the difficulty of establishing definitively the national profiles. But the pattern of domination is clear: apart from 1906, 1908, and 1936 when France, Great Britain, and Germany respectively topped the medal tables, only three nations have held that position—the USA, 16 times; the Soviet Union, 7 times, and China, for the first time in 2008. The Olympic medal table as presented here is based on the primacy of the gold medal, not the accumulated total medal haul at a Games. To look at the relative positions of the dominant nations, and other nations to break into the top four, is to see the workings of global politics on the sporting stage. Asking where, when, and how these positions were achieved are fascinating and challenging questions, at the heart of an interdisciplinary sports studies, and so these tables are included as an Appendix to invite the sports studies scholar to ask such questions about the one sporting phenomenon that provides a platform for the whole world.

Key to abbreviations

MEDALS
G	gold medals
S	silver medals
B	bronze medals

NATIONS
AUS	Australia
BEL	Belgium
BUL	Bulgaria
CAN	Canada
CHN	China
CUB	Cuba
FIN	Finland
FRA	France
GBR	Great Britain and Northern Ireland
GDR	East Germany (German Democratic Republic, 1952–88)
GER	Germany; West Germany (Federal Republic of Germany, 1952–88)
GRE	Greece
HUN	Hungary
ITA	Italy
JPN	Japan
KOR	Korea
ROM	Romania
RUS	Russia
SOV	Soviet Union (Unified Team, 1992)
SWE	Sweden
USA	United States of America

Medals tables

1896 Athens
	G	S	B
USA	11	7	2
GRE	10	16	19
GER	6	5	2
FRA	5	4	2

1900 Paris
	G	S	B
USA	21	14	15
FRA	18	27	21
GBR	12	9	7
BEL	3	3	1

1904 St Louis

	G	S	B
USA	67	72	75
GER	4	4	4
CAN	4	1	1
CUB	3	0	0

1906 Athens

	G	S	B
FRA	15	9	16
USA	12	6	6
GRE	8	13	12
GBR	8	11	5

1908 London

	G	S	B
GBR	56	51	39
USA	23	12	12
SWE	8	6	11
FRA	5	5	9

1912 Stockholm

	G	S	B
USA	25	18	20
SWE	23	24	17
GBR	10	15	16
FIN	9	8	9

1920 Antwerp

	G	S	B
USA	41	27	27
SWE	19	20	25
FIN	15	10	9
GBR	14	15	13

1924 Paris

	G	S	B
USA	45	27	27
FIN	14	13	10
FRA	13	15	10
GBR	9	13	12

1928 Amsterdam

	G	S	B
USA	22	18	16
GER	10	7	14
FIN	8	8	9
SWE	7	6	12

1932 Los Angeles

	G	S	B
USA	41	32	30
ITA	12	12	12
FRA	10	5	4
SWE	9	5	9

1936 Berlin

	G	S	B
GER	33	26	30
USA	24	20	12
HUN	10	1	5
ITA	8	9	5

1948 London

	G	S	B
USA	38	27	19
SWE	16	11	17
FRA	10	6	13
HUN	10	5	12

1952 Helsinki

	G	S	B
USA	40	19	17
SOV	22	30	19
HUN	16	10	16
SWE	12	13	10

1956 Melbourne

	G	S	B
SOV	37	29	32
USA	32	25	17
AUS	13	8	14
HUN	9	10	7

1960 Rome

	G	S	B
SOV	43	29	31
USA	34	21	16
ITA	13	10	13
GER	12	19	11

1964 Tokyo

	G	S	B
USA	36	26	28
SOV	30	31	35
JPN	16	5	8
GER	10	22	8

1968 Mexico City

	G	S	B
USA	45	28	34
SOV	29	32	30
JPN	11	7	7
HUN	10	10	12

1972 Munich

	G	S	B
SOV	50	27	22
USA	33	31	30
GDR	20	23	23
GER	13	11	16

1976 Montreal

	G	S	B
SOV	49	41	35
GDR	40	25	25
USA	34	35	25
GER	10	12	17

1980 Moscow

	G	S	B
SOV	80	69	46
GDR	47	37	42
BUL	8	16	17
CUB	8	7	5

1984 Los Angeles

	G	S	B
USA	83	61	30
ROM	20	16	17
GER	17	19	23
CHN	15	8	9

1988 Seoul

	G	S	B
SOV	55	31	46
GDR	37	35	30
USA	36	31	27
KOR	12	10	11

1992 Barcelona

	G	S	B
SOV	45	38	28

	G	S	B
USA	37	34	37
GER	33	21	28
CHN	16	22	16

1996 Atlanta

	G	S	B
USA	44	32	25
RUS	26	21	16
GER	20	18	27
CHN	16	22	12

2000 Sydney

	G	S	B
USA	38	24	32
RUS	32	28	28
CHN	28	16	15
AUS	16	25	17

2004 Athens

	G	S	B
USA	36	39	27
CHN	32	17	14
RUS	27	27	38
AUS	17	16	16

2008 Beijing

	G	S	B
CHN	51	21	28
USA	36	38	36
RUS	23	21	28
GBR	19	13	15

Appendix 3
International Federations

Summer Sports

Federation	Acronym	Formation Date	Formation City	Number of Affiliated Countries/ National Associations*	Incumbent President Name and Nationality
Fédération Internationale de Tir à l'Arc (International Archery Federation)	FITA	4 September 1931	Lwow, Poland	141	Dr Ugur ERDENER (TUR)
International Association of Athletics Federations	IAAF	1912	Stockholm, Sweden	213	Mr Lamine DIACK (SEN)
Badminton World Federation	BWF	5 July 1934	London, UK	164	Dr Young Joong KANG (KOR)
Fédération Internationale de Basketball (International Basketball Federation)	FIBA	June 1932	Geneva, Switzerland	213	Mr Bob ELPHINSTON (AUS)
Association Internationale de Boxe Amateur (International Boxing Association)	AIBA	24 August 1920 (FIBA) November 1946 (AIBA)	Antwerp, Belgium (FIBA) ND (AIBA)	196	Mr Ching-Kuo WU (TPE)
International Canoe Federation	ICF	19 January 1924	Copenhagen, Denmark	147	Mr José PERURENA (ESP)
Union Cycliste Internationale (International Cycling Union)	UCI	14 April 1900	Paris, France	173	Mr Pat MCQUAID (IRL)
Fédération Équestre Internationale (International Equestrian Federation)	FEI	1921	ND	134	HRH Princess Haya Bint AL HUSSEIN (JOR)
Fédération Internationale d'Escrime (International Fencing Federation)	FIE	29 November 1913	Paris, France	134	Mr Alisher USMANOV (RUS)
Fédération Internationale de Football Association (International Federation of Association Football)	FIFA	21 May 1904	Paris, France	208	Mr Joseph S. BLATTER (SUI)
Fédération Internationale de Gymnastique (International Gymnastics Federation)	FIG	23 July 1881	Liège, Belgium	129	Mr Bruno GRANDI (ITA)
International Handball Federation	IHF	11 July 1946	ND	166	Dr Hassan MOUSTAFA (EGY)
Fédération Internationale de Hockey (International Hockey Federation)	FIH	7 January 1924	Paris, France	127	Mr Leandro NEGRE (ESP)

(continued)

Summer Sports Cont.

Federation	Acronym	Formation Date	Formation City	Number of Affiliated Countries/ National Associations*	Incumbent President Name and Nationality
International Judo Federation	IJF	July 1951	ND	195	Mr Marius VIZER (AUT)
Union Internationale de Pentathlon Moderne (International Modern Pentathlon Union)	UIPM	1948	London, UK	103	Mr Klaus SCHORMANN (GER)
Fédération Internationale des Sociétés d'Aviron (International Federation of Rowing Associations)	FISA	25 June 1892	Turin, Italy	128	Mr Denis OSWALD (SUI)
International Sailing Federation	ISAF	October 1907	Paris, France	126	Mr Göran PETERSSON (SWE)
International Shooting Sport Federation	ISSF	17 July 1907	Zurich, Switzerland	158	Mr Olegario VÁZQUEZ RAÑA (MEX)
Fédération Internationale de Natation (International Swimming Federation)	FINA	19 July 1908	London, UK	201	Mr Julio César MAGLIONE (URU)
The International Table Tennis Federation	ITTF	1926	ND	205	Mr Adham SHARARA (CAN)
World Taekwondo Federation	WTF	28 May 1973	Seoul, South Korea	182	Dr Chungwon CHOUE (KOR)
International Tennis Federation	ITF	1 March 1913	Paris, France	205	Mr Francesco RICCI BITTI (ITA)
International Triathlon Union	ITU	1989	Avignon, France	123	Ms Marisol CASADO (ESP)
Fédération Internationale de Volleyball (International Volleyball Federation)	FIVB	1947	Paris, France	220	Mr Jizhong WEI (CHN)
International Weightlifting Federation	IWF	1905	ND	167	Mr Tamás AJÁN (HUN)
Fédération Internationale des Luttes Associées (International Federation Of Associated Wrestling Styles)	FILA	1905	Duisburg, Germany	166	Mr Raphaël MARTINETTI (SUI)

* Information taken from Federation's website

ND – Not Definitive

Winter Sports

Federation	Acronym	Formation Date	Formation City	Number of Affiliated Countries/ National Associations*	Incumbent President Name and Nationality
International Biathlon Union	IBU	2 July 1993	UK	66	Mr Anders BESSEBERG (NOR)
Fédération Internationale de Bobsleigh et de Tobog (International Bobsleigh and Skeleton Federation)	FIBT	23 November 1923	Paris, France	60	Mr Robert H. STOREY (CAN)
World Curling Federation	WCF	1 April 1966	Vancouver, Canada	44	Mr Lester M. HARRISON (CAN)
International Ice Hockey Federation	IIHF	15 May 1908	Paris, France	68	Mr René FASEL (SUI)
Fédération Internationale de Luge de Course (International Luge Federation)	FIL	25 January 1957	Davos, Switzerland	52	Mr Josef FENDT (GER)
International Skating Union	ISU	July 1892	Scheveningen, Netherlands	66	Mr Ottavio CINQUANTA (ITA)
Fédération Internationale de Ski (International Ski Federation)	FIS	2–4 February 1924	Chamonix, France	109	Mr Gian-Franco KASPER (SUI)

* Information taken from Federation's website

ND – Not Definitive

Recognized Sports

Federation	Acronym	Formation Date	Formation City	Number of Affiliated Countries/ National Associations*	Incumbent President Name and Nationality
Fédération Aéronautique Internationale (The World Air Sports Federation)	FAI	14 October 1905	Paris, France	98	Mr Pierre PORTMANN (FRA)
Federation of International Bandy	FIB	12 February 1955	Stockholm, Sweden	25	Mr Boris SKRYNNIK (RUS)
International Baseball Federation	IBAF	1938	ND	126	Riccardo FRACCARI (ITA)
World Confederation of Billiards Sports	WCBS	25 January 1992	Yverdon-les-Bains, Switzerland	148	Mr Pascal GUILLAUME (FRA)
Confédération Mondiale des Sports de Boules (Worldwide Confederation Of Boules)	CMSB	21 December 1985	Monaco	105	Mr Romolo RIZZOLI (ITA)
Fédération Internationale des Quilleurs (International Bowling Federation)	FIQ	27 January 1952	Hamburg, Germany	134	Ms Jessie PHUA (SIN)
World Bridge Federation	WBF	1958	ND	130	Mr Iosé DAMIANI (FRA)
Fédération Internationale des Échecs (World Chess Federation)	FIDE	20 July 1924	Paris, France	165	H.E. Kirsan ILYUMZHINOV (RUS)
International Cricket Council	ICC	15 June 1909	France	104	Mr David MORGAN (UK)
International Dancesport Federation	IDSF	12 May 1957	Germany	86	Mr Carlos FREITAG (ESP)
International Floorball Federation	IFF	1986	Huskvarna, Sweden	48	Mr Tomas ERIKSSON (SWE)
International Golf Federation	IGF	1958	ND	116	Mr Allan GORMLY (UK), Mr James VERNON (USA), Ms Emma VILLACIEROS (ESP)
World Karate Federation	WKF	1970	ND	189	Mr Antonio ESPINOS ORTUETA (ESP)
International Korfball Federation	IKF	11 June 1933	Antwerp, Belgium	59	Dr Jan C. FRANSOO (NED)
International Life Saving Federation	ILSF	27 March 1910	Paris, France	105	Dr Steve BEERMAN (CAN)
Fédération Internationale de Motocyclisme (International Motorcycling Federation)	FIM	21 December 1904	Paris, France	98	Mr Vito IPPOLITO (VEN)
Union Internationale des Associations d'Alpinisme (The International Mountaineering and Climbing Federation)	UIAA	August 1932	Chamonix, France	68	Mr Mike MORTIMER (CAN)

(continued)

Recognized Sports Cont.

Federation	Acronym	Formation Date	Formation City	Number of Affiliated Countries/ National Associations*	Incumbent President Name and Nationality
International Federation of Netball Associations	IFNA	1960	Sri Lanka	62	Ms Molly RHONE (JAM)
International Orienteering Federation	IOF	21 May 1961	Copenhagen, Denmark	70	Mr Åke JACOBSON (SWE)
Federación Internacional de Pelota Vasca (International Federation of Basque Pelota)	FIPV	19 May 1929	Buenos Aires, Argentina	27	Mr Dominique BOUTINEAU (FRA)
Federation of International Polo	FIP	April 1982	ND	85	Mr Patrick GUERRAND-HERMES (FRA)
Union Internationale Motonautique (International Union of Powerboating)	UIM	1922	ND	55	Dr Raffaele CHIULLI (ITA)
International Racquetball Federation	IRF	October 1979	Memphis Tennessee, USA	103	Dr Keith CALKINS (USA)
Fédération Internationale de Roller Sports (International Roller Sports Federation)	FIRS	April 1924	Montreux, Switzerland	117	Mr Sabatino ARACU (ITA)
International Rugby Board	IRB	1886	ND	122	Mr Bernard LAPASSET (FRA)
International Softball Federation	ISF	1952	ND	127	Mr Don E. PORTER (USA)
World Squash Federation	WSF	1967	ND	147	Mr RAMACHANDRAN (IND)
International Sumo Federation	IFS	10 December 1992	ND	84	Mr Hidetoshi TANAKA
International Surfing Association	ISA	1964	Sydney, Australia	51	Mr Fernando AGUERRE (ARG)
Tug of War International Federation	TWIF	1960	ND	54	Mr Cathal McKEEVER
Confédération Mondiale des Activités Subaquatiques (World Underwater Federation)	CMAS	9–11 January 1959	Monaco	126	Mr Achille FERRERO (ITA)
International Water Ski Federation	IWSF	27 July 1946	Geneva, Switzerland	92	Mr Kuno RITSCHARD
International Wushu Federation	IWUF	3 October 1990	Beijing, China	122	Mr Zaiqing YU (CHN)

* Information taken from Federation's website

ND – Not Definitive

FEDERATION CONTACT DETAILS (of federations of sports featured in the Summer Olympics, and the Winter Olympics, and those granted 'recognized' status by the International Olympic Committee)

Summer Sports

Federation	Address	Website
Fédération Internationale de Tir à l'Arc (International Archery Federation)	Maison du Sport International Av. de Rhodanie 54 1007 Lausanne Switzerland	http://www.archery.org
International Association of Athletics Federations	17, rue Princesse Florestine B.P. 359 98007 Monte-Carlo Cédex Monaco	http://www.iaaf.org
Badminton World Federation	Stadium Badminton Kuala Lumpur 3 ½ Miles Jalan Cheras 56000 Kuala Lumpur Malaysia	http://www.internationalbadminton.org
Fédération Internationale de Basketball (International Basketball Federation)	53 Avenue Louis-Casaï P.O. Box 110 1216 Cointrin/Genève Switzerland	http://www.fiba.com
Association Internationale de Boxe Amateur (International Boxing Association)	Maison du Sport International Av. de Rhodanie 54 1007 Lausanne Switzerland	http://www.aiba.org
International Canoe Federation	Maison du Sport International Av. de Rhodanie 54 1007 Lausanne Switzerland	http://www.canoeicf.com
Union Cycliste Internationale (International Cycling Union)	1860 Aigle Switzerland	http://www.uci.ch
Fédération Équestre Internationale (International Equestrian Federation)	Avenue de Rumine 37 1005 Lausanne Switzerland	http://www.fei.org
Fédération Internationale d'Escrime (International Fencing Federation)	Maison du Sport International Av. de Rhodanie 54 1007 Lausanne Switzerland	http://www.fie.ch
Fédération Internationale de Football Association (International Federation of Association Football)	FIFA-Strasse 20 P.O. Box 8044 Zurich Switzerland	http://www.fifa.com
Fédération Internationale de Gymnastique (International Gymnastics Federation)	Avenue de la Gare 12 CP 630 1001 Lausanne Switzerland	http://www.fig-gymnastics.com
International Handball Federation	P.O. Box Peter Merian-Strasse 23 4002 Basel Switzerland	http://www.ihf.info
Fédération Internationale de Hockey (International Hockey Federation)	Rue du Valentin 61 1004 Lausanne Switzerland	http://www.worldhockey.org

Summer Sports cont.

Federation	Address	Website
International Judo Federation	Roosevelt Tér 2. 1051 Budapest Hungary	http://www.ijf.org
Union Internationale de Pentathlon Moderne (International Modern Pentathlon Union)	Avenue des Castelans 13 Stade Louis II - Entrance E 98000 Monaco Monaco	http://www.pentathlon.org
Fédération Internationale des Sociétés d'Aviron (International Federation of Rowing Associations)	Maison du Sport International Av. de Rhodanie 54 1007 Lausanne Switzerland	http://www.worldrowing.com
International Sailing Federation	Ariadne House Town Quay Southampton SO14 2AQ Great Britain	http://www.sailing.org
International Shooting Sport Federation	Bavariaring 21 80336 Munich Germany	http://www.issf-sports.org
Fédération Internationale de Natation (International Swimming Federation)	Avenue de l'Avant-Poste 4 1005 Lausanne Switzerland	http://www.fina.org
The International Table Tennis Federation	Chemin de la Roche 11 1020 Renens/Lausanne Switzerland	http://www.ittf.com
World Taekwondo Federation	4th Fl., JoYang Building 113 Samseong-dong Gangnam-gu Seoul 135-090 Republic of Korea	http://www.wtf.org
International Tennis Federation	Bank Lane Roehampton London SW15 5XZ Great Britain	http://www.itftennis.com
International Triathlon Union	998 Harbourside Drive Suite 221 North Vancouver V7P 3T2 Canada	http://www.triathlon.org
Fédération Internationale de Volleyball (International Volleyball Federation)	Château Les Tourelles Ch Edouard Sandoz 2-4 1006 Lausanne Switzerland	http://www.fivb.org
International Weightlifting Federation	House of Hungarian Sports Istvanmezei ut 1-3 1146 Budapest Hungary	http://www.iwf.net
Fédération Internationale des Luttes Associées (International Federation Of Associated Wrestling Styles)	Rue du Château 6 1804 Corsier-sur-Vevey Switzerland	http://www.fila-wrestling.com

Winter Sports

Federation	Address	Website
International Biathlon Union	Peregrinstrasse 14 5020 Salzburg Austria	http://www.biathlonworld.com
Fédération Internationale de Bobsleigh et de Tobog (International Bobsleigh and Skeleton Federation)	Via Piranesi 44 B 20137 Milano Italy	http://www.bobsleigh.com
World Curling Federation	74, Tay Street Perth PH2 8NP Great Britain	http://www.worldcurling.org
International Ice Hockey Federation	Brandschenkestrasse 50 Postfach 1817 8027 Zurich Switzerland	http://www.iihf.com
Fédération Internationale de Luge de Course (International Luge Federation)	Rathausplatz 9 83471 Berchtesgaden Germany	http://www.fil-luge.org
International Skating Union	Chemin de Primerose 2 1007 Lausanne Switzerland	http://www.isu.org
Fédération Internationale de Ski (International Ski Federation)	Blochstrasse 2 3653 Oberhofen/Thunersee Switzerland	http://www.fis-ski.com

Recognized Sports

Federation	Address	Website
Fédération Aéronautique Internationale (The World Air Sports Federation)	Avenue Mon-Repos 24 1005 Lausanne Switzerland	http://www.fai.org
Federation of International Bandy	P.O. Box 91 826 23 Söderhamn Sweden	http://www.internationalbandy.com
International Baseball Federation	Case postale 6099 Avenue Mon-Repos 24 1002 Lausanne Switzerland	http://www.IBAF.org
World Confederation Of Billiards Sports	Kortrijkse Steenweg 205/6 9830 Sint-Martens-Latem Belgium	http://www.billiard-wcbs.org
Confédération Mondiale des Sports de Boules (Worldwide Confederation of Boules)	Via Vitorchiano 113-115 00189 Roma Italy	http://www.CMSBoules.com
Fédération Internationale des Quilleurs (International Bowling Federation)	100 Tyrwhitt Road 02-05 Jalan Besar Swimming Complex Singapour 207542 Singapore	http://www.fiq.org

(continued)

Recognized Sports

Federation	Address	Website
World Bridge Federation	40, rue François 1er 75008 Paris France	http://www.worldbridge.org
Fédération Internationale des Échecs (World Chess Federation)	9 Singrou Avenue 11743 Athina Greece	http://www.fide.com
International Cricket Council	Al Thuraya Tower 1, 11th floor Dubai Media City P.O. Box 500070 Dubai United Arab Emirates	http://www.icc-cricket.com
International Dancesport Federation	Calle Orient 78-84 2nd Floor, Office 15 08172 Sant Cugat Spain	http://www.idsf.net
International Floorball Federation	Alakiventie 2 00920 Helsinki Finland	http://www.floorball.org
International Golf Federation	Golf House P.O. Box 708 77 Liberty Corner Rd Far Hills NJ 07931-0708 United States of America	http://www.internationalgolffederation.org
World Karate Federation	Galeria de Vallehermoso 4 3rd Floor 28003 Madrid Spain	http://www.wkf.net
International Korfball Federation	P.O. Box 417 3700 AK Zeist Netherlands	http://www.ikf.org
International Life Saving Federation	Gemeeteplein 26 3010 Leuven Belgium	http://www.ilsf.org
Fédération Internationale de Motocyclisme (International Motorcycling Federation)	Route Suisse 11 1295 Mies Switzerland	http://www.fim.ch
Union Internationale des Associations d'Alpinisme (The International Mountaineering And Climbing Federation)	Postfach 3000 Berne 23 Switzerland	http://www.theuiaa.org
International Federation of Netball Associations	40 Princess Street Manchester M1 6DE Great Britain	http://www.netball.org
International Orienteering Federation	Radiokatu 20 00093 SLU Helsinki Finland	http://www.orienteering.org
Federación Internacional de Pelota Vasca (International Federation of Basque Pelota)	C/ Bernardino Tirapu 67 31014 Pamplona Spain	http://www.fipv.net

(*continued*)

Recognized Sports Cont.

Federation	Address	Website
Federation of International Polo	Château de Saint-Firmin 60500 Vineuil France	http://www.fippolo.com
Union Internationale Motonautique (International Union of Powerboating)	Avenue des Castelans 1 Stade Louis II - Entrée H 98000 Monaco Monaco	http://www.uimpowerboating.com
International Racquetball Federation	1631 Mesa Ave, Suite 1 Colorado Springs CO 80906 United States of America	http://www.internationalracquetball.com
Fédération Internationale de Roller Sports (International Roller Sports Federation)	Viale Tiziano 74 00196 Roma Italy	http://www.rollersports.org
International Rugby Board	Huguenot House 35-38 St Stephen's Green Dublin 2 Ireland	http://www.irb.com
International Softball Federation	1900 South Park Road Plant City FL 33563 United States of America	http://www.internationalsoftball.com
World Squash Federation	Unit 14 Innovation Centre Churchfields St. Leonards On-Sea TN38 9UH Great Britain	http://www.worldsquash.org
International Sumo Federation	1-15-20 Hyakunincho Shinjuku-ku Tokyo 169-0073 Japan	http://www.amateursumo.com
International Surfing Association	5580 La Jolla Boulevard Suite 145 La Jolla CA 92037 United States of America	http://www.isasurf.org
Tug of War International Federation	PO Box 77 Orfordville WI 53576-0077 United States of America	http://www.tugofwar-twif.org
Confédération Mondiale des Activités Subaquatiques (World Underwater Federation)	Viale Tiziano 74 00196 Roma Italy	http://www.cmas.org
International Water Ski Federation	Alte Landstrasse 19 Postbox 564 6314 Unteraegeri Switzerland	http://www.iwsf.com
International Wushu Federation	Anding Road 3 Chaoyang District 100029 Beijing China	http://www.iwuf.org

Source
http://www.olympic.org/uk/organisation/if/index_uk.asp (consulted 1 August 2009)

Appendix 4

FIFA World Cup Winners

FIFA Men's World Cup

Date	Place	Number of teams	Champion
1930	Uruguay	13	Uruguay
1934	Italy	16	Italy
1938	France	15	Italy
1950	Brazil	13	Uruguay
1954	Switzerland	16	Germany FR
1958	Sweden	16	Brazil
1962	Chile	16	Brazil
1966	England	16	England
1970	Mexico	16	Brazil
1974	Germany	16	Germany
1978	Argentina	16	Argentina
1982	Spain	24	Italy
1986	Mexico	24	Argentina
1990	Italy	24	Germany FR
1994	USA	24	Brazil
1998	France	32	France
2002	Korea/Japan	32	Brazil
2006	Germany	32	Italy

FIFA Women's World Cup

Date	Place	Number of teams	Champion
1991	China PR	12	USA
1995	Sweden	12	Norway
1999	USA	16	USA
2003	USA	16	Germany
2007	China	16	Germany

Sources

http://www.fifa.com/worldcup/archive/index.html (consulted 27 July 2009)

http://www.fifa.com/tournaments/archive/tournament=103/awards/index.html (consulted 27 July 2009)

Oxford Paperback Reference

A Dictionary of Chemistry

Over 4,700 entries covering all aspects of chemistry, including physical chemistry and biochemistry.

'It should be in every classroom and library ... the reader is drawn inevitably from one entry to the next merely to satisfy curiosity.'

School Science Review

A Dictionary of Physics

Ranging from crystal defects to the solar system, almost 4,000 clear and concise entries cover all commonly encountered terms and concepts of physics.

A Dictionary of Biology

The perfect guide for those studying biology—with over 5,500 entries on key terms from biology, biochemistry, medicine, and palaeontology.

'lives up to its expectations; the entries are concise, but explanatory'

Biologist

'ideally suited to students of biology, at either secondary or university level, or as a general reference source for anyone with an interest in the life sciences'

Journal of Anatomy

OXFORD